SALES

PROBLEMS AND MATERIALS

REVISED FIRST EDITION

LARRY BATES

BAYLOR UNIVERSITY

SAN DIEGO

Bassim Hamadeh, CEO and Publisher
Carrie Montoya, Manager, Revisions and Author Care
Kaela Martin, Project Editor
Chelsey Schmid, Production Supervisor
Jess Estrella, Senior Graphic Designer
Alexa Lucido, Licensing Manager
Natalie Piccotti, Director of Marketing
Kassie Graves, Vice President of Editorial
Jamie Giganti, Director of Academic Publishing

3970 Sorrento Valley Blvd., Ste. 500, San Diego, CA 92121

CONTENTS

Dedicated to

Carolyn Edwards

&

Zipporah Batshaw Wiseman

PREFACE

This book provides the materials I believe necessary to develop in students a basic understanding of sales transactions under Article 2 of the Uniform Commercial Code. My goal in the sales course I teach is to overcome the fear and anxiety with which many students approach codes and statutes by exposing the Code as a system of interrelated and intuitive rules working together to facilitate the sale of goods and to resolve the disputes that sometimes arise during the relationship created by a sales transaction. I'm not trying to turn out a class of experts in sales law. But, if I'm doing my job, I can provide a level of comfort and confidence when it comes to working with Article 2 and the Code that will enable my students to effectively address the needs of their clients once in practice. And, because I'm an optimist, maybe I can even convince them that Article 2 can actually be fun.

This book, like my text on Secured Transactions, is built around a series of problems that connect the cases and the original material back to the text of Article 2. The objective is to get the students to see the Code as the primary source of commercial law rather than as a source that is secondary to judicial interpretation of its provisions. The snapshots of specific provisions provided by the cases can animate the Code for students, but they can also leave students with the false impression that without the cases, the Code itself is lifeless. That was not Llewellyn's vision for his Code.

I've always preferred textbooks that did not get in the way of how I wanted to teach my classes—that provided me with the materials I needed to teach the course, but that ultimately left the teaching to me. I've tried to be true to that ideal in this book. The cases, problems, and limited text are intended to provide the materials needed to teach sales law your way.

As are all students of Article 2, I am indebted to the work of Karl Llewellyn, especially the notes and commentary he produced for the early drafts of his new sales law, many of which have been made available by Elizabeth Kelly in her multivolume work on the drafting history of the Uniform Commercial Code published by Fred B. Rothman & Company, which is referenced throughout the text. And, of course, I have been both influenced and inspired (and occasionally bemused) by the work of Jim White and Bob Summers, first as a confused law student and now as a teacher of contracts and commercial law. Their treatise on commercial law published by West is also referenced throughout the text. I had the good fortune of having two wonderful teachers as mentors during the early stages of my affliction with Article 2: Carolyn Edwards when I was at Marquette, and later Zipporah Wiseman, who hired me as her research assistant when I was at Harvard.

The team at Cognella, especially Gem Rabanera, has been exceptionally helpful and accommodating and has made putting this book together a great experience.

Finally, this project would still be only piles of cases and notes on my desk without the enthusiastic and tireless work of my two research assistants, Elizabeth Brabb and Amanda Howard. You will be a part of every sales class I teach with this book.

CHAPTER 1

IN THE BEGINNING

By the time we get to law school, most of us have done a lot of buying—and maybe even a little selling—of the products that have become a part of our everyday lives at the start of the twenty-first century.

Most of us don't think much, if we think at all, about where the wool in the sweater we bought came from, how it was made into a sweater, or where that sweater was before it ended up on display at the sweater shop. Nor do we think about who grew the peaches in the can we bought or how the peaches ended up in a can on a shelf in the supermarket. Instead, we think about things like whether the sweater fits, if it will keep us warm, whether we really need another sweater, or whether the price is right. Or whether we should buy the popular brand of canned peaches instead of the generic peaches on special this week.

But the peaches, the sweater, the ear buds, the iPhone, the snowboard, the PlayStation, the bicycle, the Gucci handbag, and the flat-screen TV did not suddenly materialize on the shelves of the stores where you bought them (or thought about buying them). Many of them have already been bought and sold multiple times before they ended up on display at Target or Walmart or Neiman Marcus, and each of them had been sold at least once before you bought them—Kroger does not grow the bananas it sells, and Target did not make the PlayStation it sold you.

But Kroger can't take delivery on January 1 of all of the bananas it thinks it can sell this year. Bananas, because they are perishable—they rot if not consumed within a limited time—have a short shelf life, so by the middle of January the bananas Kroger bought to sell in February or March or later will be rotten and not saleable. What Kroger needs is a way to ensure, on January 1, that throughout the year it will have on hand the bananas necessary to meet the anticipated demand of its customers for bananas.

One way Kroger could make the arrangements necessary for a steady supply of bananas this year is by contract—Kroger could, by contract, commit a grower or distributor of bananas to supply bananas during the year on an agreed-upon schedule.

But using a contract to get the bananas will only appeal to Kroger if it knows that the contract will be enforceable—and that it will have an appropriate remedy against the seller if the seller refuses or fails to deliver the bananas as required by the contract. Without the certainty provided by enforceability and the availability of remedies for breach, the contract does not allow Kroger to do the business planning required to keep supply matched to demand—to keep its customers happy. Target's needs are not much different from those of Kroger—it wants to have a guaranteed number of the next version of PlayStation on its shelves when it's finally released. Contract allows it to do this—to commit a seller, in advance of release, to provide the number of units it wants—but only if the consequences of making that contract are consistent with the expectations of Target and the seller.

Transactions like Kroger's bananas deal and Target's PlayStation deal are covered by Article 2 of the Uniform Commercial Code. Article 2, the focus of our study in this course, applies to sales-of-goods transactions—contracts between buyers and sellers of personal property. Article 2 carves sale-of-goods transactions out of the general law of contract on the premise that the law governing such transactions needs to reflect the actual commercial realities of the parties to the transaction and that such law should be uniform across state lines. Something that many argued the common law had been either unable or unwilling to do.

Contracts for the sale of goods have had their own rules since the Middle Ages. The *lex mercatoria*, or "law merchant," of the medieval marketplace reflected the customs and usages of the merchants who carried on the primitive commercial activities of that time. For a long time, this law merchant was developed in courts administered by the merchants themselves—outside the jurisdiction of what were becoming the courts of general jurisdiction, where the seeds of the common law were beginning to sprout and grow into the body of precedent to which the courts would look for the rules they needed to resolve the disputes before them. As specialized tribunals, the merchant courts did not have to worry about how their decisions would impact the law in general, and so their decisions could take account of the commercial realities out of which the disputes before them arose. The *lex mercatoria* really was the law of merchants.

Eventually, the merchant courts were absorbed into the courts of general jurisdiction—for the English kings and queens, the dispensation of justice was a steady source of income during these times. The law merchant—those customs and usages that were part of mercantile life—was haphazardly incorporated into the common law, and there it languished until the second half of the eighteenth century, when finally

> there appeared a judicial personality capable of accomplishing the necessary reforms and achieving a lasting synthesis in the field of commercial law.[1]

That personality was Lord Mansfield, who served for thirty years as chief justice of the King's Bench. Mansfield succeeded in "fusing the law merchant with the common law so as to meet the needs and the changing conditions of the society of his time."[2]

> The principles of Law Merchant remained in a chaotic condition until Lord Mansfield assumed the chief justiceship of the King's Bench. It was the genius of this great judge, during the thirty years or more that he presided in the King's Bench, that molded the Law Merchant into a body of law with principles as fixed and certain as those of the Common Law itself. He has justly been called the father of modern commercial law.[3]

Mansfield's revival of mercantile custom and usage to shape the rules precedent had left him to use when presiding over disputes between merchants gave courts some flexibility to adjust the law to reflect changes in commercial practice—provided judges were willing to give effect to custom and usage when it touched upon the issues before them. But the fusion of the law merchant with the common law that allowed the law merchant to influence the development of the common law also allowed the common law to influence the development of the law merchant. Common-law courts "thinking common-law thoughts in common-law ways" now controlled the development of commercial law.[4] The *lex mercatoria* was no longer only the law of merchants.

---

1   Shientag, "Lord Mansfield Revisited—A Modern Assessment," 10 *Fordham L. Rev.* 345, 350 (1941).
2   *Id.*
3   Bigelow, *Bills, Notes, and Checks,* (3rd ed. Lyle, 1928) §31.
4   Llewellyn, "Across Sale on Horseback," 52 *Harv. L. Rev.* 725, 746 (1939).

Sales law was part of the law merchant fused with the common law during this period, but it was not given its own distinctive voice. Instead, it was subsumed into the general law of contract, appearing as "isolated rules revolving about the sales transaction" rather than as a coherent system of rules developed for a specific form or type of transaction.[5] There, it was, of course, inevitably influenced by the general law of contract, since the judges were no longer merchants steeped in mercantile customs and usages.

The common law inherited by American courts included this law merchant that the English courts had folded into it. In America, sales law remained deeply buried within the general law of contract—the first work published in America treating sales as a distinct category of the law was a book published by a Harvard law professor in 1871 for use in a class he was teaching on sales. Prior to that time, sales had been given limited face time in most legal works—and almost always as part of a broader discussion of contract law.[6] And it fared no better in the opinions the courts produced to explain their decisions.

But what courts and scholars were doing did not reflect what was happening to the way business—and sales of goods—were being done as the American economy was being rapidly transformed by the Industrial Revolution during the nineteenth century. As the power of machines changed the way things were made and the railroad changed the geographic reach of business, the nature of the relationships on which business transactions were based changed as well. In an agrarian culture with limited mobility when it came to moving products, face-to-face transactions were the norm: "goods chang[ed] place and money chang[ed] hands on the spot."[7] Business was local. The uncertainties that today parties to a sales transaction control by contract were essentially nonexistent, which diminished the role that contracts—sales law—played in sales transactions.

What we might call the early law of sales that emerged as a result of these changing conditions distinguished itself from general contract law by focusing on title—sales transactions were seen as transfers of title to property. The purpose of a sales transaction was to transfer title to the goods involved from the seller to the buyer.

> Insofar as our early sales law was sales law at all—that is, law relating to the contractual transfer of property rather than a law of ownership—it focused on the manual delivery of a simple object from seller to buyer against a simultaneous payment from buyer to seller. That pattern being set, the thrust of the law was to conform increasingly intricate transactions to the simple basic formula—to construe, interpret, and project in light of this ideal bargain and sale. But the rights of the contracting parties were still described in property terms: the location of title was the key to unlock the most abstruse problems.[8]

Title transfer was not complicated in the face-to-face transactions of an agrarian society. But when the buyer of goods is located in another state or region of the country, the passing of title issue becomes more complex—when goods are transported by rail, there is a time when neither seller nor buyer has possession of the goods. Who has title during the time of transit? Title mattered because it determined which party bore the risk of loss if anything happened to the goods in transit.

> This interlocking set of legal rules which developed to clarify sales of chattel was as much property law as it was sales law. This confusion of unlike concepts had results which were to become increasingly restrictive as techniques of production and distribution grew in complexity.[9]

---

5   Friedman, "Formative Elements in the Law of Sales: The Eighteenth Century," 44 *Minn. L. Rev.* 411. 414 (1960).

6   Kimball, "Langdell on Contracts and Legal Reasoning: Correcting the Holmesian Caricature," 25 *Law & Hist. Rev.* 345, 358 (2007).

7   Friedman, 415.

8   Gilmore, "The Difficulties of Codifying Commercial Law," 57 *Yale L. J.* 1341, 1343 (1948).

9   *Id.* at 1342.

The emergence of a national market as part of this transformation of business, and with it the increase in the variety of goods available, had a profound impact on

> contract law, the area of law that arose to establish settled rules to facilitate planning for the future.... Contracting, like conversation, in earlier times had been rooted in the past. People who knew one another and who knew the local market, insulated as it was from dramatic shifts in the economy, faced little likelihood of changes in circumstances that would require elaborate agreements or provoke complex disputes. Railroads and cities, however, seemed to disrupt that past by bringing economic uncertainty into the local markets.... To compensate for the new problems and to reduce uncertainty, parties turned to new forms of contractual arrangements with increasing frequency.[10]

These new forms often lacked the specificity that courts had come to expect in an enforceable agreement, and initially the courts refused to enforce them. For example, a railroad with plans to expand its service area might not want to commit to purchase a specific quantity of the iron it would need for new tracks, but it needed to know with certainty that whatever it did need, it could get. If a seller of iron was willing to commit to sell the railroad whatever it needed in order to foreclose a portion of the market for iron from competition, the parties could agree to leave the quantity term open in their sales agreement. Open contracts allowed the parties to protect themselves against some of the uncertainties inherent in large markets for fungible goods.

But contract law required mutuality of obligation before it would enforce a contract—both parties must have actually committed to do something, and since the railroad had not actually committed to buy *any* iron, a court would not—could not—enforce the contract under controlling precedent. The unwillingness of courts to enforce such agreements, however, did not inhibit their use—they were far too useful in the new world of business to be abandoned simply because judges wedded to the old ways refused to recognize their legitimacy.

> The widespread use of open contracts did present a dilemma for courts—a dilemma that emphasized to the judges the weakening power of the past. If they adhered to precedent they would impede what appeared to be a needed contractual practice; if they were to enforce the new agreements they had to develop a new rationale.[11]

Eventually the courts gave in to social utility and allowed open-term contracts to be enforced—but not by conceding the fallibility of the mutuality doctrine; instead, for these new agreements, they discovered a place within existing doctrine that had previously been overlooked. Some—cynics—saw this "discovery" as manipulation, but if you were a merchant, this was the result you wanted. Or was it?

Even though the common law would, eventually, sometimes catch up with the evolving forms that sales transactions were taking,

a...

> [t]he object of the man of business is not to get a scientific decision on a particular point, but to avoid litigation altogether. On the whole, he would rather have a somewhat inconvenient rule clearly stated than a more convenient rule worked out by a series of protracted and expensive litigations, pending which he does not know how to act.... The mercantile view is this: [l]aw is made *by* lawyers, but not *for* lawyers, it is made for laymen, who have to regulate the conduct of their business in accordance with the rules laid down by the law.[12]

By the start of the twentieth century, there existed an

---

10   Pratt, "American Contract Law at the Turn of the Century," 39 *S. Car. L. Rev.* 415, 428, 434 (1988).
11   Pratt, 442.
12   Chalmers, "Codification of Mercantile Law," 19 *L. Q. Rev.* 10 (1903) (italics in original).

almost unbelievable discrepancy *between sales case law ... and the commercial needs current even then.* This discrepancy was the product of the failure of the case-law [sic] of Sales, since about 1850, to develop *with any consistency* a set of concepts and lines of legal analysis so built as to focus the issues that arose when the mercantile world [changed the way it did business]. Unfocused issues means blurred results and blurred rules. Blurred results and rules mean that the *results* of the law are difficult to foresee ...[13]

The other problem with the common-law approach in America was that there were, at the start of the twentieth century, forty-five jurisdictions interpreting and applying that common law. Certainty—and the predictability that follows from it—are important to businesspeople, but so, too, is uniformity when their business takes their transactions across state lines.

As more and more goods made their way from the local market into the national market, the calls for uniformity in the law that governed sales transactions grew louder. And as the common law had proven—in the view of many of those affected by it—inept (at best) or unwilling (at worst) to embrace the new forms of transactions buyers and sellers were using to move goods, the resistance to legislative intervention was not very strong. In 1892, the National Conference of Commissioners on Uniform State Laws (NCCUSL) was established to promote uniformity in state law in the areas in which it determined the law should be uniform, and shortly thereafter began work on a code of sales law for adoption by the states. England had already codified its sales law with the Sales of Goods Act of 1893, and the sales law developed by NCCUSL and presented to the states for their consideration in 1906 as the Uniform Sales Act (USA) incorporated much of the English Act.

Although the USA was well received at the time it was ready for adoption by the states, by 1920 fewer than half of the states had adopted it, and a new movement began for adoption of a federal sales act to secure the national uniformity that the USA had failed to achieve. Critics of the USA claimed that it had fallen far short of aligning sales law with the commercial world as it existed at the start of the twentieth century. One of its major flaws was that it had retained the property-based concept of a sales transaction, with its focus on the location of title that was, in the view of many, "diametrically opposed to commercial practice"[14] and had been the primary problem under the common law. Karl Llewellyn, who would become the principal draftsperson for what became Article 2 of the Uniform Commercial Code (and whom we will come to know quite well in the chapters that follow this one), claimed in 1930 that, although the USA had done some good, it was already obsolete:

> The concepts that took shape on the basis of face-to-face dealing with present goods have in a short century and a quarter been tortured into application to the nationwide indirect marketing structure of today. The Act cleared away much rubbish and produced about as workable a rebuilt machine on the old model as was humanly possible.... But I think the Act fell short of drawing the systemic conclusions called for in its own more radical (and needed) sections, much less those called for by developments since.[15]

Later, he would be less than kind in his critique of the principles on which the USA was built:

> Let us take the case of one particularly significant type of hitch: "*The buyer" goes back on "his" bargain.* The question is whether "the seller" can recover the price, or only damages. The issue is real, narrow, and, under our law, important. But it is also, as we pose it, technically silly. To a silly issue no sane answer is possible. This one we currently pose thus: Has title passed? and solve by locating a mythical—or should I say more accurately "mystical"?—essence known

---

13   I Kelly, *Uniform Commercial Code: Drafts,* (Rothman, 1984) 288–298 (italics in original).
14   Gilmore, at 1348.
15   *Id.* at 1348.

as Title, which is hung over the buyer's head *or* the seller's like a halo. Halos are, it appears, indivisible. And there is only one halo for buyer or seller to make out with. This does not, as our orthodox doctrine goes, require explanation. It is simply so.[16]

By the late1930s, Llewellyn and others who had been pushing for a federal sales act for more than a decade decided to turn the reform movement in a different direction. They began to lobby NCCUSL to prepare amendments to the USA as an alternative to the federal sales act that had never gotten traction in Congress. They eventually persuaded NCCUSL to get involved, and Llewellyn was given the charge to prepare a revised Uniform Sales Act. But Llewellyn was not interested in making repairs to an act he thought was obsolete before it was ever enacted; instead, he wanted to build a new sales law based on the realities of modern commercial practice, to "redraw the basic blueprint." What Llewellyn presented to the Conference in 1940 was a sales law reformulated "in light of his normative vision of both mercantile practice and judicial decision making" and which by 1944 had evolved into what we know today as Article 2 of the Uniform Commercial Code.[17]

---

16   Llewellyn, "Through Title to Contract and a Bit Beyond," 15 *N.Y.U. L.Q.* 159, 165 (1938).
17   This paragraph is based upon Prof. Wiseman's article, pp. 483–492. The quotes are from pp. 489 and 492.

CHAPTER 2

SCOPE

We begin our journey through Article 2 by identifying the transactions to which it actually applies. Initially, Article 2 appears to stake out a very broad claim to the territory it covers. But, like other articles of the Code, it then proceeds to carve out of that territory those transactions which at their very core are not "sales," as well as those involving "specified classes of buyers" that are regulated by other statutes. From a drafting perspective, it's more efficient and more effective to start broad and then carve out than to build scope from detailed specifics. As one member of the Code drafting team noted, it was

> a matter of vital importance that the Code as a whole be kept in terms of such generality as to allow easy and unstrained applications of its provisions to new patterns of business behavior. Commercial codification cannot successfully over particularize; the penalty for being too precise is that the statute will have to keep coming in for repairs.... or else become a dead letter.[1]

The basic scope provision of Article 2, 2-102, tells us that Article 2 cares about "transactions in goods." "Transactions" is not defined in Article 2, but "goods" is: 2-105(1) tells us that "goods" are "all things ... which are moveable at the time of identification to the contract for sale"—tangible personal property, the kind of things you can hold, hug, or pass around the room. So, "transactions" involving "goods" then would seem to include everything from your purchase of this book to a security interest in a toaster, as well as the lease of furniture for your apartment and the donation of your car to the public radio station where you live. Does Article 2 really care about all of these "transactions"? As it turns out, Article 2 only cares about transactions involving "goods" when those goods have been "identified to a contract for sale." By definition, a "sale" occurs when title to goods is passed by a seller to a buyer for a price. 2-106(1). In other words, a sale occurs when the owner of goods (the seller) transfers her rights of ownership to another person (the buyer) in return for something (the price).

So, where does that leave us in our quest to define the scope of Article 2—to identify the "transactions" that Article 2 ultimately cares about? First, the transactions Article 2 cares about take the form of sales—transactions in which one party conveys its rights of ownership in tangible personal

---

1   Gilmore, "On the Difficulties of Codifying Commercial Law," 57 *Yale L. J.* 1341, 1355 (1948).

property to another party in exchange for an agreed consideration provided by that other party. That means the security interest you granted in your toaster is not an Article 2 transaction because you did not convey your rights of ownership to the secured party.[2] Your lease of the furniture for your apartment is likewise not covered by Article 2 because all you acquired from the lessor under the lease was the right to possess the furniture for the term of the lease; you do not own the furniture during the lease term. And Article 2 does not care about the donation of your car to the public radio station: you may have conveyed title to the car to the radio station, but not for a price—you asked for and received nothing in return for your donation other than, perhaps, the thank-you phone call from the station manager. No "sale" was involved. So that leaves your purchase of this book: the bookstore transferred title of the book to you when you paid the price—we have a transaction in goods that Article 2 cares about.

What if, instead, you had ordered the book from the publisher, but the publisher could not send it to you until it printed a new edition? At the time of your order, there was no book—no tangible property, and so no "good." Does Article 2 care about your book order? Goods not yet in existence are designated as "future goods," and a present sale of future goods "operates as a contract to *sell*." 2-105 (emphasis added). The "contracts for sale" that Article 2 cares about include both "a present sale of [existing] goods" as well as "a contract to *sell* goods [not in existence] at a future time." 2-106 (emphasis added). Your contract to purchase the book is therefore a contract for sale that Article 2 cares about.

Second, Article 2 only cares about sales of "goods"—what we have characterized as tangible personal property. But where to draw the line between tangible and intangible property, especially in light of the technology that has now become an integral part of human existence, has not always been clear, and becomes less clear as that technology continues to evolve. Is your purchase of a song from iTunes for downloading onto your iPod a sale of goods covered by Article 2? And what do we do with transactions that involve more than just goods—does the service agreement you purchased along with your new television change the nature of the transaction for the purposes of Article 2? Are the braces supplied by your orthodontist covered by Article 2? What about the new website you paid a web designer to create for you? Because the answers to these and similar questions will determine the outer reaches of Article 2's scope, we explore them in detail in the following sections.

A. DOES THE TRANSACTION INVOLVE GOODS?

Article 2 cares about sales of goods and defines goods in terms of moveability, which implies that goods have a physical presence: they are tangible—things we can hold, hug, and pass around the room. Sales law had always confined its scope to transactions involving tangible things when Llewelyn began drafting Article 2 in the 1940s, and there was little reason to believe at that time that a law of sales built around the transfer of tangible personal property would work to exclude any significant amount of commercial activity in the future.[3] But an increasing amount of commercial transactions today involve things that, in their original form, have no physical presence, but which are given a tangible form to facilitate their transfer from one person to another. Computer programs are merely "1s" and "0s" in their original form, but they can be given tangible form by incorporation into a computer disc or a computer. Is the sale of a computer program a transaction in goods that Article 2 cares about? The courts have not provided consistent answers to this question or to the same question when applied to other forms of technology. As a result, a major revision of Article 2 intended to "modernize" the law

---

2   Of course, 2-102 expressly excludes a transaction that creates a security interest in goods; but, based on our examination of Article 2's definitions, such a transaction would not fall within the scope of Article 2 had it not been expressly excluded.

3   See, generally, Gilmore, "On the Difficulties of Codifying Commercial Law," 57 *Yale L. J.* 1341 (1948).

of sales was promulgated at the beginning of the twenty-first century, but it was ultimately withdrawn when it failed to gain passage in any state. A later, more limited "amendment" of Article 2 has suffered a similar fate.

So, we are left to define the outer reaches of Article 2's scope using the original goods-based (tangible property) test the drafters provided. As the following case illustrates, that process can have a metaphysical dimension to it.

GFI Wis., Inc. v. Reedsburg Util. Comm'n

United States District Court for the Western District of Wisconsin, 2010
440 B.R. 791

CRABB, *District Judge.*

Appellant GFI Wisconsin, Inc., formerly known as Grede Foundries, Inc., appeals an order of the bankruptcy court allowing appellees Reedsburg Utility Commission and Wisconsin Electric Power Company to claim administrative priority status under *11 U.S.C. §503(b)(9)* for the value of electricity they supplied to appellant during the 20 days before appellant filed for bankruptcy. Appellant contends that because electricity is not a "good" within the meaning of *§ 503(b)(9)*, the bankruptcy court should have disallowed the claim.

I agree with the bankruptcy court that appellees may claim administrative priority for the electricity they provided appellant in the 20-day period before appellant filed its bankruptcy petition. Therefore, I will affirm the decision of the bankruptcy court denying appellant's objection to the claims.

BACKGROUND

A. Facts before the Bankruptcy Court

On June 30, 2009, appellant GFI Wisconsin, formerly known as Grede Foundries, Inc., filed a chapter 11 bankruptcy petition in this district. Appellant owned several properties in Wisconsin that received electricity from appellees Reedsburg Utility Commission and Wisconsin Electric Power Company over a time period that includes the 20 days before the petition date.

On September 25, 2009, appellees submitted claims seeking administrative priority status under *§ 503(b)(9)* for the value of the electricity they provided appellant during the 20-day period. Appellant objected to the claims on several grounds, one of which was that electric services are not goods for purposes of *§ 503(b)(9)*. Appellees challenged appellant's objection and the parties agreed to submit the claims and objections to the bankruptcy court on stipulations of facts and briefs, forgoing an evidentiary hearing.

On March 29, 2010, appellant filed motions to disallow the claims, a brief in support of the motions and facts to which the parties had stipulated. Among other things, they stipulated that

- The electricity supplied by [appellees] to [appellant] during the Twenty-Day Period was metered at [appellant's] premises as it was being drawn and consumed by [appellant]; and
- Given the regulatory requirement that [appellees] make a pro rata estimate of the charges incurred during the Twenty-Day Period, [appellant] does not object to the amount of the Twenty-Day Claim.

In its brief, appellant argued that appellees' claims were for electrical services, not goods, because electricity is not movable and identifiable at the time of the contract of sale, as required under the definition of goods found in the Uniform Commercial Code, *Wis. Stat. § 402.105(1)(c)*. Appellant also argued that § 503(b)(9) claims are limited to goods capable of being reclaimed by a creditor, and electricity cannot be reclaimed.

In their responses, appellees also relied on the UCC definition of goods and argued that electricity is both movable and identifiable at the time it is metered and thus, satisfies the definition of goods under the UCC. Appellees relied heavily on *In re Erving Industries, Inc., 432 B.R. 354 (Bankr. D. Mass. Apr. 7, 2010)*, in which the bankruptcy court concluded that electricity is a good. Appellees cited specifically the following language in *Erving Industries*:

> At the time the electricity is identified to the contract [by passing through the meter], it is literally moving, and it remains movable for some period of time thereafter. The electricity continues to move through the customer's electrical wiring until it is ultimately put to use. This process may occur at speeds so imperceptible that consumption appears to occur simultaneous with identification, but logic compels the conclusion that electricity is moving (and remains in motion) until it reaches the product sought to be electrified.

Appellant filed a reply brief attempting to distinguish *Erving Industries* and discredit its conclusion. First, significant differences between the Massachusetts and Wisconsin electricity markets made the case distinguishable. Second, as a matter of physics, electricity is not movable after it has been metered. Appellant submitted the affidavit of Kevin Vesperman, an engineer, to explain the nature of electricity. Vesperman described the nature of electricity as follows:

> [N]o movement of electrons will occur until the customer's load is connected and a circuit is completed. When the load is connected, the electrons begin to flow and create electric energy, and simultaneously, the electric energy is 'consumed.' With no customer load, no electrons move and no electric current is measured. In addition, the movement of electricity (electric energy current) is virtually instantaneous from one end of the conductor to the other end ... Therefore, when it is consumed, it is simultaneously measured. Movement does not take place after measurement by the meter. The court's conclusion [in *Erving*] that electricity 'passes through' the meter and continues to the customer for use thereafter does not match the actual physics. Electric energy is not like natural gas or water where those materials physically pass through the meter and then to the consumptive use.... The electric energy is not 'movable' after metering; it does not 'move' to some other final consumptive use after metering. Instead, the consumptive use is simultaneous with the metering.

B. Bankruptcy Court Decision

In determining whether electricity qualified as a good under § 503(b)(9), the court applied the UCC definition of "goods" found in *UCC § 2-105* and found that the electricity at issue was movable when it entered the meter and moved from the power source to the meter to appellant's facilities. Because the electricity was moving, even if the movement was so fast as to be "nonexistent," it qualified as a good. The court rejected appellant's argument that electricity cannot be a good because it cannot be reclaimed under § 546(c).

OPINION

Section 503(b)(9) of the Bankruptcy Code provides administrative priority to recovery of "the value of goods received by the debtor within the 20 days before the commencement [of the bankruptcy case] in which the goods have been sold to the debtor in the ordinary course of such debtor's business." *11 U.S.C. § 503(b)(9)*. Although courts are divided on what constitutes *goods* under § 503(b)(9), the plain language of the statute does not allow creditor claims arising from the provision of *services* to a debtor.

Appellant raises three issues for review: (1) whether the bankruptcy court erred in finding that the electricity provided by appellees was a good for purposes of *§ 503(b)(9)*.

* * *

A. Electricity as a "Good"

The first question to be answered is what qualifies as a "good" under *§ 503(b)(9)*. The Bankruptcy Code does not define goods and there is no controlling case law construing the term as it is used in this section of the Bankruptcy Code. (The provision was added to the Code in 2005 as part of the Bankruptcy Abuse Prevention and Consumer Protection Act and has been analyzed by only a few bankruptcy courts.) Every bankruptcy court to consider the issue, including the court below, has applied the Uniform Commercial Code definition of goods, found in *UCC § 2-105*. The courts reason that using the UCC definition will support uniformity because forty-nine states have adopted some version of the UCC. In addition, the courts dismiss the idea that they should craft a new definition of goods because "where words are employed in a statute which had at the time a well-known meaning at common law or in the law of this country, they are presumed to have been used in that sense."

It is possible that the meaning of goods for purposes of *§503(b)(9) of the Bankruptcy Code* is different from the meaning of goods under the UCC because the laws have different purposes. *Section 503(b)(9)* is a priority provision, unique to federal law. Presumably, one of reasons *§503(b)(9)* was enacted was to prevent debtors from stockpiling "goods" in the days leading up to their bankruptcy filings. The UCC uses the term "goods" to delineate the scope of all of Article 2 and to determine whether the UCC applies to a particular transaction. *UCC § 2-102* ("[T]his Article applies to goods....").

However, the bankruptcy court below and the parties in this case assume that the UCC definition applies. Absent a different definition in the Bankruptcy Code or controlling case law, I conclude that it is reasonable to apply the definition provided by the UCC, as courts often do when interpreting Bankruptcy Code provisions. The UCC has been accepted by nearly all of the states and governs the sale of goods. Thus, most participants in the marketplace would not be surprised that the definition of "goods" that applies to ordinary transactions governed by the UCC would govern the meaning of the term in bankruptcy.

The UCC defines "goods" as "all things ... which are movable at the time of identification to a contract for sale." *UCC § 2-105*. The term includes future goods, specially manufactured goods, the unborn young of animals, growing crops and other identified things attached to realty as described in *§ 2-107*. The term does not include "information, the money in which the price is to be paid, investment securities under Article 8, the subject matter of foreign transactions, or choses in action." To constitute goods under *§ 503(b)(9)* then, the thing at issue must be identifiable, movable, have value and be received by the debtor during the 20-day period preceding the petition date.

Having decided the proper test to apply, I turn to the next question, which is whether the electricity delivered by appellees to appellant during the 20 days before its chapter 11 petition qualifies as a "good." The parties agree that the electric energy that is the subject of their contract was "identified to the contract" at the time it was metered, but they dispute whether the electricity was "movable" at the time it was metered.

Courts have reached different conclusions on whether electricity is a good under the UCC or Bankruptcy Code. Compare *In re MBS Management Services, Inc., 430 B.R. 750, 753 (Bankr. E.D. La. 2010)* (citing decision in Erving Industries for proposition that electricity is "commodity" under Bankruptcy Code), *Erving Industries, 432 B.R. at 370* (electricity is "good" under UCC and *§ 503(b)(9)*), *Enron Power Marketing, Inc. v. Nevada Power Co.*, 2004 U.S. Dist. LEXIS 20351, 2004 WL 2290486, *2 (S.D.N.Y. Oct. 12, 2004) (applying UCC Article 2 to sale of electricity), *In re Pacific Gas & Electric Co.*, 271 B.R. 626, 640 (N.D. Cal. 2002) (electricity is "good" under UCC), *Cincinnati Gas & Electric Co. v. Goebel*, 28 Ohio B. 144, 502 N.E.2d 713, 715 (Ohio Mun. Ct. 1986) (electricity that has passed through utility-owned conduits, through meters and into homes of consumers is "good" as defined in UCC), with *In re Pilgrim's Pride Corp.,* 421 B.R. 231, 239 & n.8 (Bankr. N.D. Tex. 2009) (electricity not "good" under § 503(b)(9)), *Samaritan Alliance,* 2008 Bankr. LEXIS 1830, 2008 WL 2520107, *at *4* (same), *United States v. Consolidated Edison Co. of New York, Inc.,* 590 F. Supp. 266, 269 (S.D.N.Y. 1984) (UCC not applicable directly to contracts for sale of electricity because electricity not "good"), and *Buckeye Union Fire Ins. Co. v. Detroit Edison Co.,* 38 Mich. App. 325, 196 N.W.2d 316 (Mich. App. 1972) (electricity not "good" as defined in UCC).

Appellant contends that the answer to whether electricity is a movable good requires analysis of the physical nature of electricity, as well as the provisions in the Bankruptcy Code addressing utility providers and reclamation rights. Turning first to the physical nature of electricity, appellant contends that the bankruptcy court reached a clearly erroneous conclusion that electricity is movable at the time it was metered because the facts in the record establish, as a matter of physics, that electricity is not movable when it is metered because it is consumed at the same time it is metered.

The only facts in the record were those facts stipulated by the parties and those contained in Vesperman's affidavit. The parties stipulated in the bankruptcy court that the electricity supplied by appellees to appellant during the 20-day period was "metered at [appellant's] premises *as it was being drawn and consumed* by [appellant]." Vesperman asserted that the conclusion of the court in *Erving Industries* "does not match the reality of the physics of electric energy," because "[m]ovement does not take place after measurement by the meter." Vesperman explained that "the movement of electricity (electric energy current) is virtually instantaneous from one end of the conductor to the other end. Therefore, when it is consumed, it is simultaneously measured."

Appellant contends that the only finding that could reasonably be drawn from these facts is that electricity is not moving at the time it is metered and is therefore, non-movable. In its order, however, the bankruptcy court found the following:

- "the electricity was movable when it entered the meter";
- the "meter was installed in the middle of the circuit";
- "electrons flow rapidly through the circuit from the power source to the load";
- "the movement [is] 'virtually instantaneous'";
- "electrons are moving from the power source to the meter to the load"; and
- even though electrical flow is "rapid[] and at a subatomic level," the movement is sufficient to satisfy the definition of goods in the UCC.

Arguably, some of the bankruptcy court's findings exceed the facts described in Vesperman's affidavit and the stipulations of the parties, neither of which identifies where on the circuit the meter is located or concedes that electricity flows from the power source to the meter to the load. However, it is clear that the bankruptcy court credited Vesperman's statement that "the movement of electricity (electric energy current) is virtually instantaneous from one end of the conductor to the other end." The bankruptcy court relied on this statement to conclude that although the movement of electricity may be rapid and subatomic and "so fast as to be nonexistent," an electric current is literally moving through the transmission network and continues to move until it is delivered to a customer *at the time* it is metered and consumed. The bankruptcy court found this movement sufficient for electricity to qualify as a movable good. In addition, the court noted that under the UCC, water and natural gas are considered movable goods, and "there is no principled distinction to be made between natural gas, water, or electricity." See also *UCC § 2-107(1)* ("A contract for the sale of minerals or the like (including oil and gas) … is a contract for the sale of goods within this Article….").

I conclude that the bankruptcy court ruled correctly that electricity is a "good" within the meaning of § 503(b)(9) of the Code. Determining the physical nature of electricity is complex. It requires an understanding of the nature of electrons and a grasp of quantum physics and special relativity. For the purpose of determining administrative priority under the Bankruptcy Code, the meaning of "goods" under the UCC should not depend on quantum physics, how fast electrons are moving at a particular time or even where a debtor's meter is located on an electrical circuit. Rather, determining whether a particular thing qualifies as a good and deserves administrative priority should be a straightforward assessment, taking into consideration the nature and common understanding of the thing, but also considering its similarities to goods that fall undisputedly under the UCC and would receive administrative priority under § 503(b)(9).

Few courts deciding how electricity should be treated under the UCC or other laws focus solely or even primarily on the physics of electricity; rather, they consider the general movability of electricity, common perceptions of electricity and the exchange of electricity as a commodity in the marketplace. For example, the bankruptcy court in *Erving Industries, 432 B.R. at 370*, stated that it is "logical" that electricity would be considered a good under the *§ 503(b)(9)* because it is both identifiable and moving until it reaches the intended customer. Similarly, in *Pacific Gas*, the court considered how electricity had been treated in other areas of the law and concluded that metering satisfies the identification requirement of the UCC and moving through a circuit satisfies the movability requirement. *Id.* ("Simply put, electricity in this instance is a thing movable at the time of identification to the contract for sale.")

Similarly, courts determining whether electricity is "property" or a "product" for purposes of product liability, theft or other purposes, focus on the general physical nature of electricity and its movability. E.g., *Commonwealth v. Catalano*, 74 Mass. App. Ct. 580, 908 N.E.2d 842, 845-46 (Mass. App. Ct. 2009) (electricity is "personal chattel" that may be subject of larceny because it "may be stored and conveyed ... may be transmitted through wires ... [and the] [q]uantity of consumption is measurable"); *Monroe v. Savannah Electric & Power Co.*, 267 Ga. 26, 471 S.E.2d 854, 855-56 (Ga. 1996) (electricity is product for strict liability purposes because it can be "produced, confined, controlled, transmitted, and distributed in the stream of commerce ... [and] can be measured, bought and sold, changed in quantity or quality [and] delivered wherever desired") (internal citations and quotations omitted); *Bryant v. Tri-County Electric Membership Corp.*, 844 F. Supp. 347, 349 (W.D. Ky. 1994) (electricity is product under strict liability law because it "can be made or produced ... confined, controlled, transmitted and distributed").

I agree with those courts concluding that electricity is movable, tangible and consumable, that it has physical properties, that it is bought and sold in the marketplace and thus, that it qualifies as a good for purposes of the UCC and the Bankruptcy Code. As noted by the bankruptcy court below, electricity begins flowing through power lines when a circuit is formed and continues moving at least until it is metered. The metering satisfies the identification requirement of the UCC and the movement is sufficient to satisfy the movability requirement, even if it reaches the speed of light. *Pacific Gas & Electric*, 271 B.R. at 640 (electricity is "good" because it can be moved through power lines and identified through meters); see also *Helvey v. Wabash County REMC*, 151 Ind. App. 176, 278 N.E.2d 608, 610 (Ind. App. 1972) (analogizing electricity to natural gas and finding that electricity satisfies movability and identifiability requirements of UCC as it moves into meter).

I disagree with the court in *Pilgrim's Pride*, 421 B.R. at 234, which held that electricity is not similar enough to goods that fall under the *UCC § 2-105*, because such goods occupy space, can be packaged, handled and moved. The court held that electricity is similar to television, radio, telephone, and Internet signals that would not be considered goods under the UCC. However, electricity can be moved, as explained by appellant's expert and found by the bankruptcy court; it can be consumed, as stipulated by the parties; and there is no suggestion that electricity cannot be packaged and handled, such as in a battery. In addition, as the court noted in *Erving Industries*, electricity is different from telecommunication signals because it is not merely a medium of delivering something else; it is the "thing" the customer seeks to purchase. *Erving Industries*, "[I]t is those physical properties, the very nature of electricity, that customers contract to purchase."

In sum, taking into consideration the physical properties of electricity as noted by appellant's expert and the bankruptcy court, including the fact that electricity is movable, and the parties' agreement under which the energy usage and consumption were determined by meter readings, I conclude that electricity is a good under the UCC definition and also under the Bankruptcy Code.

The *GFI Wisconsin* case aptly illustrates how "wondrously inexact and elastic" is the definition of goods provided by Article 2.[4] But that may be just how the drafters wanted the definition to work. The comment to the purpose provision of the UCC as a whole notes the drafters' intent to "make it possible for the law embodied in the Act to be developed by the courts in the light of unforeseen and new circumstances and practices." Comment 1, 1-102.

Problem 2 - 1

Every day, lots of buying and selling goes on at the supermarket Rae has been managing for her family since her father retired five years ago. Determine which, if any, of the following transactions Article 2 cares about:

1. Her agreement to purchase a truckload of canned beans for the store. The sale of a can of beans to her neighbor. The sale of a case of beans to her daughter's school for student lunches.
2. Her agreement to purchase a commercial bakery oven so the store could sell fresh, homemade bread. The sale of the bread to the store's customers.
3. Her agreement to purchase tomatoes from a grower in California. Does it matter if the tomatoes have not been planted when she orders them? 2-105.
4. Her agreement to purchase raspberries from a local grower. 2-107(2). Does the answer change if someone from the store has to pick and pack the berries? 2-107(1).
5. The sale of hamburger ground by the store's butcher department for its customers. The sale of sausage the store makes for cookouts during the summer. The sale of sandwiches made by the deli department for its customers. Does it matter whether the customers eat the sandwiches at the store or take them out? 2-314(1).
6. The sale of cakes the store makes and decorates to order for its customers during the holidays. 2-105(1).
7. The trade of the store's old shopping carts for a forklift. 2-304.
8. The sale of a side of beef for one hundred shares of Microsoft stock. 2-105(1) and 2-304(2).
9. The sale of raffle tickets at ten dollars each for a chance to win a freezer full of beef—the proceeds of ticket sales going to fund the local high school band's trip to London.
10. The local power company's agreement to supply the store with electricity.
11. The store's agreement to purchase two hundred cubic feet of dirt from the local nursery for land-scaping around the store.

Problem 2 - 2

Rae agreed to lease the store's checkout scanners from Honeywell for a term of five years. The total lease payments were equal to the purchase price of the scanners, and Rae agreed to pay any charges for service to the scanners during the term of the lease. The lease required Rae to return all of the scanners in good

---

4   Nimmer, "Images and Contract Law—What Law Applies to Transactions in Information," 36 *Hous. L. Rev.* 1 (1999).

condition at the end of the five-year term. Does Article 2 care about Rae's lease with Honeywell? Would your answer be different if the useful life of the scanners was five years? Or if Rae had the option to purchase the scanners for one dollar at the end of the lease? 1-203.

PROBLEM 2 - 3

Rae has arranged to purchase spring water from the owner of an underground artesian well located just outside of town. The water is sourced from an aquifer that has recently become pressurized and is rich in many of the minerals that experts advise are important to good health. Rae plans to sell the water from the kiosk she's had built for it in the store's parking lot. The contract provides that the seller will pump the water into fifty-gallon drums for pickup by Rae. Is Rae's contract to purchase water subject to Article 2? Would your answer be different if the contract required Rae to pump the water from the well into the fifty-gallon drums? 2-107.

B. DOES THE TRANSACTION INVOLVE MORE THAN GOODS?

Does Article 2 apply when there is more to a transaction than just a sale of goods? Section 2-102 implies only that an Article 2 transaction must include a sale of goods—it does not preclude Article 2 coverage if that sale of goods is only one part of the transaction. Does it matter that the furnace you bought for your home was installed by the vendor? Or that the sprinkler system for your yard was designed, built, and installed by the seller? Does Article 2 apply to the sale of your favorite shoe store that includes the building, inventory, accounts receivable, and goodwill? How about the contact lenses you purchased last week? Or the accounting system you purchased for your law office that included installation, six months of training, and lifetime system support? In each of these transactions, there is a goods component. Should Article 2 apply simply because somewhere in the transaction we can find a transfer of tangible property? Article 2 does not directly answer this question—and so the courts have had to work it out on their own.

Where the seller of goods also provides a service or services related to the goods—installation of a security system and subsequent monitoring, for example—we could treat the transaction as an Article 2 sale because it includes goods (the alarm system), or we could exclude it from Article 2 because it involves services (the installation and monitoring), which are subject to general contract law. Or we might apply Article 2 if the dispute involves the goods or general contract law if it involves the services. Depending on the nature of the dispute, the one we choose could be outcome determinative. Article 2 dispenses with the mirror-image rule, the absence of which could change the outcome of a formation dispute. Similarly, Article 2 substitutes the perfect-tender rule for the doctrine of material breach, which could change the consequences of a party's defective performance. So it really can matter whether we call it an Article 2 transaction or leave it to the general law of contract.

Most courts use some version of a "predominant purpose" test to determine whether Article 2 applies to a transaction that involves goods and services. If the main purpose of the transaction was the sale of the goods, then Article 2 applies. If the main purpose of the transaction was to obtain the seller's services, general contract law applies. However, as the *Audio Visual Artistry* and *Golden* cases illustrate, the test is often simpler to state than it is to apply.

AUDIO VISUAL ARTISTRY V. TANZER
COURT OF APPEALS OF TENNESSEE, 2012
403 S.W.3D 789

STAFFORD, Judge.

This is a breach of contract case. Appellant/Homeowner contracted with Appellee for the installation of a "smart home" system. After myriad problems arose, Appellant fired Appellee, who filed the instant lawsuit to collect the unpaid balance for equipment and installation. The trial court determined that the primary purpose of the parties' agreement was the sale of goods and applied Article 2 of the Uniform Commercial Code.

On or about March 26, 2004, Appellant Stephen Tanzer and Appellee Audio Video Artistry ("AVA") entered into discussions for the sale and installation of electronic and entertainment equipment in Mr. Tanzer's home. AVA is a residential entertainment and communications firm specializing in custom design projects.

Based upon their discussion, AVA submitted a proposal to Mr. Tanzer for components, parts, and installation, totaling $78,567.13.

On September 22, 2004, AVA and Mr. Tanzer entered into a written contract, which incorporates the original proposal.

* * *

As originally contemplated, the contract called for a Concierge whole-house audio system. The audio/visual items were to be integrated via the Crestron system, which would allow Mr. Tanzer to play music in the seven, independently controlled music "zones."[5] Remote control "touch-panels" would control and integrate DVD, television, music, and other smart home functions. The contract further included a Lutron automated lighting system, which would be integrated into the Crestron system, along with an intercom/phone/whole house networking system.

At the time the parties entered their contract, construction had just commenced on Mr. Tanzer's home. The home is not a usual residence; rather, it is an approximately 15,000 square foot, $3.5 million dollar build. Because of the size and scope of the project, AVA was to install certain wiring and equipment during the construction process. Mr. Tanzer and his family moved into the home in April 2006.

Mr. Tanzer eventually became unsatisfied with AVA's work. Mr. Tanzer contends that, based upon Mr. Parsley's statements, he thought that the installation, programming, and debugging of the "smart home" system would take less than three months. However, Mr. Tanzer claims that, after fifteen months, he was still having significant problems with the functionality of the system.

Both the original equipment and work and the additional work, equipment, and changes were set out in Invoice #3036, which was presented by AVA to Mr. Tanzer. This Invoice shows a total project cost of $119,402.15, and reflects an outstanding balance of $43,824.55. Mr. Tanzer disputed this balance and the instant lawsuit ensued.

On November 19, 2007, AVA filed suit against Mr. Tanzer for breach of contract. On December 31, 2007, Mr. Tanzer filed his answer, in which he denies any liability. Concurrent with the answer, Mr. Tanzer filed a counter-complaint against AVA, alleging that AVA breached the contract and seeking damages for the breach. AVA answered the counter-complaint, denying any liability.

---

5   Crestron Electronics is a company that manufactures systems for home automation and audio/video control. The hardware developed by Crestron includes programmable controllers including touch panels, keypads, and lighting control systems. It sells its products through dealers who purchase and install Crestron systems for residential and commercial automation.

I. Applicability of UCC Article 2

In his first issue, Mr. Tanzer asserts that the trial court erred in applying UCC Article 2 to his contract with AVA. Specifically, Mr. Tanzer argues that thrust of the contract is for services and not for the sale of goods such that common-law breach of contract principles apply. We begin our analysis with *67 Am. Jur. 2d Sales § 37*, which provides:

> Article 2 [of the UCC] applies to transactions in goods but does not apply to construction contracts or contracts for the rendition of services. However, the existence of a sale in and of itself does not automatically implicate the Uniform Commercial Code. In many cases, a contract or transaction may involve both the transaction of a sale and the rendition of services, presenting a "mixed" or hybrid transaction or contract. To determine whether such "mixed" or "hybrid" contracts are governed by Article 2, a court must examine the whole transaction and look to the essence or main objective of the parties' agreement or the primary or overall purpose of the transaction.
>
> Ordinarily, a court determines whether a mixed contract for goods and services is subject to Article 2 by considering whether the contract, reasonably stated, is for goods with labor incidentally involved or for services with goods incidentally involved. The question is generally one of fact, involving a consideration of the contract in its entirety. Depending upon whether the contract or transaction is predominantly for the sale of goods or the rendition of services, Article 2 applies to the entire contract or not at all.
>
> *Id.* (footnotes omitted).

As further discussed in 1 Stephen W. Ramp & Katherine Simpson Allen, Tennessee Practice: Uniform Commercial Code Forms §2-106 (2d ed. 2002):

> A sale is the passing of title from the seller to the buyer for a price. Courts will consider the substance of the transaction rather than how the parties chose to label the transaction. Where the service component of a contract for sale overrides the goods aspect of the transaction it will not fall within Article 2 once the transaction is determined to be a service and not a sale.

The question of whether UCC Article 2 or common-law contract principles apply is important in terms of available warranties and the measure of damages.

As noted above in *67 Am. Jur. 2d Sales § 37*, many transactions are neither pure sale of goods nor pure service transactions, but a combination of the two, i.e. a hybrid contract. As discussed in Barkley Clark and Christopher Smith, The Law of Product Warranties §2:19 (2012):

> When faced with these hybrids, the courts have generally employed a predominant element test: If the service aspect predominates, tort theories must control (even as to defective goods), but if the goods aspect predominates, Article 2 warranties come into play (sometimes even with respect to the service component). This is a rather mechanical approach, but the courts favor it.
>
> *Id.* (footnotes omitted).

One of the earliest cases to adopt the predominant purpose test was *Bonebrake v. Cox*, 499 F.2d 951 (8th Cir. 1974), which involved a contract for the sale and installation of pre-fabricated bowling equipment. The *Bonebrake* Court noted that such hybrid contracts are legion and then proposed its test:

> The test for inclusion or exclusion is not whether they are mixed, but granting that they are mixed, whether their predominant factor, their thrust, their purpose, reasonably stated, is the rendition of service, with goods incidentally involved (e.g., contract with artist for painting),

or is a transaction of sale, with labor incidentally involved (e.g., installation of a water heater in a bathroom).

Id. at 960.

In the case of *Pass v. Shelby Aviation*, Tennessee adopted and applied the *Bonebrake* predominant purpose test. In that case, Max E. Pass, Jr., and his wife, Martha N. Pass, were both killed when their aircraft, piloted by Mr. Pass, crashed outside of Opelika, Alabama. Approximately four-and-one-half months prior to the fatal flight, Mr. Pass had taken the aircraft to defendant, Shelby Aviation, Inc., for inspection and service. During the servicing, Shelby Aviation replaced both rear wing attach point brackets on the plane.

After the crash, the administrators of the Pass's estates filed a lawsuit against Shelby Aviation. The suit alleged that the rear wing brackets, which were sold and installed by Shelby Aviation, were defective and asserted claims for breach of common-law warranties, and for breach of express and implied warranties under Article 2 of the UCC. Shelby Aviation filed a motion to dismiss for failure to state a claim, contending that, because the contract was primarily for services, Article 2 did not apply. The motion was denied, and Shelby Aviation requested, and was granted, permission to file an interlocutory appeal to this Court. The main issue on appeal was whether the transaction between Mr. Pass and Shelby Aviation was governed by Article 2.

This Court determined that the predominant purpose test was the appropriate test to apply because it looks at the transaction as a whole. In applying the test, the Court stated:

> To determine whether the predominant thrust of a mixed contract is to provide services or goods, one looks first to the language of the contract, in light of the situation of the parties and the surrounding circumstances. Specifically one looks to the terms describing the performance of the parties, and the words used to describe the relationship between the parties.
>
> Beyond the contractual terms themselves, one looks to the circumstances of the parties, and the primary reason they entered into the contract. One also considers the final product the purchaser bargained to receive, and whether it may be described as a good or a service.
>
> Finally, one examines the costs involved for the goods and services, and whether the purchaser was charged only for a good, or a price based on both goods and services. If the cost of the goods is but a small portion of the overall contract price, such fact would increase the likelihood that the services portion predominates.

Pass, (citing Insul-Mark, 612 N.E.2d at 555 (citations omitted)).

Applying the foregoing principles, the *Pass* Court determined that "the invoice clearly emphasizes the repair and inspection aspects of the transaction, indicating that the predominant purpose was the sale of service, with the sale of goods incidental to that service." Further, the overall nature of Shelby Aviation's business was service rather than the sale of parts, and "Mr. Pass took the plane to Shelby Aviation primarily to have a service performed, i.e., the annual inspection." Finally, the court looked to allocation of costs between goods and services. The court indicated that it did not favor adding the labor charges for installing the parts to the cost of the parts as was proposed by the plaintiffs, and then the court stated that:

> Regardless of how the percentage of the cost of goods is calculated, viewing the transaction as a whole, we must conclude that the predominant purpose of the transaction was the provision of a service rather than the sale of goods.... As such, it is not subject to the warranty provisions of Article 2 of the UCC. Shelby Aviation is entitled to judgment as a matter of law on the [p]laintiffs' UCC breach of warranty claims.

The decision denying Shelby Aviation's motion for summary judgment on the UCC breach of warranty claims was reversed, and the case was remanded for further proceedings. *Id.*

From *Pass*, we understand that, in applying the predominant purpose test, the court looks to four factors:

1. the language of the contract;
2. the nature of the business of the supplier of goods and services;
3. the reason the parties entered into the contract, and
4. the amounts paid for the rendition of the services and goods, respectively.

We now turn to address each of these factors based on the evidence contained in the record to determine whether the trial court correctly found that the contract at issue in this case predominantly involves the sale of goods such that UCC Article 2 is applicable.

A. Language of the Contract

The first factor set out by the *Pass* Court requires us to look "to the language of the contract, in light of the situation of the parties and the surrounding circumstances. Specifically, [the court] looks to the terms describing the performance of the parties, and the words used to describe the relationship between the parties." Contractual language that refers to the transaction as a "purchase," for example, or identifies the parties as the "buyer" and "seller," indicates that the transaction is for goods rather than services. *See Bonebrake, 499 F.2d at 958* (stating that language referring to "equipment" is peculiar to goods rather than services); *Bailey v. Montgomery Ward & Co., 690 P.2d 1280, 1282 (Colo. Ct. App. 1984)* (holding that a contract that identifies the transaction as a "purchase" and one of the parties as the "customer" signals a transaction in goods); *Meeker v. Hamilton Grain Elevator Co., 110 Ill. App. 3d 668, 442 N.E.2d 921, 923, 66 Ill. Dec. 360 (Ill. Ct. App. 1982)* (stating that a contract that calls the parties "seller" and "purchaser" indicates a contract for goods).

Turning to the contract between Mr. Tanzer and AVA, we first note that it is titled "Systems Sale and Installation Contract." From the plain language, it is clear that this is a hybrid contract, contemplating both the sale of goods and the installation of the goods. The question, then, is whether the language, when viewed in context, indicates the predominant purpose of the contract.

Throughout the contract, Mr. Tanzer is referred to as the "purchaser," a term that connotes a sale of goods contract. In various sections, the contract states that: (1) "[p]er this contract, AVA agrees to deliver and install equipment included in the proposal;" (2) "AVA retains ownership of the equipment until contract is paid in full;" (3) "Delays ... by parties other than AVA that prohibit proper installation of delivered equipment shall not delay payment ... ;" (4) "Prices are subject to change on items ... between the time of execution of this contract and the delivery of goods;" (5) "All pre-paid goods shall be delivered at the price agreed;" (6) "Model numbers may change ... therefore Product delivered may not ... be the same model number agreed to in the Proposal;" and (7) "Final installation of most electronic hardware corresponds with purchaser['s] actual move-in date...." (Emphases added). As noted in *Bonebrake*, "equipment" is a term of art, which is "peculiar [to the sale of goods.]" Furthermore, the contract incorporates, by reference, the earlier proposal, which sets out the specific equipment that AVA would install in the Tanzer home.

In his brief, Mr. Tanzer urges this Court to read the disputed contract as a construction or building contract based, *inter alia,* upon the fact that the equipment and installation occurred during the building process and the items installed allegedly became part of the completed home. In support of his argument, Mr. Tanzer relies upon the case of *Aluminum Vinyl Sales Company v. Woerz. Woerz* involved a contract for the installation of vinyl siding on a home. In pertinent part, the *Woerz* Court stated:

"The Uniform Commercial Code does not apply to a contract for the rendition of services or to construction contracts." The subject matter of the contract before us is to furnish "all the materials and labor necessary for" the installation of vinyl siding to the entire exterior of Defendant's house.

A contract to furnish a movable thing and affix it to the freehold is not a contract for the sale of goods, but one to furnish materials and affix them to the freehold by work and labor, and, until the materials are affixed, title to the materials does not pass.

Despite Mr. Tanzer's reading of *Woerz*, we cannot extend its holding so far as to conclude that it stands for the proposition that any and all contracts that contemplate the sale of goods, which are installed in a home or affixed to realty, are to be construed as predominately service contracts. Rather, as noted in 1 Barkley Clark and Christopher Smith, The Law of Product Warranties § 2:22 (2012):

> Contracts for the installation of products that were identifiable goods before installation and that, when installed, constitute only a small portion of a total building, are covered by Article 2.... As long as the transaction involves defective products that were moveable before installation and thus once qualified as 'goods' under *§ 2-105(1)*, the courts assume that the service elements are also covered.

Id.

Accordingly, cases have held that the installation of the following are all sale of goods: (1) carpet, (2) electrical equipment, (3) trees, shrubs and sod, (4) steel lockers, (5) overhead doors, (6) water heaters, (7) a furnace, *O'Laughlin v. Minnesota Natural Gas Co.*, 253 N.W.2d 826 (Minn. 1977); (8) an air-conditioning system, and (9) interior window panels.

In *Glazer, etux v. Tri-State Tile and Marble Co., Inc.*, a suit for breach of express warranty in connection with the resurfacing of plaintiffs' patio with "prairie film," which is "a mixture of epoxy and very fine gravel," this Court noted that, in cases "involving building useful improvements out of raw materials," courts have held that these contracts are "outside the scope of the U.C.C." Such cases involved: (1) the sale and installation of blacktop, (2) construction of a house with a builder furnishing all materials and labor, and (3) construction of electrical equipment. On the other hand, in cases where the courts have found the contract to be one for the sale of goods, and thus governed by the UCC, "the items therein involved have been tangible things, movable at the time they are identified to the contract and where installation has not been a major or predominant factor in the contract." Such cases involved: (1) installation of water tank, (2) installation of a bowling alley and equipment, and (3) installation of a liner for the bottom of a swimming pool. The *Glazer* Court applied the foregoing principles in reaching its conclusion that the installation of "prairie film" is not a sale of goods. In reaching its holding, the Court noted:

> [T]his is clearly not a sale of "goods," but is closely akin to some of the cases cited above, such as, the sale and installation of a blacktop driveway, or building or painting a house. We see no difference between installing a Prairie Film system over a patio and overlaying the patio with concrete or quarry tile. Plaintiffs were contracting to obtain a service from the defendant, not to purchase a quantity of gravel.

> By the same token, materials, such as the Prairie Film, when attached to realty, such as a patio cover, lose their character as goods. *See T.C.A. §47-9-313*. Once the patio was resurfaced by defendant the resurfacing lost any characteristics of personalty and became part of an improvement of the real estate, not severable therefrom.

Tennessee Code Annotated Section 47-2-105 sets out the current definition of "goods" under the UCC. The statute provides, in relevant part, that: "'Goods' means all things (including specially manufactured goods) which are movable at the time of identification to the contract for sale...." The comments to the code section clarify that: "The definition of goods is based on the concept of movability.... It is not intended to deal with things which are not fairly identifiable as movables before the contract is performed." The comment goes on to explain that:

> The use of the word "fixtures" is avoided in view of the diversity of definitions of that term. This Article in including within its scope "things attached to realty" adds the further test that they must be capable of severance without material harm thereto. As between the parties any identified things which fall within that definition becomes "goods" upon the making of the contract for sale.

In light of the foregoing statutory provisions, the holding in *Glazer* is still applicable. Because the "prairie film" became "attached to the realty," such that it could not be removed "without material harm" to the structure, the Court correctly held that the contract was one for service, thus excluding application of the UCC. By contrast, in *Highland Rim Constructors v. Atlantic Software Corp*, this Court held that a contract involving the sale of a computer system to a construction company was a sale of goods contract. The Court noted that the contract was a hybrid contract, involving both sale of goods and service. The Court then applied the predominant purpose test to determine that the UCC applied to the transaction; in so holding, the Court stated:

> Other courts, using the predominant [purpose] test, have found that contracts for the sale of computer systems or related components, including hardware, software, training, and support services, are contracts for the sale of goods governed by Article 2. *RRX Indus., Inc. v. Lab-Con, Inc.*, 772 F.2d 543, 546 (9th Cir. 1985) (software, training, systems repairs, and upgrades); *Triangle Underwriters, Inc. v. Honeywell, Inc.*, 604 F.2d 737, 742-43 (2d Cir. 1979) (hardware and software); *Nelson Business Equip. Ctr., Inc. v. Monteleone*, 524 A.2d 1172, 1174 (Del. 1987) (computer system); *USM Corp. v. Arthur D. Little Sys., Inc.*, 28 Mass. App. Ct. 108, 546 N.E.2d 888, 894 (Mass. App. Ct. 1989) (computer system); *Communications Group, Inc. v. Warner Communications, Inc.*, 138 Misc. 2d 80, 527 N.Y.S.2d 341, 344 (N.Y. Civ. Ct. 1988) (software); *Camara v. Hill*, 157 Vt. 156, 596 A.2d 349, 351 (Vt. 1991) (computer system).

> We agree with the reasoning of these precedents. Atlantic's agreement with Highland Rim was predominately for the sale of an integrated computer system. Its obligation to provide training in the use of the system was incidental to the purchase of the system itself. Accordingly, the transaction is one involving goods, and the parties' rights are governed by Article 2.

We find the reasoning and cited cases in *Highland Rim* persuasive in the instant appeal. As set out in the contract, and in the incorporated proposal, it is clear that the contract contemplates the sale of various, moveable components, which were to be integrated via a control system. Unlike the *Glazer* case, the fact that the components were installed in the home did not result in an attachment that would change the moveability of the goods sold. Accordingly, we are not persuaded by Mr. Tanzer's argument that the integration of the components constitutes a "construction" contract. The plain language of the contract simply does not support such a finding.

B. Nature of AVA's Business

In addition to the plain language of the contract, the court may also consider the nature of the seller's business. It is not disputed in the record that AVA is in the business of design and sale of custom, state-of-the-art, home theater, multi-room music/television/lighting control, and phone/intercom systems. AVA does not manufacture or promote one brand of product; rather, it sells and installs products from various manufacturers. From our review of the record, it appears that AVA's "design" role really constitutes a determination of what goods the customer needs and what integration system(s) will work to link the various components. In this sense, the "integration" of the whole system is done by the controlling system, i.e., Escient, Concierge, Crestron, Lutron. The sale of these respective systems is, in the opinion of this Court, similar to the sale of an integrated computer system. The installation and service that AVA performs is incidental to the overarching purpose of its business, which is to sell "smart home" components.

C. Reason for the Contract

The third factor instructs the court to "consider the final product the purchaser bargained to receive, and whether it may be described as a good or a service." Whether the purchaser sought to procure a good or a service by entering into the subject contract is "a strong indication of the predominant purpose of the contract." *Stafford v. Int'l Harvester Co.,* 668 F.2d 142, 147 (2d Cir. 1981) ("underlying nature of a hybrid transaction is determined by reference to the purpose with which the customer contracted with the defendant"); *NW Equip. Inc. v. Cudmore* ("*Bonebrake* test looks to the predominant purpose or thrust of the contract as it would exist in the minds of reasonable parties."). In analyzing this factor, the *Pass* Court found guidance from the Michigan Supreme Court, in *Neibarger v. Universal Cooperatives, Inc.,* wherein the Michigan court described its analysis of the purpose of the parties' dealings as follows:

> If the purchaser's ultimate goal is to acquire a product, the contract should be considered a transaction in goods, even though service is incidentally required. Conversely, if the purchaser's ultimate goal is to procure a service, the contract is not governed by the UCC, even though goods are incidentally required in the provision of this service.
>
> *Id. at 622.*

As discussed above, even in cases where labor and services were contemplated by the parties to be an integral part of the contract, courts have still held that Article 2 applies. *See, e.g., Highland Rims Constructors,* (noting that the seller's "obligation to provide training in the use of the system was incidental to the purchase of the system itself."); *see also IBP, Inc. v. HK Sys.,* (holding that contract for purchase of a computer system was a sale of goods, with rendition of services such as design, construction, manufacturing and installation incidental); *Bonebrake,* (holding that installation of pre-fabricated bowling lanes incidental to the contract because the lanes remained "movable"); *Meyers v. Henderson Constr. Co.,* (holding that installation of pre-fabricated disassembled doors was incidental to the contract for sale of the tangible goods).

Turning to the record in the instant case, in his answer, Mr. Tanzer admits that he contracted for electronic equipment. It is not disputed that AVA orders all of the equipment it sells from the manufacturer or from the distributor. In other words, none of the equipment was "constructed" at Tanzer's home; it was merely installed there. The record further indicates that the equipment maintained its characteristics as personalty and was never rendered immovable from the residence. In support of this conclusion, Mr. Tanzer presented a spreadsheet at trial, which indicated all of the equipment he was willing to return to AVA. The fact that Mr. Tanzer could return this equipment supports a finding that it had not become a permanent improvement to his realty. The fact that the original proposal, which was incorporated into the contract, breaks apart the costs of the "equipment," i.e., tangible goods, from the cost of "cable/misc. parts," i.e., materials also supports a finding that Mr. Tanzer bargained for the purchase of equipment, and that the services rendered by AVA in connection with that sale, including delivery and installation, were necessary but incidental to the ultimate purpose of the contract, i.e, to obtain the various components and the integration system that would link them.

D. Amounts Paid for Services and Goods, Respectively

The final factor to be considered is the respective amounts charged under the contract for the goods and services. "If the cost of the goods is but a small portion of the overall contract price, such fact would increase the likelihood that the services portion predominates." Conversely, where "the charge for goods exceeds that for services, the contract is more likely to be for goods."

In this case, the trial court found that the costs of labor and services were "insignificant" compared to the cost of the equipment. As set out above, under the original contract, equipment sales constituted $56,375 of the total price of $71,915 (before taxes); on the other hand, labor accounted for only $9,880. In the final invoice, equipment totaled $89,640.03 of the total contract price of $109,830.03 (before taxes), with labor constituting only $13,260.00. Viewed as a percentage, equipment constitutes roughly 82% of the final contract price. Accordingly, this factor weighs heavily in favor of a finding that the contract was predominantly for the sale of goods.

Based upon the foregoing, we conclude that all four of the *Pass* factors favor the trial court's conclusion that the instant contract was predominantly for the sale of goods. Accordingly, we conclude that the trial court did not err in applying UCC Article 2 to this transaction.

GOLDEN V. DEN-MAT CORP.

COURT OF APPEALS OF KANSAS, 2012
47 KAN. APP. 2D 450

ATCHESON, Justice.

Plaintiff Brenda Golden purchased dental veneers—porcelain overlays meant to improve the appearance of teeth—that Defendant Den-Mat manufactured and marketed and Defendant Dr. Carissa M. Gill, a dentist, put in place. Golden contends the veneers became discolored and stained despite representations from Den-Mat and Dr. Gill that they would retain their appearance. So she sued them in Sedgwick County District Court on the grounds the veneers breached implied warranties applicable to goods sold under Article 2—Sales of the Uniform Commercial Code (UCC), K.S.A. 84-2-101 et seq., and the transaction entailed deceptive acts and practices and improper limitations of those warranties in violation of the Kansas Consumer Protection Act (KCPA), K.S.A. 50-623 et seq. The district court granted summary judgment to Den-Mat and Dr. Gill. Golden has timely appealed. We reverse and remand the case for trial, except for one claim under the KCPA on which summary judgment was properly entered.

The district court relied primarily on arguments that Golden failed to file suit within the appropriate statutes of limitations. After setting out the factual history and procedural development of the case, we first address those bases for summary judgment. The district court improperly *characterized Golden's claims as torts and, therefore, applied the incorrect limitati*ons period. The evidence does not support summary judgment on the proper limitations for UCC and KCPA claims.

FACTUAL AND PROCEDURAL HISTORY

In late 2004, Golden wanted to replace the veneers on her teeth with new ones that would give her smile what she described as a "super white" appearance. Veneers are synthetic panels cemented to the front of a person's teeth, thereby covering discoloration or other imperfections in the natural dentition. Golden saw a magazine advertisement for Cerinate veneers, a proprietary product Den-Mat manufactures. In response to her telephone call to the number in the advertisement, Den-Mat sent Golden a brochure describing the Cerinate veneers as "thin porcelain shields ... bonded to the front of" the teeth "to create dramatic changes in your smile." The brochure touted "long-term clinical research" showing the Cerinate veneers would last up to 16 years "with no discoloration" and "100% retention." The brochure also explained that the porcelain veneers "are stronger and more durable" than comparable products made from plastic. According to the brochure, "[s]ometimes plastic composites stain and discolor with age, whereas, Cerinate Veneers maintain their beautiful luster and vitality." The brochure referred several times to the durability of the veneers and promoted the "strong, patented adhesive" used to attach them.

Golden decided to get the Cerinate veneers and contacted Den-Mat for a dentist in the Wichita area. Den-Mat supplied Golden with Dr. Gill's name and contact information as the nearest professional authorized to apply Cerinate veneers. Dr. Gill worked in Wellington, some 35 miles south of Golden's home.

Dr. Gill removed the old veneers, took impressions of Golden's teeth, and ordered the new veneers from Den-Mat. On January 10, 2005, Dr. Gill attached the Cerinate veneers to Golden's upper teeth. At the end of that visit, Dr. Gill gave Golden a written warranty for the veneers.

Golden later testified in her deposition that she felt the veneers seemed darker or less white as soon as they had been affixed to her teeth. Nonetheless, Golden returned to Dr. Gill 3 weeks later and had the remaining veneers applied to her lower teeth. By then, one of the upper veneers had come loose and another appeared to have a crack in it. Dr. Gill ordered replacement veneers and later applied them; she did not charge Golden for that work.

Golden paid $9,875.25 for the Cerinate veneers.

* * *

Another veneer came off about 6 months later. Dr. Gill reapplied the veneer, again at no cost to Golden. In late March 2007, another veneer came off. Dr. Gill ordered a replacement veneer from Den-Mat. The replacement veneer was considerably whiter than the veneers Golden already had. On April 23, 2007, Dr. Gill spoke with a Den-Mat representative who said it was possible that Golden's veneers had become stained or had darkened over time. Dr. Gill recounted the conversation to Golden the same day.

In the first part of 2008, Golden went to her regular dentist to have the Cerinate veneers removed from her upper teeth and replaced with a similar product from another manufacturer. The replacements cost about $4,500. In the summary judgment materials, Golden submitted a close-up photograph of her teeth after the upper veneers had been replaced. In the photograph, the lower teeth, with the Cerinate veneers, are noticeably duller than the replacement veneers and seem to have what could be stains.

On January 9, 2008, Golden filed a petition against the Den-Mat entities and Dr. Gill alleging breach of express warranties regarding the veneers and breach of implied warranties of merchantability and fitness for a particular purpose. Golden alleged the veneers had become stained and discolored and some of them came off or cracked. Den-Mat and Dr. Gill duly filed separate answers denying liability.

The district court granted summary judgment to the defendants on all of Golden's claims. In a short letter ruling issued on August 17, 2009, without citing supporting statutes or caselaw, the district court found that warranty claims against Den-Mat were torts filed beyond the 2-year statute of limitations. As to Dr. Gill, the district court found the claims to be for professional negligence and, thus, governed by a 2-year statute of limitations that expired before Golden filed suit.

Application of UCC

Dr. Gill has fired a veritable broadside at the substance of the UCC claims Golden has asserted. Despite the numerous arguments Dr. Gill asserts, we do not find any that would support summary judgment on the factual record in this case. We address the points sequentially.

UCC Coverage

Dr. Gill contends there was "no transaction in goods" between her and Golden and, therefore, the UCC does not apply. Beneath that overstatement of the circumstances lurks an actual controversy that should be left for the jury. As we have said, Article 2 of the UCC regulates the sale of goods. The UCC defines goods expansively as meaning "all things (including specially manufactured goods) which are movable at the time of identification to the contract for sale," except for the money to be paid under the contract for the goods, investment securities, and legal rights to things or property. *K.S.A. 84-2-105(1).*

Goods—the Cerinate veneers—were plainly involved in and integral to the transaction involving Golden and Dr. Gill, as we have already indicated. Golden met with Dr. Gill, as Den-Mat's recommended dentist, and ordered the veneers through her. Dr. Gill received the veneers and then applied them to Golden's teeth. Golden paid Dr. Gill. But a sale does not come within the scope of the UCC merely because the contract includes the transfer of goods. Many contracts also entail services associated with the goods. The arrangement here was of that sort, and Dr. Gill provided services essential for Golden's use of the veneers. In UCC parlance, those transactions involving goods and services are commonly known as mixed or hybrid contracts.

The UCC does not address mixed contracts as such. So courts have created common-law rules to determine if those transactions should be treated as sales of goods covered under the UCC or service contracts outside the Code's regulation. Some 30 years ago, the Kansas Supreme Court adopted the "predominant purpose" test for classifying mixed contracts. The predominant purpose test has become the commonly accepted, if not the near universal, standard. See 1 White & Summers, Uniform Commercial Code, ch. 9, §9-2, p. 606 (5th ed. 2006). As the name suggests, the test attempts to discern the principal nature of the transaction: Is the buyer seeking services to which the goods are incidental, or is the buyer acquiring goods to which the services are auxiliary

The predominant purpose test, however, is not especially predictive in the abstract. It looks at and depends upon the factual circumstances of the transaction being litigated. Care Display, 225 Kan. at 238 ("[E]ach case must be determined on an individual basis[,] and … broad statements of principles are of little assistance in deciding a particular [case]."). The Kansas appellate courts have developed some general considerations in looking at mixed contracts.

Courts have split over whether the predominant purpose of a mixed contract presents an issue of law for the court or a question of fact for the jury. The Kansas appellate courts apparently have not directly addressed the point.

The Nebraska Court of Appeals suggested the issue should be treated as a matter of law because contract interpretation commonly presents legal rather than factual determinations. MBH, Inc., 15 Neb. App. at 348. That is true when the language of a written contract is unambiguous. But determining whether goods or services predominate in a mixed contract necessarily looks beyond the contractual language. It includes the reasons the buyer purchases the goods and the nature and extent of the integration of those goods with the related services. It likely requires detailed information about the goods and the services over and above what may be described in the contract. Given the case-specific inquiry and the factually driven nature of the determination, essentially considering all of the circumstances bearing on the transaction, we conclude the issue of predominance of goods or services in a mixed contract is fundamentally one of fact. As such, it typically should be left for the trier of fact rather than resolved on summary judgment.

Having concluded the predominant purpose of a mixed contract to be a question of fact, we turn to whether the transaction here, nonetheless, must be considered one principally for services rather than goods based on the summary judgment record. If so, the UCC would be inapplicable, as Dr. Gill argues.

Unlike most medical or dental procedures, Golden's acquisition of the veneers was purely for cosmetic purposes. She was not seeking treatment for some illness or injury. The transaction was materially different from, for example, a dentist filling a cavity. In that instance, the patient or buyer has a malady, perhaps a painful one, and seeks a cure from the dentist. The dentist may drill and fill the cavity, though there might be other treatment options, such as installing a crown or pulling the offending tooth. The patient has received services in the form of a diagnosis, a recommended course of care, and actual treatment. The patient has also received whatever material the dentist used to fill the cavity. The filling itself would likely be a form of goods under the UCC, and the contract between the patient and dentist would be a mixed one. But the services would plainly seem to predominate. The patient wanted treatment for the cavity and principally sought diagnostic and therapeutic services from the dentist to accomplish that purpose. The patient had no particular interest in what the dentist used to fill the cavity and likely left the decision to the dentist's professional judgment. We think that would be true of the vast majority of transactions between a patient and a healthcare provider for treatment of illness or injury in which there were a single contract.

Golden, however, suffered from no malady and sought no professional diagnosis or treatment. She simply wanted whiter teeth and sought replacements for the veneers she had been wearing. Golden had received information from Den-Mat containing representations about the characteristics of its Cerinate veneers making them appear to be a satisfactory choice. Although disputed in the record, there is evidence Golden shared that information with Dr. Gill and received some assurance from her as to the accuracy of a critical characteristic—the veneers, being made of porcelain, would not stain or dull over time. Golden then purchased Den-Mat's Cerinate veneers through Dr. Gill, who applied them to Golden's teeth.

Viewing the record favorably to Golden, as we must in considering her opposition to summary judgment, she did not go to Dr. Gill with a problem—dull or aesthetically unappealing teeth—for which she wanted a professional consultation about various corrective options. Golden wanted Cerinate veneers and understood from Den-Mat that Dr. Gill could provide and apply that product. To be sure, Dr. Gill also provided services in that she removed the existing veneers, sized and ordered the Cerinate veneers, and applied the new veneers to Golden's teeth. But a jury could fairly conclude Golden wanted the veneers, while the services were simply part of the means of accomplishing that purpose. That would be consistent with the notion that but for the buyer's acquisition of the goods, the services would have been unnecessary, making the contract predominately one for the goods, as the Kansas Supreme Court has suggested.

The predominance of the veneers as goods also seems plausible and, thus, within a jury's reasonable consideration when the transaction is compared with orthodontics, another form of dentistry often used for largely cosmetic purposes. To straighten the patient's teeth, the orthodontist applies braces and other devices, often over an extended time period. The goods, those devices, are an integral part of the process. But the orthodontist makes a professional judgment about the types of braces to achieve the ultimate purpose of realigning the patient's teeth. Again, the contract is a mixed one for goods and services. But the patient's purpose is not the acquisition of braces but of straight teeth. The braces are temporary appliances, used by the orthodontist, for achieving that end. In those circumstances, the orthodontist's services would seem to predominate over the goods.

The same degree of professional skill and judgment is lacking here in that Golden essentially selected the goods independently, though she sought affirmation of that selection from both Dr. Gill and representatives of Den-Mat regarding particular characteristics of the goods. And, unlike braces, the veneers themselves, once applied, provided the desired cosmetic result. The result continued only so long as the veneers remained in place and performed as Golden understood they would.

Finally, nothing in the record evidence shows Dr. Gill contracted separately with Golden for professional services apart from the purchase of the veneers. The parties do not argue there were separate or distinct contracts for the veneers, on the one hand, and Dr. Gill's services, on the other. The transaction was unitary, combining goods and services. Likewise, there is no evidence Golden was charged separately for the veneers and for Dr. Gill's services or that the services were even broken out as a distinct component or cost in the contract or in any billing. See 1 White & Summers, Uniform Commercial Code, ch. 9, §9-2, p. 606 (relative costs of goods and services and undifferentiated or itemized billing of them frequently considered in assessing predominant purpose of mixed contract); *Van Sistine v. Tollard,* 95 Wis. 2d 678, 685, 291 N.W.2d 636 (1980) (contract primarily for services where property owner supplied some of the siding to be installed on home and installer's labor costs exceeded cost of siding and other materials installer provided).

In short, the record evidence fails to support a finding as a matter of law for Dr. Gill that the transaction with Golden was one in which acquisition and use of services predominated over the purchase of goods so that the UCC would not apply. Summary judgment could not be granted to Dr. Gill on the UCC claims on that basis or on any KCPA claims dependent upon an exclusion or dilution of otherwise applicable UCC warranties.

A consequence of the all-or-nothing approach of the "predominant purpose" test is that when Article 2 applies, both the goods and services components of the transaction are subject to a system of rules built to address the special needs of sales-of-goods transactions. Should Audio Visual Artistry's failure to properly label the audio wiring it installed excuse Mr. Tanzer's obligation to pay for the entire system under Article 2's perfect-tender rule? Should Ms. Golden have a claim for breach of the implied warranty of merchantability because one of the veneers came loose? Section 2-102 tells us that Article 2 applies to transactions in goods "unless the context otherwise requires." And 1-103 commands that "[u]nless displaced by the particular provisions of this Act, the principles of law and equity ... shall supplement its provisions." A minority of courts, troubled by the incongruity of applying either Article 2 to disputes implicating the services component or the common law to disputes relating to the goods sold, have used a "gravamen of the action" test—if the dispute relates to the goods, Article 2 controls, but if the dispute involves the services provided, general contract rules control. But this approach creates its own problems. For example, applying different sources of law to the same transaction can create intractable problems of proof because it requires a court to allocate value between the goods and services for purposes of measuring damages when the parties themselves made no such allocation.[6]

PROBLEM 2 - 4

Does Article 2 apply to any of the following agreements Rae has made for the store?

1. Rae contracted to buy all of the pizzas sold at the store's deli from the gourmet pizza shop across town for the next twelve months. The pizza shop agreed to supply products and labor to produce several types of uncooked personal pizzas to the store, and the store agreed to pay $1.75 per uncooked pizza. The contract estimated monthly usage of 250 pizzas. Customers began complaining about the pizzas soon after they were put on the deli's menu, and Rae wants to cancel the contract and stop taking pizzas. 2-105(1).

2. Rae contracted to have all of the store's freezers and coolers serviced by the local refrigeration company. The refrigeration company agreed to provide all labor and parts necessary to maintain and repair the freezers and coolers in the store at rates set by the local trade association. Refrigeration service requires highly qualified technicians, and the parts used in such equipment are very expensive—sometimes it's cheaper to replace equipment than it is to repair it.

3. Rae purchased all-new checkout scanners for the store from the technology company in town, which agreed to install the scanners and train the employees who would be using them, as well as to install any software upgrades for the system released during the lives of the scanners.

4. Rae agreed to buy a mobile concessions operation from a local couple who had decided to retire. The sellers operated from a truck (equipped with refrigerators, freezers, roasters, and fountain service) that they drove to public events around town during the summer. Rae wanted the store's deli to be mobile so it could be hired out to service both public events and private parties around town. The agreement provided that in addition to the truck, Rae acquired a servicing trailer, chairs, tables, signs, and lighting equipment. She also got the right to work the events the couple had committed to service this summer. *Services Component*

---

6   You will remember from your Contracts course that Article 2 measures damages for breach differently than they are measured under common law.

As the next case illustrates, advances in technology have blurred even further the distinction between tangible and intangible property relied upon to define the outer reaches of Article 2's scope. Software was one of the original flash points that split the courts attempting to locate our new technologies on the tangible–intangible continuum, and thirty years later it remains without a true home. Internet transactions added a new twist to the problem, and smart goods—products and devices embedded with software and other intellectual property—have only widened the chasm. Efforts to amend Article 2 to deal with these issues have failed, as has an alternative uniform act—the Uniform Computer Information Transactions Act—which has been adopted by only two states. Some states have by statute prohibited their courts from relying on UCITA.[7]

Conwell v. Gray Loon Outdoor Mktg. Group

Supreme Court of Indiana, 2009
906 N.E.2d 805

SHEPARD, Chief Justice.

OPINION

As the Internet becomes a ubiquitous presence in American commerce, the nation's courts work to find satisfactory legal frameworks for resolving the disputes that inevitably arise. In this suit between a business enterprise and the marketing firm that created and hosted its website, we conclude that the Uniform Commercial Code does not apply and that the web design firm may collect for its work under principles of common law contract.

Facts and Procedural History

In November 2003, Piece of America was a limited partnership pursuing the sale of novelty packages: one-square-inch parcels of land in each of the fifty states. The general partners were F.W. Splittorff, Dennis Conwell, and Robert Aswell. To market and sell its products, Piece of America sought to establish a website. None of the partners had any sophistication in Internet technologies or website design, so they approached Gray Loon Marketing, which provides various marketing and communication services, to design and publish its website. In September 2003, Gray Loon gave POA a design proposal for the website and an estimated price of $8,080. Among other things, Gray Loon's proposal for POA's package stated, "It is Gray Loon's philosophy that clients have purchased goods and services from us and that inherently means ownership of those goods and services as well."

Piece of America agreed to the proposal and paid a 50% deposit, and design commenced. During the design process, POA asked for a few minor changes, none of which requests were written down. Gray Loon finished the site in December 2003 at a final cost of about $8,500. Once the website was running to POA's satisfaction, it paid Gray Loon in full during the first quarter of 2004. Both parties undisputedly fulfilled their obligations under the agreement of November 2003.

In April 2004, POA requested that Gray Loon make several changes, some of which required major programming work. In particular, POA wanted to allow customers to make two payments in purchasing its packages. Gray Loon agreed over the phone to make these changes, and, following its policy, Gray Loon immediately began the requested alterations. Once Gray Loon completed the modifications, Gray Loon contacted POA for approval to post the modifications. At that time, POA told Gray Loon that it did not want to implement the system for two payments by consumers. Gray Loon subsequently sent POA a bill for $5,224.50.

---

7   Site example Iowa, North Carolina, West Virginia, Vermont, Idaho.

During this period, Gray Loon was also charging POA seventy-five dollars a month for hosting the site. Once Gray Loon published the modified website, it remained available from July to September 2004. Gray Loon filed suit for non-payment, naming Splitorff, Conwell, and POA. Piece of America countersued for conversion, claiming Gray Loon had taken the original website, for which it had paid.

The trial court entered judgment for Gray Loon on its claim and against POA on its counter-claim. The Court of Appeals affirmed. *Conwell v. Gray Loon Outdoor Mktg. Group,* 873 N.E.2d 2058 (Ind. Ct. App. 2007). We granted transfer.

To resolve this case, we must determine which law applies in interpreting the agreement between the parties. Then, we must consider whether the applicable law recognizes a contract here and whether POA should be required to pay Gray Loon.

A World of Websites

We start with a short introduction of the relevant background regarding websites. As befits the subject, we begin by reference to Merriam-Webster's Online Dictionary, which defines a website as "a group of World Wide Web pages usually containing hyperlinks to each other and made available online by an individual, company, educational institution, government, or organization." It defines the World Wide Web as "a part of the Internet accessed through a graphical user interface and containing documents often connected by hyperlinks."

A web page consists of computer programming that is decoded by an Internet browser to show the "graphic user interface" that ranges from a simple combination of graphics and text to interactive applications. For our purposes, there are essentially two aspects of a website: the content that the pages on a website display and the programming that encodes it in such a way for a browser to interpret. In some web design relationships, the hiring party provides all content while the designer simply translates it into a format appropriate for viewing in the World Wide Web. On other occasions, the hiring party provides a vision and a goal for the site and the designer creates both the content and the programming. The latter characterization seems to fit the facts here, though POA provided some content.

The website at issue here was distributed by Gray Loon for free to any Internet user who directed an Internet browser to POA's domain. Piece of America paid Gray Loon to author and to distribute (or "host") the website files via its server, making it available to any computer connected through the Internet. Piece of America could have bifurcated these two tasks and hired a third party to host the site or to design it. If it had hired a third company to host the site for distribution over the Internet, it would have had to transfer the files to the other company's servers. Gray Loon could have copied them to a disk and physically delivered it or transferred the files over the Internet using any number of methods.

Inasmuch as the information technology industry runs to hundreds of billions of dollars a year in projects, it is quite ordinary that clients and providers often find themselves locked in disputes. The leading source of statistics about the industry, the Standish Group, reports in its 2009 analysis of information technology performance that 32% of engagements result in a timely product billed more or less on budget. Their historic analysis reflects outright cancellation by clients about 20% of the time and projects completed very late or substantially over budget about 50% of the time.

Contract Law

The common law of contracts governs agreements between private parties, except to the extent that it has been modified by legislation (like the Uniform Commercial Code). Piece of America argues that the contract it made with Gray Loon should be considered as one for services, such that the common law of contracts should apply. Further, it asserts that the common law strictly requires essential elements of a contract, one of which is price, in order to form an enforceable agreement, and that price was not agreed to in the instant case. For its part, Gray Loon simply advances a general contract argument that it effected the website changes at POA's request and was not paid for the work.

The trial court applied the U.C.C. in its conclusions of law. The Court of Appeals did likewise. We will begin by considering whether the U.C.C. was the right law to deploy.

Does the U.C.C. Govern this Agreement

Indiana's U.C.C. Article 2 "applies to transactions in goods." *Ind. Code. § 26-1-2-102* (2008). Goods "means all things (including specially manufactured goods) which are movable at the time of identification to the contract for sale, other than the money in which the price is to be paid, investment securities (IC 16-1-8.1) and things in action." *Ind. Code § 26-1-2-105* (2008).

Where close questions arise about whether a transaction involved the transfer of goods or performance of services, courts commonly choose one or the other by asking what was the "predominant thrust."

Arguably, software could be treated as a good, or not, depending on how it is created or transmitted. Where software is contained in a tangible medium, especially when produced on a mass scale, courts have had a difficult time placing software into the established categories. Unsurprisingly, this challenge has prompted suggestions that a new legal paradigm may be needed. The National Conference of Commissioners of Uniform State Laws has been working on this issue for some time with what was originally called U.C.C. Article 2B, later renamed the Uniform Computer Information Transaction Act after the American Law Institute withdrew from the project.

Happily, this case does not include any of the aspects (like the legal effect of an agreement to transfer software on a tangible medium) that have complicated resolution of the U.C.C.'s applicability in some cases reported in the literature. We thus can address the goods/services question rather cleanly.

Our Court of Appeals has decided at least two cases on whether software is a good. Piece of America points us to a decision from two decades ago, *Data Processing Servs., Inc. v. L.H. Smith Oil Corp. Data Processing Services* involved custom software used in the operations of an oil company. The court determined that the sale for customized computer software was not a sale for goods. It said the transaction was "more analogous to a client seeking a lawyer's advice or a patient seeking medical treatment." It further stated:

> While a tangible end product, such as floppy disks, hard disks, punch cards or magnetic tape used as a storage medium for the program may be involved incidentally in this transaction, it is the skill and knowledge of the programmer which is being purchased in the main, not the devices by which this skill and knowledge is placed into the buyer's computer. The means of transmission is not the essence of the agreement.

The Court of Appeals treated the agreement as a contract for services because that is how the language of the contract suggested the parties themselves understood it; they used terms such as "to act," and treated the object of the contract as the programmer's knowledge, skill, and ability. It also relied on common law principles of implied warranty of skill and diligence by "those who hold themselves out to the world as possessing skill and qualifications in their respective trades or professions."

In a more recent case, the Court of Appeals considered a contract that licensed one software company to use another's software modules in its own end product. In concluding that U.C.C. Article 2 applied to the contract, the Court of Appeals relied on both parties' acquiescence in that conclusion and reasoned that because the agreement involved pre-existing, standardized software modules, they were goods rather than services.

On the surface, these cases might suggest that customized software is a service while pre-made software is a good, but when courts try to pour new wine into old legal bottles, we sometimes miss the nuances. It would be a mistake, for instance, to treat software as a good simply because it was contained in a tangible medium that fits within that category. This would conflate the sale of a book with the sale of its intellectual content, suggesting that the purchaser of the book might be buying a right to general use of the expressions contained in the volume.

A website created under arrangements calling for the designer to fashion, program, and host its operation on the designer's server is neither tangible nor moveable in the conventional sense. To be sure, one can copy a website using tangible, movable objects such as hard drives, cables, and disks. These objects are in themselves just as certainly goods, but it does not necessarily follow that the information they contain classifies as goods as well. The arrangement between POA and Gray Loon contemplated a custom design for a single customer and an ongoing hosting relationship. As such, conventional "predominant thrust" doctrine suggests that the U.C.C. did not apply.

PROBLEM 2 - 5

Which of the following transactions does Article 2 care about?

1. Rae's daughter downloads the new Lady Gaga album from the iTunes website, and the website charges her PayPal account $3.98.
2. Rae pays thirty-five dollars to download a computer diagnostics program to debug her laptop, which has been freezing up lately. The program comes with free live-chat customer support.
3. Rae subscribes to the online version of *Grocer's News* for ninety-nine dollars a month.

CHAPTER 3

THE BARGAIN

Article 2 takes a very different approach to contract formation then does the common law. Article 2 looks to the practical realities of the parties trying to do a sale-of-goods deal instead of looking to see if the parties have pushed their deal through the technical hoops used by the common law to determine whether the parties have earned the right to call their agreement a contract. Llewellyn believed, generally, that the common-law rules of contract formation did not reflect the way that the people whose transactions were to be governed by the new Sales Act actually made their agreements.

> Llewellyn was concerned with the "bargain-in-fact" of the parties and believed that the identification of the factual bargain (the agreement) of the parties should not be fettered with technical rules of pre-Code classical contract law, because the application of these technical rules might well lead to a failure to recognize the true agreement or understanding of the parties.[1]

Llewellyn did not dispense with the common-law formation rules in their entirety, but instead offered an alternative basis for recognizing agreement. The common-law rules retained were, however, modified to rid them of what some had argued were their unintended consequences. For example, the mirror-image rule that was probably a part of the discussion of offer and acceptance in your Contracts course does not live on in Article 2.

Article 2 takes a two-step approach to formation. First, it asks was there in fact an agreement between the buyer and seller. Have the parties, through words or conduct, expressed or indicated that an agreement exists? If they have, then Article 2, recognizing that there is often more to the agreement as understood by the parties themselves than the words they chose to express their agreement, asks, "What is that agreement?"

A. Is There An Agreement?

Article 2 dispenses with the common-law notion that there is one way to make a contract and that any attempt at agreement that does not conform should not be enforced, regardless of what the parties have said or done. Remember the contract formation dance from your Contracts course—there must be an offer followed by an acceptance to achieve that "manifestation of mutual assent" necessary to bestow on any agreement between two people the title of enforceable contract. And the common law had little

---

1   Murray, *Murray on Contracts* (4th ed. 2001) §10 at 23.

patience for a less-than-perfect performance—a stumble at either step, no matter how inconsequential to the parties themselves, could deprive their relationship of the legal effect they assumed it had. If a court subsequently decided that the offer's commitment, completeness, or selectivity fell short of some inarticulable standard or that the acceptance was not as definite and unequivocal as it could have been, then there was no contract that could be enforced, even if the parties had been performing their "agreement" at the time the dispute before the court arose.

Llewellyn saw what he believed to be a disconnect between the common-law formation rules and the commercial reality of the usual sale-of-goods transaction. Llewellyn believed very strongly that in sales law, the application of a rule should, in most cases, produce an outcome consistent with the general expectations of commercial buyers and sellers of goods. But the outcomes in many of the cases he studied were not what the commercial community as a whole would have expected—there was a disconnect. The disconnect, by preventing the parties from predicting the legal consequences of their actions, was interfering with the efficient transaction of business—increasing the cost of doing business for both buyers and sellers and, sometimes, providing welchers—one of Llewellyn's favorite targets—a no-cost way to escape their contractual obligations when a deal turned bad.

Nowhere was this disconnect more evident than with the rules for offer and acceptance. The common law assigned great significance to the paper—the offer and acceptance—exchanged by the parties in determining whether a contract had been created. But the parties, in practice, often paid little attention to that paper; each put the paper her lawyer had drafted in play and did not worry much about the other party's paper—at least not beyond the specifically negotiated terms (e.g., price, quantity, delivery) as reflected in that paper. The legal stuff in each party's paper (e.g., warranties, disclaimers, limits on remedies, exclusions of damages, choice of law) only became important if a problem developed between them—in which case each would insist that her paper controlled. But this paper that neither party was inclined to pay much attention to in the absence of a problem ultimately controlled whether an enforceable agreement existed between the parties. It did not matter to the law that the parties believed they had an agreement and had conducted themselves as though they had a binding agreement—if there was a problem with the paper, there was no legally enforceable agreement.

Article 2 eliminates Llewellyn's disconnect by dispensing with much of the technical formalities that controlled contract formation at common law. Under Article 2, contract formation is focused on identifying the bargain the parties made—what was their actual agreement—not on sifting through piles of paper looking for that magical moment when Jupiter happens to align with Mars. 2-204. We don't need to find an offer and acceptance; if the parties act like they have an agreement, Article 2 can enforce it even if they skipped the formation dance. 2-204. If the paper they happen to exchange actually precludes formation of a contract, there can still be a contract if, by their conduct, they recognize the existence of an agreement. 2-207. A contract is not necessarily unenforceable under Article 2 because it leaves out terms the common law considered essential. 2-204. The parties can modify their contract without an exchange of additional consideration (2-209), and the entire agreement of the parties does not have to be in writing to be enforceable—as long as there is some writing indicating the parties have an agreement. 2-201.

1. Finding Agreement: 2-204

Article 2's view of contract formation is simple: if the parties act like they have a contract, the law should enforce it. The common law made the parties earn their contract by jumping through hoops that Llewellyn believed were less likely to manifest the parties' intent to be bound than what they actually did. Many, if not most, contracts for the sale of goods are made on the fly by a buyer who needs the goods and a seller who wants to sell those goods—the lawyers are not involved—and neither expects the law to get in their way down the road. Part of the problem, as Llewellyn saw it, was that by 1930 the common law had still not adapted to the new reality of commercial sales:

> The concepts that took shape on the basis of a face-to-face dealing with present goods have in a short century and a quarter been tortured into application to the nationwide indirect marketing structure of today.[2]

The commercial world had changed, but the common law had not kept pace. Rules that might have made sense when applied to a transaction in 1875 now operated to impede the objectives of the parties to the modern sale-of-goods transaction. The Uniform Commercial Code project gave Llewellyn the opportunity to restate the rules of formation for sales contracts to reflect the expectations of the parties to those transactions, based on the practical realities of the twentieth-century sale-of-goods transaction. And he seized that opportunity and more.

Article 2 gets right to the point:

> A contract for sale of goods may be made in any manner sufficient to show agreement including conduct by both parties which recognized the existence of such a contract.

2-204(1). This is the Golden Rule of contract formation under Article 2. Contract formation now reflects the expectations of parties who contract in an environment that places more value on expediency than formalism. We don't need an offer, we don't need an acceptance of an offer, we don't need any of the regalia required by the common law to create an enforceable contract. All we need is something from the parties that "shows agreement"—any "manner of expression" that shows agreement will do. And, perhaps most importantly, conduct by the parties can be sufficient to show their agreement. If the parties act like they have an agreement, Article 2 will do what the parties would expect the law to do—give their conduct legal effect. The enforceability of agreements that the parties intended to be binding is no longer controlled by obsolete rules unconnected to the actual circumstances of the parties. Substance has been liberated from form. But, as the next case makes clear, even under Article 2, the parties still can't do one thing and say another.

PCS Sales (USA), Inc. v. Nitrochem Distrib., Ltd.

United States District Court for the Southern District of New York, 2004
54 U.C.C. Rep. Serv. 2d (Callaghan) 35

SCHEINDLIN, District Judge.

PCS Sales (USA), Inc. ("PCS") brings this diversity action against Nitrochem Distribution Ltd. ("Nitrochem"), seeking a declaratory judgment that PCS had no contractual obligation to purchase ammonia from Nitrochem in 2002. Nitrochem counterclaims, arguing that there was a valid and binding contract, which PCS breached. A bench trial was held on March 31 and April 1, 2004. At the close of the trial, Nitrochem moved for judgment as a matter of law. For the reasons set forth below, Nitrochem's motion and counterclaim are denied and PCS's application for declaratory judgment is granted. Pursuant to Rule 52(a) of the Federal Rules of Civil Procedure, the Court makes the following findings of fact and conclusions of law.

---

2   Llewellyn, *Cases and Materials on the Law of Sales,* (Callaghan 1920) xvi.

Karl N. Llewellyn, Selection from *Cases and Materials on the Law of Sales.* Copyright © 1930 by Foundation Press, Inc.

I. FINDINGS OF FACT

"The facts of this case sound like the delight of a contracts professor, if no one else." PCS's primary business is the sale of fertilizer and chemical products produced by affiliated companies for use in various agricultural and industrial applications. Additionally, PCS purchases various fertilizer and chemical products, including ammonia, for resale to its affiliates or to unaffiliated customers.

Nitrochem, a Swiss corporation with its principal place of business in Binningen, Switzerland, is represented in the United States by its agent, Altus Corp. ("Altus"), a New Jersey company. Nitrochem is engaged in the business of selling anhydrous ammonia and other chemical products produced by JSC Togliattiazot, a Russian corporation.

A. The 1998–2000 Ammonia Supply Agreements

In each of the first three years of their relationship, the parties negotiated and entered into one-year written agreements. Specifically, the parties met and, by December of each year, signed an agreement for the sale and purchase of anhydrous ammonia in the following calendar year. Among other common provisions, each of the contracts provided for the calculation of the sale price solely by reference to a published index, and the delivery of the ammonia in shiploads of 35,000 metric tons. There were, however, slight differences between the contracts in terms of volume, and the presence of an automatic renewal, or "evergreen clause." Specifically, the 1999 contract contained an evergreen clause[3], but the 1998 and 2000 contracts did not.

B. The 2000-01 Contract Negotiations

In late September or early October 2000, PCS and Altus met at PCS's Illinois offices to discuss contract terms for the year 2001. In particular, the parties addressed the possibility of adding an automatic renewal clause and implementing a pricing mechanism based on negotiation, rather than published indices. The parties also agreed that it would be mutually beneficial for them to continue doing business while negotiating a contract for 2001.

Following this meeting, Altus and PCS exchanged numerous drafts, but by the end of December 2000, they had not reached an agreement that both parties were willing to sign. Nonetheless, in January 2001 Nitrochem delivered, and PCS accepted, shipments of ammonia. For each shipload of ammonia delivered to PCS in 2001, Altus prepared and transmitted to PCS a set of payment documents, including a price calculation, commercial invoice, ocean bills of lading, certificate of quantity, and certificate of quality. On each of these invoices, Nitrochem wrote the following: "Re: ... Delivery in accordance with the contract for 2001." The price for these shiploads was determined by the published index method, and the deliveries were made at regular intervals throughout the year. There were no demurrage charges applied to any of these shipments.

The parties continued to trade drafts for the 2001 contract in January and February, and on March 28, 2001, apparently growing impatient, PCS submitted to Nitrochem a signed contract. Rather than countersign the agreement, Nitrochem sent an e-mail to PCS on May 2, 2001, indicating that there were several provisions to which it would not agree.

Thereafter, the parties continued their negotiations, exchanging drafts and comments over the next several months with the objective of entering into a written, signed contract. Although the parties had almost reached an agreement by the end of June 2001, ultimately PCS and Nitrochem could not agree on contract language acceptable to both parties. In particular, they disputed the content of the force majeure and complete agreement clauses. By the end of June, active negotiations between the parties for the 2001 contract had essentially ceased. Consequently, when the parties met in Chicago on September 11, 2001,

---

3   The clause states: "The supply period shall commence on January 1, 1999, and continue through December 31, 1999, and year to year thereafter unless terminated at the end of any such period, by written notice of either party at least three months prior to the end of any applicable term."

the focus of their discussions had shifted from the 2001 contract negotiations to PCS's 2002 requirements. It was during this meeting that PCS's representatives, Rock and Dowdle, informed Nitrochem's agents (Alleyne and Spirytus) that their needs for 2002 would be reduced from prior years.—at most, PCS would require eight firm and eight optional cargoes of ammonia. Rather than argue that such a reduction was prohibited under the "terms" of their agreement, Nitrochem's representatives looked for alternative purchasers for Nitrochem's ammonia.

After the meeting, the relationship between the parties slowly deteriorated. In October 2001, Alleyne and Spirytus exchanged revised drafts of the 2001 contract, but Rock, objecting to the automatic renewal clause, would not sign the draft and negotiations stalled again. On November, 19, 2001, Rock informed Spirytus that although PCS wanted to purchase ammonia from Nitrochem in 2002, it could not do so on a contractual basis. Nitrochem did not inform PCS that its reduction to zero contract tons was barred by the notice provision in the 2001 contract drafts. One week later, Nitrochem resurrected the March 28, 2001 contract from its files, countersigned it, and mailed it to PCS.

In 2002, PCS purchased approximately two shiploads of ammonia from Nitrochem, as spot purchases. On March 26, 2003, Nitrochem served PCS with a notice of intention to arbitrate. On April 15, 2003, PCS filed its Complaint for declaratory judgment and injunctive relief to stay arbitration, and Nitrochem counterclaimed for breach of contract on July 24, 2003.

II. CONCLUSIONS OF LAW

A. Applicable Legal Standards

* * * *

2. Principles of New York Contract Law

Disputes arising from a contract for the sale of goods are governed by New York's Uniform Commercial Code ("U.C.C."), "as interpreted in light of common law principles to the extent [those principles are] not inconsistent with the U.C.C." As such, a court must consider whether the parties agreed to be contractually bound and if so, which terms govern the resulting contract. The touchstone of any valid contract is a meeting of the parties' minds. Absent a "meeting of the minds on all essential terms," there is no contract. The parties must manifest their assent to be bound by the contractual terms, either "by word, act, or conduct which evinces [their intent] to contract."

Reflecting this principle, section 2-204 of New York's U.C.C. states, in relevant part, that "[a] contract ... may be made in any manner sufficient to show agreement, including conduct by both parties which recognizes the existence of such a contract." Additionally, sections 2-206(1)and 2-207(3) "expressly allow for the formation of contracts partly or wholly on the basis of such conduct." In other words, where the parties behave as though they have a contract, courts will recognize the existence of that contract, "whether or not the precise moment of agreement may be determined." For instance, in *Otis Elevator Co. v. George A. Fuller Co.*, the court found that an agreement existed between a general contractor and a subcontractor, even though they failed to agree as to when payment would be due to the subcontractor, because both fully performed and their "course of conduct in carrying out performance under those terms upon which they agreed [made] it absolutely clear that each party recognized that a valid and enforceable contract existed, the terms of which consisted of those terms on which the writings of the parties agreed" and U.C.C. gap fillers.

"Conduct by both parties which recognizes that agreement is not yet consummated establishes the non-existence of a contract...." For example, where the parties have engaged in extensive negotiations, but "intended not to be bound until a written agreement was executed, 'no amount of negotiation or oral agreement to specific terms will result in the formation of a binding contract.'" In fact, as the court acknowledged in *Durable, Inc. v. Twin County Grocers Corp.*, during the negotiation process, parties routinely conduct business with one another:

Parties can and do conduct business relationships ... during discussion of whether ... to enter into a more binding or longer-lasting relationship. If this is kept in mind, various subsequent events are as consistent with continuing negotiations, the hope of agreement, or the possibility that some business might be done without a binding umbrella relationship, as with entry into a large-scale long-term contract....

If a contract has been formed, courts must determine the terms of that contract. To that end, section 2-207 addresses the paradigmatic "battle of the forms" situation, implicating "the all too common business practice of blithely drafting, sending, receiving, and filing unread numerous purchase orders, acknowledgments, and other diverse forms containing a myriad of discrepant terms."

Section 2-207 precludes application of common law principles, such as the so-called "mirror image" and "last shot" rules. Under section 2-207, neither party benefits from "the terms it attempted to impose unilaterally on the other.... Instead, all of the terms on which the parties' forms do not agree drop out, and the U.C.C. supplies the missing terms."

B. Discussion

* * * *

2. Contract Formation

Nitrochem argues that "the parties unquestionably engaged in conduct that recognized the existence of their contract, in that Nitrochem delivered ammonia and invoiced PCS in the manner set out in the various drafts of the contract exchanged, and PCS accepted the deliveries and duly made payment." Specifically, the following conduct purportedly establishes the existence of a 2001 contract pursuant to the terms in the drafts: (1) Nitrochem's shipment and PCS's acceptance of approximately twenty shiploads of ammonia in deliveries made at regular intervals throughout the year; (2) the parties' calculation of price in accordance with the fallback pricing mechanism from the various drafts of the 2001 contract; (3) PCS's failure to object to the phrase "in accordance with the contract for 2001" printed on the invoices transmitted in connection with the shipments; (4) PCS's apparent adherence to the six-month notification rule contained in the drafts; (5) PCS's occasional references to "contract tons" and the demurrage rate in the "purchase contract"; and (6) the alleged cessation of active negotiations by June 2001.

Nitrochem's argument lacks merit. Although a court may, under sections 2-204 and 2-207(3), recognize a contract based on conduct, this is only appropriate where the parties' undisputed actions "clearly manifest[] mutual recognition that a binding obligation was undertaken." Where there is *inconsistent* behavior that suggests the absence of mutual assent, it is inappropriate to bind the parties to an agreement. In other words, where, as here, the conduct of the parties acknowledges that an agreement has *not yet been reached*, that conduct is insufficient to establish a contract.

The parties clearly did not consider themselves bound by the terms in the 2001 drafts, as evidenced by the fact that they continued actively to negotiate until at least June. Rather than sign the drafts at the end of June, the parties continued to trade drafts, albeit sporadically, until the end of October 2001. According to both Spirytus and Rock, the parties never abandoned the objective of obtaining a *written* agreement, as they had such an agreement in the three prior years of their business relationship. Thus, the parties' decision to trade drafts throughout 2001 conflicts with Nitrochem's theory that the parties viewed themselves as contractually bound by the terms in the drafts.

Additionally, Nitrochem's retrieval and countersignature of the March draft in November runs counter to its alleged understanding that the parties had a contract governed by the terms in the drafts. Had Nitrochem believed that it had such a contract based on conduct, it would have been unnecessary to locate and sign an old, long superseded draft. Thus, because the parties' actions unequivocally demonstrate that they did not think they had a binding contractual obligation, this case is distinguishable from those in which the courts recognized the existence of contracts by virtue of the parties' conduct.

For the foregoing reasons, the ~~parties' conduct does not provide a sufficient basis for recognizing the existence of a contract base~~d on the terms common to the drafts. The evidence suggests that, at most, the parties entered into an oral contract in late 2000 under which Nitrochem would sell to PCS approximately twenty shipments of ammonia, in accordance with the delivery schedule (evenly spaced throughout the year) and pricing mechanism traditionally used by the parties.

III. CONCLUSION

For the foregoing reasons, ~~Nitrochem's motion for judgment as a matter of law is denied~~, and PCS's application for declaratory judgment is granted. PCS had no contractual obligation to purchase ammonia from Nitrochem in 2002.

Is the court's message in *PCS Sales* that, regardless of whether the parties perform as though they have an agreement, if the paper they exchange does not agree, then there can't be an enforceable agreement? That seems to fly in the face of 2-204 and also to conflict with the intent of 2-207(3):

> Conduct by both parties which recognizes the existence of a contract is sufficient to establish a contract for sale although the writings of the parties do not otherwise establish a contract. In such case the terms of the particular contract consist of those terms on which the writings of the parties agree, together with any supplementary terms incorporated under any other provisions of this Act.

But part of the "acting" we consider in determining whether the parties have recognized an agreement includes what they are saying to one another about that "agreement." Although conduct matters under 2-204 (and 2-207(3)), it matters because of what Llewellyn believed it told us about the intent of the parties. So it follows that conduct does not override the intent of the parties; rather, conduct by itself can be evidence of their intent in the absence of intent otherwise clearly expressed:

> Under the Uniform Commercial Code, if the parties have intended to contract, and if an appropriate remedy may be fashioned, a contract for sale does not fail for indefiniteness if terms, even important terms, are left open. It is no longer true that dispute over material terms inevitably prevents formation of a binding contract. What is true, and decisive in this case, is that when a dispute over material terms manifests a lack of intention to contract, no contract results.

> The basic philosophy of the sales article of the Uniform Commercial Code is simple. Practical business people cannot be expected to govern their actions with reference to nice legal formalisms. Thus, when there is a basic agreement, however manifested and whether or not the precise moment of agreement may be determined, failure to articulate that agreement in the precise language of a lawyer, with every difficulty and contingency considered and resolved, will not prevent formation of a contract. But, of equal importance, if there be no basic agreement, the code will not imply one.
>
> *Kleinschmidt Div. of SCM Corp. v. Futuronics*, 363 N.E.2d 701 (N.Y. 1977).

PROBLEM 3 - 1

When the hydraulic sausage-stuffing machine at the store broke down, Rae called a number of equipment sellers around the state, looking for a replacement machine. None of them had a new machine, but the dealer in the next town up the interstate had a lightly used machine for sale, so Rae drove up to look at it. The machine was in perfect condition, so Rae told the sales rep she would take it. While they were walking back to his office, the sales rep told a caller who was inquiring about the machine that "it had just been sold." The rep gave Rae all of the manuals and service materials for the machine, including the serial number and the number to call to get the warranty on the machine transferred to her. They agreed that the sales rep would get her the sales invoice and shipping documents for the machine as soon as possible. As she stood to leave, the sales rep shook her hand, exclaiming, "I'm so glad we were able to make this deal!" After she left, he called the sales manager to tell her he had just made a great deal for the sausage stuffer.

Back at the store, Rae emailed the rep reiterating how excited she was to get the sausage stuffer at the price they had agreed to and letting him know that the warranty has been transferred. When the documents did not arrive by the end of the next week, Rae called the sales rep and was told the machine had been sold to someone else—he explained that "we just got a much better offer than yours, so we sold it." Can Rae enforce her "deal" for the sausage machine under Article 2? 2-204(1).

PROBLEM 3 - 2

Rae saw an ad in the local restaurant association's newsletter for some of the equipment from a restaurant that had closed down. One of the items in the ad was a commercial-grade gas grill which the store needed to prepare the in-store samples it offered to customers shopping on weekends. She e-mailed the agent listed in the ad, expressing interest in the grill. The agent left Rae a voicemail asking her to return his call to discuss the sale of the grill, which was priced at $12,000. Rae e-mailed the agent, stating:

> I am interested in purchasing the grill. My offer is $8,000 delivered. If there is a good time for us to talk, let me know.

The agent e-mailed back that he had conveyed "your offer" to his boss and that he hoped to have "something concrete in the next day or so." A couple of days later, the agent e-mailed her again, stating:

> Rae: I talked with my boss today, and she gave me approval to sell the grill for the amount you offered in your e-email. Please let me know if you work through a purchase order system or if we need to put together a sales agreement.

Later that day, Rae e-mailed the agent a purchase order filled out for the sale of the grill, telling him to call if there were any problems and noting that she'd like to get the grill by the end of the week. She then called the gas company and made arrangements for a technician to hook up the grill when it arrived.

She didn't hear back from the agent, and her calls and emails went unanswered all week. Late on Friday, the agent e-mailed her, telling her that the grill had been sold to another buyer in town as part of a package deal for all of the equipment. Did Rae have an agreement under Article 2 for the purchase of the grill? 2-304.

PROBLEM 3 - 3

Rae was looking to add organic strawberries to the list of chemical-free produce the store was selling, so when she learned that a local grower was now farming organically, she emailed him and attached the following purchase order as a PDF.

> We hereby order whatever organic strawberries you have, subject to sample approval.

The PDF was on the store's letterhead (which listed her as general manager), and left the price line, delivery method, and delivery date lines blank.

The email stated:

> Heard you had organic berries—need them quickly. Strawberries will be approved for purchase upon receipt of evidence of organic certification from qualified agency.
>
> Rae
>
> Say hi to your parents for me.

Rae never heard back and refused to take the truckload of strawberries that arrived at the store several days later. The grower is threatening to sue her for breach of their agreement. Should Rae be worried? 2-206.

2. The Paper Chase

Liberating contract formation from the formalism required by the common law did not eliminate all formation disputes. Even if the facts are sufficient to show agreement between the parties, the problem of determining the terms of their agreement often remains, and 2-207 is ready to address that problem. Under Article 2, the issue is more likely to be what are the terms of the agreement rather than was there an agreement in the first place—and Llewellyn gave us 2-207 to sort out those disputes.

One reason we may have this problem is because the parties tried to form their contract using the offer–acceptance process from common law. Although Article 2 does not require that a contract be formed by offer and acceptance, an accepted offer would be "sufficient to show agreement" under 2-204(1)—it's just no longer the exclusive means of showing agreement. But should an acceptance that varies the terms of the offer be sufficient to show agreement under Article 2, when it did not create an enforceable agreement at common law? Remember the mirror-image rule from your contracts course?

Here, too, was another example of the law giving more significance to the paper than the parties, and so Llewellyn did away with the rule in Article 2. In the typical commercial transaction covered by Article 2, buyers and sellers had their own paper drafted by their lawyers to protect their own interests, and, when exchanged on the fly as a matter of course by the parties, it was unlikely to match—except as to the terms that were specific to the transaction—price, quality, quantity, delivery, and maybe a few others. Filed away, mostly unread, until a problem arose, Llewellyn was unwilling to let this paper determine whether a contract was formed in the usual case. Instead, 2-207(1) provides:

> A definite and seasonable expression of acceptance or a written confirmation which is sent within a reasonable time operates as an acceptance even though it states terms additional to or different from those offered or agreed upon, unless acceptance is expressly made conditional on assent to the additional or different terms.

The next case and the problems that follow it explore the basic application of 2-207(1).

OPTION WIRELESS, LTD. V. OPENPEAK, INC.

UNITED STATES DISTRICT COURT FOR THE SOUTHERN DISTRICT OF FLORIDA, 2012
2012 U.S. DIST. LEXIS 172478

MARRA, District Judge.

INTRODUCTION

In July 2010, Counter-Plaintiff OpenPeak Inc. was producing a computer tablet product for AT&T. Seeking embedded wireless data modules for the tablet, Counter-Plaintiff submitted a purchase order to Counter-Defendant Option Wireless, Ltd, for 12,300 units of the modules at the price of $848,700.00. Section 9 of the purchase order, labeled "BUYER'S TERMS AND CONDITIONS," provided that

> [a]ll purchase orders and sales are made only upon these terms and conditions and those on the front of this document. This document, and not any quotation, invoice, or other Seller document (which, if construed to be an offer is hereby rejected), will be deemed an offer or an appropriate counter-offer and is a rejection of any other terms or conditions. Seller, by accepting any orders or delivering any products having previously received these terms and conditions, will be deemed to have assented to these terms and conditions, notwithstanding any terms contained in any prior or later communication from Seller, and whether or not Buyer specifically or expressly objects to any of Seller's proposed terms. Buyer's failure to object to any document, communication or act of Seller will not be deemed a waiver of any of these terms and conditions. Any addition or change to these terms and conditions must be specifically agreed to in writing by a duly authorized officer of Buyer before becoming binding on Buyer.

The parties agreed that the modules would be delivered in separate shipments. After Counter-Defendant (the Seller) delivered several shipments, the parties agreed that the Seller would send the remaining units—9,840 modules totaling $678,960.00—in a final shipment to Counter-Plaintiff (the Buyer), contingent on the Buyer putting down a 12.5% deposit payment for the balance due. The Seller's invoice, which reflected these terms, also provided that

> [t]he Buyer has 14 calendar days from the date of the invoice to contest by registered letter addressed to the Seller any aspect of the invoice and the General Sales Conditions referred to therein relating to the Goods received from the Seller. The Buyer shall be deemed to have accepted the terms of any invoice (including the General Sales Conditions referred to therein) if the Seller fails to receive a notification from the Buyer within such time period.

> [Clauses followed that (1) limited buyer's remedies for breach and (2) excluded consequential damages.]

The Buyer paid the deposit, $84,870.00, and the Seller delivered the goods on January 14, 2011.

Upon inspecting "a representative sample of the modules" in the final shipment, the Buyer found several defects, and formally rejected the modules on January 24, 2011, because they failed "to conform to material product specifications." The Buyer accordingly returned the defective modules on April 12, 2011. The Seller received the goods and subsequently requested data from the Buyer to prove the modules were not defective. The Buyer complied. The Buyer maintains that the Seller has not shown that "the modules were not defective or otherwise conformed to material product specifications."

The Buyer brings four counts against the Seller, three of which are for breach of contract. These three counts allege that the initial purchase order that the Buyer submitted to the Seller is the controlling written contract between the parties, that the Seller breached the contract by delivering defective modules, and that the Seller's breach caused the Buyer harm in the form of, *inter alia*, causing the Buyer to lose its tablet project with AT&T. The Buyer seeks damages including but not limited to incidental and consequential damages as compensation.

The Seller has moved to dismiss the Buyer's breach of contract claims on the grounds that the purchase order is not the controlling contract, the terms of the controlling contract "explicitly preclude [the Seller's] liability for consequential damages," and, in any event, the Buyer has not properly pleaded its alleged entitlement to consequential damages. For the reasons that follow, the Seller's Motion to Dismiss is denied.

DISCUSSION

"The elements of a breach of contract action are (1) valid contract; (2) a material breach; and (3) damages." *Kaloe Shipping Co. Ltd v. Goltens Serv. Co., Inc.*, 315 F. App'x 877, 880 (11th Cir. 2009). At the heart of the Seller's Motion to Dismiss is the argument that the "valid contract" between the parties does not allow for consequential damages; thus, the Buyer's breach of contract claims requesting such damages cannot properly state a claim for relief. To determine what contract controls the dispute between these two parties—and by extension, whether that contract permits recovery of the consequential damages that the Buyer seeks—the Court must engage in "the battle of the forms" governed by Section 2-207 of the Uniform Commercial Code.

A. Battle of the Forms
Section 2-207 provides that

> (1) A definite and seasonable expression of acceptance or a written confirmation which is sent within a reasonable time operates as an acceptance even though it states terms additional to or different from those offered or agreed upon, unless acceptance is expressly made conditional on assent to the additional or different terms.

> (2) The additional terms are to be construed as proposals for addition to the contract. Between merchants such terms become part of the contract unless:

>> (a) The offer expressly limits acceptance to the terms of the offer;

>> (b) They materially alter it; or

>> (c) Notification of objection to them has already been given or is given within a reasonable time after notice of them is received.

> (3) Conduct by both parties which recognizes the existence of a contract is sufficient to establish a contract for sale although the writings of the parties do not otherwise establish a contract. In such case the terms of the particular contract consist of those terms on which the writings of the parties agree, together with any supplementary terms incorporated under any other provisions of this code.

Section 2-207 accounts for today's reality that the traditional common law "mirror image" rule—which foreclosed contractual formation where terms of an offer and acceptance varied—is "both unfair and unrealistic in the commercial context." While the terms of an offer and of an acceptance in today's commercial transactions will rarely "mirror" each other, § 2-207 nevertheless allows parties to form a contract in situations where they reach an agreement and subsequently exchange forms "which purport to memorialize the agreement, but which differ because each party has drafted his form to give him advantage." This is the situation before the Court.

The parties here did not enter into a formal written contract. They engaged in the common commercial practice of a buyer submitting an order, a seller filling the order, and both parties exchanging forms with self-serving boilerplate language. "This is precisely the type of situation in which Article Two of the UCC is utilized to fill the gaps." While both parties here admit that their disagreement over controlling contract terms presents the classic § 2-207 "battle of the forms" scenario, however, neither party employs the proper analysis to determine what those terms should be.

Section 2-207 lays out three ways for parties to form a contract. First, the parties can exchange forms with divergent terms; if the offeree's expression of acceptance or written confirmation is not made "expressly conditional" on the offeror's assent to the additional or different terms, a contract is formed. U.C.C. § 2-207(1). The three-part test of § 2-207(2) would then come into play to determine the precise terms of the contract. Second, if the offeree's expression of acceptance or written confirmation is made "expressly conditional" on the offeror's assent to the additional or different terms, then that acknowledgment is treated merely as a counteroffer. A contract could only be formed in that situation upon the original offeror's expression of affirmative acceptance of the counteroffer. Finally, where the first two possible avenues do not result in contract formation, a contract may nevertheless be formed via § 2-207(3) where the conduct of the parties demonstrates a belief that a contractual agreement was formed.

By the terms of § 2-207, a contract can only be formed under § 2-207(1) or § 2-207(3)—it cannot be formed under both. If a contract is properly formed under § 2-207(1), § 2-207(2) is applied merely to determine that contract's terms. Section 2-207(2) does not apply where a contract is formed by operation of § 2-207(3). Courts have applied this analysis in both possible scenarios—contract formation under § 2-207(1) that looks to §2-207(2) but not § 2-207(3), and contract formation under § 2-207(3) that does not look to either § 2-207(1) or § 2-207(2). Thus, before this Court can decide what terms govern the contractual relationship between the Buyer and the Seller, the Court must determine how the parties formed their contract.

B. Formation Under § 2-207(1)

First, the Court looks to § 2-207(1) to determine whether the writings of the parties—here the Buyer's purchase order and the Seller's invoice—established a contract. The Buyer's purchase order served as the offer in this transaction, expressing the Buyer's desire to purchase a specific number of modules at a specific price. But the application of § 2-207(1) here turns on whether the Seller's invoice constituted an acceptance such that a contract was formed.

The first clause of § 2-207(1) suggests that the invoice did constitute an acceptance of the Buyer's offer because it was "a written confirmation ... sent within a reasonable time ... even though it state[d] terms additional to or different from those offered or agreed upon." Fulfilling the first clause, however, does not end the inquiry. After the comma, Section 2-207(1) provides a restriction on contract formation where "acceptance is expressly made conditional on assent to the additional or different terms." The only provision of the Seller's invoice that could be interpreted as making acceptance "expressly conditional on assent to the different terms" reads,

> The Buyer has 14 calendar days from the date of the invoice to contest by registered letter addressed to the Seller any aspect of the invoice and the General Sales Conditions referred to therein relating to the Goods received from the Seller. The Buyer shall be deemed to

have accepted the terms of any invoice (including the General Sales Conditions referred to therein) if the Seller fails to receive a notification from the Buyer within such time period.

To determine whether this provision of the Seller's invoice prevents the formation of a contract under § 2-207(1), the Court looks to other courts that have analyzed the issue.

Provisions that have been interpreted to expressly condition acceptance on assent to additional or different terms, thus preventing contractual formation under § 2-207(1), include one that stated, "Seller's acceptance of Buyer's order and shipments made pursuant thereto are subject to and expressly conditioned upon Buyer's acceptance of the terms and conditions herein...." *See Coastal & Native Plant Specialties, Inc.*, 139 F. Supp. 2d at 1328. Another similar provision read, "Seller's acceptance of any offer by Purchaser to purchase the Products is expressly conditional upon the Purchaser's assent to all the terms and conditions herein, including any terms additional to or different from those contained in the offer to purchase." *See PCS Nitrogen Fertilizer, L.P.*, 225 F.3d at 976. Yet another stated, "Where this agreement is found to be an acknowledgment, if such acknowledgment constitutes an acceptance of an offer such acceptance is expressly made conditional upon Buyer's assent solely to the terms of such acknowledgment, and acceptance of any part of Product(s) delivered by Company shall be deemed to constitute such assent by Buyer." *See Belden Inc.*, 885 N.E.2d at 755. And finally, a provision within a purchase order provided that it was "an acceptance of such offer subject to the express condition that the Seller assent that this Purchase Order constitutes the entire agreement between Buyer and Seller with respect to the subject matter hereof and the subject matter of such offer." *See White Consol. Indus., Inc.*, 165 F.3d at 1191.

Conversely, a provision that has been interpreted to *not* expressly condition acceptance on assent to additional or different terms, thus *not* preventing contractual formation under § 2-207(1), reads, "Execution of this agreement constitutes an acceptance expressly limited to the terms herein and any additional or different terms suggested by Seller are hereby rejected unless expressly agreed to in writing by Buyer." *See Westinghouse Elec. Corp.*, 647 F. Supp. at 898. The court in *Westinghouse* reasoned that the purchase order containing this provision operated as an acceptance "because acceptance here was *not* expressly made conditional on assent to the different terms. [The] language of an 'acceptance expressly limited to the terms herein' does not invalidate the acceptance itself. Rather, that language merely qualifies the acceptance and limits its scope to those 'terms herein.'" *Id.* at 900 (emphasis in original) (citations omitted). This result, the court concluded, was consistent with the policy behind § 2-207: that large-scale business transactions are facilitated by recognizing contracts even though certain terms conflict.

A perusal of the law directs this Court to interpret narrowly the "expressly made conditional" language of § 2-207(1)'s second clause. *See Jom, Inc.*, 193 F.3d at 53 (a "seller's invoice is not deemed 'expressly conditional' under § 2-207 merely because its terms do not *match* the terms of the buyer's offer. Rather, to be deemed 'expressly conditional,' the seller's invoice must place the buyer on unambiguous notice that the invoice is a mere counteroffer.") (emphasis in original). Provisions that have prevented contract formation under § 2-207(1) have either tracked the language of the statute or expressed the intent to condition acceptance in no uncertain terms. As one court has stated,

> In order to fall within [the Subsection 2-207(1) proviso,] it is not enough that an acceptance is expressly conditional on additional or different terms; rather an acceptance must be *expressly* conditional on the offeror's *assent* to those terms. Viewing the Subsection (1) proviso within the context of the rest of that Subsection and within the policies of Section 2-207 itself, we believe that it was intended to apply only to an acceptance which clearly reveals that the offeree is unwilling to proceed with the transaction unless he is assured of the offeror's assent to the additional or different terms therein. That the acceptance is predicated on the offeror's assent must be directly and distinctly stated or expressed rather than implied or left to inference.

Dorton v. Collins & Aikman Corp., 453 F.2d 1161, 1168 (6th Cir. 1972) (citations and quotations omitted). Consequently, the Seller's invoice does not prevent the formation of a contract in this instance because the invoice does not by any terms "expressly condition" acceptance on "assent to the additional or different terms." Rather, the invoice merely requests that the Buyer contest any unwelcome terms within a specified time period (14 calendar days); otherwise, "The Buyer shall be deemed to have accepted the terms of any invoice...." The Court does not interpret this request as expressly conditioning acceptance on assent to the additional or different terms because finding otherwise would require ignoring § 2-207(1)'s specific language and inferring the Seller's intent. Moreover, in other cases dealing with provisions that set deadlines for objections to terms, courts have only found the provisions to "expressly condition" acceptance on assent to additional or different terms where the provision included "expressly conditional" language *in addition to* the deadline for objections. The Seller here included the deadline for objections, not the language that would have unequivocally expressed an intent to condition acceptance on the Buyer's assent to the conflicting terms. Thus, with the parties having formed a contract under § 2-207(1), the Court turns to § 2-207(2) to interpret that contract's terms.

* * * *

D. Formation Under § 2-207(3)

The Seller, relying on *Premix-Marbletite Manufacturing Corp. v. SKW Chemicals, Inc.*, 145 F. Supp. 2d 1348 (S.D. Fla. 2001), states that § 2-207(3) "must be applied by the Court here to determine the terms of the parties [sic] contract." For the reasons set forth above, the Court disagrees.

Section 2-207(3) allows for the formation of a contract where "[c]onduct by both parties which recognizes the existence of a contract is sufficient to establish a contract for sale *although the writings of the parties do not otherwise establish a contract.*" (emphasis added). Here, the writings of the parties do establish a contract under § 2-207(1) because the Seller's invoice does not expressly condition acceptance on the Buyer's assent to the conflicting terms. *Premix* provides no support for the Seller's position because *Premix* did not analyze whether the parties formed a contract under § 2-207(1). Rather, the court in *Premix* began its § 2-207 analysis by concluding that "[t]he parties did not enter into a formal written contract for the sale of [goods]" and that "the agreement for the sale of [goods] existed by virtue of the parties' conduct, not by the virtue of the exchange of forms." *Premix-Marbletite Mfg. Corp.*, 145 F. Supp. 2d at 1354-55. The court did not analyze whether the seller's invoice expressly conditioned acceptance on assent to different terms and instead proceeded directly to a conclusion that the parties' conduct established a contract under § 2-207(3). This Court need not address whether the conduct of the parties here formed a contract because their writings established a contract under § 2-207(1).

Problem 3 - 4

Rae's younger brother, Roy, runs the flower shop at the store. Flowers, like produce, have a short shelf life at the store, which means Roy must restock his inventory frequently to keep it fresh. Purchase orders are going out and flowers are arriving all day long every day—even on weekends—and as a result transactions are often done on the fly, with little attention paid to the details beyond the price, quantity, delivery, and type of flowers involved.

Are the following deals Roy made last week enforceable under 2-207(1)?

1. Roy sent a purchase order to the nursery across town for "ten dozen lilies at market, long cut, no white, guaranteed live on delivery, 5 percent shrinkage, receive by Tuesday our terms." The nursery replied, "Will do, terms attached."

2. Would your answer be different if the nursery had replied: "Will try—is Wednesday okay? If not, then no shrinkage guarantee" Or "Accept at cost plus 10 percent"? Why?

> Dickered terms have been described as those terms that are unique to each transaction such as price, quality, quantity, or delivery terms as compared to the usual unbargained terms on the reverse side [of a form] concerning remedies, arbitration and the like.... Section 2-207 of the UCC is designed to prescribe, by law, what nonnegotiated terms are to be considered a part of the contract—not to exclude those terms specifically negotiated and agreed upon—i.e., dickered terms.

> *Laforce v. Pioneer Gen.,* 2011 Mich. App. LEXIS 1667.

3. Roy sent a purchase order to the ceramics dealer supplying the store with flower vases, ordering "two hundred bud vases, medium, assortment colors, catalog price plus shipping, delivery by 15th." The dealer replied: "Accept your offer—terms attached." The attached terms provided that payment was due on delivery, that any disputes were subject to arbitration, and that consequential damages were excluded—matters that were not addressed in the purchase order or the store's terms.

4. Roy e-mailed the local rose grower that he "was looking for fifty to sixty dozen long-stemmed Grandiflora roses for immediate delivery—do you have any?" The grower replied: "Have roses you need at cost plus 15 percent, delivery in forty-eight hours, standard terms—see website." The "Standard Terms" on the website provided that payment was due on delivery, that any disputes were subject to arbitration, and that consequential damages were excluded. Roy sent the grower a purchase order for "sixty dozen long-stemmed Grandiflora roses at market plus 15 percent, delivery within forty-eight hours." On the back of the purchase order were the store's "Terms and Conditions," which stated "payment net 30 days."

An acceptance that varies the terms of the offer is sufficient to show agreement and a contract is formed, but what are the terms of that contract—what happens to the "additional or different" terms in the acceptance? The answer provided in 2-207(2) is deceptively simple at first glance: we are told to treat them as proposals for inclusion in the contract that has been formed. But determining whether they actually become part of the contract requires a Rube Goldberg-like construction of 2-207(2) and its Comments. What happens to the terms depends first on whether the parties are merchants. If both parties are not merchants, the terms never become part of the contract unless the nonmerchant assents to them. Assent requires, for most courts, an affirmative communication on the part of the nonmerchant—failing to object to the inclusion of the terms is not assent. When both parties are merchants, the proposed terms become a part of the contract unless excluded by 2-207(2) because:

(a) the offer expressly limits acceptance to the terms of the offer;

(b) they [the variant terms] materially alter it; or

(c) notification of objection to them has already been given or is given within a reasonable time after notice of them is received.

Most disputes about whether a term became part of the contract are based on the material alteration exclusion, which the Comments define in terms of "surprise" or "hardship," both of which have created their own issues of interpretation, as the next case illustrates.

BEARDEN V. GREAT LAKES PRODUCE & MKTG. LLC

UNITED STATES DISTRICT COURT FOR THE WESTERN DISTRICT OF MICHIGAN, 2013
2013 U.S. DIST. LEXIS 74408

QUIST, District Judge.

I. FACTUAL BACKGROUND

In July 2011, Great Lakes ordered a shipment of grape tomatoes from Bearden, doing business as J & J Tomato Farm. Bearden shipped the tomatoes on July 13, 2011. Great Lakes hired a driver to pick up the shipment, and the driver signed a bill of lading for the shipment dated July 13, 2011. The bill of lading listed the quantity (1,800 total boxes) of bulk grape tomatoes but did not include a price per unit, and indicated the total amount due was $0.00. Bearden also sent Great Lakes an invoice dated July 13, 2011 for $28,710.00, which Great Lakes alleges arrived a week later. By the time the invoice arrived, Great Lakes had already accepted the shipment and distributed the tomatoes to its customers. Both the bill of lading and invoice included the following language:

> "the perishable commodities listed on this invoice are sold subject to the statutory trust authorized by section 5 (c) of the perishable agriculture commodities act, 1930 (7 u.s.c. 499e (c) [sic], the seller of these commodities retains a trust claim over these commodities, all inventories of food or other products derived from these commodities, and any receivables or proceeds from the sale of these commodities until full payment is received."

> any claims for shortage, damage or condition will not be honored unless reported to shipper in writing within eight (8) hours of arrival and with a timely USDA inspection

> Interest shall accrue at 1.5% per month (18% per annum)

> buyer agrees to pay all costs of collection including attorney's fees.

Upon receipt of the invoice, Great Lakes did not contact Bearden to object to the contractual terms. This transaction was the first and only transaction between the parties. Bearden filed this litigation in July 2012 for violations of PACA and breach of contract. The parties now dispute whether Bearden is entitled to attorney's fees and costs of collection pursuant to their contract.

II. DISCUSSION

Entitlement to Attorney's Fees

The PACA statute allows a party to collect "all sums owing" in connection with the perishable commodities transactions at issue in a case. 7 U.S.C. § 499e(c)(2). If the parties have contracted for attorney's fees, courts have held that attorney's fees are encompassed within the language "all sums owing."

To determine whether the attorney's fees and collection costs provision is a part of the contract, this Court looks to the Uniform Commercial Code § 2-207 as adopted in Michigan. Michigan Compiled Laws § 440.2207 states:

* * * *

(2) The additional terms are to be construed as proposals for addition to the contract. Between merchants such terms become part of the contract unless:

(a) the offer expressly limits acceptance to the terms of the offer; (b) *they materially alter it*; or

(c) notification of objection to them has already been given or is given within a reasonable time after notice of them is received.

* * * *

Mich. Comp. Laws § 440.2207 (emphasis added). The Committee Comments to § 2-207 provide in pertinent part:

4. Examples of typical clauses which would normally "materially alter" the contract and so result in surprise or hardship if incorporated without express awareness by the other party are: a clause negating such standard warranties as that of merchantability or fitness for a particular purpose in circumstances in which either warranty normally attaches; a clause requiring a guaranty of 90% or 100% deliveries in a case such as a contract by cannery, where the usage of the trade allows greater quantity leeways; a clause reserving to the seller the power to cancel upon the buyer's failure to meet any invoice when due; a clause requiring that complaints be made in a time materially shorter than customary or reasonable.

5. Examples of clauses which involve no element of unreasonable surprise and which therefore are to be incorporated in the contract unless notice of objection is seasonably given are: a clause setting forth and perhaps enlarging slightly upon the seller's exemption due to supervening causes beyond his control, similar to those covered by the provision of this Article on merchant's excuse by failure of presupposed conditions or a clause fixing in advance any reasonable formula of proration under such circumstances; a clause fixing a reasonable time for complaints within customary limits, or in the case of a purchase for subsale, providing for inspection by the sub-purchaser; a clause providing for interest on overdue invoices or fixing the seller's standard credit terms where they are within the range of trade practice and do not limit any credit bargained for; a clause limiting the right of rejection for defects which fall within the customary trade tolerances for acceptance "with adjustment" or otherwise limiting remedy in a reasonable manner (see Sections 2-718 and 2-719).

Neither of the Committee Comments addresses an attorney's fee provision.

"An additional term is a material alteration if it 'results in a surprise or hardship if incorporated without the express awareness by the other party.'" *ISRA Vision, AG v. Burton Indus., Inc.,* 654 F. Supp. 2d 638, 648 (E.D. Mich. 2009). "The majority of the courts reviewing whether an additional term is a material alteration hold that it depends on the unique facts of each particular case." Michigan Courts "consider many factors in determining whether a party was unreasonably surprised by an additional term, such as prior course of dealing; the number of confirmations exchanged; absence of industry custom; whether the addition was clearly marked; and whether the addition is contained within the party's own standard contract." "With regard to hardship, the analysis of the existence of hardship focuses on whether the clause at issue would impose substantial economic hardship on the nonassenting party."

"Comment 4 to UCC 2-207 states that surprise occurs when a term is included without the express awareness of the other party." *Am. Ins. Co. v. El Paso Pipe & Supply Co.,* 978 F.2d 1185, 1190-91 (10th Cir. 1992). "[A]wareness does not necessarily require a party actually to have read the additional term. Therefore, on the issue of surprise there is both a subjective and an objective element to the inquiry." *Id.* "Courts should first make factual findings as to whether a nonassenting party subjectively knew of an added term. It must then make findings of fact concerning whether that party should have known that such a term would be included." *Id.* "'[T]he burden of proving the materiality of the alteration must fall on the party that opposes inclusion.'" *Aceros Prefabricados, S.A. v. TradeArbed, Inc.,* 282 F.3d 92, 100 (2d Cir. 2002). "This is so because the UCC presumes that between merchants additional terms will be included in a contract. Thus, 'if neither party introduced any evidence, the [proposed additional term] would, by the plain language of § 2-207(2), become a part of the contract.'" *Id.; see also Dale R. Horning,* 730 F. Supp. at 966 (finding that between merchants the nonassenting party bears the burden of showing a term materially alters a contract).

In this case, the language of § 2-207 presumes Great Lakes to have read the additional terms—and for those terms to become a part of the contract—unless Great Lakes objects within a reasonable period of time or the provision materially altered the contract. Great Lakes did not object to the contract's terms. Therefore, its only argument is that the provision materially altered the contract.

Applying the unreasonable surprise factors, Great Lakes either knew or should have known that an attorney's fees provision was in the contract. First, Great Lakes has not shown the absence of custom regarding attorney's fees provisions in produce contracts. Great Lakes concedes that it uses attorney's fees provisions in its own produce contracts and has even enforced them in court. The burden is on Great Lakes to introduce evidence in support of its argument that there is an absence of custom, thereby rendering an attorney's fees provision a material alteration. Great Lakes cites *Mikey's Choice LLC v. Fagos LLC,* for the proposition that attorney's fees provisions in produce contracts are not universal. However, its reliance on *Mikey's* is misplaced. The court in *Mikey's* held that the plaintiff could not rely on a PACA letter of intent—as opposed to a contract between the parties—to collect attorney's fees. *Id.* The court surveyed cases in which courts have granted attorney's fees in PACA cases, but the court did not make a finding on the existence or absence of an industry custom. *See id.* If anything, the case lends support to Plaintiff's argument that attorney's fees provisions are quite common in produce cases and a merchant like Great Lakes should not be surprised by such a provision. Thus, Great Lakes has failed to establish that there is an absence of industry custom, and the evidence suggests that such provisions are common in produce contracts. This factor weighs in favor of granting Bearden's motion.

Second, and similarly, there is evidence that both parties' standard contracts include attorney's fees provisions. This factor weighs strongly in favor of granting Bearden's motion.

Third, the parties do not have a prior course of dealing. "Thus, this transaction was not one involving parties familiar with the other's forms, terms, and practices." This factor weighs against granting Bearden's motion.

Fourth, the parties exchanged two written confirmations, at least one of which arrived at the time of shipping.[4] This factor does not weigh heavily in favor of either party. Although the parties lack a prior course of dealing, thus making written confirmation important, two written confirmations (with the opportunity to raise objections to the terms within a reasonable time) is sufficient to give a buyer notice of additional terms to the agreement.

Finally, whether the attorney's provision was conspicuously marked does not weigh heavily in favor of either party. The provision was in bold lettering in the center of the first and only page of the bill of lading and the separate invoice. Although the provision is at the end of a paragraph of terms that are not separated by full sentences, the terms constituted only thirteen total lines of text. They were not buried in small text on the back side of the document. *Cf. Comark,* 932 F.2d at 1202 (holding a district court did not clearly err in finding an attorney's fees clause materially altered the contract between first-time parties where the attorney's fee provisions were on the back of the price quotations).

---

4   Great Lakes argues that it cannot be bound by the terms of the bill of lading because it hired an independent driver to pick up the shipment. However, that is not the issue. Although the Court agrees that Great Lakes did not manifest any apparent authority in the driver to *alter* the contract, the bill of lading still constitutes a written confirmation of the contract between the parties that the driver was hired to deliver to Great Lakes. Thus, the Court will still look to the bill of lading, as well as the invoice, for purposes of applying U.C.C. § 2-207.

Taken together, the balance of the factors weighs in favor of granting Bearden's motion. The factors support that Great Lakes knew or should have known that attorney's fees were included in the contract and did not constitute a surprise, material term.

Great Lakes cites two additional, non-binding federal district cases in which courts have found attorney's fees provisions material under U.C.C. § 2-207. First, Great Lakes cites *Food Team International v. Unilink, LLC,* 872 F. Supp. 2d 405, 421 (E.D. Pa.). The court in *Food Team* concluded that the attorney's fees provision was material because it was not in the original contracts negotiated between the parties, and, unlike in *Herzog Oil Field Service, Inc. v. Otto Torpedo Co.,* 391 Pa. Super. 133, 137, 570 A.2d 549, 551 (Penn. 1990), the provision shifted payment of all attorney's fees—as opposed to only a portion—to defendants. However, *Food Team* is distinguishable from the present case. Although the Michigan and Pennsylvania versions of § 2-207 are nearly identical, the court did not apply the Michigan factors as enumerated in *Plastech* to determine whether the defendant knew or should have known that an attorney's fees provision was a part of the contract. Moreover, unlike here, the *Food Team* court did not have evidence that both parties routinely included attorney's fees provisions in their standard contracts. Thus, *Food Team* is distinguishable. Great Lakes also cites *Johnson Tire Service, Inc. v. Thorn, Inc.,* 613 P.2d 521, 524 (Utah 1980). However, *Johnson* is not persuasive because the Court did not conduct a factor-by-factor analysis, but merely concluded that an attorney's fee provision materially altered the offer, and thus did not fall within the "additional or different terms" provision of the U.C.C.

Therefore, in the context of the relationship between Bearden and Great Lakes, Great Lakes knew or should have known that a provision for collection costs and attorney's fees was a part of the contract. Having failed to establish that the provision for attorney's fees materially altered the contract, it cannot be said that Great Lakes was "unreasonably surprised" by the additional term.

Regarding undue hardship, the Court recognizes that the attorney's fees may impose upon Bearden some economic hardship, but an economic hardship is not equivalent to an undue hardship. A party is bound by the contract he signs, absent a valid exception.

PROBLEM 3 - 5

Rae uses a form purchase order for most of the produce the store buys. The form allows her to fill in the type of produce, the price, the quantity, and the delivery date for each order. In each of the following transactions, the seller responded to the order Rae submitted on her form with an invoice that included terms beyond those on her form. Which of the additional terms became a part of her contract with the seller? 2-207.

1. She sent the local produce distributor an order for fifty crates of cantaloupes. The seller's invoice provided that "all warranties, including the warranty of merchantability, are disclaimed."
2. Rae sent a California grower an order for "one truckload of Valencia oranges." The seller's invoice provided that "buyer's remedy for any breach of this agreement by the seller shall be limited to replacement of the nonconforming goods."
3. She ordered two pallets of "Idaho russet potatoes" from a potato broker. The broker's invoice provided that the "Seller was not liable for any failure of or delay in performance of this contract if such failure or delay is caused by acts of god, fires, floods, hurricanes, strikes or labor disputes, embargoes, war, riots, or other force majeure."

4. She ordered two hundred cases of "113 Red Delicious apples" from a Washington grower. The grower's invoice required that "all claims or complaints regarding the apples covered by this agreement shall be made in writing and delivered to seller within five days of delivery of the goods."

5. Rae sent a purchase order for one hundred cases of "Indian River grapefruit, ruby red, 56 size" to a broker in Florida. The seller's invoice "excluded all consequential damages for any breach by Seller."

6. She ordered one hundred cases of "bananas, Dole, no bruise no doubles" directly from Dole. Dole's invoice provided that "all disputes arising under or related to this Contract shall be submitted to binding arbitration before JAMS panel."

7. She sent a purchase order for "one carload, Thompson seedless grapes, extra fancy export" to a collective in Oregon. The collective's invoice included a clause stating that "Buyer shall be responsible for payment of all taxes, including sales taxes, imposed on this Sale by any local, state, or national government."

Another interpretive issue with 2-207(2) is that, by its terms, it only applies to additional terms in an acceptance—it does not tell us what happens to those terms that are different in the acceptance from the terms of the offer but don't prevent contract formation under 2-207(1). Of course, this might not matter for purposes of applying 2-207(2) if, as Judge Posner notes in the case that follows, a different term is also really an additional term—just as an additional term would also be a term different from those in the offer. Since any term not in the offer is by definition an additional term, 2-207(2) applies to all variant terms in an acceptance. But most courts have declined the invitation to adopt the sensible view, opting instead to engage in the "hairsplitting inquiry into the difference between different and additional" described by Judge Posner in the next case.

NORTHROP CORP. V. LITRONIC INDUS.

UNITED STATES COURT OF APPEALS FOR THE SEVENTH CIRCUIT, 1994
29 F.3D 1173

POSNER, Chief Judge.

"Battle of the forms" refers to the not uncommon situation in which one business firm makes an offer in the form of a preprinted form contract and the offeree responds with its own form contract. At common law, any discrepancy between the forms would prevent the offeree's response from operating as an acceptance. So there would be no contract in such a case. This was the "mirror image" rule, which Article 2 of the Uniform Commercial Code jettisoned by providing that "a definite and seasonable expression of acceptance or a written confirmation which is sent within a reasonable time operates as an acceptance even though it states terms additional to or different from those offered or agreed upon, unless acceptance is made conditional on assent to the additional or different terms." UCC § 2-207(1). Mischief lurks in the words "additional to or different from." The next subsection of 2-207 provides that if additional terms in the acceptance are not materially different from those in the offer, then, subject to certain other qualifications, they become part of the contract, § 2-207(2), while if the additional terms are materially different they operate as proposals and so have no effect unless the offeror agrees to them, UCC § 2-207, comment 3; if the offeror does not agree to them, therefore, the terms of the contract are those in the offer. A clause providing for interest at normal rates on overdue invoices, or limiting the right to reject goods because of defects falling within customary trade tolerances for acceptance with adjustment, would be the sort of additional term that is not deemed material, and hence it would become a part of the contract even if the offeror never signified acceptance of it. *Id.,* comment 5.

The Code does not explain, however, what happens if the offeree's response contains *different* terms (rather than additional ones) within the meaning of section 2-207(1). There is no consensus on that question. We know there is a contract because an acceptance is effective even though it contains different terms; but what are the terms of the contract that is brought into being by the offer and acceptance? One view is that the discrepant terms in both the nonidentical offer and the acceptance drop out, and default terms found elsewhere in the Code fill the resulting gap. Another view is that the offeree's discrepant terms drop out and the offeror's become part of the contract. A third view, possibly the most sensible, equates "different" with "additional" and makes the outcome turn on whether the new terms in the acceptance are materially different from the terms in the offer—in which event they operate as proposals, so that the offeror's terms prevail unless he agrees to the variant terms in the acceptance—or not materially different from the terms in the offer, in which event they become part of the contract. This interpretation equating "different" to "additional," bolstered by drafting history which shows that the omission of "or different" from section 2-207(2) was a drafting error, substitutes a manageable inquiry into materiality, for a hair-splitting inquiry into the difference between "different" and "additional." It is hair-splitting ("metaphysical," "casuistic," "semantic," in the pejorative senses of these words) because all different terms are additional and all additional terms are different.

Unfortunately, the Illinois courts—whose understanding of Article 2 of the UCC is binding on us because this is a diversity suit governed, all agree, by Illinois law—have had no occasion to choose among the different positions on the consequences of an acceptance that contains "different" terms from the offer. We shall have to choose.

The battle of the forms in this case takes the form of something very like a badminton game, but we can simplify it a bit without distorting the issues. The players are Northrop, the giant defense firm, and Litronic, which manufactures electronic components, including "printed wire boards" that are incorporated into defense weapon systems. In 1987 Northrop sent several manufacturers, including Litronic, a request to submit offers to sell Northrop a customized printed wire board designated by Northrop as a "1714 Board." The request stated that any purchase would be made by means of a purchase order that would set forth terms and conditions that would override any inconsistent terms in the offer. In response, Litronic mailed an offer to sell Northrop four boards for $19,000 apiece, to be delivered within six weeks. The offer contained a 90-day warranty stated to be in lieu of any other warranties, and provided that the terms of the offer would take precedence over any terms proposed by the buyer. Lynch, a purchasing officer of Northrop, responded to the offer in a phone conversation in which he told Litronic's man, Lair, that he was accepting the offer up to the limit of his authority, which was $24,999, and that a formal purchase order for all four boards would follow. Litronic was familiar with Northrop's purchase order form, having previously done business with Northrop, which had been using the same form for some time. Had Lair referred to any of the previous orders, he would have discovered that Northrop's order form provided for a warranty that contained no time limit.

Lynch followed up the phone conversation a month later with a "turn on" letter, authorizing Litronic to begin production of all four boards (it had done so already) and repeating that a purchase order would follow. The record is unclear when the actual purchase order was mailed; it may have been as much as four months after the phone conversation and three months after the turn-on letter. The purchase order required the seller to send a written acknowledgment to Northrop. Litronic never did so, however, and Northrop did not complain; it does not bother to follow up on its requirement of a signed acknowledgment.

Although Litronic had begun manufacturing the boards immediately after the telephone call from Lynch, for reasons that are unknown but that Northrop does not contend are culpable Litronic did not deliver the first three boards until more than a year later, in July of 1988. Northrop tested the boards for conformity to its specifications. The testing was protracted, either because the boards were highly complex or because Northrop's inspectors were busy, or perhaps for both reasons. At all events it was not until December and January, five or six months after delivery, that Northrop returned the three boards (the fourth had not been delivered), claiming that they were defective. Litronic refused to accept the return of the boards, on the ground that its 90-day warranty had lapsed. Northrop's position of course is that it had an unlimited warranty, as stated in the purchase order.

The parties continue to treat this as a "warranty" case. Their implicit view is that Litronic's 90-day warranty, if a term of the contract, not only barred Northrop from complaining about defects that showed up more than 90 days after the delivery of the boards but also limited to 90 days the time within which Northrop was permitted to reject the boards because of defects that rendered them nonconforming. We accept this view for purposes of deciding these appeals.

Litronic's appeal concerns the breach of its warranty on the No. 1714 boards. It wins if the warranty really did expire after only 90 days. The parties agree that Litronic's offer to sell the No. 1714 boards to Northrop, the offer made in response to Northrop's request for bids, was—the offer. So far, so good. If Northrop's Mr. Lynch accepted the offer over the phone, the parties had a contract then and there, but the question would still be on what terms. Regarding the first question, whether there was a contract, we may assume to begin with that the acceptance was sufficiently "definite" to satisfy the requirement of definiteness in section 2-207(1); after all, it impelled Litronic to begin production immediately, and there is no suggestion that it acted precipitately in doing so. We do not know whether Lynch in his conversation with Lair made acceptance of the complete contract expressly conditional on approval by Lynch's superiors at Northrop. We know that he had authority to contract only up to $24,999, but we do not know whether he told Lair what the exact limitation on his authority was or whether Litronic knew it without being told. It does not matter. The condition, if it was a condition, was satisfied and so drops out.

We do not think that Northrop's acceptance, via Lynch, of Litronic's offer could be thought conditional on Litronic's yielding to Northrop's demand for an open-ended warranty. For while Lynch's reference to the purchase order might have alerted Litronic to Northrop's desire for a warranty not limited to 90 days, Lynch did not purport to make the more extensive warranty a condition of acceptance. So the condition, if there was one, was not an express condition, as the cases insist it be.

There was a contract, therefore; further, and, as we shall note, decisive, evidence being that the parties acted as if they had a contract—the boards were shipped and paid for. The question is then what the terms of the warranty in the contract were. Lynch's reference in the phone conversation to the forthcoming purchase order shows that Northrop's acceptance contained different terms from the offer, namely the discrepant terms in the purchase order, in particular the warranty—for it is plain that the Northrop warranty was intended to be indefinite in length, so that, at least in the absence of some industry custom setting a limit on warranties that do not specify a duration (cf. UCC § 2-207, comments 4 and 5), a point not raised, any limitation on the length of the warranty in the offer would be a materially different term. Of course the fact that Northrop preferred a longer warranty than Litronic was offering does not by itself establish that Northrop's acceptance contained different terms. But Lynch did not accept Litronic's offer and leave it at that. He said that he would issue a Northrop purchase order, and both he and Lair knew (or at least should have known) that the Northrop purchase order form contained a different warranty from Litronic's sale order form. And we have already said that Lynch did not, by his oral reference to the purchase order, condition Northrop's purchase on Litronic's agreeing to comply with all the terms in the purchase order form, given the courts' insistence that any such condition be explicit. (Judges are skeptical that even businesspeople read boilerplate, so they are reluctant, rightly or wrongly, to make a contract fail on the basis of a printed condition in a form contract.) But Lynch said enough to make clear to Lair that the acceptance contained different terms from the offer.

The Uniform Commercial Code, as we have said, does not say what the terms of the contract are if the offer and acceptance contain different terms, as distinct from cases in which the acceptance merely contains additional terms to those in the offer. The majority view is that the discrepant terms fall out and are replaced by a suitable UCC gap-filler. The magistrate judge followed this approach and proceeded to section 2-309, which provides that nonconforming goods may be rejected within a "reasonable" time (see also § 2-601(1)), and she held that the six months that Northrop took to reject Litronic's boards was a reasonable time because of the complexity of the required testing. The leading minority view is that the discrepant terms *in the acceptance* are to be ignored, and that would give the palm to Litronic. Our own preferred view—the view that assimilates "different" to "additional," so that the terms in the offer prevail over the different terms in the acceptance only if the latter are not materially different, has as yet been adopted by only one state, California. Under that view, as under what we are calling the "leading" minority view, the warranty in Litronic's offer, the 90-day warranty, was the contractual warranty, because the unlimited warranty contained in Northrop's acceptance was materially different.

Because Illinois in other UCC cases has tended to adopt majority rules, and because the interest in the uniform nationwide application of the Code—an interest asserted in the Code itself (see § 1-102)—argues for nudging majority views, even if imperfect (but not downright bad), toward unanimity, we start with a presumption that Illinois, whose position we are trying to predict, would adopt the majority view. We do not find the presumption rebutted. The idea behind the majority view is that the presence of different terms in the acceptance suggests that the offeree didn't *really* accede to the offeror's terms, yet both parties wanted to contract, so why not find a neutral term to govern the dispute that has arisen between them? Of course the offeree may not have had any serious objection to the terms *in the offer* at the time of contracting; he may have mailed a boilerplated form without giving any thought to its contents or to its suitability for the particular contract in question. But it is just as likely that the discrepant terms in the offer itself were the product of a thoughtless use of a boilerplate form rather than a considered condition of contracting. And if the offeror doesn't want to do business other than on the terms in the offer, he can protect himself by specifying that the offeree must accept all those terms for the parties to have a contract. UCC § 2-207(2)(a). Now as it happens Litronic did state in its offer that the terms in the offer "take precedence over terms and conditions of the buyer, unless specifically negotiated otherwise." But, for reasons that we do not and need not fathom, Litronic does not argue that this language conditioned the existence of the contract on Northrop's acceding to the 90-day warranty in the offer; any such argument is therefore waived.

It is true that the offeree likewise can protect himself by making his acceptance of the offer conditional on the offeror's acceding to any different terms in the acceptance. But so many acceptances are made over the phone by relatively junior employees, as in this case, that it may be unrealistic to expect offerees to protect themselves in this way. The offeror goes first and therefore has a little more time for careful specification of the terms on which he is willing to make a contract. What we are calling the leading minority view may tempt the offeror to spring a surprise on the offeree, hoping the latter won't read the fine print. Under the majority view, if the offeree tries to spring a surprise (the offeror can't, since his terms won't prevail if the acceptance contains different terms), the parties move to neutral ground; and the offeror can, we have suggested, more easily protect himself against being surprised than the offeree can protect *himself* against being surprised. The California rule dissolves all these problems, but has too little support to make it a plausible candidate for Illinois, or at least a plausible candidate for our guess as to Illinois's position.

There is a further wrinkle, however. The third subsection of section 2-207 provides that even if no contract is established under either of the first two subsections, it may be established by the "conduct of the parties," and in that event (as subsection (3) expressly provides) the discrepant terms vanish and are replaced by UCC gap fillers. This may seem to make it impossible for the offeror to protect himself from being contractually bound by specifying that the acceptance must mirror his offer. But subsection (3) comes into play only when the parties have by their conduct manifested the existence of a contract, as where the offeror, having specified that the acceptance must mirror the offer yet having received an acceptance that deviates from the offer, nonetheless goes ahead and performs as if there were a contract. That is one way to interpret what happened here but it leads to the same result as applying subsection (2) interpreted as the majority of states do, so we need not consider it separately.

Given the intricacy of the No. 1714 boards, it is unlikely that Northrop would have acceded to a 90-day limitation on its warranty protection. Litronic at argument stressed that it is a much smaller firm, hence presumably unwilling to assume burdensome warranty obligations; but it is a curious suggestion that little fellows are more likely than big ones to get their way in negotiations between firms of disparate size. And Northrop actually got only half its way, though enough for victory here; for by virtue of accepting Litronic's offer without expressly conditioning its acceptance on Litronic's acceding to Northrop's terms, Northrop got not a warranty unlimited in duration, as its purchase order provides, but (pursuant to the majority understanding of UCC § 2-207(2)) a warranty of "reasonable" duration, courtesy the court. If special circumstances made a 90-day warranty reasonable, Litronic was free to argue for it in the district court.

On the view we take, the purchase order has no significance beyond showing that Northrop's acceptance contained (albeit by reference) different terms. The fact that Litronic never signed the order, and the fact that Northrop never called this omission to Litronic's attention, also drop out of the case, along with Northrop's argument that to enforce the 90-day limitation in Litronic's warranty would be unconscionable. But for future reference we remind Northrop and companies like it that the defense of unconscionability was not invented to protect multi-billion dollar corporations against mistakes committed by their employees, and indeed has rarely succeeded outside the area of consumer contracts.

AFFIRMED.

Most courts have refused to equate different with additional, even though, as Judge Posner noted, that interpretation is "possibly the most sensible" and "bolstered by drafting history which shows that the omission of 'different' from 2-207(2) was a drafting error." It's also supported by the text of the statute—we don't need to decipher the conflicting Comments to justify it. Recall that when a contract is formed by conduct under 2-207(3), the contract consists "of those terms on which the writings of the parties agree." What happens to conflicting terms—they don't become part of the contract—they are "knocked out" of the agreement recognized by Article 2. Judge Posner recognized this, but never connected it back to his most sensible interpretation:

> If no contract is established under either of the first two sections [of 2-207], it may be established by the "conduct of the parties," and in that event (as subsection (3) expressly provides) the discrepant terms vanish and are displaced by UCC gap fillers.

If the drafters intended to knock out the "different" terms in an acceptance under 2-207(2), they would have used the language used in 2-207(3) to express that intent—they would not have done so by saying nothing. And of course, this interpretation is not without support in the Comments, regardless of how convoluted they may be as a whole:

> Whether or not additional or *different* terms will become part of the agreement depends upon the provisions of subsection (2).

Comment 3, 2-207 (emphasis added).[5]

PROBLEM 3 - 6

Rae decides to replace the old (and rusted) steel-wire shopping carts at the store with new, lightweight plastic carts. The plastic carts are safer—they come with seat belts for the child's seat—and they are more friendly to the store's fixtures—shelving, freezer cases, and checkout counters. After talking with

---

5   *See, e.g.,* Murray, "The Chaos of the 'Battle of the Forms': Solutions," 39 *Vand. L. Rev.* 1305, 1355 (1986).

several sellers, she settles on a local supplier and e-mails an offer to purchase "five hundred Versacart V-Series 170-liter plastic carts with ergonomic handles at catalog price, our Standard Terms to apply, see attachment." The Standard Terms were attached to her e-mail and provided, among other terms, that the local federal district court "had exclusive jurisdiction and venue for resolution of any disputes arising out of this sale." The seller sent Rae a "Sales Invoice" confirming the sale of the five hundred Vesacarts which stated that "Seller has accepted your offer on the terms and conditions set forth on the reverse side of this invoice. You should read those terms before accepting delivery of the goods." The seller's terms required that "any disputes arising under this Agreement or related to this Agreement shall be resolved by arbitration conducted in accord with AAA rules." Rae takes delivery of the carts and places them in service at the store. Several months later, when the wheels start locking up on many of the carts and the seller refuses to remedy the problem, if Rae sues the seller in federal court, will the seller be able to compel arbitration of the dispute, based on the invoice? 2-207(2).

PROBLEM 3 - 7

If Rae's Standard Terms in the last problem had provided that "Seller warrants the goods are merchantable and fit for the purposes for which they are purchased," and the seller's invoice had stated that "Seller disclaims all warranties, including the warranties of merchantability and fitness for a particular purpose," would the warranties otherwise implied by Article 2 become a part of their deal under the knockout rule?

In *Options Wireless*, the first case we read in this section, the seller argued that its invoice was a conditional acceptance of the buyer's offer that prevented formation under the last clause of 2-207(1). Using this clause, an offeree can invoke the mirror-image rule and prevent its acceptance from forming a contract on the terms of the offer. But as the *Options Wireless* case demonstrates, courts have set an exceptionally high threshold for a party hoping to invoke the mirror-image rule with a conditional acceptance:

> a conditional acceptance must be directly and distinctly stated or expressed rather than implied or left for inference.

Options Wireless (quoting *Dorton v. Collins*). In other words, you're on your own and should not expect any help from the court.

A conditional acceptance becomes a counteroffer and can be accepted by the party who made the original offer. At common law, if the original offeror went ahead and performed, that performance was treated as an acceptance of the counteroffer, and a contract was formed on the terms of the counteroffer—the last-shot rule, which gave the party who sent the last paper (fired the last shot) a contract on his or her terms. But the "condition" that makes an acceptance "conditional" under 2-207(1) is *assent* to the counteroffer—"I accept the deal you've proposed on the condition that you 'assent to' the changes I've made." Does performance express "assent"? Most courts say no—assent requires more than just conduct by the party. See, e.g., *Mastercraft Furniture v. Saba North America*, 2015 U.S. Dist. LEXIS 41550 (D.Ore. 2015)("a party must 'specifically and unequivocally' assent to new terms of a contract … silence is not considered 'assent' to additional terms [in a conditional acceptance]").

Does performance have any effect when it follows a conditional acceptance? We know that conduct by the parties is generally sufficient to show their agreement. The conditional acceptance complicates things. We now have paper exchanged between the parties that, by its very terms, tells us there is not an agreement: my acceptance of your offer is conditional—only effective to form a contract—if you actually assent to it, and you have not. Our conduct—performing the contract—is inconsistent with our communications. Which should control whether a contract has been formed—the paper or the conduct? The next case explains why conduct trumps the paper under Article 2.

BELDEN INC. V. AM. ELEC. COMPONENTS, INC.
COURT OF APPEALS OF INDIANA, 2008
885 N.E.2D 751

BARNES, Judge.

CASE SUMMARY

Belden, Inc., and Belden Wire & Cable Company (collectively "Belden") appeal the trial court's granting of partial summary judgment in favor of American Electronic Components, Inc. ("AEC"). We affirm.

Issues

Belden raises four issues, which we consolidate and restate as:

> I.   whether the limitation on damages on the back of Belden's order acknowledgment applies to the parties' contract; and

Facts

Belden manufactures wire, and AEC manufactures automobile sensors. Since 1989, AEC, in repeated transactions, has purchased wire from Belden to use in its sensors.

In 1996 and 1997, Belden sought to comply with AEC's quality control program and provided detailed information to AEC regarding the materials it used to manufacture its wire. In its assurances, Belden indicated that it would use insulation from Quantum Chemical Corp. ("Quantum"). In June 2003, however, Belden began using insulation supplied by Dow Chemical Company ("Dow"). The Dow insulation had different physical properties than the insulation provided by Quantum.

In October 2003, Belden sold AEC wire manufactured with the Dow insulation. AEC used this wire to make its sensors, and the insulation ultimately cracked. Chrysler had installed AEC's sensors containing the faulty wire in approximately 18,000 vehicles. Chrysler recalled 14,000 vehicles and repaired the remaining 4,000 prior to sale. Pursuant to an agreement with Chrysler, AEC is required to reimburse Chrysler for expenses associated with the recall.

In 2004, AEC filed a complaint against Belden seeking consequential damages for the changes in the insulation that resulted in the recall.

ANALYSIS

Battle of the Forms

Belden first argues that the boilerplate language on the back of its "customer order acknowledgement" limited the damages available to AEC. The parties were involved in repeated transactions over many years. Prior to 1998, AEC sent all purchase orders by mail on a form that contained AEC's terms and conditions on the back. Beginning in 1998, AEC sent its purchase orders to Belden via fax. The faxed purchase orders only included the front of the form and omitted the terms and conditions printed on the back of the form.

On October 17, 2003, AEC sent Belden a purchase order containing the quantity, price, shipment date, and product specifications. Belden responded on October 22, 2003, with its order acknowledgement. The order acknowledgment referenced AEC's specific requests and contained boilerplate language on the back. At issue here is the language purporting to limit Belden's liability for special, indirect, incidental, or consequential damages. The back of order acknowledgment also stated:

1.2 Where this Agreement is found to be an acknowledgment, if such acknowledgment constitutes an acceptance of an offer such acceptance is expressly made conditional upon Buyer's assent solely to the terms of such acknowledgment, and acceptance of any part of Product(s) delivered by Company shall be deemed to constitute such assent by Buyer....

Based on these exchanges, the parties dispute whether the limitation on damages is a term of their agreement.

We start our analysis with Section 2-207 of the Uniform Commercial Code ("UCC"), which provides:

[Court quotes 2-207 in its entirety.]

The parties disagree as to whether Section 2-207(2) or Section 2-207(3) applies.

* * * *

Pursuant to Section 2-207, if a contract is formed under Section 2-207(1), the additional terms in the acceptance are considered proposals and become part of the contract unless Section 2-207(2) renders the proposed terms inoperative. "However, if an acceptance is expressly conditioned on the offerer's assent to the new terms, and no assent is forthcoming, the 'entire transaction aborts.'" In other words, if an acceptance contains a clause conditioning the acceptance on assent to the additional or different terms, the writings do not form a contract. "Yet if the parties' conduct recognizes the existence of a contract by performance it is sufficient to establish a contract for sale." The terms of such a contract are those on which the writings of the parties agree, "together with any supplementary terms incorporated under any other provisions of this act." § 2-207(3).

We applied this framework in *Uniroyal* and rejected a line of cases suggesting Uniroyal's order acknowledgement was a counter-offer that Chambers accepted by taking the delivery of the goods and failing to object to the new terms. We reasoned that such an application revives the "last-shot" doctrine under the common law "mirror-image" rule, the very rule that Section 2-207 was intended to avoid, by binding the offeror to additional terms upon the mere acceptance of goods. Further, we observed that the purpose of Section 2-207 would not be well-served by allowing an offeree's responsive document to state additional or different terms, and provide that the terms will be deemed accepted by the offeror's inaction, because Section 2-207 presumes that business people do not read exchanged preprinted forms and assumes that the offeror would not learn of such terms. We also reasoned:

> the clause placing the burden of affirmative objection on the original offeror is itself a modification of the offer to which the offeror should first have to assent, and absent its assent, any shipping and acceptance of the goods should be deemed to constitute the consummation of the contract under (Section 2-207)(3).

We concluded that the writings exchanged by Chambers and Uniroyal did not create a contract but that the parties performed their contractual obligations so as to create a contract under Section 2-207(3). Therefore, the terms of the contract consisted of the terms upon which the parties' writings agreed and the supplementary terms of the UCC.

As in *Uniroyal*, we agree here that Belden could not unilaterally include terms that were expressly conditional on AEC's assent. Thus, the parties' writings did not create a contract. Nevertheless, we conclude that the parties' actions were in recognition of the existence of a contract and were sufficient to establish a contract for the sale of wire. The terms of the contract are the written terms on which the parties agreed and the "supplementary terms incorporated under any other provisions of [the UCC]." § 2-207(3).

The parties dispute, however, what supplementary terms are incorporated into their contract. The first question we must address is Belden's argument that the terms called for in Section 2-207(2) are included in the parties contract based on Comment 6, which provides:

> If no answer is received within a reasonable time after additional terms are proposed, it is both fair and commercially sound to assume that their inclusion has been assented to. Where clauses on confirming forms sent by both parties conflict each party must be assumed to object to a clause of the other conflicting with one on the confirmation sent by himself. As a result the requirement that there be notice of objection which is found in subsection (2) is satisfied and the conflicting terms do not become a part of the contract. The contract then consists of the terms originally expressly agreed to, terms on which the confirmations agree, and terms supplied by this Act, including subsection (2). The written confirmation is also subject to Section 2-201. Under that section a failure to respond permits enforcement of a prior oral agreement; under this section a failure to respond permits additional terms to become part of the agreement.

§ 2-207 cmt. 6 (emphasis added).

Belden urges that, based on the emphasized language, we look to Section 2-207(2) to determine whether the terms in the order acknowledgement are included in the contract. Pursuant to Section 2-207(2), Belden contends that its additional terms became part of the contract unless they materially altered the contract—the only exclusionary provision of Section 2-207(2) that is relevant under these facts. Belden claims that the limitation on damages does not materially alter the contract.

We need not determine whether the limitation on damages is a material alteration because we believe that Belden's reading of Comment 6 is overbroad. As the Supreme Judicial Court of Massachusetts has observed, Comment 6 only applies where the terms conflict. Because only Belden's order acknowledgment contained a limitation on damages, there are no conflicting terms to implicate Comment 6. Further:

> the criteria in [§2-207(2)] determine what "additional or different terms" will or will not be part of a contract that is formed by the exchange of writings. Where the writings do not form a contract, [§2-207(3)] states its own criteria—"those terms on which the writings agree" plus any terms that would be provided by other Code sections. One cannot turn to subsection (2) as another Code section that would supply a term when, by its express provisions, subsection (2) simply does not apply to the transaction.

Id. at 573-74; *see also Coastal & Native Plant Specialties, Inc. v. Engineered Textile Prod., Inc.*, 139 F. Supp. 2d 1326, 1337 (N.D. Fla. 2001) ("[A] party cannot utilize section 2-207(2) to provide additional terms once a contract is formed pursuant to section 2-207(3).").

We agree with this reasoning. If we turned to Section 2-207(2) to determine the terms where the parties' writings did not create a contract, then Section 2-207(3) would be rendered meaningless. We will not do this. Thus, we rely solely on Section 2-207(3) to determine what terms are included in the contract.

Belden also argues that the parties' course of dealing is a "supplementary term" to be included by Section 2-207(3). Belden contends that the parties' course of dealing acknowledges the limitation on damages and that it is therefore included as a term of the contract.

There is a split in authorities as to whether Section 2-207(3)'s reference to "supplementary terms" includes course of performance, course of dealing, and usage of trade as defined in Section 1-205 or just the standard "gap fillers" contained in the Article 2 of the UCC. *Compare Coastal & Native Plant Specialties*, 139 F. Supp.2d at 1337 ("When a contract is formed pursuant to section 2-207(3), as here, the contract terms consist of the standard gap-filler provisions of the UCC as well as those sections relating to course of performance and course of dealing and usage of trade."), and *Dresser Industries, Inc.*,

Waukesha Engine Div. v. Gradall Co., 965 F.2d 1442, 1451 (7th Cir. 1992) (concluding that under the Wisconsin UCC, a court is not limited to the standardized gap-fillers [*759] of Article 2, but may utilize any terms arising under the entire UCC, including course of performance, course of dealing, and usage of trade), with *C. Itoh & Co. (America) Inc. v. Jordan Int'l Co.,* 552 F.2d 1228, 1237 (7th Cir. 1977) ("Accordingly, we find that the 'supplementary terms' contemplated by Section 2-207(3) are limited to those supplied by the standardized 'gap-filler' provisions of Article Two."). For the sake of argument, we assume, without deciding, that the parties' course of dealing is in fact a supplementary term for purposes of Section 2-207(3).

Belden asserts that during the more than 100 transactions between the parties from 1998 to 2003, AEC never objected to the limitation on damages and, therefore, the parties' course of dealing incorporates the limitation on damages into the contract. AEC responds, "since it is undisputed that AEC never gave its express assent to Belden's terms in any prior transaction throughout the parties' fifteen-year relationship, Belden has not established a course of dealing between the parties as a matter of law."

Pursuant to Section 1-205(1), "A course of dealing is a sequence of previous conduct between the parties to a particular transaction which is fairly to be regarded as establishing a common basis of understanding for interpreting their expressions and other conduct." Our research shows that most cases involving the repeated exchange of forms does not in and of itself establish a course of dealing between the parties that incorporates the terms of those forms into the parties' contract under Section 2-207(3). See *Step-Saver Data Sys., Inc. v. Wyse Tech.,* 939 F.2d 91, 103-04 (3rd Cir. 1991) ("While one court has concluded that terms repeated in a number of written confirmations eventually become part of the contract even though neither party ever takes any action with respect to the issue addressed by those terms, most courts have rejected such reasoning." (footnote omitted)); *see also PCS Nitrogen Fertilizer, L.P. v. Christy Refractories, L.L.C.,* 225 F.3d 974, 982 (8th Cir. 2000) ("Moreover, the fact that Christy repeatedly sent its customer acknowledgment form to PCS does not establish a course of dealing; the multiple forms merely demonstrated Christy's desire to include the arbitration clause as a term of the contract.").

We agree with the reasoning set forth in *Step-Saver*:

> For two reasons, we hold that the repeated sending of a writing which contains certain standard terms, without any action with respect to the issues addressed by those terms, cannot constitute a course of dealing which would incorporate a term of the writing otherwise excluded under § 2-207. First, the repeated exchange of forms by the parties only tells Step-Saver that TSL <u>desires</u> certain terms. Given TSL's failure to obtain Step-Saver's express assent to these terms before it will ship the program, Step-Saver can reasonably believe that, while TSL desires certain terms, it has agreed to do business on other terms—those terms expressly agreed upon by the parties. Thus, even though Step-Saver would not be surprised to learn that TSL desires the terms of the box-top license, Step-Saver might well be surprised to learn that the terms of the box-top license have been incorporated into the parties's agreement.
>
> Second, the seller in these multiple transaction cases will typically have the opportunity to negotiate the precise terms of the parties's agreement, as TSL sought to do in this case. The seller's unwillingness or inability to obtain a negotiated agreement reflecting its terms strongly suggests that, while the seller would like a court to incorporate its terms if a dispute were to arise, those terms are not a part of the parties's commercial bargain. For these reasons, we are not convinced that TSL's unilateral act of repeatedly sending copies of the box-top license with its product can establish a course of dealing

between TSL and Step-Saver that resulted in the adoption of the terms of the box-top license.

Belden's repeated sending of the order acknowledgement containing the same limitation on damages and same requirement of assent by AEC does not in and of itself establish a course of dealing between the parties showing that the parties agreed to the Belden's terms and conditions of sale. At best, it shows that Belden wanted AEC to assent to its terms and conditions, which AEC never did.

In sum, we agree with the trial court's conclusion that Section 2-207(3) applies to this case and that Section 2-207(3), not Section 2-207(2), controls the terms of the parties' agreement. We also conclude that Section 1-205 does not establish a course of dealing in which AEC agreed to the limitation on damages. The trial court properly granted summary judgment in favor of AEC as to the issue of the applicability of Belden's limitation on damages.

Most disputes about the terms of the deal will be sorted out under 2-207(1) and (2). But sometimes the parties make such a mess of the formation dance that the trail of paper they leave behind only proves that they did not have an agreement; the Zen moment—the meeting of the minds that the common law was obsessed with finding—never occurred. Since no "definite expression" of agreement exists, a contract cannot be formed under 2-207(1). In this situation, in addition to the conditional acceptance situation, 2-207(3) rides in to rescue the parties when they've gone ahead and started performing despite all of the evidence showing they never had an agreement to perform. Their conduct establishes a contract, but we still have to sort out the terms of that contract—but without the help of 2-207(2), as the court in *Beldon* explained. Instead, we pick through the paper exchanged by the parties—taking from it the terms we find in both parties' paper and adding to them "any supplementary terms" that would be supplied by Article 2 in the absence of an express term provided by the parties—to create the contract to be enforced under 2-207(3).

The supplementary terms made part of the parties' agreement under 2-207(3) are Article 2-supplied stand-ins that become part of any Article 2 contract when the parties don't provide them—default terms necessary to determine the basic obligations of the parties to a sale of goods contract. Article 2 does not require that the expression of the parties' agreement be complete to be enforceable—2-204(3)—but if we are going to enforce an agreement, we need to know the basics of what it is we are enforcing. At a minimum, we need price, delivery and payment terms, time of performance, and quantity, and Article 2 provides mechanisms—gap fillers—for determining these when the agreement is silent. And, as we will see later in this section, the parties' agreement can also include terms from any prior dealings between the parties (course of dealing) as well as any understandings about their deal reflected in how they have performed the contract at issue (course of performance). But, as the *Beldon* court noted, courts do not agree on whether the supplementary terms made part of the contract under 2-207(3) include course of dealing and course of performance.

PROBLEM 3 - 8

Recall from Problem 3 - 5 that Rae uses a form purchase order for the produce the store buys which allows her to fill in the type of produce, the price, the quantity, and the delivery date for each order. She recently discovered a new item—Star Fruit—she wants to stock in the produce department. She found an importer who sells it in the states and sent in a purchase order for "ten cases, Star Fruit, market price plus shipping." The seller e-mailed Rae its "Sales Agreement," which accepted her offer subject to the terms and conditions set out in the agreement, which disclaimed all warranties, excluded consequential damages, and provided that all disputes were subject to arbitration. It also stated: "Our acceptance of your order is subject to all of the terms and conditions on the face and reverse side hereof, including arbitration." Rae took delivery of the goods and began selling them at the store.

Under 2-207, would Rae be required to arbitrate any subsequent dispute she has with the seller? If the Star Fruit is not fit for consumption because it's full of fruit borers, will she have a claim for breach of warranty? Can she recover consequential damages for breach of the warranty? 2-207(1) and 2-207(3).

PROBLEM 3 - 9

Would your answers in Problem 3 - 8 be different if the seller's sales agreement included any of the following terms? 2-207(1).

1. This agreement is governed by the provisions on the reverse side hereof unless you notify us to the contrary within ten days or before shipment, whichever is earlier.
2. Any terms or conditions in buyer's order form which conflict with the provisions of this acceptance are deemed waived.
3. Acceptance of buyer's order is expressly limited to the terms and conditions printed on the reverse side of this acceptance.
4. This acceptance is expressly limited to the terms stated herein, including those printed on the reverse side. Any additional or different terms proposed by the Buyer are rejected unless expressly agreed to in writing.
5. Our acceptance is expressly conditioned on your assent to the additional or different terms and conditions set forth below and printed on the reverse side. If these terms and conditions are not acceptable, you must notify us at once.] — Rae would argue this undoes the cond. Acceptance

PROBLEM 3 - 10

If, in the last problem, the seller's sales agreement contained the language in Part 5, would Rae's acceptance of the Star Fruit be the express assent to the additional terms required by 2-207(1)? If it would not, does that mean there is no contract between the store and the seller? 2-207(3).

3. Technical Requirements: Statute of Frauds

The Statute of Frauds—as you remember from your Contracts course—requires a signed writing before certain contracts are enforceable. At the time of the statute's original enactment in the seventeenth century, a person falsely alleged to be contractually bound to another was not permitted by the rules governing trials to testify on his own behalf—to refute the allegations by telling his side of the story. So Parliament intervened with the Statute of Frauds, intended to prevent successful prosecution of claims based on perjured testimony. Whether it has succeeded in its intended purpose is a matter of great debate—Parliament repealed the British statute in 1954. When Llewellyn began drafting Article 2, all but nine states had enacted some form of a statute of frauds, and Article 2's predecessor, the Uniform Sales Act, had its own statute of frauds that applied to sale-of-goods transactions.

Llewellyn was concerned that the Statute of Frauds, as originally conceived, might have actually done more harm than good. He wrote in his Sales textbook:

> The litigation involving the statute in the appellate courts makes it appear at first sight an instrument of gross injustice. In the rarest cases is even a suspicion of fraudulent testimony on the part of the plaintiff to be traced. The typical picture is that of a defendant sliding out

of an honest bargain on a technicality contemplated by neither party.... the defendant has appealed to an absurd but potent rule of law to cover his welching.[6]

The "welcher" Llewellyn was worried about would agree to a deal but never put it in writing, preferring instead to wait until the time of performance to decide whether the deal was a good one—if he had paid too much or sold too dearly, he could invoke the Statue of Frauds and walk away from the bad deal. The statute had become a tool used by "evilly disposed individuals to slip their bargains." Llewellyn had no place for such a rule in his sales article.

But Llewellyn also saw "an incidental, perhaps unintended" value in the statue that made "it worth its price":

> Much business is done orally. Much always will be. Quick deals often must be. But the spread of a credit economy means the lengthening of the average period between dicker and performance.... Then a series of honest difficulties. The parties may have misunderstood each other at the outset.... Each will be sure that his understanding was correct ... Or the parties' memories may trick them. We remember, most of us, not the very language, but its import; and the import changes subtly and unconsciously in the light of subsequent events. A writing will at least maintain its wording. All of this without reference to the danger of consciously false testimony.[7]

Getting people to write down their deals was really a good idea—but only if it could be implemented in a way that did not empower the welcher. So the challenge, if a statute of frauds was to remain a part of sales law, was to craft a provision that encourages the practice of writing down agreements that could not be used by "evilly disposed" persons to escape an honest bargain that had gone bad. The next case illustrates the first step Llewellyn took to meet the challenge.

MONETTI, S.P.A. v. ANCHOR HOCKING CORP.

UNITED STATES COURT OF APPEALS FOR THE SEVENTH CIRCUIT, 1991
931 F.2D 1178

POSNER, Circuit Judge.

The district judge dismissed the suit, on the defendant's motion for summary judgment, as barred by the statute of frauds....

The plaintiffs are Monetti, an Italian firm that makes decorative plastic trays and related products for the food service industry, and a wholly owned subsidiary, Melform U.S.A., which Monetti set up in 1981 to market its products in the U.S. In 1984, Monetti began negotiations with a father-and-son team, the Schneiders, importers of food service products, to grant the Schneiders the exclusive right to distribute Monetti's products in the United States and in connection with this grant to turn over to them Melform's tangible and intangible assets. While these negotiations were proceeding, the Schneiders sold their importing firm to Anchor Hocking, the defendant, and their firm became a division of Anchor Hocking, though—at first—the Schneiders remained in charge. In the fall of 1984, the younger Schneider, who was handling the negotiations with Monetti for his father and himself, sent Monetti a telex requesting preparation of an agreement "formalizing our [i.e., Anchor Hocking's] exclusive for the United States." In response, Monetti terminated all of Melform's distributors and informed all of

---

6   Llewellyn, *Cases and Materials on the Law of Sales*, (Callaghan 1930) 916.
7   Llewellyn, *Cases and Materials on the Law of Sales*, (Callaghan 1930) 916.

Melform's customers that Anchor would become the exclusive U.S. distributor of Monetti products on December 31, 1984.

On December 18, the parties met, apparently for the purpose of making a final agreement. Monetti—which incidentally was not represented by counsel at the meeting—submitted a draft the principal provisions of which were that Anchor Hocking would be the exclusive distributor of Monetti products in the U.S., the contract would last for ten years, and during each of these years Anchor Hocking would make specified minimum purchases of Monetti products, adding up to $27 million over the entire period. No one from Anchor Hocking signed this or any other draft of the agreement. However, the record contains a memo, apparently prepared for use at the December 18 meeting, entitled "Topics of Discussion With Monetti." The memo's first heading is "Exclusive Agreement—Attachment #1"—a reference to an attached draft which is identical to the Monetti draft except for two additional, minor paragraphs added in handwriting. Under the heading appears the notation "Agree" beside each of the principal paragraphs of the agreement, with one exception: beside the first paragraph, the provision for exclusivity, the notation is "We want Canada" (i.e., exclusive distribution rights in Canada as well as in the U.S.). On the bottom of the left-hand side of the last page appears the legend "SS/mh"—indicating that the younger Schneider (Steve Schneider) had dictated the memo to a secretary.

Shortly after the December 18 meeting, Monetti—which had already, remember, terminated Melform's distributors and informed Melform's customers that Anchor Hocking would be the exclusive distributor of Monetti products in the United States as of the last day of 1984—turned over to Anchor Hocking all of Melform's inventory, records, and other physical assets, together with Melform's trade secrets and know-how.

Several months later, in May 1985, Anchor Hocking abruptly fired the Schneiders. Concerned about the possible implications of this demarche for its relationship with Anchor Hocking, Monetti requested a meeting between the parties, and it was held on May 19. Reviewing the events up to and including that meeting, a memo dated June 12, 1985, from Raymond Davis, marketing director of Anchor Hocking's food services division, to the law department of Anchor Hocking, states that "In the middle to latter part of 1984 Irwin Schneider and his company were negotiating an agreement with [Monetti and Melform] to obtain exclusive distribution rights on Melform's plastic tray product line in the United States"; "later, this distribution agreement was expanded to also include Canada, the Caribbean and Central and South America"; there had been many meetings between the parties, including the meeting of May 19 (at which Davis had been present); "Exhibit A (attached) represents the summary agreement that was reached in the meeting. You will notice that I have added some handwritten changes which I believe represents more clearly our current position regarding the agreement.... Now that we have had our 'New Management' [i.e., the management team that had replaced the Schneiders] meeting with Monetti, both parties would like to have a written and signed agreement to guide this new relationship." Exhibit A to the Davis memo is identical to Attachment #1 to Steve Schneider's memo, except that it contains the handwritten changes to which the Davis memo refers. Shortly after this memo was written, the parties' relationship began to deteriorate, and eventually Monetti sued for breach of contract.

Illinois' general statute of frauds forbids a suit upon an agreement that is not to be performed within a year "unless the promise or agreement upon which such action shall be brought, or some memorandum or note thereof, shall be in writing, and signed by the party to be charged therewith, or some other person thereunto by him lawfully authorized." The statute of frauds in Article 2 of the Uniform Commercial Code makes a contract for the sale of goods worth at least $500 unenforceable "unless there is some writing sufficient to indicate that a contract for sale has been made between the parties and signed by the party against whom enforcement is sought or by his authorized agent or broker." The differences between these formulations are subtle but important. The Illinois statute requires that the writing "express the substance of the contract with reasonable certainty." The UCC statute of frauds does not require that the writing contain the terms of the contract. In fact it requires no more than written corroboration of the alleged oral contract.

Let us postpone the question of partial performance for a moment and focus on whether there was a signed document of the sort that the statutes of frauds require. The judge, over Monetti's objection, refused to admit oral evidence on this question. He was right to refuse. The use of oral evidence to get round the requirement of a writing would be bootstrapping, would sap the statute of frauds of most of its force, and is therefore forbidden.

* * * *

We have two documents (really, two pairs of documents) to consider. The first is Steve Schneider's "Topics for Discussion" memo with its "Attachment #1." Since "signed" in statute-of-frauds land is a term of art, meaning executed or adopted by the defendant, Schneider's typed initials are sufficient. The larger objection is that the memo was written before the contract—any contract—was made. The memo indicates that Schneider (an authorized representative of the defendant) agrees to the principal provisions in the draft agreement prepared by Monetti, but not to all the provisions; further negotiations are envisaged. There was no contract when the memo was prepared and signed, though it is fair to infer from the memo that a contract much like the draft attached to it would be agreed upon—if Monetti agreed to Anchor Hocking's demand for Canada, as Monetti concedes (and the Davis memo states) it did.

Can a memo that precedes the actual formation of the contract ever constitute the writing required by the statute of frauds? Under the Uniform Commercial Code, why not? Its statute of frauds does not require that any contracts "be in writing." All that is required is a document that provides solid evidence of the existence of a contract; the contract itself can be oral. Three cases should be distinguished. In the first, the precontractual writing is merely one party's offer. We have held, interpreting Illinois' version of the Uniform Commercial Code, that an offer won't do. Otherwise there would be an acute danger that a party whose offer had been rejected would nevertheless try to use it as the basis for a suit. The second case is that of notes made in preparation for a negotiating session, and this is another plausible case for holding the statute unsatisfied, lest a breakdown of contract negotiations become the launching pad for a suit on an alleged oral contract. Third is the case—arguably this case—where the precontractual writing—the Schneider memo and the attachment to it—indicates the promisor's (Anchor Hocking's) acceptance of the promisee's (Monetti's) offer; the case, in other words, where all the essential terms are stated in the writing and the only problem is that the writing was prepared before the contract became final. The only difficulty with holding that such a writing satisfies the statute of frauds is the use of the perfect tense by the draftsmen of the Uniform Commercial Code: the writing must be sufficient to demonstrate that "a contract for sale *has been made*.... The 'futuristic' nature of the writing disqualifies it." Yet under a general statute of frauds, "it is well settled that a memorandum satisfying the Statute may be made before the contract is concluded." And while merely because the UCC's draftsmen relaxed one requirement of the statute of frauds—that there be a writing containing all the essential terms of the contract—doesn't exclude the possibility that they wanted to stiffen another, by excluding writings made before the contract itself was made, the choice of tenses is weak evidence. No doubt they had in mind, as the typical case to be governed by section 2-201, a deal made over the phone and evidenced by a confirmation slip. They may not have foreseen a case like the present, or provided for it. The distinction between what is assumed and what is prescribed is critical in interpretation generally.

In both of the decisions that we cited for the narrow interpretation, the judges' concern was with our first two classes of case; and judicial language, like other language, should be read in context. *Micromedia* involved an offer; in *American Web*, negotiations were continuing. We agree with Professor Farnsworth that in appropriate circumstances a memorandum made before the contract is formed can satisfy the statute of frauds, including the UCC statute of frauds. This case illustrates why a rule of strict temporal priority is unnecessary to secure the purposes of the statute of frauds. Farnsworth goes further. He would allow a written *offer* to satisfy the statute, provided of course that there is oral evidence it was accepted. We needn't decide in this case how far we would go with him, and therefore needn't reexamine *Bennett*.

* * * *

We need not pursue these interesting questions about the applicability and scope of the UCC statute of frauds any further in this case, because our result would be unchanged no matter how they were answered. For we have said nothing yet about the second writing in the case, the Davis memorandum of June 12. It was a writing on Anchor Hocking's letterhead, so satisfied the writing and signature requirements of the UCC statute of frauds, and it was a writing sufficient to evidence the existence of the contract upon which Anchor Hocking is being sued. It is true that "Exhibit A" does not contain all the terms of the contract; it makes no reference to the handing over of Melform's assets. But, especially taken together with the Davis memo itself (and we are permitted to connect them provided that the connections are "apparent from a comparison of the writings themselves," and they are, since the Davis memo refers explicitly to Exhibit A), Exhibit A is powerful evidence that there was a contract and that its terms were as Monetti represents. Remember that the UCC's statute of frauds does not require that the contract be in writing, but only that there be a sufficient memorandum to indicate that there really was a contract. The Davis memorandum fits this requirement to a t. So even if the partial-performance doctrine is not available to Monetti, the UCC's statute of frauds was satisfied. And since the general Illinois statute was satisfied as well, we need not decide whether, since the contract in this case both was (we are assuming) within the UCC *and* could not be performed within one year, it had to satisfy both statutes of frauds.

Section 2-201 gives the writing it requires the simplest of functions: give us a reason to believe that the party claiming a contract is not making it up. In the words of Comment 1:

> All that is required is that the writing afford a basis for believing that the offered oral evidence rests on a real transaction.

It requires some evidence "other than word of mouth that there really has been *some* deal."[8] Prior law required that the writing necessary to satisfy the Statute of Frauds contain the actual terms of the agreement alleged, and if the party asserting the statue of frauds defense could show that there was more to the parties' deal than what happened to be in the writing, the writing would not take the alleged contract out of the Statute of Frauds. So a writing, even if signed by the party claiming there was no deal, might not prevent the welcher from walking away from an honest deal. Instead of preventing fraud, the statute facilitated it:

> We regard this as commercial outrage. We think that if there was ever an instrument of fraud, that strange interpretation of the old statute which has become universal is an instrument of fraud. We turn to the exact opposite and say, as long as you are sure you have got a deal, go to the jury as in any other case ..."[9]

---

8 Llewellyn, *Stenographic Report of Hearing on Article 2 of the Uniform Commercial Code*, Report of the New York Law Revision Commission vol. 1 New York Law Revision Commission Leg. Doc. 1954 (B) Item III at 119 (55) (1954).

9 Llewellyn, Memorandum Replying to the Report and Memorandum of Task Group I of the Special Committee of the Commerce and Industry Association of New York, Inc. On the Uniform Commercial Code, 1 N.Y. State Law Revision Comm'n, 1954 Report 106, 1167-118 (1954).

By reducing the burden imposed on the writing to this bare essential—show us you're not making the transaction up—2-201 reduces the potential that the statute is used as an instrument of fraud.

The relaxed requirements of Article 2's Statute of Frauds might initially appear to undermine its effectiveness—and that would be a fair observation if the purpose of the statute was to determine whether the alleged agreement was actually enforceable. But the purpose of the statue is to prevent fraud—to prevent successful prosecution of claims based on perjured testimony. A party that overcomes a statute-of-frauds defense must still establish in fact that an enforceable contract was made between the parties. She must still persuade the fact finder that all of the requirements for an enforceable contract exist. And she must also establish the actual terms of that agreement. Overcoming a 2-201 defense does not give her a free pass to victory on her claim. It only means that she will have the opportunity to present her claim to the fact finder. So all we need 2-201 to do is to detect false claims, not unenforceable contracts, and something in writing signed by the party against whom we are trying to enforce the agreement can generally serve that purpose.

Problem 3 - 11

Which of the following agreements require something in writing in order to be enforceable under Article 2?

1. Rae's agreement with the local refrigeration company for maintenance of the store's coolers and freezers. Does it matter that the company has agreed to provide the parts necessary to maintain and repair the equipment?

2. Rae's agreement to buy all of the zucchini squash grown next year by a local farmer. Would a letter from Rae that apologized to the farmer for cancelling the agreement be sufficient under 2-201?

3. Rae's agreement to buy the following equipment from the coffee shop down the street:
     1 - Jura Latte Machine – $420
     1 - Faema Coffee Bean Grinder – $275
     1 - Cecilware Espresso Grinder – $395
     1 - Bunn Gourmet Ice System – $400
   Would an e-mail from the owner of the coffee shop thanking Rae for taking the extra equipment off of his hands be sufficient under 2-201?

4. Rae agreed to an equipment swap with the café down the street—the café would get the deli's deep fryer in exchange for the cafe's trash compactor. Would an e-mail from Rae addressed to the diner across the street agreeing to exchange the deli's deep fryer for the diner's trash compactor be sufficient under 2-201? What if Rae could show that the diner and the café were owned by the same person—and that the diner did not have a trash compactor?

5. Rae agrees to trade a paper baler to the appliance store next door for a forklift. Would an e-mail from Rae to the appliance store that stated, "Just wanted to confirm our offer to trade the paper baler for the Deere forklift that we discussed today. Let me know when you decide," be sufficient under 2-201?

The only content requirement imposed by 2-201(1) on a writing is that it show the quantity—how many or how much—the parties have agreed to buy/sell. While 2-201(1) does not explicitly require a quantity term, courts have read the last sentence of the section to so require on the basis of Comment 1, which states that

> [o]nly three definite and invariable requirements as to the memorandum are made by this subsection. First, it must evidence a contract for the sale of goods; second, it must be "signed,"

a word which includes any authentication which identifies the party to be charged; and third, it must specify a quantity.

On its own, the last sentence is at best ambiguous, but for most the comment has settled the matter.

What does it take to satisfy the "quantity" requirement of 2-201(1)? The Comments tell us that while quantity is the only term which must appear, it "needs to be accurately stated." Comment 1, 2-201. The next case canvasses various decisions that have addressed this question.

JOHNSON CONTROLS, INC. v. TRW VEHICLE SAFETY SYS.

UNITED STATES DISTRICT COURT FOR THE EASTERN DISTRICT OF MICHIGAN,
SOUTHERN DIVISION 2007
491 F. SUPP. 2D 707

II. BACKGROUND

This case involves an alleged breach of an automotive supply contract. Plaintiffs Johnson Controls, Inc., and Johnson Controls Automortriz Mexico DE RL DE CV (collectively JCI) are engaged in the business of manufacturing interior automotive component systems, notably seat assemblies. Defendant TRW Vehicle Safety Systems, Inc. (TRW), manufactures and supplies custom made automotive parts, including components to JCI's seat assemblies.

For the last several years, JCI has ordered certain component parts from TRW for the restraint systems of two General Motors vehicle platforms: the GMT 257 and the GMT 201. For the GMT 257 parts, JCI issued Purchase Orders 910-003 (Order 003) and 910-031 (Order 031).[10] For the GMT 201 parts, JCI issued Purchase Order 7002653 (Order 2653). JCI issued the purchase orders to TRW for the purchase of various parts for a period of one year. The purchase orders stated the specific price of each part but did not state the quantity. This was because JCI's need for parts depended on General Motor's production schedule. Accordingly, when JCI had a need for parts it would issue a material release to TRW, requesting that TRW ship a specified number of parts. JCI followed this practice, which is standard in the automotive industry and known as a just-in-time supply system,[11] in order to maintain a minimum inventory. JCI would periodically revise its purchase orders, which, according to the terms incorporated therein, would supercede previous purchase orders. JCI issued the latest revisions on February 21, 2006 for purchase orders 003 and 031, and on September 5, 2006, for purchase order 2653.

JCI's purchase orders detail the part number, the part description and the unit price. In the column labeled quantity, the orders state "AS REL."[12] The face of the orders also state:

> This purchase order is governed exclusively by Johnson Controls' Global Terms of Purchase (available at http://johnsoncontrols.com/asg/global-terms.htm or by calling 734-254-7500,

---

10 For the sake of clarity, the Court will refer to the Purchase Orders collectively as "the purchase orders" or "the orders" unless the context demands further specificity.

11 This type of supply system was analyzed in Omri Ben-Shahar & James J. White, "Boilerplate and Economic Power in Auto Manufacturing Contracts," 104 *Mich. L. Rev.* 953 (2006). In the article, Professors Ben-Shahar and White describe in detail the nature of contracts involved in supplying auto manufacturers with parts. These contracts are typically entered into with little or no negotiation and are primarily made up of carefully drafted boilerplate language. As in this case, the purchaser will issue a purchase order for a period of time at a fixed price that incorporates Global Terms. "General Motors, for example, enters into roughly one million procurement contracts every year, at a total amount in excess of $80 billion—all governed by a single contract form containing thirty-one paragraphs ...." *Id.* at 957.

12 Purchase Order 2653 does not have "AS REL." listed as the quantity; however, this purchase order does incorporate JCI's Global Terms.

and incorporated here by reference), except as modified provided therein. Any terms and conditions appearing on the reverse side of this purchase order form do not apply and should be disregarded. All other terms are rejected.

JCI revises the Global Terms periodically; however, the revisions do not apply retroactively to purchase orders that have already been issued.

The Global Terms identify each purchase order as an offer for the purchase of goods and further state in bold that the "Order is limited to and conditional upon Seller's acceptance of these Terms exclusively." (Def.'s Ex. F.) The agreement formed by the Order, including the Global Terms, is binding on the parties for one year. (*See id.*) Finally, under paragraph 3, labeled "Quantity; Material Releases; Delivery," the Global Terms state

> Quantities listed in each Order as estimated are Buyer's best estimate of the quantities of Supplies it might purchase from Seller for the contract term specified in the Order. If no other quantity is stated on the face of the Order or if the quantity is blank or states zero, "blanket," "see release" or similar term, then for consideration of US $10 to be paid by Buyer upon expiration or termination of the Order, Seller grants to Buyer an irrevocable option during the term of the Order to purchase Supplies in such quantities as determined by Buyer and identified as firm orders in material authorization releases, manifests, broadcasts, or similar releases ("Material Releases") that are transmitted to Seller during the term of the Order, and Seller will supply all such Supplies at the price and other terms specified in the Order; provided that the Buyer may purchase no less than a minimum quantity of at least one piece or unit of each of the Supplies and no more than 100% of Buyer's requirements for the Supplies. ... Material Releases are part of the Order, are governed by these Terms and are not independent contracts. ... Buyer is not obligated to accept early deliveries, late deliveries, partial deliveries or excess deliveries.

* * * *

JCI's complaint alleges that TRW breached the contracts embodied in Purchase Orders 003 and 031 when it threatened to stop shipping parts in October 2006. Furthermore, the complaint seeks a declaratory judgment as to Purchase Order 2653, declaring that purchase order to be a valid and enforceable contract through September 2007.

* * *

IV. ANALYSIS

A. TRW's Motion for Summary Judgment

TRW's primary argument is that it did not breach the parties' contract because no enforceable contract existed. Specifically, TRW contends that the documents presented by JCI to support a contract fail the statute of frauds' requirement that a quantity term appear in the writing. TRW further argues that even if the statute of frauds is satisfied, the contract fails for lack of consideration because JCI is not obligated to purchase any parts from TRW. In response, JCI argues that the contract sufficiently states a quantity term and is not lacking in consideration under Michigan's version of the Uniform Commercial Code (UCC), MICH. COMP. LAWS §§ 440.1101 *et seq.* As explained below, the Court finds that the statute of frauds does not bar enforcement of the parties agreement but questions of fact remain as to whether the agreement is lacking in mutuality.

1. Whether the Purchase Orders Satisfy the Statute of Frauds

Michigan's statute of frauds provides:

Except as otherwise provided in this section a contract for the sale of goods for the price of $1000.00 or more is not enforceable by way of action or defense unless there is a writing sufficient to indicate that a contract for the sale has been made between the parties and signed by the party against whom enforcement is sought or by his or her authorized agent or broker. A writing is not insufficient because it omits or incorrectly states a term agreed upon but the contract is not enforceable under this subsection beyond the quantity of goods shown in the writing.

MICH. COMP. LAWS § 440.2201(1). The writing evidencing a contract has three "definite and invariable requirements." *Id.* cmt 1. "First it must evidence of contract for the sale of goods; second, it must be 'signed'… and third, it must specify a quantity." The Michigan Supreme Court has thus found that a quantity term must appear in the writing in order to satisfy the statute of frauds. However, "[o]nce a quantity term is found to exist in the agreement, the agreement need not fail because the quantity term is not precise." *In re Estate of Frost*, 130 Mich. App. 556, 561, 344 N.W.2d 331 (1983). This is because the purpose of the writing requirement is "to provide a basis for believing that oral evidence which is offered rests upon a real transaction." *Id.* Once this purpose has been satisfied, parol evidence may be admissible to make the agreement sufficiently definite to be enforceable. *Id.* Accordingly, "[w]hen quantity is not precisely stated, parol evidence is admissible to show what the parties intended as the exact quantity, … but where the writing relied upon to form the contract of sale is totally silent as to quantity, parol evidence cannot be used to supply the missing quantity term." *Id.* Therefore, the issue in this case is whether the writings offered by JCI as evidence of the parties' contracts contain a written quantity term.

TRW argues that the writings JCI provided do not contain a quantity term. TRW points out that the quantity column on the purchase orders either states "AS REL." or does not state anything at all. Further, TRW argues that JCI's Global Terms define "AS REL." as merely granting JCI an option to purchase parts for the duration of the order, and has no connection to quantity whatsoever. On the other hand, JCI contends that its Global Terms do contain a quantity term in that the definition of "AS REL." states that TRW grants JCI an option to purchase parts at a set price for the duration of the order so long as JCI purchases at least one part but no more than 100% of its requirements. In addition, JCI notes that the Global Terms also specifically incorporate any material releases issued under the purchase orders. JCI argues that the reference to the material releases, combined with the range of quantities qualifying the option to purchase, constitutes a written quantity term.

In order to determine the sufficiency of the writing, the Court must look to Michigan law. In applying Michigan law, the Court follows the law as announced by the Michigan Supreme Court. Where the Michigan Supreme Court has not decided the issue, the Court "must ascertain the state law from 'all relevant data.'" *Garden City Osteopathic Hosp. v. HBE Corp.*, 55 F.3d 1126, 1130 (6th Cir. 1995) (quoting *Bailey v. V & O Press Co.*, 770 F.2d 601, 604 (6th Cir. 1985)). "Relevant data includes state appellate court decisions, supreme court dicta, restatements of law, law review commentaries, and [the] majority rule among other states." *Orchard Group Inc. v. Konica Medical Corp.*, 135 F.3d 421, 427 (6th Cir. 1998). While the Michigan Supreme court has clearly found that a quantity term must appear in the writing to satisfy the statute of frauds, it has not decided what is sufficient to qualify as a quantity term. Therefore, the Court will look to "all relevant data" to determine whether the writings provided in this case contain a quantity term.

The Michigan court of appeals has addressed this issue with varying results. The court first found that a quantity term must appear in the writing in *Ace Concrete Prods. Co. v. Charles J. Rogers Constr. Co.*, 69 Mich. App. 610, 245 N.W.2d 353 (1976). *Ace Concrete* involved a contract between a concrete supplier and a concrete subcontractor. The supplier sent the subcontractor a letter quoting prices for concrete in connection with a specified construction contract. *See id.* at 611. The letter referenced the specific construction contract for which the subcontractor would need concrete, "P.C.I-13 Job

1450," and stated "[m]ay we give you the following price quote on concrete for the above job." *Id.* The subcontractor argued that the contract was unenforceable under the statute of frauds because it did not state a written quantity term. The court agreed, rejecting the supplier's argument that letter's reference to the construction project in combination with the quote "for the above job" revealed a requirements contract. *Id.* at 614. The court concluded that the quantity "must appear on the [writing] without reference to parol evidence." *Id.*

The court reached the opposite result in *In re Estate of Frost*, 130 Mich. App. 556, 344 N.W.2d 331 (1983). There, the plaintiff claimed to have had a contract with the decedent for the sale of lumber. The defendant argued that the contract was not enforceable under the statute of frauds because it did not state a quantity. The court disagreed with the defendant and found that the writing's statement that the plaintiff could take "all wood sawable" was a sufficient quantity term for the statute of frauds, analogizing the contract to an output contract. *Id.* at 560-61. The court stated that the statute of frauds was satisfied even though the quantity term was not precise. *Id.*

Similarly, in *Great Northern Packaging, Inc. v. General Tire & Rubber Co.*, 154 Mich. App. 777, 399 N.W.2d 408 (1986), the court concluded that a term with no apparent reference to a specific quantity could satisfy the statute of frauds. In that case, the buyer issued a purchase order to buy 50 units that was later changed to a "Blanket Order" purportedly covering purchases for one year. *See id.* at 780. Relying on the court's holding in *Frost*, the court concluded that "the term 'blanket order' express[ed] a quantity term, albeit an imprecise one." *Id.* at 787. As the statute of frauds' purpose of providing a basis for believing a contract exists had been fulfilled, the court recognized that parol evidence should be admitted to the trier of fact to determine the precise quantity of units involved in the contract. *See id.*

In *Acemco v. Olympic Steel Lafayette*, 2005 Mich. App. LEXIS 2656, 2005 WL 2810716 (Mich. App. 2005), the court found that the writing offered to satisfy the statute of frauds did not contain a quantity term. The writing stated that "[d]uring the term of this Agreement, the Seller agrees to sell to the Buyer such quantities of the Products as the Buyer may specify in its purchase orders, which the Buyer may deliver at its discretion." 2005 Mich. App. LEXIS 2656, [WL] at *4. The court found that the above language was not a quantity term because it specified "no quantity whatsoever." *Id.* The court reasoned that the language granted the buyer complete discretion to order any amount or no amount of the seller's products and concluded that "'[a]ny' quantity is in fact no quantity at all." *Id.* The court further rejected the seller's argument that the term "blanket" on an attached document constituted a quantity term. "Blanket" appeared on a document that described the goods to be purchased. *Id.* The court concluded that, unlike *Great Northern*, where the court held that the term "blanket order" stated a quantity, [ ], "blanket" on its own was not a quantity term. The court further explained that since the term appeared on a specifications sheet and not a purchase order, and since the term was "blanket" and not "blanket order," the writing did not contain a quantity term.

Finally, the court in *Dedoes Indus. v. Target Steel*, 2005 Mich. App. LEXIS 1309, 2005 WL 1224700 (Mich. App. 2005), held that a price quote stating that the defendant "would satisfy plaintiff's steel needs" for three years did not satisfy the statute of frauds' quantity requirement. The court found the language referenced a time period and not a quantity. *See id.* Other courts have discussed Michigan's quantity requirement with differing results. Compare *Busch v. Dyno Nobel, Inc.*, 40 Fed. App'x 947 (6th Cir. 2002) (concluding that the language "up to ten million pounds" could constitute an ambiguous quantity term), with *MacSteel, Inc. v. Eramet N. Am.*, 2006 U.S. Dist. LEXIS 83339, 2006 WL 3334019 (E.D. Mich. 2006) (finding the term "additional material" was too indefinite to obligate the plaintiff to purchase any goods and, therefore, failed to satisfy the statute of frauds).

The Fourth Circuit also discussed this issue in *Thomas J. Kline, Inc. v. Lorillard, Inc.*, 878 F.2d 791 (4th Cir. 1989). In *Lorillard*, the defendant, a cigarette manufacturer, agreed to supply the plaintiff, a cigarette wholesaler, with its full line of cigarettes on a direct basis. *See id.* at 793. When the plaintiff began drastically increasing its orders, the defendant suspended a previous credit arrangement and demanded cash payments for purchases. The plaintiff sued and the defendant argued that the statute of frauds prevented enforcement of the alleged contract. The plaintiff contended that the terms "full line" and "direct basis" provided a quantity term in that they provided that the defendant would supply all of the plaintiff's requirements. *See id.* The court of appeals reviewed Maryland law and found no case in which similar terms were found to satisfy the statute of frauds quantity requirement. The court summarized those decisions:

> [I]nstructive are cases in which ambiguous terms of quantity have been deemed sufficient to prove an enforceable contract. This court, for example, recently held that quantity was adequately identified when specific language "referred to meeting the purchaser's needs." *Barber and Ross Co. v. Lifetime Doors, Inc.*, 810 F.2d 1276, 1280-81 (4th Cir. 1987). *See also Kansas Power and Light Co. v. Burlington Northern Railroad Co.*, 740 F.2d 780 (10th Cir. 1984) (writings mentioning possible maximum and minimum amounts of shipped coal sufficient to create requirements contract). It has been held that the words "the yarn" for "a potential program" could be sufficient written expression of quantity. *O. N. Jonas Co., Inc. v. Badische Corp.*, 706 F.2d 1161, 1163-64 (11th Cir. 1983). Courts have consistently found that words with some possible nexus to amount, including "all," "bags," or even customary terms such as lot numbers, can provide a basis for the admission of parol evidence. *See also Maryland Supreme Corp. v. The Blake Co.*, 279 Md. 531, 369 A.2d 1017 (1977) (written phrases "for the above mentioned project" and "throughout the job" are sufficient quantity terms).

In light of these cases, the court concluded that the terms "full line" and "direct basis" had no nexus to quantity and, therefore, did not satisfy the statute of frauds.

The Court finds little guidance in the cases discussed above but is persuaded by the reasoning in cases such as *Great Northern* and *Frost*. The Court finds these cases provide a more reasoned analysis of the issue and are consistent with the UCC's policies as well as the commercial background of the parties and the transaction involved in this case. In contrast, the Court finds that the decisions in *Ace Concrete*, *Acemco*, and *Dedoes* conflict with the UCC's goals and confuse the issue of whether the quantity term is sufficiently definite to enforce the contract with the issue of whether there is a written quantity term for the purposes of satisfying the statute of frauds. *See Riegel Fiber Corp. v. Anderson Gin Co.*, 512 F.2d 784, 789 (5th Cir. 1975) (refusing to apply the statute of frauds to bar enforcement of a contract and stating that "the real issue in this case is not whether these contracts satisfy § 2-201, but whether the quantity term in the agreement the parties undeniably made—as reflected in the signed writing—is too indefinite to support judicial enforcement"). The results reached in *Ace Concrete*, *Acemco* and *Dedoes* minimally advance the statute of frauds' purpose to provide a basis for believing a contract exists while at the same time damaging the UCC's other substantive goals of liberally incorporating trade usage, custom and practice, course of dealing, and course of performance into parties' agreements in fact.

The UCC strives to "simplify, clarify and modernize the law governing commercial transactions ... [and] to permit the continued expansion of commercial practices through custom, usage and agreement of the parties ...." MICH. COMP. LAWS § 440.1102. The "general approach" of the UCC "requires the reading of commercial background and intent into the language of any agreement and demands good faith in the performance of that agreement." MICH. COMP. LAWS § 440.2306 cmt. 1. The Court is also mindful that in determining whether a particular term is in fact a quantity term, the Court's construction of the statute of frauds' quantity requirement affects the substance and application of other code provisions. "The text of each section should be read in the light of the purpose and policy of the rule or principle in question, and also as of the Act as a whole, and the application of language should be construed narrowly or broadly, as the case may be, in conformity with the purposes and policies involved." MICH. COMP. LAWS § 440.1102 cmt. 1.

The statute of frauds expressly states that "[a] writing is not insufficient because it omits or incorrectly states a term agreed upon ...." MICH. COMP. LAWS § 440.2201(1). Furthermore, "[e]ven though one or more terms are left open a contract for sale does not fail for indefiniteness if the parties have intended to make a contract and there is a reasonably certain basis for giving an appropriate remedy." MICH. COMP. LAWS § 440.2204(3). The official comment to § 2204(3) states:

> If the parties intend to enter into a binding agreement, this subsection recognizes that agreement as valid in law, despite missing terms, if there is any reasonably certain basis for granting a remedy. *The test is not certainty as to what the parties were to do nor as to the exact amount of damages due the plaintiff.* Nor is the fact that one or more terms are left to be agreed upon enough of itself to defeat an otherwise adequate agreement. *Rather, commercial standards on the point of 'indefiniteness' are intended to be applied, this Act making provision elsewhere for missing terms needed for performance ....*

Id. cmt. 1 (emphasis added).

To this end the code specifically contemplates contracts with indefinite quantity terms. *See* MICH. COMP. LAWS § 440.2306 (defining quantity in output or requirements contracts as actual good faith output or requirements). Therefore, the Court declines to analyze the purported quantity term in this case in terms of its definiteness. Whether the quantity as provided in the writing is sufficiently definite to support an enforceable contract is to be determined under the codes' substantive provisions in light of commercial standards

In the present case, the purchase orders, in combination with the Global Terms, contain a quantity term. The face of the purchase orders state "AS REL." in the column labeled quantity. There is no dispute that this term is a reference to JCI's material releases, which it issued periodically to specify the exact quantities of parts needed. The Court finds no difference between this term and those found to be sufficient in *Great Northern* and *Frost*. The purchase orders contemplate that JCI would identify specific quantities in material releases and expressly included those releases in the orders. The term "AS REL." gives some indication that JCI intended to purchase and TRW intended to sell some quantity of parts. This is all the statute of frauds requires. Interestingly, based on the reasoning in *Acemco*, the fact that "AS REL." was listed as the quantity and was included on actual purchase orders reinforces the conclusion that some quantity term, although indefinite, was stated in the writing. Additionally, in contrast to the terms found insufficient in *Lorillard*, "AS REL." does have some nexus to the notion of amount or quantity in light of the customary practice in the automotive industry of using just-in-time supply chains and material releases.

Furthermore, the fact that the Global Terms explain that "AS REL." indicates that JCI has an option to purchase supplies does not change the fact that there is some quantity term. *See, e.g., R. A. Weaver & Assocs., Inc. v. Asphalt Construction, Inc.*, 190 U.S. App. D.C. 418, 587 F.2d 1315, 1319 (D.C. Cir. 1978) (finding that a quantity term was stated in the writing even though the language stating the quantity also spoke of the grade and quality of concrete). If anything, the precise meaning of the term is ambiguous. But as the statute of frauds specifically states, the terms need not be accurately stated. In this case, the quantity could be construed as simply referencing the amount of supplies indicated in the material releases. The releases are incorporated into the purchase orders via the Global Terms and JCI is not obligated to purchase anything that exceeds the amounts stated in the material releases. On the other hand, the fact that the Global Terms referenced an option to purchase goods at a fixed price so long as JCI's orders were within a specific range of amounts could indicate that JCI was to purchase its requirements. *See, e.g., Kansas Power & Light Co. v. Burlington N. R. Co.*, 740 F.2d 780 (writings mentioning possible maximum and minimum amounts of shipped coal sufficient to create requirements contract). That this may have been a requirements contract seems reasonable in light of the practice among automotive suppliers to enter into long-term, just-in-time production arrangements that rely on a fixed price and a variable quantity, and provide flexibility to adjust to changing commercial conditions.

Based on the foregoing analysis, the Court finds that JCI's purchase orders in combination with its Global Terms contain a satisfactory quantity term for the purposes of MICH. COMP. LAWS § 440.2201. The Court concludes that a quantity term appears in the writing, albeit an ambiguous one, and that the offered writings provide a basis for believing that a contract in fact exists. Thus, the purpose of the statute of frauds has been satisfied, particularly to the extent performance has been rendered. *See* MICH. COMP. LAWS § 440.2201(3)(c) (stating that in the absence of a writing sufficient to satisfy the statute of frauds, the parties agreement is enforceable "with respect to goods for which payment has been made and accepted or which have been received and accepted").

Problem 3 - 12

Determine whether the quantity term Rae used in the following purchase orders is sufficient under 2-201:

1. Rae sent a purchase order to a local grower agreeing to purchase "all blueberries your farm produces this growing season."
2. Rae's purchase order was for "five thousand pears at twenty-five dollars per crate."
3. Rae's purchase order agreed to "purchase a minimum of one hundred pallets, unshucked corn, burlapped." Would your answer be different if the purchase order was for "up to one hundred pallets"? Will it matter if Rae can show that it's understood in the produce business that a pallet of corn has seventy-five bags of corn?
4. Rae sent a purchase order to an orchid grower in Washington for "one carload of Bing cherries, sweet, 10.5 row." Will Rae need to show that produce cars carry fifty thousand pounds?
5. Rae's purchase order is for "all of the romaine lettuce the deli needs the next three months." Would it matter if the lettuce was for the sandwiches Rae agreed to provide for summer lunches to a local school and the purchase order added "for the summer lunch project"?

Today's world is becoming a paperless world; we've replaced the paper communication of Llewellyn's world with new forms of electronic communication—e-mails, texts, tweets, and the like. Does an e-mail or text sent by the party against whom I'm trying to enforce a contract satisfy the "writing" requirement of 2-201? Most courts were willing to read "writing" in 2-201 to include forms of electronic communication:

> Moreover, the policy motivation behind the UCC and its adoption in New York, as well as the Second Circuit's generally liberal view toward Section 2-201(2)'s construction, suggest that the electronic form of an e-mail "writing" does not as a rule preclude enforcement of the underlying agreement. The Statute of Frauds aims to guard against fraud and perjury by requiring some proof of a contract, and the UCC's sale of goods provision is designed to "require some objective guaranty, other than word of mouth, that there really has been some deal." An e-mail suffices as much as a letter, a telegram or a fax to provide such objective indication of an existing agreement. At the same time, the UCC drafters, in attempting to promote predictable and dependable business practices, endeavored to set forth clear, practical rules in line with the real pace and practices of the commercial world ... Few would dispute that e-mail is currently one of the most common forms of communication for lay-persons and merchants alike. Thus, permitting otherwise

sufficiently precise e-mails to serve as "writings" furthers the manifest intentions of the UCC's drafters.

While the possibility that a party could create a "binding contract simply by dispatching unsolicited [writings], thus unfairly disadvantaging the recipient" exists, the risk run is no greater with e-mails than with other forms of transmission. Both hand-written and typed messages are capable of fabrication.

Bazak International Corp. v. Tarrant Apparel, 378 F. Supp. 2d 377 (S.D.N.Y. 2005), Courts also adapted the "signed by" requirement of 2-201 to cover methods used to authenticate electronic documents.

But now, forty-eight states have adopted the Uniform Electronic Transactions Act (UETA), which basically provides that, in an adopting state, an electronic record satisfies the requirement of a writing called for in any state statute. It also provides that electronic authentication satisfies the requirements for a signature when required by statute. So today, a court could presume that the e-mails in *Bazak* satisfied the requirement in 2-201 that there be a "writing" signed by the defendant. In the two states which have not adopted UETA, the federal ESIGN Act passed by Congress would control and have the same effect on the "writing" and "signed by" requirements of 2-201 as the UETA.

Llewellyn's quest to prevent the Statue of Frauds from being used as an instrument of fraud did not end with the relaxation of the requirements for the writing necessary to satisfy the statute. The writing requirement—no matter how minimal—still gave the unscrupulous merchant a way to get out of an honest agreement. If the merchant never responded in writing or signed anything, she could invoke the Statute of Frauds to avoid contractual liability even if the other party had papered the transaction. So the welching merchant became the target of 2-201(2), which created an exception to Article 2's Statute of Frauds for transactions between merchants. The next case illustrates how the exception permits a party to satisfy the Statute of Frauds in the absence of a writing signed by the party asserting a 2-201(1) defense.

BAZAK INT'L CORP. V. TARRANT APPAREL GROUP
UNITED STATES DISTRICT COURT FOR THE SOUTHERN DISTRICT OF NEW YORK 2005
378 F. SUPP. 2D 377;

DECISION AND ORDER

I. BACKGROUND

On September 15, 2003, Tuvia Feldman ("Feldman"), the president of Bazak, met with Gerrard Guez ("Guez"), Tarrant's Chief Executive Officer, in Tarrant's New York office to discuss Bazak's proposed purchase of certain jeans from Tarrant. During this meeting, Guez indicated that Tarrant had 1,600,000 pairs of jeans available to sell to Bazak. The parties allegedly agreed that, subject to Bazak's receipt of a written inventory and visual inspection of the items in Tarrant's warehouses in Los Angeles, Tarrant would sell Bazak the jeans at a price of between $3.00 and $3.50 per item, provided that Bazak would buy the entire inventory and take possession of the items by the end of the year.

On September 18, 2003, an employee of Tarrant sent Feldman an inventory list that detailed the merchandise Tarrant apparently planned to sell to Bazak. Following receipt of the inventory, Feldman and Avi Jacobi ("Jacobi"), an agent of R&I Trading of New York ("R&I"),[13] flew to Los Angeles on September 29, 2003 to inspect the merchandise. Feldman and Jacobi were taken to Tarrant's office to

---

13 R&I originally planned to purchase merchandise from Tarrant jointly with Bazak. Instead, however, it entered into a separate agreement with Bazak whereby Bazak would re-sell Tarrant's goods to R&I.

meet with Guez, who indicated that they were to deal directly with Brian Buchan ("Buchan") on the transaction.

When Feldman and Jacobi inspected the merchandise at Tarrant's warehouse, they learned that approximately 700,000 of the pairs of jeans that Bazak had expected to purchase were not among the inventory and had been sold to a third party. This change in inventory altered the price Bazak was willing to pay per item. Consequently, Feldman and Jacobi spent two days spot-checking the merchandise to determine whether an agreement could still be reached. During their inspection, Feldman and Jacobi discovered that the remaining inventory varied from the description given by Tarrant during its initial conversation with Bazak. Nonetheless, Feldman offered to buy the entire inventory, consisting of 912,714 items, at $2.40 per item. Guez allegedly accepted the offer orally and told Buchan to send samples of the inventory to Bazak, along with an invoice.

According to Bazak, Feldman sent Buchan a signed letter ("Exhibit 3"), dated October 3, 2003, which purported to confirm the agreement between Guez and Feldman and detailed an inventory of 912,714 items at $2.40 per item. Tarrant contests the authenticity of Exhibit 3 and alleges it was never received by Tarrant. The disputed Exhibit 3 addressed to Buchan reads:

> As per our agreement with Mr. Gerrard Guez, we would like to inform you that Bazak International Corp. has purchased the total inventory of 912,714 pcs of assorted jeans and twills as per inventory submitted and calculated by yourself and your assistant on September 30, 2003. The total inventory purchased is 912,714 pcs at $2.40 per pcs totaling approx $2,190,513.60. Please send us a proforma invoice immediately in order for us to proceed in preparing our Letter of Credit. Please ship all the samples per your conversation with Mr. Jacobi to Bazak International Corp. at the address listed above.

The letter contains both a typed and hand-written signature of Feldman.

Bazak has also produced another letter ("October 3 e-mail"), also dated October 3, 2003, addressed to Buchan and sent via e-mail by Gali Neufeld ("Neufeld") of R&I on behalf of Feldman. The e-mail's subject line reads "Total Inventory Purchased," and the electronically attached letter sent on Bazak letterhead states:

> As per our agreement with Mr. Gerard Guez, we would like to inform you that Bazak International has bought the total inventory of 747,096 pcs per your Sep 30, 2003 inventory report less the following: Kohls men 8,000 pcs; Structure men 22,000 pcs; Express junior 10,000 pcs; Express missy 19,200 pcs. The total inventory purchased is 687,896 pcs. Please send us a proforma invoice in order for us to proceed in preparing our L/C. Please ship all samples per your conversation with Mr. Jacobi to Bazak International at the Address listed above.

The letter closes with Feldman's typed signature. Buchan claims to recall neither seeing the e-mail message nor opening its attachment. Bazak alleges that it did not receive a reply to either letter.

On October 6, 2003, Tarrant sent Bazak eleven cartons of sample inventory with accompanying documentation but no invoice. Feldman, on behalf of Bazak, then requested an invoice from Tarrant, but Bazak claims that Tarrant never sent an invoice. On October 7, 2003, Bazak was provided with a revised inventory report that deviated from the terms set down in both Exhibit 3 and the October 3 e-mail. On October 13, 2003, Guez forwarded Bazak an internal Tarrant e-mail ("GMAC e-mail") that requested the identity of the closeout buyer for credit rating purposes, though Tarrant maintains that it was not written by a Tarrant employee. Shortly thereafter, Bazak was informed that Tarrant would instead sell its inventory to another buyer, David's Place, at a higher price.

The Complaint filed by Bazak in the instant action claimed that Tarrant and Bazak had a contract for the purchase of 912,712 specific inventory items at a price of $2.40 per item and that Tarrant breached the agreement when it sold the merchandise to David's Place. The Court now considers the merits of Tarrant's motion for summary judgment on Bazak's breach of contract claim.

II. LEGAL STANDARD

Tarrant presents two grounds for its summary judgment motion. Neither is sufficiently supported by the record. First, Tarrant contends that the alleged contract violates the Statute of Frauds. Specifically, Tarrant argues both that the October 3 e-mail does not fulfill the "merchant's exception" requirements and that the Exhibit 3 letter cannot be admitted as evidence of an alternative writing. (Def. Mem. at 11.) The Court disagrees, and finds that the October 3 e-mail [**11] satisfies the New York Uniform Commercial Code ("UCC") statutory requirements that present questions of law. The remaining issues raise questions of fact as to which Bazak has produced sufficient evidence on the basis of which a reasonable jury could find in its favor.

III. DISCUSSION

A. *THE ALLEGED CONTRACT DOES NOT VIOLATE THE STATUTE OF FRAUDS*

Tarrant has failed to demonstrate the absence of any genuine issue of material fact concerning the applicability of the Statute of Frauds. The UCC sale of goods provision states:

> Except as otherwise provided in this section a contract for the sale of goods for the price of $500 or more is not enforceable by way of action or defense unless there is some writing sufficient to indicate that a contract for sale has been made between the parties and signed by the party against whom enforcement is sought or by his authorized agent or broker. A writing is not insufficient because it omits or incorrectly states a term agreed upon but the contract is not enforceable under this paragraph beyond the quantity of goods shown in such writing.
>
> N.Y. U.C.C. Law § 2-201(1).

While neither party contends that a written contract was formed, Bazak asserts that the parties' agreement falls within the UCC's "merchant's exception." This exception provides:

> Between merchants if within a reasonable time a writing in confirmation of the contract and sufficient against the sender is received and the party receiving it has reason to know its contents, it satisfies the requirements of subsection (1) against such party unless written notice of objection to its contents is given within ten days after it is received.
>
> N.Y. U.C.C. Law § 2-201(2).

In *Bazak International Corp. v. Mast Industries, Inc.*, the New York Court of Appeals directly addressed the issue of the adequacy of a writing necessary to enable an alleged oral contract to withstand the Statute of Frauds. In *Mast Industries,* the parties entered into an alleged agreement stipulating that Bazak would buy certain re-sale clothing items from Mast. The evidence put forward by Bazak of this agreement included five purchase orders signed by Bazak, telecopied to Mast, and retained by Mast without objection. The bottom of each form read, "This is only an offer and not a contract unless accepted in writing by the seller, and subject to prior sale." Mast neither signed nor returned the forms. Despite the language of the purchase orders, the court held that the documents were sufficient for the purposes of the "merchant's exception" because they "afford a basis for believing that they reflect a real transaction between the parties." Accordingly, the defendant's motion to dismiss was denied. It is against this backdrop that the Court determines the sufficiency of the documentation put forth by Bazak in the case at bar.

1. *E-mails Can Satisfy the "Writing" Requirement*

Tarrant contends that Bazak's October 3 e-mail cannot satisfy UCC Section 2-201(2)'s "writing in confirmation" requirement because the statute does not specifically mention e-mail as a recognized form of writing. However, the October 3 e-mail does, as a matter of law, satisfy this element. The UCC states that "'written' or 'writing' includes printing, typewriting or any other intentional reduction to tangible form." N.Y. U.C.C. Law § 1-201(46). Neither the Second Circuit nor the Courts of the Southern District of New York have determined conclusively whether messages sent by e-mail qualify as "writings" under this definition. Instead of stating a generally applicable rule, the Second Circuit and some courts in this District have evaluated the adequacy of e-mails on a case-by-case basis, distinguishing on account of either the absence of particular terms, or inferences from the message's language. This substantive approach implies that a writing's electronic form, alone, does not prevent it from fulfilling UCC Section 2-201(2).

Although e-mails are intangible messages during their transmission, this fact alone does not prove fatal to their qualifying as writings under the UCC. Aside from posted mail, the forms of communication regularly recognized by the courts as fulfilling the UCC "writing" requirement, such as fax, telex and telegraph, are all intangible forms of communication during portions of their transmission. Just as messages sent using these accepted methods can be rendered tangible, thereby falling within the UCC definition, so too can e-mails. Additionally, because "under any computer storage method, the computer system 'remembers' the message even after being turned off," whether or not the e-mail is eventually printed on paper or saved on the server, it remains an objectively observable and tangible record that such a confirmation exists. *Id.* at 412. Consequently, there appears to be little distinction between e-mails and other forms of communication regularly recognized under the Statute as adequate "writings."

Moreover, the policy motivation behind the UCC and its adoption in New York, as well as the Second Circuit's generally liberal view toward Section 2-201(2)'s construction, suggest that the electronic form of an e-mail "writing" does not as a rule preclude enforcement of the underlying agreement. The Statute of Frauds aims to guard against fraud and perjury by requiring some proof of a contract, and the UCC's sale of goods provision is designed to "'require some objective guaranty, other than word of mouth, that there really has been some deal.'" An e-mail suffices as much as a letter, a telegram or a fax to provide such objective indication of an existing agreement.

At the same time, the UCC drafters, in attempting to promote predictable and dependable business practices, endeavored to set forth clear, practical rules in line with the real pace and practices of the commercial world. In this spirit, the "merchant's exception" permits enforceable contracts to emerge from the common commercial practice of entering into oral agreements for the sale of goods that are only later confirmed in writing. Few would dispute that e-mail is currently one of the most common forms of communication for lay-persons and merchants alike. Thus, permitting otherwise sufficiently precise e-mails to serve as "writings" furthers the manifest intentions of the UCC's drafters. Although addressed more fully below in Part II.A.4, it merits note that whether e-mail is an appropriate form of communication for any particular set of contracting parties is a separate and subsequent question, that often presents factual questions concerning trade usage.

Arguments in favor of a more strict reading of the UCC requirements—arguments clearly rejected by the New York Court of Appeals in *Mast Industries*—are no more compelling in a case concerning e-mail confirmation than those based on more traditional forms of correspondence. While the possibility that a party could create a "binding contract simply by dispatching unsolicited [writings], thus unfairly disadvantaging the recipient" exists, the risk run is no greater with e-mails than with other forms of transmission. Both hand-written and typed messages are capable of fabrication. In fact, in holding that a telex can satisfy UCC Section 2-201, the Second Circuit in *Apex Oil* explained:

We recognize that we are permitting a substantial transaction to be consummated on fragmentary conversation and documentation. However, it is the practice in many fields to transact business quickly and with a minimum of documentation.... Parties doing business with each other in such circumstances take the risk that their conflicting versions of conversations will be resolved to their disfavor by a fact-finder whose findings, even if incorrect, are immune from appellate revision.

Apex Oil, 760 F.2d at 423.

In contrast to the e-mails rejected in *Sel-Leb* under the UCC section applicable in that case, Section 1-206, the October 3 e-mail need only be sufficient against the sender, Bazak, under the "merchant's exception." *See* N.Y. U.C.C. Law § 2-201(2). As discussed below, the October 3 e-mail satisfies this requirement. Further, that e-mail deals exclusively with the parties' transaction, explicitly refers to a specific conversation between [**22] the parties and outlines in detail the merchandise at issue. In addition, while both the October 3 e-mail and those in *Sel-Leb* omit the price term, only UCC Section 1-206, which is inapplicable in the case at bar, requires such a term.[14]

The notable lack of discussion concerning the ability of e-mail to stand as a "writing" in [other cases] may be explained in part by the adoption in 2000 of 15 U.S.C. Section 7001. The federal provision states:

> Notwithstanding any statute, regulation, or other [**23] rule of law ... with respect to any transaction in or affecting interstate or foreign commerce - (1) a signature, contract, or other record relating to such transaction may not be denied legal effect, validity, or enforceability solely because it is in electronic form; and (2) a contract relating to such transaction may not be denied legal effect, validity, or enforceability solely because an electronic signature or electronic record was used in its formation.

15 U.S.C. § 7001(a).

The widespread interest in permitting otherwise substantively sufficient e-mails to stand as "writings," as evidenced by Section 7001's adoption, supports this Court's finding to the same effect.

2. *The October 3 E-mail Satisfies the Signature Requirement*

While UCC Section 2-201(2) does not explicitly state that a signature is necessary for a writing to be "sufficient against the sender," language in *Mast Industries* hints that it may be so required. *Mast Industries,* 535 N.E.2d at 638 ("If the writings can be construed as confirming an alleged oral agreement, they are sufficient under UCC 2-201(1) against Bazak—the sender—since Bazak signed them."). Even if this is the case, the October 3 e-mail fulfills this requirement as a matter of law.

"Signed" is meant to include "any authentication which identifies the party to be charged." N.Y. U.C.C. Law § 2-201 official comments. The official commentary to the statutory language elaborates:

> The inclusion of authentication in the definition of "signed" is to make clear that as the term is used in this Act a complete signature is not necessary. Authentication may be printed, stamped or written; it may be by initials or by thumbprint. It may be on any part of the document and in appropriate cases may be found in a billhead or letterhead.... The question always is whether the symbol was executed or adopted by the party with present intention to authenticate the writing.

N.Y. U.C.C. Law § 1-201 official cmt. 39.

Since Bazak's President's typed signature appears at the signatory line of the attached letter and the letter is typed on Bazak company letterhead, the writing is "sufficient against the sender."

---

14   Compare UCC Section 1-206(1) ("at a defined or stated price") with Section 2-201(2).

3. The October 3 E-mail Can Be Construed As "In Confirmation" Of An Earlier Agreement
The October 3 e-mail also satisfies the UCC requirement of a writing "in confirmation" of an earlier agreement. To survive summary judgment, the writing need only be "sufficient to indicate that a contract for sale has been made." It is not required to precisely set forth every material term of the agreement. The writing must simply "provide a basis for belief that it rests on a real transaction—no more, no less." And while quantity is the only contractual term specifically required under the UCC, even a writing incorrectly stating this term may be sufficient. N.Y. U.C.C. Law § 2-201(1).[15]

The October 3 e-mail satisfies this legal standard in that it provides a sufficient basis for belief that its message rests on a real contract. The e-mail contains the requisite quantity term, though the parties dispute whether the figure is misstated. Additionally, while the message lacks a price quote, this omission is not fatal under Section 2-201.

4. A Jury Could Find That the Writing was Received and That the Receiving Party Had Reason to Know of Its Contents
Whether receipt of a confirmatory writing has occurred is a question of fact, inappropriately determined on summary judgment. *See Williston on Contracts* § 29:27. Though the UCC does not define "receipt" in the context of a confirmatory writing, it provides a definition of "receipt of notice." *Williston on Contracts* § 29:27. Section 1-201(26) states:

> A person "receives" a notice or notification when: (a) it comes to his attention; or (b) it is duly delivered at the place of business through which the contract was made or at any other place held out by him as the place for receipt of the communications.
>
> N.Y. U.C.C. Law § 1-201(26).

Further, the requirement of having "reason to know of its contents" is satisfied when "from all the facts and circumstances known to him at the time in question he has reason to know that it exists." N.Y. U.C.C. Law § 1-201(25)(c).

Disputes concerning both receipt and reason to know raise questions of fact. Therefore, the Court must only determine whether Bazak has presented evidence sufficient to create a genuine issue of material fact as to these elements. *See* Fed. R. Civ. P. 56. The Court is persuaded that Bazak has put forth facts that demonstrate a genuine issue of material fact as to each. Neither party disputes that the October 3 e-mail appeared in Buchan's inbox and was thereby received in the technical sense. Nonetheless, Tarrant contends that Buchan has no recollection of opening the e-mail or its attachment and that the e-mail was therefore not constructively received. However, this assertion more appropriately addresses the issue of Buchan's "reason to know" of the contents of the writing—reason to know to open the e-mail—than actual receipt of it. *See* Section 2-201(2). In spite of Tarrant's argument, the Court finds that the October 3 e-mail satisfies the UCC definition of receipt of notice set forth in UCC Section 1-201(26), as it sufficiently came "to [Buchan's] attention" and also was "duly delivered at the place of business through which the contract was made." N.Y. U.C.C. Law § 1-201(26)(a).

Nonetheless, whether e-mail is an appropriate and reasonably expected form of communication between the two particular parties before the court is a question of fact. Here, the issue's resolution requires a factual inquiry into trade usage and course of dealing. Construing facts in the light most favorable to the non-movant, Bazak has demonstrated the existence of a genuine issue of material fact concerning this question. Neither party directly addresses whether e-mail is an appropriate method of communication in the re-sale trade generally or in Tarrant and Bazak's particular relationship. Yet

---

15 But such a "contract is not enforceable under this paragraph beyond the quantity of goods shown in such a writing." N.Y. U.C.C. Law § 2-201(1).

later e-mail correspondence from Tarrant to Bazak (the "GMAC e-mail") provides evidence in light of which a reasonable jury could find that the parties did accept e-mail as an appropriate form of communication.

Further, Bazak has put forth evidence that demonstrates a genuine issue of material fact as to whether Buchan had reason to know of the October 3 e-mail's contents "from all the facts and circumstances known to him at the time in question." N.Y. U.C.C. Law § 1-201(25)(c). In particular, Bazak has offered evidence demonstrating that Buchan may have had reason to know, at least generally, what the e-mail's subject and purpose would be. A jury certainly could find the October 3 e-mail's title, "Total Inventory Purchased," sufficiently specific to put Buchan on notice of its contents given his contemporary role in the transaction, despite his alleged ignorance of the sender. Moreover, since Buchan's primary responsibility at Tarrant is to sell available merchandise, a jury could find it unlikely Buchan would think that an e-mail so titled was spam and did not require his personal attention. Buchan had also met previously with a representative from R&I, the company-sender of the e-mail, although he states he did not recognize the sender. Therefore, construing all facts in favor of Bazak, a genuine issue of material fact remains.

5. A Jury Could Find That the Writing Was Retained Without Objection

Similarly, the dispute as to whether the October 3 e-mail was retained without objection is a question of fact. In the case at bar, the parties' factual dispute as to what form of response constitutes objection requires consideration of trade usage. Bazak has provided sufficient evidence of re-sale merchant trade practices to buttress its contention that Tarrant's asserted objection was not of a recognized form. Specifically, Bazak argues that Tarrant's alleged objection manifested by the terms of its October 7, 2003 inventory report is without force. The inventory report does not express unequivocal objection and in light of trade practice in the re-sale industry, where parties allow the quantities of goods to shift continuously, Bazak would not reasonably take the sending of that report as such absent this clear expression. Thus, construing all facts in favor of Bazak, the Statute of Frauds does not, as a matter of law, preclude the Court from finding a contract to exist between Bazak and Tarrant.

PROBLEM 3 - 13

As part of her "Go Green" campaign at the store, Rae decided to switch from plastic to paper shopping bags and placed an order by phone with an East Coast paper mill for ten thousand bales of 1/6 barrel recycled paper bags at thirty-nine dollars per bale plus shipping to the store. Immediately after she got off the phone, she sent the following e-mail to the mill:

> Art: Just wanted to confirm my bag order—5,000 bales 1/6 barrel bags at $39 each bale. Let me know when the bags ship. Thanks.
>
> P.S. I'll need more next month—what volume discounts are available?

She left the "Re" line of the e-mail blank.

After three weeks and no word from the mill about her bags, she called the mill and was told her order had been rejected. When she told the rep that they had a deal and the mill was obligated to fill the order, the rep explained that since the mill had not signed a contract with her, there was nothing she could do. Is the rep right—without something in writing signed by the mill that evidences their agreement, the mill has no obligation to send her the bags? 2-201(2).

PROBLEM 3 - 14

A regular customer of the store called today to order two hundred pounds of ground bison for a block party her neighborhood was planning. Rae agreed to sell her the bison at a discounted price of $6.50 per pound, which the customer was happy to pay. The store did not keep that much bison on hand, so Rae had to special order it from the regional bison distributor. After she placed the order for the bison, Rae texted the customer to confirm the order. The text mirrored the terms they had agreed to over the phone. The customer responded with her own text thanking Rae for helping out. If the customer cancels the order, can Rae use her text to the customer to enforce the agreement under 2-201? 2-201(2).

We've already noted how Article 2's formation rules emphasize the conduct of the parties—conduct often trumps paper—and 2-201(3) allows for the use of conduct as a surrogate for the writing otherwise required to satisfy the statute in three limited situations. If conduct affords a basis similar to a writing for believing that oral evidence rests on a real transaction, the purpose of the statute has been served, and it should not bar enforcement of a contract simply because there doesn't happen to be anything in writing. Manufacturing goods to a buyer's specifications is conduct that might afford a basis for believing that seller's claim of an oral agreement rested on a real transaction when the goods were not otherwise saleable in the ordinary course of the seller's business. 2-201(3)(a). Sellers usually don't produce specialized goods they cannot sell to anyone else in the absence of at least an oral commitment from a buyer. The goods themselves provide a basis for believing that there really was an oral agreement. So too might the buyer's acceptance and use of goods delivered by the seller who claims she was acting pursuant to an oral agreement with the buyer. 2-201(3)(c). Partial performance "constitutes an unambiguous overt admission by both parties that a contract actually exists." Comment 2, 2-201. Buyers and sellers don't "ordinarily confer gratuitous benefits on others, except perhaps at Christmas or during other holidays,"[16] and a party's admission under oath during litigation that a contract was made confirms that the alleged oral agreement rests on a real transaction. 2-201(3)(b). Welchers can't have it both ways.

Section 2-201 recognizes an exception to its writing requirement in each of these situations because the conduct of a party is consistent with the claim that a contract was made by the parties. The cases and problems that follow examine these exceptions to 2-201's writing requirement in more detail.

CO. IMAGE KNITWARE, LTD. V. MOTHERS WORK, INC.

SUPERIOR COURT OF PENNSYLVANIA, 2006
909 A.2D 324

TODD, Judge.

In this breach of contract action, Mothers Work, Inc., appeals the judgment entered in favor of Company Image Knitware, Ltd. ("CIK") and Perma Lift Corseteria, S.A. De C.V. ("PLC") (collectively "Appellees"), and Appellees cross-appeal. We affirm.

The extensive factual background of this case, based on the detailed factual findings of the Honorable Marilyn J. Horan, is as follows. CIK is a U.S. garment manufacturing company owned and operated by Clarence B. Williams. PLC is a Mexican garment manufacturing company, with its business headquarters in Mexico City, Mexico, and is owned and operated by Carlos Sandoval. Mothers Work, a Pennsylvania corporation with headquarters in Philadelphia, is a "knock off" maternity garment company that produces clothing by copying the designs of other leading manufacturers.

---

16   White and Summers, *Uniform Commercial Code* (West, 6th ed. 2010) 102.

In February 1999, Don Oaks, Mothers Work's then-executive vice president, asked Williams, with whom Oaks had a long-standing business relationship in the garment industry, to come to Philadelphia to discuss a business venture with Mothers Work wherein Williams would manufacture garments for Mothers Work in Mexico. Williams was asked to locate the appropriate mills and manufacturing centers in Mexico City.

According to the testimony at trial, at this meeting, Mothers Work and Williams' company, CIK, reached an oral agreement whereby CIK agreed to specially manufacture maternity garments in Mexico according to the standards set and approved by Mothers Work regarding fabric, color, style, and pattern, and Mothers Work agreed to pay CIK a set price, 50% after fabric cutting, and 50% on delivery. The trial court set forth the agreed upon production routine as follows:

a. [Mothers Work] would provide a sample material to CIK, which represented the fabric texture, content, and "feel" desired by [Mothers Work]. These fabric samples were generally taken from a garment of a competitor of [Mothers Work], which [Mothers Work] wanted CIK to reproduce.

b. CIK, through Mr. Williams, would negotiate with mills in Mexico City for the production of this specific fabric to meet the requirements of [Mothers Work].

c. Once sample fabrics were produced, they were sent to [Mothers Work] in Philadelphia for approval. Upon approval by [Mothers Work], [Mothers Work] would then send specific color swatches to CIK for exact matching in the manufacture of the fabric.

d. Mr. Williams would take the color swatches to the mill. CIK, through Mr. Williams, would obtain matching colors in sample quantities from the mill and forward the same to [Mothers Work] for approval. Upon approval by [Mothers Work], [Mothers Work] would instruct CIK to order production of a designated quantity of said fabric and color according to [Mothers Work's] specifications.

e. After [Mothers Work] approved the dyed fabric and while the fabric was in production, [Mothers Work] would make a garment fit and pattern, and [Mothers Work] would send those to CIK for purposes of cutting and manufacturing sample garments pursuant to [Mothers Work's] instructions and specifications.

f. CIK would have the Mexican factory make the final fit sample garments from the approved fabric and send the same to [Mothers Work] for final approval. Upon final approval, [Mothers Work] would send CIK the patterns and specifications for the findings, i.e., trim, buttons, etc., manufacturing directions, and instructions to proceed with production.

g. After receiving a written or oral order, CIK, through Mr. Williams, would order the specially made and specially dyed fabric from the mill. The findings were also specially ordered to match the fabric and [Mothers Work] specifications.

PLC, a manufacturer of ladies lingerie and maternity tops to the local Mexican market and for export, was selected by CIK as the Mexican clothing manufacturer, and PLC was also interviewed and approved by Mothers Work. With approval of Mothers Work, and following Mothers Work's inspection of PLC's facilities, Appellees entered into a joint venture for the manufacture of garments pursuant to orders placed by Mothers Work.

In 1999, Appellees began manufacturing garments for Mothers Work. Mothers Work placed its orders for fabric and garments by purchase order, telephone, fax, and some e-mail communications. When garments were delivered to Mothers Work, invoices were issued by CIK or PLC. According to Williams, Appellees produced about 150,000 units for Mothers Work in 1999, about 500,000 units in 2000, and about 200,000 units in the early months of 2001.

Mothers Work terminated its relationship with Appellees in the spring of 2001 by failing to place any further orders for garment production or fabric manufacture. After Mothers Work refused to pay sums Appellees asserted were due for goods already shipped and materials and goods in the process of manufacture, in June 2002, Appellees sued Mothers Work, asserting claims for breach of oral contract, promissory estoppel, and quasi-contract, and seeking damages of nearly $2 million.

In response to Appellees' suit, Mothers Work, *inter alia*, denied the existence of an oral contract between the parties, and asserted that, in any case, Appellees' claims were barred by the statute of frauds. It also counterclaimed for damages related to unfulfilled purchases orders of $300,000.

Following a nonjury trial.... the trial court found in favor of Appellees in the amount of $603,848.40. Judgment was entered against Mothers Work on October 5, 2005, Mothers Work timely appealed, and Appellees cross-appealed.

On appeal, Mothers Work asks:

> Whether the trial court erred as a matter of law in holding that the goods at issue fell within the specially manufactured goods exception to the Statute of Frauds?

Mothers Work argues that, even assuming an oral contract was formed between the parties, it was barred by the statute of frauds. The statute of frauds in the UCC, Section 2201, provides:

[Court quotes 2-201(1).]

None of the parties disputes that Section 2201(a) otherwise bars enforcement of the oral agreement at issue in this case. However, Appellees argued, and the trial court agreed, that the agreement herein fell within the exception to the statute of frauds for specially manufactured goods under Section 2201(c)(1):

> (c) Enforceability of contracts not satisfying general requirements.—A contract which does not satisfy the requirements of subsection (a) but which is valid in other respects is enforceable:

> (1) if the goods are to be specially manufactured for the buyer and are not suitable for sale to others in the ordinary course of the business of the seller and the seller, before notice of repudiation is received and under circumstances which reasonably indicate that the goods are for the buyer, has made either a substantial beginning of their manufacture or commitments for their procurement;

There is a paucity of caselaw interpreting this specially-manufactured—goods exception from the courts of this Commonwealth, thus we look to other jurisdictions for guidance. In *Impossible Elec. Techniques, Inc. v. Wackenhut Protective Sys., Inc.*, 669 F.2d 1026 (5th Cir. 1982), one of the leading specially-manufactured-goods cases, the court explained that the UCC exempts such goods from the writing requirement because "in these cases the very nature of the goods serves as a reliable indication that a contract was indeed formed." *Id.* at 1037; *see also Colorado Carpet Installation, Inc. v. Palermo*, 668 P.2d 1384, 1390 (Colo. 1983) ("It is a reasonable assumption ... that a seller will not make or procure goods not suitable for sale to others in the normal course of the seller's business unless a purchaser has contracted with the seller to purchase these goods."). The *Impossible Elec. Techniques* court further explained:

> Where the seller has commenced or completed the manufacture of goods that conform to the special needs of a particular buyer, and thereby are not suitable for sale to others, not only is the likelihood of a perjured claim of a contract diminished, but denying enforcement to such a contract would impose substantial hardship on the aggrieved party (i.e., a seller is left with goods that are difficult or impossible to sell to others; a buyer may have difficulty locating an alternative supply of the goods). The unfairness is especially acute where, as in the present case, the seller has incurred substantial, unrecoverable expense in reliance on the oral promise of the buyer.

Thus, the term "specially manufactured" refers to "the nature of the particular goods in question," *Impossible Elec. Techniques*, 669 F.2d at 1037, and whether they are "specially made *for a particular buyer*, and not to whether they were 'specially made' in the usual course of the seller's business," *Colorado Carpet Installation*, 668 P.2d at 1390 (emphasis original). *See also Webcor Packaging Corp.*, 158 F.3d at 357 ("[T] he exception requires the presence of circumstances which reasonably indicate that the goods are for the buyer."

The "crucial inquiry," however, is

> whether the manufacturer could sell the goods in the ordinary course of his business to someone other than the original buyer. If with slight alterations the goods could be so sold, then they are not specially manufactured; if, however, essential changes are necessary to render the goods marketable by the seller to others, then the exception does apply.

Impossible Elec. Techniques, 669 F.2d at 1037; *see also Colorado Carpet Installation*, 668 P.2d at 1390 ("There is no unfairness in nonenforcement, however, when the goods are of a class customarily sold by the seller and are readily marketable to others in the ordinary course of the seller's business."); *Contours, Inc. v. Lee*, 10 Haw. App. 368, 874 P.2d 1100, 1105 (Haw. App. 1994) (mandating that the trial court on remand apply the *Impossible Electronic Techniques* "crucial inquiry" of whether manufacturer could sell goods in the ordinary course of business to someone other than the original buyer to determine if the goods at issue were specially manufactured). Furthermore, the unsalable quality of the goods "'must be found in their characteristics of special manufacture and not in such tests as lost markets, passed seasons, or the objective inability of the particular seller to dispose of the goods for reasons unrelated to their nature as prescribed by the buyer.'"

In the instant case, the trial court concluded that the goods were specially manufactured by Appellees for Mothers Work:

> The record clearly established that all fabric, findings and garments were specially manufactured for [Mothers Work]. The colors had to be very specific and exact, the fabric had to have specific content, hand feel and processing, the findings had to be manufactured to match the colors of the fabric, the garments had to have a certain feel, and the sizes of the garments were manufactured to fit American women. The garments and fabric were not suitable for market re-sale in the ordinary course of [Appellees'] business.

> Given that these were specially manufactured goods, that [Appellees] had made substantial commitments for their manufacture, and the past conduct and course of dealing between the parties, this oral agreement, although well beyond $500.00, is valid and enforceable as an exception to the Statute of Frauds. All of the garments, findings and fabric were specially manufactured.

For the following reasons, we agree. First, the trial court made extensive findings of fact, which we find are supported by the record, concerning the detailed specifications set forth by Mothers Work concerning the size, color, feel, and composition of the goods, and the related fabric and findings. Indeed, it is undisputed that the garments were designed to be as identical as possible to garments made by other manufacturers and already on the market in the United States. Contrary to Mothers Work's argument that this fact makes the goods non-unique and thus not specially manufactured (*see, e.g.*, Appellant's Brief at 19 (asserting that the trial court "lost sight of the undisputed ... fact that the garments manufactured for Mothers Work were manufactured to be knock-offs")), we find the peculiar nature of the specifications—to be "knock-offs"—idiosyncratically ties these goods to Mothers Work, a self-described "'knock off' maternity company that designs maternity clothing by copying the designs of other leading manufacturers." Thus, Mothers Work does not dispute, nor can it reasonably dispute, that these goods were specially manufactured for it in the sense that they were made specifically for a particular buyer, Mothers Work.

Section 2201(c)(1) also requires, however, that the goods be "not suitable for sale to others in the ordinary course of the business of the seller," and Mothers Work argues that Appellees have failed to prove this was the case. The trial court found, however, that "there was credible testimony by Carlos Sandoval that these garments could not be sold in Mexico; the feel, fit and sizing were not appropriate for such market as they were specially manufactured for [Mothers Work] and the American market." Although Mothers Work proffers Sandoval's general statements that exports to the United States remain a part of PLC's business, we do not find this possibility sufficient to undermine a conclusion that these goods fall within Section 2201(c)(1), in light of the strong evidence that these goods were specifically tailored for Mothers Work's needs; here, the nature of the goods "serves as a reliable indication that a contract was indeed formed."

PROBLEM 3 - 15

The store bought all of the ice that it used and sold to its customers from the ice company in town based on a long-term agreement Rae had with its owner. The store used large amounts of ice in the produce and meat departments, as well as the deli. It also had bags of ice available for purchase by shoppers. Because of the large quantity of ice the store needed, the ice company had built a storage unit next to the loading dock to store extra ice. Rae decided that she could cut costs if the store made its own ice, so she purchased the equipment necessary to make ice. When the store was finally making enough ice to meet its needs, she stopped ordering from the ice company. When the owner protested, she apologized for the change but insisted she had no continuing obligation to the company.

Rae and the ice company had never put their agreement in writing, but the owner of the ice company claims Rae agreed to buy ice from him for another five years—that's why he built the storage unit, at his expense, at the store. The attorney for the ice company claims that the agreement is enforceable under 2-201(3)(c) even though nothing was ever put in writing. Is she right?

4. And Now for Something Completely Different

During this class one day last week, your laptop shut down, and because you were not able to revive it, you called Dell and ordered a new one. After you told the sales rep the model you wanted and the features you wanted added to it, she quoted you a price for the laptop that you were happy with, so you gave her your credit card info, and she promised that Dell would ship it the next day. It arrived today, and you were excited about the new machine until you noticed a pamphlet in the shipping container. On the cover of the pamphlet was printed:

THIS IS YOUR CONTRACT
READ IT NOW!

Browsing through the pamphlet, you noticed that Dell disclaimed all warranties (except the limited warranty it provided for thirty days), excluded your right to recover damages if anything went wrong with the laptop, required you to arbitrate any dispute you have with Dell at Dell's headquarters in Texas, and provided that if you lost in arbitration you had to pay Dell's legal expenses. It also explained that if you did not agree to the terms, you had to send the laptop back to Dell within ten days, and that your failure to do so would be consent to the terms. You need the laptop for classes, and your seminar paper is due this week, but you don't want to accept the terms Dell has added now that it has your payment. Can Dell change the terms of the transaction you had agreed to over the phone?

The Seventh Circuit (and a few other courts) thinks it can. In *ProCD, Inc. v. Zeidenberg*, 86 F.3d 1447 (1996) and *Hill v. Gateway*, 105 F.3d 1147 (2000), the Seventh Circuit, borrowing from a famous twentieth-century philosopher, declared that contract formation wasn't over until it was over or, at least in your case, until Dell said it was over. In opinions that one writer has called "a swashbuckling tour de force that dangerously misinterpret[s] legislation and precedent," the court turned formation, as we've come to know it under both the common law and Article 2, on its head:[17]

> *ProCD, Inc. v. Zeidenberg*, 86 F.3d 1447 (7th Cir. 1996), holds that terms inside a box of software bind consumers who use the software after an opportunity to read the terms and to reject them by returning the product. Likewise, *Carnival Cruise Lines, Inc. v. Shute*, 499 U.S. 585 (1991), enforces a forum-selection clause that was included amoung three pages of terms attached to a cruise ship ticket. *ProCD* and *Carnival Cruise Lines* exemplify the many commercial transactions in which people pay for products with terms to follow; *ProCD* discusses others. The district court concluded in *ProCD* that the contract is formed when the consumer pays for the software; as a result, the court held, only terms known to the consumer at that moment are part of the contract, and provisos inside the box do not count. Although this is one way a contract could be formed, it is not the only way: "A vendor, as master of the offer, may invite acceptance by conduct, and may propose limitations on the kind of conduct that constitutes acceptance. A buyer may accept by performing the acts the vendor proposed to treat as acceptance." Gateway shipped computers with the same sort of accept-or-return offer *ProCD* made to users of its software.
>
> Payment preceding the revelation of full terms is common for air transportation, insurance, and many other endeavors. Practical considerations support allowing vendors to enclose the full legal terms with their products. Cashiers cannot be expected to read legal documents to customers before ringing up sales. If the staff at the other end of the phone for direct-sales operations such as Gateway's had to read the four-page statement of terms before taking the buyer's credit card number, the droning voice would anesthetize rather than enlighten many potential buyers. Others would hang up in a rage over the waste of their time. And oral recitation would not avoid customers' assertions (whether true or feigned) that the clerk did not read term X to them, or that they did not remember or understand it. Writing provides benefits for both sides of commercial transactions. Customers as a group are better off when vendors skip costly and ineffectual steps such as telephonic recitation, and use instead a simple approve-or-return device. Competent adults are bound by such documents, read or unread.
>
> Next the Hills insist that *ProCD* is irrelevant because Zeidenberg was a "merchant" and they are not. Section 2-207(2) of the UCC, the infamous battle-of-the-forms section, states that "additional terms [following acceptance of an offer] are to be construed as proposals for addition to a contract. Between merchants such terms become part of the contract unless ...". Plaintiffs tell us that *ProCD* came out as it did only because Zeidenberg was a "merchant" and the terms inside *ProCd's* box were not excluded by the "unless" clause. This argument pays scant attention to the opinion in *ProCD*, which concluded that, when there is only one form," § 2-207 is irrelevant." The question in *ProCD* was not whether terms were added to a contract after its formation, but how and when the contract was formed—in particular, whether a vendor may propose that a contract of sale be formed, not in the store (or over the phone) with the payment

---

17   Murray, "Contract Theories and the Rise of Neoformalism," 71 *Fordham L. Rev.* 896, 905 (2002).

of money or a general "send me the product," but after the customer has had a chance to inspect both the item and the terms. *ProCD* answers "yes," for merchants and consumers alike.

As the Seventh Circuit sees it, formation is a process that occurs over a period of time. It starts with the initial contact—the phone call to the seller—but does not end with the buyer's payment or the seller's shipment of the computer. It ends when it says it ends, which, in the *Hill* case, was when the Hills did not return the computer within thirty days of receiving it. During the process, Gateway can add terms to the transaction initiated by the phone call, and by declaration can make anything it wants—breathing—acceptance, as long as the buyer has the option of packing it all up and sending it back.

As for your deal with Dell, *ProCD* and *Hill* appear to put you between a rock and a hard place—finish your paper on Dell's terms or ask your professor for an extension. Of course, if the Seventh Circuit really means what it says, you might have another option: you could send Dell a note rejecting its offer (since, under *ProCD*, Dell has made you the offer) and make a counteroffer—you'll keep the laptop and Dell will provide an all-inclusive lifetime warranty, and you'll assume that's the deal unless Dell objects within five days. If it works for Gateway, it should work for you.[18]

Of course, not all courts have been as contemptuous toward Article 2 as the Seventh Circuit when presented with your dilemma. Some, as the next case illustrates, have actually read Article 2.

KLOCEK V. GATEWAY, INC.
UNITED STATES DISTRICT COURT FOR THE DISTRICT OF KANSAS, 2000
104 F. SUPP. 2D 1332

VRATIL, District Judge.

William S. Klocek brings suit against Gateway, Inc. and Hewlett-Packard, Inc. on claims arising from purchases of a Gateway computer and a Hewlett-Packard scanner. This matter comes before the Court on the Motion to Dismiss ... which Gateway filed November 22, 1999.

Gateway's Motion to Dismiss

Plaintiff brings individual and class action claims against Gateway, alleging that it induced him and other consumers to purchase computers and special support packages by making false promises of technical support. Individually, plaintiff also claims breach of contract and breach of warranty, in that Gateway breached certain warranties that its computer would be compatible with standard peripherals and standard internet services.

Gateway asserts that plaintiff must arbitrate his claims under Gateway's Standard Terms and Conditions Agreement ("Standard Terms"). Whenever it sells a computer, Gateway includes a copy of the Standard Terms in the box which contains the computer battery power cables and instruction manuals. At the top of the first page, the Standard Terms include the following notice:

NOTE TO THE CUSTOMER:

> This document contains Gateway 2000's Standard Terms and Conditions. By keeping your Gateway 2000 computer system beyond five (5) days after the date of delivery, you accept these Terms and Conditions.

---
18   Murray, "The Dubious Status of the Rolling Contract Formation Theory," 50 *Duq. L. Rev.* 35, 56 (2012).

The notice is in emphasized type and is located inside a printed box which sets it apart from other provisions of the document. The Standard Terms are four pages long and contain 16 numbered paragraphs. Paragraph 10 provides the following arbitration clause:

> DISPUTE RESOLUTION. Any dispute or controversy arising out of or relating to this Agreement or its interpretation shall be settled exclusively and finally by arbitration. The arbitration shall be conducted in accordance with the Rules of Conciliation and Arbitration of the International Chamber of Commerce. The arbitration shall be conducted in Chicago, Illinois, U.S.A. before a sole arbitrator. Any award rendered in any such arbitration proceeding shall be final and binding on each of the parties, and judgment may be entered thereon in a court of competent jurisdiction.[19]

Gateway urges the Court to dismiss plaintiff's claims under the Federal Arbitration Act ("FAA"), 9 U.S.C. § 1 *et seq.* The FAA ensures that written arbitration agreements in maritime transactions and transactions involving interstate commerce are "valid, irrevocable, and enforceable." 9 U.S.C. § 2. Federal policy favors arbitration agreements and requires that we "rigorously enforce" them.

Before evaluating whether the parties agreed to arbitrate, the Court must determine what state law controls the formation of the contract in this case.

The parties do not address the choice of law issue, and the record is unclear where they performed the last act necessary to complete the contract. Gateway presents affidavit testimony that it shipped a computer to plaintiff on or about August 31, 1997, but it provides no details regarding the transaction. Plaintiff's complaint alleges that plaintiff lives in Missouri and, if Gateway shipped his computer, it presumably shipped it to Missouri. In his response to Gateway's motion, however, plaintiff states that on August 27, 1997 he purchased the computer in person at the Gateway store in Overland Park, Kansas, and took it with him at that time. Depending on which factual version is correct, it appears that the parties may have performed the last act necessary to form the contract in Kansas (with plaintiff purchasing the computer in Kansas), Missouri (with Gateway shipping the computer to plaintiff in Missouri), or some unidentified other states (with Gateway agreeing to ship plaintiff's catalog order and/or Gateway actually shipping the order).[20]

The Uniform Commercial Code ("UCC") governs the parties' transaction under both Kansas and Missouri law. *See* K.S.A. § 84-2-102; V.A.M.S. § 400.2-102 (UCC applies to "transactions in goods."); Kansas Comment 1 (main thrust of Article 2 is limited to sales); K.S.A. § 84-2-105(1) V.A.M.S. § 400.2-105(1) ("'Goods' means all things ... which are movable at the time of identification to the contract for sale...."). Regardless whether plaintiff purchased the computer in person or placed an order and received shipment of the computer, the parties agree that plaintiff paid for and received a computer from Gateway. This conduct clearly demonstrates a contract for the sale of a computer. Thus the issue is whether the contract of sale includes the Standard Terms as part of the agreement.

State courts in Kansas and Missouri apparently have not decided whether terms received with a product become part of the parties' agreement. Authority from other courts is split. *Compare*

---

19 Gateway states that after it sold plaintiff's computer, it mailed all existing customers in the United States a copy of its quarterly magazine, which contained notice of a change in the arbitration policy set forth in the Standard Terms. The new arbitration policy afforded customers the option of arbitrating before the International Chamber of Commerce ("ICC"), the American Arbitration Association ("AAA"), or the National Arbitration Forum ("NAF") in Chicago, Illinois, or any other location agreed upon by the parties. Plaintiff denies receiving notice of the amended arbitration policy. Neither party explains why—if the arbitration agreement was an enforceable contract—Gateway was entitled to unilaterally amend it by sending a magazine to computer customers.

20 While Gateway may have shipped the computer to plaintiff in Missouri, the record contains no evidence regarding how plaintiff communicated his order to Gateway, where Gateway received plaintiff's order or where the shipment originated.

Step-Saver, 939 F.2d 91 (printed terms on computer software package not part of agreement); *Arizona Retail Sys., Inc. v. Software Link, Inc.*, 831 F. Supp. 759 (D. Ariz. 1993) (license agreement shipped with computer software not part of agreement); *and U.S. Surgical Corp. v. Orris, Inc.*, 5 F. Supp. 2d 1201 (D. Kan. 1998) (single use restriction on product package not binding agreement); [*1338] *with Hill v. Gateway 2000, Inc.*, 105 F.3d 1147 (7th Cir.), *cert. denied*, 522 U.S. 808 (1997) (arbitration provision shipped with computer binding on buyer); *ProCD, Inc. v. Zeidenberg*, 86 F.3d 1447 (7th Cir. 1996) (shrinkwrap license binding on buyer); *and M.A. Mortenson Co., Inc. v. Timberline Software Corp.*, 140 Wn.2d 568, 998 P.2d 305 (Wash. 2000) (following *Hill* and *ProCD* on license agreement supplied with software). It appears that at least in part, the cases turn on whether the court finds that the parties formed their contract *before* or *after* the vendor communicated its terms to the purchaser. *Compare Step-Saver*, 939 F.2d at 98 (parties' conduct in shipping, receiving and paying for product demonstrates existence of contract; box top license constitutes proposal for additional terms under § 2-207 which requires express agreement by purchaser); *Arizona Retail*, 831 F. Supp. at 765 (vendor entered into contract by agreeing to ship goods, or at latest by shipping goods to buyer; license agreement constitutes proposal to modify agreement under § 2-209 which requires express assent by buyer); *and Orris*, 5 F. Supp. 2d at 1206 (sales contract concluded when vendor received consumer orders; single-use language on product's label was proposed modification under § 2-209 which requires express assent by purchaser); *with ProCD*, 86 F.3d at 1452 (under § 2-204 vendor, as master of offer, may propose limitations on kind of conduct that constitutes acceptance; § 2-207 does not apply in case with only one form); *Hill*, 105 F.3d at 1148-49 (same); *and Mortenson*, 998 P.2d at 311-314 (where vendor and purchaser utilized license agreement in prior course of dealing, shrinkwrap license agreement constituted issue of contract formation under § 2-204, not contract alteration under § 2-207).

Gateway urges the Court to follow the Seventh Circuit decision in *Hill*. That case involved the shipment of a Gateway computer with terms similar to the Standard Terms in this case, except that Gateway gave the customer 30 days—instead of 5 days—to return the computer. In enforcing the arbitration clause, the Seventh Circuit relied on its decision in *ProCD*, where it enforced a software license which was contained inside a product box. In *ProCD*, the Seventh Circuit noted that the exchange of money frequently precedes the communication of detailed terms in a commercial transaction. Citing UCC § 2-204, the court reasoned that by including the license with the software, the vendor proposed a contract that the buyer could accept by using the software after having an opportunity to read the license. Specifically, the court stated:

> A vendor, as master of the offer, may invite acceptance by conduct, and may propose limitations on the kind of conduct that constitutes acceptance. A buyer may accept by performing the acts the vendor proposes to treat as acceptance.

The *Hill* court followed the *ProCD* analysis, noting that "practical considerations support allowing vendors to enclose the full legal terms with their products."

The Court is not persuaded that Kansas or Missouri courts would follow the Seventh Circuit reasoning in *Hill* and *ProCD*. In each case the Seventh Circuit concluded without support that UCC § 2-207 was irrelevant because the cases involved only one written form. *See ProCD*, 86 F.3d at 1452 (citing no authority); *Hill*, 105 F.3d at 1150 (citing *ProCD*). This conclusion is not supported by the statute or by Kansas or Missouri law. Disputes under § 2-207 often arise in the context of a "battle of forms," *see, e.g., Daitom, Inc. v. Pennwalt Corp.*, 741 F.2d 1569, 1574 (10th Cir. 1984), but nothing in its language precludes application in a case which involves only one form. The statute provides:

[Court quotes from 2-207(1) and (2).]

By its terms, § 2-207 applies to an acceptance or written confirmation. It states nothing which requires another form before the provision becomes effective. In fact, the official comment to the section specifically provides that §§ 2-207(1) and (2) apply "where an agreement has been reached orally ... and is followed by one or both of the parties sending formal memoranda embodying the terms so far agreed and adding terms not discussed." Official Comment 1 of UCC § 2-207. Kansas and Missouri courts have followed this analysis. *See Southwest Engineering Co. v. Martin Tractor Co.*, 205 Kan. 684, 695, 473 P.2d 18, 26 (1970) (stating in dicta that § 2-207 applies where open offer is accepted by expression of acceptance in writing or where oral agreement is later confirmed in writing); *Central Bag Co. v. W. Scott and Co.*, 647 S.W.2d 828, 830 (Mo. App. 1983) (§§ 2-207(1) and (2) govern cases where one or both parties send written confirmation after oral contract). Thus, the Court concludes that Kansas and Missouri courts would apply § 2-207 to the facts in this case.

In addition, the Seventh Circuit provided no explanation for its conclusion that "the vendor is the master of the offer." *See ProCD*, 86 F.3d at 1452 (citing nothing in support of proposition); *Hill*, 105 F.3d at 1149 (citing *ProCD*). In typical consumer transactions, the purchaser is the offeror, and the vendor is the offeree. *See Brown Mach., Div. of John Brown, Inc. v. Hercules, Inc.*, 770 S.W.2d 416, 419 (Mo. App. 1989) (as general rule orders are considered offers to purchase); *Rich Prods. Corp. v. Kemutec Inc.*, 66 F. Supp. 2d 937, 956 (E.D. Wis. 1999) (generally price quotation is invitation to make offer and purchase order is offer). While it is possible for the vendor to be the offeror, *see Brown Machine*, 770 S.W.2d at 419 (price quote can amount to offer if it reasonably appears from quote that assent to quote is all that is needed to ripen offer into contract), Gateway provides no factual evidence which would support such a finding in this case. The Court therefore assumes for purposes of the motion to dismiss that plaintiff offered to purchase the computer (either in person or through catalog order) and that Gateway accepted plaintiff's offer (either by completing the sales transaction in person or by agreeing to ship and/or shipping the computer to plaintiff).[21] *Accord Arizona Retail*, 831 F. Supp. at 765 (vendor entered into contract by agreeing to ship goods, or at latest, by shipping goods).

Under § 2-207, the Standard Terms constitute either an expression of acceptance or written confirmation. As an expression of acceptance, the Standard Terms would constitute a counter-offer only if Gateway expressly made its acceptance conditional on plaintiff's assent to the additional or different terms. "The conditional nature of the acceptance must be clearly expressed in a manner sufficient to notify the offeror that the offeree is unwilling to proceed with the transaction unless the additional or different terms are included in the contract." *Brown Machine*, 770 S.W.2d at 420. Gateway provides no evidence that at the time of the sales transaction, it informed plaintiff that the transaction was conditioned on plaintiff's acceptance of the Standard Terms. Moreover, the mere fact that Gateway shipped the goods with the terms attached did not communicate to plaintiff any unwillingness to proceed without plaintiff's agreement to the Standard Terms. *See, e.g., Arizona Retail*, 831 F. Supp. at 765 (conditional acceptance analysis rarely appropriate where contract formed by performance but goods arrive with conditions attached); *Lighton Indus., Inc. v. Callier Steel Pipe & Tube, Inc.*, 1991 WL 18413, *6, Case No. 89-C-8235 (N.D.Ill. Feb. 6, 1991) (applying Missouri law) (preprinted forms insufficient to notify offeror of conditional nature of acceptance, particularly where form arrives after delivery of goods).

Because plaintiff is not a merchant, additional or different terms contained in the Standard Terms did not become part of the parties' agreement unless plaintiff expressly agreed to them. *See* K.S.A. §

---

21   UCC § 2-206(b) provides that "an order or other offer to buy goods for prompt or current shipment shall be construed as inviting acceptance either by a prompt promise to ship or by the prompt or current shipment ..." The official comment states that "either shipment or a prompt promise to ship is made a proper means of acceptance of an offer looking to current shipment." UCC § 2-206, Official Comment 2.

84-2-207, Kansas Comment 2 (if either party is not a merchant, additional terms are proposals for addition to the contract that do not become part of the contract unless the original offeror expressly agrees).[22] Gateway argues that plaintiff demonstrated acceptance of the arbitration provision by keeping the computer more than five days after the date of delivery. Although the Standard Terms purport to work that result, Gateway has not presented evidence that plaintiff expressly agreed to those Standard Terms. Gateway states only that it enclosed the Standard Terms inside the computer box for plaintiff to read afterwards. It provides no evidence that it informed plaintiff of the five-day review-and-return period as a condition of the sales transaction, or that the parties contemplated additional terms to the agreement.[23] *See Step-Saver*, 939 F.2d at 99 (during negotiations leading to purchase, vendor never mentioned box-top license or obtained buyer's express assent thereto). The Court finds that the act of keeping the computer past five days was not sufficient to demonstrate that plaintiff expressly agreed to the Standard Terms. *Accord Brown Machine*, 770 S.W.2d at 421 (express assent cannot be presumed by silence or mere failure to object). Thus, because Gateway has not provided evidence sufficient to support a finding under Kansas or Missouri law that plaintiff agreed to the arbitration provision contained in Gateway's Standard Terms, the Court overrules Gateway's motion to dismiss.

In *Klocek*, the court, relying on 2-206, determined that a contract was formed when Gateway, in response to the offer the buyer made to purchase the computer at its store or over the phone, completed the transaction or promised to ship the computer. Section 2-206 provides that "unless unambiguously indicated by the language or the circumstances,"

> (b) an order or other offer to buy goods for prompt or current shipment shall be construed
> as inviting acceptance either by a prompt promise to ship or by the prompt or current
> shipment ...

Comment 2 to 2-206 tells us that shipment or a promise to ship is a proper means of acceptance in such cases. Presumably, Gateway does not randomly ship computers to people around the country; it ships them in response to some form of contact made by the recipient—what most of us would call an order, if not an offer to buy. The Seventh Circuit never mentioned 2-206, even though it obviously applied to the phone order placed by the Hills—they contacted Gateway presumably to offer to purchase a computer, not for the current weather conditions in California—and Gateway promised to ship the computer. The Hills must have gotten something in return for providing their credit card information. When their phone call with Gateway ended, then, the Hills had an enforceable contract with Gateway under 2-206.

That means that the surprise in the box the Hills received from Gateway—the Standard Terms—could only become part of the contract if 2-207 let them in or if the Standard Terms were a modification (under 2-209) of the contract formed during the phone call. Since there was only one piece of paper, 2-207 did not apply, according to the Seventh Circuit. But even though modifications do not require additional consideration under Article 2, they do require consent—a *unilateral* modification is not effective with or without consideration. And the Hills never consented to the modification—silence is not consent and cannot be deemed consent by the party proposing to modify the contract.

Since these provisions prevent terms supplied later by a seller from becoming part of the parties' agreement absent consent, the Seventh Circuit had to ignore them or disingenuously dismiss them.

---

22 The Court's decision would be the same if it considered the Standard Terms as a proposed modification under UCC § 2-209. *See, e.g., Orris*, 5 F. Supp. 2d at 1206 (express assent analysis is same under §§ 2-207 and 2-209).
23 The Court is mindful of the practical considerations which are involved in commercial transactions, but it is not unreasonable for a vendor to clearly communicate to a buyer—at the time of sale—either the complete terms of the sale or the fact that the vendor will propose additional terms as a condition of sale, if that be the case.

Problem 3 - 16

Determine whether a contract was formed under 2-206 in each of the following cases: 2-206.

1. Rae mailed a purchase order for "five hundred pounds of salmon at market price plus transport" to a fishery on the East Coast. When the fishery received the order, it immediately e-mailed its acceptance of the order to Rae.

2. Rae left a voice mail ordering "two hundred dozen organic eggs, free-range," from the local organic poultry farm. The farm texted her its acceptance of her order after listening to her message. The next day, before the farm had filled her order, Rae e-mailed the farm cancelling the order.

3. Rae e-mailed an order for "twenty-five cases of Artesa 2011 Limited Release Rive Gauche Cabernet Sauvignon, Napa Valley at $498 case plus transport" to the Artesa Winery in California. Artesa immediately mailed a sales invoice accepting the order and promising delivery within ten days. Before the invoice arrived, Rae e-mailed the winery cancelling her order.

4. Rae texted an order for "twenty-five Irish cream cheesecakes and twenty-five white chocolate cheesecakes" to New Skete Monastery in upstate New York. The monks boxed up the cheesecakes and turned them over to FedEx for delivery to the store. While they were in transit, Rae sent a follow-up text cancelling her order.

B. What is the Agreement?

Article 2 makes the parties' *agreement* the touchstone of a contract for the sale of goods—"a contract for the sale of goods may be made in any manner sufficient to show agreement" (2-204(1)), and that *agreement* "is to be found in their language or inferred from other circumstances, including course of performance, course of dealing, or usage of trade." 1-201(3). A contract for the sale of goods is not created in a vacuum—the agreement of the parties must be understood in light of what Llewellyn called the "background" of a transaction, which was, as between merchants, as much a part of their agreement as what they happened to have put in writing. An early draft of the revised Sales Act seems intended to actually give primacy to this "background" over the language of the parties:

> *Section 1-D. Usage of Trade an Course of Dealing.* Between merchants, the usage of trade or of a particular trade, and any course of dealing between the parties, are presumed to be the background which the parties have presupposed in their bargaining and have intended to read into the particular contract; and express words are to be construed, where that is reasonable, as consistent with, rather than as a displacement of, such usage and course of dealing.[24]

The final version of Article 2 restored the primacy of express terms over this "background," or what Article 2 today would treat as implied terms (1-303), but preserved the presumption from the early drafts that the parties intended to make usage of trade, course of performance, and course of dealing a part of their agreement. The agreement Article 2 gives effect to is "the bargain of the parties in fact," which includes both express and implied terms.

1. Express Terms

For Llewellyn, the "express" terms of a sale-of-goods transaction were the "dickered terms"—the terms the parties actually haggled over during the negotiations that gave rise to their agreement—not the endless stream of print that happened to be part of a preprinted form onto which they scribed their deal:

---

24   I Kelly, *Uniform Commercial Code: Drafts,* (Rothman 1984) 334–335.

The principle of freedom of bargain is a principle of freedom of *intended* bargain. It requires what the parties have bargained out to stand as the parties have shaped it, ... "Written" bargains, in the days when the rules about them crystallized, were bargains whose detailed terms the two parties had looked over; and the rule was proper, that a signature meant agreement.... [D]eliberate intent is not shown by a lop-sided form whose very content suggests that it has not been, carefully read, and the circumstances of whose execution suggest that the matters under discussion and consideration were only the matters written or typed in.[25]

But contract law had been built upon the principle of freedom of contract, and so too would the revised Sales Act. Llewellyn ultimately conceded the primacy of the terms expressly provided by the parties in their agreement. Section 1-303 provides that "express terms prevail over course of performance, course of dealing, and usage of trade" when express terms cannot be reasonably construed as consistent with terms Article 2 would otherwise make part of an agreement by implication. The parties' agreement was to be "found in their language." As we will see, when the parties speak, Article 2 defers to them in all but the most exceptional of circumstances.

2. Implied Terms: Parol-Evidence Rule

For Llewellyn, the parol-evidence rule was another archaic rule of law that, because it elevated form over substance, did more harm than good. It removed from consideration by the trier of fact evidence essential to discovering the true agreement between the parties—evidence that reflected the actual circumstances within which they made their contract. Commercial transactions do not take place in a vacuum—the understanding of the parties often extends beyond the paper they created to record their agreement. This is especially so when the parties have dealt with each other in the past or when the parties are members of a trade or industry that has its own customs or practices for transacting business. At common law, the parol-evidence rule gave primacy over all extrinsic facts to the paper the parties created—even though those extrinsic facts were just as much a part of the parties' understanding as what they happened to put down on paper. Instead of protecting the actual agreement of the parties, the parol-evidence rule prevented a court from giving effect to the true agreement the parties had made.

We've already noted that bridging the disconnect between sales law and the realities of commercial transactions was one of Llewellyn's goals—maybe the primary goal—when he sat down to draft a new sales code. So the parol-evidence rule was an early target, and it took a direct hit in the first drafts Llewellyn produced.

Unlike prior law, Article 2 presumes that there is more to the parties' agreement than the paper they produced to record it. As Llewellyn explained in the notes to his second draft:

between merchants, the usage of trade or a particular trade and any course of dealing between the parties are presumed to be the background which the parties have presupposed in their bargain and have intended to read into the particular contract.[26]

Under Article 2, it's the "agreement" of the parties that creates contractual obligations (1-201(b)(12)), and the parties' agreement is "the bargain of the parties in fact, as found in their language or *inferred from other circumstances, including course of performance, course of dealing, or trade usage* ..." (1-201(b) (3)) (emphasis added). Because the Code presumes the parties intended any applicable course of performance, course of dealing, or usage of trade to be a part of their agreement, it follows then that Article 2 should presume that there is more to their agreement than they happened to have put down in writing. Any written agreement is

---

25 I Kelly, *Uniform Commercial Code: Drafts*, (Rothman, 1984) 332–333 (emphasis in original).
26 I Kelly, *Uniform Commercial Code: Drafts*, (Rothman 1984) 334–335.

to be read on the assumption that the course of prior dealings between the parties and the usages of trade were taken for granted when the document was phrased.

Comment 2, 2-202. An Article 2 contract for the sale of goods, then, consists of the terms expressly provided by the parties in any written agreement, the terms Article 2 implies as part of that written agreement based on any applicable course of dealing or usage of trade, and on any implications that can be drawn from the actual performance by the parties. Article 2 also provides that course of dealing, trade usage, and course of performance can be used to give meaning to the words they used in their written agreement.

But the evidence necessary to show that there was more to the agreement than what the parties put in writing was inadmissible in many cases under the parol-evidence rule that applied to sales transactions. Without some evidence of an additional term, a court could not find that the parties' agreement included terms that were not in the writing that recorded their deal. If a court determined that the writing of the parties was final—that the parties did not intend to create any more paper to record their deal—the parties could not use evidence outside the writing to prove terms that were inconsistent with or that contradicted anything they had put in that writing. And if a court determined that the writing was also the complete expression of the parties' agreement—that there was no more to the deal because they wrote down everything they had agreed to—the parties could not use evidence outside the writing to show otherwise. So the parol-evidence rule prevented the parties from presenting the evidence necessary to prove that there was more to their agreement than they wrote down. Which meant, of course, that the parol-evidence rule had to go—or at least be remade so it did not get in the way of a party trying to prove terms beyond those in the writing.

What remains of the parol-evidence rule—it did survive—is set out in 2-202. It gives effect to the presumption that course of performance, course of dealing, and usage of trade are part of the parties' agreement by allowing the court to consider any evidence of those circumstances presented by the parties, as long as it does not contradict the express terms of their written agreement. Under 2-202, course of performance, course of dealing, and usage of trade are always admissible to explain or supplement a writing—even if the court finds that the parties intended the writing to be the final, complete, and exclusive statement of their agreement. The rule no longer prevents the parties from presenting evidence to prove there was more to their deal than they wrote down when that "more" is based on what Llewellyn considered the "background which the parties have presupposed in their bargain and have intended to read into the particular contract." This background is necessary "in order that the true understanding of the parties as to the agreement can be reached." Comment 2, 2-202. Evidence of consistent additional terms—terms the parties agreed to orally but did not put in their writing—can also be used to explain or supplement the terms in a final writing, unless the court determines that the parties intended the writing to be the "complete and exclusive statement of the terms" of their agreement. 2-202(b).

The next case illustrates the basic application of 2-202.

C-THRU CONTAINER CORP. v. MIDLAND MFG. CO.

SUPREME COURT OF IOWA, 1995
533 N.W.2D 542

TERNUS, Justice.

This case requires us to interpret and apply the trade-usage exception to the parol evidence rule embodied in Iowa Code chapter 554, Iowa's Uniform Commercial Code (U.C.C.). The trial court held that parol evidence of trade usage was inadmissible and granted summary judgment to the defendant, Midland

Manufacturing Company. We agree with the contrary decision of the court of appeals that the challenged evidence was admissible and generated a question of fact that prevented summary judgment. Therefore, we affirm the decision of the court of appeals and reverse the judgment of the district court.

BACKGROUND FACTS AND PROCEEDINGS.

C-Thru Container Corporation entered into a contract with Midland Manufacturing Company in March of 1989. In this contract, Midland agreed to purchase bottle-making equipment from C-Thru and to make commercially acceptable bottles for C-Thru. Midland was to pay for the equipment by giving C-Thru a credit against C-Thru's bottle purchases. The contract stated that C-Thru expected to order between 500,000 and 900,000 bottles in 1989. Finally, the contract also provided that if Midland failed to manufacture the bottles, C-Thru could require Midland to pay the entire purchase price plus interest within thirty days.

Midland picked up the equipment as agreed and later sent a notice to C-Thru that it was ready to begin production. C-Thru never ordered any bottles from Midland, but instead purchased its bottles from another supplier at a lower price. C-Thru claims that in numerous phone conversations between the parties Midland indicated that it was unable to produce commercially acceptable bottles for C-Thru.

In 1992, Midland gave C-Thru notice that it was rescinding the 1989 contract based on C-Thru's failure to order any bottles. C-Thru did not respond to this notice. Midland later sent C-Thru notice that it was claiming an artisan's lien for the expenses of moving, rebuilding and repairing the machinery. Midland eventually foreclosed the artisan's lien and sold the machinery.

Approximately one month later, C-Thru notified Midland that Midland had failed to comply with the terms of the contract and that the full purchase price plus interest was due and payable within thirty days. When Midland failed to pay C-Thru the amount requested, C-Thru Filed a petition alleging that Midland had breached the contract by being incapable of producing the bottles as agreed to in the contract.

Midland filed a motion for summary judgment. It contended that the contract did not require that it demonstrate an ability to manufacture commercially acceptable bottles as a condition precedent to C-Thru's obligation to place an order. Midland asserted that the contract merely required that it manufacture commercially acceptable bottles in response to an order from C-Thru. Because C-Thru never placed an order, Midland argued that it had not breached the contract by failing to manufacture any bottles.

C-Thru resisted Midland's motion. It argued that a material issue of fact existed on whether Midland was unable to manufacture the bottles, thereby excusing C-Thru's failure to place an order. As proof that Midland could not manufacture the bottles, C-Thru pointed to Midland's failure to provide sample bottles. C-Thru relied on deposition testimony that the practice in the bottle-making industry was for the bottle manufacturer to provide sample bottles to verify that it could make commercially acceptable bottles before the purchaser placed any orders.

In ruling on Midland's motion for summary judgment, the trial court found no sample container requirement in the written contract. The court also held that the parol evidence rule precluded consideration of any evidence that the practice in the trade was to provide sample bottles before receiving an order. It concluded that no genuine issue of material fact existed and granted Midland summary judgment. The court of appeals reversed the district court's ruling, concluding that evidence regarding the trade practice should have been considered. We granted Midland's application for further review.

Should Usage-of-Trade Evidence Be Allowed?
Under the common law of Iowa, parol evidence is admissible to shed light on the parties' intentions but it may not be used to modify or add to the contract terms. Nevertheless, sale-of-goods contracts, such

as the agreement here, are governed by Iowa Code chapter 554, the Iowa Uniform Commercial Code. Section 554.2202 contains the applicable U.C.C. parol evidence rule and it states:

> Terms with respect to which the confirmatory memoranda of the parties agree or which are otherwise set forth in a writing intended by the parties as a final expression of their agreement with respect to such terms as are included therein may not be contradicted by evidence of any prior agreement or of a contemporaneous oral agreement but may be *explained or supplemented*
>
> a. by course of dealing or *usage of trade* (section 554.1205) or by course of performance (section 554.2208); and
>
> b. by evidence of consistent additional terms unless the court finds the writing to have been intended also as a complete and exclusive statement of the terms of the agreement.

Iowa Code § 554.2202 (1993) (emphasis added). Thus, unlike the common law, parol evidence may be used to supplement a fully integrated agreement governed by the U.C.C. if the evidence falls within the definition of usage of trade.

The Iowa U.C.C. includes the following definition of usage of trade:

> 2. A usage of trade is any practice or method of dealing having such regularity of observance in a place, vocation or trade as to justify an expectation that it will be observed with respect to the transaction in question. The existence and scope of such a usage are to be proved as facts....

Section 554.1205 goes on to provide that any usage of trade of which the parties are or should be aware supplements their agreement.

Midland does not dispute that a trier of fact could find that the alleged practice in the bottling industry of providing samples to a prospective purchaser is a usage of trade. However, Midland argues usage-of-trade evidence may not be used to add a new term to a contract that is complete and unambiguous.

We first reject Midland's argument that evidence of trade usage is admissible only when the contract is ambiguous. There is no such requirement in section 554.2202. Moreover, the official comment to section 2-202 of the Uniform Commercial Code, which is identical to section 554.2202, states that this section "definitely rejects" a requirement that the language of the contract be ambiguous as a condition precedent to the admission of trade-usage evidence.

We also hold that even a "complete" contract may be explained or supplemented by parol evidence of trade usages.[27] As the official comment to section 2-202 states, commercial sales contracts "are to be read on the assumption that the course of prior dealings between the parties and the usages of trade were taken for granted when the document was phrased." Therefore, even a completely integrated contract may be supplemented by practices in the industry that do not contradict express terms of the contract.

That brings us to the remaining argument made by Midland—that C-Thru may not use parol evidence to add a new term to the agreement. Section 554.2202 says that when parol evidence shows a usage of trade that does not contradict a contract term[28], the evidence is admissible to "supplement" the contract. We look to the common meaning of the word "supplement." *State v. Simmons*, 500 N.W.2d 58, 59 (Iowa 1993) (we give 1words used in a statute their ordinary meaning, including reference to the

---

27   The contract here stated that "this agreement constitutes the entire agreement between C-Thru and Midland and supersedes any and all prior agreements between them."

28   Midland makes no argument that the sample requirement contradicts a term of the contract. In fact, the contract is silent on whether Midland must verify its ability to manufacture commercially acceptable bottles prior to C-Thru's placement of an order.

dictionary definition). "Supplement" means "to add ... to." *Webster's Third New Int'l Dictionary 2297* (1993). Consequently, the trade-usage evidence upon which C-Thru relies is admissible even though it adds a new term to the contract. White & Summers, § 3-3 (usage of trade may itself constitute a contract term).

SUMMARY

The usage-of-trade evidence offered by C-Thru does not contradict any explicit contractual term. It supplements the written agreement which is permitted under section 554.2202. Taking this evidence in a light most favorable to C-Thru, we conclude there exists a genuine issue of fact concerning the performance required of Midland as a prerequisite to C-Thru's obligation to place an order. Therefore, summary judgment is not appropriate.

PROBLEM 3 - 17

During the first week of November, one aisle of the store is converted into a Christmas village which displays seasonal items—artificial Christmas trees, inflatable Santas, and the like—for sale in the store. This year, the store did not sell twenty-five of the artificial trees Rae had ordered for the village, and so Rae shipped them back to the seller with a request for a credit to the store's account. The seller refused to take them back or credit the account because neither Rae's purchase order nor the seller's invoice required the seller to accept returns of unsold goods—both were silent on the issue. Has the seller breached their agreement if Rae can show that in each of the last four years the seller accepted unsold returns and credited the store's account, even though there was nothing in their writings that required it to do so? 2-326(3).

PROBLEM 3 - 18

What if, in the last problem, Rae had never ordered holiday items from the seller, but she could prove that it was standard practice for sellers of seasonal merchandise to accept unsold returns and credit the buyer's account at the end of the holiday season—has the seller breached their agreement by refusing to take back the trees?

PROBLEM 3 - 19

A local grain merchant has supplied all of the bulk cereal products sold by the store for the past fifteen years under an agreement Rae's father made when he was running the store. The agreement was for one year, but it has automatically renewed every year since the first because neither party has exercised its right to prevent renewal by giving the other thirty days' notice prior to the end of the term—until last week, when the seller told Rae he did not want to renew the agreement for another year. Can Rae argue that the parties' course of dealing or performance over the fifteen years has invalidated the termination provision in the agreement? 1-303(e).

When do course of performance, course of dealing, or trade usage "contradict" the express terms of the parties' agreement so as to preclude their inclusion in that agreement? When do such terms merely explain or supplement express terms? If the terms of the writing expressly exclude a usage of trade that would otherwise become part of the agreement, a conflict appears to exist. Does any usage of trade that touches—no matter how tangentially—on a subject addressed in the written agreement necessarily contradict the writing? Comment 2 to 2-202 and section 1-303(e) suggest that something more than some overlap between express terms and course of performance, course of dealing, or usage of trade is required to create an exclusionary contradiction. Comment 2 to 2-202 tells us that the extrinsic terms become part of the agreement "unless carefully negated." And 1-303(e) commands that express terms "must be construed whenever reasonable as consistent with course of performance, course of dealing, or trade usage." The message seems to be that doubts are resolved against exclusion, and the next case constructs the most sensible analysis for dealing with this issue.

NANAKULI PAVING & ROCK CO. V. SHELL OIL CO.
UNITED STATES COURT OF APPEALS FOR THE NINTH CIRCUIT, 1981
664 F.2D 772

HOFFMAN, Judge.

Appellant Nanakuli Paving and Rock Company (Nanakuli) initially filed this breach of contract action against appellee Shell Oil Company (Shell) in Hawaiian State Court in February, 1976. Nanakuli, the second largest asphaltic paving contractor in Hawaii, had bought all its asphalt requirements from 1963 to 1974 from Shell under two long-term supply contracts; its suit charged Shell with breach of the later 1969 contract. The jury returned a verdict of $220,800 for Nanakuli on its first claim, which is that Shell breached the 1969 contract in January, 1974, by failing to price protect Nanakuli on 7200 tons of asphalt at the time Shell raised the price for asphalt from $44 to $76. Nanakuli's theory is that price-protection, as a usage of the asphaltic paving trade in Hawaii, was incorporated into the 1969 agreement between the parties, as demonstrated by the routine use of price protection by suppliers to that trade, and reinforced by the way in which Shell actually performed the 1969 contract up until 1974. Price protection, appellant claims, required that Shell hold the price on the tonnage Nanakuli had already committed because Nanakuli had incorporated that price into bids put out to or contracts awarded by general contractors and government agencies. The District Judge set aside the verdict and granted Shell's motion for judgment n. o. v., which decision we vacate. We reinstate the jury verdict because we find that, viewing the evidence as a whole, there was substantial evidence to support a finding by reasonable jurors that Shell breached its contract by failing to provide protection for Nanakuli in 1974.

Nanakuli offers two theories for why Shell's failure to offer price protection in 1974 was a breach of the 1969 contract. First, it argues, all material suppliers to the asphaltic paving trade in Hawaii followed the trade usage of price protection and thus it should be assumed, under the U.C.C., that the parties intended to incorporate price protection into their 1969 agreement. This is so, Nanakuli continues, even though the written contract provided for price to be "Shell's Posted Price at time of delivery," F.O.B. Honolulu. Nanakuli points out that Shell had price protected it on the two occasions of price increases under the 1969 contract other than the 1974 increase. In 1970 and 1971 Shell extended the old price for four and three months, respectively, after an announced increase. This was done, in the words of Shell's agent in Hawaii, in order to permit Nanakuli's to "chew up" tonnage already committed at Shell's old price.[29]

Nanakuli's second theory for price protection is that Shell was obliged to price protect Nanakuli, even if price protection was not incorporated into their contract, because price protection was the commercially reasonable standard for fair dealing in the asphaltic paving trade in Hawaii in 1974. Observance of those standards is part of the good-faith requirement that the Code imposes on merchants

---

29   Price protection was practiced in the asphaltic paving trade by either extending the old price for a period of time after a new one went into effect or charging the old price for a specified tonnage, which represented work committed at the old price. In addition, several months' advance notice was given of price increases.

in performing a sales contract. Shell was obliged to price protect Nanakuli in order to act in good faith, Nanakuli argues, because such a practice was universal in that trade in that locality.

Shell presents three arguments for upholding the judgment n. o. v. or, on cross appeal, urging that the District Judge erred in admitting certain evidence. First, it says, the District Court should not have denied Shell's motion in limine to define trade, for purposes of trade usage evidence, as the sale and purchase of asphalt in Hawaii, rather than expanding the definition of trade to include other suppliers of materials to the asphaltic paving trade. Asphalt, its argument runs, was the subject matter of the disputed contract and the only product Shell supplied to the asphaltic paving trade. Shell protests that the judge, by expanding the definition of trade to include the other major suppliers to the asphaltic paving trade, allowed the admission of highly prejudicial evidence of routine price protection by all suppliers of aggregate. Asphaltic concrete paving is formed by mixing paving asphalt with crushed rock, or aggregate, in a "hot-mix" plant and then pouring the mixture onto the surface to be paved.

* * * *

Shell's final argument is that, even assuming its prior price protection constituted a course of performance and that the broad trade definition was correct and evidence of trade usages by aggregate suppliers was admissible, price protection could not be construed as reasonably consistent with the express price term in the contract, in which case the Code provides that the express term controls.

We hold that the judge did not abuse his discretion in defining the applicable trade, for purposes of trade usages, as the asphaltic paving trade in Hawaii, rather than the purchase and sale of asphalt alone, given the unusual, not to say unique, circumstances: the smallness of the marketplace on Oahu; the existence of only two suppliers on the island; [and] the long and intimate connection between the two companies on Oahu, including the background of how the development of Shell's asphalt sales on Oahu was inextricably linked to Nanakuli's own expansion on the island;....

Lastly we hold that, although the express price terms of Shell's posted price of delivery may seem, at first glance, inconsistent with a trade usage of price protection at time of increases in price, a closer reading shows that the jury could have reasonably construed price protection as consistent with the express term. We reach this holding for several reasons. First, we are persuaded by a careful reading of the U.C.C., one of whose underlying purposes is to promote flexibility in the expansion of commercial practices and which rather drastically overhauls this particular area of the law. The Code would have us look beyond the printed pages of the contract to usages and the entire commercial context of the agreement in order to reach the "true understanding" of the parties. Second, decisions of other courts in similar situations have managed to reconcile such trade usages with seemingly contradictory express terms where the prior course of dealings between the parties, trade usages, and the actual performance of the contract by the parties showed a clear intent by the parties to incorporate those usages into the agreement or to give to the express term the particular meaning provided by those usages, even at times varying the apparent meaning of the express terms. Third, the delineation by thoughtful commentators of the degree of consistency demanded between express terms and usage is that a usage should be allowed to modify the apparent agreement, as seen in the written terms, as long as it does not totally negate it. We believe the usage here falls within the limits set forth by commentators and generally followed in the better-reasoned decisions. The manner in which price protection was actually practiced in Hawaii was that it only came into play at times of price increases and only for work committed prior to those increases on non-escalating contracts. Thus, it formed an exception to, rather than a total negation of, the express price term of "Shell's Posted Price at time of delivery." Our decision is reinforced by the overwhelming nature of the evidence that price protection was routinely practiced by all suppliers in the small Oahu market of the asphaltic paving trade and therefore was known to Shell; that it was a realistic necessity to operate in that market and thus vital to Nanakuli's ability to get large government contracts and to Shell's continued business growth on Oahu; and that it therefore constituted an intended part of the agreement, as that term is broadly defined by the Code, between Shell and Nanakuli.

Scope of Trade Usage

The validity of the jury verdict in this case depends on four legal questions. First, how broad was the trade to whose usages Shell was bound under its 1969 agreement with Nanakuli: did it extend to the Hawaiian asphaltic paving trade or was it limited merely to the purchase and sale of asphalt, which would only include evidence of practices by Shell and Chevron? Second, were the two instances of price protection of Nanakuli by Shell in 1970 and 1971 waivers of the 1969 contract as a matter of law or was the jury entitled to find that they constituted a course of performance of the contract? Third, could the jury have construed an express contract term of Shell's posted price at delivery as reasonably consistent with a trade usage and Shell's course of performance of the 1969 contract of price protection, which consisted of charging the old price at times of price increases, either for a period of time or for specific tonnage committed at a fixed price in non-escalating contracts? Fourth, could the jury have found that good faith obliged Shell to at least give advance notice of a $32 increase in 1974, that is, could they have found that the commercially reasonable standards of fair dealing in the trade in Hawaii in 1974 were to give some form of price protection?

The Code defines usage of trade as "any practice or method of dealing having such regularity of observance in a place, vocation or trade as to justify an expectation that it will be observed with respect to the transaction in question." We understand the use of the word "or" to mean that parties can be bound by a usage common to the place they are in business, even if it is not the usage of their particular vocation or trade. The drafters' Comments say that trade usage is to be used to reach the ".... commercial meaning of the agreement...." by interpreting the language "as meaning what it may fairly be expected to mean to parties involved in the particular transaction in a given locality or in a given vocation or trade." The inference of the two subsections and the Comment, read together, is that a usage need not necessarily be one practiced by members of the party's own trade or vocation to be binding if it is so commonly practiced in a locality that a party should be aware of it. A party is always held to conduct generally observed by members of his chosen trade because the other party is justified in so assuming unless he indicates otherwise. He is held to more general business practices to the extent of his actual knowledge of those practices or to the degree his ignorance of those practices is not excusable: they were so generally practiced he should have been aware of them.

[E]ven if Shell did not "regularly deal" with aggregate supplies, it did deal constantly and almost exclusively on Oahu with one asphalt paver. It therefore should have been aware of the usage if Nanakuli and other asphaltic pavers to bid at fixed prices and therefore receive price protection from their materials suppliers due to the refusal by government agencies to accept escalation clauses. Therefore, we do not find the lower court abused its discretion or misread the Code as applied to the peculiar facts of this case in ruling that the applicable trade was the asphaltic paving trade in Hawaii. An asphalt seller should be held to the usages of trade in general as well as those of asphalt sellers and common usages of those to whom they sell. Certainly, under the unusual facts of this case it was not unreasonable for the judge to extend trade usages to include practices of other material suppliers toward Shell's primary and perhaps only customer on Oahu. He did exclude, on Shell's motion in limine, evidence of cement suppliers. He only held Shell to routine practices in Hawaii by the suppliers of the two major ingredients of asphaltic paving, that is, asphalt, and aggregate. Those usages were only practiced towards two major pavers. It was not unreasonable to expect Shell to be knowledgeable about so small a market. In so ruling, the judge undoubtedly took into account Shell's half-million dollar investment in Oahu strictly because of a long-term commitment by Nanakuli, its actions as partner in promoting Nanakuli's expansion on Oahu, and the fact that its sales on Oahu were almost exclusively to Nanakuli for use in asphaltic paving. The wisdom of the pre-trial ruling was demonstrated by evidence at trial that Shell's agent in Hawaii stayed in close contact with Nanakuli and was knowledgeable about both the asphaltic paving market in general and Nanakuli's bidding procedures and economics in particular.

Shell argued not only that the definition of trade was too broad, but also that the practice itself was not sufficiently regular to reach the level of a usage and that Nanakuli failed to show with enough precision how the usage was carried out in order for a jury to calculate damages. The extent of a usage is ultimately a jury question. The Code provides, "The existence and scope of such a usage are to be proved as facts." The practice must have "such regularity of observance … as to justify an expectation that it will be observed…." Id. The Comment explains:

> The ancient English tests for "custom" are abandoned in this connection. Therefore, it is not required that a usage of trade be "ancient or immemorial," "universal" or the like…. (Full) recognition is thus available for new usages for usages currently observed by the great majority of decent dealers, even though dissidents ready to cut corners do not agree.
>
> Id., Comment 5.

The Comment's demand that "not universality but only the described "regularity of observance' "is required reinforces the provision only giving "effect to usages of which the parties "are or should be aware' …." Id., Comment 7. A "regularly observed" practice of protection, of which Shell "should have been aware," was enough to constitute a usage that Nanakuli had reason to believe was incorporated into the agreement.

Nanakuli went beyond proof of a regular observance. It proved and offered to prove that price protection was probably a universal practice by suppliers to the asphaltic paving trade in 1969.

Shell next argues that, even if such a usage existed, its outlines were not precise enough to determine whether Shell would have extended the old price for Nanakuli for several months or would have charged the old price on the volume of tonnage committed at that price. The jury awarded Nanakuli damages based on the specific tonnage committed before the price increase of 1974. Shell says the jury could not have ascertained with enough certainty how price protection was carried out to calculate such an award for Nanakuli. The argument is not persuasive. Nanakuli got advance notices of each but the disputed increase by Shell, as well as an extension of several months at the old price in 1970, 1971, 1977, and 1978. Shell protests that in 1970 and 1971 Nanakuli's protected tonnage only amounted to 3,300 and 1,100 tons, respectively. Chevron's price protection of H.B. in 1969 however, is also part of the trade usage; H.B.'s protection amounted to 12,000 tons. The increase in Nanakuli's tonnage by 1974 is explained by its growth since the 1970 and 1971 increases.

Summers and White write that a usage, under the language of 1-205(2), need not be "certain and precise" to fit within the definition of "any practice or method of dealing." White & Summer, supra, § 3-3 at 87. The manner in which the usage of price protection was carried out was presented with sufficient precision to allow the jury to calculate damages at $220,800.

Express Terms as Reasonably Consistent With Usage In Course of Performance
Perhaps one of the most fundamental departures of the Code from prior contract law is found in the parol evidence rule and the definition of an agreement between two parties. Under the U.C.C., an agreement goes beyond the written words on a piece of paper. "'Agreement' means the bargain of the parties in fact as found in their language or by implication from other circumstances including course of dealing or usage of trade or course of performance as provided in this chapter (sections 490:1-205 and 490:2-208)." Express terms, then, do not constitute the entire agreement, which must be sought also in evidence of usages, dealings, and performance of the contract itself. The purpose of evidence of usages, which are defined in the previous section, is to help to understand the entire agreement.

> (Usages are) a factor in reaching the commercial meaning of the agreement which the parties have made. The language used is to be interpreted as meaning what it may fairly be expected

to mean to parties involved in the particular commercial transaction in a given locality or in a given vocation or trade…. Part of the agreement of the parties … is to be sought for in the usages of trade which furnish the background and give particular meaning to the language used, and are the framework of common understanding controlling any general rules of law which hold only when there is no such understanding.

Id. § 490:1-205, Comment 4.

A commercial agreement, then, is broader than the written paper and its meaning is to be determined not just by the language used by them in the written contract but "by their action, read and interpreted in the light of commercial practices and other surrounding circumstances. The measure and background for interpretation are set by the commercial context, which may explain and supplement even the language of a formal or final writing." Performance, usages, and prior dealings are important enough to be admitted always, even for a final and complete agreement; only if they cannot be reasonably reconciled with the express terms of the contract are they not binding on the parties. "The express terms of an agreement and an applicable course of dealing or usage of trade shall be construed wherever reasonable as consistent with each other; but when such construction is unreasonable express terms control both course of dealing and usage of trade and course of dealing controls usage of trade."

Our study of the Code provisions and Comments, then, form the first basis of our holding that a trade usage to price protect pavers at times of price increases for work committed on nonescalating contracts could reasonably be construed as consistent with an express term of seller's posted price at delivery. Since the agreement of the parties is broader than the express terms and includes usages, which may even add terms to the agreement, and since the commercial background provided by those usages is vital to an understanding of the agreement, we follow the Code's mandate to proceed on the assumption that the parties have included those usages unless they cannot reasonably be construed as consistent with the express terms.

Federal courts usually have been lenient in not ruling out consistent additional terms or trade usage for apparent inconsistency with express terms. The leading case on the subject is *Columbia Nitrogen Corp. v. Royster Co.*, 451 F.2d 3 (4th Cir. 1971). Columbia, the buyer, had in the past primarily produced and sold nitrogen to Royster. When Royster opened a new plant that produced more phosphate than it needed, the parties reversed roles and signed a sales contract for Royster to sell excess phosphate to Columbia. The contract terms set out the price that would be charged by Royster and the amount to be sold. It provided for the price to go up if certain events occurred but did not provide for price declines. When the price of nitrogen fell precipitously, Columbia refused to accept the full amount of nitrogen specified in the contract after Royster refused to renegotiate the contract price. The District Judge's exclusion of usage of the trade and course of dealing to explain the express quantity term in the contract was reversed. Columbia had offered to prove that the quantity set out in the contract was a mere projection to be adjusted according to market forces. Ambiguity was not necessary for the admission of evidence of usage and prior dealings. Even though the lengthy contract was the result of long and careful negotiations and apparently covered every contingency, the appellate court ruled that "the test of admissibility is not whether the contract appears on its face to be complete in every detail, but whether the proffered evidence of course of dealing and trade usage reasonably can be construed as consistent with the express terms of the agreement." The express quantity term could be reasonably construed as consistent with a usage that such terms would be mere projections for several reasons: (1) the contract did not expressly state that usage and dealings evidence would be excluded; (2) the contract was silent on the adjustment of price or quantities in a declining market; (3) the minimum tonnage was expressed in the contract as Products Supplied, not Products Purchased; (4) the default clause of the contract did not state a penalty for failure to take delivery; and (5) apparently most important in the court's view, the parties had deviated from similar express terms in earlier contracts in times of declining market. As here, the contract's merger clause said that there were no oral agreements.

The court explained that its ruling "reflects the reality of the marketplace and avoids the overly legalistic interpretations which the Code seeks to abolish." The Code assigns dealing and usage evidence "unique and important roles" and therefore "overly simplistic and overly legalistic interpretation of a contract should be shunned."

Numerous state courts have interpreted their own state's versions of the Code in line with the weight of federal authority on the U.C.C. to admit freely evidence of additional terms, usages, and prior dealings and harmonize them in most instances with apparently contradictory express terms. The only Hawaiian case on the subject dealt with the parol evidence rule in dicta. *Cosmopolitan Financial Corp. v. Runnels*, 2 Haw. App. 33, 625 P.2d 390 (Haw. App. 1981), cert. denied, (Hawaii S. Ct. 4/20/81). The rule did not bar evidence of an additional oral term between an officer of a financial institution and the guarantors of a promissory note that the latter would not be liable in the event the promissor defaulted. Because the additional term was fraudulent and thus invalidated the entire agreement, "the parol evidence rule was inapplicable." Id. at 396. The court's discussion of the rule, however, is pertinent as an indication of the approach it would take in this case. It wrote, id. at 395:

> Historically, in an action to determine the parties' contractual rights under an agreement, the court's only inquiry would center around whether the written agreement was a total integration of the parties' intent. If so, absent evidence of mistake or fraud, the rule barred introduction of any extrinsic evidence that varied or altered the terms.... However, since the advent of the adoption of the (Code) in practically every state, rigid adherence to the exclusionary effects of the parol evidence rule has seen a relaxation of its application by the courts in many jurisdictions. This has been largely attributed to a combination of the U.C.C.'s intent to facilitate the flow in business and commercial transactions, and the widespread use of standard business forms to evidence the existence of contractual relationships between parties. For example, article 2 of the U.C.C. permits the court to consider a far wider range of extrinsic evidence to discern the intent of the parties than has been permitted under contract law.... (W)e think that expansion of the liberal approach toward the receipt of extrinsic evidence, in the face of the proliferation of standard form contracts and commercial paper, gives the courts a wider insight into the real intent of the parties.

The district judge, "in his refusal to bar evidence of the circumstances surrounding the transaction, was applying this modern principle," which was the "same view adopted" in a law review article cited by the court:

> As between immediate parties, however, all evidence whether written or oral, whether of conditions precedent or subsequent, should be admitted to determine what the parties understood the true contractual relationship to be. Any inherent improbability, such as a contradiction between what allegedly was agreed upon and what was signed will naturally affect the weight to be accorded such evidence, but procedural wrangles can be avoided by allowing the fact finder to hear all the evidence which either party wishes to bring to bear.

Some guidelines can be offered as to how usage evidence can be allowed to modify a contract. First, the court must allow a check on usage evidence by demanding that it be sufficiently definite and widespread to prevent unilateral post-hoc revision of contract terms by one party. The Code's intent is to put usage evidence on an objective basis

Although the Code abandoned the traditional common law test of nonconsensual custom and views usage as a way of determining the parties' probable intent, thus abolishing the requirement that common law custom be universally practiced, trade usages still must be well settled.

Evidence of a trade usage does not need to be protected against perjury because, as one commentator has written, "an outside standard does exist to help judge the truth of the assertion that the parties intended the usage to control the particular dispute: the existence and scope of the usage can be determined from other members of the trade."

[As one writer notes] "Astonishing as it will seem to most practicing attorneys, under the Code it will be possible in some cases to use custom to contradict the written agreement.... Therefore usage may be used to "qualify' the agreement, which presumably means to "cut down' express terms although not to negate them entirely." Here, the express price term was "Shell's Posted Price at time of delivery." A total negation of that term would be that the buyer was to set the price. It is a less than complete negation of the term that an unstated exception exists at times of price increases, at which times the old price is to be charged, for a certain period or for a specified tonnage, on work already committed at the lower price on nonescalating contracts. Such a usage forms a broad and important exception to the express term, but does not swallow it entirely. Therefore, we hold that, under these particular facts, a reasonable jury could have found that price protection was incorporated into the 1969 agreement between Nanakuli and Shell and that price protection was reasonably consistent with the express term of seller's posted price at delivery.

The message hidden between the lines in both *C-Thru Container* and *Nanakuli*—and what we need to remember—is that the parol-evidence rule only comes into play if something goes wrong with the transaction and the parties end up in a dispute about the terms of their agreement. They may disagree about the meaning of a term in their written agreement, or they may not agree about what terms were actually a part of that agreement. If the parties dispute the meaning of the words they used in their agreement, Article 2 tells us those words can mean what they have come to mean in the parties' trade, what they meant in prior dealings between the parties, or what the parties' performance of the contract indicates they mean. And 2-202 allows the parties to introduce the evidence necessary to show those meanings.

If the parties disagree about which terms were a part of their agreement, Article 2 tells us to include in their agreement terms that were a part of their prior dealings, terms that members of their trade would expect to be part of their agreement, and any terms that appear to have become a part of that agreement based on how they performed it before the dispute. But we can't include any of these terms if they contradict the express terms in the writing the parties made to record their agreement. To determine whether an unwritten term contradicts an express term, we ask whether including the unwritten term will have the effect of completely negating the express term—will it be made inoperable for the duration of the contract. If the unwritten term merely qualifies the operation of the express term or shrinks the possible scope of its application, the term becomes part of the agreement. Reducing the scope of an express term does not negate the term. If the unwritten term reduces the scope of the express term to zero—completely negates it—then we cannot add the unwritten term to the parties' agreement.

In *Nankuli*, the contract included a term that set the price the buyer was to pay for asphalt under the contract: posted price (essentially current market price) at delivery. The buyer wanted the court to add a term, based on trade usage, requiring the seller to use a price different from that required by the contract in certain situations: the price in effect when the buyer bid on asphalt jobs (old price). The seller argued that any term that would set a price different from the price set by the express term contradicted the express term and could not be added to the agreement under 2-202. Would the unwritten term completely negate the express term if it were added to the contract? Would it make the express term inoperable at all times during the contract period? Or did it merely qualify the operation of the express term—shrink the scope of its application? Adding the term would not make the express term inoperable at all times—the express term would set the price the buyer paid for asphalt except when the asphalt was delivered to fill a contract the buyer had committed to before an increase in the price of asphalt. The buyer would still have to pay the posted price at delivery—current market price—unless it was taking asphalt it needed to fill a contract it had made before the current market price went into effect. Since the unwritten term did not contradict the express term, it could be added to the parties' agreement.

3. Open Terms and Good Faith

As we've noted, the parties don't have to tell us everything about their deal to create an enforceable contract under Article 2. Sometimes they omit details because they intend to provide them later—but the relationship sours before they agree on the missing details (or because they can't agree on them), and the omissions remain. Or they just never get around to filling in the missing terms because neither expects any problems—but then something does go wrong that can't be fixed without the missing terms. Sometimes the parties don't realize they've left something out until a dispute arises between them that can't be resolved on the basis of the terms they did provide. And sometimes the parties' agreement will empower one of them to provide the term—set the price, for example—but the other party objects when the power is exercised.

Many times these missing terms will be supplied by the parties' course of performance, course of dealing, or by trade usage, which, as we discussed earlier in this chapter, Article 2 makes a part of the parties' agreement. But when it can't be supplied on one of those grounds, Article 2 itself provides a basis for filling in certain terms when omitted by the parties—whether deliberately or by inattention. So when the parties leave out of their deal terms like price, specific quantity, time for performance, delivery requirements, or payment details, Article 2 provides the courts with a basis for filling these open terms in the parties' agreement.

As the following case illustrates, the parties to a sales-of-goods contract may decide the interests of each are best served if the contract does not fix the quantity of goods covered by the contract, and so they leave the quantity term open. The buyer may only be willing to commit to purchase as many of the goods as she will need in her business during the contract period—a requirements contract—or the seller may be willing to supply the goods only if the buyer agrees to take all the seller is able to produce—an output contract. An open-quantity contract provides flexibility that allows the parties to allocate some of the risks inherent in a relationship intended to include more than a single delivery and receipt of goods. A buyer committed to taking only what he needs can control his costs if the demand for his product drops during the contract period—Rae only commits to buy as many boxes of oranges as she is able to sell at the store so she's not stuck with rotting oranges she can't sell if her customers stop eating breakfast. Or if the latest health craze is to consume an orange at every meal, Rae has a source for all the oranges she needs—at a price below the current market price, which has been inflated by the increased demand for oranges. The grower's upside in his deal with Rae is that he has no competition for Rae's business—whatever Rae needs, she buys from him, regardless of what other growers might offer Rae. He also saves the costs of finding a buyer for the oranges Rae takes.

You may remember from your Contracts course that for a long time the common-law courts refused to enforce agreements that did not include a specific quantity. They considered Rae's promise to be illusory—since she had committed to buy only what she needed, if it turned out she did not need any oranges, she had not committed to buy anything. But as the utility of these arrangements in the modern marketplace became obvious, the courts rethought their analysis and, based on the duty of good faith they read into all contracts, discovered that Rae had actually made a commitment—she had obligated herself to take as many oranges as were needed in the good-faith operation of her store. That was enough to remove the illusory-promise cloud over the contract, and so requirements contracts became enforceable. Article 2 incorporates the good-faith rationale to approve output and requirements contracts in 2-306.

KEYES HELIUM CO. v. REGENCY GAS SERVS., L.P.

COURT OF APPEALS OF TEXAS, FIFTH DISTRICT, DALLAS, 2012
393 S.W.3D 858

O'NEILL, Justice.

In this U.C.C. breach of contract case, a jury returned an 11-1 verdict in favor of appellee Regency Gas Services, L.P., ("Regency"), finding it had not breached its contract with appellant Keyes Helium Company ("Keyes"). The trial court further rendered a directed verdict in favor of Regency on Keyes's unreasonable variation and best efforts claims.

Keyes raises four issues on appeal. It first argues the jury charge improperly defined "good faith" under the U.C.C., which caused the jury to reach an incorrect verdict.

* * *

Third, the trial court erred by directing a verdict in favor of Regency on Keyes's unreasonable variation claim. And lastly, the trial court erred by directing a verdict in favor of Regency on Keyes's best efforts claim. We affirm the trial court's judgment.

BACKGROUND

The Hugoton Basin spans several states and is the largest and one of the oldest natural gas fields in the country. Both Keyes and Regency have operations in the region. Regency owns a natural gas processing plant in the Hugoton Field area known as the Lakin Plant. Regency is considered a "midstream" company in the oil and gas field, meaning it moves and processes natural gas and associated products like crude helium for its customers. It does not own the products it transports for its customers but gets paid a fee for moving and processing the product for its clients.

Keyes owns a helium processing plant in Oklahoma that refines crude helium into pure helium. Keyes acquires the crude helium from midstream companies like Regency. On August 1, 1996, Keyes entered into a contract for the sale and purchase of crude helium with Regency that forms the basis of this lawsuit. The contract provided that from August 1, 1996 through December 31, 2008, "Seller [Regency] shall sell and Buyer [Keyes] shall purchase all volumes of Crude Helium produced at the Lakin Plant," up to 120 millions of cubic feet in any year. After December 31, 2008, Keyes's purchase obligation was zero.

In 2003, Regency began receiving complaints about the high costs of processing gas at the Lakin Plant from its largest customer, Oxy USA, Inc. ("Oxy"). The contracts between Oxy and Regency were expiring in 2003. Regency had reason to believe, based on discussions with Oxy, that Oxy had better alternatives for processing its gas. Because Oxy accounted for roughly one-third of the volume of Regency's system in the Hugoton Field, losing it would result in a thirty percent loss in business. Regency also recognized that losing Oxy would mean the Lakin Plant would be dangerously close to "turndown," which is a term referring to the minimum gas volume required to extract crude helium. After considering its options, and despite its contract with Keyes, Regency decided to close the Lakin Plant and move its gas processing to a nearby plant owned by its competitor, Duke Field Services.

Keyes claimed that despite hearing rumors Duke and Regency were building a pipeline to connect Regency's system to Duke's plant, Regency never told Keyes it planned to shut down the Lakin Plant. Rather, Keyes alleged Regency said it would take care of Keyes and the shutdown was temporary. However, the reality was that shutting down the Lakin Plant meant shutting off crude helium that flowed to Keyes. Essentially, Keyes would lose the main source of its crude helium. Regency shut down the Lakin Plant on August 1, 2005.

Keyes sued Regency for breach of contract claiming that Regency did not act in good faith, that it unreasonably varied from the stated estimates in the contract, and that it did not use its best efforts to supply Keyes with crude helium as required under the contract.

At the conclusion of the jury trial, the court submitted a single liability question asking, "Did Regency fail to comply with the Contract by failing to act in good faith in reducing its output of crude helium to zero at the Lakin Plant?" Included in the definition of "good faith" was whether Regency had a "legitimate business reason for eliminating its output under the Contract." Keyes argued the trial court erred in including the "legitimate business reason" because that strays from "good faith" as defined by the U.C.C.

The jury found in favor of Regency by an 11-1 vote. This appeal followed.

Jury Charge Error

In its first issue, Keyes argues the trial court erroneously defined "good faith" in the jury charge, and the error probably caused the rendition of an improper verdict. Regency responds the trial court's definition was correct and even if it was erroneous, it is irrelevant under these facts because there is no reversible error based on Keyes's arguments.

The trial court has considerable discretion to determine necessary and proper jury instructions. When a trial court refuses to submit a requested instruction on an issue raised by the pleadings and evidence, the question on appeal is whether the request was reasonably necessary to enable the jury to render a proper verdict. The omission of an instruction is reversible error only if the omission probably caused the rendition of an improper judgment. On the record before us, we agree with Regency that Keyes has failed to establish the definition of "good faith" in the jury charge probably caused the rendition of an improper judgment.

Question 1 asked, "Did Regency fail to comply with the Contract by failing to act in good faith in reducing the output of crude helium to zero at the Lakin Plant?" The charge included the following instruction and definition:

> You may find that Regency failed to comply with the Contract only if you find that Regency's decision to shut down the Lakin Plant was not made in good faith.

> "Good faith" means that Regency acted in accordance with commercial standards of fair dealing in making its decisions, including whether Regency had a legitimate business reason for eliminating its output under the Contract, as opposed to a desire to avoid the Contract.

The jury answered "No" to this question. Keyes argues the Uniform Commercial Code defines "good faith" as "honesty in fact and the observance of reasonable commercial standards in fair dealing in the trade." Because this definition was statutory, it contends the trial court's definition of "good faith" should have closely tracked the statute. *See Trinity Fire Ins. Co. v. Kerrville Hotel Co.*, 129 Tex. 310, 321, 103 S.W.2d 121, 126 (1937) ("It is true that ordinarily where the statute defines a legal term the court should confine his charge to the statutory definition."). Instead, Keyes argues that by expanding the definition of "good faith" to include whether Regency had a legitimate business reason for eliminating its output under the contract, the court's submitted charge was erroneous. Accordingly, Keyes argues this led to the rendition of an improper verdict. We disagree.

First, Keyes's argument that the trial court's definition makes "legitimate business reason" equivalent to "good faith" is incorrect. Rather, use of the word "including" in the definition means the jury could consider a legitimate business reason as a factor in Regency's decision to close the plant. However, the definition does not provide that a "legitimate business reason" is the only consideration for the jury or that good faith is the same as a legitimate business reason.

Further, Keyes has failed to cite to any evidence that Regency's decision to take its output to zero was not made honestly. The evidence Keyes cites is not relevant to the liability question. It argues Regency told Keyes (1) it was "neutral" on crude helium; (2) it would take care of Keyes; (3) it would keep Keyes whole; (4) any shut down of the Lakin Plant would only be temporary; (5) Regency was going to refill the Lakin Plant with other gas; and (6) Regency would work with Duke to make sure Keyes continued to receive streams of crude helium.

Section 4-1-304 of the Colorado Revised Statutes Annotated provides that "every contract or duty within this title imposes an obligation of good faith in its performance and enforcement." However, comment 1 makes it clear that the good faith obligation has to be tied to a particular provision in the contract.

> This section does not support an independent cause of action for failure to perform or enforce in good faith. Rather, this section means that a failure to perform or enforce, in good faith, a specific duty or obligation under the contract, constitutes a breach of that contract or makes unavailable, under the particular circumstances, a remedial right or power. This distinction makes it clear that the doctrine of good faith merely directs a court towards interpreting contracts within the commercial context in which they are created, performed, and enforced, and does not create a separate duty of fairness and reasonableness which can be independently breached.

Here, the contract between Keyes and Regency provided that "Seller shall sell and Buyer shall purchase all volumes of Crude Helium produced at the Lakin Plant." None of the above statements cited by Keyes to support its claim of Regency's alleged dishonesty are tied to its obligation to provide volumes of helium under the contract. Rather, the statements go towards what Regency allegedly claimed it would do *after* the shutdown of the Lakin Plant. These statements do not support any dishonesty on Regency's part in deciding to shut down the plant. To conclude otherwise would write obligations into the contract that do not exist. Thus, because Keyes has failed to provide any evidence tying the good faith obligation required under section 4-1-304 to a particular contract provision, the trial court's instructions to the jury regarding good faith probably did not cause the rendition of an improper verdict. Accordingly, we overrule Keyes's second issue.

Directed Verdicts in Favor of Regency

In its third issue, Keyes argues the trial court erred by directing a verdict on its unreasonable variation claim because it presented legally sufficient evidence to support it. It contends the plain language of the U.C.C. prohibited Regency from unreasonably reducing the Lakin Plant's output (in this case to zero) from the contract's stated estimates. Regency contends the trial court properly directed a verdict because, as a matter of law, the U.C.C. exception concerning unreasonably disproportionate increases in quantity does not apply to it as a seller under an output contract.

The U.C.C. provides the following regarding output and requirements contracts:

> (1) A term which measures the quantity by the output of the seller or the requirements of the buyer, means such actual output or requirements as may occur in good faith; except that no quantity unreasonably disproportionate to any stated estimate or, in the absence of a stated estimate, to any normal or otherwise comparable prior output or requirements, may be tendered or demanded.

U.C.C. § 2-306(1) (West 2012).

The majority of courts to interpret this portion of the statute and address the issue of whether a party to an output or requirements contract under U.C.C. section 2-306(1) may reduce its output or requirements, even to zero, despite stated estimates in the contract, have concluded a party may do so as long as the reduction is made in good faith. Although neither Texas nor Colorado has addressed this issue, Regency urges this Court to follow the majority view and apply it to the present facts. Keyes, however, urges this Court to follow the minority view expressed only by the Supreme Court of Alabama.

The leading and most cited case on this issue is *Empire Gas Corporation v. American Bakeries Company*, 840 F.2d 1333 (7th Cir. 1988). In that case, American Bakeries (AB) sought to convert its fleet of delivery vehicles from gasoline to propane. Consequently, AB executed a contract with Empire Gas (Empire) obligating AB to purchase "three thousand ... [conversion] units, more or less depending upon [AB's] requirements...." The contract also obligated AB to purchase its propane motor fuel requirements solely from Empire. The contract was to last four years. AB never ordered any equipment or propane from Empire after deciding not to convert its fleet to propane. Consequently, Empire filed suit, claiming that AB breached the contract by eliminating its requirements. The jury returned a verdict in favor of Empire.

On appeal, the Seventh Circuit rejected the notion that AB breached the contract simply because it failed to purchase any conversion units or propane from Empire. The court concluded that, pursuant to U.C.C. § 2-306(1), a buyer may "reduce his requirements to zero if he was acting in good faith, even though the contract contained an estimate of those requirements." Thus, the court determined that Empire could not recover under its contract claim unless the evidence established that AB reduced its requirements in bad faith. *Id.* at 1339. In reaching this conclusion, the Empire Gas court reasoned that the "unreasonably disproportionate" proviso of U.C.C. § 2-306(1) merely explains the term "good faith" with respect to disproportionately large demands.

According to the *Empire Gas* court, in promulgating this statute, the drafters of the U.C.C. were concerned that when the market price rose above the contract price, a requirements contract might allow a buyer to increase disproportionately his requirements and resell the product on the open market at a profit. The drafters intended the proviso to establish clearly that such actions constituted bad faith. However, "there is no indication that the draftsmen were equally, if at all, concerned about the case where the buyer takes less than his estimated requirements, provided, of course, that he does not buy from anyone else." Thus, the Empire Gas court held that U.C.C. § 2-306(1) does not proscribe unreasonably disproportionate reductions in a buyer's requirements if done in good faith.

Similar to the majority of courts who have addressed this issue, we find the reasoning in *Empire Gas* persuasive. Accordingly, although no Colorado authority has addressed this issue, we believe Colorado courts would adopt a similar interpretation for Colorado's version of U.C.C. § 2-306(1). Thus, we hold that under Colorado law, an output contract allows a seller to reduce the quantity produced to any amount, including zero, so long as it does so in good faith. If the seller wishes to reallocate some of the inherent risks in such a contract, it may specify some minimum requirement.

In reaching this conclusion, we reject Keyes's reliance on *Simcala, Inc. v. American Coal Trade, Inc.*, 821 So.2d 197 (Ala. 2001). Since its publication, no other court has followed its holding.

In its final issue, Keyes contends the trial court erred by granting a directed verdict in favor of Regency on Keyes's best-efforts claim. Regency responds the trial court correctly determined, as a matter of law, the Contract was not an exclusive dealing contract under the U.C.C.; therefore, Regency was not required to use best efforts to supply Keyes with crude helium.

U.C.C. section 2-306(1)-(2) provides the following regarding output, requirements, and exclusive dealings contracts:

* * *

(2) A lawful agreement by either the seller or the buyer for exclusive dealing in the kind of goods concerned imposes unless otherwise agreed an obligation by the seller to use best efforts to supply the goods and by the buyer to use best efforts to promote their sale.

U.C.C. § 2-306(1)-(2) (West 2012); *see also* Colo. Rev. Stat. Ann. § 4-2-306(1)-(2) (West 2012).

The contract here provides that "Seller shall sell and Buyer shall purchase all volumes of Crude Helium produced at the Lakin plant." The contract requires Regency to sell all of its output to Keyes; however, the contract does not require Keyes to purchase crude helium exclusively from Regency. When a buyer agrees to buy the seller's entire output of production, it is called an output contract. Such contracts are governed by U.C.C. section 2-306(1), which does not include the best efforts requirement in U.C.C. section 2-306(2).

However, the contract also appears to involve an exclusive dealings agreement because Regency agreed to exclusively sell crude helium to Keyes. We acknowledge the agreement is not mutually exclusive because Keyes is not required to purchase only from Regency. With this in mind, we consider the application of section 2-306(2).

While U.C.C. section 2-306(2) applies to exclusive dealing contract, we conclude under these facts the trial court correctly directed a verdict on Keyes's best efforts claim. The "best efforts" doctrine was created to protect the party who is at the complete mercy of another party in an exclusive dealing contract. *Tigg Corp. v. Dow Corning Corp.*, 962 F.2d 1119, 1125 (3d Cir. 1992) ("The obligation to use best efforts to resell a product is imposed upon those buyers engaged in 'exclusive dealing in the kind of goods concerned....'").

On its face, courts have noted this provision could be interpreted to mean that any party to such a contract has an implied obligation to use best efforts. However, comment 5 of section 2.306(2) indicates the duty to use best efforts applies only to those who receive the benefit of an exclusive commitment. *See* U.C.C. § 2.306 cmt. 5 ("Under such contracts the exclusive agent is required, although no express commitment has been made, to use reasonable effort and due diligence in the expansion of the market or the promotion of the product, as the case may be."). Here, Regency was at the complete mercy of Keyes because it agreed to sell all its output of crude helium only to Keyes. It could not attempt to sell its product to others, whereas, Keyes could take all of Regency's product and still seek out crude helium from other resources. As such, Keyes was in the position of receiving the benefit from the exclusive commitment. Thus, the obligation of best efforts was not on Regency.

Although Keyes argues "when constructing its business model and its marketing for its purified helium," it is just as entitled "to rely on Regency's obligation to use its best efforts to draw from the gas stream and furnish the crude helium," it has not provided authority to support a different interpretation of section 2-306(2). Accordingly, we conclude Regency established as a matter of law that Keyes's best efforts claim under section 2-306(2) fails, and the trial court properly granted a directed verdict in favor of Regency. We overrule Keyes's final issue.

PROBLEM 3 - 20

Article 2 anticipates, as we've noted, that the parties might leave things out of their agreement—2-204(3) tells us that an agreement does not fail for indefiniteness "even though one or more terms are left open" if the parties have intended to make a contract "and there is a reasonably certain basis for giving an appropriate remedy." Determine whether the omissions in the following cases will eliminate the reasonably certain basis necessary for giving a remedy:

1. Rae agreed to buy all of the gas the store sells at the fuel kiosks it built at the far end of the store's parking lot from the local unbranded independent distributor at a price to be determined thirty days before each delivery. The first delivery is scheduled for today, and Rae and the distributor have not yet agreed on the price. Will Rae have a claim for breach if the seller does not deliver? 2-305, 2-306.

2. Rae sent a purchase order to the local supplier for one hundred rolls of the plastic film the produce department uses to wrap product for sale. The supplier returned a sales invoice accepting Rae's order. Neither the purchase order nor the sales invoice contained a delivery time or schedule. If the seller never delivers the film, will Rae have a claim for breach without a delivery date in the contract? 2-309.

3. Rae agreed to buy all of the bottled water the store sells during the next twelve months from the local water distributor. She estimated in the agreement that she would need one hundred thousand cases of water for the contract period, and delivery was to begin within seven days. The agreement did not include a delivery schedule, and this morning eight semi-trailers loaded with one hundred thousand cases of bottled water showed up at the loading dock. She has nowhere to store that much water, so she called the seller, but he refused to hold any of it for her—she ordered the water, and he delivered as required by the contract. Does Rae have to take all of the water? Will she breach the contract if she refuses to take any of it? 2-307.

Parties to long-term agreements—especially those involving commodities—often use some form of open pricing rather than a fixed price in their agreements. Remember the contract between Shell and Nanakuli which set the price of asphalt Shell was to provide at what was, in effect, the current market price as determined by Shell at the time Nanakuli took delivery? Neither Shell nor Nanakuli wanted to lock in a fixed price for the entire term of their agreement because the price of petroleum, the major component of asphalt, was so volatile. If the parties had set a fixed price for the term, Shell would not have been able to pass along to Nanakuli any increase in the cost of producing asphalt. Nor would Nanakuli have been entitled to benefit if Shell's cost of producing asphalt declined. A fixed price in a long-term agreement can become an all-or-nothing proposition for the parties, depending on what happens in the market for the contract goods. When the parties leave the contract price open, Article 2 provides a basis for determining the price if the parties are unable to agree. 2-305(1).

Of course, in Nanakuli the parties did not leave the contract price open—they specified how the price was to be determined during the term of their agreement, but the method they choose failed to prevent the dispute that arose when Shell refused to price protect Nanakuli. As it turned out, the pricing mechanism did not fail once the court interpreted it in light of the applicable trade usage, but if it had, Article 2 would have provided a basis for determining the price Nanakuli paid for asphalt under the agreement. 2-305(2).

In the next case, Shell again retains the power to set the price its buyers pay, this time for the gas Shell sells its franchisees under long-term franchise agreements. The plaintiff-franchisees claim the pricing mechanism in the franchise agreements has failed because Shell has improperly exercised its discretion when setting the price of gas. Their argument is similar to the alternative argument Nanakuli made when it challenged the price set by Shell for asphalt.

CASSERLIE V. SHELL OIL CO.

SUPREME COURT OF OHIO, 2009
121 OHIO ST. 3D 55

MOYER, Justice.

I

Appellants' proposition of law proposes that "[t]he definition of Good Faith under the [Uniform Commercial Code] incorporating an 'honesty in fact' component requires a subjective inquiry." We disagree and affirm the judgment of the court of appeals.

II

Appellants, Donald Casserlie and others, are a group of independent Shell lessee-dealers in the greater Cleveland area (collectively, "the dealers"). The appellees in this case are Shell Oil Company, its partners, and its successors (collectively, "Shell"), who at various times between 1995 and the time the complaint was filed sold Shell-branded gasoline to the dealers in the greater Cleveland area. The dealers leased gas stations, including equipment and land, from Shell and operated them as franchisees. The parties' contracts obligated the dealers to buy gasoline only from Shell at a wholesale price set by Shell at the time of delivery. This type of term in a contract is known as an open-price term.

The price paid by the dealers is referred to as the dealer-tank-wagon ("DTW") price because it includes the cost of delivery to the stations. Shell charged the dealers a DTW price that was based on market factors including the prices offered by its major competitor, British Petroleum ("BP"), and the street price within areas of Cleveland. In each area of the city, called a price administration district ("PAD"), Shell charged all dealers the same DTW price.

In 1998, Shell, Texaco, and Saudi Aramco formed Equilon Enterprises L.L.C.; Shell's agreements with service stations in Cleveland were assigned to Equilon. In November 1999, Equilon and appellee Lyden Company entered into a joint venture called True North Energy, L.L.C. True North became the distributor of Shell-branded gasoline in the Cleveland area, including to the stations operated by the dealers. True North set the DTW price as the wholesale price it had paid Equilon for gasoline plus six or seven cents per gallon.

Shell also sold gasoline to "jobbers," which were independent companies operating non-Shell-owned gas stations. Jobbers purchased gasoline directly at the oil company's terminal and paid the "rack" price, which was the cost of purchasing gasoline at the oil company's terminal and thus did not include delivery costs.

In 1999, the dealers filed suit against Shell, alleging, among other claims, that Shell had engaged in bad faith when it set the DTW price. The dealers alleged that the rack price was often substantially lower than the DTW price. This allowed jobbers, including Lyden Company, to offer wholesale DTW prices that were substantially lower than the DTW price charged to the dealers. The dealers contend that this pricing is unreasonable and is part of a marketing plan proposed by Shell that was designed to drive them out of business. The dealers assert that Shell's goal was to eliminate them so that Shell could take over operation of the gas stations, thus profiting from all of the sales, including nonfuel sales, at the stations, and not just from wholesale gasoline sales to and rental income from the dealers.

The parties agreed to bifurcate the proceedings and move forward only on the bad-faith claim. On April 13, 2005, the trial court granted summary judgment for Shell. The court found that Shell did not violate R.C. 1302.18, which codifies Uniform Commercial Code ("UCC") section 2-305 and requires a price to be fixed in good faith, when it set the DTW price and that the dealers had not proven that the price had been set in a commercially unreasonable manner.

The dealers appealed, arguing that bad faith may be shown either by evidence of a party's intent, a subjective standard, or by evidence of its commercial unreasonableness, which is an objective standard. The court of appeals affirmed the trial court's ruling and adopted an objective standard based on *Tom-Lin Ents. v. Sunoco, Inc.* (R&M) (C.A.6, 2003), 349 F.3d 277. The court determined that the dealers failed to show that Shell's prices were not commercially reasonable. The cause is before this court upon our acceptance of a discretionary appeal.

III

The parties agree that Shell has authority pursuant to the dealer agreements to set the price of gasoline at the time of delivery. They agree that the price must be set subject to R.C. 1302.18, which requires the price to be "reasonable." R.C. 1302.18(A). Pursuant to R.C. 1302.18(B) (UCC section 2-305(2)), the price must be set "in good faith." "Good faith" is defined generally as "honesty in fact in the conduct or transaction concerned," [1-201(20)], but in the case of a merchant, "'good faith' * * * means honesty in fact and the observance of reasonable commercial standards of fair dealing in the trade." [1-201(20)]. It is undisputed that Shell is a "merchant," as defined in [2-104(1)].

Shell argues that good faith requires an objective inquiry and is demonstrated when a seller's price is within the range of its competitors and the seller has not discriminated between similarly situated buyers. Shell also contends that "an inquiry into the seller's subjective intent is neither permitted nor required." The dealers argue that good faith requires a subjective inquiry and ask, "[H]ow can an open price, specifically calculated to drive a contractual partner out of business, be a 'good faith' price."

The trial court and court of appeals agreed with Shell, relying on *Tom-Lin Enters.*, 349 F.3d 277. In *Tom-Lin*, the court confronted an agreement nearly identical to the one between the dealers and Shell and concluded, applying Ohio law, that an inquiry into good faith required "an *objective* analysis of the merchant-seller's conduct." Thus, neither the trial court nor the court of appeals considered whether an examination into "good faith" required a subjective inquiry, and neither court engaged in a subjective inquiry.

It is not disputed that the latter half of the definition of good faith, "the observance of reasonable commercial standards of fair dealing in the trade," requires only an objective analysis. The issue before us is whether there is room for a subjective inquiry within the honesty-in-fact analysis in these circumstances.

The UCC does not define the term "honesty in fact." It should also be noted that "[c]ourts and commentators have recognized that the meaning of 'good faith' is not uniform throughout the [UCC]." See also *Martin Marietta Corp. v. New Jersey Nat'l Bank* (C.A.3, 1979), 612 F.2d 745, 751 (noting that good faith is considered subjective in Article 1 but objective in Article 2). Thus, case law defining good faith in other areas of the UCC, such as the Article 1 covenant of good faith and fair dealing, is of somewhat limited value here. Non-UCC cases defining good faith are of even less relevance.

Official Comment 3 to UCC section 2-305 does provide some guidance. That comment provides, in full:

> "[UCC section 2-305(2)], dealing with the situation where the price is to be fixed by one party rejects the uncommercial idea that an agreement that the seller may fix the price means that he may fix any price he may wish by the express qualification that the price so fixed must be fixed in good faith. Good faith includes observance of reasonable commercial standards of fair dealing in the trade if the party is a merchant. (Section 2-103). But in the normal case a 'posted price' or a future seller's or buyer's 'given price,' 'price in effect,' 'market price,' or the like satisfies the good faith requirement."

Comment 3 explains that the purpose of R.C. 1302.18(B) is to restrict the price a seller or buyer may set when the contract price has been left open, by requiring the price to be fixed in good faith. The second sentence of the comment does not remove honesty in fact from the definition of good faith in this context, because it uses the nonexclusive term "includes." The last sentence, however, is not limited to part of the good-faith definition but rather provides a safe harbor where a "posted price" satisfies good faith in its entirety.

A number of cases from other jurisdictions considering open-price terms have relied on the posted-price comment. This court has noted in the past that "it is desirable to conform our interpretations of the Uniform Commercial Code to those of our sister states." Relying on the Official Comments to the UCC helps to achieve this uniformity, as does reviewing case law that has previously interpreted particular provisions.

The Supreme Court of Texas addressed the very issue before us here in an essentially identical fact pattern in *Shell Oil Co. v. HRN, Inc.* (Tex.2004), 144 S.W.3d 429. Independent gasoline dealers brought suit against Shell, alleging that the prices were not set in good faith under UCC section 2-305(2) because Shell had set the prices intending to put them out of business. The court held that Shell did not violate its duty of good faith, because the posted price was both commercially reasonable and nondiscriminatory. It noted that "'[i]t is abundantly clear * * * that the chief concern of the UCC Drafting Committee in adopting § 2-305(2) was to prevent discriminatory pricing.'" A subjective good-faith inquiry "injects uncertainty into the law of contracts and undermines one of the UCC's primary goals—to 'promot[e] certainty and predictability in commercial transactions.'" The drafters of the UCC, therefore, incorporated the posted-price safe harbor to prevent extensive litigation involving any open-price term, "while seeking 'to avoid discriminatory prices.'" The court concluded that subjective intent was not intended to stand alone as a basis for liability: "[A]llegations of dishonesty under this section must also have some basis in objective fact which at a minimum requires some connection to the commercial realities of the case."

A few cases note the posted-price comment but conclude that it does not provide a safe harbor where there is subjective bad faith. Those cases contend that the comment is limited to the "normal case," which does not include a situation where the seller is purposefully trying to drive the buyer out of business.

This interpretation would eviscerate the safe harbor in any action in which the plaintiff alleges circumstantial evidence of an improper motive, leading to drawn-out litigation "even if the prices ultimately charged were undisputedly within the range of those charged throughout the industry." If a subjective inquiry could determine bad faith, a seller charging a fair price, even exactly the same price as another, good-faith seller, could be deemed to be acting in bad faith.

There appear to be five other cases, besides *HRN*, that directly address the issue of subjectivity. Two, each holding in favor of a subjective inquiry, were decided under Massachusetts law. *Mathis*, 302 F.3d 448, the only other case proposing subjectivity, is no longer good law, as it was decided by the Fifth Circuit Court of Appeals under Texas law before the Texas Supreme Court issued its ruling in *HRN*. The final two cases, including one from the Sixth Circuit applying Ohio law, conclude that UCC section 2-305 requires only an objective inquiry. There are a number of other cases discussing similar open-price-term contracts under UCC section 2-305 that conduct only an objective analysis, although those cases do not directly state that a subjective inquiry is inappropriate. In total, prior to this court's opinion today, at least three jurisdictions found that the test could be met only with objective evidence of bad faith, while only one concluded that evidence of intent was sufficient.

All of this is not to say that intent is necessarily irrelevant to an analysis of good faith under UCC section 2-305(2), but only that a subjective inquiry is not permitted when the posted-price safe harbor applies. By its language, the safe harbor does not apply when it is not the "normal case" or when the price setter is not imposing a "posted price," "given price," "price in effect," "market price," or the like. As long as a price is commercially reasonable, it qualifies as the "normal case." The touchstone of prices set through open-price term contracts under UCC section 2-305 is reasonableness. A price that is nondiscriminatory among similarly situated buyers correspondingly qualifies as a "posted price" or the like. A discriminatory price could not be considered a "posted" or "market" price, because, in effect, the seller is not being "honest in fact" about the price that it is charging as a posted price, since it is charging a different price to other buyers.

Therefore, a price that is both commercially reasonable and nondiscriminatory fits within the limits of the safe harbor and complies with the statute's good-faith requirement. Given our conclusion below that the safe harbor applies to the facts of this case, we are not required to precisely define good faith as it is used in section 2-305(2). We offer no opinion, in particular, on the role of subjective intent within the good-faith analysis beyond the safe harbor.

IV

The facts of this case demonstrate that the prices set by Shell were both commercially reasonable and nondiscriminatory. Aside from claiming that Shell's goal in setting prices was to drive the dealers out of business, the only evidence of bad faith was that the prices set were too high for dealers to remain profitable and compete with jobbers in the Cleveland area. However, Shell is not required to sell gasoline at a price that is profitable for buyers. "A good-faith price under section [2-305] is not synonymous with a fair market price or the lowest price available." As noted by the court of appeals: "The trial court * * * found that Shell submitted expert testimony which established that the DTW prices set by the company were within the range set by its competitors." The dealers failed to rebut this evidence.

The dealers also point out that Shell's prices varied throughout the area because of PAD pricing. But the fact that Shell's DTW prices varied by PADs does not itself demonstrate unreasonable or discriminatory pricing. It is reasonable for Shell to adjust according to competition, and there is no evidence that Shell discriminated among similarly situated buyers, such as dealers within a given PAD or dealers in similar PADs.

Finally, the only other argument of discrimination put forth by the dealers is that jobbers were charged significantly less, specifically, the rack price rather than the DTW price. Jobbers and dealers are not, however, similarly situated buyers. The price difference is partially explained by the fact that the DTW price includes a delivery charge, while the rack price does not. We further find the Sixth Circuit Court of Appeals analysis comparing jobbers and dealers in *Tom-Lin instructive*, just as the lower courts did. *Tom-Lin* noted that jobbers perform additional functions compared to dealers, such as maintaining the properties they own and bearing the risk of environmental liability. Because jobbers relieve Shell of these obligations, they are charged a lower price. The dealers have not challenged these differences. The disparate pricing between jobbers and dealers is not evidence of discrimination.

V

When a price that has been left open in a contract is fixed at a price posted by a seller or buyer, and the posted price is both commercially reasonable and nondiscriminatory, the price setter has acted in good faith as required by R.C. 1302.18(B), and a subjective inquiry into the motives of the price setter is not permitted. In this case, the dealers have not provided any evidence that the prices set by Shell were commercially unreasonable or discriminatory. The posted-price safe harbor therefore applies, and we affirm the judgment of the court of appeals.

Judgment affirmed.

PFEIFER, dissenting.

The majority opinion's reliance on the safe-harbor presumption is misplaced, as shown by one simple fact: Official Comment 3 to Uniform Commercial Code ("UCC") section 2-305, which introduced the concept of a safe-harbor presumption, has never been adopted by the General Assembly. The safe-harbor presumption is not part of the law of Ohio, despite the majority opinion's insouciant belief to the contrary.

"Good faith" is generally treated as incorporating both subjective and objective standards. Although R.C. 1302.18 deals exclusively with open-price terms, it does not define "good faith" differently from its customary meaning. Many different jurisdictions in many different contexts, including in the context of an open-price term, define "good faith" as requiring both subjective and objective analysis. I am more persuaded by the bulk of these cases than by the fact that three out of four jurisdictions (one of which, in my view, mistakenly applied Ohio law) have decided that an open-price term is susceptible only of objective analysis. See *Bhatia v. Debek* (2008), 287 Conn. 397, 412, 948 A.2d 1009, quoting *Kendzierski v. Goodson* (1990), 21 Conn.App. 424, 429-430, 574 A.2d 249 ("In common usage, the term good faith has a well-defined and generally understood meaning, being ordinarily used to describe that state of mind denoting honesty of purpose, freedom from intention to defraud, and, generally speaking, means being faithful to one's duty or obligation. * * * Whether good faith exists is a question of fact to be determined from all the circumstances"); *Tonka Tours, Inc. v. Chadima* (Minn.1985), 372 N.W.2d 723, 728 (determining good faith "necessarily involves factual findings. * * * It is for the trier of fact to evaluate the credibility of a claim of 'honesty in fact' and, in doing so, to take account of the reasonableness or unreasonableness of the claim"); *Smalygo v. Green* (Okla.2008), 2008 OK 34, 184 P.3d 554, 559 ("By requiring good faith, the Legislature did not create an ambiguity nor did it render the provision vague. Rather, it employed a well-known legal concept that applies to a variety of situations and transactions. For example, the Uniform Commercial Code defines 'good faith' as 'honesty in fact and the observance of reasonable commercial standards of fair dealing.' * * * Similarly, the concept of subjective honesty combined with objective reasonableness is found in an insurer's 'implied-in-law duty to act in good faith and deal fairly with the insured to ensure that the policy benefits are received.' *Christian v. Am. Home Assurance Co.*, 1977 OK 141, P 8, 577 P.2d 899, 901"); *Simmons v. Jenkins* (1988), 230 Mont. 429, 435, 750 P.2d 1067 ("the *breach* of a duty of good faith is a question of fact not susceptible to summary judgment" [emphasis sic]); *Miller Brewing Co. v. Ed Roleson, Jr., Inc.* (2006), 365 Ark. 38, 45, 223 S.W.3d 806 (in determining whether the Miller Brewing Company violated the Arkansas Franchise Practices Act, Ark.Code Ann. 4-72-201 et seq., the Supreme Court of Arkansas stated that "[w]hether Miller dealt with the franchise in a commercially reasonable manner and in good faith is a fact question for the jury"); *Garrett v. BankWest, Inc.* (S.D.1990), 459 N.W.2d 833, 841 ("Good faith is derived from the transaction and conduct of the parties. Its meaning varies with the context and emphasizes faithfulness to an agreed common purpose and consistency with the justified expectations of the other party"); and *Brunswick Hills Racquet Club, Inc. v. Route 18 Shopping Ctr. Assocs.* (2005), 182 N.J. 210, 224-225, 864 A.2d 387, quoting 4 Williston on Contracts (3d Ed.1961), Section 610B ("The covenant of good faith and fair dealing calls for parties to a contract to refrain from doing 'anything which will have the effect of destroying or injuring the right of the other party to receive' the benefits of the contract").

The majority opinion dismisses these cases as being of "limited value" because they do not specifically address open-price terms. But "good faith" does not have a different meaning in Ohio, which has not adopted the UCC comments, when used with open-price terms than when used in any other context. Although the cases mentioned above discussed "good faith" in a variety of contexts, the courts agree that it is not possible to determine whether a party acted in "good faith" without a subjective inquiry. See *Allapattah Servs., Inc. v. Exxon Corp.* (S.D.Fla.1999), 61 F.Supp.2d 1308, 1322, fn. 24 (The UCC "imposes a duty on merchants to meet good faith requirements that are measured both subjectively and objectively").

We have had little occasion to discuss "good faith" in Ohio other than to parrot the Revised Code. See *Master Chem. Corp. v. Inkrott* (1990), 55 Ohio St.3d 23, 28, 563 N.E.2d 26 ("'Good faith' is defined in UCC 1-201(19), R.C. 1301.01(S), as 'honesty in fact in the conduct or transaction concerned'"); *Arcanum Natl. Bank v. Hessler* (1982), 69 Ohio St. 2d 549, 554, 23 O.O.3d 468, 433 N.E.2d 204 (same). But we have defined "bad faith" as "'that which imports a dishonest purpose and implies wrongdoing or some motive of self-interest.'" See Black's Law Dictionary (8th Ed.2004) 713 ("good faith" is defined as the "absence of intent to defraud or to seek unconscionable advantage"). *Tom-Lin Ents., Inc. v. Sunoco, Inc.* (R&M) (C.A.6, 2003), 349 F.3d 277, on which the majority opinion relies, clearly misinterpreted *Master Chem.* in concluding that "good faith" requires only objective inquiry. The definition of "bad faith" in *Master Chem.* is the closest that opinion came to addressing the issue before us, and it does not support the conclusion reached by the court in *Tom-Lin* or the conclusion reached by the majority in this case.

Although Shell cited several cases from federal courts to support its contention that prices set pursuant to an open-price term are subject to only objective inquiry, none of them are persuasive. *Ajir v. Exxon Corp.* (May 26, 1999), C.A. 9 Nos. 97-17032 and 97-17134, 1999 U.S. App. LEXIS 11046, 1999 WL 393666, did not address "good faith" but only whether the price charged was "commercially reasonable." 1999 U.S. App. LEXIS 11046, [WL] at *7. *Schwartz v. Sun Co., Inc.* (C.A.6, 2002), 276 F.3d 900, 905, does not support Shell's contention, because the court addressed only the "commercially reasonable" aspect of "good faith." *USX Corp. v. Internatl. Minerals & Chems. Corp.* (Feb.8, 1989), N.D.Ill. No. 86 C 2254, 1989 U.S. Dist. LEXIS 1277, 1989 WL 10851, *1, does not support Shell's contention, because the court emphasized only that the obligation to fix a price in good faith does not "impose a requirement for a seller to match the lowest price available," an issue that is not before us. *Adams v. G.J. Creel & Sons, Inc.* (1995), 320 S.C. 274, 279, 465 S.E.2d 84, does not support Shell's contention, because the court stated only that the plaintiff did not produce evidence that the price fixed by the defendant was unreasonable. *Richard Short Oil Co., Inc. v. Texaco, Inc.* (C.A.8, 1986), 799 F.2d 415, 422-423, also does not speak directly to subjective or objective inquiry; the court concluded that Short had not presented sufficient evidence to support a claim that Texaco did not act in good faith when it set a cap on rebates, in part because Short did not show that Texaco was dishonest or had a bad motive to injure Short. *Wayman v. Amoco Oil Co.* (D.Kan.1996), 923 F. Supp. 1322, 1349, does not support Shell's contention. In *Wayman*, the court concluded that the plaintiffs could not establish that Amoco had set its price in bad faith. That court stated, however, that "[i]f there was evidence that Amoco had, for example, engaged in discriminatory pricing or tried to run plaintiffs out of business, then the court's decision might be different." *T.A.M., Inc. v. Gulf Oil Corp.* (D.C.Pa.1982), 553 F.Supp. 499, 509, does not support Shell's contention. The court stated, with respect to "good faith," that "[t]he plaintiffs have not alleged that the prices they were asked to pay differed from those demanded of other Gulf dealers." In short, none of these cases provide a reason to conclude that the analysis of whether a defendant acted in good faith in setting a price under an open-price term is amenable only to objective inquiry.

The majority opinion also relies on *Shell Oil Co. v. HRN, Inc.* (Tex.2004), 144 S.W.3d 429, in which the Supreme Court of Texas considered the issue that is before us and concluded that open-price terms are subject only to objective inquiry. Because the court in *HRN* relied on the readily distinguishable federal cases discussed above and on the safe-harbor presumption, which Ohio has not adopted, this court should not rely on *HRN*. See *Bob's Shell, Inc. v. O'Connell Oil Assoc., Inc.* (Aug. 31, 2005), D.Mass. No. 03-30169, 2005 U.S. Dist. LEXIS 21318, 2005 WL 2365324 (the court rejected the logic and conclusion of *HRN* and stated that it agreed "with Plaintiffs' assertion that [UCC] section 2-305's purpose of preventing price discrimination should bar a supplier from trying to drive its dealers out of business").

"Good faith" in the context of open-price terms should be subject to both objective and subjective inquiry. Even courts and commentators who have written in favor of the safe-harbor presumption have concluded that an intent to drive a contractual partner out of business might overcome the presumption. Berry, Byers, and Oates, Open Price Agreements: Good Faith Pricing in the Franchise Relationship (2007), 27 Franchise L.J. 45, 51. See *Wilson v. Amerada Hess Corp.* (2001), 168 N.J. 236, 247, 773 A.2d 1121 ("various courts have stated that a party must exercise discretion reasonably *and with proper motive* when that party is vested with the exercise of discretion under a contract" [emphasis added]). I can conceive of situations in which nondiscriminatory pricing could violate "good faith." For instance, in this case, it is alleged that Shell charged all of its similarly situated franchisees the same price, and it is alleged that that price was set too high for them to profitably operate a gas station. In that situation, even though the pricing was nondiscriminatory, it was designed to drive a contractual partner out of business. So much for the concept of a partnership.

I believe that "good faith" as defined in R.C. 1302.01 requires parties to act both honestly in fact and according to reasonable commercial standards. A court's analysis of a merchant's good faith, then, should be both subjective and objective. Furthermore, the safe-harbor presumption, even though not part of the law of Ohio, only applies in the normal case; at a minimum, the appellants should be allowed to attempt to establish that this is not a normal case. I would reverse the judgment of the court of appeals and remand the cause for further consideration consistent with this opinion. After this opinion becomes public, all franchisees in Ohio should watch their wallets very carefully because their franchisors will no longer be held to subjective good-faith standards. Instead, the law of the ocean applies: the big fish are free to consume smaller fish at will. Apparently, not until the waters are exclusively inhabited by a few great white sharks will the majority decide they need a bigger boat or a more robust interpretation of the UCC.

Setting aside the issue of whether the comments can amend the text of Article 2, it's difficult to square the majority's holding in *Casserlie* with the generally accepted view that good faith, as used in the UCC, has both a subjective and an objective component. When compared to the Fifth Circuit's detailed analysis of the Article 2 sections in play, the majority's analysis of the issue in *Casserlie* seems almost superficial:

> To decide whether comment 3 creates an exception, we turn first to the text of the comment and the related sections of the Texas version of the UCC.
>
> [Court quotes Comment 3]
>
> The bare text offers little to resolve the question. First, the comment notes that good faith "includes" reasonable commercial standards. This implies that the good faith required of a merchant setting an open price term encompasses both objective and subjective elements. The comment also creates a good faith safe harbor for such merchants when they use various sorts of fixed prices. But this safe harbor is applicable only in the "normal case." This suggests the safe harbor is not absolute, but it does nothing to define what takes a case out of the safe harbor.
>
> As we will explain, we conclude that the "normal case" of comment 3 is coextensive with a merchant's residual "honesty in fact" duty embodied in §§ 1.201(19) and 2.103. Thus, the comment embraces both the objective (commercial reasonableness) and subjective (honesty in fact) senses of good faith; objective good faith is satisfied by a "price in effect" as long as there is honesty in fact (a"normal case"). This conclusion finds support in three sources: the structure of the UCC, its legislative history, and the caselaw.
>
> Reading comment 3 to embody two different meanings of "good faith" tracks the general structure of the UCC. Courts and commentators have recognized that the meaning of "good faith" is not uniform throughout the code. The cases and commentary treat the "good faith" found in article 1 as subjective and the good faith found only in article 2 as objective. Thus, there is nothing inconsistent in comment 3's using "good faith" in both the objective and the subjective senses.
>
> The history of comment 3 bolsters this conclusion. Some drafters of the UCC worried that for the "great many industries where sales are not made at fixed prices," such as the steel industry, where "practically every contract" is made at "the seller's price in effect," if § 2-305 "is to apply … it means that in every case the seller is going to be in a lawsuit … or he could be, because there isn't any outside standard at all." The drafters considered wholly exempting such contracts from § 2-305, or stating that for a price in effect, the only test is whether the merchant engaged in price discrimination. One drafter explained that the steel industry wanted to make "clear that we do not have to establish that we are fixing reasonable prices, because that gets you into the rate of return of profit, whether you are using borrowed money, and all those questions."

The committee responded to these worries with the current comment 3: "In the normal case a 'posted price' or a future seller's or buyer's 'given price,' 'price in effect,' 'market price,' or the like satisfies the good faith requirement." The drafter's solution was to avoid objective good faith challenges to prices set by reference to some "price in effect," while preserving challenges to discriminatory pricing. Nothing in the proceedings leading to the addition of comment 3 suggests that the overall *subjective* good faith duty of §§ 1-201 and 2-103 was to be supplanted; the evidence is quite to the contrary.

The drafters ultimately rejected two suggested addendums to §2-305:

An agreement to the effect that the price shall be or be adjusted to, or be based upon, or determined by reference to the seller's going price, price in effect, regular price, market price, established price, or the like, at the time of the agreement or at any earlier or later time, is not an agreement to which this subsection is applicable ...

An agreement such as this is an agreement under which the seller or the buyer does not have any burden of showing anything other than that he has not singled out the particular other party for discrimination.

Both of these recommendations are more sweeping than is the language ultimately adopted. The first would have omitted any mention of the good faith duty for open price provisions; the second would have limited the duty of the price-setter to that of avoiding discrimination.

The existing comment, however, avoids challenges to prices set according to an open price term unless that challenge is outside the normal type of case. Although price discrimination was the type of aberrant case on the minds of the drafters, price discrimination is merely a subset of what constitutes such an aberrant case. Any lack of subjective, honesty-in-fact good faith is abnormal; price discrimination is only the most obvious way a price-setter acts in bad faith—by treating similarly-situated buyers differently.

                                                    Mathis v. Exxon Corp., 302 F.3d 448 (2002).

The majority in *Casserlie* may not have been persuaded by the plaintiff's evidence that there was an evil motive behind Shell's pricing, but that's a proof issue, not a question of statutory interpretation. The plaintiffs in the *Mathis* case provided more than mere speculation to back up their claim of bad motive:

Like the plaintiffs in *Nanakuli*, *Allapattah*, and *Wayman*, the franchisees here are alleging a breach of good faith grounded not in Exxon's failure to price in accord with an established schedule, but in its failure to set the price in good faith. Suits recognizing such a cause of action are rare, and with good reason: We would be ill-advised to consider a case to be outside the norm based only on an allegation of improper motive by the party setting the price.

Plaintiffs produced enough evidence to escape comment 3's "normal case" limitation. They showed, for example, that Exxon planned to replace a number of its franchises with [Exxon operated stores], that the DTW price was higher than the sum of the rack price and transportation, that Exxon prevented the franchisees from purchasing gas from jobbers after 1994, and that a number of franchisees were unprofitable or non-competitive.

For example, one Exxon document stated that the company's "marketing Strategy for 1992–1997 is to reduce Dealer stores (est. 30%)." Another document set forth Exxon's plans to reduce dealer stations in Houston from 95 to 45, and to increase [Exxon operated stores] from 83 to 150, between 1997 and 2003. James Carter, the Regional Director of the Exxon/ Mobile Fuels Marketing Company, testified that Exxon made more of a profit from a [Exxon operated stores] than from an independent lessee store. These plans and observations were validated by the fact that the number of dealer stations steadily declined.

Exxon's answer on appeal is that these documents "say nothing about *using pricing* to accomplish a 'plan' to eliminate dealers." Although that is so, there was sufficient evidence on this issue to go to the jury, which was free to, and apparently did, draw the inference connecting pricing to the elimination of dealer-lessees. The consequence of the jury's decision is that this case exceeds the "normal case" limit of § 2.305 comment 3.

C. Unenforceable Terms: Unconscionability

When Llewellyn began drafting his new sales law, he was determined that it should address what he thought was the inability of current law to deal with the problems caused by the ever-increasing use of form contracts in sales transactions. Courts trying to adapt the old rules in the Uniform Sales Act or the common law to the issues raised by standard form contracts appeared to be aimlessly flailing away and making matters worse—the decisions were inconsistent and confusing, making it difficult for parties to predict the outcome of many disputes. And unpredictability is the bane of a merchant's existence.

Llewellyn's goal was not to banish the use of form contracts—he lived in a world where freedom of contract reigned—but rather to restore the "balance" that he thought the use of form contracts had disrupted. For Llewellyn, free contract was not a completely abstract concept:

> *The principle of freedom of bargain* is a principle of freedom of *intended* bargain. It requires what the parties have bargained out to stand as the parties have shaped it, subject only to certain overriding rules of public policy. "Written" bargains, in the days when the rules about them crystallized, were bargains whose detailed terms the two parties had looked over; and the rule was proper, that a signature meant agreement. When, however, parties bargain today, they *think* and *talk* of such matters as price, credit, date of delivery, description and quantity. These are the bargained terms. The unmentioned background is assumed without mention to be fair and balanced general law and the fair and balanced usage of the particular trade. Displacement of these balanced backgrounds is not to be assumed as intended unless deliberate intent is shown that they shall be displaced; and deliberate intent is not shown by a lopsided form whose very content suggests that it has not been carefully read, and the circumstances of whose execution suggest that the matters under discussion and consideration were only the matters written or typed in.

Comment to section 1-C [withdrawn], Revised Uniform Sales Act, Second Draft (1941) (emphasis in original).[30]

Llewellyn's effort to restore the balance evolved into what is now 2-302—Unconscionable Contract or Clause—which is not limited to form contracts. "Unconscionability" is not defined in 2-302 or anywhere else in Article 2—the courts are left to do the heavy lifting when a party raises the issue. And

---

30   Kelly I *Uniform Commercial Code: Drafts,* (Rothman 1984).

the cases make it seem like there are as many definitions of unconscionability as there are courts that have construed 2-302. Some claim it's undefinable:

> It is not possible to *define* unconscionability. It is *not a concept*, but a determination to be made in light of a variety of factors not unifiable into a formula.[31]

But that has not stopped anyone or any court from trying to define it. Llewellyn had promised those opposed to using the new sales law to restore the balance he claimed had been disrupted by form contracts that a statutory provision would not cause uncertainty; instead, it would lessen the existing uncertainty. But courts "have groped for a guide" through unconscionability just as they had groped for guidance with the form contract problem under the Uniform Sales Act.

The following case illustrates generally how courts today are applying 2-302.

SIMPSON V. MSA OF MYRTLE BEACH, INC.

SUPREME COURT OF SOUTH CAROLINA, 2007
373 S.C. 14

TOAL, Chief Justice.

This case arises out of an arbitration clause in an automobile trade-in contract between an automobile dealership and a customer. The automobile dealership filed a motion for protective order and/or to stay and to compel arbitration in response to the customer's civil action. The trial court denied the dealership's motion on the grounds that the arbitration clause was unconscionable. This appeal followed.

FACTUAL/PROCEDURAL BACKGROUND

Appellant MSA of Myrtle Beach, Inc d/b/a Addy's Harbor Dodge ("Addy"), a car dealership, and Respondent Sherry H. Simpson ("Simpson") entered into a contract whereby Simpson traded in her 2001 Toyota 4Runner for a new 2004 Dodge Caravan. Directly above the signature line on the first page of the contract, the signee was instructed in bold to "SEE ADDITONAL TERMS AND CONDITIONS ON OPPOSITE PAGE." The additional terms and conditions contained an arbitration clause stating the following:

> 10. ARBITRATION Any and all disputes, claims or controversies between Dealer and Customer or between any officers, directors, agents, employees, or assignees of Dealer and Customer arising out of or relating to: (a) automobile warranty, workmanship, or repair; (b) the terms or enforceability of the sale, lease, or financing of any vehicle; (c) any claim of breach of contract, misrepresentation, conversion, fraud, or unfair and deceptive trade practices against Dealer or any officers, directors, agents, employees, or assignees of Dealer; (d) any and all claims under any consumer protection statute; and (e) the validity and scope of this contract, shall be settled by binding arbitration in accordance with the Commercial Arbitration Rules of the American Arbitration Association. The parties expressly waive all rights to trial by jury on such claims. Provided, however, that nothing in this contract shall require Dealer to submit to arbitration any claims by Dealer against customer for claim and delivery, repossession, injunctive relief, or monies owed by customer in connection with the purchase or lease of any vehicle and any claims by Dealer for these remedies shall not be stayed pending the outcome of arbitration.

---

31   White and Summers, *Commercial Law* (West, 6th ed. 2010).

* * *

Any arbitration under this agreement shall take place in Horry County, South Carolina and Customer agrees that the courts of Horry County, South Carolina shall have exclusive jurisdiction over enforcement of this contract and any award made by any arbitrator pursuant to this contract. In no event shall the arbitrator be authorized to award punitive, exemplary, double, or treble damages (or any other damages which are punitive in nature or effect) against either party. Unless otherwise agreed in writing, no claims against Dealer shall be consolidated with other claims in the nature of a class action.

Six months later, Simpson filed a complaint in the Horry County court of common pleas alleging Addy violated the South Carolina Unfair Trade Practices Act and the South Carolina Manufacturers, Distributors, and Dealers Act by misrepresenting the trade-in value of the vehicle, artificially increasing the purchase price, and failing to provide all rebates promised. Simpson sought damages consistent with the maximum statutory remedies permitted for violations of these statutes.

Addy's answer denied Simpson's allegations and asserted that the contract between the parties contained an arbitration clause such that the matter should be stayed and that Simpson's only remedy was to file for arbitration. Addy contemporaneously filed a motion for protective order and/or to stay and compel arbitration. Thereafter, Simpson filed a memorandum in opposition to Addy's motion alleging that the arbitration clause was unconscionable and unenforceable.

At the motion hearing, the trial court ordered the parties to attempt mediation. After the parties notified the trial court that mediation failed, the trial court issued an order denying Addy's motion on the grounds that the arbitration clause was unconscionable. Addy filed this appeal.

LAW/ANALYSIS

Denial of Addy's motion for protective order and/or to stay and compel arbitration.
Addy argues that the trial court erred in denying Addy's motion for protective order and/or to stay and compel arbitration. We disagree.

There is a strong presumption in favor of the validity of arbitration agreements because both state and federal policy favor arbitration of disputes. The South Carolina Uniform Arbitration Act (UAA) provides that in any contract evidencing a transaction involving commerce, a written provision to settle by arbitration shall be valid, irrevocable, and enforceable.

General contract principles of state law apply in a court's evaluation of the enforceability of an arbitration clause. In South Carolina, unconscionability is defined as the absence of meaningful choice on the part of one party due to one-sided contract provisions, together with terms that are so oppressive that no reasonable person would make them and no fair and honest person would accept them. If a court as a matter of law finds any clause of a contract to have been unconscionable at the time it was made, the court may refuse to enforce the unconscionable clause, or so limit its application so as to avoid any unconscionable result.

In analyzing claims of unconscionability in the context of arbitration agreements, the Fourth Circuit has instructed courts to focus generally on whether the arbitration clause is geared towards achieving an unbiased decision by a neutral decision-maker. It is under this general rubric that we determine whether a contract provision is unconscionable due to both an absence of meaningful choice and oppressive, one-sided terms.

A. Absence of meaningful choice
Addy argues that the facts do not show that Simpson had no meaningful choice in agreeing to arbitrate. We disagree.

Absence of meaningful choice on the part of one party generally speaks to the fundamental fairness of the bargaining process in the contract at issue. In determining whether a contract was "tainted by an absence of meaningful choice," courts should take into account the nature of the injuries suffered by the plaintiff; whether the plaintiff is a substantial business concern; the relative disparity in the parties' bargaining power; the parties' relative sophistication; whether there is an element of surprise in the inclusion of the challenged clause; and the conspicuousness of the clause. *Holler v. Holler*, 364 S.C. 256, 269, 612 S.E.2d 469, 476 (Ct. App. 2005) ("A determination whether a contract is unconscionable depends upon all the facts and circumstances of a particular case."(quoting 17A Am.Jur.2d *Contracts* § 279 (2004))).

There are many cases in this jurisdiction and others involving the enforceability of arbitration clauses in adhesion contracts between commercial entities and consumers. Each transaction is analyzed on its own particular facts in conjunction with the federal and/or state policies favoring arbitration. We begin our inquiry with a focus on the decisions of courts in Ohio, which have heard numerous cases in the very recent past specifically addressing issues of unconscionability of arbitration clauses embedded in adhesion contracts between automobile retailers and consumers.

The Ohio courts characterize automobiles as a "necessity" and factor this characterization into a determination of whether a consumer had a "meaningful choice" in negotiating the arbitration agreement. In this same context, the Ohio courts have adhered to the idea that sales agreements between consumers and retailers "are subject to considerable skepticism upon review, due to the disparity in bargaining positions of the parties." Under the Ohio courts' rationale, "the presumption in favor of arbitration clauses is substantially weaker when there are strong indications that the contract at issue is an adhesion contract, and the arbitration clause itself appears to be adhesive in nature. In this situation there arises considerable doubt that any true agreement ever existed to submit disputes to arbitration."

Turning to the instant case, we first note that under general principles of state contract law, an adhesion contract is a standard form contract offered on a "take-it-or-leave-it" basis with terms that are not negotiable. Neither party disputes that the contract entered into by Simpson and Addy was an adhesion contract as such contracts are standard in the automobile retail industry. Adhesion contracts, however, are not per se unconscionable. Therefore, finding an adhesion contract is merely the beginning point of the analysis.

We agree with the rationale of the Ohio courts and proceed to analyze this contract between a consumer and automobile retailer with "considerable skepticism." Under this approach, we first observe that the contract between Simpson and Addy involved a vehicle intended for use as Simpson's primary transportation, which is critically important in modern day society. Applying the factors considered by the Fourth Circuit in analyzing arbitration clauses, we also acknowledge Simpson's claim that she did not possess the business judgment necessary to make her aware of the implications of the arbitration agreement, and that she did not have a lawyer present to provide any assistance in the matter. Similarly, we note Simpson's allegation that the contract was "hastily" presented for her signature.

Moreover, regardless of the general legal presumptions that a party to a contract has read and understood the contract's terms, we also find it necessary to consider the otherwise inconspicuous nature of the arbitration clause in light of its consequences. The loss of the right to a jury trial is an obvious result of arbitration. However, this particular arbitration clause also required Simpson to forego certain remedies that were otherwise required by statute.[32] While certain phrases within other provisions of the additional terms and conditions were printed in all capital letters, the arbitration clause in its entirety was written in the standard small print, and embedded in paragraph ten (10) of sixteen (16) total paragraphs included on the page. Although this Court acknowledges that parties are always free to contract

---

32   Specifically, the arbitration clause prohibited an arbitrator from awarding double or treble damages.

away their rights, we cannot, under the circumstances, ignore the inconspicuous nature of a provision, which was drafted by the superior party, and which functioned to contract away certain significant rights and remedies otherwise available to Simpson by law.

Accordingly, we find that when considered as a whole and in the context of an adhesion contract for a vehicle trade-in, the circumstances reveal that Simpson had no meaningful choice in agreeing to arbitrate claims with Addy.

B. Oppressive and one-sided terms

1. Limitation on statutory remedies in an arbitration clause

Addy contends that the arbitration clause's limitation on statutory remedies was not oppressive and one-sided. We disagree.

The arbitration clause in Simpson's contract with Addy provides that "[i]n no event shall the arbitrator be authorized to award punitive, exemplary, double, or treble damages (or any other damages which are punitive in nature or effect) against either party." Simpson's underlying complaint filed in civil court alleged, among other things, that Addy violated the South Carolina Uniform Trade Practices Act (SCUPTA) and the South Carolina Regulation of Manufacturers, Distributors, and Dealers Act (Dealers Act). The SCUPTA requires a court to award treble damages for violations of the statute.[33] Similarly, the Dealers Act requires a court to award double damages for violations of the statute.[34]

In arguing that this provision was not oppressive and one-sided, **Addy relies on** *Carolina Care Plan*. In that case, this Court held that the issue of whether an arbitration clause prohibiting an arbitrator from awarding "punitive damages" violated the public policy of the SCUTPA was not ripe for review. The Court explained that "an arbitrator may or may not choose to award treble damages in accordance with the SCUTPA, depending upon whether an arbitrator finds the SCUPTA was violated and whether the arbitrator finds that statutory treble damages are punitive or compensatory damages."

Addy's comparison falls short. In fact, the present case requires the *Carolina Care Plan* analysis to be taken one step further because the arbitration clause at issue here goes beyond banning "punitive" damages generally and specifically prohibits an arbitrator from awarding statutorily required treble or double damages. Therefore, an arbitrator's ultimate classification of an award as "compensatory" or "punitive" is no longer relevant in an analysis of whether this particular clause is unconscionable: under this arbitration clause, treble and double damages—whether classified as compensatory or punitive—are prohibited outright.

The general rule is that courts will not enforce a contract which is violative of public policy, statutory law, or provisions of the Constitution. In our opinion, this rule has two applications in the present case. First, this arbitration clause violates statutory law because it prevents Simpson from receiving the mandatory statutory remedies to which she may be entitled in her underlying SCUTPA and Dealers Act claims. Second, unconditionally permitting the weaker party to waive these statutory remedies pursuant to an adhesion contract runs contrary to the underlying statutes' very purposes of punishing acts that adversely affect the public interest. Therefore, under the general rule, this provision in the arbitration clause is unenforceable.

---

33   *See* S.C. Code Ann. § 39-5-140(a) (1976) (providing that a "court *shall* award three times the actual damages sustained and may provide such other relief as it deems necessary or proper" [emphasis added]).
34   *See* S.C. Code Ann. § 56-15-110(1) (2006) (providing that an individual "*shall* recover double the actual damages by him sustained" [emphasis added]).

Accordingly, we find the provision prohibiting double and treble damages to be oppressive, one-sided, and not geared toward achieving an unbiased decision by a neutral decision-maker. In conjunction with Simpson's lack of meaningful choice in agreeing to arbitrate, this provision is an unconscionable waiver of statutory rights, and therefore, unenforceable.

2. Dealer's remedies not stayed pending outcome of arbitration

Addy argues that the arbitration clause's provision reserving certain judicial remedies to the dealer and authorizing the award of the dealer's remedies even if the consumer's arbitration proceedings have not concluded is not oppressive and one-sided. We disagree.

While stating that "all disputes, claims or controversies between Dealer and Customer" are to be settled in binding arbitration, the arbitration clause notes several exceptions. Specifically, the clause provides:

> Nothing in this contract shall require the Dealer to submit to arbitration any claims by Dealer against Customer for claim and delivery, repossession, injunctive relief, or monies owed by Consumer in connection with the purchase or lease of any vehicle and *any claims by Dealer for these remedies shall not be stayed pending the outcome of arbitration.* [emphasis added].

Our courts have held that lack of mutuality of remedy in an arbitration agreement, on its own, does not make the arbitration agreement unconscionable.

* * *

However, the essence of Simpson's unconscionablity claim is not the general lack of mutuality of remedy, but rather the arbitration agreement's express stipulation that the dealer may bring a judicial proceeding that completely disregards any pending consumer claims that require arbitration. The clauses at issue in *Munoz* and *Lackey* contained no such directives. To this effect, we can easily envision a scenario in which a dealer's claim and delivery action is initiated in court, completed, and the vehicle sold prior to an arbitrator's determination of the consumer's rights in the same vehicle. As the arbitration agreement between Simpson and Addy is written, the dealer collects on a judgment awarded in a judicial proceeding regardless of any protections for the collateral afforded by law.

Addy's suggestion that there are procedural motions available to the consumer which offset any potentially inconsistent effects of this provision, in our opinion, shows an informal acknowledgement on the part of Addy that such a provision on its face is indeed one-sided. These procedural mechanisms only act to place an additional burden on the consumer to ensure that the vehicle in controversy is not disposed of in a court proceeding initiated by the dealer before the adjudication of the consumer's claims in arbitration.

We continue to abide by our previous holdings in *Munoz* and *Lackey* that lack of mutuality of remedy will not invalidate an arbitration agreement. However, we find that the provision in the arbitration clause dictating that the dealer's judicial remedies supersede the consumer's arbitral remedies is one-sided and oppressive and does not promote a neutral and unbiased arbitral forum. Accordingly, in light of Simpson's lack of meaningful choice in agreeing to arbitrate, the provision is unconscionable and unenforceable.

Severability

In the alternative to its argument that the arbitration clause is not unconscionable, Addy suggests that any provision found by this Court to be unconscionable may be severed from the clause and arbitration allowed to otherwise proceed. In fact, it seems as though the "Additional Terms and Conditions" section of the contract anticipated just such a scenario. Paragraph fifteen (15) articulates a severability clause providing that:

> In the event any provision of this contract shall be held invalid, illegal, or unenforceable, the validity, legality, and enforceability of the remaining provisions shall not be affected or impaired thereby.

We disagree.

In consideration of the federal and state policies favoring arbitration agreements, severability clauses have been used to remove the unenforceable provisions in an arbitration clause while saving the parties' overall agreement to arbitrate.

* * *

Additionally, legislation permits this Court to "refuse to enforce" any unconscionable clause in a contract or to "limit its application so as to avoid an unconscionable result."

At the same time, courts have acknowledged that severability is not always an appropriate remedy for an unconscionable provision in an arbitration clause. Although, "a critical consideration in assessing severability is giving effect to the intent of the contracting parties," the D.C. Circuit recently cautioned, "If illegality pervades the arbitration agreement such that only a disintegrated fragment would remain after hacking away the unenforceable parts, the judicial effort begins to look more like rewriting the contract than fulfilling the intent of the parties." Similarly, the general principle in this State is that it is not the function of the court to rewrite contracts for parties.

In this case, we find the arbitration clause in the adhesion contract between Simpson and Addy wholly unconscionable and unenforceable based on the cumulative effect of a number of oppressive and one-sided provisions contained within the entire clause. While this Court does not ignore South Carolina's policy favoring arbitration, we hold that the intent of the parties is best achieved by severing the arbitration clause in its entirety rather than "rewriting" the contract by severing multiple unenforceable provisions.

PROBLEM 3 - 21

The scales built into the new scanners have not functioned properly since installation, and the seller has not been very responsive to Rae's demands that the problem be solved. She's had to set the old self-service scales out in the produce department so shoppers can weigh their purchases—which they invariably manage to do incorrectly—before proceeding to checkout. This, then, slows up checkout, and to avoid long lines, Rae has to keep more checkers on duty. She fears this is going to end up in litigation, and she is greatly troubled by one of the terms in the store's contract with the seller:

> COSTS, DAMAGES, AND ATTORNEYS' FEES. You agree to be liable to Seller for any loss, costs, or expenses, including, without limitation, reasonable attorneys' fees, the costs of litigation, and the costs to prepare or respond to subpoenas, depositions, or other discovery that the Seller incurs as a result of any dispute involving your purchase.

The contract she signed was a twelve-page form contract that the seller presented to her with the price, delivery date, and options they had agreed to filled in on the first page. The seller also represented that this was an industry-approved contract, but there are only two other companies that sell bioptic in-counter scanners with scales like those she purchased. If Rae ends up in litigation with the seller, will she really have to pay all of the seller's litigation expenses, even if she wins? 2-302.

PROBLEM 3 - 22

Would your answer in the last problem be different if Rae used the same contract terms in the agreements the store's customers sign when they apply for a store credit card?

Most courts today use some form of the two-factor test for unconscionability that was applied by the South Carolina Supreme Court in the Simpson case. Where they differ is in how they characterize the relationship between "bargaining naughtiness," or procedural unconscionability, and the harshness of the "lopsided terms," or substantive unconscionability. Most courts require some showing of both procedural and substantive unconscionability, with many treating the relationship between the two as inversely proportional—a little procedural naughtiness requires lots of substantive unconscionability, and a lot of procedural unconscionability requires less lopsidedness.

But these are generalizations, and the concepts can be very nuanced from state to state, so one has to tread carefully through the decisions to find what Llewellyn might have called the "situation sense" of the different courts.

A determination that a contract term is unconscionable does not necessarily mean the contract as a whole cannot be enforced. A court can enforce the rest of the contract or it can limit the application of the clause to eliminate its unconscionable effects.

CHAPTER 4

CHANGED CIRCUMSTANCES

It should come as no surprise that, no matter how careful or thoughtful they may be, the parties to a sale-of-goods agreement cannot predict the future with absolute certainty. Things can happen after agreement is reached that neither anticipated and that may adversely affect the bargain they made or, worse, actually prevent performance of their agreement. Sometimes the parties can ameliorate the consequences of changed circumstances by adjusting the terms of the contract. Article 2 anticipates that the parties may need to do this and eliminates the barriers to contract modification imposed by the common law. 2-209(1). But, sometimes, simply adjusting the terms of the contract will not solve the problem caused by the changed circumstances—as when one party's performance has been made impossible by the changed circumstances. Article 2 anticipates such situations as well and may excuse nonperformance so caused. 2-615.

A. MODIFICATION

For centuries, the common law has been deeply suspicious of unilateral concessions made by a party during the performance of a contract. The courts presumed that such concessions were more likely the result of coercion or even extortion than of commercial practicality. They took it upon themselves to police contract modifications by requiring that the beneficiary of a modification give something to the other party in return—what you called consideration in your Contracts course. Today this policing of adjustments to the terms of a contract is known as the preexisting-legal-duty rule (PELD). Although PELD may discourage sailors from coercing a pay increase from the ship's captain while a ship is at sea (assuming one of them has some legal training), it also prevents contracting partners from making midcourse adjustments that ultimately might benefit both in a long-term relationship:

> Often it is neither unreasonable nor unjust to allow a party to benefit from a modification without paying anything further. For example, the parties may modify and set a date for contract performance earlier than in the prior agreement, and this may benefit one party without imposing any burden whatsoever on the other. When so, there is no reason why the beneficiary should have to pay for the change.[1]

---

1   White and Summers, *Uniform Commercial Code*, (6th ed., 2010), at 77–78.

As the following case illustrates, Article 2 rejects the notion that unilateral contract concessions are usually the product of coercion by expressly providing that "an agreement modifying a contract within this Article needs no consideration to be binding." 2-209(1). The parties to an Article 2 transaction are free to make on-the-fly adjustments to their agreement, constrained only by the admonition in comment 2 to 2-209 that modifications "must meet the test of good faith imposed by this Act." The "good faith" test removes the barrier on consensual modifications imposed by PELD while at the same time protecting against the coercion/extortion that animated PELD as "the extortion of a 'modification' without legitimate commercial reason is ineffective as a violation of the duty of good faith." Comment 2, 2-209. But as the case also makes clear, eliminating the consideration requirement does not eliminate the requirement that modifications must actually be agreed to by the parties.

LOGAN & KANAWHA COAL CO., LLC v. DETHERAGE COAL SALES, LLC

UNITED STATES DISTRICT COURT FOR THE SOUTHERN DISTRICT OF WEST VIRGINIA, 2012
841 F. SUPP. 2D 955

GOODWIN, Chief District Judge.

* * *

3. Contract Modification Under W. Va. § Code 46-2-209

Logan also argues that its May 11, 2010 letter constituted a contract modification proposal, which Detherage accepted through its silence and by beginning performance under the contract. Specifically, Logan asserts that the May 11, 2010 letter proposed additional contract terms, and Detherage accepted the additional terms because it manifested assent through silence and by beginning performance. Thus, according to Logan, Detherage's silence and delivery of coal after receipt of the May 11, 2010 letter constituted its acceptance of the additional terms, and the arbitration provision became part of the agreement.

West Virginia Code § 46-2-209 is the UCC provision governing contract modification. Section 2-209 applies once the contract is formed, and it establishes the requirements for a valid contract modification. Section 46-2-209 provides in pertinent part that:

> (1) An agreement modifying a contract within this article needs no consideration to be binding ... .

> (3) The requirements of the statute of frauds section of this article (section 2-201) [§ 46-2-201] must be satisfied if the contract as modified is within its provisions.

A valid contract modification under § 46-2-209 requires that the parties agree to modify the contract. One party cannot modify the contract without the other party's consent. ("Mutual assent is required to establish the existence of a modification of the sales contract.") Mutual assent requires a "meeting of the minds" between the two parties and may be evidenced by "word, act or conduct which evince the intention of the parties to contract." Some courts have found that silence by one party can indicate assent and have held that a valid contract existed when the silence of one party constituted acceptance of the proposal.

In West Virginia, silence plus the offeree beginning performance can constitute acceptance. *See First Nat'l Bank of Gallipolis v. Marietta Mfg. Co.*, 151 W. Va. 636, 641–42, 153 S.E.2d 172 (1967) ("That an acceptance may be effected by silence accompanied by an act of the offeree which constitutes a performance of that requested by the offeror is well established."). However, silence alone is usually insufficient to establish consent to an agreement. *See Quincy Dairy Co. v. Hartford Accident & Indem.*

Co., 57 F. Supp. 899, 903 (S.D.W. Va. 1944) ("Mere silence on the part of an offeree, or his failure to accept the offer promptly can never be construed as an acceptance, unless there is some duty resting on the offeree to reply or accept.").

Acceptance through silence accompanied by beginning performance under the contract raises additional concerns in the context of contract modification. When a party proposes to modify a contract, by definition, a contract between the parties already exists and the offeree is obligated to perform under the existing agreement. Thus, it is difficult to discern whether the offeree's performance is conduct manifesting assent to the proposed modification or if the performance is simply the offeree fulfilling its preexisting duty under the contract. Doubt exists as to whether performance constitutes acceptance when there is a contract modification proposal under UCC § 2-209, and the offeree is silent as to the proposed modification and later performs under the contract, but the party's performance was already required under the original contract.

Some courts have responded to such concerns by requiring that offerees expressly assent to contract modification proposals and that assent "cannot be inferred merely from a party's conduct in continuing with the agreement." The courts' holdings relied on the reasoning found in *Step-Saver Data Systems, Inc. v. Wyse Technology*, an opinion by the Court of Appeals for the Third Circuit. *Step-Saver* involved the question of whether a "Limited Use License Agreement" included on the packaging of a software program was part of a software contract under UCC § 2-207. The Third Circuit stated that:

> [P]roceeding with a contract after receiving a writing that purports to define the terms of the parties's contract is not sufficient to establish the party's consent to the terms of the writing to the extent that the terms of the writing either add to, or differ from, the terms detailed in the parties' earlier writings or discussions.

The Third Circuit reasoned that a party must expressly consent to additional terms, and its consent cannot be inferred by the offeree fulfilling its already-existing obligation. Although *Step-Saver* involved questions of assent and performance under UCC § 2-207, courts have applied its reasoning when evaluating assent to a contract modification under UCC § 2-209. *See, e.g., U.S. Surgical Corp.*, 5 F. Supp. 2d at 1206 ("The express assent analysis is the same under §§ 2-207 and 2-209.").

This court finds the reasoning of *Step-Saver* and its application to UCC § 2-209 convincing. This court also believes that the West Virginia Supreme Court of Appeals would be persuaded by such reasoning. Therefore, I conclude that an offeree's silence and continuation of its course of performance is insufficient to demonstrate assent to the proposed modification. Specifically, an offeree must expressly consent to a contract modification under § 46-2-209 when it is already obligated to perform, and continuing the course of performance is not express consent. This principle is consistent with the court's understanding of the general principle of contract law that there must be a "meeting of the minds" for a contract to be formed. The court cannot determine if there was a meeting of the minds regarding a contract modification proposal if the offeree merely acts in accordance with its preexisting obligations.

In this case, Detherage did not respond to Logan's May 11, 2010 letter, but it began performing under the parties' agreement approximately one month later. However, Detherage was already obligated to deliver the coal under the parties' March 2010 agreement. Detherage's delivery of the coal does not manifest assent to the contract modification proposals in the May 10, 2010 letter because Detherage was acting consistently with its preexisting obligations. Based on this reasoning, I **FIND** that Detherage did not accept Logan's contract modification proposals contained in the May 11, 2010 letter. Accordingly, the court **FINDS** the parties did not form a modified contract that contained the arbitration provision.

PROBLEM 4 - 1

Last spring, a local grower agreed to supply all of the tomatoes the store required for the month of August at twenty-five cents per pound. In June, Rae e-mailed the grower and asked if she could start delivering tomatoes by July 15. The grower replied to Rae's e-mail, agreeing to the July 15 delivery date. When no tomatoes were delivered on the fifteenth of July, Rae called the grower and was told the tomatoes would be delivered on August 1 as required by the contract. The grower claimed that because Rae had not offered additional compensation for early delivery, she was not required to deliver before the time specified in the contract. Is the grower right? 2-209(1).

PROBLEM 4 - 2

Would your answer be different in Problem 4 - 1 if instead Rae had e-mailed the grower that unless tomato delivery began by July 15, the store would not accept any tomatoes delivered in August and the grower agreed to early delivery of the tomatoes but then did not deliver by July 15? Would it matter if Rae knew the growing season made it impossible for tomatoes to be ready for harvesting by the middle of July? Or that the tomato harvest had exceeded expectations and as a result the current market price for tomatoes was fifteen cents per pound? 2-209(1).

PROBLEM 4 - 3

A local farmer agreed to supply the store each week with one hundred dozen eggs. The agreement provided that the eggs would be delivered by "Monday noon" each week. The eggs have never been delivered before Tuesday of any week, but Rae has not refused to accept the late deliveries. Last week Rae e-mailed the farmer that she was terminating the contract because he had not complied with the delivery terms during the first six months of the agreement. The farmer's lawyer told Rae today that the delivery date had been modified by her continued acceptance of the late deliveries and that she would breach the agreement if she terminated it. Is the lawyer right? 2-209(1). See 1-303(f).

B. MODIFICATION AND THE STATUTE OF FRAUDS

The enlightened approach to contract modification Article 2 takes in 2-209(1) by eliminating consideration as a requirement for an enforceable modification is potentially undermined by 2-209(3), which provides that

> the requirements of the statute of frauds [in section 2-201] must be satisfied if the contract as modified is within its provisions.

The informal, on-the-fly adjustments made possible by the abrogation of the preexisting-legal-duty rule become illusory if they must be memorialized in a writing to be enforceable. But does 2-209(3) require that *all* modifications be in writing? Or does it only require that some modifications be reduced to writing, and if so, how do the parties determine whether their modification requires a writing to be enforceable? As the *Costco* case illustrates, the courts have not agreed on the intended scope of the "statute of frauds" requirement imposed by 2-209(3).

COSTCO V. WORLD WIDE

COURT OF APPEALS OF WASHINGTON, 1995
78 WN. APP. 637

WEBSTER, Justice.

This case involves modifications allegedly made to a contract for the sale of jewelry. Costco Wholesale Corporation contends that the price it agreed to pay Worldwide Licensing Corporation was modified when Worldwide's agent agreed, in writing, to rebate part of the purchase price. Worldwide alleges Costco orally modified the contract by promising to buy more jewelry. Each party contends that the modification alleged by the other is barred by the statute of frauds, which requires certain contracts to be written. We hold that the contract's initial satisfaction of the statute passes through to the modification, but that the contract as modified can only be enforced up to the quantity stated. Thus, the statute of frauds bars the oral promise to purchase additional jewelry, but not the rebate claim.

FACTS

Worldwide Licensing Corporation sells jewelry to wholesale buyers. Worldwide's sales are negotiated by independent sales representatives known as brokers. When Worldwide decided to pursue Costco as a potential buyer, it contacted Loren Coleman, an independent sales representative. Ed Dose, a Worldwide division president, flew to Seattle to meet Coleman. Coleman and Dose met with Megghan Harruff, a Costco division manager.

At the meeting, Coleman presented Worldwide's merchandise, including its packaging. Costco agreed to purchase 5 pallets of 416 boxes each, for a total of $74,880.00, and paid by check. After Harruff described the purchase as "test marketing", and expressed the opinion that the merchandise would quickly sell out, the parties discussed the possibility of subsequent orders. Dose told Harruff that reordering would take eight weeks. Outside of the meeting and Harruff's hearing, Coleman urged Dose to produce more than the five pallet loads ordered. Although the jewelry was a specialty item not easily marketed, Dose reluctantly agreed to manufacture three additional pallets.

In Costco's opinion, the jewelry it received was poorly packaged, and not the quality it expected. Subsequently, Costco did not sell the jewelry as quickly as it had hoped. Coleman told Worldwide about Costco's displeasure. Although Worldwide believed in the quality of its product, it was concerned about selling Costco the already manufactured three pallet loads of jewelry. Dose told Coleman to "approach Costco with an $8 per box adjustment in price *providing they agreed to purchase the remaining 3 pallets at the adjusted price*". According to Dose, Coleman "indicated" that Costco "had agreed to the additional order". Coleman's declaration, on the other hand, asserts that Dose authorized an $8 per unit rebate, but it says nothing about the alleged additional order, or any instruction to make the rebate contingent on a promise to buy the other three pallets. Costco agreed to the rebate amount, and sent a rebate form to Coleman. Coleman signed it and faxed a copy to Worldwide. Worldwide entered the rebate in its accounting system, pending Dose's approval. When Costco did not order the three additional pallets, Worldwide refused to pay the rebate. When Worldwide paid Coleman's sales commission, however, it was based on the rebated sales price.

Costco sued Worldwide, seeking $16,640 (2,080 boxes at $8 per box). Worldwide denied the rebate agreement and alleged the statute of frauds as an affirmative defense. The trial court entered summary judgment in favor of Costco.

DISCUSSION

We review the trial court's grant of summary judgment de novo. *Finkelstein v. Security Properties, Inc.,* 76 Wn. App. 733, 736, 888 P.2d 161, review denied 127 Wn.2d 1002, 898 P.2d 307 (1995). The only cause of action alleged is breach of a promise to rebate $16,640. Worldwide asserts three alternative defenses. First, Worldwide contends the rebate modification is unenforceable because it does not satisfy the Uniform Commercial Codes statute of frauds.

Statute of Frauds

This case addresses the interplay between the statute of frauds and contract modifications under the U.C.C. The statute of frauds denies enforcement of a contract for the sale of goods worth more than $500 when no writing evidences the agreement. When a contract is modified, U.C.C. § 2-209(3) requires the statute of frauds to be satisfied if the contract as modified falls within the provisions of the statute of frauds.[2] The Costco/Worldwide contract, as modified, involved a sale of goods for more than $500 and is within the statute of frauds. Therefore, the only issue is whether the statute has been satisfied.

The original contract satisfied the statute of frauds. The plain language of U.C.C. § 2-209(3) only requires a satisfaction of the statute if the contract as modified is within the statute; it does *not* require a satisfaction for the modification itself. We hold that the original satisfaction of the statute passes through to the contract as modified. Thus, a modification to a contract, which initially satisfied the statute, does not require a new memorandum.[3] This interpretation respects plain statutory language and the common commercial practice of oral modifications.

Assuming the contract in this case was modified to include the rebate (a price modification) and the additional purchase (a quantity modification), the pass-through power of the original contract's satisfaction infuses the contract as modified with the characteristic of enforceability. The rebate, which modified the price, did not require an additional writing to satisfy the statute of frauds. *But,* under the statute of frauds, a contract can only be enforced up to the quantity shown in the writing. Without a writing showing the three additional pallet load order, the quantity modification is not enforceable by way of action or defense, despite the pass-through nature of the original satisfaction of the statute. *RCW 62A.2-201(1); see also RCW 62A.2-201(3)(b);* and U.C.C. § 2-209, comment 3 (an authenticated "memo is limited in its effect to the quantity of goods set forth in it").

Therefore, Worldwide cannot avoid summary judgment on the rebate claim by arguing that Costco breached an oral promise to purchase more jewelry.

---

2   RCW 62A.2-209(3) provides: "The requirements of the statute of frauds section of this Article (RCW 62A.2-201) must be satisfied if the contract as modified is within its provisions". Although the contract, as modified, includes some terms from the original contract, and some terms from the modification, "the new contract is viewed as a whole" when applying the statute. Restatement (Second) of Contracts § 149, comment a (1979). The following examples help clarify when a "contract as modified" is within the statute. A sales contract originally for a $400 television, but modified to include a second $400 television is, as modified, within the statute of frauds because the price now exceeds $500. A contract for a $1,000 stereo later modified to exclude all components except a $200 tuner is, as modified, outside of the statute because the price is less than the $500 threshold.

3   We disagree with decisions that require every modification to be in writing. *See, e.g. Van Den Broeke v. Bellanca Aircraft Corp.,* 576 F.2d 582, 584 (5th Cir. 1978); *Cooley v. Big Horn Harvestore Systems, Inc.,* 767 P.2d 740, 744 (Colo. Ct. App. 1988), *aff'd in part, rev'd in part,* 813 P.2d 736 (Colo. 1991); and *Green Constr. Co. v. First Indemnity of Am. Ins. Co.,* 735 F. Supp. 1254, 1261 (D.N.J. 1990), *aff'd,* 935 F.2d 1281 (3d Cir. 1991). "There is not a scintilla of support in the drafting history of § 2-209(3) for the notion that § 2-209(3) was designed to require a formalistic validation for unsupported modifications and to incorporate the requirements of § 2-201 for all modifications". John E. Murray, Jr., "The Modification Mystery: Section 2-209 of the Uniform Commercial Code," 32 *Vill. L. Rev.* 1, 15 (1987); see also James J. White & Robert S. Summers, *Uniform Commercial Code* § 1-6 (3d ed. 1988).

In summary, we hold that the contract, as modified to include a rebate, has satisfied the statute of frauds, but the alleged promise to purchase additional jewelry is barred. The court's summary judgment order was proper insofar as its effect was to strike Worldwide's affirmative defense.

Under *Costco*, the writing that satisfied the statute of frauds for the original contract would "shelter" a subsequent modification for purposes of 2-209(3). The court's spin on 2-209(3) greatly reduces its impact on the modifications liberated from the consideration requirement by 2-209(1). Under *Costco*, it would appear that only a modification to the quantity term in the original contract would need to be in writing in order to be enforceable. Recall that the writing required by Article 2's statute of frauds must merely "evidence" the existence of an agreement—other than the quantity involved, the actual terms of the agreement need not be reduced to writing. 2-201(1). Reading 2-209(3) to require that modifications affecting anything other than the quantity term be reduced to writing would require more of a modification than Article 2 requires of the original agreement. Nonetheless, as footnote 3 in *Costco* notes, some courts have interpreted 2-209(3) to apply to all modifications. These courts require that modifications to terms such as price, time of performance, and place of performance be in writing, even though the writing necessary to evidence the original agreement would satisfy 2-201 without them.

The 2-209(3) writing requirement, by its express terms, would also seem to apply where an agreement originally not subject to the Article 2 statute of frauds would be subject to the statute of frauds as modified. If the original contract price was less than $500, 2-201 would not require it be evidenced by a writing. If, after modification, the contract price was $500 or more, "the contract as modified is within" 2-201, and "the requirements of the statute of frauds section of this Article must be satisfied." 2-209(3). This is consistent with the "shelter principle" in *Costco*—if no writing was initially produced for statute-of-fraud purposes because 2-201 did not require the original agreement to be evidenced by a writing, no writing sufficient under 2-201 presently exists that could shelter the agreement as modified.

Problem 4 - 4

The principal of the elementary school across town called the store's deli and ordered one hundred sandwich boxes for the "School's Out" party for the second grade. Each box held a sandwich, chips, and a cookie, and was priced at $4.25. Which, if any, of the following changes made by the principal to her original order would require a writing to be enforceable under 2-209(3)?

Case 1: She orders an additional ten sandwich boxes.
Case 2: She orders an additional twenty-five sandwich boxes.
Case 3: She substitutes gluten-free brownies for the cookies at an additional cost of twenty-five cents per box.

Problem 4 - 5

Rae sends a purchase order for one hundred cases of pulp produce trays, size 10H, at fifty dollars per case to the packaging company across town. The PO requires delivery within fifteen days. Which, if any, of the following changes to her order would require a writing to be enforceable under 2-209(3)?

Case 1: She orders an additional twenty-five cases.
Case 2: She changes the tray size to 5H for twenty-five of the one hundred cases.
Case 3: She changes the delivery requirement to ten days.

C. No Oral Modification Clauses

Article 2 authorizes the parties to a sale-of-goods transaction to incorporate their own statute of frauds into the contract. 2-209(2) provides that

> a signed agreement which excludes modification ... except by a signed writing cannot be otherwise modified ...

Parties to a sales-of-goods transaction can agree that, notwithstanding the requirements of Article 2, only modifications reduced to a writing signed by the parties will be enforceable. On its face, 2-209(2) seems simple to apply: if the parties include a "no oral modification" clause (NOM) in their contract, then only modifications that are reduced to a writing signed by the parties should be enforced in a subsequent dispute between the parties. But when 2-209(2) is read together with 2-209(4), things get more complicated—at least, the courts have made it more complicated. 2-209(4) provides that

> Although an attempt at modification ... does not satisfy the requirements of subsection (2) or (3), it can operate as a waiver.

In other words, regardless of a provision that precludes modification without a writing signed by the parties (and regardless of whether the modification satisfied Article 2's statute of frauds), an otherwise unenforceable oral modification might be given effect by calling it a waiver.

VALSPAR REFINISH, INC. v. GAYLORD'S, INC.

Supreme Court of Minnesota, 2009
764 N.W.2d 359

DIETZEN, Justice.

Respondent Valspar Refinish, Inc. (Valspar) commenced this action to recover damages arising out of an alleged breach by Gaylord's, Inc. (Gaylord's) of the parties' refinish-coat supply agreement.

Valspar is a wholly-owned subsidiary of Valspar Corporation, a paint-coating supplier headquartered in Minneapolis, Minnesota. Gaylord's is a California corporation that manufactures and sells fiberglass truck-bed lid covers for light trucks, located in Santa Fe Springs, California.

In the spring of 2003, a Valspar representative approached Gaylord's to discuss a possible supply agreement in which Valspar would provide the automobile paint coverings for Gaylord's truck-bed lid accounts. Gaylord's indicated that it would be interested if Valspar could provide a quality product and meet its pricing requirements.

In October 2003, Valspar and Gaylord's entered into a five-year contract. The agreement provided, among other things, that Valspar would be the exclusive supplier for Gaylord's truck-bed lid business and that Valspar would pay $400,000 in the form of a rebate to Gaylord's upon execution of the agreement.

[During the first year of the contract, Gaylord claimed that problems with Valspar's products that it had identified during a testing period prior to the execution of the contract were never resolved despite attempts by Valspar to address them after the contract had been made.]

On November 12, 2004, Gaylord's sent an e-mail to Valspar documenting the problems it experienced with the Valspar products. Gaylord's then stopped buying Valspar products and switched to another supplier, claiming it was losing business and costs were increasing because of corrections needed to resolve problems with the products. In December 2004, Valspar sent a representative to Gaylord's facility in an attempt to resolve the problems. That effort was unsuccessful.

In April 2005, Valspar sued Gaylord's, alleging that Gaylord's breached the contract and seeking return of the rebate, payment of unpaid invoices, and other damages. Gaylord's denied the allegations in the complaint and asserted various counterclaims against Valspar.

Valspar moved for summary judgment, alleging that Gaylord's failed to give written notice of default as required by the contract, and therefore it breached the contract when it stopped purchasing Valspar paint products in November 2004.

* * *

B. Waiver

Alternatively, Gaylord's argues that Valspar waived its right to receive written notice of its various alleged defaults. Specifically, Gaylord's argues that when Valspar met with Gaylord's production personnel to resolve its oral complaints, Valspar tacitly acknowledged its default under the contract and waived its right to receive written notice. Valspar counters that eliminating the requirement of written notice of default is a modification of the contract and is not effective unless it is in writing and signed by both parties. Paragraph 10(a) of the contract states that "[t]his Agreement may be changed only in a written document signed by both parties."

A sales contract clause that requires all contract changes to be in writing is enforceable. *See* Minn. Stat. § 336.2-209(2) ("A signed agreement which excludes modification or rescission except by a signed writing cannot be otherwise modified … ."). But Minn. Stat. § 336.2-209(4) sets forth an exception, providing that "[a]lthough an attempt at modification or rescission does not satisfy the requirements of subsection (2) … it can operate as a waiver." Comment 4 to U.C.C. § 2-209(4) (2004) states "[this section] is intended, despite the provisions of subsection 2 … , to prevent contractual provisions excluding modification except by a signed writing from limiting in other respects the legal effect of the parties' actual later conduct."

Many other courts, including the Minnesota Court of Appeals, have interpreted U.C.C. § 2-209(4) to mean that parties to a sales contract may waive a requirement that any changes to the contract must be in writing and, as a result, waive other contractual requirements without a written agreement. We agree with this interpretation, and conclude that Minn. Stat. § 336.2-209(4) modifies Minn. Stat. § 336.2-209(2). Under subsection 2-209(4), parties to a contract for the sale of goods may waive a contract's requirement that any modification must be in a writing signed by both parties. This exception is narrow, however, and any waiver under subsection 2-209(4) must satisfy the rules and principles of Minnesota law regarding waiver. Minn. Stat. § 336.1-103(b) (2008) ("Unless displaced by the particular provisions of the Uniform Commercial Code, the principles of law and equity … supplement its provisions.").

Minnesota law provides that waiver is "the 'intentional relinquishment of a known right.'" "[I]t is the expression of an intention not to insist on what the law affords." Waiver generally is a question of fact, and "[i]t is rarely to be inferred as a matter of law."

Waiver "is essentially unilateral and results as a legal consequence from some act or conduct of the party against whom it operates, without any act of the party in whose favor it is made being necessary to complete it." Knowledge and intent are essential elements of waiver. But "[t]he requisite knowledge may be actual or constructive and the intent to waive may be inferred from conduct." When a party acts in a way that is inconsistent with the terms of a contract, a fact finder can reasonably conclude that a party waived those contractual provisions.[4]

---

4 There is a split of authority as to whether a party must show detrimental reliance, in addition to the intentional relinquishment of a known right, to establish waiver under UCC 2-209(4). *See, e.g., Wis. Knife Works,* 781 F.2d at 1286-87 (holding that detrimental reliance is necessary to show waiver under section 2-209(4)). *But see BMC Indus., Inc.,* 160 F.3d at 1333 (holding that detrimental reliance is not necessary to show waiver under section 2-209(4)). But that issue is not before us and, therefore, we decline to reach it.

To avoid summary judgment, Gaylord's must present specific facts showing that there is a genuine issue of waiver for trial. Minn. R. Civ. P. 56.05; *see also DLH*, 566 N.W.2d at 71. Gaylord's does not point to any specific statements made by Valspar representatives that it intended to waive the written notice requirements of the contract. And Valspar's conduct does not create a genuine issue of material fact on the issue of waiver. It is true that Valspar employees met with Gaylord's representatives in an effort to correct the paint product problems. But cooperation between businesses to resolve product performance issues under a contract, without more, is insufficient to raise an issue of fact regarding waiver of express terms of an agreement. In short, Valspar's attempts to satisfy its customer, without more, do not indicate an intention to surrender its rights under the contract that all modifications to the contract be in writing. Even when viewed in a light most favorable to Gaylord's, a reasonable jury could not conclude that Valspar waived the contractual requirements that any written changes be in writing and that it receive written notice of any alleged default or breach of warranty. Thus, we conclude that summary judgment was properly entered for Valspar.

Does 2-209(4) mean that *any* oral modification—whether it would operate to "impose an onerous new term" on one party or allow a party to "wiggle out of an onerous term" in the original agreement—can be enforced? *See Wisconsin Knife Works v. National Metal Crafters*, 781 F.2d 1280. If so, 2-209(3) (and 2-209(2) as well) seems superfluous, which, as one court has warned, returns us to the common law "with not even a requirement of consideration to reduce the likelihood of fabricated or unintended oral modifications." *Wisconsin Knife Works*.

As the *Valspar* court notes, Article 2 does not define the term "waiver," and so courts have looked to the common law for answers. But Article 2 also does not define the term "modification" other than to suggest that a modification might also be a waiver—even though waiver and modification are distinct concepts under the common law. As the Supreme Judicial Court of Massachusetts noted:

> common law defines waiver as the "intentional relinquishment of a known right," or, as one commentator has explained, "the excuse of the nonoccurrence of or a delay in the occurrence of a condition of a duty." 2 E.A. Farnsworth, Contracts § 8.5. A modification "is the changing of the terms of the agreement which may diminish or increase the duty of either party." R.A. Anderson, Uniform Commercial Code. While a waiver may be effectuated by one party, a modification "is the result of the bilateral action of both parties to the sales transaction." *Id. Cochran v. Quest Software, Inc.*, 328 F.3d 1, 9 (1st Cir. 2003) ("Under Massachusetts law, the parties to a contract must agree to a modification"). By the plain terms of § 2-209 (5), a waiver is retractable in the absence of reliance. A modification, in contrast, cannot be retracted unilaterally. *BMC Indus., Inc. v. Barth Indus., Inc.*, 160 F.3d 1322, 1334 (11th Cir. 1998), ("while a party that has agreed to a contract modification cannot cancel the modification without giving consideration for the cancellation, a party may unilaterally retract its waiver of a contract term provided it gives reasonable notice"). See 2A R.A. Anderson, Uniform Commercial Code, ("Unilateral action by a party cannot restore the contract to its original premodified form").
>
> *Dynamic Machine Works, Inc. v. Mach. & Elec. Consultants, Inc.*, 444 Mass. at 771–72.

But 2-209(4) only applies to "attempted" modifications. I could unilaterally "attempt" to modify a contract to which I am a party—could my unilateral "attempt" operate as a waiver and be used against me? At least one court has rejected this proposition:

> The term "attempt at modification" has the potential to mislead in this context. One might construe this phrase to mean that a mere effort to modify a contract is an "attempt at

modification." However, we believe the better construction of the phrase "attempt at modification" is that it contemplates a completed oral modification of a written contract which
prohibits oral modification. In other words, because [2-209(2)] requires contract modifications be in writing, a completed oral agreement to modify a written contract is viewed as
an "attempt" to modify the contract; the statutes uses the word "attempt" only in the sense
that an oral agreement to modify may or may not be recognized as a binding modification.

Royster-Clark, Inc. v. Olsen's Mill, Inc., 2005 Wisc. App. LEXIS 584.

Such a restrictive view of modifications which may become waivers may not be justified in light of
Comment 4 to 2-209, which affirms the primacy that Article 2 generally gives conduct over the paper
created by the parties:

> Subsection (4) is intended, despite the provisions of subsections (2) and (3), to prevent
> contractual provisions excluding modification except by a signed writing from limiting in
> other respects the legal effect of the parties' actual later conduct.

Valspar did not address another issue that has split the courts: must there be reliance on an attempted
modification before it can operate as a waiver? Subsection 4 does not expressly require reliance to make
a waiver enforceable, but courts have inferred such a requirement based on 2-209(5), which permits
retraction of a subsection 4 waiver

> unless the retraction would be unjust in view of a material change of position in reliance on
> the waiver.

The better view—indeed, the only view based on the plain language of 2-209, is that reliance is not
required for a failed modification to be effective as a waiver. As the Eleventh Circuit in *BMC Industry v.
Barth Industry* explained:

> Although other courts have held that waiver requires reliance under the UCC, those courts
> have ignored the UCC's plain language. The leading case espousing this view of waiver is
> *Wisconsin Knife Works* in which a panel of the Seventh Circuit addressed a contract that
> included a term prohibiting oral modifications, and considered whether an attempted oral
> modification could instead constitute a waiver. Writing for the majority, Judge Posner
> concluded that the UCC's subsection (2), which gives effect to "no oral modification" pro-
> visions, would become superfluous if contract terms could be waived without detrimental
> reliance. Judge Posner reasoned that if attempted oral modifications that were unenforce-
> able because of subsection (2) were nevertheless enforced as waivers under subsection (4),
> then subsection (2) is "very nearly a dead letter." According to Judge Posner, there must
> be some difference between modification and waiver in order for both subsections (2) and
> (4) to have meaning. This difference is waiver's detrimental reliance requirement. Judge
> Posner, however, ignores a fundamental difference between modifications and waivers:
> while a party that has agreed to a contract modification cannot cancel the modification
> without giving consideration for the cancellation, a party may unilaterally retract its waiver
> of a contract term provided it gives reasonable notice. The fact that waivers may unilater-
> ally be retracted provides the difference between subsections (2) and (4) that allows both
> to have meaning.

The Court went on to hold

> that the UCC does not require consideration or detrimental reliance for waiver of a contract
> term. Our conclusion follows from the plain language of subsections [2-209(4) and (5)].

While subsection (4) states that an attempted modification that fails may still constitute a waiver, subsection (5) provides that the waiver may be retracted *unless* the non-waiving party relies on the waiver. Consequently, the statute recognizes that waivers may exist in the absence of detrimental reliance—these are the retractable waivers referred to in subsection (5). Only this interpretation renders meaning to subsection (5), because reading subsection (4) to require detrimental reliance for all waivers means that waivers would *never* be retractable. *See Wisconsin Knife Works* (Easterbrook, J., dissenting) (noting that reading a detrimental reliance requirement into the UCC would eliminate the distinction between subsections (4) and (5)). Subsection (5) would therefore be meaningless.

160 F.3d 1333–34.

PROBLEM 4 - 6

Rae agreed to purchase a Hobart PS40 labeling scale for the meat department at the store. The contract with Hobart provided that "claims for extras positively will not be allowed unless ordered in writing." Before the scale was delivered, Rae called Hobart and asked if it would "throw in" a bottom-label applier and a one-year supply of the company's ITW special labels. The Hobart representative said, "Sure, you've been such a good customer over the years, it's the least we can do." The scale was delivered without the label applier, and the labels supplied were not ITW labels. When Rae called and asked when the label applier and labels the company had promised her would be delivered, the representative told her that since the "extras" were not part of the written agreement, the company was not obligated to provide them, even though the representative had agreed to "throw them in" with the scale. Can Rae enforce the oral promise for extras? 2-209(2).

D. EXCUSE

At their most basic level, contracts are about the future. By agreeing today what they will do for each other in the future, the parties to a contract are trying to exercise some form of control over their future—or at least what they are today predicting that future will look like. And of course, their predictions about the future will be based on their expectations—their assumptions—about what will happen between today and that future time of performance. But what if things don't go as expected—their assumptions turn out to be wrong—and as a result the deal turns out much better for one party and much worse for the other party: should the law intervene and reset the bargain struck by the parties? Are failed assumptions part of the risk assumed by the parties when they try to predict the future? Should it matter whether the party adversely affected could have contractually protected itself from the risk that its assumptions might be wrong?

Common-law courts eventually decided to intervene, but only in limited situations—where the failed assumption or changed circumstances made it impossible for the party adversely affected to perform. Thus, when performance became unlawful as a result of a change in the law after the contract was made, when the subject matter of the contract was destroyed by no fault of the party, or when the promisor had passed away before the time for her performance, the courts would step in and relieve the adversely affected party of her contractual obligations, but only when performance had become physically impossible. And the impossibility alleged had to be objective rather than subjective: it was not enough to show merely that you could not do it—you had to show that no one could do it.

By the time Article 2 was in the works, some courts had moved away from the requirement of actual physical impossibility:

A thing is impossible in legal contemplation when it is not practicable; and a thing is impracticable when it can only be done at an excessive and unreasonable cost.

Mineral Park Land co. v. Howard, 172 Cal. At 293.

Article 2 openly embraces the move from impossibility to impracticability in 2-615. The Comments explain:

This section excuses a seller from timely delivery of goods contracted for, where his performance has become commercially impracticable because of unforeseen supervening circumstances not within the contemplation of the parties at the time of contracting … . The additional test of commercial impracticability (as contrasted with "impossibility," …) has been adopted to call attention to the commercial character of the criterion chosen by this Article.

Comments 1 and 3, 2-615.

The following case explains the basics of impracticability under 2-615.

MISHARA CONSTR. CO. V. TRANSIT—MIXED CONCRETE CORP.

SUPREME JUDICIAL COURT OF MASSACHUSETTS, 1974
365 MASS. 122

REARDON, Justice.

In this action of contract a verdict was returned for the defendant. The case is here on the plaintiff's exceptions.

The plaintiff Mishara Construction Company, Inc. (Mishara) was the general contractor under contract with the Pittsfield Housing Authority for the construction of Rose Manor, a housing project for the elderly. In September, 1966, the plaintiff negotiated with the defendant Transit-Mixed Concrete Corp. (Transit) for the supplying of ready-mixed concrete to be used on the project. An agreement was reached that Transit would supply all the concrete needed on the project at a price of $13.25 a cubic yard, with deliveries to be made at the times and in the amounts as ordered by Mishara. This agreement was evidenced by a purchase order signed by the parties on September 21, 1966. That purchase order identified the Rose Manor project and indicated that delivery was to be made "[a]s required by Mishara Construction Company." Performance under this contract was satisfactory to both parties until April, 1967. In that month a labor dispute disrupted work on the job site. Although work resumed on June 15, 1967, a picket line was maintained on the site until the completion of the project in 1969. Throughout this period, with very few exceptions, no deliveries of concrete were made by Transit notwithstanding frequent requests by Mishara. After notifying Transit of its intention, Mishara purchased the balance of its concrete requirements elsewhere. Mishara sought in damages the additional cost of concrete incurred by virtue of the higher price of the replacement product, as well as the expenses of locating an alternate source.

The remainder of the plaintiff's exceptions relate to the proffered defense of the impossibility of performance.

* * *

We are asked to decide as matter of law and without reference to individual facts and circumstances that "picket lines, strikes or labor difficulties" provide no excuse for nonperformance by way of impossibility. This is too sweeping a statement of the law and we decline to adopt it.

The excuse of impossibility in contracts for the sale of goods is controlled by the appropriate section of the Uniform Commercial Code, G. L. c. 106, § 2-615.[5] That section sets up two requirements before performance may be excused. First, the performance must have become "impracticable." Second, the impracticability must have been caused "by the occurrence of a contingency the nonoccurrence of which was a basic assumption on which the contract was made."

With respect to the requirement that performance must have been impracticable, the official Code comment to the section stresses that the reference is to "commercial impracticability" as opposed to strict impossibility. This is not a radical departure from the common law of contracts as interpreted by this court. Although a strict rule was originally followed denying any excuse for accident or "inevitable necessity," e.g., *Adams* v. *Nichols*, 19 Pick. 275 (1837), it has long been assumed that circumstances drastically increasing the difficulty and expense of the contemplated performance may be within the compass of "impossibility." By adopting the term "impracticability" rather than "impossibility" the drafters of the Code appear to be in accord with Professor Williston who stated that "the essence of the modern defense of impossibility is that the promised performance was at the making of the contract, or thereafter became, impracticable owing to some extreme or unreasonable difficulty, expense, injury, or loss involved, rather than that it is scientifically or actually impossible."

The second criterion of the excuse, that the intervening circumstance be one which the parties assumed would not occur, is also familiar to the law of Massachusetts. The rule is essentially aimed at the distribution of certain kinds of risks in the contractual relationship. By directing the inquiry to the time when the contract was first made, we really seek to determine whether the risk of the intervening circumstance was one which the parties may be taken to have assigned between themselves. It is, of course, the very essence of contract that it is directed at the elimination of some risks for each party in exchange for others. Each receives the certainty of price, quantity, and time, and assumes the risk of changing market prices, superior opportunity, or added costs. It is implicit in the doctrine of impossibility (and the companion rule of "frustration of purpose") that certain risks are so unusual and have such severe consequences that they must have been beyond the scope of the assignment of risks inherent in the contract, that is, beyond the agreement made by the parties. To require performance in that case would be to grant the promisee an advantage for which he could not be said to have bargained in making the contract. "The important question is whether an unanticipated circumstance has made performance of the promise vitally different from what should reasonably have been within the contemplation of both parties when they entered into the contract. If so, the risk should not fairly be thrown upon the promisor." The emphasis in contracts governed by the Uniform Commercial Code is on the commercial context in which the agreement was made. The question is, given the commercial circumstances in which the parties dealt: Was the contingency which developed one which the parties could reasonably be thought to have foreseen as a real possibility which could affect performance? Was it one of that variety of risks which the parties were tacitly assigning to the promisor by their failure to provide for it explicitly? If it was, performance will be required. If it could not be so considered, performance is excused. The contract cannot be reasonably thought to govern in these circumstances, and the parties are both thrown upon the resources of the open market without the benefit of their contract.

With this backdrop, we consider Mishara's contention that a labor dispute which makes performance more difficult never constitutes an excuse for nonperformance. We think it is evident that in some

---

5   "Excuse by Failure of Presupposed Conditions." Except so far as a seller may have assumed a greater obligation and subject to the preceding section on substituted performance "(a) Delay in delivery or non-delivery in whole or in part by a seller who complies with paragraphs (b) and (c) is not a breach of his duty under a contract for sale if performance as agreed has been made impracticable by the occurrence of a contingency the non-occurrence of which was a basic assumption on which the contract was made or by compliance in good faith with any applicable foreign or domestic governmental regulation or order whether or not it later proves to be invalid."

situations a labor dispute would not meet the requirements for impossibility discussed above. A picket line might constitute a mere inconvenience and hardly make performance "impracticable." Likewise, in certain industries with a long record of labor difficulties, the nonoccurrence of strikes and picket lines could not fairly be said to be a basic assumption of the agreement. Certainly, in general, labor disputes cannot be considered extraordinary in the course of modern commerce. Admitting this, however, we are still far from the proposition implicit in the plaintiff's requests. Much must depend on the facts known to the parties at the time of contracting with respect to the history of and prospects for labor difficulties during the period of performance of the contract, as well as the likely severity of the effect of such disputes on the ability to perform. From these facts it is possible to draw an inference as to whether or not the parties intended performance to be carried out even in the face of the labor difficulty. Where the probability of a labor dispute appears to be practically nil, and where the occurrence of such a dispute provides unusual difficulty, the excuse of impracticability might well be applicable. Thus in discussing the defense of impossibility, then Chief Judge Cardozo noted an excuse would be provided "conceivably in some circumstances by unavoidable strikes." The many variables, which may bear on the question in individual cases, were canvassed by Professor Williston in Williston, and he concluded that the trend of the law is toward recognizing strikes as excuses for nonperformance. We agree with the statement of the judge in *Badhwar* v. *Colorado Fuel & Iron Corp.* 138 F. Supp. 595, 607 (S. D. N. Y. 1955), on the same question: "Rather than mechanically apply any fixed rule of law, where the parties themselves have not allocated responsibility, justice is better served by appraising all of the circumstances, the part the various parties played, and thereon determining liability." Since the instructions requested by the plaintiff and the exclusion of the evidence objected to would have precluded such a factual determination, the requests were more properly refused, and the evidence was properly admitted.

Exceptions overruled.

Courts applying 2-615 generally agree that a party claiming excuse under 2-615 must establish some combination of the following:

> (1) that an unforeseeable event occurred; (2) the nonoccurrence of the event was a basic assumption underlying the agreement; (3) the event rendered performance impracticable; and (4) the party seeking to be excused was not responsible for the occurrence of the event..

See, e.g., Chainworks, Inc. v. Webco Industries, 2006 U.S. Dist. LEXIS 9194. But, as in the *Mishara* case, the foreseeability factor tends to dominate the focus of their analysis. In *Waldinger Corp. v. Ashbrook-Simon-Hartley*, the court proclaimed:

> The applicability of the defense of commercial impracticability ... . turns largely on foreseeability. The relevant inquiry is whether the risk of the occurrence of the contingency was so unusual or unforeseen and the consequences of the occurrence of the contingency so severe that to require performance is to grant the buyer an advantage he did not bargain for in the contract.
>
> 775 F.2d at 786.

These courts seem to presume that if a risk was foreseeable but not addressed in the contract, it was assumed by the party against whom it operates and therefore its occurrence is not grounds for excusing the party's performance under 2-615.

> This, however, is an incomplete and sometimes misleading test. Anyone can foresee, in some general sense, a whole variety of potential calamities, but that does not mean he or she will

deem them worth bargaining over. The risk may be too remote, the party may not have suffi-cient bargaining power, or neither party may have any superior ability to avoid the harm ... . So, while the risk of an unforeseeable event can safely be deemed not to have been assumed by the promisor, the converse is not necessarily true. Properly seen, then, foreseeability, while perhaps the most important factor, is at best one fact to be considered in resolving first how likely the occurrence of the event in question was and, second, whether its occurrence, based on past experience, was of such reasonable likelihood that the obligor should not merely foresee the risk but, because of the degree of its likelihood, the obligor should have guarded against it or provided for non-liability against the risk.

Specialty Tires of America v. CIT Group/Equipment Financing, 82 F. Supp. 2d at 438–39.

Excuse under 2-615 is most commonly invoked by sellers whose costs of performance have radically increased or whose source of supply has failed. Source-of-supply failures have fared slightly better than increased-cost-of-performance claims under 2-615. Increased cost of performance is an inherent risk in most fixed-price contracts—and therefore not usually a contingency the nonoccurrence of which can be claimed as a basic assumption of the parties:

> [A] fixed-price contract is an explicit assignment of the risk of market price increases to the seller and the risk of market price decreases to the buyer, ... If ... the buyer forecasts the market incorrectly and therefore finds himself locked into a disadvantageous contract, he has only himself to blame and so cannot shift the risk back to the seller by invoking impos-sibility.... Since "the very purpose of a fixed-price contract is to place the risk of increased costs on the promisor (and the risk of decreased costs on the promisee)", the fact that costs decrease steeply cannot allow the buyer to walk away from the contract.
>
> *Northern Indiana Public Services v. Carbon County Coal Co.*, 799 F.2d at 278.

Conversely, source-of-supply failures directly implicate a basic assumption of the parties, at least where the circumstances show that a particular source of supply was contemplated or assumed by the parties at the time of contracting. 2-615 Comments 5 and 6 (2-615 applies "where a particular source of supply is exclusive under the agreement and fails through casualty"). Even then, "there is no excuse under [2-615] unless the seller has employed all due measures to assure himself that his source will not fail." 2-615 Comment 5.

PROBLEM 4 - 7

Rae contracted with a California winemaker to purchase one thousand cases of red wine made from Pinot Noir grapes grown in the winemaker's vineyard in Napa Valley during the 2015 growing season. Because of the severe drought in California, the 2015 yield of Pinot Noir grapes from the seller's Napa Valley property was 80 percent less than usual. As a result, the seller was only able to deliver two hundred cases of the wine it had agreed to sell to the store. The seller could have purchased the Pinot Noir grapes it needed to produce the other eight hundred cases of wine from vineyards in northern California or Oregon, but it chose not to do so. Is the seller excused from delivering the other eight hundred cases of wine because of the drought? What if supplemental irrigation that would have prevented the diminished yield was not available because the Napa Valley Water Authority had shut off water to the vineyard because the winemaker refused to comply with local conservation regulations? 2-615.

PROBLEM 4 - 8

Would your answer in Problem 4 - 7 be different if the seller had been a wine broker rather than a winemaker and had contracted to sell Rae one thousand cases of red wine made from Pinot Noir grapes grown by the same vineyard, but was unable to procure one thousand cases of the wine because of the drought? What if the contract only required that the wine be made from grapes grown in Napa Valley? Would it matter if the wine required under the broker's contract with Rae was available, but at a price that exceeded the price Rae was required to pay for it under the contract? 2-615.

PROBLEM 4 - 9

The local produce warehouse agreed to sell the store five hundred cases of bananas to be delivered by September 1. Bananas are imported from various locations in Central America through the port of Los Angles. The warehouse could not deliver the bananas on September 1 because a strike by dock workers in Los Angles prevented bananas and all other fruit from being unloaded off of any ship docked at the port of Los Angles. Is the warehouse excused from performing because of the dock workers' strike? Would your answer be different if the contract with the warehouse provided:

> Neither party is liable for failure to perform its obligations where such failure is the result of an act of God, including, but not limited to, flood, hurricane, fire, earthquake or other natural disaster, civil war, military invasion, embargo, labor dispute or strike, failure of electricity or other public services.

As the problems illustrate, 2-615 does not create any bright lines or categories that might guide courts in its application. But the Comments provided fair warning:

> The present section deliberately refrains from any effort at an exhaustive expression of contingencies and is to be interpreted in all cases sought to be brought within its scope in terms of underlying reason and purpose.
>
> 2-615 Comment 2.

Instead, 2-615

> seeks to accommodate the law to sound commercial sense and practice. Courts must decide the point at which the community's interest in predictable contract enforcement shall yield to the fact that enforcement of a particular contract would be commercially senseless and unjust. The spirit of the Code is that such decisions cannot justly derive from legal abstractions. They must derive from courts sensitive to the mores, practices and habits of thought in the respectable commercial world.
>
> *ALCOA v. Essex Group*, 499 F. Supp. At 72.

Unfortunately, as White and Summers have noted, these "sensitivities" of the courts have resulted in cases that "are full of weasel words such as 'severe' shortage, 'marked' increase, 'basic' assumptions, and 'force majeure'," and "it remains impossible to predict with accuracy how the law will apply to a variety of relatively common cases."[6] Others have described the doctrine of impracticability developed by the courts under 2-615 as "largely incoherent."[7]

---

6 White and Summers, *Uniform Commercial Code*, (6th ed., 2010) at 181.

7 Sirianni, "The Developing Law of Contractual Impracticability and Impossibility: Part 1," 14 *UCC L. J.* 30 (1981).

Consequently, according to White and Summers:

> Students who have concluded a first-year contracts course in confusion about the doctrine of impossibility and have since had difficulty mastering 2-615 or have found the that cases somehow slip through their fingers when they try to apply them to new situations, may take comfort in knowing that they are in good company.[8]

---

8 *Uniform Commercial Code* at 181.

CHAPTER 5

REMEDIES FOR BREACH

Once parties have an enforceable agreement, each becomes legally obligated to perform the obligations it has undertaken in the agreement. Failure to do so will constitute a breach of the agreement, and under Article 2 will give the nonbreaching party a claim for relief—often in the form of a claim for damages—but relief can take other forms. In this chapter, we examine the relief—the remedies—Article 2 provides to the nonbreaching party in the event of a breach.

A contract for the sale of goods requires the seller to transfer and deliver goods to the buyer and the buyer to accept those goods and pay for them as required by the contract. 2-301. A seller breaches a sale-of-goods contract when it does not transfer and deliver the goods called for in the contract to the buyer when required by the contract. A buyer breaches a sales contract when it takes the goods and does not pay for them. A buyer also can breach a sales contract by wrongfully refusing to take the goods when delivered by the seller. But a breach can also occur before the time for performance set by the contract if one of the parties announces it will not perform as required when the time arrives. Prospective nonperformance—what we call anticipatory repudiation—if accepted by the other party, is treated the same under the remedial provisions of Article 2 as failure to perform at the time required by the contract. And a breach also can occur, even though a party has performed, when that performance is not in accord with the requirements of the contract—if the seller delivers goods that do not conform to the requirements of the contract or are defective, the seller has breached the contract.

In this chapter, we will examine the remedies available under Article 2 for nonperformance and prospective nonperformance. We will examine the remedies for defective performance in Chapters 7 and 8.

Part 7 of Article 2 is where we find the remedies for breach and the rules for using them. Buyers and sellers each have their own sets of remedies which, for the most part, mirror one another. Here again, we see the guiding hand of Llewellyn at work, shaping the remedies and their measures of damages to reflect the commercial realities present when breach occurs. This meant not only putting the nonbreaching party in the position it would have been in had there not been a breach—remember your Contracts course—but also doing so quickly and efficiently, with speed and efficiency requiring different metrics depending on whether the nonbreaching party was the buyer or the seller. Breach by the seller means the buyer does not have the goods it expected to get from the seller's performance. A system of remedies that does not provide the buyer a meaningful opportunity to get the goods from the seller or to purchase substitute goods without penalty would not meet Llewellyn's objectives for the modern commercial transaction. Breach by the buyer means the seller is stuck with goods it did not expect to have beyond the time for its performance under the contract. A system of remedies that does not allow the seller to dispose of those goods without penalty—especially the lost volume seller, also would not meet Llewellyn's objectives for the commercial realities to which the new sales law would apply.

Article 2 does all of this and more, as we will see in this chapter. Part 7 empowers the nonbreaching party—whether buyer or seller—to call off the contract, to require the other party to perform, or to recover damages for the breach. It also allows the parties to contract out of Article 2 remedies—to provide their own remedies and measures of damages for a breach of their agreement.[1] Article 2 gives both buyers and sellers the option of obtaining substitute performance from a third party without penalty when the other party breaches. It provides specific formulae for calculating both buyers' and sellers' damages; these are intended to replicate, for sales-of-goods transactions, the expectancy measure of common law and take into account which party ends up with the goods. And the parties also may limit or alter how damages are calculated under Article 2 itself.

Of course, standing watch over Article 2's remedial provisions is 1-305(a), which commands:

> The remedies provided by [the Uniform Commercial Code] must be liberally administered to the end that the aggrieved party may be put in as good a position as if the other party had fully performed ...

In a preamble to the remedies section of his second draft of what became Article 2, Llewellyn set out the basic principles upon which he built the system of remedies we now find in Article 2. They reflect "Llewellyn's belief that legal rules must relate to the facts and must fit the realities of the transactions they govern."[2] They also provide a background against which Article 2's remedial provisions must be interpreted:

> (1) The principles which underlie the sections and particular provisions on remedies ... are that the remedy shall be adequate, flexible, and as direct and speedy as may be, and that the party entitled to remedy shall be protected in the exercise of reasonable judgment in good faith.

> (2) On the other hand, the remedy shall not be oppressive; unnecessary waste, loss, or expense are to be eliminated or reduced.

> (3) (a) The seller's remedies are founded on the principle that his contract entitles him to rely on receiving, net, the value to him of the price, in return for conforming goods, duly delivered.

> (b) the buyer's remedies are founded on the principle that his contract entitles him to rely on receiving, net, the value to him of conforming goods duly delivered for use or resale, in return for the price.

> Section 56-A, Revised Uniform Sales Act (1941, Second Draft).[3]

---

1   Peters, "Remedies for Breach of Contract Relating to the Sale of Goods Under the Uniform Commercial Code: A Roadmap for Article 2," 73 *Yale L.J.* 199, 204 (1963).

2   Wiseman, "The Limits of Vision: Karl Llewellyn and the Merchant Rules," 100 *Harvard L. Rev.* 465, 469 (1986).

3   I Kelly, *Uniform Commercial Code: Drafts,* (Rothman 1984) 513.

A. Prospective Nonperformance: Anticipatory Repudiation and Insecurity

The doctrine of anticipatory repudiation—that a party could breach a contract before the time it was required to perform under that contract—was hardly new when Llewellyn was drafting his sales law. And it was a good fit in a law that was, in part, intended to accommodate the practical needs of parties engaged in the buying and selling of goods.

When the seller repudiates, the uncertainty created for the buyer disrupts its business plan—it's not going to have the goods it planned to use or pass along to its customers. If the buyer cannot immediately act to protect its interests without risk of liability to the breaching seller, it loses the opportunity to mitigate its losses by finding substitute goods and avoiding additional costs under the broken contract. A seller's business is also disrupted by the uncertainty that follows from a buyer's repudiation. A buyer's repudiation leaves the seller holding goods it did not expect to have but now has to deal with and without the money it expected would be available to pay its costs and fund its operations. Like the buyer, the seller needs the flexibility to act quickly without fear of liability to protect its interests. The doctrine of anticipatory repudiation empowers the nonrepudiating party to terminate the contract and move on with its life.

Article 2's predecessor, the Uniform Sales Act, did recognize anticipatory repudiations but made it difficult for an aggrieved party to predict how a court might interpret any action it took, and it also protected sellers better than buyers. Llewellyn's reformulation of anticipatory repudiation for sales-of-goods contracts is set out in 2-610. It gives both buyers and sellers the right to claim a repudiation by the other party and requires that the performance repudiated substantially impair the value of the contract to the nonrepudiating party. It also makes clear what the aggrieved party's options are for responding to a repudiation. As the next case notes, 2-610 leaves it to the courts to determine what constitutes a "repudiation" and when the loss of a repudiated performance "substantially impairs" the value of the contract to the nonrepudiating party.

Upton v. Ginn

Court of Appeals of Kentucky, 2007
231 S.W.3d 788

ABRAMSON, Judge.

Upton, on behalf of Lloyd's of London, appeals from the April 5, 2005 Findings of Fact and Conclusions of Law entered by the Montgomery Circuit Court finding that Elden Ginn and Elden Ginn Tobacco Warehouses, Inc. (collectively "Ginn") did not repudiate a contract to purchase tobacco from Lloyd's, and further adjudging Lloyd's liable to Ginn for wrongfully selling a portion of that tobacco to a third party after it had previously been sold to Ginn. Finding no error, we affirm.

On February 6, 1998, the weight of new-fallen snow caused the roof of the Farmers Tobacco Warehouse in Mt. Sterling, Kentucky, to collapse. At the time, the warehouse was filled with hundreds of thousands of pounds of tobacco awaiting sale. Both the warehouse and its contents were insured by Lloyd's. In an attempt to salvage at least some of the tobacco, Lloyd's held a sealed-bid auction ten days following the warehouse collapse. Ginn was among the bidders.

Following an inspection of the tobacco, Ginn successfully submitted the high bid for the tobacco, $0.71 per pound. On February 20, 1998, Ginn tendered a check to Lloyd's in the amount of $177,500.00, representing advance payment of one-half of the estimated value of the damaged tobacco. When Ginn arrived three days later to begin the process of removing the tobacco, he concluded that between 10,000 and 12,000 pounds of "good tobacco" had already been removed from the warehouse and replaced with poor quality "junk" tobacco. Nonetheless, Ginn's employees began preparing and removing the tobacco using pallets, a forklift and a tobacco press that were brought in for the task. The process continued between February 23–28, 1998, with an additional load being removed on March 3. Ginn then advised Lloyd's that he would not be able to remove any tobacco during the period March 4–8, 1998, due to a previously scheduled machinery show in Maysville, Kentucky, that he was sponsoring. Ginn also indicated that removal had to cease during the show because his equipment was needed for use in conjunction with the show, and further because his available storage space for the tobacco was temporarily filled with show-related equipment. When Ginn removed his employees and his equipment from the Mt. Sterling warehouse to Maysville, he left behind approximately forty-three pallets of tobacco (approximately 90,000 pounds) that were ready for removal as well as numerous additional empty pallets and thousands of pounds of stacked but not yet palleted tobacco.

Upon the return of Ginn's representative to the tobacco warehouse following the conclusion of the machinery show, he discovered that the doors were chained and locked. Ginn subsequently learned that during his absence, Lloyd's had sold the remaining tobacco to a third party, Mack Bailey, at the rate of $0.05 per pound. Lloyd's subsequently initiated this action against Ginn, contending that it was forced to sell the tobacco because Ginn repudiated his contract and abandoned the remaining tobacco.

Lloyd's sought to recover from Ginn the difference between the unpaid contract amount and the amount actually received from Bailey.

Following a bench trial, the trial court rendered Findings of Fact and Conclusions of Law on April 5, 2005, in which it found that Ginn did not abandon its contract and Lloyd's had no authority to resell to Bailey any of the tobacco Ginn had previously purchased. The trial court further found that Lloyd's sale to Bailey was not commercially reasonable because Lloyd's failed to provide any notice of it to Ginn. Ginn was awarded $16,506.79, representing the amount that Ginn had paid for tobacco that he did not receive. This appeal followed.

Lloyd's argues that the trial court's findings were erroneous in that Ginn himself testified that he repudiated the contract. According to Lloyd's, Ginn testified at trial that he refused to remove all of the tobacco he had purchased unless Lloyd's agreed to adjust the price to reflect the alleged disappearance of approximately 12,000 pounds of high quality tobacco shortly after the auction. Characterizing Ginn's testimony as proof of his intention to repudiate the contract, Lloyd's contends that it was justified in treating the tobacco remaining in the warehouse as abandoned and, consequently, in offering it for sale to a third party.

Whether a contract has been anticipatorily repudiated is a question of fact. However, in making that factual determination, the fact-finder must be guided by Kentucky law regarding anticipatory repudiation.

KRS 355.2-610 provides:

> When either party repudiates the contract with respect to a performance not yet due the loss of which will substantially impair the value of the contract to the other, the aggrieved party may
>
> (a) for a commercially reasonable time await performance by the repudiating party;
>
> or
>
> (b) resort to any remedy for breach (KRS 355.2-703 or 355.2-711), even though he has notified the repudiating party that he would await the latter's performance and has urged retraction; and

(c) in either case suspend his own performance or proceed in accordance with the provisions of this article on the seller's right to identify goods to the contract notwithstanding breach or to salvage unfinished goods

The Official Comment to this section states that "anticipatory repudiation centers upon an overt communication of intention or an action which renders performance impossible or demonstrates a clear determination not to continue with performance." The words or facts alleged to constitute the anticipatory repudiation must be "unequivocal."

Turning then to the record, we first note that Ginn, in fact, did testify during the trial that he wanted an adjustment of the contract price due to his belief that over 10,000 pounds of high quality tobacco had been removed from the warehouse subsequent to the auction but before he began removal. Ginn also testified that without the price adjustment he would not remove the poor quality tobacco he termed "junk," *i.e.*, that tobacco he believed was placed in the location where the missing high quality tobacco originally was located. Despite the disagreement over the alleged missing tobacco and the price adjustment, however, Ginn also repeatedly stated during his testimony that he never intended to repudiate the contract or abandon the almost 100,000 pounds of tobacco remaining at the warehouse when he removed his equipment for use in his machinery show. Several times during his testimony he noted that between 40 and 50 pallets were fully loaded with good tobacco and awaiting transport when the previously scheduled machinery show temporarily halted the removal work. In addition to the palleted tobacco, Ginn also testified that he left in the warehouse a quantity of empty pallets that were intended for use after the machinery show as well as tens of thousands of additional pounds of tobacco that had not yet been placed on them.

Clearly, the evidence before the trial court does not reflect an unequivocal intent on Ginn's part to repudiate his contract. On the contrary, Ginn's testimony demonstrates a dispute over a small percentage—less than 2%—of the tobacco purchased by him at the auction. His testimony also reveals that he did not intend to abandon the vast majority of the tobacco that was ultimately sold by Lloyd's to Bailey. Thus, because there is "substantial and credible evidence" supporting the trial court's findings, we are foreclosed from setting them aside on appeal.

Lloyd's next asserts that, even if Ginn did not expressly admit in his testimony that he abandoned the tobacco in the warehouse, his conduct constituted an anticipatory repudiation as a matter of law. According to Lloyd's, because Ginn expressly refused to remove the poor quality tobacco without an adjustment in the selling price, he necessarily breached the entire contract which required him to remove *all* of the tobacco. We disagree.

Under Kentucky law, the doctrine of anticipatory repudiation "requires unequivocal words or conduct evidencing an intent to repudiate the contract." As discussed above, the evidence before the trial court does not indicate Ginn's "unequivocal" intent to repudiate his contract with Lloyd's. Rather, both his testimony and his actions (*e.g.*, leaving palleted tobacco and empty pallets in the tobacco warehouse during the machinery sale and returning thereafter to continue with the removal) indicate an intent on his part to continue performance of his contractual obligations by removing the vast majority of the remaining tobacco from the warehouse.

Moreover, as quoted, *supra*, KRS 355.2-610 provides that in order for a party to a contract to take action based upon the alleged anticipatory repudiation of the contract by the other party, the other party's failure of performance must "substantially impair the value of the contract" to the party claiming the breach. There is *no* evidence in the record that had Ginn refused to remove the small quantity of allegedly substituted poor quality tobacco the value of the contract to Lloyd's would have been "substantially impair[ed]." There is also nothing in the record suggesting that if Lloyd's had refused to agree to a price adjustment that Ginn would have then refused to pay the full contract amount; Ginn simply refused to load and transport away the small percentage of poor quality tobacco—less than

2%—that he believed was substituted for good quality tobacco. Moreover, to the extent Lloyd's asserts that rejection of the poor quality tobacco substantially impaired the value of the contract, its position is undermined by the fact that Bailey, the subsequent purchaser, also did not remove the disputed poor quality tobacco but left it to be buried when the damaged warehouse was demolished. Under these circumstances we do not find that, as a matter of law, Ginn's actions constituted an anticipatory repudiation of the contract.

At common law, a repudiation requires a definite and unequivocal statement of intent not to perform when the time for performance arrives. Like the *Upton* court, most courts have read the language of Comment 1 as incorporating a similar standard into 2-610:

> anticipatory repudiation centers upon an overt communication of intention or an action which renders performance impossible or demonstrates a clear determination not to continue with performance.

Comment 1, 2-610. *See, e.g., Mextel, Inc. v. Air-Shields, Inc.*, 2005 U.S. Dist. LEXIS 1281, *53 (E.D. Pa. 2005) (Hill-Rom's December 16 letter did not manifest a definite and unequivocal refusal to perform an obligation not yet due); *Solow v. NW Airlines (in re Midway Airlines)*, 180 B.R. 851, 924 (Bankr. N.D. Ill. 1995) (intent to repudiate must be definite and unequivocal; doubtful and indefinite statements that performance may or may not take place are not enough to constitute anticipatory repudiation); *Roussalis v. Wyo. Med. Ctr., Inc.*, 4 P.3d 209, 254 (Wyo. 2000) (repudiation consists of a statement that the repudiating party cannot or will not perform and must be sufficiently positive to be reasonably understood as meaning that the breach will actually occur); *Inamed Corp. v. Kuzmak*, 275 F. Supp. 2d 1100, 1130 (C.D. Cal. 2002) (an anticipatory breach occurs when a party expressly and unequivocally refuses to perform); *Moncrief v. Williston Basin Interstate Pipeline Co.*, 880 F. Supp. 1495, 1506 (D. Wyo. 1995) (in order to predicate a cause of action upon an anticipatory breach, the words or conduct evidencing the breach must be unequivocal and positive in nature); *in re Asia Global Crossing, Ltd.*, 326 B.R. 240, 249 (Bankr. S.D.N.Y. 2005) (for a statement to constitute an anticipatory breach, the announcement of an intention not to perform [must be] positive and unequivocal); *Am. Bronze Corp. v. Streamway Products*, 8 Ohio App. 3d 223, 228, 456 N.E.2d 1295, 1301 (1982) (indication of determination not to perform must be definite and unequivocal); *Gilmore v. Duderstadt*, 1998-NMCA-086, ¶ 16, 125 N.M. 330, 335, 961 P.2d 175, 180 (repudiation must rise to the level of a distinct, unequivocal, and absolute refusal to perform). Whether a party's statement of intent not to perform rises to the level of definiteness and unequivocalness required will depend on the circumstances—a demand by one party that the other do more than required under the contract by itself is not a repudiation, but if the party demanding more conditions its continued performance on acquiescence to the demand, a repudiation occurs. Comment 2, 2-610. The line between chiseling and repudiation cannot be drawn in the abstract.

Repudiation by conduct is subject to a different standard—although not the impossibility standard suggested in Comment 1, in part because Comment 2 qualifies it by noting that

> [i]t is not necessary for repudiation that performance be made literally and utterly impossible.
>
> Comment 2, 2-610.

So, what are we looking for when assessing whether conduct—the action of a party—results in a repudiation? In a prior draft of Article 2, what became Comment 2 to 2-610 went on to explain:

> The core of the matter is action which reasonably indicates repudiation of the continuing obligation, as, for example, where the seller of the future crop of a given orchard sells the

orchard without making appropriate arrangements, or where a buyer lets pass an agreed time limit for giving necessary instructions.

Kelly, 2 *Uniform Commercial Code: Drafts,* (Rothman, 1984), 267.

For a moment there's hope—but upon further reflection, that hopes fades again, and we understand that determining when unlikely gets close enough to impossible to become a repudiation will depend on the facts of each case

The following problems illustrate how difficult it can be to determine whether a party has repudiated the contract under 2-610.

Problem 5 - 1

Rae wants to add an organic vegetable section to the produce department at the store, selling locally grown products under the store's "Sun-Rae" brand. Earlier this year, a local farm that has applied to the state for "organic producer" certification agrees to supply organic lettuce, peppers, cucumbers, and carrots to the store beginning June 1. Since committing to provide organic produce to the store, the farmer has said and done things that have brought into question both his intent and ability to deliver product as promised by June 1, and Rae wants to know which, if any, of the following incidents would allow her to cancel the contract under 2-610:

Incident 1: A month after agreeing to supply product to the store, the farmer told Rae he wasn't "sure this organic thing is the way to go—it just doesn't seem like it's worth all of the effort to make it happen."

Incident 2: In March the farmer warned Rae that, because of the certification expenses, he might not be able to plant any vegetables this year without an advance payment under the contract from the store.

Incident 3: In mid-March, another local grower told Rae that, based on a conversation she had with the farmer, she did not think he had submitted the application for organic certification, even though planting time was only weeks away. Produce planted before certification cannot be sold as organic. The grower had recently sued the farmer for breach of a contract involving the sale of a tractor.

Incident 4: Several weeks ago, Rae received notice that the farmer had filed for bankruptcy.

Incident 5: The farmer e-mailed her last week, asking whether she would forgive him if he did not make the change to organic farming this year.

Incident 6: Yesterday when she stopped by the farmer's place, the person who answered the door claimed to have leased the farm for two years with an option to buy at the end of the lease.

Even if we have conduct or a statement that we can confidently label a repudiation, that's not enough to act on under 2-610. Not getting the performance repudiated must "substantially impair the value of the contract" to the aggrieved party. When does a repudiated performance substantially impair the value of the contract? Here, again, 2-610 doesn't tell us much about what it's looking for—the Comments equate substantial impairment with "material inconvenience or injustice," the classic statutory bait-and-switch that nobody finds very helpful. Many courts equate substantial impairment with material breach and adopt the five-factor test of materiality from Section 241 of RESTATEMENT

OF CONTRACTS (Second) to determine whether the repudiation causes the substantial impairment required by 2-610:

1. Extent to which the injured party will be denied the benefit it expected to receive. 2. Extent to which injured party can be adequately compensated for benefit lost. 3. Extent to which breaching party will suffer forfeiture. 4. Likelihood of cure by breaching party. 5. Good faith of breaching party.

And there is evidence in the early drafts of Article 2 that supports equating the term "substantial" with material breach. Section 11-A of the 1941 Draft substituted a "substantial defect" standard for the perfect-tender rule which excused the buyer from taking goods that were defective in even the most trivial way. A defect was not substantial under 11-A (b)(1)

if the delivered lot is of such character as not in a *material* manner to increase the risks or burdens which would rest on the buyer under exact performance …

Kelly, *Uniform Commercial Code: Drafts,* (Rothman 1984) 380 (emphasis added). Section 11-A(c) further explained:

The principle of mercantile performance [no substantial defect] is that a contract between merchants calls for a performance having the expected substance, but that discrepancies are not to interfere with the flow of goods in commerce unless they are in mercantile fact *material* discrepancies, and unless an appropriate money-allowance against the price can give no adequate compensation for failure of exact performance.

Id. (emphasis added). The last part of 11-A(c) actually incorporates the second factor of the restatement materiality test.

Problem 5 - 2

In which of the following cases does the repudiation substantially impair the value of the contract to the non-repudiating party?

Case 1: Rae agreed to purchase all of the apples grown by a local orchard each year for the next ten years. The shelf life of most apples is two years if stored in a controlled-atmosphere cooler like the one Rae had installed at the store. Rae has refused to accept delivery of any apples during the second year of the contract because the CA cooler is full and she has no alternative storage facility for apples. Would your answer be different if the contract was for five years rather than ten?

Case 2: Each year, Rae orders five thousand frozen turkeys from the turkey farm up the inter-state, for delivery twenty-one days before Thanksgiving. Yesterday the turkey farm informed Rae that because of equipment issues at its processing plant, the turkeys will not be delivered until November 23, three days before Thanksgiving.

Case 3: Every summer, the store holds an "Ice Cream Social" on the weekend before the Fourth of July. Arctic Chill always provides the ice cream for the event and agreed to provide all of the ice cream for this year's event as it had in the past. The agreement provided Arctic Chill would deliver chocolate, vanilla, and three designer flavors selected by Rae in what-ever quantities were needed for the event. Five weeks before this year's social, Arctic Chill informed Rae that it could not supply any chocolate ice cream because salmonella had been found at the plant where the chocolate ice cream was made. But it offered to supply another designer flavor in whatever quantity Rae needed. Arctic Chill Chocolate Supreme was always the best-selling flavor during the social—it alone accounted for 60% of sales on average. The combined sales of the designer flavors never topped 15% of total sales—when it came to ice cream, Rae's customers preferred the traditional flavors: chocolate and vanilla. 2-610.

Ultimately, whether a repudiation meets the substantial impairment requirement in 2-610 will, like the question of whether a statement is a repudiation, turn on the facts of the case—which side the facts favor when examined under the material-breach factors. And of course this raises the stakes for the party thinking about calling a repudiation. A repudiation under 2-610 permits the aggrieved party to treat the repudiation as a breach and invoke any remedy available for the breach—including cancelling the contract. 2-610(b). It can also suspend its own performance under the contract and cut its losses in the face of the uncertainty created by the repudiation. 2-610(c). But, if it's wrong about the repudiation—a court subsequently determines that no definite and unequivocal statement of intent not to perform had been made—then the "aggrieved" party has itself anticipatorily repudiated by suspending performance or declaring breach.

Article 2 offers the repudiating party with second thoughts an opportunity to take back the repudiation—to retract it. 2-611. But the window to act is short—it must act before the other party cancels the contract or otherwise indicates that it considers the repudiation final, or materially changes its position on account of the repudiation. If the repudiation is the result of the repudiating party's failure to provide adequate assurance of performance after a demand by the other party under 2-609, the retraction, to be effective, must include the necessary assurances of performance. The following problems illustrate the requirements for retraction under 2-611.

Problem 5 - 3

The ice cream for this year's Ice Cream Social was to be supplied by the handcrafted ice cream company that had recently begun operating just outside of town. Two weeks before the social, the ice cream company notified Rae that it could not supply ice cream for the event because the FDA had found traces of salmonella in some of its ice cream.

Which of the following would preclude the company from retracting its repudiation if it is subsequently determined that the bad ice cream was not made by the company:

Case 1: She sends offers to purchase the ice cream for the event to several other ice cream companies.

Case 2: She runs new ads in the local paper and on TV for the social, omitting the name of the ice cream company.

Case 3: She has new banners made for the event that do not include the brand of ice cream to be served.

Case 4: One of the ice cream companies she contacted accepts her offer to purchase ice cream but can only supply half of the ice cream she needs for the event.

Case 5: Another ice cream company agrees to provide the rest of the ice cream she needs for the event.

Section 2-609 offers a ray of light to the party—perhaps more likely, the lawyer—unwilling to risk everything by asserting repudiation under 2-610:

> A contract for sale imposes an obligation on each party that the other's expectation of receiving due performance will not be impaired. When reasonable grounds for insecurity arise with respect to the performance of either party, the other may in writing demand adequate assurance of due performance and until he receives such assurance may, if commercially reasonable, suspend any performance for which he has not already received the agreed return.

While 2-610 offers full protection to a party worried that it will not receive the return performance it's expecting under the contract when the time arrives—suspend performance, cancel the contract, and recover damages—for many, that protection will not outweigh its attendant risks. Section 2-609 offers the risk-averse party a way to resolve uncertainty about the other party's future intentions without risking a breach on its own part, along with an opportunity to avoid the expense of continuing to perform until the uncertainty is resolved. It also—and this was always important to Llewellyn—preserves the chance that the deal might be saved.

But, as the next case illustrates, a party that fails to comply with the requirements of 2-609 will be no better off than the party who guessed wrong under 2-610.

Scott v. Crown

Court of Appeals of Colorado, 1988
765 P.2d 1043

PLANK, Judge.

In this breach of contract action, defendant, Dennis Crown d/b/a Crown Company (Buyer), appeals from a judgment entered in favor of plaintiffs, Larry and Vera Scott, and from the dismissal of Buyer's counterclaim against them. We reverse.

During February 1983, Larry Scott (Seller) and Buyer entered into contract No. 76 for the sale of 16,000 bushels of U.S. No. 1 wheat. Pursuant to the contract, Buyer paid Seller $2,000 as an advanced payment. With respect to payment of the contract balance, the agreement reads in part:

> "Payment by Buyer is conditioned upon Sellers [sic] completion of Delivery of total quantity as set forth in this contract. Any payment made prior to completion of delivery is merely an accommodation. In making such accommodation, Buyer does not waive any condition of this contract to be performed by Seller."

Elsewhere, the contract provided that the full balance would be paid 30 days after shipment of the total contract quantity of grain.

By March 13, 1983, Seller had delivered all the wheat called for in the contract. Payment of the full contract balance of approximately $49,000 was due on April 13, 1983.

On March 1, 1983 Seller and Buyer executed contract 78-2 for the sale of 13,500 bushels of U.S. No. 1 wheat and contract No. 81-3 for the sale of approximately 30 truckloads of U.S. No. 1 wheat. These contracts are the subject of this action. With the exception of quantity, the contracts had identical terms and conditions as those in contract No. 76, including the above-quoted provision and the provision for full payment by Buyer 30 days after complete performance by Seller.

In early March 1983, Seller commenced performance of contract No. 78-2. By March 15, 1983, he had delivered to Buyer approximately 9,086 bushels of wheat. However, he ceased performance because of his belief that Buyer could not pay for the wheat.

Seller was contracting with other grain dealers while working with Buyer. Seller suffered a loss on an unrelated contract. When reviewing this loss with his banker, Seller was told that Buyer was not the "best grain trader" and was advised to contact an agent from the Department of Agriculture for additional information about Buyer. The agent, Mr. Witt, indicated there was an active complaint against Buyer concerning payments to other farmers.

The next day, one of Buyer's trucks appeared at Seller's farm to take another load of grain. Seller refused to deliver the grain. Instead, he testified that he told the driver:

> "that we had the grain, but were trying to get in touch with Mr. Crown, and my attorney advised me not to load until we had made contact with Mr. Crown to settle some questions that we had."

Seller and Witt testified that during the period of March 21 through April 6, 1983, they and Seller's attorney had attempted to contact Buyer several times by telephone, but were not successful.

By a letter dated March 23, 1983, Buyer responded to Seller's refusal to load the wheat. Buyer stated that he had not breached the contracts; however, Seller had breached the agreements. Buyer pointed out the payment terms requiring shipment of the full quantity before payment was due and requested that Seller resume performance. Otherwise, Buyer would be forced to "resort to cover."

Buyer followed up the letter with a April 4, 1983, correspondence in which he notified Seller that he was cancelling the contracts. However, he assured Seller that, if the contracts were performed, his company would pay according to the contract terms.

Through counsel, Seller replied by an April 6, 1983, letter. Counsel informed Buyer that his client had not been paid on the contracts and that Seller had received information that Buyer had been paid by his buyers. Counsel demanded assurances of performance that Buyer would pay for the grain shipped on the fully performed contract 76 and the partially performed contract 78-2. However, under the contract terms, payment was not due on contract 76 until April 13, 1983, and was not due on contract 78-2 until 30 days after full performance.

Buyer cancelled contracts 78-2 and 81-3 on April 7, 1983. He had previously contacted grain sellers in Denver and Salt Lake City to effect cover, but by this date the grain was no longer available.

Seller instituted suit on April 25, 1983, alleging breach of contract by Buyer in not paying in full for the grain prior to delivery pursuant to his demand for adequate assurance of performance.

The circumstances at issue bring this action within the scope of § 4-2-609(1), C.R.S., of the Uniform Commercial Code. That section provides:

> "A contract for sale imposes an obligation on each party that the other's expectation of receiving due performance will not be impaired. When reasonable grounds for insecurity arise with respect to the performance of either party, the other may in writing demand adequate assurance of due performance and, until he receives such assurance, may if commercially reasonable suspend any performance for which he has not already received the agreed return."

By the express language of this provision, reasonable grounds for insecurity about the performance of either party must exist in order for the other party to exercise further rights.

Buyer alleges that Seller did not have reasonable grounds for insecurity and, further, that the demand for assurance of due performance was defective. We disagree that there were no reasonable grounds for insecurity, but agree that the demand for assurance of due performance was defective.

Whether Seller had reasonable grounds for insecurity is a question of fact. Since trial was to the court, we will not disturb the court's findings that Seller had reasonable grounds for insecurity unless it was clearly erroneous and not supported by the record.

The trial court found that reasonable grounds for insecurity existed because: 1) Seller recently had had an unfortunate experience similar to the incident at issue with another grain dealer (i.e., a pattern of unreturned phone calls culminating in nonpayment for a grain delivery); 2) Investigator Witt had informed Seller that his office had active complaints by other farmers against Buyer; and 3) Buyer failed to make personal contact after Seller refused to load the wheat. This evidence supports the trial court's conclusion of reasonable grounds for insecurity.

There are, however, serious problems with the timing, form, and content of Seller's demand for assurances of performance. The court found that Seller had made an oral demand for assurances by his refusal load the grain and his conversation with the [**7] driver on March 22, 1983. However, Seller did not make the written demand until his counsel's letter of April 6, 1983, some two weeks after he had suspended performance.

Generally, the express language of the statute is followed such that a demand for assurances of performance must be in writing in order to be effective. However, in some cases an oral demand for assurances has sufficed. In such cases, there appears a pattern of interaction which demonstrated a clear understanding between the parties that suspension of the demanding party's performance was the alternative, if its concerns were not adequately addressed by the other party.

In *AMF, Inc., v. McDonald's Corp. supra,* for example, McDonald's had ordered 23 computerized cash registers from AMF. However, a prototype machine installed at a McDonald's franchise performed poorly. McDonald's personnel then met with AMF and demanded that the order for their 23 units be held up pending resolution of the problems experienced in the prototype. AMF failed to resolve the problem, and McDonald's cancelled the order. The court expressly rejected AMF's argument that McDonald's had not made a written demand, and held that McDonald's had properly invoked the pertinent Uniform Commercial Code provision.

Here, Seller made only the oral statement to Buyer's driver before he suspended performance. In our view, that was insufficient to make that suspension justified under § 4-2-609.

Also, there was not a subsequent pattern of interaction between the parties that would clearly demonstrate that Buyer understood that Seller had requested assurances of performance. Indeed, Buyer's letter of March 23, and April 4, 1983, demonstrated that he thought that Seller had inexcusably refused to perform the contracts. Hence, we conclude that the conditions necessary to validate an oral demand were not met here.

Moreover, even if we were to conclude that an oral demand would have been permissible here, the content of the alleged demand is deficient. In contrast to *AMF,* Seller did not communicate clearly to Buyer that he was demanding assurances of performance. He simply told Buyer's driver that he wanted to "settle" some questions with Buyer. A mere demand for meeting to discuss the contracts, even if it had been in writing, would not be sufficient to constitute a proper demand for assurances.

Finally, a demand for performance assurances cannot be used as a means of forcing a modification of the contract.

When Seller's counsel made the demand for assurances of performance, he demanded performance beyond that required by the contracts. In the April 6, 1983, letter, counsel requested payment in full of contract 76 and payment for the grain delivered on contract 78-2. At that time, Buyer was not obligated under the terms of the contracts to make such payments.

Under these facts, we conclude that Seller did not have the right to suspend performance because he failed to act in a manner that would bring him within the scope of § 4-2-609. Instead, Seller's actions constituted an anticipatory repudiation which gave Buyer the right to cancel the contracts and resort to the buyer's remedies as provided in § 4-2-713, C.R.S.

This matter is remanded to the trial court to determine the following factual issues relating to Buyer's damages: (1) whether the grain being delivered was U.S. No. 1 wheat or a lesser quality; (2) the date Buyer first learned of the breach; and (3) the fair market value of the wheat on the date Buyer learned of the breach. Seller is entitled to all credit for grain sold and delivered and for which payment was not received. Accordingly, the judgment is reversed and the cause is remanded with directions that the court enter judgment for Buyer after making findings on these issues.

PROBLEM 5 - 4

Do any of the incidents set out in Problem 5 - 1 entitle Rae to demand adequate assurance of performance from the would-be organic farmer? Would her demand for assurance be effective if the farmer received it in a voicemail she left when he did not answer her call? Would it be effective if the farmer received it as a text message on his iPhone?

Whether a party has reasonable grounds for insecurity "is to be determined according to commercial standards" when both parties are merchants, which means it's a fact-intensive inquiry that, in the end, may turn more on the advocacy of the parties than legal abstractions. The Comments to an early draft of the section noted:

> the issue is to be both posed and determined in terms of factual conditions existing: does a threat to one party's security exist in fact ...

II Kelly, *Uniform Commercial Code: Drafts,* (Rothman, 1984) 258 (May 1944 Proposed Final Draft No. 1). And, as we saw in the *Crown* case, it can be the cumulative effect of several facts, each of which alone would not have given reasonable grounds for insecurity, that justifies the demand for assurances.

Beyond "reasonable grounds for insecurity," 2-609 does not require a lot, but as the *Crown* case demonstrates, some courts are not very forgiving when a party strays from its requirements, and noncompliance will result in a repudiation by the party demanding assurances if it suspends its own performance. By its terms, 2-609 requires the demand for assurances be in writing—a few courts have ignored this explicit requirement, but their justifications are suspect. The writing must alert the other party to the fact that you are asking for assurances that it intends to perform—an ambiguous communication won't do it. The demand must precede any suspension of performance—as we also saw in the *Crown* case, if the party invoking its right under 2-609 stops performing before it makes the demand, it has repudiated the contract, and the assurance demanded cannot effect a modification of the contract; courts distinguish between the demand for assurances which itself requires the other party to do something it did not undertake to do in the contract—provide assurance of performance—and a demand inconsistent with the express terms of the contract. A demand for modification is ineffective to trigger the right to suspend performance granted by 2-609.

B. BUYER'S REMEDIES WHEN SELLER BREACHES

A seller breaches by repudiating its performance before it's due, failing to perform by the time required in the contract, or performing defectively. We will address the remedies for defective performance by sellers in Chapters 7 and 8.

When a seller breaches, the buyer may be able to call off the deal (cancel the contract), compel the seller to perform (deliver the goods called for by the contract), and/or recover damages for loss caused by the breach. Section 2-711 catalogs the remedies available under Article 2 to the buyer on the seller's breach. When a seller breaches by repudiating or by failing to perform when required, the buyer does not get the goods she was expecting from the seller's performance, so which of these alternatives works best to put the buyer in the position she was expecting to be in will depend on the particular circumstances of each buyer, and Article 2 leaves it to the buyer to determine which way to proceed. Of course, sometimes the reason for a seller's breach may limit the buyer's alternatives—if the seller has gone out of business, the buyer is probably not going to be able to compel performance. And whichever alternative the buyer chooses, she must comply with any requirements imposed by Article 2 to obtain that relief.

1. Substitute Transaction: Buyer's Right to Cover

Llewellyn believed that, if given the choice between money damages and a new transaction in place of one that had ended in breach, most merchants—whether buyer or seller—would prefer the replacement transaction as the remedy for breach of a sale-of-goods contract, so a sales law intended to reflect modern commercial practice needed to

> make it possible, in transactions between professionals in the market, for the justified claimant, be he buyer or seller, to fix his rights with speed, after a breach, and then to *move*, with safety, in such manner as to get in fact the agreed benefit under the contract, or so much of it as is still available.[4]

For the seller, "moving safely to get the agreed benefit under the contract" means finding another buyer for the goods she's stuck with because of breach. For the buyer, it means purchasing the goods she was expecting to get from the breaching seller from someone else. The replacement transaction—what Llewellyn called "cover"—contained the damages caused by the breach by limiting the disruptive effect of the breach on the nonbreaching party. If Rae can buy the grapefruit you were supposed to deliver from someone else, she won't lose any grapefruit sales at the store.

Under prior law, the buyer who acted immediately to purchase substitute goods did so at great risk if she paid more for them than she had agreed to pay the breaching seller, because her damages were not measured on the basis of the price of the substitute goods. Damages were based on what the trier of fact later determined was the market value of the goods at the time they were to be delivered under the breached contract. That might turn out to be the price she paid, but it might not, especially where the buyer was covering for a repudiation made long before the time for delivery. And it did not matter that the buyer had acted in good faith or that the cover transaction was by all measures a reasonable transaction under the circumstances. In effect, the buyer was punished for doing what professional traders thought was the best practice, and so the new sales law—Article 2—had to redress the wrong.

Article 2 empowers the buyer to make a substitute transaction when the seller breaches:

> After breach … the buyer may "cover" by making in good faith and without unreasonable delay any reasonable purchase of or contract to purchase goods in substitution for those due from the seller.

> 2-712(1).

It then protects the buyer who does so by measuring her damages for the seller's breach by the difference between "the cost of cover and the contract price." 2-712(2). Although Llewellyn had originally put substitute transactions by both buyers and sellers under the "cover" umbrella, by the time Article 2 was ready for adoption by the states, a seller's substitute transaction was known instead as a "resale" in Article 2. Cover was what the buyer did when it bought replacements for the goods it did not get because of the seller's breach.

Under Article 2, the focus shifted from the market value of the substitute goods in a hypothetical market to the conduct of the buyer when she bought substitute goods. That she paid more for the substitute goods than what, in hindsight, might have been their market value is not controlling. If the substitute transaction meets the general norms of commercial practice, she's entitled to the difference between the cost of cover and the contract price.

Are there any limits on what the buyer can substitute for the goods due from the seller under 2-712? Surely a buyer cannot substitute refrigerators for toasters. If the Chevy dealer tells me I can't have the Spark that just arrived and that he had promised to sell me, can I buy a BMW (car) and recover the

---

4 I Kelly, *Uniform Commercial Code: Drafts,* (Rothman, 1984) 522 (Second Draft, Revised Uniform Sales Act, Sept. 1941) (emphasis in original).

difference between the price of the Chevy Spark and the price of the BMW? A car is a car is a car, right? The Comments tell us that the cover remedy "is aimed at enabling [the buyer] to obtain the goods he needs." Comment 1, 2-712. I was promised a car, I needed a car, and I bought a car. My BMW purchase looks like it falls within the objective stated for 2-712 (thank you Chevrolet dealer!).

But the Comments go on to note that 2-712 cover envisages "goods not identical with those involved, but commercially usable as reasonable substitutes under the circumstances of the particular case." Comment 2. My BMW is not identical to the Spark, but it's certainly usable as a substitute for it—I can make it work, really.

As the next case illustrates, courts have not given covering buyers *carte blanche* under 2-712. All Article 2 remedies are subject to the proscription in 1-305 that UCC remedies are to be

> administered to the end that the aggrieved party may be put in as good a position as if the other party had fully performed ...

The command is to put the aggrieved party in as good a position—not a better position—and courts have been mindful of this oracle when assessing whether a covering buyer has overindulged. The good faith requirement in 2-712 limits how much a buyer can get away with as well. Even if the Chevy Spark my dealer refused to deliver was the last of the breed, a nice little Ford Fiesta would have done everything the Spark could for about one-third the price of the BMW. Could it be that I bought the BMW to increase my claim against the dealer? And of course the cover must be a "reasonable purchase" under 2-712. Does that mean that if my choice for substitute goods is between cheaper goods of lesser quality and more expensive goods of better quality, I have to buy the cheap goods or my cover is unreasonable?

The next case and the problems that follow it explore these questions and others that are buried within the seemingly simple text of 2-712.

CETKOVIC v. BOCH, INC.

STATE OF MASSACHUSETTS, APPELLATE DIVISION, SOUTHERN DISTRICT
2003 MASS. APP. DIV. 1

WELSH, Judge.

Following negotiations with a salesperson employed by Boch Mitsubishi, the plaintiff (buyer) agreed to purchase and the defendant agreed to sell a used 1998 Mitsubishi Diamante LS with approximately 25,000 miles for the sum of $18,300.00. Within two days after signing the contract, the salesman learned that the vehicle which had been the subject of the contract had been sold by another sales representative of Boch to a third party. The deposit of $1,000 that had been given was promptly returned to the plaintiff. The plaintiff was disappointed and displeased, insisting that Boch make good on the contract. Various attempts to locate a like vehicle satisfactory to the buyer were made by Boch, but no vehicle could be found that the buyer was willing to accept. After several weeks of looking for a vehicle at other dealerships, the plaintiff acquired a new 2000 Nissan Maxima at a price $8,400 more than that agreed upon for the 1998 Mitsubishi Diamante. The plaintiff sued for damages....

After a 3-day trial, the judge awarded damages reckoned by trebling the $8,400, plus an attorneys fee of $11,760, plus interest, totaling $39,210.95.

The defendant appeals, contending that the judge erred in determining that the purchase of the new Nissan Maxima was reasonable "cover" as a matter of law.... We vacate the award of damages for cover.... and remand the case for a redetermination of damages.

The Uniform Commercial Code's fundamental injunction is to render such damages to the aggrieved party as to place that party in as good a position as if the other party had performed the contract. See

§ 1-106(1). The Code provides an aggrieved buyer two alternative remedies when the seller breaches the contract by failing to deliver the goods agreed upon. The buyer may recover his economic loss calculated by the difference between the market price and the agreed contract price, sometimes called the "benefit of the bargain" rule. § 2-711 [sic]. The buyer may eschew this remedy and instead "cover" by procuring substitute goods. In such a case, the damages will be the difference between the "cover" price and the contract price. Whichever option is chosen, the buyer may also recover incidental and foreseeable consequential damages occasioned by the breach. § 2-715. Perhaps to avoid a windfall, the buyer's damage recovery is to be reduced by the expenses the buyer avoids by not having to perform. §§ 2-712(2), 2-715(1).

Calculation of "cover" damages involves three elements. First, the trier of fact should determine the aggregate difference between the cover price and the contract price. Second, the damage award should be increased by the incidental and consequential damages found. Third, the award should be reduced by the expenses avoided by the buyer because of the seller's breach. Although at least one appellate court has held in circumstances not unlike those in the instant case that "cover" is applicable only to transactions in a commercial context, the prevailing view is that "cover" is applicable to consumer transactions. Comment 4 ("cover" not limited to merchants: it is a vital and important remedy for the consumer buyer also). We perceive no reason to deny the remedy of "cover" to a consumer buyer.

> The test of proper cover is whether at the time and place the buyer acted in good faith and in a reasonable manner, and it is immaterial that hindsight may later prove that the method of cover used was not the cheapest or most effective. § 2-712, Comment 2.

One aid for determining reasonableness in this context is the Code's injunction: put the buyer in the position that performance would have done. The buyer has the burden to show that the goods procured are a reasonable substitute. While courts are rightly reluctant to declare a buyer's good faith acts unreasonable, a court ought not affix its imprimatur to the transaction with a blind eye, and defer obsequiously to the buyer's choice as to "cover." While no exclusive test exists, a helpful guide is to pose the question how, when and where would the buyer have procured the goods had he not been covering and had no prospect of a court recovery from another. If a buyer can truthfully answer he would have spent his own money in that way with no prospect of reimbursement, the court should not demand more.

It needs to be stressed that the goods obtained as cover need not be identical with those called for in the contract so long as they are commercially usable as a reasonable substitute. The recovery for "cover" goods ought not to be denied merely because there exists a possibility of a windfall unless the seller demonstrates persuasively the likelihood of a significant windfall due to the superior quality of the cover goods. Occasionally, a windfall might occur by overcompensating a buyer due to seller's inability to prove that buyer specifically benefited from the added quality of the cover goods. A buyer may not utilize cover to put himself in a better position than he would have been in had the contract been performed. In *Freitag v. Bill Swad Datsun*, 3 Ohio App. 3d 83, the court held that the buyer's purchase of a 1980 Datsun was not a reasonable substitute for a differently equipped 1979 Datsun. Compare: *Mueller v. McGill*, 870 S.W.2d 673 (Tex. App. 1994), where the court held that it was a jury question whether a 1986 Porsche Targa 911 was a reasonable substitute for a 1985 Porsche Targa 911. There was evidence that the two cars were virtually identical. We conclude that the instant case is more in line with the *Bill Swad Datsun* case, *supra*, and is distinguished from *Mueller v. McGill, supra*, in that the substitute goods were virtually identical and it was practically difficult if not impossible to obtain the exact year and type of Porsche. We hold that the acquisition of a new Nissan Maxima as a substitute for a used 1998 Mitsubishi Diamante is unreasonable under the circumstances of this case.

PROBLEM 5 - 5

Black Ivory coffee is the latest craze among the caffeine addicts in town, so Rae ordered ten thousand pounds of Black Ivory coffee beans from the local coffee broker at three dollars a pound. The broker agreed to deliver one thousand pounds of the beans every six weeks. The broker informed Rae when he delivered the second thousand pounds that this would be the last delivery under the contract because his supplier had gone out of business. The market price of the beans at the time of the second delivery was six dollars a pound and rising rapidly as demand for the beans accelerated across the country. In the months that followed, Rae purchased the remaining eight thousand pounds of beans in eight separate transactions at prices that ranged from $6.50 a pound to $9.75 a pound. The store could only take one thousand pounds at a time because space was limited in the coffee cooler, where the beans had to be stored to prevent bean rot. And sellers were unwilling to sell beans for delivery more than a couple of weeks out because of the rising prices. Will Rae be able to recover the difference between the cover price and the contract price for each of the eight purchases she made after the broker refused to deliver any more of the beans under 2-712? What are the arguments that the broker is likely to make against measuring her damages in this way?

PROBLEM 5 - 6

Rae ordered a new paper baler for the stockroom at the store from the local equipment distributor. The baler was to be delivered and installed by the first of June. When no baler had been delivered by the beginning of June, Rae called the seller, who told her that the manufacturer refused to deliver any more balers, and so he had none to deliver under the contract. While Rae was looking for a substitute purchase, she noticed that a new model of the baler was to go on sale at the end of summer, and she decided to wait and purchase the new model because it had additional features she liked—even though it was priced 15 percent higher than the baler she had ordered. The announcement of the new model had caused the price of the old model to fall by more than 30 percent. The new baler was delivered mid-September. Will Rae be able to recover from the local equipment distributor the difference between the cost of the substitute baler she purchased and the contract price under 2-712?

PROBLEM 5 - 7

Rae decided to start selling ice at the store, and so she ordered a large industrial ice machine from a national manufacturer of such equipment. The machine was to be delivered by the beginning of May, when sales of ice picked up as the weather improved. The machine was not delivered by May because a labor dispute with no end in sight had forced the manufacturer to shut down its factory. She immediately began looking for a substitute machine and found one that could be delivered within seven days, but it was priced 25 percent higher than the price she had agreed to pay the breaching seller, although she would save the cost of shipping the machine that she was to pay under the breached contract. She could order the identical machine for about the same price she was to pay under the original contract but could not get it delivered before the end of summer—the peak season for ice sales. She decided to pay the premium for immediate delivery, and the machine was delivered the second week of May. Will she be able to recover the difference between the purchase price of the substitute ice machine and the contract price under 2-712?

PROBLEM 5 - 8

The regional distributor of grocery products had offered to sell Rae five hundred pallets of canned vegetables that had been returned by a grocery store that had gone out of business, at an 80 percent discount-to-market price. Rae accepted the offer and made plans for a major sale based on the discounted vegetables. She advertised the sale in the local papers and ran ads for it on TV. A week before the sale was to start, the distributor notified Rae that it had sold the vegetables to another grocer willing to pay more for the goods. To avoid the public relations disaster calling off the sale would have caused, Rae substituted the store's current inventory of canned vegetables for the discounted vegetables she was supposed to get from the distributor—even though she had paid market price for the cans in inventory. She later replenished the store's inventory of canned vegetables at current market price, which was 10 percent less than she had paid for the vegetables she used in the sale. Under 2-712, will she be able to recover the difference between the price of the inventory she substituted at the sale and the contract price from the distributor? Can she use the purchase price of the replacement inventory to measure her damages, under 2-712?

2. Alternative to Cover: Market Price Damages

What happens if the buyer does not cover or cannot cover? Cover is an option—Article 2 does not require that a buyer cover when her seller breaches, as 2-712 and its Comments make clear:

> Failure of the buyer to effect cover within this section does not bar him from any other remedy. 2-712(3).

> Subsection (3) expresses the policy that cover is not a mandatory remedy for the buyer. The buyer is always free to choose between cover and damages for nondelivery under [2-713]. Comment 3, 2-712.

The drafters may have assumed—even preferred—that cover would be the choice of most buyers, but they did not condition all of the other buyers' remedies on showing inability to cover (except consequential damages as discussed later). Section 2-713 provides the alternative to cover for buyers not in possession of the contract goods:

> the measure of damages for nondelivery or repudiation by the seller is the difference between the market price at the time when the buyer learned of the breach and the contract price ...

The measure of damages in 2-713—like the measure set out in 2-712—is deceptively simple. But as the next case illustrates, there are several issues buried within its simple text that only come to light when we try to apply it to the facts of our client's case.

UNLIMITED EQUIP. LINES V. GRAPHIC ARTS CENTRE

COURT OF APPEALS OF MISSOURI, EASTERN DISTRICT, DIVISION THREE, 1994
889 S.W.2D 926

CRANE, Judge.

The seller [GAC/HGK] and the buyer [UEL] entered into a first and second agreement under which the buyer purchased a five-color printing press from the sellers. As part of the agreements, the sellers gave the buyer a right of first refusal for 12 months on the remainder of the sellers' assets. Without notifying the buyer, the sellers sold the entire operation to a third party [Jefferson Printing]. The lower court awarded the buyer $410,000 in damages which represented the difference between the contract price of $690,000 and the orderly liquidation value of $1.1 million, and $89,171 in prejudgment interest for the sellers' breach of the right of first refusal with the buyer.

On appeal defendants challenge ... the award of damages and prejudgment interest.

* * * *

IV. DAMAGES

A. Computation of Actual Damages

Defendants argue that the trial court erred in holding that UEL was entitled to recover $410,000 in damages as the difference between the contract price and the liquidation value of the equipment sold to Jefferson Printing. In its point challenging damages, it contends that UEL was not entitled to that amount of damages under § 400.2-713, because

> (1) [UEL] failed to prove a contract price, an appropriate market, and a market price, all as required under 400.2-713; (2) the judgment reflected a windfall to [UEL] and a profit of almost 60%, when the record and available evidence established a much lower profit margin and, therefore, the award put [UEL] in a better position than it would have been had [UEL] purchased the equipment from GAC; (3) the judgment constituted an award of lost profits to [UEL], without [UEL] being required to prove an available buyer of the equipment or inability to cover, or to present evidence sufficient to allow lost profits to be estimated with reasonable certainty; (4) the judgment was not based on the equipment actually sold to Jefferson but rather was based on an incorrect list provided to [UEL]'s appraiser by Geissler, which list contained more and different equipment than had been purchased by Jefferson Printing; (5) the damages were not based on requiring UEL to assume Jefferson Printing's position in the transaction with Keeler-Morris, which included assumption of an expensive lease; and (6) the award was based on invalid and incompetent expert testimony offered by [UEL].

With respect to UEL's damages the trial court made the following finding of fact:

> 19. There was expert testimony that the fair market value of GAC and HGK's equipment sold to Jefferson Printing was in excess of $1.5 million, and that the equipment's value on an orderly liquidation sale basis was $1.1 million. The difference between the fair market value and the price paid by Jefferson Printing is $860,000. The difference between the fair market value and the orderly liquidation value is $410,000.

The court concluded:

> 13. UEL is entitled to recover $410,000 in damages which represents the difference between the contract price ($690,000) and the orderly liquidation value ($1.1 million).... There is no proof that Plaintiff could obtain the fair market value price or any amount greater than the orderly liquidation value, and, therefore, it would be unjust and inappropriate and a windfall to Plaintiff to make an award based upon the fair market value.

Both parties treat the award of damages as made under § 400.2-713(1) RSMo (1986), which provides:

> Subject to the provisions of this article with respect to proof of market price (section 400.2-723), the measure of damages for nondelivery or repudiation by the seller is the difference between the market price at the time when the buyer learned of the breach and the contract price together with any incidental and consequential damages provided in this article (section 400.2-715), but less expenses saved in consequence of the seller's breach.

Comment 3 to this section reads as follows:

> 3. When the current market price under this section is difficult to prove the section on determination and proof of market price is available to permit a showing of a comparable market price or, where no market price is available, evidence of spot sale prices is proper. Where the

unavailability of a market price is caused by a scarcity of goods of the type involved, a good case is normally made for specific performance under this Article. Such scarcity conditions, moreover, indicate that the price has risen and under the section providing for liberal administration of remedies, opinion evidence as to the value of the goods would be admissible in the absence of a market price and a liberal construction of allowable consequential damages should also result.

Section 400.2-723(2) RSMo (1986) further provides:

> If evidence of a price prevailing at the times or places described in this article is not readily available the price prevailing within any reasonable time before or after the time described or at any other place which in commercial judgment or under usage of trade would serve as a reasonable substitute for the one described may be used, making any proper allowance for the cost of transporting the goods to or from such other place.

1. Contract Price and Market Price

Defendants first argue that UEL failed to establish a contract price, a market, and a market price under § 400.2-713. We disagree.

They assert that the court improperly used $690,000 as the contract price. They contend that this figure represented a reduced price because the buyer also agreed to assume a lease and there was no evidence what this price would have been in the absence of the lease assumption. Defendants offered no evidence to support their contention that the lease assumption depressed the contract price of the equipment.

It was undisputed that defendants sold HGK's equipment, name, and customer lists to Jefferson Printing Company for $691,000. The Assets Purchase Agreement allocated this price as follows: $680,000 for the equipment and assumption of lease, $1,000 for the name and customer lists, and $10,000 (not specifically allocated) to be paid upon execution of the agreement. Geissler testified that the press which was the subject of the lease was a very saleable item in the marketplace and the assumption of the lease would not result in a net economic disadvantage to the buyer. The written contract was sufficient evidence of a contract price. The trial court was entitled to defer to Geissler's credibility and accept his testimony that the lease assumption would not have created an economic disadvantage. This was sufficient evidence that the price in the contract was the contract price of the equipment.

Defendants next argue that UEL failed to prove a market or a market price for the equipment sold to Jefferson Printing. Geissler testified that he has personally conducted equipment appraisals for companies in bankruptcy, finance companies, borrowers, and his own business. He has testified to his appraisals in court. In connection with his business, he habitually monitors market prices on printing and graphic arts equipment by checking guide books which average selling prices, manufacturers, dealers, customers and trade publications. He routinely consults the Fair Market Guide which shows the average selling price of particular equipment on the market place at that time. Geissler defined the elements of both a fair market value and a liquidation value. He viewed the equipment defendants eventually sold to Jefferson Printing in 1990. He gave his opinion that its fair market value was between 1.5 and 1.7 million dollars. Corbett, UEL's expert, testified that he was in the business of buying and selling printing machinery. He appraised equipment for his own business and did some outside appraisals for banks. He monitored the market for used printing equipment by reading weekly trade magazines and monitored other sales through dealers and manufacturers. He had liquidated printing companies and had appraised incidental equipment and furniture used by printing companies.

Corbett defined fair market value and testified that he used the Fair Market Value Guide to establish fair market values for the equipment as of summer 1990. Corbett also defined liquidation value and testified that he had established liquidation values for the equipment. His appraisals based on both values were offered and received into evidence.

Defendants' contend that proof of a "market"[5] was required. Without deciding whether such proof was required, we find that there was substantial evidence on which the court could find there was a market for used printing presses and equipment. Geissler and Corbett were both dealers in used printing equipment. Used printing equipment has a value capable of appraisal. Geissler and Corbett used a reference guide which shows average selling prices of used printing equipment as well as other trade publications which followed the market for used printing equipment.

Further, there was evidence that much of the equipment was unique and a buyer would have to use a dealer network to locate a particular piece of equipment. Under Comment 3 to § 400.2-713(1), opinion evidence as to the value of goods was admissible in lieu of a specific market price.

Geissler's and Corbett's testimony and appraisals constituted sufficient evidence from which the court could have found a fair market value and a liquidation value. Accordingly, there was evidence of a contract price and fair market or liquidation value from which damages could be calculated under § 400.2-713.

2. Windfall/Lost Profits

In their second subpoint defendants assert the judgment reflected a "windfall" to UEL because it gave UEL a better profit than its usual profit margin. In their third subpoint defendants contend the judgment constituted an award of lost profit without the required proof. These arguments ignore the facts that UEL did not seek lost profits and the trial court did not award lost profits, but awarded damages under § 400.2-713, which provides the measure of damages as the difference between the contract price and the liquidation value. This measure of damages is not limited by lost profits.

Defendants argue that damages should be limited to actual loss suffered under § 400.1-106 RSMo (1986) and that UEL failed to prove that it would have obtained a benefit equal to the damages awarded under § 400.2-713. In support of this argument, defendants rely on two cases in which the reviewing courts affirmed awards of damages based on actual loss rather than UCC § 2-713. *H-W-H Cattle Co., Inc. v. Schroeder*, 767 F.2d 437 (8th Cir. 1985) and *Allied Canners & Packers, Inc. v. Victor Packing Co.*, 162 Cal. App. 3d 905 (Cal. App. 1984). In *H-W-H Cattle*, the buyer's actual loss from the breached contract was the loss of the commission on his resale contract. 767 F.2d at 440. The appellate court affirmed a judgment in favor of buyer based on buyer's actual losses (the lost commission) rather than the market-contract price differential damages award of UCC § 2-713. In *Allied Canners*, the appellate court affirmed a judgment in the amount of actual loss to buyer where buyer had a resale contract, seller knew of the resale contract, the breaching seller did not act in bad faith and the buyer would not be

---

5   "The word 'market,' in some connections, may be a technical term, but it also may be used without any technical meaning since it is not a term of fixed legal significance. In ordinary language it is a common word of the most general import having many meanings, and varying in its significance with the particular objects to which the language is directed and covering a variety of possible forms. It is derived from the Latin 'mercatus,' which signifies trade or traffic, or buying and selling. Thus the term 'market' conveys the idea of selling, and it assumes the existence of trade and implies competition, and also implies the existence of supply and demand, for, without the existence of either factor, no market is shown. A market is not a mere name without substance, and ordinarily a casual sale does not establish or create a market, but in some situations a single actual buyer would become a market.

* * *

"*As a noun.* When employed as a noun the word 'market' may mean simply purchase and sale, or it may mean the exchange of goods or provisions for money, purchase, or it may mean the rate of purchase and sale, or the demand there is for any particular article. It is also said that the term is used to denote that phase of commercial activity in which articles are bought and sold. * * * "

Sitzes v. Raidt, 335 S.W.2d 690, 699 (Mo. App. 1960) (quoting 55 C.J.S. *Market*, at 784, 785).

liable for damages on its resale contract. Both courts found that UCC § 2-713 would result in a windfall to buyers and recovery should be limited to actual loss. In each of these cases, buyer's actual loss could be proved by buyer's resale contract.

Before addressing the application of these cases to this appeal, we first note that these cases are controversial. Professors White and Summers approve the result, but they assert this result should be limited to those cases in which the breaching seller proves that the buyer's expected resale profit was less than the market-contract price differential of § 2-713. 1 WHITE & SUMMERS, UNIFORM COMMERCIAL CODE § 6-4, at 306 (3rd ed. 1988). On the other hand, the Kansas Supreme Court has held that the market-contract price differential of § 2-713 is the appropriate measure of damages regardless of whether the award is in excess of buyer's actual losses. *Tongish v. Thomas,* 251 Kan. 728 (Kan. 1992). In *Tongish* the buyer had a resale contract in which the only profit expected was a handling fee. *Id.* The buyer argued the correct measure of damages for seller's breach was § 2-713. The breaching seller argued that damages should be measured by the actual loss contending that § 1-106 required only that the buyer be placed in as good a position as it would have been had the breaching seller performed. The court reviewed the *Allied* decision and law journal articles discussing *Allied* and held that § 2-713 prevails not only because it is the more specific statute on calculating damages, but also because, as a matter of policy, damages computed under § 2-713 "encourage the honoring of contracts and market stability."

Section 2-713 damages are not necessarily intended to reflect actual loss. 1 WHITE & SUMMERS, *supra,* at 294-304. Section 2-713 is explained as a substitute remedy for those buyers that do not "cover" in that it would approximate the same amount of damages as those provided to a covering buyer under § 2-712. Section 2-713 is also explained as a statutory liquidated damages clause to inhibit breach so that § 2-713 damages need not bear close relation to the actual loss suffered by the buyer. *See also Tongish,* 840 P.2d at 474-76.

We do not need to resolve the conflict over whether and when actual damages may substitute for § 2-713 damages because in this case defendants did not prove actual damages. There was no evidence that UEL had an existing resale contract on any of the equipment subject to the first right of refusal. Defendants could not prove UEL's resale profit would be less than the market-contract price differential of § 2-713. Accordingly, the trial court did not err by awarding § 2-713 damages instead of actual damages.

PROBLEM 5 - 9

Rae ordered 250 pounds of black tiger prawns at nineteen dollars a pound, peeled, from an itinerant fishmonger for a prawn and fennel bisque she want to add to the deli's menu. The prawns were to be delivered yesterday (when the market price was $22.50 a pound) but never arrived. The seller has not returned her calls. After several weeks of calling around, she was able to purchase the prawns from a seller on the East Coast at $16.50 per pound. Can she use 2-713 to measure her damages if she sues the fishmonger for breach?

PROBLEM 5 - 10

Several years ago, Rae built a gas station at the far end of the store's parking lot so customers can buy cheap gas for their cars. The store sells its gas at cost plus three cents per gallon, which is significantly less than the price standalone stations are able to charge for their gas. When oil prices were low last year, Rae put contracts on several tankers of gas that were to be delivered last month. Since then, the price of oil has risen steadily—almost 50 percent by the time the gas was supposed to be delivered under the contracts. The seller refused to deliver the gas last month at the contract price, and Rae has not purchased substitute gas. At a resale price of cost plus three cents, the store expected to make $270 per tanker. But because the difference between the market price at the time Rae learned of the seller's breach and the contract price was eighty-five cents per gallon, the store would recover more than $7,500 per tanker under 2-713—a windfall of $7,200 on each tanker under contract. Is Rae entitled to recover the extra $7,200 per tanker under Article 2 because the seller breached the contracts? See 1-305.

PROBLEM 5 - 11

Rae is always looking for new items to sell that will interject a bit of excitement into the customers' shopping experience at the store. Earlier this year, she read an article about pepinos—a South American fruit resembling a cross between a melon and a pear—and decided to introduce the fruit to her customers. She found a California grower of pepinos and placed an order for one hundred crates at $300 per crate, delivery by April 1. She planned to have a new display case built for the pepinos in the produce department of the store. In early March, the seller notified Rae that his entire crop of pepinos had been destroyed by mosaic virus, and so he would not be able to deliver the one hundred crates she had ordered. In early March, imported pepinos were selling for $450 per crate—she could not find another US grower. By April 1, the price had dropped to $275 per crate for imported pepinos. Rae decides to forget about the pepinos for this year and does not order the new display case. How should the court measure her damages under 2-713 if she sues the seller for breach of the pepinos contract?

When the buyer chooses 2-713 to measure damages for the seller's breach, 2-713(1) tells us to calculate those damages using the market price of the goods "at the time when the buyer learned of the breach." When does the buyer "learn" of the seller's breach if the seller anticipatorily repudiates? At the moment of repudiation? When the date for the seller's performance passes without delivery of the goods? Or some other time? A buyer can treat a seller's repudiation as a breach—but that suggests that "repudiation" does not mean "breach." If it did, the buyer would not need to treat repudiation as breach. If the seller breaches in a rising market, the time at which the buyer is determined to have learned of the seller's breach will affect how much the seller pays as damages under 2-713. The next case shows how some courts have answered this question.

COSDEN OIL & CHEMICAL CO. V. KARL O. HELM AKTIENGESELLSCHAFT

UNITED STATES COURT OF APPEALS FOR THE FIFTH CIRCUIT, 1984
736 F.2D 1064

REAVLEY, Circuit Judge.

We must address one of the most difficult interpretive problems of the Uniform Commercial Code—the appropriate time to measure buyer's damages where the seller anticipatorily repudiates a contract and the buyer does not cover. The district court applied the Texas version of Article 2 and measured buyer's damages at a commercially reasonable time after seller's repudiation. We affirm, but remand for modification of damages on another point.

I. CASE HISTORY

This contractual dispute arose out of events and transactions occurring in the first three months of 1979, when the market in polystyrene, a petroleum derivative used to make molded products, was steadily rising. During this time Iran, a major petroleum producer, was undergoing political turmoil.

Karl O. Helm Aktiengesellschaft (Helm or Helm Hamburg), an international trading company based in Hamburg, West Germany, anticipated a tightening in the world petrochemical supply and decided to purchase a large amount of polystyrene. Acting on orders from Helm Hamburg, Helm Houston, a wholly-owned subsidiary, initiated negotiations with Cosden Oil & Chemical Company (Cosden), a Texas-based producer of chemical products, including polystyrene.

Rudi Scholtyssek, general manager of Helm Houston, contacted Ken Smith, Cosden's national sales coordinator, to inquire about the possibility of purchasing quantities of polystyrene. Negotiating over the telephone and by telex, the parties agreed to the purchase and sale of 1250 metric tons of high impact polystyrene at $.2825 per pound and 250 metric tons of general purpose polystyrene at $.265 per pound. The parties also discussed options on each polystyrene type. On January 18, 1979, Scholtyssek met with Smith in Dallas, leaving behind two purchase confirmations. Purchase confirmation 04 contained the terms for high impact and 05 contained the terms for general purpose. Both confirmations contained the price and quantity terms listed above, and specified the same delivery and payment terms. The polystyrene was to be delivered during January and February in one or more lots, to be called for at Helm's instance.

As Helm had expected, polystyrene prices began to rise in late January, and continued upward during February and March.

Late in January Cosden notified Helm that it was experiencing problems at its production facilities and that the delivery under 04 might be delayed. On February 6, Smith telephoned Scholtyssek and informed him that Cosden was cancelling orders 05, ... because two plants were "down" and it did not have sufficient product to fill the orders. Cosden, however, would continue to honor order 04. Smith confirmed the cancellation in a letter dated February 8, which Scholtyssek received on or about February 12. After Helm Hamburg learned of Cosden's cancellation, Wolfgang Gordian, a member of Helm's executive board, sent an internal memorandum to Helm Houston outlining a strategy. Helm would urge that Cosden continue to perform under 04 and, after receiving the high impact polystyrene, would offset amounts owing under 04 against Helm's damages for nondelivery of the balance of polystyrene. Gordian also instructed Helm Houston to send a telex to Cosden. Following instructions, Scholtyssek then requested from Cosden "the relevant force majeure certificate" to pass on to Helm Hamburg. Helm also urged Cosden to deliver immediately several hundred metric tons of high impact to meet two February shipping dates for which Helm had booked shipping space.

In mid-February Cosden shipped approximately 1,260,000 pounds of high impact to Helm under order 04. This shipment's invoice, which also included the force majeure provision on the reverse side, specified that Helm owed $355,950, due by March 15 or 16. After this delivery Helm requested that Cosden deliver the balance under order 04 for shipment on a vessel departing March 16. Cosden informed Helm that a March 16 delivery was not possible. On March 15, citing production problems with the 04 balance, Cosden offered to sell 1000 metric tons of styrene monomer at $.41 per pound. Although Cosden later lowered the price on the styrene monomer, Helm refused the offer, insisting on delivery of the balance of 04 polystyrene by March 31 at the latest. Around the end of March, Cosden informed Scholtyssek by telephone that it was cancelling the balance of order 04.

Cosden sued Helm, seeking damages for Helm's failure to pay for delivered polystyrene. Helm counterclaimed for Cosden's failure to deliver polystyrene as agreed. The jury also found that Cosden anticipatorily repudiated orders 05, ... and that Cosden cancelled order 04 before Helm's failure to pay for the second 04 delivery constituted a repudiation. The jury fixed the per pound market prices for polystyrene under each of the four orders at three different times: when Helm learned of the cancellation, at a commercially reasonable time thereafter, and at the time for delivery.

The district court ... determined that Helm was entitled to recover $628,676 in damages representing the difference between the contract price and the market price at a commercially reasonable time after Cosden repudiated its polystyrene delivery obligations and that Cosden was entitled to an offset of $355,950 against those damages for polystyrene delivered, but not paid for, under order 04.

II. TIME FOR MEASURING BUYER'S DAMAGES

Both parties find fault with the time at which the district court measured Helm's damages for Cosden's anticipatory repudiation of orders 05 ...[6] Cosden argues that damages should be measured when Helm learned of the repudiation. Helm contends that market price as of the last day for delivery—or the time of performance—should be used to compute its damages under the contract-market differential. We reject both views, and hold that the district court correctly measured damages at a commercially reasonable point after Cosden informed Helm that it was cancelling [the order].

Article 2 of the Code has generally been hailed as a success for its comprehensiveness, its deference to mercantile reality, and its clarity. Nevertheless, certain aspects of the Code's overall scheme have proved troublesome in application. The interplay among sections 2.610, 2.711, 2.712, 2.713, and 2.723, Tex. Bus. & Com.Code Ann. (Vernon 1968), represents [**10] one of those areas, and has been described as "an impossible legal thicket." J. White & R. Summers, *Uniform Commercial Code* § 6-7 at 242 (2d ed. 1980). The aggrieved buyer seeking damages for seller's anticipatory repudiation presents the most difficult interpretive problem.[7] Section 2.713 describes the buyer's damages remedy:

> Buyer's Damages for Non-Delivery or Repudiation
>
> (a) Subject to the provisions of this chapter with respect to proof of market price (Section 2.723), the measure of damages for non-delivery or repudiation by the seller is the difference between the market price *at the time when the buyer learned of the breach* and the contract price together with any incidental and consequential damages provided in this chapter (Section 2.715), but less expenses saved in consequence of the seller's breach.

(emphasis added).

Courts and commentators have identified three possible interpretations of the phrase "learned of the breach." If seller anticipatorily repudiates, buyer learns of the breach:

(1) When he learns of the repudiation;

(2) When he learns of the repudiation plus a commercially reasonable time; or

(3) When performance is due under the contract.

We would not be free to decide the question if there were a Texas case on point, bound as we are by *Erie* to follow state law in diversity cases. We find, however, that no Texas case has addressed the Code question of buyer's damages in an anticipatory repudiation context.

Fredonia Broadcasting Corp. v. RCA Corp., 481 F.2d 781 (5th Cir. 1973) (*Fredonia I*), contains dicta on this question. The court merely quoted the language of the section and noted that the time for measuring market price—when buyer learns of the breach—was the only difference from pre-Code

---

6   The damages measurement problem does not apply to Cosden's breach of order 04, which was not anticipatorily repudiated. The time Helm learned of Cosden's intent to deliver no more polystyrene under 04 was the same time as the last date of performance, which had been extended to the end of March.

7   The only area of unanimous agreement among those that have studied the Code provisions relevant to this problem is that they are not consistent, present problems in interpretation, and invite amendment.

Texas law.[8] We have found no Texas case quoting or citing *Fredonia I* for its dicta on damages under section 2.713. Although *Fredonia I* correctly stated the statutory language, it simply did not address or recognize the interpretive problems peculiar to seller's anticipatory repudiation.

Since *Fredonia I,* four Texas courts have applied section 2.713 to measure buyer's damages at the time he learned of the breach. In all of these cases the aggrieved buyer learned of the breach at or after the time of performance.

Two recent Texas cases indicate that appropriate measure for buyer's damages in the anticipatory repudiation context has not been definitively decided. In *Aquamarine Associates v. Burton Shipyard,* 645 S.W.2d 477 (Tex.App.—Beaumont 1982), seller anticipatorily repudiated its obligation to construct and deliver ships. After seller learned of the repudiation, it covered by contracting with another party to complete the vessels. Since buyer covered under section 2.712, the jury's answer to the section 2.713 damages issue was properly disregarded. Referring to comment 5 of section 2.713, however, the Texas Court of Civil Appeals cited two cases that measured buyer's damages for anticipatory repudiation at different times. *Cargill, Inc. v. Stafford,* 553 F.2d 1222 (10th Cir. 1977), held that buyer's damages for anticipatory repudiation should be measured at a commercially reasonable time after he learned of the repudiation if he should have covered, and at the time of performance if buyer had a valid reason for failure or refusal to cover. In *Ralston Purina Co. v. McFarland,* 550 F.2d 967 (4th Cir. 1977), the court measured buyer's damages at the market price prevailing on the day seller anticipatorily repudiated. The two citations in *Aquamarine* reveal uncertainty concerning the applicable time for measuring damages.

Hargrove v. Powell, 648 S.W.2d 372 (Tex.App.—San Antonio 1983, no writ), also indicates that the interpretation of section 2.713 in an anticipatory repudiation case has not been settled in Texas. In referring to the hypothetical case of seller's repudiation, the *Hargrove* court cited *Cargill* and Professor Anderson's article, which presents the argument that "time when the buyer learned of the breach" means the time for performance or later.

We do not doubt, and Texas law is clear, that market price at the time buyer learns of the breach is the appropriate measure of section 2.713 damages in cases where buyer learns of the breach at or after the time for performance. This will be the common case, for which section 2.713 was designed. In the relatively rare case where seller anticipatorily repudiates and buyer does not cover, the specific provision for anticipatory repudiation cases, section 2.610, authorizes the aggrieved party to await performance for a commercially reasonable time before resorting to his remedies of cover or damages.

In the anticipatory repudiation context, the buyer's specific right to wait for a commercially reasonable time before choosing his remedy must be read together with the general damages provision of section 2.713 to extend the time for measurement beyond when buyer learns of the breach. Comment 1 to section 2.610 states that if an aggrieved party "awaits performance beyond a commercially reasonable time he cannot recover resulting damages which he should have avoided." This suggests that an aggrieved buyer can recover damages where the market rises during the commercially reasonable time he awaits performance. To interpret 2.713's "learned of the breach" language to mean the time at which seller first communicates his anticipatory repudiation would undercut the time that 2.610 gives the aggrieved buyer to await performance.

---

8   Before Texas adopted the Code, its courts applied the traditional time-of-performance measure of damages in repudiation cases. *See, e.g., Henderson v. Otto Goedecke, Inc.,* 430 S.W.2d 120, 123-24 (Tex.Civ.App.—Tyler 1968, writ ref'd n.r.e.); Anderson, *Learning of Breaches Under Section 2-713 of the Code,* 40 Tex. B. J. 317, 318 & n. 7 (1977). By interpreting the time buyer learns of the breach to mean a commercially reasonable time after buyer learns of the repudiation, we depart from pre-Code law, although in a different manner than suggested by the dicta of *Fredonia I.* This panel, however, is not bound by dicta of a previous panel. *Curacao Drydock Co. v. M/V AKRITAS,* 710 F.2d 204 (5th Cir. 1983).

The buyer's option to wait a commercially reasonable time also interacts with section 2.611, which allows the seller an opportunity to retract his repudiation. Thus, an aggrieved buyer "learns of the breach" a commercially reasonable time after he learns of the seller's anticipatory repudiation. The weight of scholarly commentary supports this interpretation. *See* J. Calamari & J. Perillo, *Contracts* § 14-20 (2d ed. 1977); Sebert, *Remedies Under Article Two of the Uniform Commercial Code: An Agenda for Review*, 130 U.Pa. L. Rev. 360, 372-80 (1981); Wallach, *Anticipatory Repudiation and the UCC*, 13 U.C.C. L.J. 48 (1980); Peters, *supra*, at 263-68.

Typically, our question will arise where parties to an executory contract are in the midst of a rising market. To the extent that market decisions are influenced by a damages rule, measuring market price at the time of seller's repudiation gives seller the ability to fix buyer's damages and may induce seller to repudiate, rather than abide by the contract. By contrast, measuring buyer's damages at the time of performance will tend to dissuade the buyer from covering, in hopes that market price will continue upward until performance time.

Allowing the aggrieved buyer a commercially reasonable time, however, provides him with an opportunity to investigate his cover possibilities in a rising market without fear that, if he is unsuccessful in obtaining cover, he will be relegated to a market-contract damage remedy measured at the time of repudiation. The Code supports this view. While cover is the preferred remedy, the Code clearly provides the option to seek damages. *See* § 2.712(c) & comment 3. If "the buyer is always free to choose between cover and damages for non-delivery," and if 2.712 "is not intended to limit the time necessary for [buyer] to look around and decide as to how he may best effect cover," it would be anomalous, if the buyer chooses to seek damages, to fix his damages at a time before he investigated cover possibilities and before he elected his remedy. *See id.* comment 2 & 3. Moreover, comment 1 to section 2.713 states, "The general baseline adopted in this section uses as a yardstick the market in which the buyer would have obtained cover had he sought that relief." *See* § 2.610 comment 1. When a buyer chooses not to cover, but to seek damages, the market is measured at the time he could have covered—a reasonable time after repudiation. *See* §§ 2.711 & 2.713.

Persuasive arguments exist for interpreting "learned of the breach" to mean "time of performance," consistent with the pre-Code rule. *See* J. White & R. Summers, *supra*, § 6-7; Anderson, *supra*. If this was the intention of the Code's drafters, however, phrases in section 2.610 and 2.712 lose their meaning. If buyer is entitled to market-contract damages measured at the time of performance, it is difficult to explain why the anticipatory repudiation section limits him to a commercially reasonable time to await performance. *See* § 2.610 comment 1. Similarly, in a rising market, no reason would exist for requiring the buyer to act "without unreasonable delay" when he seeks to cover following an anticipatory repudiation. *See* § 2.712(a).

The interplay among the relevant Code sections does not permit, in this context, an interpretation that harmonizes all and leaves no loose ends. We therefore acknowledge that our interpretation fails to explain the language of section 2.723(a) insofar as it relates to aggrieved buyers. We note, however, that the section has limited applicability—cases that come to trial before the time of performance will be rare. Moreover, the comment to section 2.723 states that the "section is not intended to exclude the use of any other reasonable method of determining market price or of measuring damages...." In light of the Code's persistent theme of commercial reasonableness, the prominence of cover as a remedy, and the time given an aggrieved buyer to await performance and to investigate cover before selecting his remedy, we agree with the district court that "learned of the breach" incorporates section 2.610's commercially reasonable time.[9]

---

9 We note that two circuits arrived at a similar conclusion by different routes. In *Cargill, Inc. v. Stafford*, 553 F.2d 1222 (10th Cir. 1977), the court

   conclude[d] that under § 4-2-713 a buyer may urge continued performance for a reasonable time. At the end of a reasonable period he should cover if substitute goods are readily available. If substitution is readily available

In *Cosden Oil*, the court noted that a different interpretation of the "learned of the breach" language in 2-713 was possible based on 2-723(1), but dismissed that interpretation because of the "limited applicability" of 2-723(1)—it only applies to the "rare" case that comes to trial before the date for performance of the breached contract. More recent cases have not been as dismissive of the importance of 2-723(1). In *Hess Energy v. Lightning Oil*, Lightning repudiated its long-term contract to sell natural gas to Hess and argued, based on cases like *Cosden Oil*, that the market price on the date Hess learned of Lightning's repudiation should be used to measure Hess's damages under 2-713. The Fourth Circuit rejected that argument, relying in part on the language of 2-723:

> While [2-713] might be susceptible to multiple interpretations, we conclude that the drafters of the Uniform Commercial Code made a deliberate distinction between the terms "repudiation" and "breach," and to blur these two words by equating them would render several related provisions of the Uniform Commercial Code meaningless.

[Court explains same problem with 2-610 that *Cosden Oil* court identified]

> In another example, if the date of the seller's repudiation is equated with the time when the buyer learns of the seller's breach as used in [2-713], then [2-723(1)] would become meaningless. Section [2-723(1)] provides:

> > If an action based on anticipatory repudiation comes to trial before the time for performance with respect to some or all of the goods, any damages based on market price (2-708 or 2-713) shall be determined according to the price of such goods prevailing at the time when the aggrieved party learned of the repudiation.

> This section moves the date that the seller learned of the *breach* under [2-713] to the date that the seller learned of the *repudiation* in circumstances where the case has come to trial before the performance date. To give meaning to [2-723(1)], when the case does *not* come to trial before the performance date, as here, damages are *not* measured when the aggrieved party learned of the repudiation. *See* White & Summers, *supra*, § 6-7, at 341 (commenting that a reading that equates the date of breach with the date of repudiation "makes the portion of 2-723(1) which refers to 2-713 superfluous" and concluding that the drafters "must have thought 'learned of the repudiation' had a different meaning than 'learned of the breach'").

> Thus, we conclude that the better reading of [2-713] is that an aggrieved buyer's damages against a repudiating seller are based on the market price on the date of performance—i.e., the date of delivery. This reading also harmonizes the remedies available to aggrieved buyers and aggrieved sellers when faced with a repudiating counterpart. Faced with a repudiating buyer, an aggrieved seller is entitled to "recover damages for nonacceptance"

---

and buyer does not cover within a reasonable time, damages should be based on the price at the end of that reasonable time rather than on the price when performance is due.

Id. at 1227. The *Cargill* court would employ the time of performance measure only if buyer had a valid reason for not covering.

In *First Nat'l Bank of Chicago v. Jefferson Mortgage Co.*, 576 F.2d 479 (3d Cir. 1978), the court initially quoted with approval legislative history that supports a literal or "plain meaning" interpretation of New Jersey's section 2-713. Nevertheless, the court hedged by interpreting that section "to measure damages within a commercially reasonable time after learning of the repudiation." *Id.* at 492.

under [2-708]. Under [2-708], "the measure of damages for nonacceptance or repudiation by the buyer is the difference between the market price *at the time and place for tender* and the unpaid contract price together with any incidental damages." *Id.* [2-708] (emphasis added). There is nothing in the Uniform Commercial Code to suggest that the remedies available to aggrieved buyers and sellers in the anticipatory repudiation context were meant to be asymmetrical. Indeed, the lead-in clause to [2-610], relating to anticipatory repudiation, addresses both parties: "When either party repudiates the contract with respect to a performance not yet due...."

Because our interpretation of [2-713] avoids rendering other sections of the Uniform Commercial Code meaningless or superfluous and harmonizes the remedies available to buyers and sellers, we are persuaded that in this case "the time when the buyer learned of the breach" was the scheduled date of performance on the contract, i.e., the agreed-upon date for the delivery of the natural gas, not the date that the seller informed the buyer that it was repudiating the contract.

3. Other Damages: Consequential and Incidental

The loss suffered by the buyer from the seller's breach of a contract for the sale of goods often goes beyond the loss of the goods themselves. This is especially so for a buyer who is not the end user of the goods or has purchased the goods for use in a business. Rae adds fifty cents a quart to the price she pays the local grower for the strawberries she sells at the store. If the grower does not deliver the strawberries as promised, Rae loses the profit she expected to make on resale of the strawberries. The local print shop can't charge your professor for the materials she ordered for this class if it cannot print those materials because the new press it had ordered never arrives. And there will be no iPads to sell for a profit if Apple does not get the touch screens its supplier agreed to provide. The market price measure alone will not put these buyers in the position they would have been in had their sellers not breached. Nor will covering for a seller's breach always put the buyer in the position it would have been in—if the print shop cannot purchase a substitute press for several days or weeks, it will still have lost the business of its customers who had to take their print jobs to another shop during that period.

Market price and cover measure what the common law referred to as direct or general damages—they compensate the buyer for the lost value of the seller's performance under the contract, the harm we would expect to follow from the breaching party's failure to perform. But the common law also recognized that sometimes the nonbreaching party lost more than just the performance it was expecting under the breached contract—sometimes, because of the particular circumstances of the nonbreaching party, the failure to perform caused other loss, what the common law called special or consequential damages. And so does Article 2—when the nonbreaching party is the buyer. The buyer's full measure when it covers is the difference between the cover price and the contract price "together with any incidental or *consequential damages.*" 2-712(2). The buyer's full measure under the market price remedy is the difference between the market price and the contract price "together with any incidental or *consequential damages.*" 2-713(1).

The following case examines the scope of the buyer's right to consequential damages under Article 2.

REXNORD INDUS., LLC V. BIGGE POWER CONSTRUCTORS

UNITED STATES DISTRICT COURT FOR THE EASTERN DISTRICT OF WISCONSIN, 2013
947 F. SUPP. 2D 951

ADELMAN, District Judge.

This is a breach of contract case involving two commercial entities, Rexnord Industries, LLC ("Rexnord") and Bigge Power Constructors ("Bigge"). Bigge manufactures and sells cranes and similar equipment for use in heavy industry. In 2009, Bigge agreed to supply a company named Shaw Constructors, Inc. ("Shaw") with two large derricks, which Shaw intended to use to construct nuclear power plants in Georgia and South Carolina. The derricks Shaw ordered are among the largest in the world. After Bigge and Shaw entered into the contract for the derricks, Bigge entered into a separate contract with Rexnord, which is in the foundry business, for the production of twenty-eight steel castings (components made by pouring liquid metal into molds) that Bigge intended to incorporate into the derricks. The contract consists of two purchase orders and a set of "commercial terms" printed on Bigge letterhead.

The purchase price for the castings was approximately $4.5 million. Rexnord manufactured and delivered the castings, and Bigge ultimately accepted them, incorporated them into the derricks, and received full payment from Shaw (less a holdback that is not relevant here). However, Bigge refuses to pay Rexnord the balance that remains due, which is approximately $1 million. Rexnord filed this suit in state court to recover that amount. Bigge removed the case to this court under the diversity jurisdiction, and in addition it filed a counterclaim alleging that Rexnord breached certain provisions of the commercial terms, causing it approximately $1.6 million in damages.

Rexnord's alleged breaches can be divided into two categories. The first category encompasses breaches of the commercial terms relating to Rexnord's promise to deliver the castings in accordance with a schedule incorporated into the contract. Bigge contends that Rexnord's delay in delivering the castings caused it to incur additional expenses. Bigge generally describes these as "time-related expenses" associated with "personnel" and "equipment rental." Bigge also states that it had to pay additional compensation to one of its subcontractors, Schuff Steel, because Rexnord's delay required Schuff to "reschedule and re-order its work."

The other category of breach involves Rexnord's alleged failure to properly perform a "root cause analysis," as required by the commercial terms. "Root cause analysis" is not defined in the terms, but the parties agree that it is a detailed engineering analysis of the cause of a defect and the impact it would have on the product's performance. Here, the parties agree that Rexnord's duty to perform a root cause analysis was triggered when Rexnord discovered that three of the castings, which were the mast feet for the derricks, had developed internal cracks. Rexnord conducted a root cause analysis, but Bigge thought that Rexnord's analysis was unsatisfactory. Bigge thus hired separate consultants to advise it on the condition of the mast feet and also devoted "significant internal resources (both management and engineering)" to solving the problem with the mast feet.

Rexnord and Bigge have each filed motions for partial summary judgment. Rexnord has moved for summary judgment on Bigge's counterclaim, contending that even if Rexnord had committed the alleged breaches, Bigge would not be entitled to recover anything because all of its alleged damages constitute incidental and consequential damages, which the parties have agreed to exclude pursuant to the following provision in the commercial terms:

> Neither party (including its subcontractors, agents, assignees and affiliates) shall be liable to the other for special, consequential or incidental damages of any kind, and regardless of whether such liability arises in contract, in tort, or by operation of law.

Bigge has moved for summary judgment on the question of Rexnord's liability for breach of contract. Bigge does not seek summary judgment as to the amount of damages it is entitled to recover in connection with Rexnord's breaches, but it does seek summary judgment in its favor on the question of whether any damages flowing from the breach constitute nonrecoverable incidental and consequential damages. The parties agree that California law, including California's version of the Uniform Commercial Code, applies to their dispute.

I begin with the question of whether summary judgment should be granted on Bigge's counterclaim on the ground that all of Bigge's claimed damages fall within the contract's exclusion of incidental and consequential damages. Initially, I note that Bigge eventually "accepted" all the castings, and so the starting point for an analysis of the remedies available to Bigge is UCC § 2-714, which in California is codified as Cal. Com. Code § 2714. That provision provides that where the buyer has accepted goods "he or she may recover as damages for any nonconformity of tender, the loss resulting in the ordinary course of events from the seller's breach as determined in any manner that is reasonable." Id. § 2714(1). Comment 2 to 2-714 states that the "non-conformity" referred to in 2-714(1) includes "any failure of the seller to perform according to his obligations under the contract." In the present case, Bigge alleges that Rexnord failed to perform two of its obligations under the contract—the obligation to deliver the castings in accordance with the schedule, and the obligation to perform a root cause analysis. Assuming that Bigge proves that Rexnord failed to perform these obligations, Bigge may recover "the loss resulting in the ordinary course of events from" each failure. Damages that flow in the ordinary course from the breach are usually referred to as "direct" or "general" damages. These damages may be contrasted with incidental and consequential damages, which are available under 2-714(3) unless they have been excluded, as they have been here.

In the present case, it is relatively easy to dispose of the argument that Bigge's damages are incidental. The text of 2-715(1) enumerates a list of damages that a buyer may recover as incidental damages, but the actual definition of incidental damage appears in Comment 1 to 2-715. The comment states that the damages listed in the text "are merely illustrative of the typical kinds of incidental damage" and that incidental damages fall into one of three categories: (1) reasonable expenses incurred in connection with the handling of rightfully rejected goods; (2) reasonable expenses incurred in connection with the handling of goods whose acceptance may justifiably be revoked; and (3) reasonable expenses incurred in connection with effecting cover. Bigge's damages do not fall into any of these categories. Bigge did not reject the castings, revoke acceptance of the castings, or effect cover by purchasing substitute castings, and thus none of its expenses could be deemed to have been incurred in connection with those acts.

Rexnord points out that the text of 2-715(1) lists "any other reasonable expense incident to the delay" as an example of incidental damage and contends that any damages caused by its failure to deliver the castings in accordance with the schedule falls within this language. However, delay damages of this sort do not fit within any of the categories identified in Comment 1, and thus they do not appear to be among the kinds of damages the drafters of the UCC had in mind when drafting 2-715(1). Moreover, the phrase "any other reasonable expense incident to the delay" is vague. Use of the definite article "the" before "delay" suggests that the reader is being referred to some exact delay that is identified earlier in 2-715(1), yet no such delay is identified there or anywhere else. Thus, it is not clear what "the delay" refers to. However, given that the preceding forms of incidental damage identified in 2-715(1) and the kinds of incidental damage identified in Comment 1 relate to expenses associated with rejecting goods and effecting cover, the most reasonable interpretation is that "the delay" refers to some delay associated with those acts. Again, in the present case, Bigge did not reject the castings or effect cover by purchasing substitute castings, and so Bigge's delay-related damages do not constitute incidental damages. I thus proceed to the question of whether Bigge's damages are consequential rather than direct.

As noted, the UCC provides that a buyer's remedy includes direct damages, which are those that flow in the ordinary course from the breach. The UCC does not define consequential damages, which are sometimes referred to as "special" damages. Instead, the Code relies on the principles relating to consequential damages that have been developed in contract law generally. In contract law generally, the leading case concerning consequential damages is the famous *Hadley v. Baxendale*, 9 Ex. 341, 156 Eng. Rep. 145 (1854). In that case, the plaintiffs owned a mill and experienced a broken crank shaft. They needed to send the broken shaft to the manufacturer so that the manufacturer could use it as a model for a new one. The plaintiffs contracted with the defendants, who were common carriers, to transport the shaft to the manufacturer. The plaintiffs informed the defendants that they were in a hurry, and the defendants promised that the shaft could be delivered to the manufacturer in a day's time. However, due to the carrier's neglect, delivery of the shaft was delayed, with the result that the mill's replacement shaft arrived several days later than expected. The plaintiffs did not have a spare shaft on hand, and so the plaintiffs could not operate their mill during the period of delay caused by the carrier's neglect. The plaintiffs thus sought to recover, as damages for the carrier's breach of contract, the lost profits for the period of delay. The court held that the plaintiffs could not recover lost profits, and this holding was based on the distinction between direct and consequential damages (although the court did not use those terms). In making this distinction, the court first identified the general rule governing damages:

> Where two parties have made a contract which one of them has broken, the damages which the other party ought to receive in respect of such breach of contract should be such as may fairly and reasonably be considered either arising naturally, i.e., according to the usual course of things, from such breach of contract itself, or such as may reasonably be supposed to have been in the contemplation of both parties, at the time they made the contract, as the probable result of the breach of it.

The court then identified a subset of these damages—now known as consequential damages—as those that would ordinarily follow from a breach of contract under "special circumstances." The court reasoned that if the defendant knew about the plaintiff's special circumstances at the time of entering the contract, then the defendant should be liable for the damages ordinarily following a breach of contract under those circumstances; however, if the defendant did not know about the plaintiff's special circumstances, then the defendant should not be liable for those damages. With respect to the mill's lost profits, the court observed that the carrier had no reason to know that the mill would not be able to operate and generate profits while the shaft was in transit, since one would ordinarily expect a mill to have a spare shaft on hand so that it could continue operations in the event that the shaft in use broke. Because the carrier did not know about the mill's "special circumstances"—i.e., that it did not keep a spare shaft on hand—the carrier could not be held liable for the damages attributable to those special circumstances.

Like most courts, those in California follow *Hadley v. Baxendale*. Thus, for purposes of the present case, the distinction between direct and consequential damages can be stated as follows: Direct damages are those that Rexnord, at the time of contracting, would reasonably have expected to follow from its breaches, assuming that it did not have knowledge of any circumstances peculiar to Bigge—circumstances analogous to the mill's not having a spare shaft on hand. Thus, Bigge's direct damages are those that Rexnord would reasonably have expected an ordinary purchaser of metal castings to incur in the event that Rexnord delivered the castings late or failed to carry out its obligation to perform a root cause analysis. In contrast, Bigge's consequential damages are those that Rexnord, at the time of contracting, would reasonably have expected to follow from its breaches under any circumstances that are peculiar to Bigge. Under the rule of *Hadley*, Rexnord would be liable for such consequential damages if Bigge had communicated its special circumstances to Rexnord at the time of contracting. However, because in this case the parties have agreed to exclude all consequential damages, Rexnord is not liable for consequential damages even if Bigge is able to prove that Rexnord knew about its special circumstances. Thus, the key question is whether the damages Bigge claims are those that Rexnord would reasonably have expected an ordinary purchaser of metal castings to incur as a result of its breaches.

With respect to Rexnord's alleged failure to perform an adequate root cause analysis, it is clear that the expenses Bigge reasonably incurred in hiring separate consultants to perform the analysis, as well as any of its own, internal resources reasonably incurred in performing the analysis, would be direct damages. This is so because, at the time of contracting, Rexnord would have known that if it did not properly perform a needed root cause analysis, an ordinary purchaser of metal castings would have to incur expenses in connection with either performing that analysis itself or hiring someone else to perform the analysis. In other words, there was nothing special about Bigge's circumstances that caused it to incur such expenses. Thus, any expenses Bigge reasonably incurred to obtain the root cause analysis called for by the contract are recoverable, assuming of course that Bigge is able to establish that Rexnord breached the root cause analysis provision of the contract in the first place.

However, whether Rexnord is liable for the expenses Bigge incurred because of Rexnord's breach of its scheduling obligations cannot be decided now. To decide whether such expenses are direct or consequential, I would need to know whether Rexnord should have expected an ordinary purchaser of metal castings to incur them or whether they were the result of Bigge's special circumstances. For example, Bigge claims that it incurred "personnel" and "equipment" expenses as a result of the delay. Should Rexnord have expected an ordinary purchaser of metal castings to incur these expenses, or would Rexnord have been justified in assuming that the purchaser would have arrange its affairs such that it could have used its personnel and equipment on other projects while it waited for Rexnord to deliver the castings, thereby avoiding any wasted expense? The record does not shed any light on that question. Similarly, the record does not enable me to determine whether an ordinary purchaser of castings would have incurred the additional expenses that Bigge paid to Schuff Steel. Accordingly, given the present state of the record, I cannot grant summary judgment to either party on the question of whether Bigge's delay-related expenses constitute consequential damages.

CONCLUSION

IT IS FURTHER ORDERED that Bigge's motion for partial summary judgment is GRANTED IN PART and DENIED IN PART. It is established that Rexnord breached the contract by delivering the castings late; that none of Bigge's claimed damages constitute incidental damages; and that the expenses Bigge reasonably incurred in hiring separate consultants to perform the root cause analysis, as well as any other expenses reasonably incurred in performing the analysis, are direct damages stemming from any breach by Rexnord of its obligation to perform a root cause analysis. In all other respects, Bigge's motion is denied.

As the court in *Rexnord* noted, consequential damages in Article 2 are subject to the same limitations the courts applied to them at common law—not only the "foreseeability" requirement from *Hadley v. Baxendale* applied in *Rexnord*, but also the requirements that they were caused by the breach, that they be proved with reasonable certainty, and that they are not barred by the doctrine of mitigation. Mitigation, under Article 2, includes the additional requirement that the buyer cover when possible—a buyer cannot recover consequential damages it could have prevented by a substitute purchase. Damages the seller had "reason to know" of are foreseeable, and although the "particular needs of the buyer must generally be made known to the seller,"

> [i]n the case of sale of wares to one in the business of reselling them, resale is one of the requirements of which the seller has reason to know within the meaning of subsection (2)(a).

Comments 2, 3, and 6, 2-715. The buyer retains the burden of proving the reasonable certainty of any loss, but the section on liberal administration of remedies rejects any doctrine of certainty which requires almost mathematical precision in the proof of loss. Loss may be determined in any manner which is reasonable under the circumstances.

Comment 4, 2-715. The next case applies the three limits to a buyer's claim for lost profits he claimed when the seller breached a contract for the sale of restaurant and bar equipment.

GERWIN v. SOUTHEASTERN CAL. ASSN. OF SEVENTH DAY ADVENTISTS
COURT OF APPEAL OF CALIFORNIA, FOURTH APPELLATE DISTRICT, 1971
14 CAL. APP. 3D 209

TAMURA, Judge.

Plaintiff brought an action seeking specific performance and damages for breach of an alleged contract for the sale from defendant to plaintiff of certain restaurant and bar equipment. Following a nonjury trial the court found in favor of plaintiff and entered judgment which, (1) decreed specific performance, or, in the event defendant fails or is unable to deliver the property, ordered payment of damages in the sum of $15,000 in lieu of specific performance, and (2) awarded plaintiff consequential damages for loss of anticipated profits in the sum of $20,000. Defendant appeals from the judgment.

Plaintiff had recently acquired a hotel in Beaumont and needed equipment for a proposed bar and restaurant which he planned to operate in conjunction with the hotel. In late November 1964 he learned of the availability of the equipment of the Azure Hills Country Club. He called defendant's office and was informed that the sale was being handled through Harty. Plaintiff went to the Club and spoke to Harty. Harty took plaintiff on a tour of the Club bar and cocktail lounge and showed him generally the items to be sold. Plaintiff made several other visits to the Club to view the equipment. On one of these visits he obtained from someone a purported inventory of items to be sold and, in addition, made note of the serial numbers of several cash registers he saw in the bar.

Upon his return home that day (December 18) plaintiff's wife told him someone called indicating that plaintiff would have to bid $4,000 or more for the property. Plaintiff thereupon contacted a Mr. Cunningham for the purpose of having him submit a bid on plaintiff's behalf. Either plaintiff or Cunningham called defendant's office to determine whether it was too late in the day to submit a bid. They were informed that it was but that bids would still be received through the following Monday, December 21, 1964. Thereafter, under plaintiff's direction, Cunningham typed out a bid for $4,126 for certain described items, including cash registers. The bid was made out in the name of "Richard Cunningham and Associates," dated December 21, 1964, and was signed by Cunningham. On the afternoon of December 21 Cunningham took the bid to the Club and asked a secretary in one of the offices for Harty, stating he wished to leave a bid with him. The secretary stated Harty was out but that she would deliver the bid to him when he came in the following day. Cunningham left the bid with the secretary.

On July 12, 1965, plaintiff and Cunningham went to the Club to pick up the equipment. A dispute arose as to the items to be delivered. The parties were unable to settle their differences and as a consequence defendant refused to deliver any of the items.

* * * *

II

We next consider the damage issues. As heretofore noted the court awarded ... $20,000 consequential damages for loss of anticipated profits. Defendant contends ... that the award of consequential damages based upon loss of anticipated profits was improper.

As noted earlier herein, if a buyer elects not to "cover" and sues for damages for breach, the measure of damages is the difference between market value and the contract price (Com. Code, § 2713), and any consequential damage "resulting from general or particular requirements and needs of which the seller at the time of contracting had reason to know and which could not reasonably be prevented by cover or otherwise.... " (Com. Code, § 2715.) Paragraph 2 of the Uniform Commercial Code comment to section 2715 states: "Although the older rule at common law which made the seller liable for all consequential damages of which he had 'reason to know' in advance is followed, the liberality of that rule is modified by refusing to permit recovery unless the buyer could not reasonably have prevented the loss by cover or otherwise...." Thus, in order to recover consequential damages other than those which could not have been avoided by cover or otherwise, the buyer must have made a good faith attempt to mitigate his losses by "cover." The concept of "cover" thus serves two purposes; it enables the buyer to make reasonable substitute purchases and to recover the cost thereof rather than the difference between market value and contract price and, at the same time, protects the seller from consequential damages which could have been mitigated by the purchase of substitute goods.

In the present case plaintiff did not cover. But it does not follow that he was thereby precluded from recovering consequential damages. Plaintiff was unable to purchase substitute items because of their unavailability at prices within his financial ability. Ordinarily a duty to mitigate does not require an injured party to take measures which are unreasonable or impractical or which require expenditures disproportionate to the loss sought to be avoided or which are beyond his financial means. That principle should govern in determining whether a buyer acted reasonably in failing to cover or otherwise mitigate his losses. In the circumstances here presented plaintiff's failure to purchase substitute goods did not, in and of itself, preclude his recovery of consequential damages. By ordering specific performance, the court impliedly found that after reasonable effort plaintiff was either unable to effect cover or the circumstances reasonably indicated that such effort would be unrewarding. (Com. Code, § 2716, subd. (3).) There was substantial evidence to support such an implied finding.

Nevertheless the evidence in the instant case is insufficient to support the award of damages for loss of prospective profits. The Commercial Code permits recovery of consequential damages for "[any] loss resulting from general or particular requirements and needs of which the seller at the time of contracting had reason to know...." Paragraph 3 of Uniform Commercial Code comment to section 2715 states in part: "Particular needs of the buyer must generally be made known to the seller while general needs must rarely be made known to charge the seller with knowledge." In substance, the section codifies the rule enunciated in *Hadley* v. *Baxendale*, 9 Exch. 341 [156 Eng. Reprint 145]; the test is one of reasonable foreseeability of probable consequences. Foreseeability, however, is to be determined as of the time the contract was entered into and not as of the time of the breach or some other subsequent event.

In the present case the court found that defendant knew "that plaintiff intended to use the assets to run a restaurant, hotel and cocktail lounge." However, there was no evidence to show that defendant accepted Cunningham's bid with knowledge that plaintiff was interested in it. There was nothing in Cunningham's bid showing plaintiff's interest in it or that Harty or any of defendant's representatives knew that Cunningham was submitting the bid on behalf of plaintiff. The bid was signed only by Cunningham; Cunningham personally submitted it; Cunningham made the required deposits with his checks; the confirmation of acceptance of the bid and receipt for the deposit referred to the bid by Cunningham; and all communications from defendant concerning that bid were with Cunningham. It was only after Cunningham requested that the proposed option agreement submitted to him be revised to show plaintiff as one of the optionees that defendant was made aware of plaintiff's interest in that bid. The record discloses that plaintiff attempted to conceal his identity as a bidder by submitting through Turner and Cunningham to avoid payment of a commission to Mr. Katz of All State Furniture. He testified that he agreed to pay Katz a commission for submitting a bid and was afraid the commission would have been payable on any successful bid submitted by plaintiff. At the time it accepted the bid, defendant could not reasonably have foreseen the probable consequences of its breach upon plaintiff when it didn't even know it was contracting with him. Although plaintiff made known to defendant his particular need for the equipment when he went to pick up the items on July 12, 1965, knowledge on the part of the seller at the time of breach is insufficient.

Apart from the foregoing, the evidence discloses deficiency in proof of anticipated profits.

It has been frequently stated that if a business is new, it is improper to award damage for loss of profits because absence of income and expense experience renders anticipated profits too speculative to meet the legal standard of reasonable certainty necessary to support an award of such damage. However, the rule is not a hard and fast one and loss of prospective profits may nevertheless be recovered if the evidence shows with reasonable certainty *both* their *occurrence* and the *extent* thereof. 5 Corbin, Contracts (1964), *supra*, § 1023, pp. 150–151. In the present case the question is whether the evidence of loss of prospective profits meets that standard.

The evidence on loss of anticipated profits in the present case may be summarized as follows:

Plaintiff acquired a hotel in Beaumont in June 1964. It was a two-story structure; the second floor consisted of some 25 guest rooms and the first floor a few additional guest rooms, a kitchen, banquet hall, space for a cocktail lounge and coffee shop. The hotel was vacant when plaintiff acquired it and had not been in operation for some time. There were no furnishings or furniture in it other than that provided for guest rooms. Plaintiff commenced renting some rooms in the fall of 1964.

In December 1964, Mr. and Mrs. Turner, whom plaintiff had employed to manage the hotel, signed a proposed three-year lease covering the entire hotel at a rental of $1,500 per month. Under the proposal, plaintiff was required to furnish and equip the kitchen, coffee shop and cocktail lounge. Plaintiff did not sign the lease because he was unable to obtain the necessary furnishings and equipment.

Plaintiff testified he had never before operated a hotel but that he had owned and operated bars in Los Angeles and that in his opinion the Turners would have been able to pay the $1,500 per month rental. Plaintiff also testified that he had an offer to lease only the banquet room and restaurant space for a monthly rental of $450 provided he furnished and equipped them.

The foregoing evidence fails to measure up to that degree of reasonable certainty required to support the award for loss of anticipated profits. The business being new, plaintiff was obviously unable to produce evidence of operating history of the proposed venture. But neither did he introduce even evidence of operating history of comparable businesses in the locality. Although plaintiff expressed his opinion that Turners could have paid the $1,500 per month rental for the operation of the hotel, bar and restaurant, plaintiff had no prior experience in the operation of a hotel or of a bar in the locality in question. In these circumstances it was speculative and conjectural whether the venture would have generated the business necessary to enable the Turners to pay the $1,500 per month.

Moreover, there was no showing that the rental income from the lease would have constituted net profit to plaintiff. Under the terms of the proposed lease plaintiff was required to provide and install the necessary equipment, furniture and furnishings. Amortization of such costs as well as interest on his capital investment, taxes, and cost of maintenance should have been deducted. When loss of anticipated profits is an element of damages, it means net and not gross profits. As the court noted in *Coates, supra*, at p. 119: "To allow plaintiff to recover a judgment based in part on his gross profits would result in his unjust enrichment. If he is entitled to recover at all, because of his loss of profits, such recovery must be confined to his net profits. Net profits are the gains made from sales 'after deducting the value of the labor, materials, rents, and all expenses, together with the interest of the capital employed." In the instant case the evidence, at the very most, showed loss of gross revenue, not loss of net pecuniary gain. An award of consequential damages based on loss of anticipated profits, particularly in a new venture, may not be sustained on such evidence.

III

Defendant urges that the court erred in decreeing specific performance insofar as two cash registers were concerned because they had been returned to the conditional seller long before the present action was instituted. Since the judgment afforded defendant the alternative of paying damages, the error, if any, was nonprejudicial.

For the foregoing reasons that portion of the amended judgment awarding plaintiff $20,000 as consequential damages (paragraph II of judgment) is reversed; the remainder of the judgment is affirmed.

Buyers can also recover "incidental damages" caused by a seller's breach, which include

> expenses reasonably incurred in inspection, receipt, transportation and care and custody of goods rightfully rejected, any commercially reasonable charges, expenses or commissions in connection with effecting cover, and any other reasonable expenses incident to the delay or other breach.
>
> 2-715(1).

The line between incidental expenses and consequential damages is not, as one court observed, "crystal clear," in part because what are claimed as incidental expenses in one case will be claimed as consequential damages in the next. Attorneys' fees incurred in breach-of-contract litigation have been claimed as consequential damages in some cases, as incidental expenses in others. Often the classification game is the result of contract terms that exclude certain damages. If the contract excludes consequential damages, the nonbreaching party may argue that what look like consequential damages are really incidental expenses in order to get around the damage exclusion clause. This is even more likely when a seller is claiming damages for a buyer's breach because, as we'll see in the next section of this chapter, Article 2 does not allow sellers to recover consequential damages. 2-710. So sellers frequently try to dress up their consequential damages as incidental expenses.

Although the line between incidental and consequential damages may be hazy, the courts have tried to sharpen the edges a bit:

> While the distinction between the two is not an obvious one, the Code makes plain that incidental damages are normally incurred when a buyer (or seller) repudiates the contract or wrongfully rejects the goods, causing the other to incur such expenses as transporting, storing, or reselling the goods. On the other hand, consequential damages do not arise within the scope of the immediate buyer–seller transaction, but rather stem from losses incurred by the nonbreaching party in its dealings, often with third parties, which were a proximate result of the breach, and which were reasonably foreseeable by the breaching party at the time of contracting.
>
> *Superior Inc. v. Behlen Mfg. Company,* 738 N.W.2d 19 (N.D. 2007), (quoting *Petroleo Brasileiro, S.A., Petro. v. Ameropan Oil Corp.,* 372 F. Supp. 503, 508 (E.D.N.Y. 1974).

We can simplify further. Incidental damages represent money the nonbreaching party spends dealing with the effects of breach, and consequential damages represent income the nonbreaching party did not receive because of the breach. When the seller breaches, as we've noted, the buyer does not get the goods it needs—was expecting to get when the seller performed. The buyer's incidental damages are what she has to spend because she does not have the goods—including what she spends to get substitute goods (aside from the actual purchase price of the substitutes). When the local print shop does not get the press it had ordered, it might be able to rent another press while it tries to purchase a substitute. Or maybe it pays another print shop to run the jobs it had committed to fill in anticipation of additional capacity the new press would provide. Maybe it has to rent a storage locker to store the extra paper and ink it won't need without the new press and has nowhere to store. These out-of-pocket expenses are incidental damages recoverable under 2-715(1). So, too, are extra shipping costs of the substitute press and the commission the shop paid to the broker who located the press. These are charges, expenses, or commissions incurred "in connection with effecting cover" and can be recovered by the buyer.

The following problem explores these and other issues raised by 2-715.

PROBLEM 5 - 12

Rae decided to add a section of upscale, gourmet frozen foods to the frozen foods department in the store. The additional inventory for the new section required additional cold storage space, so Rae purchased a second walk-in subzero freezer for the store. The new freezer was supposed to be delivered and installed at the store by July 1. Anticipating the availability of the new cold storage space, Rae had ordered an additional truckload of frozen foods for delivery on July 2. The freezer was not delivered on July 1, and so when the extra frozen food was delivered on July 2, Rae had nowhere to keep it at the store. She was able to locate additional cold storage space in a warehouse across town to which she transported the extra frozen food in a refrigerated truck she rented for moving the food. A dozen employees worked overtime to get all of the food moved as quickly as possible, but they were unable to save all of the food—about $1,000 of food thawed out before it could be relocated and had to be tossed out. Rae kept the refrigerator truck she rented until all of the additional food stored across town had been brought back to the store and sold. On one of the trips to the cold storage space across town to retrieve food for sale in the store, the driver clipped a parked car, causing damage to both the car and the truck. Rae purchased a substitute freezer which was installed several weeks later, but it is less energy efficient than the freezer that was never delivered, and as a result it costs 15 percent more to operate. What will Rae be able to recover as damages from the seller under 2-715?

4. Specific Performance

Specific performance as a remedy for breach of contract has been around a long time—but has been of limited utility as a remedy for breach of contracts for the sale of goods because, at common law, it was only available if the legal remedy for breach—money damages—would not do what contract damages were supposed to do: put the nonbreaching party in the position it would have been in had there not been a breach. Money was inadequate to do that only when the goods were unique. In the commercial world of contracts for fungible goods—peaches, plastics, aluminum, capacitors, bottled water, even toasters and washing machines—not much is unique, however we define that term. Personal property, unlike land—which is presumptively unique, is presumptively not unique. You might feel a special connection with the Keurig coffeemaker that gets your day started, but if you can buy it at Walmart, it's not unique—there's nothing special about it. It's not an heirloom or one of a kind—what makes personal property unique at common law.

But fungible goods can be functionally unique when, for example, the buyer's finances prevent it from covering at the current market price and it cannot continue to operate without the goods. Or where the buyer's operations will be significantly disrupted if it must resort to multiple purchases on the spot market when the seller breaches a long-term supply contract. The Uniform Sales Act tried to liberate specific performance from the uniqueness requirement by providing that a court could, "if it thinks fit," order specific performance of a contract for the sale of goods, assuming that courts would take the hint and be more flexible in their use of specific performance to remedy breach. They did not, and so Llewellyn, as the next case illustrates, decided that his new sales law would need to do more to overcome the inherent bias against the use of specific performance as a remedy for breach of a contract for the sale of goods.

KING AIRCRAFT SALES V. LANE

COURT OF APPEALS OF WASHINGTON, 1993
68 WN. APP. 706

PEKELIS, Judge.

The Lane Company, and Lane Aviation, Inc. (Lane) appeal the judgment of the trial court awarding King Aircraft Sales, Inc., d.b.a. King Aviation Services (King) $338,280.60 in damages, prejudgment interest, attorney fees, and statutory costs for its breach of a contract to sell two airplanes to King. The principal issue presented in this appeal, one of first impression in Washington, is whether the trial court may award money damages as a remedy in a claim for specific performance under the Uniform Commercial Code (UCC), RCW 62A.2-716. The trial court found King was entitled to specific performance and, because the planes were no longer available, awarded relief in the form of "value". The trial court determined value by using a lost expectation of profit approach resulting in an award of $157,010 plus return of the $10,000 deposit. In addition, the trial court awarded prejudgment interest of $35,688.60 and attorney fees in the amount of $135,454 and statutory costs of $128.

FACTS

The trial court found that in October 1988, King made a written offer to purchase two "quality, no damage" aircraft from Lane for $870,000. The offer was accompanied by a $10,000 deposit. Lane accepted the King offer both in writing and by depositing the $10,000 deposit. The acceptance created a contract of sale between the parties. King was to perform certain requirements but prior to the expiration of the time to perform, Lane advised King it was backing out of the agreement and that it had reached agreement with another party, Western Aircraft (Western), for the sale of the planes. Because at the time Lane backed out of the contract the time for King's performance had not yet expired, the trial court concluded that Lane's action was a breach of the contract.

King made it clear to both Lane and Western that it intended to enforce its contract with Lane and filed suit in Texas state court, seeking a temporary restraining order (TRO) to prohibit the sale of the aircraft to anyone other than King. The Texas state court issued the TRO. However, the case was later removed to a federal court in Texas, which denied King's motion to extend the TRO.

Lane then rescinded the Western contract and returned Western's deposit. Although Lane refused to honor the original contract with King, in settlement attempts pending litigation, it offered to sell the planes to King for the same price, but "as is", rather than "quality, no damage" airplanes as required in the original contract. King refused to purchase the planes under the terms of Lane's proposal and insisted on compliance with the original contract. At this time King had tentatively arranged to resell the planes for a profit of approximately $165,000.

After the federal court in Texas refused to extend the TRO, King brought this action in Washington and sought a TRO to prohibit the sale of the planes. In addition, King's complaint sought specific performance of the contract and other appropriate relief. After the King County Superior Court granted the TRO, King dismissed its federal court action. Subsequently, in December 1988, the King County Superior Court dissolved the previously granted TRO and sanctioned King for having misled the court and for failing to give proper notice of hearing to the other parties.

In January of 1989, long before trial, Lane sold both planes "as is" to Priester Aviation (Priester) for $870,000. Priester put the planes on the market and resold them separately in a series of transactions.

King's claim for specific performance and "other appropriate relief" was tried before the court without a jury.

* * * *

The trial court entered findings of fact that a contract was formed and that Lane breached the contract before the time for King's performance expired. In addition, the trial court found the planes were fairly characterized as "one of a kind" or "possibly the best" in the United States; however, it was not proved that the planes were "unique" because there were others of the same make and model available. However, the planes were so rare in terms of their exceptional condition that King had no prospect to cover its anticipated resales by purchasing alternative planes, because there was no possibility of finding similar or better planes.

Therefore, the trial court concluded that under the total surrounding circumstances this case appropriately fell within the "other proper circumstances" clause of the specific performance statute, RCW 62A.2-716(1), and therefore King was entitled to specific performance. Relying on the official comments to RCW 62A.2-716, the trial court noted that the inability to cover was strong evidence of "other proper circumstances" [**554] for an action/award of specific performance. Because the planes were no longer available the trial court concluded that specific performance should take the form of the value of the aircraft at the time of the breach. The trial court concluded this value could be measured either by the blue book value, including increased price adjustments for the prime condition of the planes, or by King's expectation of profit. The trial court chose the latter and awarded judgment to King as set forth above.

I

Lane's principal claim on appeal is that because this was solely an action for specific performance under the UCC, and because the goods had been sold and thus were inaccessible, no remedy was available to King. Lane contends the trial court had no authority to make a dollar value award. Its argument is as follows: Because King failed to plead a claim for monetary damages in its original complaint and had twice been denied permission by the court to add such a claim, no right to a damages remedy existed. However, because an adequate remedy at law existed, albeit not one available to King, specific performance was not proper here either.

We disagree and find that the remedy fashioned by the trial court was proper under the UCC and Washington common law.

The UCC, § 2-716, codified in Washington as RCW 62A.2-716, provides:

62A.2-716 Buyer's right to specific performance or replevin. (1) *Specific performance may be decreed where the goods are unique or in other proper circumstances.*

(2) The decree for specific performance may include such terms and conditions as to payment of the price, *damages*, or other relief as the court may deem just.

(3) The buyer has a right of replevin for goods identified to the contract if after reasonable effort he is unable to effect cover for such goods or the circumstances reasonably indicate that such effort will be unavailing or if the goods have been shipped under reservation and satisfaction of the security interest in them has been made or tendered.

(Italics ours.)

The UCC, like its predecessor, the Uniform Sales Act, does not expressly require that the remedy at law be inadequate in order to invoke specific performance. However, the stated intent of the drafters of the UCC was to continue "in general prior policy as to specific performance and injunction against breach", and also "to further *a more liberal attitude* than some courts have shown" toward specific performance. (Italics ours.) Official Comment 1, RCWA 62A.2-716.

Nevertheless, there is a split of authority among those jurisdictions which have considered whether a buyer's remedy at law must be inadequate before specific performance can be granted. *Compare Beckman v. Vassall-Dillworth Lincoln-Mercury, Inc.*, 321 Pa. Super. 428 (1983) (requiring inadequacy of remedy at law) *and Klein v. PepsiCo, Inc.*, 845 F.2d 76 (4th Cir. 1988) *with Dexter Bishop Co. v. B. Redmond & Son, Inc.*, 58 A.D.2d 755 (1977) (specific performance does not preclude a claim for damages) *and Sedmak v. Charlie's Chevrolet, Inc.*, 622 S.W.2d 694 (Mo. Ct. App. 1981) (taking "liberal" approach to code and allowing specific performance even though no absence of legal remedy).

We find the *Sedmak* case particularly instructive both on its facts and on the law. There, Mr. and Mrs. Sedmak were told they could buy a limited edition "pace car" when it arrived at the dealership for the suggested retail price of approximately $15,000. Factory changes were made to the car at the Sedmaks' request before delivery to the dealer. When the car arrived at the dealership the Sedmaks were told they could *bid* on the car, but its popularity had increased the price. The Sedmaks did not bid, but sued for specific performance. The court held that the pace car was not unique in the traditional legal sense, however, its "mileage, condition, ownership and appearance" did make it difficult, if not impossible, to obtain the replication without considerable expense, delay, and inconvenience. The court ordered specific performance even though the legal remedy of damages may have been available to make the Sedmaks "whole".

The *Sedmak* court also addressed the UCC's adoption of the term "in other proper circumstances" and Official Comment 2, RCWA 62A.2-716:[10]

> The general term "in other proper circumstances" expresses the drafters' intent to "further a more liberal attitude than some courts have shown in connection with the specific performance of contracts of sale." § 400.2-716, U.C.C., Comment 1. This Comment was not directed to the courts of this state, for long before the Code, we, in Missouri, took a practical approach in determining whether specific performance would lie for the breach of contract for the sale of goods and did not limit this relief only to the sale of "unique" goods.

We agree with the *Sedmak* court's interpretation of § 2-716 and, like that court, find the liberal interpretation urged by the UCC drafters to be entirely consistent with the common law of our state. Prior to adoption of the UCC, our cases did not always require the absence of a legal remedy before awarding specific performance nor did these cases require the goods to be absolutely "unique". Hence, the liberal approach to "other proper circumstances" suggested in Official Comment 2, RCW 62A.2-716 is not a departure from our law.

The trial court here expressly relied on *Welts v. Paddock*, 139 Wash. 668 (1926). In *Welts*, a car was bargained for but was no longer available, and thus specific performance in the form of the car itself was impossible. Nevertheless, the court held that the trial court correctly awarded specific performance in the form of a judgment for the value of the particular car.

---

10   Official Comment 2 states:
"In view of this Article's emphasis on the commercial feasibility of replacement, a new concept of what are 'unique' goods is introduced under this section. Specific performance is no longer limited to goods which are already specific or ascertained at the time of contracting. The test of uniqueness under this section must be made in terms of the total situation which characterizes the contract.... [U]niqueness is not the sole basis of the remedy under this section for the relief may also be granted 'in other proper circumstances' and inability to cover is strong evidence of 'other proper circumstances'."

The decision of the trial court is also supported by the case of *Zastrow v. W.G. Platts, Inc.*, 57 Wn.2d 347 (1960), in which the court held that "once a court of equity has properly acquired jurisdiction over a controversy, such a court can and will grant whatever relief the facts warrant, including the granting of legal remedies." In *Zastrow* the prayer for relief not only requested specific performance, but also "'such other and further relief as to the court seems meet and proper.'" The *Zastrow* court also found significant the fact that it was because of the appellant's own acts in relation to the property that the awarding of specific performance became impractical.

Nevertheless, Lane claims that King has not met the requirements of § 2-716 because it has not shown an inability to cover. Lane contends that King could have covered by accepting Lane's "as is" proposal of November 4. King's failure to do so, argues Lane, was "commercially unreasonable". Lane cites RCW 62A.1-203, .2-103(1)(b) for the proposition that the buyer has the duty to act reasonably and to mitigate damages. Lane contends that King should have "covered" with the "as is" offer of November 4 and if there were additional repair costs or other expenses, it could have sued for the difference. Furthermore, Lane argues that even if the trial court was correct in finding that King did not have to cover by accepting its November 4 proposal, RCW 62A.2-713 sets forth the measure of damages for a buyer who does not cover—the difference between the market price when the buyer learned of the breach and the contract price. In addition, however, a buyer for resale cannot recover more than his expected profit.

Here, the trial court held in conclusion of law 4 that King was under no obligation to purchase the planes on terms other than as contained in the contract. Specifically, the trial court found that King was under no obligation to accept the new November 4 proposal, which the trial court deemed to be considerably different from the original contract agreement.

We conclude the trial court properly determined that specific performance was an appropriate remedy here. At the time King commenced its action for specific performance Lane was still in possession of the planes; thus, the court properly acquired equity jurisdiction. The airplanes, although not necessarily "unique", were rare enough so as to make the ability to cover virtually impossible. Furthermore, Lane, by its own act of selling the planes, incapacitated itself from performance. Under these circumstances, the court of equity did not err in finding that "other proper circumstances" were present for issuance of relief under a claim of specific performance under the UCC. The trial court had the discretion to award the legal remedy of damages or other relief deemed just by the trial court. For the reasons above, we conclude that under RCW 62A.2-716 and Washington common law the trial court's determination that "other proper circumstances" existed is correct and permitted it to fashion the relief it did.

As the court noted in *King Aircraft*, not all courts have read "other proper circumstances" in 2-716(1) as eliminating uniqueness as a requirement for a decree of specific performance, despite the admonition in Comment 2 that "uniqueness is not the sole basis of the remedy under this section." Comment 2 also states that "inability to cover is strong evidence of 'other proper circumstances,'" which some courts have read as meaning that 2-716(1) requires the party asking for specific performance to show the goods are unique. But if other proper circumstances means unique, then it's redundant in 2-716—specific performance may be decreed when the goods are unique or when they are unique. That reading also seems inconsistent with the message that the Comments to 2-716 as a whole convey that things are supposed to be different now—specific performance is available when it would not have been available under the old rules. And, as we've noted, the inability of a buyer to cover is not necessarily a result of the uniqueness of the goods—the particular circumstances of the buyer may impair her ability to cover even if the contract goods were fungible. Since inability to cover is not proof of uniqueness, the other proper circumstances of which inability to cover is evidence must be something other than uniqueness. The drafting history supports this view as well. The 1941 draft of what became Article 2 expressly conditioned a decree of specific performance on an "unsuccessful resort to cover."[11] By the 1944 draft, the condition was gone, other proper circumstances had become a basis for specific performance, and inability to cover was not mentioned.[12]

PROBLEM 5 - 13

After reading news stories about the age-reversing effects of a South American fruit known as the Inka berry, Rae decided to see if she could order some for the healthy-foods campaign she was planning to run at the store. She found a small produce vendor in California who imported the berries and ordered three hundred pints at two dollars a pint for delivery in April. By March, the Inka berry had become the *cause célèbre* of the spring after Martha Stewart interviewed a Peruvian woman on her show who claimed to be 118 years old and to have eaten a pint of Inka berries every day of her adult life. When the seller called to tell Rae she would not be getting the Inka berries he had promised her in April, they were selling for more than one hundred dollars a pint. She could not find another vendor who would sell her berries at any price because the entire spring crop was under contract. Can Rae use 2-716 to compel the seller to deliver the Inka berries in April as promised?

C. SELLER'S REMEDIES

A buyer breaches by repudiating its performance before it's due, by failing to pay when the seller has completed its performance, or by improperly rejecting the seller's performance or revoking its acceptance.

When a buyer breaches, the seller may be able to call off the deal—cancel the contract, recover the price, and/or recover damages for loss caused by the breach. Section 2-703 catalogs the remedies available under Article 2 to the seller on the buyer's breach. When the buyer breaches, the seller is stuck with the goods it expected the buyer would take, so which of the alternatives offered by Article 2 works best to put the seller in as good a position as the buyer's performance would have will depend on the particular circumstances of each seller, and Article 2 leaves it to the seller to determine which way to proceed. Of course, whichever way the seller chooses to proceed, it must comply with any requirements imposed by Article 2 to obtain the relief chosen.

1. Substitute Transaction: Seller's Right to Resell

Article 2 presumes that sellers, like buyers, if given a choice between a new sale to replace the failed transaction and a claim for money damages, would prefer the replacement transaction, and 2-706 empowers a seller to resell the goods it's stuck with because of the buyer's breach and measure its damages for that breach as the difference between the resale price and the contract price. The seller's right to resell the goods is the analogue to the buyer's right to cover under 2-712. Reselling the goods allows a seller to quickly fix her loss and to avoid the risks inherent in proving a hypothetical market price later at trial. It also lessens the disruption to cash flow that results when the breaching buyer does not pay for the goods as expected, and abates the unbudgeted costs of dealing with the goods (e.g., storing and insuring the goods). And if the breach occurs in a declining market, a quick resale will mitigate the liability of the buyer for its breach as well.

---

11   I Kelly, *Uniform Commercial Code: Drafts,* (Rothman, 1984) 562 (Section 67A of Second Draft).
12   II Kelly, *Uniform Commercial Code: Drafts,* (Rothman 1984) 74 (Section 118 of Proposed Final Draft).

As the next two cases illustrate, the seller's right to measure her damages as the difference between the resale price and the contract price is conditioned on a resale made in good faith and in a commercially reasonable manner.

COOK COMPOSITES V. WESTLAKE STYRENE CORP.

COURT OF APPEALS OF TEXAS, FOURTEENTH DISTRICT, HOUSTON, 2000
15 S.W.3D 124

FROST, Judge.

This is a breach of contract case arising out of a written agreement between two companies for the purchase and sale of goods. At issue is the propriety of the trial court's granting of the seller's motion for summary judgment notwithstanding the buyer's assertion of various affirmative defenses, both under common law and arising under the Uniform Commercial Code.

FACTUAL BACKGROUND

In January of 1995, [Cook Composites or "CCP"] and Westlake entered into a three-year contract for the purchase and sale of styrene monomer. Under the parties' contract, CCP agreed to buy a set quantity of product from Westlake through the end of 1997, at an agreed formula price. CCP was to purchase the product in equal monthly installments in the following volumes: (i) 12 million pounds in 1995; (ii) 14 million pounds in 1996; and (iii) 16 million pounds in 1997. Because the market price for styrene monomer fluctuates on a daily basis, the parties included in the contract a "meeting competition" clause in an effort to buffer the effects of market price movements. The clause reads in part:

> If Buyer [CCP] furnishes Seller [Westlake] satisfactory written evidence of a legitimate price, which is lower than Seller's effective price to buy, offered by a recognized domestic manufacturer on standard products of like quantity and quality on substantially similar terms and conditions, Seller agrees to meet such lower price on the base volume as long as such competitive offer is valid over the term of this contract.

Beginning in December of 1996, CCP refused to honor the Westlake/CCP contract formula price. Westlake filed suit against CCP for breach of contract. To mitigate its damages, Westlake sold the styrene monomer CCP had agreed to purchase on the spot market at prices well below the price specified in the Westlake/CCP contract. Westlake did not give CCP advance notice of the sale. At trial, the court found in favor of Westlake and awarded damages for the difference between the contract price and the spot market sales price, plus prejudgment and post judgment interest and attorney's fees.

FAILURE TO ESTABLISH ELEMENTS OF *PRIMA FACIE* CASE

In its fourth issue, CCP claims the trial court erroneously granted summary judgment because Westlake did not prove the elements of its *prima facie* case for recovery of damages under either UCC section 2.706 or UCC section 2.708, as adopted in the Texas Business and Commerce Code. A plaintiff must offer legally sufficient proof on every element of its case to entitle it to summary judgment. Westlake's first response is that it was not required to do so because the matters CCP raised under UCC sections 2.706 and 2.708 are affirmative defenses. We now examine these UCC provisions to determine if they are in the nature of affirmative defenses, which would place the burden on CCP, or part of the claimant's *prima facie* case, which would place the burden on Westlake.

Recovery of Damages Under UCC § 2.706

UCC section 2.706, as adopted in Texas, authorizes an aggrieved seller to resell the contract goods and to measure its damages by the difference between the contract price and the resale price. Where, as here, the seller chooses to resell privately, section 2.706 sets out three simple steps the seller must follow:

(1) identify the resale contract to the broken contract;
(2) give the buyer reasonable notice of the seller's intention to resell; and
(3) resell in good faith and in a commercially reasonable manner.

CCP claims that because Westlake failed to prove (1) presale notice and (2) commercial reasonableness, it cannot recover under section 2.706. Texas has not decided whether recovery under section 2.706 is precluded in the absence of strict compliance with its terms. However, several other UCC states have considered the matter and concluded that recovery under section 2.706 is precluded if the seller does not prove each of the elements. *See Larsen Leasing, Inc. v. Thiele, Inc.*, 749 F. Supp. 821, 823 (W.D. Mich. 1990) (finding party seeking damages must plead and prove sale was made in good faith and in a commercially reasonable manner); *Sprague v. Sumitomo Forestry Co., Inc.*, 104 Wn.2d 751, 709 P.2d 1200, 1204 (Wash. 1985) (finding party seeking damages must show notice of intent to resell); *Anheuser v. Oswald Refractories Co.*, 541 S.W.2d 706, 711 (Mo. Ct. App.1976) (finding party seeking damages must plead and prove compliance with notice requirements). Therefore, characterizing the terms of section 2.706 as essential elements of a seller's *prima facie* case is consistent with the characterization adopted in other UCC states.

Finally, in making the determination, we note that the seller is in the best position to know what affirmative steps were taken to ensure the sale was conducted in a commercially reasonable manner and whether notice of intent to resell was given to the buyer. It would make no sense to impose the burden on the buyer to prove a negative as an affirmative defense, i.e., to prove the seller's failure to satisfy the elements of section 2.706. Considering the plain language of the statute and other UCC states' characterizations, and applying traditional notions of Texas jurisprudence, we find that presale notice and commercial reasonableness are elements of a *prima facie* claim for damages and not affirmative defenses.

Westlake, anticipating this possibility, next argues that because it pled that the conditions precedent to recovery had been satisfied, under Texas Rule of Civil Procedure 54, it was merely required to offer summary judgment proof on those conditions CCP specifically denied. Because CCP failed to specifically deny that any conditions precedent had been satisfied, Westlake contends its failure to plead presale notice and commercial reasonableness as part of its *prima facie* case is inconsequential. The record, however, does not support Westlake's factual assertions. Westlake did not plead that all conditions precedent to its recovery on the contract had been performed or had occurred, but only that all "conditions precedent to Westlake's recovery of *attorney's fees* have been performed." Pleading the performance of conditions precedent to the recovery of attorney's fees merely relieved Westlake of the burden of proof, in the absence of a specific denial, on those conditions precedent to the recovery of attorney's fees. A statement that conditions precedent to the recovery of attorney's fees have been performed is not tantamount to pleading that all conditions precedent to recovery on the breach of contract claim have occurred or have been performed. Consequently, Westlake's reliance on Rule 54 is misplaced.

Even if its pleading were sufficient, Westlake still would not be able to prove the *prima facie* elements of section 2.706 because Westlake did not give CCP notice of intent to resell the product. Therefore, Westlake could not recover under section 2.706 in any event.

Westlake's inability to prevail under section 2.706, however, is not necessarily fatal to its recovery of damages on a breach of contract claim. The comments to section 2.706 provide that failure to comply with the procedural provisions of that section still leaves the seller its remedy under UCC section 2.708.

SMITH V. PAOLI POPCORN CO.

SUPREME COURT OF NEBRASKA, 2000
260 NEB. 460

WRIGHT, Judge.

NATURE OF CASE

This is an action for damages arising from the alleged wrongful rejection of goods. In the first trial, the court granted summary judgment in favor of Stan Smith (Smith) on the issue of liability. Prior to submitting the issue of damages to the jury, the trial court granted a directed verdict in the amount of $28,542.37. We reversed the judgment and remanded the cause for further proceedings. In the second trial, a jury returned a verdict in favor of Smith in the amount of $31,175.19. Paoli Popcorn Co. (Paoli) appeals.

FACTS

In March 1994, Smith and Paoli entered into a contract in which Paoli agreed to purchase popcorn grown by Smith during the 1994 growing season for 10 cents per pound. Smith harvested the popcorn in late September or early October 1994. During the harvest, it began to mist, and Smith's son Steve Smith noticed that smut had attached to one of the loads of popcorn.

Tom Harmon, an agent of Paoli's, visited the grain bins to which the popcorn was delivered on the day of the harvest. Harmon took two samples of the popcorn, one about a foot below the surface of the bin and the second at a greater depth. In the process of taking those samples, Harmon noticed smut attached to the kernels. It was Harmon's belief that the smut could not be cleaned off and that, therefore, the popcorn would be difficult to market. While at the site, Harmon had a discussion with Rob Smith, another of Smith's sons. Although Harmon expressed concerns with the quality of the popcorn, he did not reject the popcorn at that time. Instead, Harmon conveyed that he intended to try to market the popcorn as best he could.

From the time the popcorn was harvested until early April 1995, the parties had several discussions regarding its marketability. On April 4, 1995, Harmon called Smith and rejected the popcorn. Two days later, the rejection was formalized by a letter from Paoli to Smith.

Paoli claims that after it rejected the popcorn, it offered to pay 8 cents per pound for the popcorn plus interest and storage, and that this offer was rejected by Smith. Steve Smith does not recall Paoli making this offer.

After Smith received the letter of rejection, he and Steve Smith attempted to resell the popcorn. Steve Smith testified that he contacted several popcorn companies that were likely to be in the market for popcorn. If a company showed any interest at all, Steve Smith sent them a sample of the popcorn and requested a bid. He sent these companies the "worst part" of the popcorn because "they weren't interested in seeing what the best [was], they wanted to know what the worst was." When the samples were sent, Steve Smith also informed the companies that most of the popcorn was fine.

Bids of 5 cents per pound were obtained from three separate companies. These 5-cent bids were communicated to Paoli, which responded with a bid of 5.25 cents per pound. Smith relayed Paoli's 5.25-cent offer to the three companies, but only Colorado Cereal, Inc., showed further interest by offering 6 cents per pound. This offer was communicated to Paoli, which offered 6.25 cents per pound. Smith agreed to accept this offer if he could retain the right to collect the difference between the contract price of 10 cents per pound and the current bid of 6.25 cents and if Paoli would pay the balance by certified check. Paoli refused, and in May 1995, Smith sold the popcorn to Colorado Cereal for 6 cents per pound.

Smith sued Paoli for wrongful rejection of the popcorn, seeking damages for the reduced price of the popcorn, storage fees, and interest.

ASSIGNMENTS OF ERROR

Paoli asserts, summarized and restated, that the trial court erred (1) in directing a verdict in favor of Smith on the issue of the commercial reasonableness of the resale....

ANALYSIS

On remand, the issues presented were whether Smith acted in good faith and in a commercially reasonable manner in reselling the popcorn, and what damages, if any, to which Smith was entitled. The trial court determined as a matter of law that Smith acted in a commercially reasonable manner, and the remaining issues were submitted to the jury.

On appeal, Paoli first argues that the trial court erred in directing a verdict that Smith resold the popcorn in a commercially reasonable manner.

Paoli contends that Smith did not act in a commercially reasonable manner because Smith (1) sent samples of the "worst part" of the popcorn to potential buyers, (2) denied Paoli an independent sampling of the popcorn after Paoli's rejection, (3) refused Paoli's offer of 6.25 cents per pound, (4) sold the popcorn for 6 cents per pound, and (5) asked one of the potential buyers for a bid for "low quality type popcorn" in order to give Smith leverage in dealing with Paoli.

The phrase "commercially reasonable" is not specifically defined in Neb. U.C.C. § 2-706 (Reissue 1992). Assuming a buyer has wrongfully rejected goods, § 2-706 provides that where resale is made in good faith and in a commercially reasonable manner, the seller may recover the difference between the resale price and the contract price together with any incidental damages allowed. Section 2-706(2) requires that every aspect of the sale, including the method, manner, time, place, and terms, must be commercially reasonable.

We conclude that the trial court did not err when it determined as a matter of law that Smith resold the popcorn in a commercially reasonable manner. Upon notification that the popcorn was rejected, Steve Smith contacted several companies which were in the business of purchasing popcorn from farmers. Three bids were received for 5 cents per pound. These bids were communicated to Paoli, which then offered 5.25 cents per pound. Colorado Cereal increased its offer to 6 cents per pound, and this bid was communicated to Paoli. Paoli then offered to pay 6.25 cents per pound, which Smith was willing to accept if Paoli would agree that the sale would not preclude Smith from pursuing any additional remedies he might have under the contract. Paoli refused to agree to these terms, and Smith sold the popcorn to Colorado Cereal.

With regard to the method and manner used by Smith to resell the popcorn, Harmon (Paoli's agent) stated that if he were a farmer selling popcorn, he would call different popcorn companies to see if they were bidding. If they were, he would provide samples and would then get bids and negotiate for the best price. This method was similar to the one used by Smith in negotiating the sale to Colorado Cereal. Harmon also testified that short of directly marketing the popcorn, there was nothing else a farmer could do to sell the product.

With regard to the price ultimately obtained by Smith, Bernard Blach, an agent for Colorado Cereal, testified that 6 cents per pound was a fair value for Smith's popcorn and that the price paid to Smith ended up being more than Colorado Cereal had paid other producers for popcorn in the same time period. He also testified that the transaction between Smith and Colorado Cereal was made in good faith and in a commercially reasonable manner. Furthermore, Dennis Kunnemann, who had been involved in selling and processing popcorn in the Imperial, Nebraska, area for 13 to 14 years, stated that the market price for popcorn in the area during the summer of 1995 was 6 to 7 cents per pound. Even Paoli's agent, Harmon, testified that if there had been a market for less than premium popcorn in the fall of 1994 through the winter of 1995, the price would have been 3 to 4 cents per pound. In addition, a letter from the president of Paoli to Smith dated April 18, 1995, indicated that 8 cents per pound was substantially more than the market price.

Paoli also argues that Steve Smith did not act in a commercially reasonable manner by sending potential buyers samples of the "worst part" of the popcorn. Steve Smith testified that this was the part of the crop the companies wanted to see. He also told the companies that the sample reflected one truckload placed on the top of the bin and that the rest of the popcorn was fine.

Paoli further contends that Smith's asking for a bid for "low quality type popcorn" was not commercially reasonable. It is undisputed that this bid was conveyed to Paoli, which then submitted another bid.

Giving every reasonable inference to Paoli, we conclude as a matter of law that Smith's actions in reselling the popcorn were commercially reasonable and that the trial court did not err in directing a verdict on this issue.

PROBLEM 5 - 14

Every April, the store promoted the arrival of spring with its "Strawberry Festival," a month-long event that took advantage of the California strawberry harvest and used strawberries as a loss leader for many other spring promotions at the store. This year, Rae ordered one thousand pallets of strawberries from a California grower at fifty cents per quart, to be delivered over a thirty-day period beginning April 1. After the first one hundred pallets had been delivered, a local TV station did a story on the pesticides used by California strawberry growers to increase yields and the connection of these pesticides to children's health problems. People stopped buying strawberries—when Rae called the grower to cancel the rest of the store's order, she told him that "the store wouldn't be able to give the strawberries away if it wanted to." The story broke nationally a week later, and although the grower was able to sell all of the strawberries he produced—more than five hundred thousand pallets in all—he did so only by continuously slashing prices during the strawberry harvest. He sold the last twenty-five thousand pallets at ten cents per quart. Can the seller use the resale price of the last twenty-five thousand pallets he sold to measure his damages under 2-706 for Rae's cancellation of her order?

PROBLEM 5 - 15

Would your answer to the last problem be different if, after selling 475,000 pallets of strawberries for more than ten cents a quart, the strawberry grower had actually designated nine hundred of the last twenty-five thousand pallets he sold as the pallets that were meant for Rae's store? Does it matter that the strawberries on the last twenty-five thousand pallets were not ripe enough to harvest at the time Rae cancelled her order? 2-706(2).

"Commercially reasonable" is not defined in Article 2 or anywhere else in the UCC. Earlier drafts of what became 2-706 did not use the term, but they did reject the "reasonable care and judgment" standard the Uniform Sales Act applied to a seller's resale, replacing it with "reasonable mercantile usage in the circumstances." The Comments explain that "mercantile reasonableness" (today's "commercially reasonable"?) was not used for fear that it might suggest a one-size-fits-all interpretation even where there were "a dozen lines which are mercantilely possible and reasonable." Instead, by "reasonable mercantile usage" the drafters intended

> reasonable leeway and absence of penalization where the judgment made was such as a reasonable merchant might make at the time and in the circumstances.

The goal was to make the trier of fact decide the case while standing in the shoes of the seller who resold and to avoid the "hindsight judgment" that had impaired commercial practice under the Uniform Sales Act.[13] The Comments to 2-706 indicate that the substitution of "commercially reasonable" for "reasonable mercantile usage in the circumstances" did not change the original intent of the drafters:

> Other meticulous conditions and restrictions of the prior uniform statutory provisions are
> disapproved by this Article and are replaced by standards of commercial reasonableness.
>
> Comment 1, 2-706.

2. Alternative to Resale: Market Price

A seller can use 2-708(1) to measure its damages for a buyer's breach, which, as the analogue to the buyer's measure in 2-713, will give it the difference between the market price and the contract price. Here, the market price we use to measure damages is the price of the goods at the time of "tender"—we don't use the "learned of the breach" timing, as 2-713 required, when measuring a buyer's damages based on the market price. The time for tender will turn on the delivery requirements of the contract, as we will see in Chapter 6, but for now we can think of it very generally as the time the goods were to be made available to the buyer. The following problems illustrate the basic application of 2-708(1).

PROBLEM 5 - 16

Rae recently began acting as a distributor for a number of local produce growers. Rae markets their produce she does not need for the store to buyers located through the region. Some of the buyers are located in neighboring states. Occasionally, some of these buyers, like the buyers in the following trans-actions, cancel their orders or refuse to take delivery of the goods. Determine, in each of the following transactions, how Rae's damages should be measured under 2-708(1):

> Transaction 1: A small grocery up the interstate ordered one of the last pallets of early-season, vine-ripened tomatoes at $0.75 per pound to be delivered at the buyer's store, with the buyer to pay for shipping. The buyer refused to take the tomatoes when the carrier Rae used to ship them attempted delivery several days later. When the carrier picked up the tomatoes for delivery from Rae, the market price for similar tomatoes was $0.90 per pound. By the time the tomatoes had arrived at the buyer's store, a new crop of tomatoes had flooded the buyer's market, and the price had dropped to $0.65 a pound.

> Transaction 2: An independent grocer in the next state down the interstate ordered 500 bushels of green beans at $2.75 per bushel to be delivered at the buyer's store, with the buyer to pay for shipping. When the carrier picked the beans up at Rae's place, Rae was paying $2.00 per bushel for the beans, which had become available in the buyer's local market for $2.35 a bushel. Unbeknownst to Rae, the seller had bought beans from a local farmer at the better price, and so he refused to take delivery of Rae's beans. At the time the carrier attempted to deliver the beans, Rae was paying $2.15 per bushel for the same quality of green beans that the buyer could purchase locally for $2.25.

> Transaction 3: Would your answer be different in the last transaction if the contract had provided that the buyer would pick up the beans at the grower's farm using his own truck?

---

13   All of the early drafts details mentioned here can be found in II Kelly, *Uniform Commercial Code: Drafts,* (Rothman 1984) 524–526.

Transaction 4: Rae agreed to sell 100 cases of butter lettuce to a cafeteria doing business in a large metropolitan area in a state adjacent to Rae's. The price was "$35 per case, shipping included F.O.B. cafeteria." When it was time for the carrier to pick up the lettuce from Rae for delivery, Rae was only paying $25 per case, but the same lettuce was selling for $35 per case in the metro area around the cafeteria. When the carrier arrived at the cafeteria to deliver the lettuce, the cafeteria was not open, and there was a sign in the window: "Out of Business—Too Many Cheapskates." Rae directed the carrier to deliver the goods to a produce wholesaler not far from the cafeteria that had agreed to take the lettuce for $20 a case. Rae could have gotten $40 a case for the lettuce from restaurants in town, but by the time it got back to her, it would have started to rot, so she had to sell it quickly.

Like buyers, sellers are free to choose how they measure their damages—a seller can resell the goods and measure her damages using 2-706, or, because she does not have to resell the goods, she can use the market price measure in 2-708(1). Can a buyer who resells the goods still use 2-708(1) to measure her damages? Should it matter that she was able to resell the goods at a later date for more than the market price of the goods at the time of tender—that her damages measured under 2-708(1) will be greater than her damages if measured under 2-706? Does the UCC's golden rule for remedies—remedies shall be administered to put the nonbreaching party in the position it would have been in—take away the seller's right to choose her measure in such a case? 1-305. The text of 2-708 does not address this issue, so it should not surprise us that the courts have given different answers to the question. The next case expresses one view of what the answer should be.

PEACE RIVER SEED CO-OPERATIVE, LTD. v. PROSEEDS MKTG.

SUPREME COURT OF OREGON, 2014
355 ORE. 44

BALMER, Chief Justice.

In this breach of contract case, we examine the availability of different remedies under the Uniform Commercial Code (UCC) for an aggrieved seller of goods after a buyer breaches a contract to purchase those goods. Specifically, we consider the relationship between ORS 72.7080(1), which measures a seller's damages as the difference between the unpaid contract price and the *market* price at the time and place for tender, and ORS 72.7060, which measures a seller's damages as the difference between the contract price and the *resale* price. We examine those provisions to determine whether an aggrieved seller who has resold goods can recover a greater amount of damages using the market price measure of damages than the seller would recover using the resale price measure of damages.

Plaintiff, a seller seeking damages from a buyer that breached contracts to purchase goods, argued at trial that it was entitled to recover its market price damages. The trial court determined that plaintiff was entitled to the lesser of its market price damages or its resale price damages, and the court ultimately awarded plaintiff its resale price damages. The Court of Appeals reversed and remanded, because the court determined that plaintiff could recover its market price damages, even though it had resold some of the goods at issue. For the reasons that follow, we agree that plaintiff was entitled to recover its market price damages, even if those damages exceeded plaintiff's resale price damages.

FACTS AND PROCEEDINGS BELOW

The facts material to our discussion are mostly undisputed. Peace River Seed Co-Operative ("plaintiff") is a Canadian company that buys grass seed from and sells grass seed for grass seed producers. Proseeds

Marketing ("defendant") is an Oregon corporation that purchases grass seed from various sources to resell to end users. A broker prepared and the parties agreed to multiple contracts for defendant to purchase from plaintiff the total production of grass seed from a certain number of acres for a fixed price over a period of two years.

Under the contracts, defendant was to provide shipping and delivery instructions to plaintiff. During the contract period, however, the price of grass seed fell dramatically. Although defendant initially provided shipping instructions and plaintiff shipped conforming seed, defendant eventually refused to provide shipping instructions for delivery of additional seed under the contracts. After multiple requests for shipping instructions, and defendant's continued refusal to provide them, plaintiff cancelled the contracts. Over the next three years, plaintiff was able to sell at least some of the seed that defendant had agreed to purchase to other buyers.

In the subsequent bench trial, the court concluded that defendant had breached the contracts and that plaintiff had been entitled to cancel the contracts and seek damages. When the trial court awarded plaintiff its damages, the court noted that the parties had entered into fixed price contracts, "regardless of the market price at the time of harvest and shipment," and the court explained that "[e]ach party takes certain risks and hopes for certain benefits in this type of a contract." Nonetheless, the court concluded that plaintiff had an "obligation to mitigate damages" and was "not entitled to recover damages in an amount greater than actually incurred." Accordingly, the trial court awarded plaintiff the lesser of two measures of damages: the difference between the unpaid contract price and the market price (the measure under ORS 72.7080(1)) or the difference between the contract price and the resale price (the measure under ORS 72.7060). The trial court directed plaintiff to submit calculations of each measure of damages.

[The Court goes on to explain that the evidence, on the whole, showed that the Plaintiff's damages as calculated under 2-706 using the resale price measure would be less than Plaintiff's damages as calculated under 2-708 using the market price measure.]

1

The Court of Appeals reversed and remanded. On the first issue, the court noted that, at least on its face, the UCC allows a seller to recover damages as calculated under either ORS 72.7060 (contract price less resale price) or ORS 72.7080(1) (contract price less market price). After reviewing the relevant statutory provisions, the court went on to conclude that, "[i]n the absence of a restriction within the UCC that precludes an aggrieved seller from seeking its remedy pursuant to ORS 72.7080 if the seller has resold, we would decline to impose such a restriction."

AN AGGRIEVED SELLER'S REMEDIES UNDER THE UCC

The UCC provides a variety of remedies to an aggrieved seller. *See* ORS 72.7030 (providing an index of a seller's remedies). As noted, the issue in this case is whether an aggrieved seller who has resold goods can recover the difference between the unpaid contract price and the market price under ORS 72.7080(1), even when market price damages would exceed resale price damages under ORS 72.7060.

Commentators and courts have taken two different approaches to this issue. Relying on the text and context of the sellers' remedies provisions, some commentators have argued that the drafters of the UCC intended for sellers to be able to recover either market price damages or resale price damages, even if the seller resold the goods for more than the market price. *See, e.g.*, Henry Gabriel, *The Seller's Election of Remedies Under the Uniform Commercial Code: An Expectation Theory*, 23 Wake Forest L Rev 429, 429 (1988) (arguing that an aggrieved seller "should be allowed to elect between the two remedies regardless of the seller's good faith post-breach activities concerning the non-accepted goods"); Ellen A. Peters, *Remedies for Breach of Contracts Relating to the Sale of Goods Under the Uniform Commercial Code: A Roadmap for Article Two*, 73 Yale LJ 199, 260 (1963) (arguing for a "non-restrictive reading of the various remedies sections to preserve full options to use or to ignore substitute transactions as a measure of damages"). On the other hand, Professors White and Summers, whose view has been adopted by a number of courts, have argued that the UCC's general policy is that damages should put a seller only in "as good a position as if the other party had fully performed," meaning a seller who has resold should not be allowed to recover more in market price damages than it could recover in resale price damages. James J. White, Robert S. Summers and Robert A. Hillman, 1 *Uniform Commercial Code* § 8:13, 689 (6th ed 2012) (so stating). We agree with those commentators who have observed that the drafters did not clearly resolve this issue. Nonetheless, we conclude that the text, context, and legislative history of the sellers' remedies provisions support a seller's right to recover either market price damages or resale price damages, even if market price damages lead to a larger recovery.

We begin by examining the statute's text and context to determine the legislature's intent regarding a seller's remedies under the UCC. Because the relevant statutes are part of the UCC, we also consider the official UCC comments as an indication of the legislature's intent. In addition, "the legislative intent to make the UCC a uniform code makes relevant the decisions of other courts that have examined these questions and the discussions of the questions by scholars in the field, especially those scholars who participated in drafting the UCC." We also examine legislative history. The Oregon legislature enacted the UCC in 1961 "with little debate or discussion of the legislative intent," but the UCC was proposed so that Oregon could "obtain the same advantages that other states had gained from the adoption of a uniform and comprehensive set of commercial statutes." Given "the legislative intent to make the UCC a uniform code," we consider prior drafts of the UCC, as drafted by the National Conference of Commissioners on Uniform State Laws (NCCUSL), as part of the legislative history.

Before examining the statutory scheme, however, we briefly review the law as it existed prior to the enactment of the UCC in Oregon. At common law, an aggrieved seller

> "ha[d] the election of three remedies: (1) To hold the property for the purchaser, and to recover of him the entire purchase money; (2) to sell it, after notice to the purchaser, as his agent for that purpose, and recover the difference between the contract price and that realized on the sale; (3) to retain it as his own, and recover the difference between the contract and market prices at the time and place of delivery[.]"

Krebs Hop Co. v. Livesley, 59 Ore. 574, 588, 118 P 165 (1911). *Krebs Hop Co.* suggests that, before Oregon adopted the UCC, an aggrieved seller had to elect between remedies, and if the seller resold the goods, it had elected its remedy and could recover only resale price damages, but not market price damages. Although the UCC retained some aspect of each of the remedies available at common law, as explained below, it specifically rejected the doctrine of election of remedies.

When a buyer breaches a contract for the sale of goods, ORS 72.7030 provides a seller with an index of remedies:

> "Where the buyer wrongfully rejects or revokes acceptance of goods or fails to make a payment due on or before delivery or repudiates with respect to a part or the whole, then with respect to any goods directly affected and, if the breach is of the whole contract as provided in ORS 72.6120, then also with respect to the whole undelivered balance, the aggrieved seller may:
>
> "* * * *
>
> "(4) Resell and recover damages as provided in ORS 72.7060.

"(5) Recover damages for nonacceptance as provided in ORS 72.7080 or in a proper case the price as provided in ORS 72.7090.

"(6) Cancel."

That section lists the seller's remedies, which, as relevant here, include resale price damages, ORS 72.7060, and market price damages, ORS 72.7080. Moreover, it lists those remedies without any limiting conjunction, such as "or," that might suggest that the remedies are mutually exclusive. In contrast, a similar index of a buyer's remedies after a seller's breach provides that the buyer may "(a) 'Cover' and have damages * * * *or* (b) Recover damages for nondelivery." ORS 72.7110(1) (emphasis added.) Thus, although the buyer's index of remedies suggests that a buyer who covers may be precluded from seeking market price damages, the seller's index of remedies does not contain a similar limitation if the seller chooses to resell. It follows that the text of ORS 72.7030 supports plaintiff's argument that a seller who has resold is not necessarily limited to its resale price damages under ORS 72.7060, but has the option of seeking to recover market price damages under ORS 72.7080.

The UCC comments to the statute describing a seller's remedies confirm that interpretation. Although the comments acknowledge that, in a particular case, the pursuit of one remedy may prevent a seller from obtaining certain damages, the comments also state that the UCC chapter on sales "reject[s] any doctrine of election of remedy as a fundamental policy and thus the remedies are essentially cumulative in nature and include all of the available remedies for breach." Legislative Comment 1 to ORS 72.7030 at 101; *id.* ("Whether the pursuit of one remedy bars another depends entirely on the facts of the individual case."). In contrast, the comments to the statute describing a buyer's market price remedy explain that that remedy "is completely alternative to 'cover' under ORS 72.7120 and applies *only when and to the extent that the buyer has not covered.*" Legislative Comment 5 to ORS 72.7130 at 110 (emphasis added). Thus, while the comments to the statute describing a seller's remedies expressly reject the doctrine of election of remedies, the comments to the statute describing a buyer's market price remedy appear to adopt that doctrine. Those comments further indicate that a seller who resells goods after a buyer's breach would not be considered to have "elected" the resale remedy and thus would not be precluded from seeking a larger damage recovery using the market price measure of damages.

The text of ORS 72.7060, which sets forth the seller's resale remedy, similarly suggests that a seller who resells goods is not necessarily precluded from using the market price measure of damages, even if it leads to a larger recovery. ORS 72.7060(1) states that "the seller *may* resell the goods concerned or the undelivered balance thereof," which suggests that an aggrieved seller is not required to resell. (Emphasis added.) Similarly, the text of ORS 72.7060 indicates that a seller who resells is not required to seek damages using the resale remedy. *See* ORS 72.7060(1) ("Where the resale is made in good faith and in a commercially reasonable manner the seller *may* recover the difference between the resale price and the contract price * * *." (Emphasis added.)). In fact, the unqualified text of ORS 72.7080(1) seems to suggest that market price is in fact the default measure of damages. *See* ORS 72.7080(1) ("Subject to * * * the provisions of ORS 72.7230 with respect to proof of market price, *the* measure of damages for nonacceptance or repudiation by the buyer is the difference between the market price at the time and place for tender and the unpaid contract price * * *." (Emphasis added.)). Thus, the text of the remedy provisions does not limit a seller who resells to its resale price damages.

As defendant notes, however, one of the comments to ORS 72.7060 does indicate that the drafters intended ORS 72.7060 to be a seller's primary remedy, and did not intend to allow a seller to recover more under the market price remedy. Comment 2 to ORS 72.7060 explains that "[f]ailure to act properly under ORS 72.7060 *deprives* the seller of the measure of damages there provided and *relegates* him to that provided in ORS 72.7080 [market price damages]." That language suggests that the comment drafters viewed market price damages as less favorable, but it does not indicate *why* they viewed them that way. The pejorative language used in the comments does not necessarily lead to the conclusion that a seller who resells cannot use the market price remedy or must use the resale price remedy if it would yield the same or a smaller amount of damages than the market price remedy. That language instead could indicate that market price damages are considered less favorable because market price is often hard to prove, as many commentators have noted. As a result, that comment language is not dispositive, particularly in light of the text of the remedy provisions.

Turning to legislative history, prior drafts of the UCC provide additional insight into the drafters' intent to allow a seller to recover its market price damages, even if the seller has resold. In particular, in an earlier draft of the section describing the resale price remedy, section 2-706, one of the comments stated that that section provided

> "'the *exclusive* measure of the seller's damages where the resale has been made in accordance with the requirements of this section. Evidence of market or current prices at any particular time or place is relevant *only* on the question of whether the seller acted with commercially reasonable care and judgment in making the resale.'"

Under that version of the UCC, a seller who had met the resale requirements would be required to use the resale price measure of damages. That comment later was revised, however, and when Oregon adopted the UCC, the comment included language that also had been in the 1949 draft comment, but the mandatory language had been removed, leaving only the permissive wording: "If the seller complies with the prescribed standard of duty in making the resale, he *may* recover from the buyer the damages provided for in subsection (1)." Legislative Comment 3 to ORS 72.7060 at 104 (emphasis added). That shift, from resale as the exclusive remedy to resale as a permissible remedy, indicates that the drafters intended for a seller to be able to choose to recover market price damages, even after reselling under ORS 72.7060.

Defendant argues, however, that even if a seller who resells can recover market price damages under ORS 72.7080(1), those damages cannot exceed the seller's resale price damages. Defendant primarily relies on the general policy statement set forth in ORS 71.3050 to support its argument. ORS 71.3050(1) provides,

> "The remedies provided by the Uniform Commercial Code must be liberally administered to the end that the aggrieved party may be put *in as good a position as if the other party had fully performed* but consequential damages, special damages or penal damages may not be had except as specifically provided in the Uniform Commercial Code or by other rule of law."

(Emphasis added.) Defendant reasons that the reference in ORS 71.3050(1) to putting an aggrieved party "in as good a position as if the other party had fully performed" acts as a limit on the damages that a party can receive. Commentators and courts likewise have relied on that provision in concluding that a seller's market price damages should be limited to the actual loss suffered, by taking into account any goods that have been resold. *See, e.g., Tesoro Petroleum Corp. v. Holborn Oil Co.*, 145 Misc. 2d 715, 547 NYS2d 1012, 1016-17 (NY Sup Ct 1989) (adopting approach of White and Summers and limiting seller to resale price damages because higher market price damages would create a "windfall" inconsistent with the general policy of the UCC).

The text of ORS 71.3050(1) indicates that the drafters of the UCC intended a seller's remedies to be compensatory. The text of that section, however, also provides that the remedies in the UCC are to be "liberally administered." Nonetheless, we agree with defendant that the general policy of compensation provided in ORS 71.3050(1) must be taken into account.

We do not agree, however, that that policy necessarily limits an aggrieved seller who has resold to its resale price damages. Defendant argues that if it had fully performed, plaintiff could expect to recover only the contract price, and that limiting plaintiff to the difference between the contract price and the resale price therefore gives it the benefit of its bargain. As Professor Gabriel notes, however, limiting a seller to its resale price damages does not account fully for either party's expectations upon entering into the contract. He explains that a seller expects to be able to recover the difference between the contract price and the market price because it is the "logical and expected measure of damages," and because the ability to recover market price damages "is the natural assumption the seller makes in return for the risk inherent in the contract that the sale may not turn out to be economically beneficial to the seller. That the seller then resells the goods in no way diminishes this expectancy regarding the first contract." From the buyer's perspective, he argues that "the [buyer] has specific obligations and will suffer the consequences of the failure to perform these obligations because this is the [buyer's] expectation." In other words, contrary to defendant's argument, an aggrieved seller expects to be able to recover market price damages under the contract, and a breaching buyer expects to have to fulfill its obligation to the seller—even if a seller resells and recovers market price damages, "the buyer's obligation is no more than the right the buyer originally conferred upon the seller."

Moreover, limiting an aggrieved seller to its resale price damages ignores the risk for which the parties bargained. When parties bargain for fixed price contracts, each party assumes the risk of market price fluctuations. The parties are willing to take that risk because of the benefits that they might receive: if the market price decreases, the seller benefits, and if the market price increases, the buyer benefits. In a fixed price contract, therefore, market price damages represent the risk for which both parties bargained. For those reasons, we conclude that a seller can recover market price damages, even if the seller resells some of the goods at above the market price at the time and place for tender.

Defendant argues, however, that that conclusion does not account for an aggrieved party's duty to mitigate, which is consistent with the UCC's policy of minimizing damages. We do not understand the duty to mitigate to be a limit on a seller's market price damages because, as noted, the text demonstrates and commentators agree that a seller is not required to resell goods after a buyer's breach. If the duty to mitigate does not require the aggrieved seller to resell its goods, we do not think that the duty to mitigate can require the seller to use the resale price measure of damages. The comments to the resale remedy provision also acknowledge that the seller who resells does so for its own benefit, and not for the benefit of the breaching party as mitigation. *See* ORS 72.7060(6) ("The seller is not accountable to the buyer for any profit made on any resale."). Therefore, the principle of mitigation does not appear to limit an aggrieved seller's recovery to resale price damages under ORS 72.7060; the seller may instead seek market price damages under ORS 72.7080(1).

In sum, when viewed in light of the bargained-for market risks and the UCC's rejection of the doctrine of election of remedies, the text, context, and legislative history of the sellers' remedy provisions demonstrate that an aggrieved seller can seek damages under either ORS 72.7080(1) or ORS 72.7060. That means that an aggrieved seller can seek damages under ORS 72.7080(1) even if the seller has resold the goods and market price damages exceed resale price damages.

Returning to the facts of this case, the trial court limited plaintiff's damages to resale price damages under ORS 72.7060. We have determined that plaintiff is entitled to market price damages under ORS 72.7080(1).

The trial court did not award plaintiff its market price damages under ORS 72.7080(1), presumably because the court concluded that plaintiff was not entitled to that measure of damages—defendant's calculation of resale price damages was the "lesser of the two calculations offered. Thus, because we have concluded that plaintiff is entitled to recover its market price damages, on remand, the trial court should award plaintiff its market price damages as calculated in Exhibit 409.

In *Tesoro Petroleum v. Holborn Oil,* 547 N.Y.S.2d 1012 (Sup. Ct. 1989), one of the cases relied on by the defendant in *Peace River,* the New York court invoked the golden rule and denied the seller's claim under 2-708(1) for nearly twice the recovery it was entitled to under 2-706 based on its resale of the contract goods. The court's reasoning is representative of those courts that have rejected the view expressed in *Peace River*.

Although the Official Comment to section 2-703 states that the "Article rejects any doctrine of election of remedy as a fundamental policy and thus the remedies are essentially cumulative in nature", it concludes that "[w]hether the pursuit of one remedy bars another depends entirely on the facts of the individual case."

In 1 White and Summers, Uniform Commercial Code [Practitioner's 3d ed 1988]), the distinguished authors indicate that the Code and Comments in this area are "equivocal", and that "[w]hether the drafters intended a seller who has resold to recover more in damages under 2-708 * * * is not clear." On this question, White and Summers conclude that: "a seller who resells goods reasonably identified to the broken contract for a price above the 2-708(1) market price should be limited to the difference between the contract price and his actual resale price. We believe that this is an exact measure of his expectation and that he should not recover more than that. As indicated above, the buyer bears the burden of showing that the seller was not a lost volume seller, and that the goods which in fact were resold were those that would have been delivered to him, the breaching buyer." In so concluding the authors expressed the following caveat: "All of the foregoing discussion assumes that the buyer who wishes to limit the seller to the difference between the contract and the resale price can show that the goods resold were in fact the goods contracted for. If the seller could have fulfilled the buyer's contract by buying on the market or by a choice among a variety of fungible goods, the buyer will be unable to limit the seller to 2-706 damages. The buyer will not be able to prove that the resale is 'reasonably identified as referring to the broken contract.' Put another way, the difference between the contract and a specific resale price is not the proper measure of the seller's expectation damages unless that resale is a substitute for the one actually conducted."

The foregoing position has generally been that enunciated by the courts that have considered the issue. In *Nobs Chem. v Koppers Co.* (616 F2d 212, 215 [5th Cir 1980]), the court (after observing the lack of "any law directly on point") limited damages on a breach of contract for the sale of chemicals to that provided in UCC 2-706. It heavily relied on the policy provision set forth in UCC [1-305] that "[t]he remedies provided by this Act shall be liberally administered to the end that the aggrieved party may be put in as good a position as if the other party had fully performed", concluding that: "No one insists, and we do not think they could, that the difference between the fallen market price and the contract price is necessary to compensate the plaintiffs for the breach. Had the transaction been completed, their 'benefit of the bargain' would not have been affected by the fall in market price, and they would not have experienced the windfall they otherwise would receive if the market price-contract price rule contained in § 2.708(a) is followed."; *accord, H-W-H Cattle Co. v Schroeder*, 767 F2d 437, 440 [8th Cir 1985] [where the admonition of UCC [1-305] carried the day, the court finding that the section suggested that it "should look through the form of a transaction to its substance when necessary to fulfill the parties' expectations expressed in the contract"]; *Coast Trading Co. v Cudahy Co.*, 592 F2d 1074 [9th Cir 1979]; *Union Carbide Corp. v Consumers Power Co.*, 636 F Supp 1498, 1501 [ED Mich 1986] [where it was stated that UCC 2-708 did "not authorize awards of damages which put the seller in a better position than performance would have put them"].

Plaintiff asserts that the foregoing cases are inapposite because New York legislative history calls for a different result. This argument is based on the 1956 New York Law Revision Commission recommendation to delete language in the draft of UCC 2-703(e) that would have limited UCC 2-708 to situations where the "'goods have not been resold' ". This recommendation was apparently accepted by the Commissioners on Uniform State Laws, and hence the Code in New York, and elsewhere does not contain such language. This is hardly reason to call for an interpretation of the Code in New York different from that in other States.

In explaining this deletion, White and Summers state: "It is possible that the New York Law Revision Commission had in mind the seller who would not receive a windfall by suing under 2-708(1) and simply wanted to make it clear that a seller who makes a good faith attempt to comply with 2-706 but fails may then resort to 2-708(1). Nothing in their report suggests that they considered the case in which 2-706 recovery would be small because the seller sold at a price very near to the contract price yet the contract-market differential under 2-708 would be large."

Further, Official Comment 2 under UCC 2-706 states that "[f]ailure to act properly under this section deprives the seller of the measure of damages here provided and *relegates* him to that provided in Section 2-708" (emphasis supplied), thus implying that it was contemplated that UCC 2-708 recoveries would be less than the contract-resale price differential authorized in UCC 2-706.

If plaintiff's damages are measured in accordance with UCC 2-706, it would be receiving the benefit reasonably to be expected when it entered into the alleged contract with defendant. Granting it the approximately $3,000,000 additional recovery that it seeks would result in a windfall which cannot be said to have been in the contemplation of the parties at the time of their negotiations, and would be inconsistent with the policy of the Code as expressed in UCC [1-305].

The New York court seems to take a more superficial view of the seller's bargain than the court did in *Peace River*, focusing mainly on the differences in price instead of looking below the surface of the agreement at the more complex nature of a seller's expectation interest in a contract for the sale of goods, especially the sale of a commodity like gasoline. There is often a lot more to the bargain of the parties to a sale-of-goods contract than meets the eyes of a court.

3. Not All Sellers Are Equal: Lost Profits

Sales law has long recognized that a measure of damages based on the difference between the market price and the contract price will not put all sellers in the position they would have been in had the buyer not breached the contract. The Uniform Sales Act measured the seller's damages in terms of the profit the seller would have made if the contract had been fully performed when the buyer breached before the seller had done what was necessary to fulfill its obligations under the contract and the labor or expense necessary to complete its performance were material. USA Section 64. The lost-profits measure was carried over into the early drafts of Article 2 and eventually made available to any seller who could show, based on her circumstances, that the market-price measure was not adequate "to put the seller in as good a position as performance would have done." 2-708(2).

But what circumstances did the drafters have in mind that would make the market price measure inadequate—and how would measuring damages in terms of profits lost do for the seller what the market price measure could not? The Comments tell us that the lost-profits alternative was designed to eliminate the unfair and uneconomically wasteful results arising under the older law when fixed prices were involved. This section permits the recovery of lost profits in all appropriate cases, which would include all standard priced goods …

Comment 2, 2-708.

Which obfuscates more than it clarifies for anyone not in the room at the time it was drafted. Fortunately, the courts have managed to decipher the text and the Comments, as the next case demonstrates.

Neri v. Retail Marine Corp.

Court of Appeals of New York, 1972
30 N.Y.2d 393

GIBSON, Judge.

The appeal concerns the right of a retail dealer to recover loss of profits and incidental damages upon the buyer's repudiation of a contract governed by the Uniform Commercial Code. This is, indeed, the correct measure of damage in an appropriate case and to this extent the code (§ 2-708, subsection [2]) effected a substantial change from prior law, whereby damages were ordinarily limited to "the difference between the contract price and the market or current price". Upon the record before us, the courts below erred in declining to give effect to the new statute and so the order appealed from must be reversed.

The plaintiffs contracted to purchase from defendant a new boat of a specified model for the price of $12,587.40, against which they made a deposit of $40. They shortly increased the deposit to $4,250 in consideration of the defendant dealer's agreement to arrange with the manufacturer for immediate delivery on the basis of "a firm sale", instead of the delivery within approximately four to six weeks originally specified. Some six days after the date of the contract plaintiffs' lawyer sent to defendant a letter rescinding the sales contract for the reason that plaintiff Neri was about to undergo hospitalization and surgery, in consequence of which, according to the letter, it would be "impossible for Mr. Neri to make any payments". The boat had already been ordered from the manufacturer and was delivered to defendant at or before the time the attorney's letter was received. Defendant declined to refund plaintiffs' deposit and this action to recover it was commenced. Defendant counterclaimed, alleging plaintiffs' breach of the contract and defendant's resultant damage in the amount of $4,250, for which sum defendant demanded judgment. Upon motion, defendant had summary judgment on the issue of liability tendered by its counterclaim; and Special Term directed an assessment of damages, upon which it would be determined whether plaintiffs were entitled to the return of any portion of their down payment.

Upon the trial so directed, it was shown that the boat ordered and received by defendant in accordance with plaintiffs' contract of purchase was sold some four months later to another buyer for the same price as that negotiated with plaintiffs. From this proof the plaintiffs argue that defendant's loss on its contract was recouped, while defendant argues that but for plaintiffs' default, it would have sold two boats and have earned two profits instead of one. Defendant proved, without contradiction, that its profit on the sale under the contract in suit would have been $2,579 and that during the period the boat remained unsold incidental expenses aggregating $674 for storage, upkeep, finance charges and insurance were incurred. Additionally, defendant proved and sought to recover attorneys' fees of $1,250.

The trial court found "untenable" defendant's claim for loss of profit, inasmuch as the boat was later sold for the same price that plaintiffs had contracted to pay; found, too, that defendant had failed to prove any incidental damages; further found "that the terms of section 2-718, sub section 2(b), of the Uniform Commercial Code are applicable and same make adequate and fair provision to place the sellers in as good a position as performance would have done" and, in accordance with paragraph (b) of subsection (2) thus relied upon, awarded defendant $500 upon its counterclaim and directed that plaintiffs recover the balance of their deposit, amounting to $3,750. The ensuing judgment was affirmed, without opinion, at the Appellate Division and defendant's appeal to this court was taken by our leave.

The issue is governed in the first instance by section 2-718 of the Uniform Commercial Code which provides, among other things, that the buyer, despite his breach, may have restitution of the amount by which his payment exceeds: (a) reasonable liquidated damages stipulated by the contract or (b) absent such stipulation, 20% of the value of the buyer's total performance or $500, whichever is smaller (§ 2-718, subsection [2], pars. [a], [b]). As above noted, the trial court awarded defendant an offset in the amount of $500 under paragraph (b) and directed restitution to plaintiffs of the balance. Section 2-718, however, establishes, in paragraph (a) of subsection (3), an alternative right of offset in favor of the seller, as follows: "(3) The buyer's right to restitution under subsection (2) is subject to offset to the extent that the seller establishes (a) a right to recover damages under the provisions of this Article other than subsection (1)".

Among "the provisions of this Article other than subsection (1)" are those to be found in section 2-708, which the courts below did not apply. Subsection (1) of that section provides that "the measure of damages for non-acceptance or repudiation by the buyer is the difference between the market price at the time and place for tender and the unpaid contract price together with any incidental damages provided in this Article (Section 2-710), but less expenses saved in consequence of the buyer's breach." However, this provision is made expressly subject to subsection (2), providing: "(2) If the measure of damages provided in subsection (1) is inadequate to put the seller in as good a position as performance would have done then the measure of damages is the profit (including reasonable overhead) which the seller would have made from full performance by the buyer, together with any incidental damages provided in this Article (Section 2-710), due allowance for costs reasonably incurred and due credit for payments or proceeds of resale."

The provision of the code upon which the decision at Trial Term rested (§ 2-718, subsection [2], par. [b]) does not differ greatly from the corresponding provisions of the prior statute (Personal Property Law, § 145-a, subd. 1, par. [b]) except as the new act includes the alternative remedy of a lump sum award of $500. Neither does the present reference (in § 2-718, subsection [3], par. [a]) to the recovery of damages pursuant to other provisions of the article differ from a like reference in the prior statute to an alternative measure of damages under section 145 of that act; but section 145 made no provision for recovery of lost profits as does section 2-708 (subsection [2]) of the code. The new statute is thus innovative and significant and its analysis is necessary to the determination of the issues here presented.

Prior to the code, the New York cases "applied the 'profit' test, contract price less cost of manufacture, only in cases where the seller [was] a manufacturer or an agent for a manufacturer." Its extension to retail sales was "designed to eliminate the unfair and economically wasteful results arising under the older law when fixed price articles were involved. This section permits the recovery of lost profits in all appropriate cases, which would include all standard priced goods." Additionally, and "[in] all cases the seller may recover incidental damages." The buyer's right to restitution was established at Special Term upon the motion for summary judgment, as was the seller's right to proper offsets, in each case pursuant to section 2-718; and, as the parties concede, the only question before us, following the assessment of damages at Special Term, is that as to the proper measure of damage to be applied. The conclusion is clear from the record—indeed with mathematical certainty—that "the measure of damages provided in subsection (1) is inadequate to put the seller in as good a position as performance would have done" (Uniform Commercial Code, § 2-708, sub section [2]) and hence—again under subsection (2)—that the seller is entitled to its "profit (including reasonable overhead) * * * together with any incidental damages * * *, due allowance for costs reasonably incurred and due credit for payments or proceeds of resale."

It is evident, first, that this retail seller is entitled to its profit and, second, that the last sentence of subsection (2), as hereinbefore quoted, referring to "due credit for payments or proceeds of resale" is inapplicable to this retail sales contract.[14] Closely parallel to the factual situation now before us is that hypothesized by Dean Hawkland as illustrative of the operation of the rules: "Thus, if a private party agrees to sell his automobile to a buyer for $2,000, a breach by the buyer would cause the seller no loss (except incidental damages, i.e., expense of a new sale) if the seller was able to sell the automobile to another buyer for $2,000. But the situation is different with dealers having an unlimited supply of standard-priced goods. Thus, if an automobile dealer agrees to sell a car to a buyer at the standard price of $2,000, a breach by the buyer injures the dealer, even though he is able to sell the automobile to another for $2,000. If the dealer has an inexhaustible supply of cars, the resale to replace the breaching buyer costs the dealer a sale, because, had the breaching buyer performed, the dealer would have made two sales instead of one. The buyer's breach, in such a case, depletes the dealer's sales to the extent of one, and the measure of damages should be the dealer's profit on one sale. Section 2-708 recognizes this, and it rejects the rule developed under the Uniform Sales Act by many courts that the profit cannot be recovered in this case."

The record which in this case establishes defendant's entitlement to damages in the amount of its prospective profit, at the same time confirms defendant's cognate right to "any incidental damages provided in this Article (Section 2-710)."[15] From the language employed it is too clear to require discussion that the seller's right to recover loss of profits is not exclusive and that he may recoup his "incidental" expenses as well. Although the trial court's denial of incidental damages in the uncontroverted amount of $674 was made in the context of its erroneous conclusion that paragraph (b) of subsection (2) of section 2-718 was applicable and was "adequate * * * to place the sellers in as good a position as performance would have done", the denial seems not to have rested entirely on the court's mistaken application of the law, as there was an explicit finding "that defendant completely failed to show that it suffered any incidental damages." We find no basis for the court's conclusion with respect to a deficiency of proof inasmuch as the proper items of the $674 expenses (being for storage, upkeep, finance charges and insurance for the period between the date performance was due and the time of the resale) were proven without objection and were in no way controverted, impeached or otherwise challenged, at the trial or on appeal. Thus the court's finding of a failure of proof cannot be supported upon the record and, therefore, and contrary to plaintiffs' contention, the affirmance at the Appellate Division was ineffective to save it.

The trial court correctly denied defendant's claim for recovery of attorney's fees incurred by it in this action. Attorney's fees incurred in an action such as this are not in the nature of the protective expenses contemplated by the statute (Uniform Commercial Code, § 1-106, subd. [1]; § 2-710; § 2-708, subsection [2]) and by our reference to "legal expense" in *Procter & Gamble Distr. Co.* v. *Lawrence Amer. Field Warehousing Corp.* (16 N Y 2d 344, 354-355, *supra*), upon which defendant's reliance is in this respect misplaced.

---

14   The concluding clause, "due credit for payments or proceeds of resale", is intended to refer to "the privilege of the seller to realize junk value when it is manifestly useless to complete the operation of manufacture." The commentators who have considered the language have uniformly concluded that "the reference is to a resale as scrap under * * * Section 2-704." Another writer, reaching the same conclusion, after detailing the history of the clause, says that "'proceeds of resale' previously meant the resale value of the goods in finished form; now it means the resale value of the components on hand at the time plaintiff learns of breach."

15   "Incidental damages to an aggrieved seller include any commercially reasonable charges, expenses or commissions incurred in stopping delivery, in the transportation, care and custody of goods after the buyer's breach, in connection with return or resale of the goods or otherwise resulting from the breach" (Uniform Commercial Code, § 2-710).

It follows that plaintiffs are entitled to restitution of the sum of $4,250 paid by them on account of the contract price less an offset to defendant in the amount of $3,253 on account of its lost profit of $2,579 and its incidental damages of $674.

The order of the Appellate Division should be modified, with costs in all courts, in accordance with this opinion, and, as so modified, affirmed.

Ordered accordingly.

PROBLEM 5 - 17

Rae has carried forward a tradition her father began shortly after he opened the store: making and selling fruitcakes during the winter holiday season. By the time Rae took over store operations from her father, the store was selling thousands of fruitcakes nationwide every year—and had orders for more cakes than it could make every holiday season. Seventy-five percent of fruitcake sales were to other stores and shops who resold the cakes to their customers. The fruitcakes are very profitable—the cakes cost less than two dollars to make but sell for twenty-five dollars or more. Last week, a confectionary shop in Vermont cancelled its order for one hundred deluxe fruitcakes. Rae quickly resold all one hundred cakes at the current market price, which was 10 percent above the contract price, to other shops around the country. What are Rae's damages, as measured under 2-706, for the buyer's breach? What are her damages if we measure them under 2-708(1)? If her damages as measured under 2-706 and 2-708(1) are zero dollars, can she recover for the profits she lost, under 2-708(2)? See 2-723(1).

PROBLEM 5 - 18

Earlier this year Rae, ordered five powered shopping carts for the store, each with a standard-size basket, keyless operation, extended run time, smart-charge battery system, and anti-tip casters. The carts were priced at $1,700 each, and the manufacturer promised to deliver them the following week. After she placed the order, Rae saw an ad for five used carts for a package price of $4,000. She checked out the used carts and decided that for half the price of the new carts she had ordered, they were all she needed for the store. She purchased them and immediately cancelled her order for the new carts. A few months later, the seller resold the carts Rae had ordered, along with ten older models the company had not been able to sell, to another grocery store for $1,800 each after adding quick-change battery covers and rear steel bumpers to each. The carts Rae ordered were built by the seller at its Minnesota plant, with parts and labor for each cart totaling $1,000. What damages will the seller be entitled to recover from Rae for cancelling her order? 2-708(2).

PROBLEM 5 - 19

The local chamber of commerce ordered one hundred seafood dinners from the store's deli for its fall banquet, to be delivered to the chamber's headquarters across town. The dinners would include a salmon steak with prawns, saffron rice medley, local vegetables medley, butter rolls, and chocolate parfait. The dinners were priced at twenty dollars each, but each cost the deli only $3.50. Before the deli had ordered any of the food for the banquet dinners, the chamber cancelled the order—moving the banquet to a local restaurant instead. What damages will the store be entitled to recover from the chamber—what measure should the court use if the store sues the chamber for breach? 2-708(1).

The courts agree that 2-708(2) applies to the lost-volume seller, which the court in *Neri* defined simply in terms of supply exceeding demand. When the seller has or can get more of the contract goods than it can sell, a buyer's breach makes the market price measure inadequate to put the seller in as good a position as the buyer's performance would have. The seller has "lost volume" and the seller needs to recoup the profits it would have made on the lost sale in order to be returned to the position it would have been in had the buyer not breached. But not all courts agree that supply exceeding demand necessarily establishes that the market-price measure is inadequate and justifies measuring the seller's damages by profits lost. In *R.E. Davis Chemical v. Diasonics*, 826 F.2d 678 (1987), the Seventh Circuit explained why more than supply exceeds demand is required:

> Concluding that Diasonics is entitled to seek damages under 2-708, however, does not automatically result in Diasonics being awarded its lost profit. Two different measures of damages are provided in 2-708. Subsection 2-708(1) provides for a measure of damages calculated by subtracting the market price at the time and place for tender from the contract price. The profit measure of damages, for which Diasonics is asking, is contained in 2-708(2). However, one applies 2-708(2) only if "the measure of damages provided in subsection (1) is inadequate to put the seller in as good a position as performance would have done...." [2-708(2)]. Diasonics claims that 2-708(1) does not provide an adequate measure of damages when the seller is a lost volume seller. To understand Diasonics' argument, we need to define the concept of the lost volume seller. Those cases that have addressed this issue have defined a lost volume seller as one that has a predictable and finite number of customers and that has the capacity either to sell to all new buyers or to make the one additional sale represented by the resale after the breach. According to a number of courts and commentators, if the seller would have made the sale represented by the resale whether or not the breach occurred, damages measured by the difference between the contract price and market price cannot put the lost volume seller in as good a position as it would have been in had the buyer performed. The breach effectively cost the seller a "profit," and the seller can only be made whole by awarding it damages in the amount of its "lost profit" under 2-708(2).

> We agree with Diasonics' position that, under some circumstances, the measure of damages provided under 2-708(1) will not put a reselling seller in as good a position as it would have been in had the buyer performed because the breach resulted in the seller losing sales volume. However, we disagree with the definition of "lost volume seller" adopted by other courts. Courts awarding lost profits to a lost volume seller have focused on whether the seller had the capacity to supply the breached units in addition to what it actually sold. In reality, however, the relevant questions include, not only whether the seller could have produced the breached units in addition to its actual volume, but also whether it would have been profitable for the seller to produce both units. As one commentator has noted, under

> > the economic law of diminishing returns or increasing marginal costs[,] ... as a seller's volume increases, then a point will inevitably be reached where the cost of selling each additional item diminishes the incremental return to the seller and eventually makes it entirely unprofitable to conclude the next sale.

> Shanker, *supra* p. 7 n.6, at 705. Thus, under some conditions, awarding a lost volume seller its presumed lost profit will result in overcompensating the seller, and 2-708(2) would not take effect because the damage formula provided in 2-708(1) does place the seller in as good a position as if the buyer had performed. Therefore, on remand, Diasonics must establish, not only that it had the capacity to produce the breached unit in addition to the unit resold, but also that it would have been profitable for it to have produced and sold both.

Article 2's drafters may have constructed 2-708(2) with lost-volume sellers in mind, but the courts have found it a good fit for two other types of sellers—the sellers of assembled goods and sellers who are "jobbers," sellers who don't have the goods and never acquire them once the contract is breached. Section 2-708(1)'s market-price measure will not be adequate to put either type of seller in as good a position as the buyer's performance would have done.

For example, I agree to sell you a pallet of sod for $1,000 which I know that I can purchase at a wholesale price of nine hundred dollars from the sod grower up the interstate. The $1,000 you agree to pay me covers my cost of acquiring the sod and the one-hundred-dollar profit I want to make on the deal. If, before I acquire the sod, you inform me that you don't need it and won't take delivery of it, and I don't get the sod after you breach, measuring my damages by the difference between the market price and the contract price will not put me in as good a position as I would have been in had you performed, unless the market price has fallen one hundred dollars between the time we contracted and the time I was supposed to deliver the grass to you. If the market price for sod on the measuring date is $950, 2-708(1) will give me fifty dollars, but that's only half of what I expected to make on our deal. And since I don't have a pallet of sod that I can sell for $950—fifty dollars above my cost—I'm not in as good a position as I would have been had you performed. The seller who never gets the goods cannot sell the goods to make up the difference between the market value and her cost—the part of her profit not covered by the difference between the contract price and the market price. The market price measure is inadequate—measuring her damages by the profit she lost is what it takes to put her in as good a position as the buyer's performance would have put her.

The seller of assembled goods faces a problem similar to that of the lost-volume seller when the buyer breaches before the goods are completed. These sellers have to assemble what they've agreed to sell—buying and/or making the parts needed for the finished product. The products are not specially manufactured goods—they are the same things they sell to others—they just don't put them together until the buyer orders them. If the goods are not built when the buyer breaches, and the seller does not finish them after the breach, the seller loses a sale—there is no product to sell. There probably is no market for partially assembled goods either, so no market value to use in the 2-708(1) formula.

PROBLEM 5 - 20

Rae ordered 1000 cases of the plastic film used by both the produce and meat departments to package their products. The rolls were priced at $200 per case and were to be delivered the following month. Shortly after Rae placed the order, the produce manager discovered several hundred cases of the plastic film in a storage container—somehow it had not been counted in the last storewide inventory. Rae refused to accept delivery of the plastic rolls she had ordered explaining the inventory problem to the seller. The seller was later able to resell the rolls Rae had refused to take for $800 per roll—the price of plastic film had quadrupled after the rolls were returned to the seller. The seller expected to make a $100 profit on each of the cases of film Rae ordered. What are the seller's damages under 2-706 or 2-708(1)? If the seller's supply usually exceeds demand for plastic film, should the seller be able to recover the $100 profit per case it was expecting to make on the deal with Rae?

The next case addresses this issue.

WESTLAKE PETROCHEMICALS, L.L.C. v. UNITED POLYCHEM, INC.

UNITED STATES COURT OF APPEALS FOR THE FIFTH CIRCUIT, 2012
688 F.3D 232

WIENER, Circuit Judge.

I. FACTS & PROCEEDINGS

A. Facts

UPC is a distributor of petrochemicals and plastics. In 2008, it sought to enter the market for ethylene, a petroleum product used in making plastics, with the intention of buying and reselling the compound. To facilitate UPC's acquisition of ethylene, Van Der Wall, as UPC's President, gave permission to a bilateral broker, Lawson Brice, to bid for five million pounds of ethylene per month during calendar year 2009 at a fixed price of $0.54 per pound. On July 2, 2008, Brice matched UPC's bid with an offer from Westlake, and Westlake agreed to the transaction …

* * *

Westlake presented evidence indicating that the market price for ethylene dropped sometime in the fall of 2008, thus turning against UPC's ethylene position. On October 30, 2008, Chappelle sent an email to Van Der Wall, informing him that Westlake was setting up billing in its system for the sale. Later that day, Van Der Wall informed Westlake that UPC would not perform under the contract because Westlake had not confirmed credit. After UPC repudiated, Westlake decided not to proceed with acquiring ethylene from a supplier in anticipation of delivering ethylene to UPC, although it had procured ethane, the feedstock of ethylene, for the purpose of supplying one of its subsidiaries in addition to meeting its obligation to UPC.

B. Proceedings

As noted, Westlake filed suit in state court against UPC and Van Der Wall on November 10, 2008, claiming that UPC breached its contract by refusing to perform and that Van Der Wall breached the Guaranty by refusing to satisfy UPC's obligations. UPC removed the case to federal court under diversity jurisdiction pursuant to 28 U.S.C. § 1332 and counterclaimed that Westlake had breached the agreement.

At the conclusion of a two-week trial in April 2010, the jury found that UPC and Westlake had formed a binding contract in July of 2008 and that UPC had breached that contract. The jury awarded Westlake $6.3 million in damages and $633,199.67 in attorney's fees. The jury did not decide whether Van Der Wall had breached the Guaranty because the parties had agreed to have the presiding judge decide this issue.

* * *

III. DAMAGES

* * *

B. Analysis

The determinative issue relating to the proper quantum of damages is whether to apply subsection (a) or subsection (b) of Tex. Bus. & Com. Code. § 2.708. Subsection (a) states:

Subject to Subsection (b) and to the provisions of this chapter with respect to proof of market price (Section 2.723), the measure of damages for non-acceptance or repudiation by the buyer is the difference between the market price at the time and place for tender and the unpaid contract price together with any incidental damages provided in this chapter (Section 2.710), but less expenses saved in consequence of the buyer's breach.

Subsection (b) states:

If the measure of damages provided in Subsection (a) is inadequate to put the seller in as good a position as performance would have done then the measure of damages is the profit (including reasonable overhead) which the seller would have made from full performance by the buyer, together with any incidental damages provided in this chapter (Section 2.710), due allowance for costs reasonably incurred and due credit for payments or proceeds of resale.

In this dichotomy, § 2.708(a) provides damages in the amount of the difference between the contract and the market price at the time and place of tender, and § 2.708(b) provides damages in the amount that the non-breaching party would have realized under the contract had the breaching party fully performed. At trial, Chappelle testified for Westlake that its lost profits under the contract with UPC amounted to $2 million. In contrast, Westlake's damages expert testified that the average price for ethylene in 2009 was 26.81 cents per pound, so that, applying this price, Westlake should be awarded $16.3 million in damages, i.e., the difference between the contract price and the market price.

After discussion at trial, the district court agreed with Westlake to instruct the jury to award damages under § 2.708(a), the difference between contract and market prices. Without elaboration or explanation, the jury awarded Westlake $6.3 million in damages, and the district granted Westlake the jury amount $6.3 million in damages in its Final Judgment.

Appellants insist that the proper measure of damages in this case should be calculated pursuant to § 2.708(b). They emphasize that Westlake never actually purchased ethylene in anticipation of fulfilling the contract. According to Appellants, then, awarding more than Westlake's lost profit would constitute a windfall. Westlake counters that, before UPC breached the contract, Westlake purchased enough ethane, the feedstock for ethylene, to cover its obligation to UPC. To this, Appellants respond that Westlake purchased the ethane for a dual purpose: to make ethylene for UPC *and* to supply its own subsidiary.

We have previously ruled on this issue in a case involving similar circumstances. In *Nobs Chem., U.S.A., Inc., v. Koppers Co., Inc.*, the plaintiffs contracted to sell cumene, a substance used in high octane motor fuel, to the defendant. The plaintiffs arranged to acquire cumene from a supplier. After the defendant repudiated the contract, however, the plaintiffs cancelled plans to acquire the cumene. The district court determined that the plaintiffs were entitled to recover lost profits under § 2.708(b) as opposed to damages under § 2.708(a) because they had never actually acquired the cumene.

In affirming, we noted that the UCC intends for § 2.708(b) to apply to particular types of sellers, one being a "jobber." A jobber is a seller who (1) never acquired the contracted goods, and (2) the seller's decision not to acquire those goods "after learning of the breach was not commercially unreasonable." In applying subsection (b) in *Nobs*, we made special note of the fact that the plaintiffs in that case never acquired the goods from the supplier after they learned of the defendant's repudiation; thus, there could be no action for either the purchase price or resale. Such a conclusion is commensurate with the basic UCC policy embodied in § 1.305(a), which provides that "the aggrieved party may be put in as good a position as if the other party had fully performed but not in a better position." Observing this underlying policy in our application of subsection (b), we stated:

No one insists, and we do not think they could, that the difference between the fallen market price and the contract price is necessary to compensate the plaintiffs for the breach. Had the transaction been completed, their "benefit of the bargain" would not have been affected by the fall in market price, and they would not have experienced the windfall they otherwise would receive if the market price-contract price rule contained in s 2.708(a) is followed.

The circumstances in *Nobs* are sufficiently similar to those of the instant case to warrant application of § 2.708(b), rather than § 2.708(a). Westlake originally intended to procure ethylene from a supplier to meet its contractual obligation to deliver ethylene to UPC. After UPC repudiated, Westlake reasonably chose not to acquire the ethylene. Westlake's actions make it tantamount to a "jobber". Although Westlake contends that it *also* purchased enough *ethane* to meet its obligation to UPC, this fact is inapposite because (1) the parties contracted for the delivery of ethylene, not ethane, and (2) Westlake's acquisition of the ethane was also for the purpose of supplying one of its subsidiaries. We agree with Appellants that, under these circumstances, awarding Westlake more than the profit it would have made under the contract would constitute a windfall by placing it in a better position than if both parties had fully performed. As with the plaintiff in *Nobs*, had the instant transaction been completed, Westlake's "benefit of the bargain" would not have been affected by the fall in market price, and thus it would not have experienced the windfall it otherwise would receive if subsection (a)'s market price/contract price rule were followed.

We conclude that the proper measure of damages in this case is Westlake's lost profits under § 2.708(b). We therefore vacate the damages award as determined by the jury and accepted by the district court, and we remand this issue for the district court to calculate the damages under subsection (b).

---

4. Seller's Incidental Damages

Sellers are entitled to recover incidental damages caused by a buyer's breach. 2-710. When the buyer breaches, the seller is stuck with the goods it was expecting the buyer to take and the costs of dealing with those goods: the out-of-pocket expenses of storing them, preserving them and insuring them, and any costs incurred in reselling the goods or otherwise disposing of them. But Article 2 does not let sellers recover for consequential damages caused by a buyer's breach—and so sellers are forced to try and disguise their consequential damages as incidental damages if they hope to recover for loss not compensated by the measures for direct damages provided by Article 2. The constant testing of the limits of incidental damages under 2-710 blurs the line between consequential and incidental damages for sellers—the line between the two is less clear for sellers than it is for buyers, as we noted earlier in this chapter.

Interestingly, Section 70 of the Uniform Sales Act, which the Comments to 2-710 cite as its statutory predecessor, seemed to contemplate that sellers were entitled to consequential damages:

> Nothing in this act shall affect the right of the buyer *or the seller* to recover interest or special damages in any case where by law interest or special damages may be recoverable ...

(Emphasis added). By the 1941 second draft of what became Article 2, this section of the Uniform Sales Act had been rewritten in the form of what is now 2-710, with no comment explaining the change.

PROBLEM 5 - 21

Which, if any, of the following would the seller in Problem 5 - 18 (the sale of powered shopping carts) be entitled to recover on account of Rae's breach under 2-710?

1. The rent the seller paid for the space in which it stored unsold carts.
2. The cost of moving the carts to a new space when the lease expired on the original storage space.
3. The cost of insuring the carts it had in storage.
4. The additional shipping costs it paid to ship the carts to the substitute buyer.
5. The cost of keeping the carts in working condition—if the batteries were allowed to completely discharge from non-use, they would require replacement.
6. The cost of replacing the batteries that completely discharged because of non-use.
7. The commission paid to the employee that found the new buyer.
8. The attorneys' fees it incurred recovering damages from Rae for her breach.

5. Specific Performance: Seller's Action for the Price

Sales law has been reluctant to compel breaching buyers to perform—to pay the contract price for the goods—unless the buyers have chosen to retain possession of the goods. Usually, the seller is in a better position than is the buyer to find the goods an alternative home—a seller in the business of selling goods already has resources committed to that purpose as well as contacts with those who might need or might be interested in buying the goods. And of course the economist types tell us it is wasteful to make people take things they don't want, so letting the seller force the goods onto the buyer has been the remedy of last resort—it's always been conditioned on some showing by the seller that no one else will take the goods. The Uniform Sales Act allowed the seller to recover the price upon showing that the goods could not "be readily resold for a reasonable price," and the early drafts of what became Article 2 raised the bar by requiring that the not readily resalable for a reasonable price determination be based on "an effort in good faith [by the seller] to resell the goods."

The requirement that the seller actually demonstrate that the goods were not resalable was carried over into 2-709, which allows the seller to recover the price

> of goods identified to the contract if the seller is unable after reasonable effort to resell them at a reasonable price or the circumstances reasonably indicate that such effort will be unavailing.
>
> 2-709(1)(b).

The Comments emphasize the drafters' intent to raise the bar:

> This section substitutes an objective test by action for the former "not readily resalable" standard. An action for the price under subsection (1)(b) can be sustained only after a "reasonable effort to resell" the goods at a "reasonable price" has actually been made or where the circumstances "reasonably indicate" that such an effort will be unavailing.
>
> Comment 3, 2-709.

Section 2-709 makes clear that only the exceptionally reasonable seller will have an action for the price, but then shrouds in obscurity what a seller must do to earn exceptionally reasonable status. What is it that distinguishes the "reasonable effort at resale" from the unreasonable effort at resale? What is a reasonable resale price? And what sort of circumstances "reasonably indicate" when a seller's effort to resell the goods would be a waste of her time?

The following case attempts to answer some of these questions.

Precision Mirror & Glass v. Nelms

Civil Court of the City of New York, 2005
797 N.Y.S.2d 720

DIDOMENICO, Judge.

At the trial of this case on March 21, 2005, both parties were represented by legal counsel. Mr. Thomas Basile, president of Precision Mirror & Glass, testified on behalf of plaintiff and submitted one document (plaintiff's exhibit 1). Defendant Bobby Nelms testified on his own behalf and submitted two documents (defendant's exhibits A, B). The court makes the following findings of fact and conclusions of law based on the testimony and evidence adduced at trial.

Precision is a manufacturer of custom-made glass products, such as shower doors, mirrors and glass tabletops. It has a retail store in Staten Island. Precision's regular business practice is to give immediate attention to customers' orders and begin production on the same day an order is placed, if possible.

On July 9, 2003, defendant Mr. Bobby Nelms brought Precision a pattern, drawn on paper, he had made of the top of an antique table. Defendant gave the pattern to the Precision employee at the customer service desk and indicated that he wanted to cover his table with three-quarter-inch glass conforming to the pattern. After some discussion, it was decided that the tabletop would be made with three-eighths-inch glass at a cost, including sales tax, of $684.33. Defendant left a $100 deposit, leaving a balance of $584.33 payable upon pickup of the tabletop.

At the time the order was placed, defendant signed a document entitled "Proposal" (plaintiff's exhibit 1; defendant's exhibit A). Among other terms, this document: (i) specified that the item ordered by defendant was: "1 -36 × 48 3/8 glass ... Pol [polished] edges ... As per pattern"; (ii) recited the total cost of the order, the deposit paid and the $584.33 balance due; and (iii) further contained, immediately above defendant's signature, an "Acceptance of Proposal" which provided that "the above prices, specifications and conditions are satisfactory and are hereby accepted. You are authorized to do the work as specified. Payment will be as specified." (Plaintiff's exhibit 1; defendant's exhibit A; hereinafter the contract.)

In addition, the contract contained the following noncancellation clause:

> "No Cancellations. ALL ORDERS ARE FINAL SALE. In the event collection of this account or accepted proposal becomes necessary, all discounts will be negated, purchaser will be responsible for any and all costs associated with same, including attorneys; fees costs and assessments including interest of 24% per annum ... Personally Guaranteed. I waive my right to cancellation" (defendant's exhibit A; plaintiff's exhibit 1).

Notwithstanding this no cancellation policy, Precision's regular business practice is to allow a customer to cancel an order as long as it occurs prior to the start of production. The rationale for this policy is that once a custom item is made to a customer's unique specifications, it rarely has any resale value.

On July 11, 2003 at approximately 9:15 in the morning, defendant called Precision stating he wanted to cancel the order because he believed the three-eighths-inch glass ordered would not be suitable for his purposes. Precision responded that the sale could not be cancelled as the glass had already been cut and was awaiting his pickup. Defendant never picked up the tabletop, notwithstanding Precision's demands that he do so. On or about February 2, 2005, Precision brought this action to recover money damages in the amount owed on the contract ($584.33).

Precision established that it had a valid contract with Mr. Nelms to make the custom glass tabletop ordered in exchange for the price Mr. Nelms agreed to pay. (See UCC 2-204 [1] ["A contract for sale of goods may be made in any manner sufficient to show agreement, including conduct by both parties which recognizes the existence of such a contract"]; see also Jeppestol v Alfa-Laval, Inc., 293 AD2d 575,

576, 740 NYS2d 136 [2d Dept 2002] [buyer's proposal constituted the offer and seller's purchase order the acceptance resulting in an enforceable contract].)

To justify his refusal to accept delivery, Mr. Nelms does not allege that the custom-made piece was in any way nonconforming to what was agreed to by the parties. Rather, after the order was placed, Mr. Nelms had reservations about the weight of the three-eighths-inch glass he agreed would be used. This change of heart does not excuse Mr. Nelm's refusal to accept delivery. Accordingly, defendant's failure to accept delivery of the tabletop is a breach of contract for which he is liable to plaintiff for damages. (*See* UCC 2-301 [obligation of the seller is to transfer and deliver and obligation of the buyer is to accept and pay in accordance with contract]; *International Paper Co. v Margrove, Inc.*, 75 Misc 2d 763, 764, 348 NYS2d 916 [Sup Ct, Monroe County 1973] [summary judgment granted in favor of seller where buyer no longer needed seller's goods because of change in buyer's machinery when no claim was made that seller's product was defective].)

Here, the court finds that the custom glass top was made prior to the time defendant sought to cancel the contract on July 11, 2003. However, even if the glass had not been cut, Precision, when faced with Mr. Nelm's anticipatory breach, had the right to either accept the repudiation or continue to perform its contractual obligations and sue for breach. (*See* 22A NY Jur 2d, Contracts §448, at 135 ["Where one party has repudiated an executory contract, the adverse party thus has an election to treat the contract as broken or not so to treat it"]; *see also Greenspan v Amsterdam*, 145 AD2d 535, 536, 536 NYS2d 90 [2d Dept 1988] [plaintiff's election not to waive breach was evidenced by his filing of a mechanic's lien only days after the breach].)

Pursuant to UCC 2-703, where a buyer wrongfully rejects or revokes acceptance of goods or fails to make payment when due, a seller may, among other available remedies: (i) withhold delivery; (ii) resell and recover damages pursuant to UCC 2-706; or (iii) recover damages for nonacceptance pursuant to UCC 2-708, or, in the appropriate case, recover the price set by the contract pursuant to UCC 2-709. Where, as here, the subject of the contract is a custom-made product allegedly having no resale value, the seller may be entitled to recover the amount owed on the contract. (UCC 2-703, 2-709 [1]; *see also Safety Cover Specialist v Marmurek*, 2003 NY Slip Op 50846[U], 2003 NY Misc LEXIS 484 [App Term, 9th & 10th Jud Dists 2003] [where buyer repudiated contract to purchase a custom-made swimming pool cover, seller was entitled to recover the price of the cover].) The burden is on the seller to establish that the subject piece has no resale value. (*Creations by Roselynn v Costanza*, 189 Misc 2d 600, 601, 734 NYS2d 803 [App Term, 2d Dept 2001] [seller entitled to contract damages where seller establishes that "resale is impracticable or unavailing under the circumstances"].)

The court finds that it is impracticable for Precision to locate another consumer who possesses a table of the exact dimensions to whom it could sell the custom glass tabletop defendant ordered. Defendant clearly recognized the unique shape and design of this table because he created a pattern to capture its exact characteristics. For these reasons, and as the lack of a resale market for this piece was not rebutted by defendant, this court finds Precision has credibly established it is entitled to recovery of the $584.33 owed on the contract.

CHAPTER 6

RISK OF LOSS

What happens if, after the parties have agreed on a sale of goods but before the buyer has become obligated to pay for those goods under the code[1], the goods are lost, damaged, or destroyed? Which party—the buyer or the seller—should bear the risk that the goods will be lost, damaged, or destroyed during this period? Should it matter whether, at the time of loss, damage, or destruction, the goods were still in the possession of the seller, had been turned over to a carrier for transport to the buyer, or had been delivered to the buyer? Should it matter whether, prior to the loss, damage, or destruction, that either the buyer or the seller had breached the agreement? How we answer these questions is important to the parties because under Article 2, if we decide that the seller should bear the risk, the seller's failure to provide the goods will be a breach by the seller; alternatively, if we decide that the buyer should bear the risk, the buyer will have to pay for the goods even if the goods were never delivered or were damaged when delivered.

We might expect the parties to address such risks as part of their agreement, and Article 2 contemplates that they will in fact do so: the parties are "free to readjust their rights and risks … in any manner agreeable to them." Comment 5, 2-509. But if the parties do not address the issue in their agreement, then the law—in our case, Article 2—must provide the rules for allocating those risks. Prior law used the concept of title as the basis for allocating the risk of loss between a buyer and a seller: whoever owned the goods at the time of casualty should bear the risk of their loss. But the party who just happened to have title was not always the party in the best position to prevent or to insure against the loss, and determining which party actually had title at a particular moment had surrealistic undertones that would have confounded the likes of Breton and Duchamp.

Article 2's basic risk-of-loss rules are set out in sections 2-509 and 2-510. These rules reject the title concept and instead follow from the drafters' suppositions that (1) a party in breach should bear the risk of loss, and (2) in the absence of breach, the party in *control* of the goods at the time of casualty should bear the risk of loss. We will consider the effect that a party's breach should have on our risk of loss assessment later in this chapter.

It would be perfectly reasonable to allocate the risk of loss for goods to the party that has actual possession of the goods. The party in possession is in the best position to manage the destiny of those goods—to take the steps necessary to preserve and protect those goods—and has an incentive to protect

---

1   As we will learn in Chapter 7, the buyer is not obligated to pay for the goods, even though in possession of the goods, until it has accepted the goods under 2-606.

its own interests by insuring the goods against loss. But Article 2's risk-of-loss rules are based on "control" of the goods rather than mere physical possession because in many, if not most, sales transactions there is a period during which neither party has actual possession of the goods. 2-509 Comment 3. If the goods have to be shipped from the seller to the buyer, the parties in most cases will use a shipping company—think UPS or FedEx—in which case the goods, during transport, will be in possession of the shipping company, not the seller or the buyer. If the goods are lost, damaged, or destroyed in transit, a risk-of-loss rule based only on actual possession would not provide a basis for allocating that loss to either the seller or the buyer. By emphasizing control rather than possession, Article 2 aims to identify, with the certainty lacking under pre-Code law, the point in time at which the risk of loss passes from the seller to the buyer in the absence of either party's possession of the goods.

But when does a party have this "control" that determines risk of loss under Article 2? We know what possession looks like; what does control look like? As it turns out, there is not a definitive description, and courts that have noted the control concept underlying 2-509 have simply asserted it and have not attempted to develop its contours. The Comments seem to equate control with the ability to preserve and protect the goods from casualty or the incentive to insure them against loss. Obviously, the party in possession has the ability to preserve and protect as well as an incentive to insure against loss. But there are times when a party not in possession may have the power to preserve and protect or the incentive to insure. A buyer who has paid for the goods will have an incentive to insure them against loss once the seller has turned them over to the shipping company for delivery to the buyer. This buyer would then have "control" over the goods, and Article 2 would allocate the risk of loss to the buyer, even though the buyer did not have possession of the goods.

A. RISK OF LOSS WHEN GOODS ARE NOT SHIPPED

Fortunately, 2-509 provides specific rules for determining which party had the risk of loss at the time of casualty to the goods, and these rules can be applied independently of the control theory. Which risk-of-loss rule applies will depend, in most cases, on whether the contract requires the seller to ship the goods to the buyer. If the seller is not required to ship the goods—what we might think of as a face-to-face transaction—2-509(3) provides:

> [where the contract does not require the seller to ship the goods] the risk of loss passes to the buyer on his receipt of the goods if the seller is a merchant; otherwise the risk passes to the buyer on tender of delivery.

If the seller is a merchant—a professional seller—risk of loss passes on the buyer's receipt—when the buyer takes physical possession of the goods. 2-103(1)(c).[2] These rules generally follow from the premise that risk of loss should be allocated on the basis of which party has the ability to preserve and protect the goods and/or the incentive to insure against loss. The seller initially has possession (and with it the risk of loss), but eventually, the buyer is going to get possession of the goods—that's presumably the goal of the contract. We would not expect the seller to assume the risk of loss after the buyer takes possession of the goods—the seller would no longer have the power to preserve or protect the goods or the incentive to insure them against loss. Once the buyer has possession, it should also have the risk of loss, since it now has the power to preserve and protect the goods (and the incentive to insure them against loss). And that's how 2-509(3) treats risk of loss in face-to-face transactions when the seller is

---

2   If the seller is not a merchant, then risk of loss passes to the buyer when the seller tenders delivery—offers the goods to the buyer—which means the risk of loss will pass to the buyer *before* the buyer has physical possession of the goods.

a merchant—transactions where there's no shipping company involved and consequently no period during which neither party is in possession.

The following case and problems illustrate Article 2's risk-of-loss rules when the contract does not require the seller to ship the goods to the buyer and the seller is not a merchant.

CAPSHAW V. HICKMAN

COURT OF APPEALS OF OHIO, 2007
173 OHIO APP. 3D 677

BRYANT, J.

Defendant-appellant, Rachel Hickman, appeals from a judgment of the Franklin County Municipal Court granting judgment on the pleadings pursuant to *Civ.R. 12(C)* to plaintiffs-appellees, Charles W. Capshaw (individually, "plaintiff") and Donna M. McClure. Because the pleadings do not entitle plaintiffs to judgment as a matter of law, we reverse.

According to the allegations in the parties' pleadings, plaintiff entered into a written contract with defendant to purchase defendant's 1996 Honda Civic EX for the purchase price of approximately $5,025. According to the contract, "the title will be surrendered upon the new owner's check clearing." After making a cash down payment of $80, plaintiff gave defendant a personal check for the balance. Defendant provided plaintiff with the keys to the vehicle. She also complied with plaintiff's request to sign the certificate of title over into the name of plaintiff's father. They agreed the vehicle was to remain parked in defendant's driveway until the check cleared.

Unfortunately, before defendant was notified that the check cleared, a hailstorm heavily damaged the vehicle. Due to the damage the vehicle sustained, plaintiffs decided they no longer wanted the vehicle and requested that defendant return their money. Defendant refused, believing the sales transaction was complete and the vehicle belonged to plaintiffs. Defendant requested that plaintiffs remove the vehicle from her driveway.

In response, plaintiffs filed a complaint against defendant, alleging conversion, breach of contract, and "quasi-contract and unjust enrichment—promissory estoppel." Defendant denied plaintiffs' allegations and filed two counterclaims requesting compensation for storing the vehicle on her driveway. Defendant also sought to recover her costs, attorney fees and expenses arising out of plaintiffs' conversion claim because it was frivolous pursuant to *R.C. 2323.51*.

Plaintiffs filed a motion and an amended motion for judgment on the pleadings, and defendant filed a response to both. Plaintiffs asserted the risk of loss remained with defendant until the check cleared; because it had not cleared at the time the hail damaged the car, defendant sustained the loss. Relying on *[2-509(3)]*, defendant maintained the risk-of-loss for non-merchant sellers such as her passes to the buyer after a non-merchant seller tenders delivery. Defendant contended that because a material issue of fact exists as to whether she tendered delivery of the vehicle to plaintiffs, judgment on the pleadings was improper.

Based upon the pleadings, the trial court found the parties agreed to the following facts: (1) plaintiffs offered to purchase the vehicle for $5,025, minus an $80 down payment; (2) plaintiffs tendered a check to defendant for the remaining balance due; (3) until the check cleared the vehicle would remain on defendant's property; (4) before the check cleared, hail damaged the vehicle while it still was in defendant's driveway; and (5) because of the damage, plaintiffs never took possession of the vehicle, no longer wanted it, and asked defendant to return the purchase price.

Premised on those facts, the trial court concluded the parties agreed the transfer of title and delivery of the vehicle would occur only after the successful transfer of funds. In reaching its decision, the trial court applied *[2-401(2)]* which provides that "[u]nless otherwise explicitly agreed, title passes to the buyer at the time and place at which the seller completes performance with reference to the physical delivery of the goods, despite any reservation of security interest and even though a document of title is to be delivered at a different time or place." Because the agreed facts demonstrated no delivery of the title or vehicle occurred at the time of the hailstorm, the trial court granted plaintiffs' motion and entered judgment for plaintiffs on their complaint and on defendant's counterclaims.

Defendant appeals, assigning two errors:

Assignment of Error No. 1
The Trial Court erroneously granted judgment on the pleadings in favor of Plaintiffs-Appellees and against Defendant-Appellant because material issues of fact existed which precluded judgment on the pleadings with respect to delivery of the 1996 Honda Civic EX and/or tender of delivery of the 1996 Honda Civic EX to Plaintiffs-Appellees by Defendant-Appellant.

Assignment of Error No. 2
The Trial Court erroneously granted judgment on the pleadings in favor of Plaintiffs-Appellees and against Defendant-Appellant because Plaintiffs-Appellees were not entitled to judgment as a matter of law with respect to the causes of action asserted in Plaintiffs-Appellees' Complaint and Defendant-Appellant's Counterclaim.

I. First Assignment of Error
In her first assignment of error, defendant contends the trial court erred in granting judgment on the pleadings to plaintiffs, as a material issue of fact exists about whether defendant tendered delivery of the vehicle.

Where a motor vehicle identified to a purchase contract is damaged, lost or destroyed prior to the issuance of a certificate of title in the buyer's name, the risk of such damage, loss or destruction lies with either the seller or buyer as determined under the rules set forth in [2-509]. In relevant part, [2-509] states "the risk of loss passes to the buyer on his receipt of the goods if the seller is a merchant; otherwise the risk passes to the buyer on tender of delivery." The parties here agree that defendant is not a merchant. Thus, if defendant tendered delivery, plaintiff bore the risk of the loss; if defendant did not tender delivery, the risk of loss remained with her.

Although the trial court concluded defendant did not tender delivery, it incorrectly focused on ownership and legal title in reaching its decision. Title is no longer "of any importance in determining whether a buyer or seller bears the risk of loss." Rather, tender of delivery "requires that the seller put and hold conforming goods at the buyer's disposition and give the buyer any notification reasonably necessary to enable him to take delivery." [2-503(1)]. In this context, disposition means "doing with as one wishes: discretionary control." Webster's Third New International Dictionary (1966) 654. Delivery thus does not consist in the mere transfer of location or custody of property. The parties concurring to a transfer per the contract must intend one to deliver and the other to receive.

When tendering delivery, the seller must not limit the buyer's disposition of the goods. *Burnett v. Purtell. Burnett* upheld the trial court's allowing rescission because no tender of delivery occurred when the seller did not remove personal possessions from a mobile home after title passed to the buyer. After the mobile home was destroyed in a fire, the buyer sought rescission of the contract. As the personal property inside the mobile home fettered the buyer's disposition of the mobile home, *Burnett* held that the requirements for tender of delivery were not met.

When, however, limitations upon a buyer's disposition of personal property do not result from the seller's activity, then the requirements for tender of delivery are met. The buyer in *Semler v. Prescott*, was not permitted to rescind the contract even though the seller damaged the item purchased, a $36,000 Lalique crystal table. In *Semler*, the seller's tender of delivery was effective even though he remained in possession of the table, as he placed no restrictions on the buyer's disposition of the table. The table remained with the seller simply because the buyer failed to arrange shipping. Risk of loss passed to the buyer upon the seller's effective tender of delivery. See, also, *Akin v. Continental Ins. Co.* (Dec. 26, 2000), Licking App. No. 00-CA-00064, 2000 Ohio App. LEXIS 6148 (concluding tender of delivery occurred when the buyer took physical possession of the vehicle by accepting the keys, starting the vehicle and driving it, even though he drove it on the seller's property).

Defendant contends she fulfilled the statutory requirements for tendering delivery by turning over the keys to the vehicle and, after signing the certificate of title over to plaintiffs' father per plaintiffs' request, by placing the certificate of title in the vehicle's glove box. She asserts plaintiffs chose to leave the vehicle at her residence in order to induce her to take a personal check. Defendant argues that "for all intents and purposes" plaintiffs "possessed and controlled the Vehicle when the keys were given to them." She thus claims not only that she tendered delivery of the vehicle, but also that plaintiffs were in actual possession of the vehicle at the time it was damaged. Describing the fact that the vehicle remained parked in her driveway as a "red herring," defendant assets she could have done "absolutely nothing else" to complete her performance with respect to physical delivery of the vehicle.

The vehicle's continued presence in defendant's driveway is not a red herring. Under Ohio law, a purchaser's performance under a contract generally is complete when the purchaser tenders the check. [2-511(2)] states "[t]ender of payment is sufficient when made by any means or in any manner current in the ordinary course of business unless the seller demands payment in legal tender and gives any extension of time reasonably necessary to procure it.." Thus, upon tendering the plaintiffs ordinarily would be free to drive away in the vehicle. Understanding why the car remained in the driveway is central to determining whether the defendant tendered delivery.

The difficulty in applying the law to this case lies in determining why the car remained on defendant's property, as the pleadings do not disclose that information. If plaintiffs paid by check but defendant refused to consider payment made until the check cleared, then plaintiffs were not free to remove the vehicle from defendant's driveway until the check cleared. Under those circumstances, defendant did not tender delivery under *[2-503]*, as plaintiffs lacked the discretionary control over the vehicle. As a result, the risk of loss would not have passed to plaintiffs. By contrast, if to induce defendant to accept payment by check plaintiffs offered to allow the vehicle to remain on defendant's driveway until the check cleared, then the risk of loss passed to plaintiffs who in their discretion volunteered to leave the car on defendant's driveway in order to pay in tender most convenient to them. Because the pleadings do not reveal the underlying reasons for leaving the car in the driveway until plaintiffs' check cleared, judgment on the pleadings is inappropriate.

In the final analysis, the pleadings do not entitle plaintiffs to judgment as a matter of law as to whether defendant tendered delivery of the vehicle, including why the vehicle remained on defendant's property. Accordingly, we sustain defendant's first assignment of error.

PROBLEM 6 - 1

On her way home from work, Rae stopped by the dealer to pick up her new car. Just after she had signed the sales agreement committing to pay for the car, another sales rep accidentally stepped on the accelerator instead of the brake while demonstrating another car, ramming into Rae's new car sitting on the lot. The car was totaled. Does Rae still have to pay for the car? 2-509(3) and 2-103(c).

Would your answer be different if the sales rep had signed the car's title over to Rae before the crash?

What if the sales rep had just offered her the keys to the new car, but she had not taken them from the rep when the other car crashed into hers? Would she have to pay for the car?

What if she had taken the keys from the rep right before the other car crashed into hers—would she have to pay for the car?

PROBLEM 6 - 2

Would any of your answers in Problem 6 - 1 be different if, instead of purchasing the car from a dealer, Rae was buying the car from a neighbor, and while backing his own car out of the garage, the neighbor's child stepped on the accelerator instead of the brake, ramming his car into the car Rae was buying and totaling it? 2-509(3).

B. RISK OF LOSS WHEN GOODS SHIPPED

If the contract requires the seller to ship the goods to the buyer, 2-509(1) allocates risk of loss based on the specific obligation imposed on the seller. When the seller is obligated to ship the goods to a specific destination—a "destination contract" in Article 2 terms—risk of loss passes from the seller to the buyer when the goods are delivered to the buyer at the specific destination identified. Shipping, of course, presumes that the goods will be delivered somewhere—carriers don't usually offer perpetual shipping—so we might assume, then, that all contracts requiring the seller to ship the goods would be destination contracts. But to create a destination contract, Article 2 requires more than just an obligation to deliver to a designated location; the contract must also reflect that the parties intended the seller to carry the risk of loss during transit and until the goods were delivered to the location designated. In the absence of such intent, Article 2 presumes that a contract requiring transport by carrier is a "shipment contract" and shifts the risk of loss to the buyer when the seller delivers the goods to the carrier for shipment to the buyer—hands them to the FedEx agent at the counter.

So, which party has the risk of loss at a particular moment turns on whether we have a shipment contract—in which case risk of loss passes from the seller to the buyer when the goods are delivered to the carrier for transport—or a destination contract, in which case risk of loss does not pass to the buyer until the goods have been delivered to the designated location. If the goods are lost, damaged, or destroyed in transit under a shipment contract, the buyer is still obligated to pay for the goods because the risk of loss passed to the buyer when the goods were delivered to the carrier. If the goods are lost, damaged, or destroyed in transit under a destination contract, the seller must still deliver the goods called for by the contract in order to avoid a claim for breach, because the risk of loss had not yet passed to the buyer.

The following cases illustrate how the basic risk-of-loss rules apply when the contract contemplates shipment of the goods by the seller and how courts determine whether the parties have overcome Article 2's presumption that agreements requiring transit by carrier are shipment rather than destination contracts.

STAMPEDE PRESENTATION PRODS. V. PRODUCTIVE TRANSP., INC.

UNITED STATES DISTRICT COURT FOR THE WESTERN DISTRICT OF NEW YORK 2013
2013 U.S. DIST. LEXIS 72236

REPORT, RECOMMENDATION AND ORDER

This matter was referred to the undersigned by the Hon. Richard J. Arcara, in accordance with *28 U.S.C. § 636(b)*, for all pretrial matters and to hear and report upon dispositive motions. Dkt. #5.

Plaintiff Stampede Presentation Products, Inc. ("*Stampede*"), brought this action against defendants Productive Transportation, Inc., Productive Transportation Carrier Corp. (collectively, "Productive"), and 1SaleADay L.L.C., seeking money damages based on an alleged loss of an interstate shipment of 960 flat screen TVs.

Pending for report and recommendation is defendant 1SaleADay's motion to dismiss the complaint against it for failure to state a claim upon which relief can be granted. Upon consideration of the pleadings and submissions presented, and for the reasons that follow, it is recommended that defendant's motion be granted.

BACKGROUND

As alleged in the original Verified Complaint, Stampede is in the business of distributing presentation equipment, including flat panel display units and projectors, to audio/visual, computer, and home theater resellers. Pursuant to a "Purchase Invoice" dated February 10, 2012, Stampede purchased 960 thirty-two-inch flat screen TVs from 1SaleADay, an Internet discount retailer, for a total price of $205,440.00. Stampede pre-paid the purchase price in cash by wire transfer on January 2, 2012.

Pursuant to a "Uniform Straight Bill of Lading" dated February 2, 2012, Stampede hired Productive for a fee of $3,475 to pick up the TVs at the manufacturer's warehouse in California, "FOB Origin," and deliver them to Stampede's customer, TigerDirect (also referred to as "SYX Distribution"), located in Napierville, Illinois. Productive in turn subcontracted with another carrier, MML Transport, Inc. ("MML") of Chicago, Illinois, to pick up the TVs in California and deliver them to Stampede's customer in Illinois. As alleged in the original Verified Complaint, "[t]he [TVs] were in fact picked up at the California warehouse, but they were never delivered to [Stampede]'s customer. Instead, they were stolen and/or lost by the trucker who picked them up at the warehouse." Stampede claims that Productive engaged MML as its agent to perform the obligations of the contract without authenticating MML's qualifications, resulting in the loss of the shipment and causing Stampede to suffer damages in the amount paid to 1SaleADay, along with the profits it would have made in the resale of the TVs to its customer. Stampede asserts causes of action against Productive based on theories of breach of contract.... Stampede also seeks recovery of the contract price and lost resale profits from 1SaleADay based on theories of breach of contract....

On June 19, 2012, defendant 1SaleADay filed a motion to dismiss the claims asserted against it, on the following grounds:

> 1. Stampede fails to state a claim against 1SaleADay for breach of contract because, under the Uniform Commercial Code ("UCC"), the Purchase Invoice governing the sale of the TVs was a "shipment" contract, not a "destination" contract, and the risk of loss passed from the seller to the buyer upon delivery of the goods to the carrier;

On July 9, 2012, following entry of a scheduling order for briefing on the motion to dismiss, Stampede filed an Amended Complaint containing new allegations in an effort to remedy the pleading defects addressed by 1SaleADay's motion. Specifically, with regard to the delivery of the TVs to the carrier at the manufacturer's warehouse, Stampede now alleges in the Amended Complaint that:

> 20. Possession of the Goods was in fact turned over at the California warehouse. However, the Goods were not turned over to MML. Instead, SaleADay turned them over to an unauthorized stranger, to whom defendant Productive had apparently provided a bill of lading.

> 21. The Goods were never delivered to plaintiff's customer. Instead, they were stolen by the unauthorized stranger to whom defendant SaleADay delivered them.

In response to the motion to dismiss, Stampede asserts that the Amended Complaint has clarified the claims against 1SaleADay by alleging that 1SaleADay breached the contract by delivering the TVs to someone other than the carrier authorized by plaintiff. According to Stampede, 1SaleADay has mischaracterized the transaction at issue as a UCC "shipment contract/risk of loss" case, and the Amended

Complaint sufficiently alleges that the breach occurred at the time the TVs were delivered by 1SaleADay to the "unauthorized stranger."

DISCUSSION AND ANALYSIS

Breach of Contract

1SaleADay contends that Stampede has failed to state a breach of contract claim against it because the Purchase Invoice for the sale of the TVs is a "shipment contract" governed by *§2-504 of New York's Uniform Commercial Code*, pursuant to which to the risk of loss of or damage to the goods passed from the seller to the buyer upon delivery of the goods to the carrier at the warehouse in California. *UCC §2-504* provides:

> Where the seller is required or authorized to send the goods to the buyer and the contract does not require him to deliver them at a particular destination, then unless otherwise agreed he must:
>
> (a) put the goods in the possession of such a carrier and make such a contract for their transportation as may be reasonable having regard to the nature of the goods and other circumstances of the case; and
>
> (b) obtain and promptly deliver or tender in due form any document necessary to enable the buyer to obtain possession of the goods or otherwise required by the agreement or by usage of trade; and
>
> (c) promptly notify the buyer of the shipment. Failure to notify the buyer under paragraph (c) or to make a proper contract under paragraph (a) is a ground for rejection only if material delay or loss ensues.

N.Y.U.C.C. §2-504. In contrast, a "destination contract" is covered by *UCC §2-503*; it arises where "the seller is required to deliver at a particular destination." *N.Y.U.C.C. §2-503(3)*. Allocation of the risk of loss is addressed by *UCC §2-509(1)*, which provides:

> Where the contract requires or authorizes the seller to ship the goods by carrier
>
> (a) if it does not require [the seller] to deliver them at a particular destination, the risk of loss passes to the buyer when the goods are duly delivered to the carrier ....
>
> (b) if it does require him to deliver them at a particular destination and the goods are there duly tendered while in the possession of the carrier, the risk of loss passes to the buyer when the goods are there duly so tendered as to enable the buyer to take delivery.
>
> *N.Y.U.C.C. §2-509(1)*.

Based on this Court's reading of the documents governing Stampede's purchase of the TVs from 1SaleADay in this case, and considering the undisputed logistics of the transaction, it is clear that the contractual arrangement required or authorized 1SaleADay to ship the TVs by carrier, designated by Stampede to be Productive Transportation. The Purchase Invoice contains no express requirement that 1SaleADay deliver the TVs "at a particular destination." The invoice simply identifies 1SaleADay as the "Vendor," and directs that the purchased items are to be shipped to Stampede's resale customer, TigerDirect, in Napierville, Illinois. The Uniform Straight Bill of Lading, prepared on a "Productive Transportation" form designating Productive as the "delivering carrier," clearly indicates that the TVs were to be shipped "FOB Origin" by the "Shipper," identified as Stampede, from their origin at the warehouse in California to TigerDirect in Illinois.

As recognized by the Second Circuit, "[w]here the terms of an agreement are ambiguous, there is a strong presumption under the U.C.C. favoring shipment contracts. Unless the parties 'expressly specify' that the contract requires the seller to deliver to a particular destination, the contract is generally construed as one for shipment." *Windows, Inc. v. Jordan Panel Systems Corp.*, 177 F.3d 114, 117 (2d Cir. 1999) citing *Dana Debs, Inc. v. Lady Rose Stores, Inc.*, 65 Misc. 2d 697, 319 N.Y.S.2d 111, 112 (N.Y.City Civ.Ct. 1970) ("The word 'require' means that there is an explicit written understanding to that effect for otherwise every shipment would be deemed a destination contract."). Here, the terms of the agreement clearly express the parties' understanding that the buyer (Stampede) designated a carrier (Progressive) to make the shipment of the TVs from the manufacturer's warehouse to the customer. There is no express language anywhere in the contract documents specifying that the seller (1SaleADay) was itself required to deliver the TVs to a particular destination. Even if these terms of agreement were to be somehow construed as ambiguous, "the strong presumption favoring shipment contracts" would lead the Court to conclude that UCC §2-509(1)(a) should apply to allocate the risk of loss to Stampede upon 1SaleADay's delivery of the TVs to the carrier at the warehouse in California.

This conclusion is strengthened by the clearly printed indication on the Bill of Lading that the goods were to be shipped by Stampede, and delivered by Productive, "FOB Origin" from the warehouse in California to the resale customer in Illinois. "The general rule is that upon a sale 'f.o.b. the point of shipment,' title passes from the seller at the moment of delivery to the carrier, and the subject of the sale is thereafter at the buyer's risk." *Sara Corp. v. Sainty Intern. America Inc.*, 2008 U.S. Dist. LEXIS 58049, 2008 WL 2944862, at *7 (S.D.N.Y. Aug. 1, 2008). Under the ordinary application of this rule, "delivery to the carrier is delivery to the buyer." *Chase Manhattan Bank v. Nissho Pacific Corp.*, 22 A.D.2d 215, 254 N.Y.S.2d 571, 577 (App. Div. 1964), see also UCC §2-319(1)(a) ("Unless otherwise agreed the term f.o.b. (which means 'free on board') at a named place ... is a delivery term under which ... when the term is the place of shipment, the seller must at that place ship the goods in the manner provided in this Article (Section 2-504) and bear the expense and risk of putting them into the possession of the carrier").

Stampede contends that 1SaleADay's reliance on the UCC provisions dealing with allocation of risk of loss is a "pure red herring", since the facts pleaded in the Amended Complaint clearly set forth a plausible claim that 1SaleADay breached the contractual arrangement by delivering the TVs to an unauthorized carrier. To the contrary, since the parties are merchants as that term is defined in UCC §2-104(1), and the transaction at issue is for the sale of goods as defined in UCC §2 105(1), it cannot be disputed that the allocation of the risk of loss to the goods during the transaction is covered by UCC Article 2.

Applying the UCC's allocation of risk of loss provisions, because the contract documents clearly identify Stampede as the party to the transaction responsible for hiring an authorized carrier to ship the goods from the point of origin to its customer in Illinois, and because there is otherwise no express indication that 1SaleADay itself was required to deliver the goods at a particular destination, the contract governing the transaction at issue must be construed as a shipment contract under UCC §2-504(a), and the risk of loss passed to Stampede when the goods were delivered to the carrier, under UCC §2-509(1)(a). As indicated by the signatures on page one1 of the Bill of Lading, the TVs were picked up by the carrier on February 2, 2012, and there is nothing in the pleadings or in the contract documents attached as exhibits thereto to indicate that the goods were non-conforming or were otherwise not duly delivered within the requirements of UCC Article 2.

Accordingly, since 1SaleADay had already fulfilled its contractual obligations, and Stampede had assumed the risk, at the time the goods were lost, there can be no set of facts pleaded that would allow the Court to draw the reasonable inference that 1SaleADay is liable for breach of contract.

~~Based on this analysis, accepting the material facts alleged in the complaint as true and drawing all reasonable inferences in the plaintiff's favor, this Court finds that Stampede has failed to plead sufficient factual content to state a breach of contract claim against 1SaleADay that is plausible on its face.~~ It is therefore recommended that Stampede's breach of contract claim against 1SaleADay be dismissed.

BERRY V. LUCAS

COURT OF APPEALS OF OREGON, 2006
210 ORE. APP. 334

CRAMER, J. pro tempore

This appeal arises from a contract dispute regarding a manufactured home placed on a lot in Bandon, Oregon. Following a bench trial, the trial court entered a judgment in favor of plaintiffs and awarded damages of $6,535. Defendant appeals and, for the reasons discussed below, we affirm.

We take the facts—which are undisputed—from the record and the trial court's findings in its letter opinion. Defendant is in the business of the retail sale of manufactured homes. In September 2002, plaintiffs and defendant entered into a contract in which plaintiffs agreed to purchase a Redman manufactured home for $69,040. As the trial court explained:

> "The contract consisted of a printed form (front and back) and three exhibits. Defendant agreed as part of the contract to deliver and set up the manufactured home on a lot owned by plaintiffs in Bandon, Oregon. The parties contemplated that plaintiffs would be receiving a home suitable for occupancy. The contract provided that plaintiffs would pay 50% down and the balance on delivery. * * *

> "As part of the contract, the parties certified that the terms printed on the back side of the contract were part of the contract, and furthermore, plaintiffs acknowledged by signing the contract that they had read and understood the contract and received a copy of the contract."

Plaintiffs mailed a check for one-half of the purchase price to defendant in September 2002 and mailed a check for the remaining balance in early November.

The manufactured home was delivered in two sections to plaintiffs' lot on November 15, 2002, and placed on concrete slab that had been constructed by plaintiffs' contractor. About a month later—before the home had been completed and prepared for occupancy—it suffered severe storm damage. The trial court found:

> "As of that date, the carpet inside the home had not been laid, railings remained to be installed, sheet rock still needed to be installed and exterior siding on the west end had not yet been installed. * * * [T]he home was not ready to be moved into because set up work remained to be done by the defendant, and its agent, both inside and outside the home. The carpet work, the railings, the sheet rock and the exterior siding were the responsibility of defendant. Neither party had insurance on the manufactured home as of the date of the storm damage. Plaintiffs paid a contractor $6535 to repair the damage."

In a second count, plaintiffs alleged that the damage to the manufactured home "was sustained after the manufactured home was shipped to the specified destination but before Defendants could tender delivery or Plaintiffs could inspect and potentially accept the goods." Plaintiffs alleged that defendant refused to repair the wind and rainwater damage and that plaintiffs therefore had to incur the expense of having the repair performed.

The trial court ... entered a money judgment in favor of plaintiffs on the contract claim. Defendant appeals, arguing that the trial court erred in finding in plaintiffs' favor and awarding damages. Because we agree with the trial court that the risk of loss was on defendant at the time the storm damage occurred, we affirm.

As a general matter, Oregon's codification of the Uniform Commercial Code (UCC) governs sales contracts of the type involved here. But, "[t]he effect of provisions of the Uniform Commercial Code may be varied by agreement, except as otherwise provided in the Uniform Commercial Code." *ORS 71.1020(3); see also ORS 72.5090(4)* (regarding the provision addressing risk of loss in the absence of breach, "[t]he provisions of this section are subject to contrary agreement of the parties"). Defendant acknowledges the general applicability of the UCC, but argues that a provision of the contract governs the risk of loss in this case and is dispositive. We begin with that argument.

Paragraph 12 of the sales contract states:

"INSURANCE. Buyer understands that Buyer is <u>not</u> covered by insurance on the unit purchased until accepted by an insurance company, and Buyer agrees to hold Dealer harmless from any and all claims due to loss or damage prior to acceptance of insurance coverage by an insurance company."

(Underscoring and boldface in original.) Defendant argues that paragraph 12 addresses risk of loss and that resort to the UCC provisions regarding risk of loss therefore is unnecessary. It argues that paragraph 12 "effectively allocates the risk of loss to the buyer before complete performance of the contract." According to defendant, the risk of loss under paragraph 12 had passed to plaintiffs at the time of the storm damage.

In interpreting a contract, we first examine the text and context to determine if the contract is ambiguous. Whether a contract is ambiguous presents a question of law. In addition to examining the text and context of the provision, the court, in determining whether the contract is ambiguous, is also to consider extrinsic evidence of "the circumstances underlying the formation of the contract." Finally, if the "provision remains ambiguous after the first two steps have been followed, the court relies on appropriate maxims of construction" to determine the provision's meaning.

Paragraph 12 does not, on its face, address risk of loss. It follows a heading that reads, "Insurance." Its text focuses on the effect of insurance coverage, not a time in the transaction that will shift the risk of loss from seller to buyer. Moreover, as plaintiff points out, at the time the parties entered into the contract, the manufactured home had not yet been constructed by the manufacturer. According to plaintiff,

"it seems nonsensical and illogical to force the Plaintiff to bear the risk of loss for a manufactured home that had yet to be manufactured and yet to be placed in the control of the Defendant. * * * It also seems untenable to force the Plaintiff to bear the risk of loss when the Defendant and Defendant's agents are still working on setting up the manufactured home, in accordance with their contractual duties."

Although we are not convinced that paragraph 12 addresses risk of loss, the provision arguably is ambiguous in that regard. That is, it could be read to place the risk of loss on the buyer from the time the contract is signed. Or, as plaintiff argues, it could be read to simply not address risk of loss at all. The parties point to no extrinsic evidence that resolves the ambiguity or that sheds light on the parties' intention. In light of the provision's ambiguity, we proceed, then, to ascertain the provision's meaning by applying maxims of construction.

Two maxims apply to the provision at issue here. First, it is a basic tenet of contract law that ambiguous language in a contract is construed against the drafter of the contract. Here, the form contract was provided by defendant, and applying that maxim leads to the conclusion that the parties did not intend to reallocate the risk of loss by the paragraph relating to insurance.

The second relevant maxim is one that is more specific to the situation involved here. That maxim is that, to allocate risk of loss in a manner different from that contemplated by the UCC, "the parties must expressly shift the risk of loss and such a shift will not readily be inferred." *Galbraith v. American Motorhome Corporation,* 14 Wn App 754, 757-58, 545 P.2d 561, 563 (1976); *see also McKenzie v. Olmstead,* 587 N.W.2d 863, 865 (Minn Ct App 1999) ("The implications of any contrary agreement regarding allocation of the risk of loss * * * should be explicit and understood by both parties."). Moreover, insurance provisions in a contract—such as a provision that the buyer must insure a yacht while the seller was installing options after receiving the boat from the manufacturer—have been held not to allocate the risk of loss contrary to the relevant UCC provision. *Hayward v. Postma,* 31 Mich. App. 720, 724, 188 N.W.2d 31, 33 (1971). Rather, as the *Hayward* court held, "we feel that a contract which shifts the risk of loss to the buyer before he receives the goods is so unusual that a seller who wants to achieve this result must make his intent very clear to the buyer."

Applying those two maxims, and considering the text in context, we conclude that the parties did not intend to vary the risk of loss from that provided in the UCC. We turn, accordingly, to the UCC provision governing risk of loss.

Risk of loss in this case is governed by [2-509], which provides, in part:

"(1) Where the contract requires or authorizes the seller to ship the goods by carrier:

"* * * *

"(b) *If it does require the seller to deliver them at a particular destination and the goods are there duly tendered while in the possession of the carrier, the risk of loss passes to the buyer when the goods are there duly so tendered as to enable the buyer to take delivery.*

"* * * *

(Emphasis added.) The contract between plaintiffs and defendant required defendant to deliver the manufactured home to plaintiffs' lot and to set it up. The transaction thus is governed by [2-509(1)(b)]. In short, the "goods" that plaintiffs purchased consisted of a complete manufactured home, placed on their lot, and ready for occupancy.

At the time of the storm damage, defendant had not supplied the goods that it had agreed to tender. Rather, it had provided an as-yet incomplete manufactured home. Under [2-509(1)(b)], risk of loss passes to the buyer only after the goods are "duly so tendered as to enable the buyer to take delivery." [2-503(1)] provides, in part, that "[t]ender of delivery requires that the seller put and hold *conforming goods* at the buyer's disposition and give the buyer any notification reasonably necessary to enable the buyer to take delivery." (Emphasis added.) And under [2-106 (2)], "Goods or conduct including any part of a performance are 'conforming' or conform to the contract when they are in accordance with the obligations under the contract."

Here, although defendant had partially performed under the contract, it had not tendered delivery of a completed manufactured home by putting conforming goods at plaintiffs' disposition. Simply put, defendant had not—at the time that the damage occurred—tendered delivery of the goods for which plaintiffs had contracted. And because, under [2-509(1)(b)], the risk of loss is on the seller until such tender has occurred, the risk remained on defendant at the time the storm damaged the manufactured home. It follows that the trial court correctly entered judgment in favor of plaintiffs.

Courts applying other states' versions of the UCC have reached the same conclusion—although not necessarily following the exact route we have. *Moses v. Newman,* 658 S.W.2d 119 (Tenn Ct App 1983), is the case most factually similar to this one. As in this case, the seller had agreed to provide a mobile home and to set it up on the buyer's lot. As in this case, the home was delivered to the lot but, before the seller could complete the set-up, a windstorm destroyed the home. Although the court analyzed the liability issue under UCC 2-510 its analysis was analogous to ours. It concluded that, although the buyer had placed certain items of personal property in the home before it was destroyed, the buyer had not accepted delivery of the home at that time. Moreover, the court explained that the risk of loss had not passed from the seller to the buyer at the time the goods were destroyed:

> "In this case, plaintiff contracted for a habitable mobile home plus the installation. Accordingly, since the loss occurred before the installation was complete, the defendant had not delivered conforming goods which would shift the risk of loss to plaintiff."

Similarly, in *Southland Mobile Home Corporation v. Chyrchel,* 255 Ark 366, 500 S.W.2d 778 (1973), the plaintiff purchased a mobile home from the defendant. After delivering the mobile home and placing it in position, the defendant hooked up the sewer and gas connections, but did not complete other connections. Before the connections were completed, an explosion occurred and extensively damaged the mobile home. In addressing the risk of loss issue, the Arkansas Supreme Court rejected the argument "that the sale was complete before the fire and the risk of loss had passed to the buyer." The court concluded that the risk of loss never passed to the buyer because the seller had not delivered conforming goods.

Other courts, albeit in somewhat different factual contexts, have reached the same result. *See, e.g., In re Thomas,* 182 BR 347, 349 (SD Fla 1995) (buyer purchased pool heater under contract that included installation; seller dropped heater off on buyer's driveway, from where it was stolen; United States Bankruptcy court concluded that unit never was "delivered," so that risk of loss remained on seller); *William F. Wilke, Inc. v. Cummins Diesel Engines, Inc.,* 252 Md 611, 618, 250 A.2d 886, 890 (1969) (contract called for purchase, installation, and field testing of diesel generator; damage occurred after generator was installed, but before other obligations were performed; the court held, "[W]e have no difficulty in holding that the delivery of the generator to the job site, while identifying the goods to the contract, did not amount to a delivery of goods or the performance of obligations conforming to the contract. It could not constitute such a delivery and performance until the generator had been installed, started up, and field tests completed.").

In sum, because plaintiffs contracted for a completed manufactured home and no such home had been delivered at the time the windstorm damage occurred, the risk of loss was still on defendant at that time. Accordingly, the trial court correctly found in favor of plaintiffs and awarded damages.

Affirmed

In the *Stampede* case, the buyer was not able to overcome Article 2's presumption that a contract requiring the seller to transport the goods to the buyer is a shipment contract, but the court is less than clear as to what exactly it takes to overcome that presumption—what would "'expressly specify' that the contract requires the seller to deliver to a particular destination."

One judge has suggested that the key to distinguishing a shipment contract from a destination contract lies in the text of the Code itself:

I agree with the majority opinion's conclusion that there is a strong presumption under the N.Y.U.C.C. favoring "shipment" contracts. The question then arises as to what it takes to overcome the presumption. While the opinion appropriately suggests that a commonly recognized industry term would do it, it fails to emphasize the importance of the distinction between delivery *to* a destination versus delivery *at* a destination.

Every sales contract entails a "delivery." See N.Y.U.C.C. § 2-503. Further, to the extent that a shipment contract is one that requires or authorizes the seller to "send the goods to the buyer," N.Y.U.C.C. § 2-504, such contract contemplates "delivery," in the colloquial sense, *to* a designated location. Accordingly, contractual language that requires goods to be "delivered to" a location does not by itself create a destination contract. This is not to say that a contract containing a term requiring delivery "to" a location is necessarily a shipment contract. The parties may, of course, create a destination contract by the use of language making it clear that the seller's obligation continues to the point of delivery at a particular destination. Rather, the point is that, standing alone, "delivered to" does not constitute a specific agreement designating where the seller will perform its obligation to deliver goods. See N.Y.U.C.C. § 2-503 official cmt. 5 ("The seller is not obligated to deliver at a named destination and bear the concurrent risk of loss until arrival, unless he has specifically agreed so to deliver....").

By contrast, contractual language that requires the seller to "deliver at" a particular location designates a location at which the seller must effect delivery. Until the goods are tendered at that location, delivery has not occurred and the seller has not performed its duties under the contract.

I do not view this distinction between "to" and "at" as technical or as a trap for the unwary. Parties should be able to create unambiguous destination contracts by employing the precise text of the controlling statute. They may also do so by using other language but should be aware that deviation from the text risks confusion. In sum, "delivered to" and "delivered at" are not, in this context, synonymous.

In my view had the contract in this case tracked the language of § 2-503 (3) by specifying that Windows was required to deliver *at* a particular location in New York City, it would have been a destination contract. The fact that instead Windows was required to deliver *to* a particular location in New York City (absent any additional language) was insufficient to overcome the presumption.

Windows, Inc. v. Jordan Panel Sys. Corp., 177 F.3d 114
(2nd Circuit, 1999)(Parker, Concurring).

Fortunately, long before Article 2 was enacted, merchants regularly involved in the shipping of goods had developed their own shorthand form for expressing their intent about the respective obligations (i.e., risk of loss, as well as who pays for shipping and insurance if procured) of sellers and buyers when goods were shipped under a sales contract. These mercantile terms and their meanings were incorporated into Article 2 and can be used by the parties to eliminate any ambiguity as to whether the parties intended a shipment or a destination contract. See, e.g., 2-319 (FOB and FAS), 2-320 (CIF and C&F). For example, "FOB[3] place of delivery" communicates that the parties intended a destination contract, with the seller assuming the risk of loss until the goods are delivered to the location designated by the buyer. "FOB place of shipment" communicates that the parties intended a shipment contract, with the risk of loss passing to the buyer when the seller delivers the goods to the carrier.

---

3   Free On Board.

These mercantile terms can also shift the risk of loss at other times—"FOB car, vessel, or other vehicle" shifts the risk of loss to the buyer when the goods are actually loaded onto the carrier, as opposed to an ordinary shipment contract, where the risk passes when the goods are simply delivered to the carrier, before the goods are loaded on the carrier. Similarly, CIF (Cost, Insurance, Freight) and C&F (Cost and Freight) both designate shipment contracts, but with each the risk of loss does not pass to the buyer until the goods are transferred to the carrier and loaded. A term commonly used in maritime transport, "FAS vessel,"[4] requires the seller to deliver the goods alongside the named vessel, the risk of loss passing when the goods are delivered to the dock alongside the vessel within reach of the ship's lifting tackle.

Mercantile terms also communicate details about which party is responsible for expenses incurred in transporting the goods—most commonly the cost of shipping and insurance, if required. For example, in a CIF contract, the seller pays the cost of shipping the goods as well as the cost of insuring them during transport, whereas in a C&F contract, the seller pays the costs of shipping but the buyer pays to insure the goods. The following table classifies for 2-509 purposes the most commonly used domestic shipping terms.

Mercantile Term	2-509 Classification	When Risk of Loss Passes	Who Pays Freight	Who Pays Insurance
F.O.B. Place of Shipping	Shipment Contract	Upon Transfer to Carrier	Buyer	Buyer
F.O.B. Place of Delivery	Destination Contract	Upon Tender Of Delivery to Buyer at Destination	Seller	Seller
F.O.B. Car, Vessel, or Vehicle	Shipment Contract	When Goods Loaded on Car, Vessel, or Vehicle	Buyer	Buyer
C.I.F.	Shipment Contract	When Goods Loaded	Seller	Seller
C. & F.	Shipment Contract	When Goods Loaded	Seller	Buyer
F.A.S. Vessel	Shipment Contract	When Goods Delivered Alongside Vessel	Buyer	Buyer

Many of these terms are included in the International Commercial Terms (referred to as Incoterms) that have been published periodically by the International Chamber of Commerce since the 1930s for use in international transactions, where they can have different meanings for risk-of-loss purposes.[5]

As the table illustrates, whether a contract is a shipment or destination contract is not necessarily based on which party pays for shipping or for any insurance procured. Comment 5 to 2-503 explains:

> [T]here is omitted from this Article the rule under prior uniform legislation that a term requiring the seller to pay the freight or cost of transportation to the buyer is equivalent to an agreement by the seller to deliver to the buyer or at an agreed destination. This omission is with the specific intention of negating the rule, for under this Article the "shipment" contract is regarded as the normal one and the "destination" contract as the variant type.

---

4   Free Alongside.
5   See: www.iccwbo.org/products-and-services/trade-facilitation/incoterms-2010/.

This Comment precludes a buyer from asserting, in the absence of a mercantile term reflecting the intent of the parties to create a destination contract, that a provision requiring the seller to pay the cost of shipping is the equivalent of a destination provision, and as such, is sufficient to overcome the shipment contract presumption.

Finally, 2-509 must be read in connection with 2-503 and 2-504, which impose additional conditions in both shipment and destination contracts on the shipping seller that must be satisfied before risk of loss actually passes. In a shipment contract, risk of loss passes to the buyer when the goods are turned over to the carrier only if the contract for shipping is reasonable under the circumstances, the goods conform to the requirements of the contract, and the seller both notifies the buyer that the goods have been shipped and provides the buyer with whatever documents will be necessary for the buyer to get the goods from the carrier. 2-504. In a destination contract, risk of loss passes when the goods are delivered by the carrier to the specified location only if the goods conform to the contract and the seller both notifies the buyer that the goods are available and provides the buyer with whatever documents are necessary for the buyer to obtain immediate possession of the goods. 2-503.

PROBLEM 6 - 3

Rae decided to offer fresh-baked "homemade" bread for sale in the store's bakery, so she ordered two new Doyon Jet Air Electric Oven Proofer Combos from the manufacturer in upstate New York. The ovens were priced at $21,100 each and had to be transported interstate to the store. Determine when the risk of loss passed to Rae in each of the following cases and whether Rae will have to pay for the ovens:

Case 1: The contract required the seller to ship the ovens to "Buyer at 111 First Street North, City, State, ZIP." The seller delivered the ovens to UPS for shipment. The UPS semi carrying the ovens caught fire at a rest stop, and the ovens were destroyed. 2-509(1).

Case 2: The contract required the seller to ship the goods to Rae, "FOB seller's factory." The seller delivered the goods to UPS for shipment. The UPS trailer loaded with the ovens was stolen en route to Rae. 2-509(1) and 2-319.

Case 3: The contract provided that the ovens would be shipped to the store, "FOB buyer's vehicle." Rae sent the store's delivery truck to pick up the ovens. The seller's forklift dropped the ovens while loading them onto the store's truck. The ovens were damaged beyond repair. 2-509(1) and 2-319.

Case 4: The contract provided that the ovens would be shipped to the store, "FOB buyer's vehicle." Rae sent the store's delivery truck to pick up the ovens. The ovens were on the store's truck when it ran off the highway and rolled into the river on the way back to the store. The truck and the ovens were destroyed. 2-509(1) and 2-319.

Case 5: The contract required the seller to ship the ovens "FOB Buyer's store." The seller delivered the ovens to UPS for shipment. The UPS semi loaded with the ovens was involved in a multi-vehicle wreck en route to Rae, and the ovens sustained significant damage. 2-509(1) and 2-319.

Case 6: The contract stated the price of the ovens as "$42,200 CIF" and required the seller to ship them to Rae at the store. The seller delivered the ovens to UPS for shipment to the buyer. The UPS truck backed over the ovens, destroying them before they were loaded onto the UPS semi. 2-509(1) and 2-320.

Case 7: The contract required the seller to ship the ovens "FAS, SS Howdy, NY, NY." The crate with the ovens in it fell into the harbor while being lifted onto the ship. The ovens were damaged beyond repair. 2-509(1) and 2-319.

C. EFFECT OF BREACH ON RISK OF LOSS

The risk-of-loss rules set out in 2-509 only apply in the absence of breach:

> The scope of the present section ... is limited strictly to those cases where there has been no breach by the seller. Where for any reason his delivery or tender fails to conform to the contract, this present section does not apply and the situation is governed by the provisions on effect of breach on risk of loss.

Comment 1, 2-509. Section 2-510 alters how risk of loss is allocated when one of the parties has breached the contract by delaying when the risk passes or by allowing the nonbreaching party to put it on the breaching party. When the seller fails to deliver goods that conform to the requirements of the contract or otherwise fails to perform in accord with the contract (for example, time, place, or manner of delivery), the buyer is not obligated to take (accept) the goods, and so Article 2 leaves the risk of causality to of the goods with the seller, regardless of whether the parties intended a shipment or destination contract. If the goods the seller delivers to the carrier under a shipment contract don't conform to the contract, 2-510 prevents the risk of loss from passing to the buyer on delivery to the carrier as it otherwise would under 2-509. Similarly, if the goods don't conform to the contract when delivered to the buyer under a destination contract, 2-510 prevents the risk from passing to the buyer even though the buyer has the goods. Risk of loss will not pass to the buyer in these situations until the seller "cures" (brings the goods into conformity with the contract or provides substitute goods that conform to the contract) or the buyer "accepts" the nonconforming goods (agrees to take them and pay for them even though they don't meet the requirements of the contract).

If the buyer repudiates (or is otherwise in breach) before the seller ships the goods (under a shipment contract), or before the goods are delivered to the buyer (under a destination contract), 2-510 allows the seller to put the risk of loss on the buyer even though it would not have passed to the buyer under 2-509—but only if, at the time of the repudiation, the seller has actually identified (designated) the specific goods to be provided to the buyer under the contract and the goods so identified conform to the requirements of the contract, and only to the extent that the seller's insurance does not cover the loss. The *Multiplastics* case illustrates how 2-510 works when the buyer breaches.

MULTIPLASTICS, INC. v. ARCH INDUSTRIES, INC.
SUPREME COURT OF CONNECTICUT
1974

Reporter: 166 Conn. 280; 348 A.2d 618; 1974 Conn. LEXIS 893

The plaintiff, Multiplastics, Inc., brought this action to recover damages from the defendant, Arch Industries, Inc., for the breach of a contract to purchase 40,000 pounds of plastic pellets. From a judgment rendered for the plaintiff, the defendant has appealed to this court.

The facts may be summarized as follows: The plaintiff, a manufacturer of plastic resin pellets, agreed with the defendant on June 30, 1971, to manufacture and deliver 40,000 pounds of brown polystyrene plastic pellets for nineteen cents a pound. The pellets were specially made for the defendant, which agreed to accept delivery at the rate of 1000 pounds per day after completion of production. The defendant's confirming order contained the notation "make and hold for release. Confirmation." The plaintiff produced the order of pellets within two weeks and requested release orders from the defendant. The defendant refused to issue the release orders, citing labor difficulties and its vacation schedule. On August 18, 1971, the plaintiff sent the defendant the following letter: "Against P. O. 0946, we produced 40,000 lbs. of brown high impact styrene, and you have issued no releases. You indicated to us that you would be using 1,000 lbs. of each per day. We have warehoused these products for more than forty days, as we agreed to do. However, we cannot warehouse these products indefinitely, and request that you send us shipping instructions. We have done everything we agreed to do." After August 18, 1971, the plaintiff made numerous telephone calls to the defendant to seek payment and delivery instructions. In response, beginning August 20, 1971, the defendant agreed to issue release orders but in fact never did.

On September 22, 1971, the plaintiff's plant, containing the pellets manufactured for the defendant, was destroyed by fire. The plaintiff's fire insurance did not cover the loss of the pellets. The plaintiff brought this action against the defendant to recover the contract price.

The trial court concluded that the plaintiff made a valid tender of delivery by its letter of August 18, 1971, and by its subsequent requests for delivery instructions; that the defendant repudiated and breached the contract by refusing to accept delivery on August 20, 1971; that the period from August 20, 1971, to September 22, 1971, was not a commercially unreasonable time for the plaintiff to treat the risk of loss as resting on the defendant under General Statutes § 42a-2-510 (3); and that the plaintiff was entitled to recover the contract price plus interest.

General Statutes § 42a-2-510, entitled "Effect of breach on risk of loss," reads, in pertinent part, as follows: "(3) Where the buyer as to conforming goods already identified to the contract for sale repudiates or is otherwise in breach before risk of their loss has passed to him, the seller may to the extent of any deficiency in his effective insurance coverage treat the risk of loss as resting on the buyer for a commercially reasonable time." The defendant contends that § 42a-2-510 is not applicable because its failure to issue delivery instructions did not constitute either a repudiation or a breach of the agreement. The defendant also argues that even if § 42a-2-510 were applicable, the period from August 20, 1971, to September 22, 1971, was not a commercially reasonable period of time within which to treat the risk of loss as resting on the buyer. The defendant does not claim that the destroyed pellets were not "conforming goods already identified to the contract for sale," as required by General Statutes § 42a-2-510 (3), nor does it protest the computation of damages. With regard to recovery of the price of goods and incidental damages, see General Statutes §42a-2-709 (1) (a).

The trial court's conclusion that the defendant was in breach is supported by its finding that the defendant agreed to accept delivery of the pellets at the rate of 1000 pounds per day after completion of production. The defendant argues that since the confirming order instructed the plaintiff to "make and hold for release," the contract did not specify an exact delivery date. This argument fails, however, because nothing in the finding suggests that the notation in the confirming order was part of the agreement between the parties. Since, as the trial court found, the plaintiff made a proper tender of delivery, beginning with its letter of August 18, 1971, the plaintiff was entitled to acceptance of the goods and to payment according to the contract. General Statutes §§ 42a-2-507 (1), 42a-2-307.

The remaining question is whether, under General Statutes § 42a-2-510 (3), the period of time from August 20, 1971, the date of the breach, to September 22, 1971, the date of the fire, was a "commercially reasonable" period within which to treat the risk of loss as resting on the buyer. The trial court concluded that it was "not, on the facts in this case, a commercially unreasonable time," which we take to mean that it was a commercially reasonable period. The time limitation in § 42a-2-510 (3) is designed to enable the seller to obtain the additional requisite insurance coverage. The trial court's conclusion is tested by the finding. Although the finding is not detailed, it supports the conclusion that August 20 to September 22 was a commercially reasonable period within which to place the risk of loss on the defendant. As already stated, the trial court found that the defendant repeatedly agreed to transmit delivery instructions and that the pellets were specially made to fill the defendant's order. Under those circumstances, it was reasonable for the plaintiff to believe that the goods would soon be taken off its hands and so to forgo procuring the needed insurance.

We consider it advisable to discuss one additional matter. The trial court concluded that "title" passed to the defendant, and the defendant attacks the conclusion on this appeal. The issue is immaterial to this case. General Statutes § 42a-2-401 states: "Each provision of this article with regard to the rights, obligations and remedies of the seller, the buyer, purchasers or other third parties applies irrespective of title to the goods except where the provision refers to such title." As one student of the Uniform Commercial Code has written: "The single most important innovation of Article 2 [of the Uniform Commercial Code] is its restatement of ... [the parties'] responsibilities in terms of operative facts rather than legal conclusions; where pre-Code law looked to 'title' for the definition of rights and remedies, the Code looks to demonstrable realities such as custody, control and professional expertise. This shift in approach is central to the whole philosophy of Article 2. It means that disputes, as they arise, can focus, as does all of the modern law of contracts, upon actual provable circumstances, rather than upon a metaphysical concept of elastic and endlessly fluid dimensions." Peters, "Remedies for Breach of Contracts Relating to the Sale of Goods under the Uniform Commercial Code: A Roadmap for Article Two," 73 Yale L.J. 199, 201.

There is no error.

———————————

Article 2's allocation of risk of loss after a breach has been sharply criticized, and revisions to Article 2 proposed for adoption by the states several years ago would have eliminated most of what is now in 2-510. One author explained:

> The Drafting Committee concluded that the effect of breach on risk of loss rules is largely irrelevant and the notion that risk of loss should be reallocated in breach situations is dubious at best, particularly where there is no causal connection between the breach and casualty to the goods. Moreover, the application of reallocation rules based upon the extent of insurance coverage is unclear in original sections 2-510(2) and (3). The underlying concept that these subsections operated as "anti-subrogation" provisions has not been shown to have had any effect on insurance companies or calculated premiums.

Murray, The Emerging Article 2: The Latest Iteration, 35 *Duq. L. Rev.* 533 (1997). Those revisions were never adopted and now have been withdrawn, so 2-510 continues to control risk allocation when one of the parties has breached the contract.

CHAPTER 7

PERFORMANCE

When the time comes for the parties to perform their sale-of-goods contract, the expectations of the parties are pretty basic: the buyer expects the seller to deliver the goods to the buyer, and the seller expects the buyer to pay for those goods. And so it's no surprise that 2-301 restates these expectations as obligations of the parties to a sale-of-goods contract:

> The obligation of the seller is to transfer and deliver and that of the buyer is to accept and pay in accordance with the contract.

And of course the buyer, in the usual case, will not expect to pay for the goods until they have been delivered by the seller. So it's also not a surprise that Article 2 conditions the buyer's obligation to pay on the seller's delivery of the goods:

> Tender of delivery is a condition to the buyer's duty to accept the goods and, unless otherwise agreed, to his duty to pay for them.

2-507. But what happens if the goods delivered are defective or are not identical to the goods described in the contract? What if the delivery is late—the seller delivers the goods after the time provided in the contract? Or what if the seller only delivers ninety-five toasters instead of the one hundred required under the contract? Does the buyer have to take the goods and pay for them even though the seller's performance is not what the contract required—not what the buyer was expecting under the contract—and then sue the seller for breach later? What if the buyer does not realize the goods are defective until after she has used the goods for some time—is she stuck with the goods and a claim for breach? Should it matter that, as a result of her use of the goods before discovery of the defect, the condition of the goods has changed in some significant respect? Should it matter that the seller persuaded her to take the goods even though it was obvious they were not what the contract promised? Should it matter that the seller's defective performance results in little, if any, loss or harm to the buyer? And should the seller be given an opportunity to remedy its failure to perform regardless of the circumstances?

We will explore the answers to these and other questions in the materials that follow.

A. Acceptance: The Buyer Takes the Goods

Acceptance is the term of art applied by Article 2 to the buyer's decision to take the goods and to pay for them:

> Under this Article "acceptance" … means that the buyer, pursuant to the contract, takes particular goods … as his own … whether he does so by words, actions, or silence when it is time to speak. If the goods conform to the contract, acceptance amounts only to the performance by the buyer of one part of his legal obligation.

Comment 1, 2-606. If the buyer wants the goods promised by the seller, the buyer must "accept" them when delivered. Acceptance has specific legal consequences under Article 2.[1] First, acceptance obligates the buyer to pay for the goods at the contract price. 2-607(1). Second, acceptance prevents the buyer from returning the goods to the seller—rejecting the goods—simply because the goods do not conform in all respects to the requirements of the contract. Accepted goods can only be returned to the seller if, among other things, any defect or other problem with the goods substantially impairs their value to the buyer. 2-607(2) and 2-608(1).

Acceptance usually occurs when the buyer tells—signifies to—the seller that the goods conform to the requirements of the contract or that she will take or retain the goods even though they do not conform to the requirements of the contract. 2-606(1)(a). But acceptance can also occur if the buyer fails to inform the seller that she is not going to take the goods because they are not what the contract required the seller to deliver. As we will see in the next section, Article 2 does not require the buyer to take whatever the seller delivers. 2-601. The buyer can refuse to take the goods—"reject" the goods—if they are not what the seller promised to deliver. But the buyer can't wait forever to exercise its right to refuse the goods. Article 2 gives the buyer a "reasonable" time after the goods are delivered to make up its mind. If the buyer does not act within that reasonable period of time, the buyer loses its right to reject the goods—the buyer is deemed to have accepted the goods by failing to act. 2-606(1)(b). How long does the buyer have to decide whether to refuse the goods? It depends—what is reasonable will turn on the buyer's ability to inspect the goods after delivery. She must have a "reasonable" opportunity to inspect the goods—enough time to examine the goods and discover any defects in them. We will examine the relationship between inspection and timely rejection in the next section.

The buyer also accepts the goods if it "does any act inconsistent with the seller's ownership" of the goods—even though the buyer never tells the seller it will take the goods, or even if the buyer intended to reject the goods. 2-606(1)(c). Using, installing, or altering the goods after delivery are generally acts that would be inconsistent with the seller's ownership of the goods, and could also be inconsistent with a claim by the buyer that it had rejected the goods. As the courts have discovered, though, it is difficult to draw a definitive line that marks the point beyond which a buyer's treatment of the goods becomes inconsistent with the seller's ownership of the goods or a buyer's claim that it rejected the goods. Is the buyer who lives in the defective mobile home she has rejected acting inconsistently with the seller's ownership (or her claim of rejection) when she cannot afford alternative housing without a return of the down payment she made on the mobile home? Courts have struggled with these questions, and their decisions have been inconsistent at best.

The *Henley Supply* case addresses acceptance by affirmative act of the buyer under 2-606(1)(a)—what conduct operates to "signify" to the seller that the buyer is going to take the goods, whether conforming or not.

---

1   Allocation of the risk of loss is *not* one of the legal consequences of acceptance.

HENLEY SUPPLY CO. v. UNIVERSAL CONSTRUCTORS, INC.

COURT OF APPEALS OF TENNESSEE, MIDDLE SECTION 1989
1989 TENN. APP. LEXIS 260

WILLIAM C. KOCH, JR., judge

This appeal involves a dispute between a contractor and a material supplier concerning metal bi-fold doors that were rejected by the owner after they had been installed in a large apartment project. The supplier sued the contractor and others in the Chancery Court for Davidson County after the contractor refused to pay for the doors. The trial court dismissed the supplier's complaint pursuant to Tenn. R. Civ. P. 41.02(2). The supplier has appealed, insisting that the trial court erred by finding that it was not entitled to recover because it had failed to furnish shop drawings and because the project architect had not approved the doors. We agree and, therefore, vacate the order dismissing the supplier's complaint.

I.

In October, 1984, Rivergate Associates, Ltd. ("owner") entered into a contract with Universal Constructors, Inc. ("contractor") for the construction of Rivergate Meadows, a 200-unit apartment complex in Goodlettsville. The contract specifications called for metal bi-fold closet doors manufactured by either Slimfold Manufacturing Company or National Industries and prefinished in the "Manufacturer's White Painted finish."[2]

In November, 1984, Henley Supply, Inc. ("supplier") submitted its proposal to sell the contractor the metal bi-fold doors manufactured by National Industries. The contractor accepted the proposal and, in January, 1985, issued a purchase order for 1,280 doors. The purchase order required the supplier to "submit five copies of shop drawings for approval on each door to be used."

The supplier ordered 640 doors and requested National to ship them to the job site. The doors were delivered on February 4, 1985, and the contractor stored them at the project until they were installed. They were packaged in clear plastic with cardboard and styrofoam boots on each end, leaving five to six feet of each door plainly visible.

The supplier sent its invoice to the contractor on February 14, 1985. A representative of Clark and Associates Architects, Inc. ("architect") saw the doors and on March 1, 1985, certified on the contractor's request for payment that "all prior work labor, and materials, to be paid under this Request for Payment are satisfactory and in accordance with the Contract Drawings." On March 11, 1985, the contractor paid the supplier for the National doors.

The contractor began to install the National doors in May, 1985. During a routine inspection sometime in July, 1985, a representative of the owner commented to the contractor and the architect that the doors seemed to have a greenish tint. No one communicated the owner's observation to the supplier, and the contractor continued to install the doors without objection from the architect or the owner.

When the contractor requested the remaining doors, the supplier informed the contractor that there would be an eight to ten week delay in delivery. Since it was already behind schedule, the contractor asked the supplier to find out whether Slimfold could deliver its doors sooner. After receiving the supplier's assurance that Slimfold could deliver its doors more quickly and that Slimfold's navajo white color matched the color of the National doors, the contractor directed the supplier to obtain the remaining doors from Slimfold.

---

2 National Industries manufactured only one prefinished white metal bi-fold door. Slimfold manufactured prefinished white doors in two colors—"windsor white" and "navajo white."

The supplier ordered the Slimfold doors in early September, 1985. They were delivered to the job site several weeks later, packed in clear plastic. The contractor began installing the doors in late September, 1985 and completed its work within a very short period of time.

Representatives of the owner, the contractor, and the architect inspected the completed apartments in October, 1985 after the Slimfold doors had already been installed. The owner decided that the color of the National doors was unacceptable after seeing the doors "in the context of the apartment" and in contrast to Slimfold's navajo white doors.

At a project meeting held on November 20, 1985, the owner, architect, and contractor decided that the color of both types of doors was unacceptable and that "improper procedures had been utilized with respect to the doors." The owner decided that the National doors and the Slimfold navajo white doors should be replaced with Slimfold windsor white doors. Accordingly, the contractor was directed to remove all the doors that had already been installed and to replace them with new doors.

On the day following the project meeting, the contractor sent a mailgram to the supplier pointing out for the first time that the supplier had not submitted shop drawings for the doors. It told the supplier that the color of the doors was unacceptable and that the owner was insisting that the doors be replaced with Slimfold windsor white doors. The contractor also requested "clarification as to the order of these doors" and stated that it would make no payments to the supplier "until this matter is resolved."

The supplier responded to the contractor's mailgram through its lawyer. It declined to accept responsibility for the "color problem," stating that the shop drawings would not have depicted the color of the doors. It also declined to ship additional doors until it received payment for the doors it had already delivered. However, in order to avoid a "judicial confrontation," it offered to share the cost of repainting the doors.

The supplier's offer to assist in repainting the doors was unacceptable to the architect … [A]ccordingly, the architect instructed the contractor to "provide the doors of the proper color as soon as possible for the completed units" and to "replace those in units which have already been installed."

In December, 1985, the contractor ordered replacement Slimfold windsor white doors from another supplier. It took down all the original National and Slimfold navajo white doors and, when the supplier refused to take the doors back, sold them as salvage for less than one thousand dollars.[3]

[*7] The contractor refused to pay for the Slimfold navajo white doors. The supplier placed a materialmen's lien on the project in January, 1986 and filed this action three months later. The owner filed a third-party claim against the contractor's bonding company. The contractor filed a third-party claim against the architect. The trial court heard the proof without a jury and, on March 18, 1988, entered an order dismissing the supplier's complaint pursuant to Tenn. R. Civ. P. 41.02(2).

* * *

IV.

The contractor asserts that it was not required to pay for the Slimfold doors furnished by the supplier because the architect rejected them. The supplier, on the other hand, insists that the contractor accepted the doors and that the architect's eventual rejection of the doors does not affect the contractor's obligation to pay for them. We agree with the supplier. Under the facts of this case, the contractor, not the supplier, must bear the risk of installing the doors without first obtaining the architect's approval. The contractor accepted the doors by installing them and thus should be required to pay for them.

---

3   The retail value of the doors exceeded $33,000. The supplier could have returned the unused doors for credit if it had been informed of the owner's dissatisfaction with the doors before they were installed.

A.

The contract between the contractor and the supplier is a transaction in goods and is, therefore, governed by the sales article of the Uniform Commercial Code [Tenn. Code Ann. §§ 47-2-101 through 47-2-725 (1979)]. Under the U.C.C., a buyer has a positive duty to accept goods that conform to the contract. However, if the goods or the tender of delivery[4] fail to conform to the contract, Tenn. Code Ann. § 47-2-601 (1979) permits the buyer (a) to reject the goods, (b) to accept the goods, or (3) [sic] to accept any commercial unit and reject the rest.

Tenn. Code Ann. § 47-2-602(1) (1979) requires the buyer to reject nonconforming goods "within a reasonable time after their delivery or tender" and to "seasonably" notify the seller of its decision. These requirements are designed to minimize the parties' aggregate economic loss. They also give the seller the opportunity to take protective action like withdrawing the goods and tendering conforming goods, proposing a cure, or beginning negotiations to settle the dispute.

The U.C.C. uses "acceptance" as a term of art. It has no relationship to the passing of title and only tangential relationship to the buyer's possession of the goods. 1 J. White & R. Summers, Uniform Commercial Code § 8-2, at 391 (3d ed. 1988). It also has no relationship to whether the goods conform to the contract.

Tenn. Code Ann. § 47-2-606(1) provides that acceptance of the goods occurs when the buyer:

(a) after a reasonable opportunity to inspect the goods signifies to the seller that the goods are conforming or that he will take or retain them in spite of their non-conformity; or

(b) fails to make an effective rejection (subsection (1) of § 47-2-602), but such acceptance does not occur until buyer has had a reasonable opportunity to inspect them; or

(c) does any act inconsistent with the seller's ownership; but if such act is wrongful as against the seller it is an acceptance only if ratified by him.

Once a buyer accepts goods, Tenn. Code Ann. § 47-2-607(1) (1979) requires it to pay for them at the contract rate, and Tenn. Code Ann. § 47-2-607(2) prevents it from subsequently rejecting them.[5]

As a general rule, a buyer who, after a reasonable opportunity to inspect the goods, uses them to construct a building is deemed to have accepted the goods. *Clow Corp. v. Metro Pipeline Co.*, 442 F. Supp. 583, 587 (N.D. Ga. 1977); In re Barney Schogel, Inc., 12 Bankr. 697, 712 (S.D.N.Y. 1981); *Engel Mortgage Co. v. Triple K Lumber Co.*, 56 Ala. App. 337, 321 So. 2d 679, 683 (1975); *Art Metal Prods. Co. of Chicago v. Royal Equip. Co.*, 670 S.W.2d 152, 157 (Mo. Ct. App. 1984); *Meland v. International Sys., Inc.*, 712 P.2d 1295, 1297 (Mont. 1985); *V. Zappala & Co. v. Pyramid Co. of Glens Falls*, 81 A.D.2d 983, 439 N.Y.S.2d 765, 767 (1981).[6]

B.

The contractor does not quarrel with these general principles. However, it insists that the parties modified the normal application of Tenn. Code Ann. § 47-2-606 by agreeing that the doors would not be deemed accepted until the architect approved them. While the parties can agree on reasonable variations

---

4   Tenn. Code Ann. § 47-2-503(1) (1979) described a "tender of delivery" as putting and holding conforming goods at the buyer's disposition and giving reasonable notice to enable the buyer to take delivery.

5   Acceptance of the goods does not prevent a later revocation of acceptance pursuant to Tenn. Code Ann. § 47-2-608 (1979).

6   Acceptance does not occur when the buyer's inspection can only take place after the goods have been used or installed. *Barrett Paving Materials, Inc. v. U.S.F. & G.*, 118 A.D.2d 1039, 500 N.Y.S.2d 413, 414 (1986); *United Air Lines, Inc. v. Conductron Corp.*, 69 Ill. App. 3d 847, 387 N.E.2d 1272, 1282 (1979). This situation is not present here because the doors could have been easily inspected before they were installed.

of the U.C.C.'s standards, we have determined that their agreement did not alter the contractor's duty under Tenn. Code Ann. § 47-2-602(1) to reject the doors within a reasonable time after delivery.

The U.C.C. preserves the parties' freedom of contract. Accordingly, Tenn. Code Ann. § 47-1-102(3) (1979) permits the parties to vary the standards by which their performance will be measured. Similarly, Tenn. Code Ann. § 41-1-204(1) (1979) permits the parties to agree on a reasonable time within which an action must be taken.

Other courts have held that statutes similar to Tenn. Code Ann. § 47-1-102(3) enable the parties to determine when an effective rejection can occur. *Intervale Steel Corp. v. Borg & Beck Div., Borg-Warner Corp.*, 578 F. Supp. at 1088; *United Air Lines, Inc. v. Conductron Corp.*, 69 Ill. App. 3d 847, 387 N.E.2d 1272, 1281-82 (1979).

While buyers and sellers are normally free to make the buyer's obligation to pay depend upon the acceptance of the goods by a third party the time within which the goods must be accepted or rejected must remain reasonable in light of the parties' course of dealing, the usage of the trade, and the circumstances of the particular case. Tenn. Code Ann. §§ 47-1-204(2) (1979) & 47-1-205 (1979)[.])

The terms of the agreement concerning the doors are contained in a series of documents prepared by the parties between November, 1984 and September, 1985. Thus, in accordance with Tenn. Code Ann. § 47-2-207(3) (1979), our task is to review the documents and to give effect to "those terms on which the writings of the parties agree."

* * *

While the parties agreed that the doors could be inspected and approved by the architect, nothing in the credit agreement, purchase order, invoice, or statement provides that they agreed to delay acceptance of the doors until the architect approved the doors or that they agreed to alter the contractor's and architect's obligation to inspect the doors within a reasonable period of time after delivery. Accordingly, we will determine the legal effect of the contractor's conduct using the standards in Tenn. Code Ann. §§ 47-2-602 & 47-2-606.

C.

The U.C.C. imposes a duty on the buyer to discover and to take timely action concerning non-conforming goods within a reasonable time. *EPN-Delaval, S.A. v. Inter-Equip., Inc.*, 542 F. Supp. 238, 247 (S.D. Tex. 1982). Tenn. Code Ann. § 47-2-606(1)(b) provides that a buyer will be deemed to have accepted the goods if it fails to inspect them and to notify the seller of discrepancies within a reasonable time.

The question of whether the buyer's rejection occurred within a reasonable time can best be answered by considering four factors: (1) the difficulty of discovering the defect, (2) the terms of the agreement, (3) the relative perishability of the goods, and (4) the course of the buyer's performance after the sale and before the formal rejection. 1 J. White & R. Summers, Uniform Commercial Code § 8-3, at 408 (3d ed. 1988).

The timeliness of a rejection is not merely based upon the amount of time between the delivery and the rejection. According to Tenn. Code Ann. § 47-1-204(2), timeliness depends upon the "nature, purpose and circumstances" of the action. Just as a long delay may, by itself, be sufficient to render a rejection ineffective, a rejection occurring only a short period of time after delivery may be ineffective if the buyer's intervening acts render the rejection too late.

Both the contractor and the architect had ample time to inspect the doors before they were installed. Any defect in color, if there was a defect, could have been easily discovered because the doors were plainly visible through their plastic wrapping. However, the contractor installed the doors without first obtaining the architect's approval and did not reject them until after they had been installed. The attempted rejection came too late. We find that the contractor accepted the doors because it failed to make an effective rejection. Tenn. Code Ann. § 47-2-606(1)(b).

The Contractor's installation of the doors in Henley Supply would also seem to be an act inconsistent with the seller's ownership of the doors and constituting an acceptance by the buyer under 2-606(1)(c) but the seller did not make that argument. In *Trinity Industries v. McKinnon Bridge Co.*, 77 S.W.3d 159, another Tennessee court noted that "[o]ur courts have attempted to balance a reasonable time to inspect against use by the buyer holding that the statute gives the buyer a right to possession and some possible use of the goods without having accepted them." Installing hundreds of doors as the contractor did in Henley Supply would seem to go far beyond what the courts had surely contemplated as "some possible use."

Just as paying for the goods is not, by itself, an act that signifies that the buyer has decided to accept the goods, mere possession of the goods after the seller's delivery to the buyer is not an act of acceptance.

> This language [2-606(1)], in defining what constitutes an acceptance, clearly contemplates an act of the buyer beyond taking delivery or possession of the goods. Possession during the time necessary for the "reasonable opportunity" to inspect is contemplated prior to acceptance. Similarly, § 2-602 of the code allows a rejection of goods for nonconformance "within a reasonable time *after their delivery*". Thus, while transfer of possession or title may be acts bearing on the question of acceptance, they are not in themselves determinative thereof. White & Summers, Handbook of the Law Under the Uniform Commercial Code (2d ed), § 8-2, p 296.
>
> *Capital Dodge Sales v. Northern Concrete Pipe*, 346 N.W.2d 535
> (Mich. App. 1983)(emphasis in original).

Some cases suggest that possession by the buyer is not necessarily a condition for acceptance. For example, when the buyer of propane gas immediately resold the gas it had purchased before the seller actually delivered the gas, the resale was an act "so inconsistent with the seller's ownership as to constitute acceptance" under 2-606. *Commonwealth Propane v. Petrosol Int'l*, 818 F.2d 522 (6th Cir. 1987). *Contra, Badger Produce v. Prelude Foods International*, 130 Wis. 2d 230. But 2-606 seems to assume the buyer will have possession before it accepts—acceptance cannot occur until after the buyer has had a reasonable opportunity to inspect the goods, and inspection implies possession. The right to inspect the goods before becoming obligated to pay for them is one the courts have emphasized. In *First Nat'l Bank of Litchfield v. Miller*, the buyers signed a purchase agreement for a boat. The agreement stated that the buyers had inspected the boat and were satisfied with the boat. At the time they signed the agreement, the boat was in dry dock and could not be test driven. Later, but before the buyers took possession of the boat, a problem with the motor was discovered, and the buyers ultimately rejected the boat and cancelled the sale. The seller argued, based on the language in the purchase agreement, that the buyers had accepted the boat and could not reject it. The court disagreed:

> Professors White and Summers provide an illustration that is very similar to the present case where acceptance could not occur until there was a reasonable opportunity to inspect the goods: "Suppose a purchaser signs a contract which contains a clause to the effect that she has inspected the automobile or other merchandise and found it to be conforming. A few cases to the contrary notwithstanding, the prevailing view is that one who buys complex goods such as an automobile and signs a contract for purchase after only a short demonstration ride should not be held to have had a 'reasonable opportunity to inspect' and therefore not be held to have accepted the goods." J. White & R. Summers, Uniform Commercial Code (5th Ed. 2000) § 8-2, p. 308. Here, the demonstration ride occurred *after* the Millers signed the contract that stated that they had inspected the boat and were satisfied with it. "[A] buyer must be afforded a reasonable opportunity to inspect goods to determine whether they

should be rejected ... ." (Citation omitted.) *Bead Chain Mfg. Co. v. Saxton Products, Inc.,* 183 Conn. 266, 271, 439 A.2d 314 (1981); General Statutes § 42a-2-513 (1). Under the facts of this case, we conclude that the evidence admits of one conclusion and that is that the Millers were not given a reasonable opportunity to inspect the boat and, therefore, acceptance could not have occurred at the time of the signing of the retail installment contract under § 42a-2-606 (1) (a).

For the same reasoning, we further conclude that acceptance could not have occurred under § 42a-2-606 (1) (b) because acceptance under that provision cannot occur "until the buyer has had a reasonable opportunity to inspect [the goods] ... ." General Statutes § 42a-2-606 (1) (b).

904 A.2d 1282 (Conn. App. 2006).

What if the "inspection" necessary to determine whether the goods conform to the requirements of the contract—whether they function as promised—requires the buyer to use the goods? Is the buyer's use of the goods an "act inconsistent with the seller's ownership" causing acceptance under 2-606(1) (c), which is not expressly conditioned on any buyer's right to inspect? Not necessarily—a buyer cannot tell whether a printing press conforms to the contract—is capable of printing things—without at least trying to print something on the press. If, however, the initial test reveals the press is defective, the buyer's continued use might become more than just inspection. If the press is a novel design or new model, continued use might fall within the right to inspect, where the buyer's use is a good-faith attempt to work out the bugs in the new design/model—especially if it was encouraged by the seller in an effort to save the deal. *Can-Key Industries v. Industrial Leasing,* 593 P.2d 1125 (Ore. 1979). On the other hand, commingling the goods with other goods for the purpose of testing them is an act inconsistent with the seller's ownership. *Johnson v. Holdrege Cooperative,* 293 N.W.2d 863 (Neb. 1980).

On a more general level, a buyer acts inconsistently with the seller's ownership when the buyer does something with or to the goods that it would not be entitled to do unless it owned the goods. *Oda Nursery v. Garcia Tree & Lawn,* 708 P.2d 1039 (N.M. 1985). Deceptively simple in its application, this standard covers a broad spectrum of conduct, from reselling the goods to removing the goods to replanting the goods to insuring the goods (and then making a claim under that insurance) to repairing the goods and then using them. The buyer is more likely to move into "inconsistent with the seller's ownership" territory when she does any of these things (or others) with knowledge that the goods do not conform to the contract.

PROBLEM 7 - 1

Determine in each of the following cases whether Rae has accepted the goods—signified her acceptance—under 2-606:

Case 1: Rae ordered a truckload of Santa Rosa plums from a California grower she has done business with for years. After the plums were unloaded from the truck, she texted the grower: "Plums are here today. Thanks." 2-606(1)(a).

Case 2: While the pallet of raspberries Rae had ordered was being unloaded from the delivery truck, Rae told the grower/driver, "Stuff looks good—can't wait to put it out for the customers." 2-606(1)(c).

Case 3: Because space was tight in the produce cooler when the bananas she had ordered were delivered, Rae put twenty cases in the dairy cooler. She forgot about them until the dairy manager called them to her attention the following week, by which time they were slightly overripe and could not be sold at the regular price. 2-606(1)(b).

Case 4: Last month, Rae began stockpiling canned soup for a sale she was planning at the store this month. Over the course of several weeks, she took delivery of twenty-five pallets, each pallet holding fifty cases of soup. When the stockers began building the soup display yesterday, they noticed that the "use by" date on all of the soup had passed before it had been delivered to the store.

Case 5: Rae ordered two sides of venison for the store. When the meat was delivered, the butcher shop sliced the sides into traditional meat cuts (chuck, loin, top round, tips, etc.), packed and priced it, and put it on display for purchase. The next day, a customer returned with a pack of the "venison" complaining that it was bison. Upon closer examination, the chief butcher determined that it was, in fact, bison not venison.

Case 6: Rae ordered a Tennant T2 Walk Behind Floor Scrubber for the store. Rae never thought the T2 lived up to its billing after the maintenance crew began using it to clean the floor, and two months later she now knows why: the model delivered was the T200, a lightweight version of the T2.

Acceptance and rejection are interdependent concepts under Article 2, at least in the sense that if the buyer accepts the goods, there can be no rejection, or if the buyer (properly, as we will see) rejects the goods, there can be no acceptance. When a court decides that the buyer accepted the goods, it is also deciding (by implication, at least) that the buyer failed to properly reject the goods. When a court decides that the buyer has rejected the goods, it is also deciding (again, by implication, at least) that the buyer has not accepted the goods. Our discussion of rejection, then, will inevitably be a continuation of the conversation we have begun in this section about acceptance.

B. Rejection: The Buyer Refuses to Take the Goods

When the seller delivers goods that do not conform to the requirements of contract, the buyer has two options: it can take the goods—"accept" the goods—and obligate itself to pay for them even though they do not conform to the requirements of the contract, or it can refuse to take the goods—"reject" the goods"—in which case it does not become obligated to pay for the goods. 2-601. As the *Ramirez* case explains, the buyer's power to reject a seller's nonconforming performance follows from the drafters' decision to incorporate into Article 2 what at common law was known as the "perfect-tender rule."

> if the goods or the tender of delivery fail in any respect to conform to the contract, the buyer may (a) reject the whole …

2-601. The seller's performance must *conform* to the commitments it made in the contract *in all respects*—the buyer's obligation to take the goods and to pay for them is conditioned on "perfect" performance of each and every one of the seller's obligations under the contract. In theory, this means that any nonconformity, no matter how trivial in light of the rest of the seller's obligations under the contract, will entitle the buyer to reject the seller's performance and avoid becoming obligated to pay for the goods. An unscrupulous buyer might invoke its right to reject nonconforming goods for a trivial defect in order to escape from a deal that has turned bad since its making. But as *Ramirez* also notes, Article 2 ameliorates the potential harshness of the perfect-tender rule by providing sellers with the right to remedy—to "cure"—a nonconforming performance and eliminate the grounds for the buyer's rejection.

RAMIREZ V. AUTOSPORT

SUPREME COURT OF NEW JERSEY, 1982
440 A.2D 1345

POLLOCK, Justice.

This case raises several issues under the Uniform Commercial Code ("the Code" and "UCC") concerning whether a buyer may reject a tender of goods with minor defects and whether a seller may cure the defects. We consider also the remedies available to the buyer, including cancellation of the contract. The main issue is whether plaintiffs, Mr. and Mrs. Ramirez, could reject the tender by defendant, Autosport, of a camper van with minor defects and cancel the contract for the purchase of the van.

The trial court ruled that Mr. and Mrs. Ramirez rightfully rejected the van and awarded them the fair market value of their trade-in van. The Appellate Division affirmed in a brief *per curiam* decision which, like the trial court opinion, was unreported. We affirm the judgment of the Appellate Division.

I

Following a mobile home show at the Meadowlands Sports Complex, Mr. and Mrs. Ramirez visited Autosport's showroom in Somerville. On July 20, 1978 the Ramirezes and Donald Graff, a salesman for Autosport, agreed on the sale of a new camper and the trade-in of the van owned by Mr. and Mrs. Ramirez. Autosport and the Ramirezes signed a simple contract reflecting a $14,100 purchase price for the new van with a $4,700 trade-in allowance for the Ramirez van, which Mr. and Mrs. Ramirez left with Autosport. After further allowance for taxes, title, and documentary fees, the net price was $9,902. Because Autosport needed two weeks to prepare the new van, the contract provided for delivery on or about August 3, 1978.

On that date, Mr. and Mrs. Ramirez returned with their checks to Autosport to pick up the new van. Graff was not there so Mr. White, another salesman, met them. Inspection disclosed several defects in the van. The paint was scratched, both the electric and sewer hookups were missing, and the hubcaps were not installed. White advised the Ramirezes not to accept the camper because it was not ready.

Mr. and Mrs. Ramirez wanted the van for a summer vacation and called Graff several times. Each time Graff told them it was not ready for delivery. Finally, Graff called to notify them that the camper was ready. On August 14 Mr. and Mrs. Ramirez went to Autosport to accept delivery, but workers were still touching up the outside paint. Also, the camper windows were open, and the dining area cushions were soaking wet. Mr. and Mrs. Ramirez could not use the camper in that condition, but Mr. Leis, Autosport's manager, suggested that they take the van and that Autosport would replace the cushions later. Mrs. Ramirez counteroffered to accept the van if they could withhold $2,000, but Leis agreed to no more than $250, which she refused. Leis then agreed to replace the cushions and to call them when the van was ready.

On August 15, 1978 Autosport transferred title to the van to Mr. and Mrs. Ramirez, a fact unknown to them until the summer of 1979. Between August 15 and September 1, 1978 Mrs. Ramirez called Graff several times urging him to complete the preparation of the van, but Graff constantly advised her that the van was not ready. He finally informed her that they could pick it up on September 1.

When Mr. and Mrs. Ramirez went to the showroom on September 1, Graff asked them to wait. And wait they did—for one and a half hours. No one from Autosport came forward to talk with them, and the Ramirezes left in disgust.

On October 5, 1978 Mr. and Mrs. Ramirez went to Autosport with an attorney friend. Although the parties disagreed on what occurred, the general topic was whether they should proceed with the deal or Autosport should return to the Ramirezes their trade-in van. Mrs. Ramirez claimed they rejected the new van and requested the return of their trade-in. Mr. Lustig, the owner of Autosport, thought, however, that the deal could be salvaged if the parties could agree on the dollar amount of a credit for the Ramirezes. Mr. and Mrs. Ramirez never took possession of the new van and repeated their request for the return of their trade-in. Later in October, however, Autosport sold the trade-in to an innocent third party for $4,995. Autosport claimed that the Ramirez' van had a book value of $3,200 and claimed further that it spent $1,159.62 to repair their van. By subtracting the total of those two figures, $4,159.62, from the $4,995.00 sale price, Autosport claimed a $600–700 profit on the sale.

On November 20, 1978 the Ramirezes sued Autosport seeking, among other things, rescission of the contract. Autosport counterclaimed for breach of contract.

II

Our initial inquiry is whether a consumer may reject defective goods that do not conform to the contract of sale. The basic issue is whether under the UCC, adopted in New Jersey as *N.J.S.A.* 12A:1-101 *et seq.*, a seller has the duty to deliver goods that conform precisely to the contract. We conclude that the seller is under such a duty to make a "perfect tender" and that a buyer has the right to reject goods that do not conform to the contract. That conclusion, however, does not resolve the entire dispute between buyer and seller. A more complete answer requires a brief statement of the history of the mutual obligations of buyers and sellers of commercial goods.

In the nineteenth century, sellers were required to deliver goods that complied exactly with the sales agreement. *See Filley v. Pope*, 115 *U.S.* 213, 220, 6 *S.Ct.* 19, 21, 29 *L.Ed.* 372, 373 (1885) (buyer not obliged to accept otherwise conforming scrap iron shipped to New Orleans from Leith, rather than Glasgow, Scotland, as required by contract); *Columbian Iron Works & Dry-Dock Co. v. Douglas*, 84 Md. 44, 47, 34 *A.* 1118, 1120-1121 (1896) (buyer who agreed to purchase steel scrap from United States cruisers not obliged to take any other kind of scrap). That rule, known as the "perfect tender" rule, remained part of the law of sales well into the twentieth century. By the 1920's the doctrine was so entrenched in the law that Judge Learned Hand declared "[t]here is no room in commercial contracts for the doctrine of substantial performance." *Mitsubishi Goshi Kaisha v. J. Aron & Co., Inc.*, 16 *F.*2d 185, 186 (2 Cir. 1926).

The harshness of the rule led courts to seek to ameliorate its effect and to bring the law of sales in closer harmony with the law of contracts, which allows rescission only for material breaches. Nevertheless, a variation of the perfect tender rule appeared in the Uniform Sales Act. *N.J.S.A.* 46:30-75 (purchasers permitted to reject goods or rescind contracts for any breach of warranty); *N.J.S.A.* 46:30-18 to -21 (warranties extended to include all the seller's obligations to the goods). The chief objection to the continuation of the perfect tender rule was that buyers in a declining market would reject goods for minor nonconformities and force the loss on surprised sellers.

To the extent that a buyer can reject goods for any nonconformity, the UCC retains the perfect tender rule. Section 2-106 states that goods conform to a contract "when they are in accordance with the obligations under the contract". *N.J.S.A.* 12A:2-106. Section 2-601 authorizes a buyer to reject goods if they "or the tender of delivery fail in any respect to conform to the contract". *N.J.S.A.* 12A:2-601. The Code, however, mitigates the harshness of the perfect tender rule and balances the interests of buyer and seller. *See Restatement (Second), Contracts*, § 241 comment (b) (1981). The Code achieves that result through its provisions for revocation of acceptance and cure. *N.J.S.A.* 12A:2-608, 2-508.

Initially, the rights of the parties vary depending on whether the rejection occurs before or after acceptance of the goods. Before acceptance, the buyer may reject goods for any nonconformity. *N.J.S.A.* 12A:2-601. Because of the seller's right to cure, however, the buyer's rejection does not necessarily discharge the contract. *N.J.S.A.* 12A:2-508. Within the time set for performance in the contract, the seller's right to cure is unconditional. *Id.*, subsec. (1); *see id.*, Official Comment 1. Some authorities recommend granting a breaching party a right to cure in all contracts, not merely those for the sale of goods. *Restatement (Second), Contracts*, ch. 10, especially §§ 237 and 241. Underlying the right to cure in both kinds of contracts is the recognition that parties should be encouraged to communicate with each other and to resolve their own problems. Id., Introduction p. 193.

The rights of the parties also vary if rejection occurs after the time set for performance. After expiration of that time, the seller has a further reasonable time to cure if he believed reasonably that the goods would be acceptable with or without a money allowance. *N.J.S.A.* 12A:2-508(2). The determination of what constitutes a further reasonable time depends on the surrounding circumstances, which include the change of position by and the amount of inconvenience to the buyer. *N.J.S.A.* 12A:2-508, Official Comment 3. Those circumstances also include the length of time needed by the seller to correct the nonconformity and his ability to salvage the goods by resale to others. Thus, the Code balances the buyer's right to reject nonconforming goods with a "second chance" for the seller to conform the goods to the contract under certain limited circumstances. *N.J.S.A.* 12A:2-508, New Jersey Study Comment 1.

After acceptance, the Code strikes a different balance: the buyer may revoke acceptance only if the nonconformity substantially impairs the value of the goods to him. *N.J.S.A.* 12A:2-608. This provision protects the seller from revocation for trivial defects. *Herbstman, supra*, 68 *N.J.* at 9. It also prevents the buyer from taking undue advantage of the seller by allowing goods to depreciate and then returning them because of asserted minor defects. *See* White & Summers, *Uniform Commercial Code*, § 8-3 at 391 (2 ed. 1980). Because this case involves rejection of goods, we need not decide whether a seller has a right to cure substantial defects that justify revocation of acceptance.

Other courts agree that the buyer has a right of rejection for any nonconformity, but that the seller has a countervailing right to cure within a reasonable time.

One New Jersey case, *Gindy Mfg. Corp. v. Cardinale Trucking Corp.*, suggests that, because some defects can be cured, they do not justify rejection. Nonetheless, we conclude that the perfect tender rule is preserved to the extent of permitting a buyer to reject goods for any defects. Because of the seller's right to cure, rejection does not terminate the contract. Accordingly, we disapprove the suggestion in *Gindy* that curable defects do not justify rejection.

A further problem, however, is identifying the remedy available to a buyer who rejects goods with insubstantial defects that the seller fails to cure within a reasonable time. The Code provides expressly that when "the buyer rightfully rejects, then with respect to the goods involved, the buyer may cancel." *N.J.S.A.* 12A:2-711. "Cancellation" occurs when either party puts an end to the contract for breach by the other. *N.J.S.A.* 12A:2-106(4). Nonetheless, some confusion exists whether the equitable remedy of rescission survives under the Code.

The Code eschews the word "rescission" and substitutes the terms "cancellation", "revocation of acceptance", and "rightful rejection". *N.J.S.A.* 12A:2-106(4); 2-608; and 2-711 & Official Comment 1. Although neither "rejection" nor "revocation of acceptance" is defined in the Code, rejection includes both the buyer's refusal to accept or keep delivered goods and his notification to the seller that he will not keep them. Revocation of acceptance is like rejection, but occurs after the buyer has accepted the goods. Nonetheless, revocation of acceptance is intended to provide the same relief as rescission of a contract of sale of goods. *N.J.S.A.* 12A:2-608 Official Comment 1; N.J. Study Comment 2. In brief, revocation is tantamount to rescission. Similarly, subject to the seller's right to cure, a buyer who rightfully rejects goods, like one who revokes his acceptance, may cancel the contract. *N.J.S.A.* 12A:2-711 & Official Comment 1. We need not resolve the extent to which rescission for reasons other than rejection or revocation of acceptance, *e.g.* fraud and mistake, survives as a remedy outside the Code. Accordingly, we approve *Edelstein* and *Sudol*, which recognize that explicit Code remedies replace rescission, and disapprove *Ventura* and *Pavesi* to the extent they suggest the UCC expressly recognizes rescission as a remedy.

Although the complaint requested rescission of the contract, plaintiffs actually sought not only the end of their contractual obligations, but also restoration to their pre-contractual position. That request incorporated the equitable doctrine of restitution, the purpose of which is to restore plaintiff to as good a position as he occupied before the contract. In UCC parlance, plaintiffs' request was for the cancellation of the contract and recovery of the price paid. *N.J.S.A.* 12A:2-106(4), 2-711.

General contract law permits rescission only for material breaches, and the Code restates "materiality" in terms of "substantial impairment". The Code permits a buyer who rightfully rejects goods to cancel a contract of sale. *N.J.S.A.* 12A:2-711. Because a buyer may reject goods with insubstantial defects, he also may cancel the contract if those defects remain uncured. Otherwise, a seller's failure to cure minor defects would compel a buyer to accept imperfect goods and collect for any loss caused by the nonconformity. *N.J.S.A.* 12A:2-714.

Although the Code permits cancellation by rejection for minor defects, it permits revocation of acceptance only for substantial impairments. That distinction is consistent with other Code provisions that depend on whether the buyer has accepted the goods. Acceptance creates liability in the buyer for the price, *N.J.S.A.* 12A:2-709(1), and precludes rejection. *N.J.S.A.* 12A:2-607(2); *N.J.S.A.* 12A:2-606, New Jersey Study Comment 1. Also, once a buyer accepts goods, he has the burden to prove any defect. *N.J.S.A.* 12A:2-607(4). By contrast, where goods are rejected for not conforming to the contract, the burden is on the seller to prove that the nonconformity was corrected.

Underlying the Code provisions is the recognition of the revolutionary change in business practices in this century. The purchase of goods is no longer a simple transaction in which a buyer purchases individually-made goods from a seller in a face-to-face transaction. Our economy depends on a complex system for the manufacture, distribution, and sale of goods, a system in which manufacturers and consumers rarely meet. Faceless manufacturers mass-produce goods for unknown consumers who purchase those goods from merchants exercising little or no control over the quality of their production. In an age of assembly lines, we are accustomed to cars with scratches, television sets without knobs and other products with all kinds of defects. Buyers no longer expect a "perfect tender". If a merchant sells defective goods, the reasonable expectation of the parties is that the buyer will return those goods and that the seller will repair or replace them.

Recognizing this commercial reality, the Code permits a seller to cure imperfect tenders. Should the seller fail to cure the defects, whether substantial or not, the balance shifts again in favor of the buyer, who has the right to cancel or seek damages. *N.J.S.A.* 12A:2-711. In general, economic considerations would induce sellers to cure minor defects. Assuming the seller does not cure, however, the buyer should be permitted to exercise his remedies under *N.J.S.A.* 12A:2-711. The Code remedies for consumers are to be liberally construed, and the buyer should have the option of cancelling if the seller does not provide conforming goods. *See N.J.S.A.* 12A:1-106.

To summarize, the UCC preserves the perfect tender rule to the extent of permitting a buyer to reject goods for any nonconformity. Nonetheless, that rejection does not automatically terminate the contract. A seller may still effect a cure and preclude unfair rejection and cancellation by the buyer. *N.J.S.A.* 12A:2-508, Official Comment 2; *N.J.S.A.* 12A:2-711, Official Comment 1.

III

The trial court found that Mr. and Mrs. Ramirez had rejected the van within a reasonable time under *N.J.S.A.* 12A:2-602. The court found that on August 3, 1978 Autosport's salesman advised the Ramirezes not to accept the van and that on August 14, they rejected delivery and Autosport agreed to replace the cushions. Those findings are supported by substantial credible evidence, and we sustain them. *See Rova Farms Resort v. Investors Ins. Co.,* 65 N.J. 474, 483-484 (1974). Although the trial court did not find whether Autosport cured the defects within a reasonable time, we find that Autosport did not effect a cure. Clearly the van was not ready for delivery during August, 1978 when Mr. and Mrs. Ramirez rejected it, and Autosport had the burden of proving that it had corrected the defects. Although the Ramirezes gave Autosport ample time to correct the defects, Autosport did not demonstrate that the van conformed to the contract on September 1. In fact, on that date, when Mr. and Mrs. Ramirez returned at Autosport's invitation, all they received was discourtesy.

On the assumption that substantial impairment is necessary only when a purchaser seeks to revoke acceptance under *N.J.S.A.* 12A:2-608, the trial court correctly refrained from deciding whether the defects substantially impaired the van. The court properly concluded that plaintiffs were entitled to "rescind"—*i.e.*, to "cancel"—the contract.

PROBLEM 7 - 2

Determine in each of the following cases whether the seller's tender was nonconforming under 2-601:

Case 1: Rae ordered one hundred pounds of ocean-fresh scallops for the deli, to be delivered June 1. The scallops were for the Big Brothers/Big Sisters banquet the deli was catering on June 2. The scallops were delivered on June 2.

Case 2. Rae ordered two hundred pounds of ground bison for the butcher shop. The order called for the meat to be transported "at all times a refrigerated environment." The truck that delivered the bison did not have a refrigeration unit.

Case 3: Rae ordered a new employee time clock, to be shipped "FedEx, overnight early delivery." The next afternoon, UPS delivered the clock to the store.

Case 4: The store's produce manager ordered one thousand pounds US No.1 russet potatoes for the holiday season. The seller delivered one thousand pounds of US Extra No. 1 russet potatoes instead. Extra No. 1 potatoes are considered superior to No. 1 potatoes by the US Department of Agriculture.

Case. 5: Would your answer be different in Case 4 if the price of potatoes had declined by 50 percent between the time the order was placed and the potatoes were delivered?

Case 6: Rae ordered one hundred cases of "Indian River Ruby Red grapefruit #30, FOB buyer's store." The grapefruit delivered were Indian River Deep Red grapefruit #30. Deep Red grapefruit are slightly less pulpy than Ruby Red and a tad bit sweeter. The average consumer would not be able to notice the difference.

Case 7: The produce manager ordered five hundred large Crimson Sweet watermelons. The produce manager inspected the melons after they had been delivered to the store by the seller and found twenty-five melons that were cracked or soft. The order did not expressly address spoilage, but trade usage allows for 5 percent spoilage of produce.

Case 8: Would your answer in Case 7 be different if the seller had only delivered 495 melons to the store?

As the court noted in *Rameriz*, the rejecting buyer can "cancel"—put an end to—the contract, relieving itself of any future obligations under the contract, including the obligation to pay any part of the unpaid purchase price. But rejection also means that the seller breached the contract, giving the buyer a claim for any damages it sustained as a result of the seller's nonconforming performance. 2-711. The buyer also gets a security interest in the rejected goods in its possession for any payment it made under the contract prior to rejection.

The seller's right to cure limits the buyer's right to reject and can ameliorate the harsh consequences to the seller that can follow from the perfect-tender rule, especially where the buyer's rejection was merely strategic—an attempt to get out of what had become a bad deal. But the right to cure might also encourage strategic seller behavior—it can reduce the seller's incentive to live up to its end of the bargain. If a seller knows that it will get a second chance to satisfy the buyer, there's little risk in cutting a few corners, especially in light of the fact that it is the buyer who bears the burden of invoking the perfect-tender rule.[7]

The seller's right to cure a nonconforming performance is not without its own limits. The seller has an absolute right to cure only if the time for its performance under the contract has not passed. 2-508(1). If the seller delivers nonconforming goods before the time provided for delivery in the contract, the seller has an absolute right to redeliver conforming goods, but must do so before the time specified for delivery in the contract. The seller's right to cure after the time for its performance has passed is conditional—the seller must show there was a reason to believe that the buyer would accept the less-than-perfect performance required by the perfect-tender rule. The buyer's prior acceptance of nonconforming goods or a trade practice of accepting limited deviations in quantity or quality might prove a seller's reasonable belief that a nonconforming performance would be acceptable to the buyer. The seller might also be able to establish this reason to believe by delivering goods that are the functional equivalent of—or are better than—those required by the contract. The seller's conditional right to cure is not indefinite; it extends the time for the seller to provide a conforming performance for only a "reasonable time." And in the case of either the absolute right to cure or the conditional right to cure, the seller must give "seasonable notice" or "seasonably notify" the buyer of its intention to cure a nonconforming performance.

Ramirez also briefly introduced the concept of revocation of acceptance as another way that a buyer might be able to cancel the contract when a seller delivers nonconforming goods. We will develop the revocation alternative to rejection later in this chapter, where will see that revocation, unlike rejection, is not derived from the perfect-tender rule incorporated into Article 2.

As we noted earlier in this chapter, a buyer is deemed to have accepted goods if it waits too long to exercise its right to reject. The buyer that does not reject within a "reasonable time" and provide "seasonable" notice of rejection to the seller has waited too long. How do we determine whether a buyer rejected within a "reasonable time"? How does the buyer's right to inspect the goods affect what is a "reasonable time"? The next case addresses these questions.

La Villa Fair v. Lewis Carpet Mills, Inc.

Supreme Court of Kansas, 1976
219 Kan. 395

MILLER, Judge.

This is an action for rescission of a portion of a contract for the purchase of carpet and for the recovery of the purchase price, interest thereon, incidental damages and loss of profit. Plaintiff (the purchaser) is a wholesaler and retailer of carpet and other furnishings specializing in apartment projects and commercial buildings.

Defendant is a carpet manufacturer, incorporated in Georgia with its principal place of business in Cartersville, Georgia.

---

7   Goetz and Scott, "The Mitigation Principle: Toward a General Theory of Contractual Obligation," 69 *Va. L. Rev.* 967 (1983).

The genesis of the business dealings of these parties was the solicitation of the plaintiff by the defendant's agent and representative in Kansas, Cla-Mar, Inc. during the winter months of 1966, 1967. These solicitations took place at the plaintiff's office in Lawrence, Kansas, and through telephone conversations between Cla-Mar in Topeka, Kansas and the plaintiff in Lawrence. As a result of these dealings plaintiff placed an order for the purchase of approximately 12,000 square yards of carpet, which order was accepted by the defendant by letter dated May 29, 1967. The carpet ordered, described as $2.80 per yard F. O. B. mill, 25 oz. face weight—100% acrylic cut pile of first quality (no seconds) was to be delivered on defendant's truck to either Kansas City, Missouri, or Lawrence, Kansas, at six cents per square yard.

The carpet which gave rise to this action is twenty-one of the forty-five rolls shipped by the defendant to the plaintiff on April 26, 1968. These rolls averaged about 180 square yards each. Due to a construction strike in Kansas City in the spring of 1968, the plaintiff's purchaser, Stanley Christopher Investment Company of Lawrence, an apartment builder, was not ready to receive the carpet. Plaintiff therefore arranged with the defendant to have the defendant transport and deliver the carpet to Wagner Cartage Company, Kansas City, Missouri, for storage in their bonded warehouse until Christopher was in a position to make use of it.

By January 2, 1969, Christopher Investment Company, plaintiff's purchaser, had collapsed financially and had been taken over by its financier, James B. Nutter Company. Nutter was aware of Christopher's intention to purchase carpet from the plaintiff. It was also aware that the carpet was stored in the bonded warehouse. Both Christopher and Nutter paid part of the storage charges. Nutter gave the plaintiff assurances that it would honor the Christopher contract, and would pay for the carpet as soon as it was cut and laid at the apartment project site. On or about January 2, 1969, Nutter indicated to the plaintiff that it was ready to receive the carpet. Plaintiff therefore arranged for the carpet to be moved from Wagner Cartage to Lay-Rite Carpet Company, which company was employed by Nutter to cut the carpet and to install it in the apartment complex. Employees of Lay-Rite inspected several rolls of the carpet, but were unable to find 23 feet of carpet that matched so as to lay carpet in one display apartment. Lay-Rite informed Nutter, who also inspected the carpet. Nutter rejected the carpet and refused to pay to the plaintiff the purchase price of $10,791.10. Plaintiff then informed the defendant that it, too, rejected the carpet. After the exchange of some correspondence, this action was filed August 1, 1969. In its supplemental memorandum opinion filed September 10, 1973, the trial court found in favor of the plaintiff in the amount of $11,805.44 plus the costs of the action, less a $202 judgment in favor of the defendant against the plaintiff.

The district court made numerous findings of fact and conclusions of law upon which it based its ruling. It found that the carpet in question was part of a 12,000 yard order by plaintiff accepted by the defendant's letter of May 29, 1967. That letter fixed the price of the carpet at "$2.80 yard F. O. B. Mill", "25 oz. face weight—100% acrylic cut pile", "Carpet will be 1st quality (no seconds)." The court found that the 21 rolls complained of in this action were moved from Wagner to Lay-Rite Carpet for cutting for plaintiff's purchaser. The court determined that Lay-Rite examined three or four 100-foot rolls in an attempt to get a piece 23 feet long that would match in order to lay carpet in a "show" apartment. Lay-Rite, the trial court found, considered the carpet defective in that it was extensively patched, delaminated in places, and was not 25 oz. face weight. Lay-Rite's owner, the court stated, opined that some damage had resulted from storage, but that this was limited to only the outer four or five feet of some of the rolls.

The court concluded that the plaintiff showed that 21 rolls shipped by the defendant was the same carpet handled and inspected as set forth above. The court also concluded that the defendant had been advised that the carpet would be stored in a bonded warehouse due to a building trades strike to await plaintiff's purchaser's requirements and that therefore plaintiff's inspection at the time of cutting for installation was not unreasonable. The court ruled that the carpet was not in conformity with the specifications of plaintiff's order, of which the defendant was seasonably notified by the plaintiff as provided by K. S. A. 84-2-602.

Defendant's brief is divided into four parts, with each part having several divisions, but when boiled down the defendant's theory of the case is this: that even if all that the plaintiff says is true, plaintiff's action was unreasonable and amounted to commercial bad faith in that it failed to make a timely inspection of the carpet, thereby effectively depriving the defendant of any opportunity to invoke its statutory right to cure the nonconformity.

Having disposed of the nonconformity issue, it is now necessary to turn to what, by stipulation, was supposed to be the sole issue on appeal. That is: Notwithstanding the carpet's nonconformity, was plaintiff's rejection, or revocation of its acceptance of the same, timely?

Appellant relies heavily on *Cervitor Kitchens v. Chapman,* 7 Wn. App. 520, 500 P. 2d 783, in support of its position that plaintiff's delayed inspection was unreasonable as a matter of law. That case sets forth the rule to be applied to determine whether the question of rejection within a reasonable time is one of fact or of law:

"If the facts are disputed, the question of what is a reasonable time is for the trier of the fact. ...

"If the facts are undisputed concerning the duration of the time for inspection, the question of whether the goods were retained for an unreasonable time becomes one for the court to decide ... ." (pp. 522, 523.)

Defendant contends that a failure by plaintiff to inspect is only justified where such inspection is wholly impracticable, not just inconvenient or time-consuming and thus it argues that the plaintiff had a reasonable opportunity to inspect and that its failure to do so amounts to acceptance under K. S. A. 84-2-606.

Cervitor was a case in which a plumbing contractor, Chapman, was working on the construction of a college dormitory. Chapman purchased from Cervitor Kitchens, Inc., a merchandising business, four kitchen units to be installed in a dormitory. On May 4, 1967, Chapman received from Cervitor four kitchen units enclosed in shipping crates or cartons. Chapman did not inspect the units on delivery, although Chapman's manager was present when the units arrived and noticed some minor exterior shipping damage on two of the crates. The units remained in their shipping crates and were stored in a separate room at the dormitory then under construction. No inspection was made of the units until shortly before installation on or about August 5, 1967. A few days later Chapman notified the engineer that the units had been installed. Somewhat later the engineer informed Chapman that the units were of poor quality and did not comply with specifications. Chapman in turn notified Cervitor that the units did not comply with the specifications and would be rejected. Chapman shipped the units to Cervitor, who refused them. They were later sold for storage charges. The sole question in *Cervitor* was whether Chapman was deemed to have accepted the four kitchen units because of his failure to inspect and reject them for a period of approximately three months after delivery and because of his installation of the units without prior inspection and rejection. Cervitor contended that Chapman waited too long to inspect and reject the units, and his installation of the units without inspection further precluded him from rejecting them. The Washington Court of Appeals, with one dissent, agreed with both contentions. Not noted in defendant's brief, however, is the Washington Supreme Court's reversal of the intermediate appellate court as to Cervitor's first point, that is, that Chapman's inspection was not timely. The Washington Supreme Court in *Cervitor Kitchens, Inc. v. Chapman* [*Cervitor* II], 82 Wn. 2d 673, 513 P. 2d 25, stated:

"... We ... cannot agree with the Court of Appeals that, as a matter of law, the 3-month time delay in failing to inspect and accept or reject the goods constituted an acceptance." (p. 676.)

The dissent in the appeals court decision had noted that there was evidence that suppliers that deal in commercial fixtures such as these units recognize that their merchandise will frequently be stored on job sites and that when delivery is made, the purchasers may not be ready to install the units immediately. The supreme court's opinion also noted this testimony and concluded that the trial court's finding that the units were timely inspected was supported by substantial competent evidence in the record. The supreme court did, however, affirm the appeals court's ruling that Chapman's *installation* of the units without inspection after over 3 months' delay was inconsistent with the seller's ownership as a matter of law and amounted to acceptance where the deficiencies claimed were readily apparent upon inspection after the units were taken from the crates and before installation.

Applying *Cervitor* II to the facts of this case it would seem that it cannot be said that plaintiff's nine-month delay in inspecting and accepting or rejecting the carpet is itself an acceptance as a matter of law, but rather should be left to the trier of fact. As in *Cervitor* II there was evidence in the instant case that the defendant was aware that plaintiff's purchaser was not ready to use the goods it shipped (because of the construction strike) and that it was aware that the goods were to be shipped to a warehouse for storage. There was also evidence that no set time for inspection exists but that the industry practice is not to inspect until a purchaser is found and is ready to use the goods. There was further evidence that the carpet, when received in a large order such as this one, is stocked until ready for use rather than unrolled for inspection of concealed defects. Under all the evidence the carpet was timely and reasonably inspected and the trial court's finding to that effect is supported by substantial competent evidence.

There is a further question, however, whether or not the acts of the carpet installer for plaintiff's purchaser, Lay-Rite, were so inconsistent with the seller's ownership as to amount to the exercise of ownership and dominion by the plaintiff thereby constituting acceptance. Once again applying *Cervitor* II to the facts of this case, it would appear that the actions of the installer for plaintiff's purchaser were not inconsistent with seller's ownership and could not be said to amount to acceptance as a matter of law. In *Cervitor* there was no evidence that installation of the units was necessary to enable a proper inspection to take place, particularly where the deficiencies complained of were readily apparent upon inspection after the units were taken from the crates and before installation. In the instant case there would appear to be evidence that it was necessary to unroll and cut into three or four rolls of carpet in order to determine that the carpet was extensively patched, was delaminated in places, that it varied in width and in hue, and that it was not 25 oz. face weight. That is analogous to the uncrating of the units in *Cervitor*. After unrolling three or four rolls of carpet it became obvious that the carpet was defective since Lay-Rite could not find 23 feet in the several hundred feet of carpet that would match for installation in a "show" apartment. Had Lay-Rite installed the carpet in the "show" apartment or other apartments before rejecting it, *Cervitor* II might be in point. Here, however, the deficiencies complained of were readily apparent upon inspection after the carpet was unrolled, and rejection preceded installation. It cannot be said that the unrolling and cutting of the carpet in an attempt to match portions for installation was inconsistent with the seller's ownership as a matter of law so as to constitute an acceptance of the carpet.

Problem 7 - 3

Rae ordered a new digital scale for the deli—most of the products in the deli are sold and priced by weight. The scale arrived on time and, once it was unboxed and set up according to the instructions that came with it, appeared to be working properly. During the first couple of months of its use in the deli, the scale would occasionally shut down and require rebooting. By the end of the second month, the scale was shutting down several times each day. This caused considerable disruption in the deli, increasing the time necessary to process customers' orders and causing long lines at the deli during peak demand periods. Although Rae had complained to the seller about the problem multiple times, she was assured that the operating program used in the scale required a period of time to adapt to the usage patterns of the operator—in this case, the deli. Earlier this week, the scale shut down and refused to reboot. Rae summoned the seller's representative to the store, and after performing several tests on the scale, he discovered that it had been shipped with a faulty processor that could only be replaced at the factory. Rae told the rep that she was cancelling the transaction and to get the scale out of the store. Today the seller called to tell her it was too late to cancel the transaction and that he was sending the repaired scale back to her. Is it too late for Rae to reject the scale?

PROBLEM 7 - 4

Rae purchased a new delivery truck for the deli—the deli was getting more and more catering work, and the store did not really have a vehicle outfitted for delivering food to and setting up the kind of events for which the deli was being hired. The first time she drove the truck, she had difficulty shifting it into park, but she was able to get it into park by jiggling the steering wheel. She assumed the problem would go away once the truck was broken in. After six months (and eleven thousand miles), the problem had not gone away, so she took the truck back to the dealer, who determined that the torque converter in the transmission had failed, and so the entire transmission had to be replaced. Rae told the dealer she was cancelling the transaction and that it should keep the truck and return the payments the store had made on the truck. The dealer refused to accept her cancellation of the transaction. Can Rae reject the truck, or has she accepted it and become obligated for the price under 2-709?

PROBLEM 7 - 5

Rae ordered one hundred cases of "Sunkist Valencia oranges #113" from the local produce warehouse. The seller delivered one hundred cases of Del Monte Valencia oranges #88. Rae called the seller, and when the call rolled over to voicemail, she told him, "These are not what I ordered. I'm not going to take them—you need to come pick them up now." Is Rae's voicemail effective to reject the oranges and prevent acceptance? 2-602.

As several of the problems illustrated, whether the seller's performance conforms to the requirements of the contract will not necessarily be based exclusively on the express terms of the contract. As we learned earlier, under Article 2, the parties' agreement is often more than what they happened to write down as their deal—it includes course of performance, course of dealing, and usage of trade—so the fact that the goods delivered are not identical to their description in the contract might not establish a nonconformity. In *Intermeat, Inc. v. American Poultry, Inc.*, 575 F, 2d 1017 (2nd Cir. 1978), the contract required the seller to deliver "Richardson Production," but the goods delivered were marked "Tasmeats." The buyer rejected the goods on the ground that they did not conform to the contract, and the seller later sued for wrongful rejection. The Second Circuit agreed with the seller, explaining:

> There is no doubt that the perfect tender rule applies to measure the buyer's right of initial rejection of goods under U.C.C. § 2-601. Neither the broker's confirmation nor the contract of sale, however, called for any particular markings on the cartons. The District Court found that in the trade in which both parties are engaged as merchants, it is common knowledge that Tasmeats is the equivalent of Richardson Production, and concluded that Intermeat had delivered the exact product called for by its agreement with American Poultry. This conclusion was amply supported by the evidence in the record, which included evidence that Richardson Production is only available in the United States under the brand name of its

wholly-owned subsidiary, Tasmeats. We affirm its holding that rejection of the shipment by American Poultry was wrongful.

A rejection in the absence of any nonconformity in the seller's performance is considered, as the Second Circuit noted, "wrongful" and constitutes a breach by the buyer which gives the seller a claim for damages against the buyer:

> If the seller has made a tender which in all respects conforms to the contract, the buyer has a positive duty to accept and his failure to do so constitutes a "wrongful rejection" which gives the seller immediate remedies for breach.

Comment 3, 2-602. What the Second Circuit did not address is whether a wrongful rejection can operate to prevent a buyer's acceptance which would otherwise follow from a buyer's failure to reject the seller's performance in a timely manner under 2-606(1)(a). The next case recognizes that rejection under Article 2 has both procedural and substantive components and explores the effect each has on acceptance under 2-606.

INTEGRATED CIRCUITS UNLIMITED, INC. v. E. F. JOHNSON CO.

UNITED STATES DISTRICT COURT FOR THE EASTERN DISTRICT OF NEW YORK, 1988
691 F. SUPP. 630

WEINSTEIN, District Judge.

Plaintiff seeks to recover damages in the sum of $160,725, allegedly the balance due on invoices for microprocessors ordered by defendant. Uniform Commercial Code § 2-709. Defendant contends that certain of the microprocessors were defective … . It counterclaims for refunds and credits totaling more than the invoices on which it has withheld payment. The case was tried without a jury.

I. FACTS

Plaintiff Integrated Circuits Unlimited, Inc. ("ICU") is a New York-based distributer of electronic components. Defendant E. F. Johnson Company ("Johnson") is a Minnesota-based manufacturer of two-way taxi radios. In the winter and spring of 1984, a shortage developed of a particular microprocessor, known as model no. 8748, needed by Johnson to fulfill certain of its contracts. Unable to obtain it from its usual sources, Johnson purchased the part from ICU. In March of 1984, Johnson placed three purchase orders with ICU: WO4746 for 2,500 UPD8748 microprocessors at $85.00 each, WO4747 for 2,500 D8748H microprocessors at $87.50 each, and WO4750 for 1,100 D8749 microprocessors at $120.00 each.

Between March 21, 1984 and April 13, 1984, ICU delivered to Johnson 1,709 UPD8748 microprocessors pursuant to purchase order number WO4746, about 70% of the total order. The deliveries were made in four shipments. Johnson received shipments containing 130 and 150 on March 21 and 22 respectively, for which it gave ICU payment in full of $23,800.00 on March 30. It subsequently received 829 on April 11, and 600 on April 13. Between March 23 and April 7, Johnson received all 1100 ordered under purchase order WO4750, for which it paid in full $132,000.00.

On April 24, Johnson sent ICU a letter rejecting the 130 parts from the March 21 WO4746 shipment based on tests indicating that the devices were of substandard quality. The letter said that Johnson's acceptable quality level ("AQL")—the number of devices which can be defective without rendering the entire shipment unacceptable—was 1%. It attached a memorandum summarizing results of laboratory tests in which six of the devices, or 4.6%, had failed. The next day Johnson sent ICU a similar letter regarding the WO4750 units. It stated that out of 115 devices tested 113 had failed, and offered their return for credit. The attached memorandum summarizing the test results indicated that 113 had failed when subjected to temperatures higher than the maximum required by commercial standards and Johnson's own procurement specifications.

Three devices had failed at the agreed-upon standard temperature, a failure rate of 2.6%. All tests were conducted by an independent laboratory.

On May 8, Johnson sent ICU an itemized list of 1,973 parts it wished to return based on the laboratory tests. Not all of these parts had been individually tested. Rather, the rejections were premised on the laboratory results previously summarized in the memoranda sent to ICU. These results were based on tests of a sampling of each type of device. Under separate cover it sent to ICU 18 samples of the rejected devices so that ICU could conduct its own tests, and issued debit memoranda for the value of these parts.

From May until August, Johnson wrote and called ICU repeatedly requesting authorization to return the rejected parts. ICU declined to accept the returns. It continued to press for payment of its invoices. On May 21, Johnson sent ICU a check for $70,465, payment in full for the 829 parts received on April 11. On July 25, ICU reported to Johnson that its own tests had found that only one device out of 19 failed at commercial tolerances.

Johnson informed ICU on August 15 that it was returning the rejected parts "no matter what." It shipped them back to ICU, debited ICU's account $170,450.00 (the value of the rejected parts minus the 18 samples already sent back and debited), and withheld payment on two ICU invoices: the $51,000 allegedly owed for the 600 parts received on April 13 and $109,725 owed for parts shipped pursuant to purchase order WO4747, a total of $160,725. ICU refused delivery of the rejected parts. They were returned to Johnson, which has since held them on ICU's account.

II. FINDINGS OF FACT AND CONCLUSIONS OF LAW

A buyer is entitled under the U.C.C. to reject goods which fail to conform to the contract. U.C.C. § 2-601. The court concluded preliminarily on the trial record that Johnson's rejection of 1,973 parts was wrongful because less than five percent of the microprocessors from each order, proportional to the percent which had proven defective during testing, were nonconforming. Upon further consideration of the relevant testimony, however, the court finds that the defects rendered the shipments which contained defective parts nonconforming in their entirety.

A. Johnson's rejection was effective regardless of whether it was justified

The seller's remedies for a rejection of goods which is "ineffective" because the buyer failed to follow proper procedures are distinct from the remedies for a rejection which is "wrongful" because it was unjustified. If Johnson's rejection had been wrongful but nevertheless effective, ICU would not be entitled to maintain an action for the price.

Section 2-709 allows an action for the price only if the goods have been "accepted" (or are lost, damaged, or non-resalable, none of which are true in this case). Section 2-606, in turn, defines acceptance as "failure to make an *effective* rejection" (emphasis added). It is cross-referenced to § 2-602 (1), which provides that a rejection of goods must be made "within a reasonable time after their delivery or tender," and is "*ineffective* unless the buyer seasonably notifies the seller" (emphasis added). Thus, the remedy for an ineffective rejection—one which is procedurally defective under § 2-602 (1)—is an action for the price.

By contrast, a *wrongful* rejection may still be an effective rejection, and does not in itself entitle the seller to the price. Since an ineffective rejection constitutes an acceptance, by negative inference any effective rejection—whether or not it is justified—bars acceptance and protects the buyer from §

2-709 damages. Subsection (3) of § 2-602, which is *not* cross-referenced to the § 2-606 definition of acceptance as ineffective rejection, makes separate mention of goods "wrongfully" rejected. It provides that the remedies in cases of wrongful rejection are contained in § 2-703, entitled "Seller's Remedies in General." Subsection (e) of § 2-703 states that the measure of damages for goods wrongfully rejected is the difference between the contract price and the market price (§ 2-708), or "in a proper case the price" under § 2-709. Thus, a seller whose goods have been wrongfully rejected will be entitled to the price only if that measure of damages is "proper" under § 2-709 because the rejection was also procedurally ineffective.

This interpretation is supported by both the U.C.C. commentaries and by the authorities. The official commentary to § 2-602, the section setting forth procedures for an effective rejection, states that subsection (3) on wrongful rejections was included only to emphasize the "sharp distinction" between the rules governing procedures for making an effective rightful rejection and those governing "non-acceptance which is a breach"—*i.e.*, procedurally effective rejection (non-acceptance) which is wrongful. Professors White and Summers, in their treatise on the U.C.C., analyze the issue as follows:

> All commentators agree that the Code drafters contemplated effective *rejections* which might be substantively wrongful and intended that all such rejections forestall acceptance without regard to their substantive wrongfulness. Writing for the New York Law Revision Commission, Professor Honnold stated: "buyer may have the power to make an 'effective' rejection even though his action is in breach of contract and subjects buyer to liability for damages."

> .... .

> It is important to distinguish between "wrongful" rejections and "ineffective" rejections. As we use the term (and as we believe the drafters intended the term to be used), a rejection of a conforming tender would be a wrongful rejection. Nevertheless if timely notice was sent and if the buyer lived up to his post rejection obligations under section 2-602 and those following, the rejection though "wrongful" would be "effective" and would so preclude his acceptance of the goods and foreclose a consequent liability for the price under 2-709 (1) (a).

J. White & R. Summers, *Uniform Commercial Code*, 258, 314 (2d Ed. 1980) (footnotes omitted). One court has specifically held:

> The trial court's statement during trial that "a wrongful rejection ... would constitute an acceptance" is not correct. The remedies for wrongful rejection are separately set out and do not include treating that action as an acceptance. An *ineffective* rejection may be an acceptance.

Johnson's rejection of the microprocessors was effective. It met the requirement in § 2-602 that a rejection be made within a reasonable time after delivery or tender, and that the buyer seasonably notify the seller.

Time to test complex electronic parts must be afforded. Here testing by the independent laboratory retained by Johnson was prompt and thorough. Immediately after learning that the test results had revealed excessive flaws in the microprocessors, Johnson notified ICU of these results and of its intent to reject the parts. Less than two weeks later, it sent ICU an itemized list of parts being rejected. Its letter of May 8 satisfied the requirement of § 2-605 that the buyer set forth the nature of the defect with sufficient particularity to allow the seller to cure it.

The fact that Johnson took temporary physical possession of the microprocessors and even used some of them before rejecting them does not mean that it accepted them. Those actions were taken during the time required to complete the tests. Section 2-606 provides that acceptance of goods does not occur until the buyer has had a "reasonable opportunity to inspect them." *See Barrett Paving Materials, Inc. v. United States Fidelity and Guaranty Company*, 118 A.D.2d 1039, 500 N.Y.S.2d 413 (3rd Dept. 1986) (whether use of product constituted acceptance was a question of fact because of the substantial time and special conditions needed to test it). *Cf. Shokai Far East Ltd. v. Energy Conservation Systems, Inc.*, 628 F. Supp. 1462 (S.D.N.Y. 1986) (use of goods *subsequent* to testing them constituted acceptance under the U.C.C.).

Nor did Johnson waive any rights by paying for the microprocessors after it had rejected them. The payments represented an effort on the part of Johnson to resolve the dispute amicably. *See Barrett Paving Materials, Inc. v. United States Fidelity and Guaranty Company, supra* (payment for goods is not dispositive of whether they were accepted).

Thus, even if Johnson's rejection of the microprocessors were substantively wrongful, ICU would not be entitled to maintain an action for the price. The proper measure of damages would be the difference between the contract price and market price at the time of delivery plus incidental damages. U.C.C. § 2-708.

B. Johnson's actions following the rejection were proper.

Section 2-602 requires that a buyer hold rejected goods with reasonable care at the seller's disposition for a time sufficient to permit the seller to remove them. Johnson fulfilled this duty. It held the microprocessors in storage for three months, during which time they remained in good condition, without physical deterioration as a result of the testing or the passage of shelf time. Throughout those months it unsuccessfully sought authorization from ICU for return of the microprocessors. When it attempted to ship them back without such authorization, ICU sent them back. Thus, although the market price of the parts began to fall in September of 1984, Johnson is not liable to ICU for any damages incurred as a result of that subsequent price fluctuation.

Johnson was not required under § 2-603 to resell the rejected parts. Since Johnson received no instructions from ICU with respect to disposition of the parts after it gave notice of rejection, it was not required to take any further action. The parts were not "perishable" and did not, when the dispute arose, "threaten to decline in value speedily." ICU is a dealer in microprocessors and would have been able to sell them far more readily than Johnson. Johnson is a manufacturer and assembler; it had no ready access to the seller's market for these components.

Had ICU accepted Johnson's timely attempts to return the parts and resold them, it would not have suffered any loss. Johnson cannot now be held responsible for ICU's unjustified refusal to mitigate damages.

As the court explained, a rejection might be wrongful, but it still has legal significance under Article 2 if both the rejection and notice to the seller are timely. There may be no substantive basis for the buyer's rejection (no defect in the goods), but as long as the buyer follows the procedure for rejection under 2-602, the rejection counts—which means it prevents the seller from claiming the goods were accepted under 2-606(1)(b). The seller has a claim for breach against the buyer and is entitled to invoke the remedies Article 2 provides sellers when their buyers breach (2-703), but because the rejection means there is no acceptance, the seller does not have a claim against the buyer for the price under 2-709. A procedurally defective rejection—an untimely rejection or notice of rejection, on the other hand, has no effect and will not prevent acceptance from occurring.

Rejection can still be wrongful even where the buyer has a substantive basis for the rejection if the buyer does not identify for the seller the nonconformities on which the rejection is based. The buyer has an obligation to particularize the grounds for its rejection and waives any nonconformity it does not identify in its notice of rejection if (1) at the time of rejection the seller was entitled to cure the nonconformity under Article 2's provisions for cure, or (2) the parties are both merchants and the buyer fails to particularize its grounds after receiving from the seller a request for a "full and final written statement of all defects on which the buyer proposes to rely." 2-605(1). If, under 2-605, the buyer loses her right to assert the defects on which she based her rejection, the rejection becomes wrongful, and now the buyer is in breach, even though the seller has failed to perform as promised. The rejection, if timely, would still prevent acceptance, but the seller would still be entitled to invoke the remedies provided in 2-703 for a buyer's breach.

Finally, what happens after a buyer rejects a seller's performance? If the goods have been delivered and the rejection is made after the buyer's inspection, what does the buyer do with the goods still in its possession? The buyer must still be careful to avoid taking any act inconsistent with the seller's ownership of the goods to prevent deemed acceptance under 2-606(1)(c). The following case maps out the rights and responsibilities of a rejecting buyer.

DESIGN PLUS STORE FIXTURES, INC. V. CITRO CORP.

COURT OF APPEALS OF NORTH CAROLINA, 1998
508 S.E.2D 825

MARTIN, Judge.

Plaintiff, Design Plus Store Fixtures, Inc., (Design), entered into a contract with defendant, Citro Corporation (Citro), to buy display tables in three installments to be delivered to Design's primary customer, Springmaid, in Oregon, Kansas, and New Mexico. Citro sub-contracted with the third party defendant, Decolam, Inc., (Decolam), to "edge-tape" and bore holes in the parts according to plaintiff's specifications and a pattern approved by Citro.

The tables for the first two orders were delivered late, and a number of non-conformities made the tables impossible to assemble. When Design notified Citro of the defects, Citro offered no cure. Despite the non-conformities, Design eventually re-drilled the holes and assembled the tables. Design consummated the sale to Springmaid with the understanding that the tables would ultimately be replaced. Design covered the cost of the replacement tables, and refused to pay Citro for the defective tables. After Design provided replacement tables to Springmaid, Design gave the defective tables to charity. Design canceled the New Mexico installment after the table parts were cut and before they were bored or taped.

Design sued for expenses incurred due to Citro's breach. Citro counterclaimed for breach of contract and unjust enrichment, and filed a third party complaint against Decolam for breach of warranties and contract. The trial court found that Design had accepted the goods and awarded Citro $19,404.00 as damages for Design's breach of contract, less $18,420.17, which the court offset as Design's damages occasioned by Citro's breach of warranty. The trial court also awarded Citro $9,404.64 as damages for Design's anticipatory repudiation of the New Mexico installment, and awarded Citro $7,407.84 for Decolam's breach of subcontract and breach of warranty. Plaintiff Design and third party defendant Decolam appeal.

I. PLAINTIFF'S ASSIGNMENTS OF ERROR

Design contends it never accepted the Oregon and Kansas orders despite its repair, continued use, and ultimate discarding of the defective tables.

A. Acceptance of Oregon and Kansas Installments

Design's transaction with Citro is governed by the Uniform Commercial Code (Code), N.C. Gen. Stat. §§ 25-2-102, 25-2-105 (1995). Specifically, this is an installment contract subject to the provisions of G.S. § 25-2-612(1) (1995) ("An 'installment contract' is one which requires or authorizes the delivery of goods in separate lots to be separately accepted ... ").

Initially, Design properly rejected the tables by providing reasonable notice of the nonconformity to Citro. The trial court found that the non-conformities "made it impossible to properly assemble the table,"... . The trial court also noted that Design "arguably communicated a valid intent to reject the goods to [Citro]." Design notified Citro of significant non-conformities on 10 November 1993; and after Citro made no offer to cure the defects, Design refused to pay for the defective tables on 21 November 1993. Thus, Design's actions after discovery of the non-conformities were consistent with a rightful rejection of the tables. Nevertheless, the trial court concluded that Design had accepted the tables by actions "inconsistent with [Citro's] ownership," including: consummating the sale of the tables to Springmaid with concessions, and "failure to replace the Oregon tables for eleven months and the Kansas tables for nineteen months, and the Plaintiff's disposal of the tables after their replacement without notifying or attempting to obtain the consent" of Citro.

"Acceptance of goods occurs when the buyer ... does any act inconsistent with the seller's ownership; but if such act is wrongful against the seller, it is an acceptance only if ratified by him." N.C. Gen. Stat. § 25-2-606(1)(c) (1995). "Acts inconsistent with the seller's ownership" can best be understood in light of the buyer's statutory options and duties with respect to rightfully rejected non-conforming goods. The buyer's options and duties upon rejection are described in G.S. §§ 25-2-602 to -604 (1995). For most buyers, there is a general duty to hold goods with reasonable care "for a time sufficient to permit the seller to remove them." N.C. Gen. Stat. § 25-2-602(2)(b) (1995). Merchant buyers have a more specific duty when the seller has no agent or place of business in the market of rejection:

> a merchant buyer is under a duty after rejection of goods in his possession or control to fol-
> low any reasonable instructions received from the seller with respect to the goods and in the
> absence of such instructions to make reasonable efforts to sell them for the seller's account if
> they are perishable or threaten to decline in value speedily.
>
> N.C. Gen. Stat. § 25-2-603(1) (1995).

In this case, Design is a merchant dealing in tables, G.S. § 25-2-104(1) ("'Merchant' means a person who deals in goods of the kind ... "); and Citro had no place of business or agent in the markets of rejection, Oregon and Kansas. In addition, the tables are not "perishables" such that "the value of the goods is threatened and the seller's instructions do not arrive in time to prevent serious loss." N.C. Gen. Stat. § 25-2-603(1) Official U.C.C. Comment 1 (1995). Thus Design's duty, upon rejection, was to follow Citro's reasonable instructions with respect to Citro's tables. However, no instructions from Citro were forthcoming.

Absent such instructions, the statute presents three options for a buyer who has given reasonable notification rejecting non-conforming goods: (1) store the rejected goods on the seller's account, (2) re-ship them to seller, or (3) resell them on the seller's account with reimbursement for expenses incurred in caring for and selling them. N.C. Gen. Stat. § 25-2-604 (1995). These potential courses of action are "intended to be not exhaustive but merely illustrative." N.C. Gen. Stat. § 25-2-604 Official U.C.C. Comment 1 (1995).

The basic purpose of this section is twofold: on the one hand it aims at reducing the stake in dispute and on the other at avoiding the pinning of a technical "acceptance" on a buyer who has taken steps towards realization on or preservation of the goods in good faith. N.C. Gen. Stat. § 25-2-604 Official U.C.C. Comment (1995).

A merchant buyer in possession of rejected goods, and without instructions from the seller, is in the somewhat difficult position of having a choice of reasonable options but no clear affirmative duties with respect to those goods, G.S. § 25-2-604; yet, the buyer must avoid acts "inconsistent with the seller's ownership" in order to avoid accepting the non-conforming goods. N.C. Gen. Stat. § 25-2-606(1)(c) (1995). The issue is whether Design's actions constitute good faith steps toward "realization on or preservation of the goods," on the one hand, or "acts inconsistent with ownership" on the other. *Compare,* N.C. Gen. Stat. § 25-2-604 Official U.C.C. Comment (1995) and N.C. Gen. Stat. § 25-2-606(1)(c) (1995). Whether actions taken with respect to rejected non-conforming goods, beyond those suggested by statute, are "inconsistent with the seller's ownership," depends on the circumstances and the buyer's steps towards realization on or preservation of the goods in good faith.

The repair and continued use of the non-conforming, rejected goods constitutes a reasonable good faith effort to preserve the goods while mitigating damages. *Accord Hajoca Corp. v. Brooks,* 249 N.C. 10, 15, 105 S.E.2d 123, 127-28 (1958) (retention and use of defective machine by purchaser did not waive rejection because "purchaser does not waive his right to rescind the contract for breach of warranty 'where the retention was at the instance and request of the seller and for the benefit of the seller in his endeavors to remedy the defective machine so that it would properly perform the functions for which it was warranted and sold.'") (citation omitted)*; Romy v. Picker Int'l Inc.,* 1992 U.S. Dist. LEXIS 3995, 1992 W.L. 70403, 3 (E.D.Pa. 1992), *affirmed,* 986 F.2d 1409 (3rd Cir. (Pa) 1993) ("use of nonconforming goods, however, does not constitute, per se, a waiver of revocation; … rather, a court will annul a revocation and conclude that a re-acceptance has occurred only where the buyer's actions with respect to the goods are deemed 'unreasonable.'")*; Fablok Mills, Inc., v. Cocker Machine & Foundry Co.,* 125 N.J. Super. 251, 257-58, 310 A.2d 491, 494-95, *cert. denied,* 64 N.J. 317, 315 A.2d 405 (1973) ("We conceive that in certain situations continued use of goods by the buyer may be the most appropriate means of achieving mitigation, i.e., where the buyer is unable to purchase a suitable substitute for the goods.").

Thus it has been frequently held that under certain circumstances a buyer rejecting goods or revoking his acceptance may continue to use the goods … particularly where such use is a direct result of the oppressive conduct of the seller … or where no prejudice is shown (citations omitted). *Frank's Maintenance & Engineering, Inc., v. C.A. Roberts Co.,* 86 Ill. App. 3d 980, 986-87, 408 N.E.2d 403, 408, 42 Ill. Dec. 25 (1980).

In this case, Citro entered into the contract with the understanding that manufacturing and delivering the tables in a timely manner was necessary to serve Design's primary customer, Springmaid. Citro delivered the tables late, and the tables were defective. According to the trial court's findings of fact, the plaintiff "performed corrective measures" on the tables, and provided them to Springmaid with the understanding they would be replaced and "replacement of the tables could not affect any of the scheduled store openings;" and, Citro "offered neither explanation nor solution." Design bore the expense of repairing the tables for temporary use by Springmaid. Citro offered no instructions as to the disposal or return of the tables. Under these circumstances, we hold that repairing the tables and allowing Springmaid the continued use of the tables were reasonable actions in good faith and did not constitute acceptance of the tables.

However, after allowing Springmaid the reasonable continued use of the repaired tables, Design gave the nonconforming tables away, contending they had no market value. The trial court concluded, *inter alia,* that "disposal of the tables after their replacement without notifying or attempting to obtain the consent of [Defendant] Corporation constituted acceptance of the goods under the code as acts inconsistent with Defendant's ownership." We agree.

As discussed above, reasonable repair and use of the tables to temporarily satisfy a contract contemplated at the time of the transaction is not inconsistent with ownership; thus those actions did not constitute an acceptance. However, discarding the tables without notifying Citro is an unreasonable act, inconsistent with ownership, where the tables had some salvageable value. Underlying the issue of acceptance, in this context, is the question of whether Design acted inconsistently, by rejecting the goods and then disposing of these goods as an owner. Giving the tables to charity without notifying Citro was such an act of ownership.

There are some circumstances where it might be reasonable to discard rejected goods when there is no salvageable value. N.C. Gen. Stat. § 25-2-608, Official U.C.C. Comment 6 (1995) ("Worthless goods, however, need not be offered back … ."); *Askco Engineering Corp., v. Mobil Chemical Corp.*, 535 S.W.2d 893 (Tex. Civ. App. 1976). In this case, however, the court found that the un-bored, un-edged, parts for the New Mexico installment had a salvage value of $15.60 per table; and its finding is supported by the evidence. Plaintiff concedes in its brief that the assembled and used tables of the Kansas and Oregon installments had the same salvage value as the unassembled, unedged parts of the New Mexico installment; and so these tables were not worthless. Discarding these goods constituted an act inconsistent with Citro's ownership, and so Design is deemed to have accepted the goods. N.C. Gen. Stat. § 25-2-606(1)(c), 25-2-604, Official U.C.C. Comment (1995). We therefore affirm the trial court's conclusion that Design accepted the Kansas and Oregon installments and its award of damages to Citro in the amount of the contract price for those goods, less an offset for damages sustained by Design by reason of the defects. N.C. Gen. Stat. § 25-2-607(1) (1995).

PROBLEM 7 - 6

Rae ordered one hundred cases of red seedless grapes from the produce distributor up the interstate. When the grapes were delivered, the produce manager noticed they were not the seedless variety Rae had ordered and immediately notified Rae, who e-mailed the store's rejection of the grapes to the seller. By the time the seller came by to pick up the rejected grapes, they were no longer useable—they were covered with bunch rot, a mold that grows on grapes when they are not refrigerated. The produce manager had left the grapes on the loading dock (after Rae had e-mailed her rejection) instead of putting them in the produce cooler. The seller claims the store's failure to refrigerate the grapes negated the rejection. Is he right? 2-603 and 2-604.

PROBLEM 7 - 7

Would your answer in the last problem be different if, after receiving Rae's e-mail rejecting the grapes, the seller had called and told her to leave the grapes on the loading dock so his driver could pick them up after hours? 2-603.

PROBLEM 7 - 8

Rae ordered a heavy-duty stand mixer for the deli. The mixer was unable to knead the bread dough the bakery made for its homemade bread, and last Friday, after using the mixer for several days, Rae e-mailed the seller that she was rejecting the mixer because it was not able to do the work for which she bought it. The seller told Rae it would come by for the mixer on Monday. The deli manager decided to use the mixer for other projects over the weekend (since it had not been disassembled and removed from the deli work room), but the shaft locked up and would no longer turn. Can the seller refuse to take back the mixer because the store continued to use it after sending notice of rejection? 2-603.

C. Revocation: Buyer Returns the Goods

Although acceptance prevents a buyer from rejecting the goods and putting them back on the seller, acceptance does not stick the buyer with the goods forever if they turn out to be defective. Article 2 gives a buyer a second chance to return the goods to the seller and relieve itself of the obligation to pay for them by allowing a buyer to revoke—take back—its acceptance. 2-608. But Article 2 ups the ante for a buyer using its second chance by requiring a more compelling justification for revocation than it does for rejection. The tougher standard for revocation is not surprising in light of the disruptive effect it has on the understandable expectation of the seller that, after acceptance, the goods will not be coming back. And the goods may have depreciated significantly through passage of time or their use by the buyer, so not just any nonconformity will justify revoking acceptance—the nonconformity on which revocation is based must "substantially impair the value" of the goods to the buyer. 2-608(1). Inconvenience, preference, or the like are not enough to upset the status quo after the goods have been accepted. And the buyer must also have an excuse for not addressing the problem sooner by rejecting the goods: the buyer must not have known about the nonconformity at the time of acceptance, or, if it did know, must show that it accepted the goods anyway because the seller promised to fix the problem—to cure the nonconformity. 2-608(1)(a) and (b). And if the buyer was unaware of the nonconformity at the time of acceptance, it must have a good reason for its ignorance.

In addition to showing substantial impairment and excuse, the revoking buyer must decide to revoke before the condition of the goods has changed substantially and within a reasonable time after she discovered or should have discovered the nonconformity, and she must notify the seller of her revocation within a reasonable time after deciding to revoke her acceptance. 2-608(2).

The following case maps out the basic requirements for a buyer's revocation under Article 2.

HEMMERT AGRICULTURAL AVIATION, INC. v. MID-CONTINENT AIRCRAFT CORP.

UNITED STATES DISTRICT COURT FOR THE DISTRICT OF KANSAS, 1987
663 F. SUPP. 1546

MEMORANDUM AND ORDER

Wesley E. Brown

This is a diversity action wherein plaintiff seeks to revoke acceptance and to recover damages arising from its purchase of an agricultural spray plane from the defendant.

FINDINGS OF FACT

1. Hemmert Agricultural Aviation, Inc. ("Hemmert Ag"), is a Kansas corporation engaged in the business of agricultural spraying, primarily commercial crop dusting and fertilizer application.
2. Mark Hemmert (Hemmert) is the President and sole stockholder of Hemmert Ag.
3. Defendant, Mid-Continent Aircraft Corporation (Mid-Continent), is a Missouri corporation in Hayti, Missouri, engaged in the business of commercial crop dusting and aircraft sales. Mid-Continent is an authorized dealer of Ag-Cat spray planes.
4. Richard Reade is the President and principal stockholder of Mid-Continent.

5. In 1980, Hemmert purchased a 1977 used "B" model Schweizer Ag-Cat.

6. In 1984, Hemmert called Mid-Continent, as he was interested in trading in his 1977 "B" Ag Cat for a new and bigger plane, Super "B".

7. In August 1985, Hemmert again contacted Mid-Continent, in particular Richard Reade, about purchasing the Super "B". While satisfied with the performance of his 1977 "B" Ag Cat, he had been having a good year and wanted a plane that was faster to the field, more maneuverable and more productive. Hemmert's trade-in was in good condition other than needing some routine maintenance. Hemmert purchased the Super "B" believing it would make his work easier, safer and more profitable. Another reason for the timing of the purchase was that Hemmert hoped to take advantage of the investment tax credit.

8. Hemmert's belief that a Super "B" was more maneuverable than his 1977 Ag-Cat "B" was based in part on an advertisement for the 450 "B", which stated in part: "New raised wing design means more maneuverability; more visibility; more speed." The 450 "B" described in defendant's Exhibit 38 differs from the Super "B" 600 hp. only in horsepower, hopper size, and length (4 inches). In fact, defendant's Exhibit 39, a Schweizer advertisement brochure stamped with defendant's name and address, explains the Super "B" is powered by either a 450 or 600 horsepower engine. The 450 "B" is identical to the 600 hp. Super "B" in almost all relevant respects, except for engine size and hopper capacity.

9. Hemmert testified that during the telephone conversation in early August 1985, Richard Reade represented the Super "B" to be faster, more maneuverable, and having better visibility than his 1977 Ag-Cat "B". Reade denied that these representations were made and stated that he only represented the Super "B" as more productive.

10. The parties struck their bargain over the telephone on August 6, 1985. Reade promised Hemmert that the Super "B" would be delivered in Oakley, Kansas, on or before August 9,1985, and that the Super "B" would be ready to spray when it was delivered. Hemmert also believed the Super "B" would arrive equipped with aileron servos, an EGT gauge and a push-to-talk switch. The plane was sold to plaintiff for $128,000.00 total, $75,500.00 in cash plus Hemmert's trade-in. On August 6, 1985, Hemmert instructed the bank to wire the defendant the sum of $40,000.00.

12. Ed Zeeman, a ferry pilot, delivered the Super "B" to Hemmert Ag in Oakley, Kansas, on August 20, 1985. Zeeman arrived in Oakley late in the afternoon, and he was in a hurry to return that afternoon with plaintiff's trade-in.

13. Even though his bank was closed, by the time Zeeman arrived on August 20, 1985, Hemmert was able to get a cashier's check for $35,000.00 payable to Mid-Continent. Zeeman asked Hemmert to sign the purchase order and delivery receipt, which he did after looking over the plane. Zeeman left early the next morning around 5:30 A.M. Due to time and inclement weather conditions, plaintiff was unable to try the plane before Zeeman's departure.

16. Prior to August 6, 1985, Hemmert had not flown the particular Super "B" he purchased nor flown any Super "B". Hemmert made no inquiries to other spray pilots who were using a Super "B". Reade acknowledged that it is not unusual for agricultural spray planes to be sold before the purchaser has actually flown them.

17. On August 20, 1985, the actual delivery date, Hemmert called Reade saying he was happy but that the aileron servos and EGT gauge were not on the aircraft.

18. Around August 23, 1985, Hemmert flew the Super "B" with a small load of water in an effort to calibrate the spraying system. Hemmert noticed that the shut-off valve was not developing adequate "suck back" to shut off the flow of water. After his adjustments failed to correct the situation, Hemmert called Reade and told him the valve was defective. Read said a new valve would be sent and it could be installed at Mid-Continent's expense.

19. At about the same time, Hemmert complained about the performance of the Super "B". Hemmert noted that the plane was unresponsive in pitch, rolled excessively to the right, and

lost air speed in turns, giving the pilot the sensation that the aircraft was "falling out from under him". Reade suggested the performance problems could be simply due to a bad engine. Hemmert said he was not satisfied and instructed Reade not to sell his trade-in. Reade represented that the trade-in had been sold. While the sale of the trade-in was not completed until September 6, 1985, at the time of Reade's representation to plaintiff there was an outstanding offer on the plane.

20. When the second spray valve arrived within a couple of days of August 23, 1985, plaintiff and an airport mechanic installed the second valve which also proved to be defective. When Hemmert called Reade about the defective second valve, Reade said additional valves would be sent until an operative one was found.

21. Reade directed Dan Westbrook, a mechanic with Mid-Continent, to drive to Oakley, Kansas, and to replace the engine with the original Aero engine from the manufacturer. On or about August 26, 1985, Westbrook checked over the plane and replaced the engine. Westbrook then flew the plane empty for 30–40 minutes. Westbrook detected nothing glaringly wrong with the plane's flight characteristics. He believed the plane "flew well" and that it had a "personality of its own."

22. Still dissatisfied with the plane's flight characteristics, Hemmert contacted four other agricultural spray pilots and asked them to fly the Super "B". Each of these four spray pilots were highly experienced, but none had previously flown a Super "B". Each pilot flew the plane before Hemmert related any of his negative feelings regarding the plane. The four spray pilots were Jim Bussen of Sharon Springs, Kansas; Steven Kistler of Colby, Kansas; Kelly Henry of Augusta, Kansas; and Ken Bixeman of Colby, Kansas.

28. Hemmert is dissatisfied with his Super "B" and has lost his confidence in it. Each pilot that testified at trial acknowledged that a spray pilot's confidence in his aircraft is very important. Because of a spray pilot's maneuvers close to the ground, his confidence is extremely essential.

29. In the Spring of 1986, Hemmert purchased another Ag-Cat, a 1982 600 horsepower "B" plus. This model did not have a raised wing design as found on the Super "B". Hemmert paid $78,000.00 for this plane and is still using it.

30. Hemmert was never satisfied with the Super "B". On October 30, 1985, Hemmert's attorney sent a certified letter notifying Mid-Continent of Mr. Hemmert's intent to revoke acceptance of the Super "B" under the Uniform Commercial Code. Reade admitted the plaintiff's complaints in that letter were not new to him.

CONCLUSIONS OF LAW

3. Plaintiff seeks to employ the remedy of revocation of acceptance set forth at *K.S.A. 84-2-608*:

(1) The buyer may revoke his acceptance of a lot or commercial unit whose nonconformity substantially impairs its value to him if he has accepted it

(a) on the reasonable assumption that its nonconformity would be cured and it has not been seasonably cured; or

(b) without discovery of such nonconformity if his acceptance was reasonably induced either by the difficulty of discovery before acceptance or by the seller's assurances.

(2) Revocation of acceptance must occur within a reasonable time after the buyer discovers or should have discovered the ground for it and before any substantial change in condition of the goods which is not caused by their own defects. It is not effective until the buyer notifies the seller of it.

(3) A buyer who so revokes has the same rights and duties with regard to the goods involved as if he had rejected them.

To revoke acceptance is to refuse the delivered goods after they have been accepted and after the time for their rejection has run. While a buyer may nominally reject for any defect, acceptance cannot be revoked absent a substantial nonconformity. The purpose of this remedy is to restore the buyer to the economic status quo which would have been enjoyed if the goods had not been delivered.

4. *Notice.* K.S.A. 84-2-608(2) (hereinafter 2-608) requires revocation to occur within a reasonable time after the buyer discovers or should have discovered the grounds for it. What is a reasonable time is obviously a function of circumstances. Typically, the notice of revocation will be given after the general notice of breach required under *K.S.A. 84-2-607(3)(a)*, as the purchaser's wish to revoke is frequently the last resort after the seller's attempts to cure have failed. Because one purpose behind the notice provisions is to allow the seller the chance to cure, the outer limits of the reasonable time period should be flexible to encourage both the buyer and seller to cooperate in an effort to cure. Official Comment 4 to 2-608. Similarly, if the seller continuously assures the buyer that the defects will be remedied, the notice period should be accordingly suspended.

Plaintiff gave notice of revocation within a reasonable time. Plaintiff properly relied on defendant's assurances that any defects would be corrected, and on defendant's subsequent efforts to cure. Hemmert promptly discovered the defects and immediately advised Reade of his complaints.

5. *Elements of Revocation Remedy.* Under 2-608, the buyer has the burden to prove:

(1) the nonconformity of the machine to the needs and circumstances of the purchaser when purchase was made; (2) that such nonconformity in fact substantially impaired the value of the machine to the purchaser, and (3) that the purchaser accepted the machine under circumstances which bring him within either paragraph (1)(a), reasonable assumption of cure, or paragraph (1)(b), difficulty of discovery.

As discussed more fully later in this order, the primary issue in this case is whether a substantial impairment exists when the plane's handling characteristics create fear and apprehension in the pilot for the first 50 hours of flying during the execution of maneuvers considered normal for other models of Ag-Cat planes. Substantial impairment is not defined in the Uniform Commercial Code. What constitutes a substantial impairment is considered to be a common sense determination. Kansas courts have followed the interpretation of other courts and have given substantial impairment both a subjective and an objective element. In *McGilbray*, the Kansas Supreme Court adopted the two-step inquiry found in *Jorgensen v. Pressnall*, 274 Ore. 285, 545 P.2d 1382, 1384-1385 (1976), which is:

Since *ORS 72.6080(1)* provides that the buyer may revoke acceptance of goods 'whose nonconformity substantially impairs its value *to him*,' the value of conforming goods *to the plaintiff* must first be determined. This is a subjective question in the sense that it calls for a consideration of the needs and circumstances of the plaintiff who seeks to revoke; not the needs and circumstances of an average buyer. The second inquiry is whether the nonconformity in fact substantially impairs the value of the goods to the buyer, having in mind his particular needs. This is an objective question in the sense that it calls for evidence of something more than plaintiff's assertion that the nonconformity impaired the value to him; it requires evidence from which it can be inferred that plaintiff's needs were not met because of the nonconformity. In short, the nonconformity must *substantially* impair the value of the goods to the plaintiff buyer. The existence of substantial impairment depends upon the facts and circumstances in each case. (Emphasis in original.)

The fact-finder determines from the evidence the questions of nonconformity, the needs and circumstances of a purchaser, and impairment of value to a purchaser. Leading commentators have noted:

> The only element of objectivity the *Jorgensen* court required was evidence from which it could be inferred that the buyer's needs were not met because of the nonconformity; that evidence must be something more than the buyer's mere assertion of substantial impairment. The language of cases like *Jorgensen*, coupled with the subjective phrase "to him" in *Section 2-608* and official Comment 2 to that section, gives an aggrieved buyer a strong argument that he has the right to revoke acceptance because of his special sensitivity to the breach of warranty, even though the defects would be considered insubstantial to the average buyer.

Clark and Smith, *The Law of Product Warranties*, Para. 7.03(3)(a)(1984). While the evidence in this case establishes that not just Hemmert experienced discomfort and fear from the handling characteristics of the Super "B", if Hemmert's sensitivity to the Super "B" had been unique and there had been objective evidence that his needs were not met, revocation would still be consistent with the purpose and interpretation of 2-608. In considering the subjective element, the courts have employed a term, "shaken faith." In determining whether value was substantially impaired, the courts have weighed the cost of repairs, the inconvenience resulting from the nonconformities, and the entire impact the defects had on the buyer's confidence in the goods purchased. Lost confidence has been adopted by a number of courts and labelled as the "shaken faith" doctrine. Where the buyer's confidence in the dependability of the machine is shaken because of the defects and possibly because of seller's ineffective attempts to cure, revocation appears justified.

Kansas appellate courts have not specifically addressed whether a buyer's lost confidence is a relevant factor for determining substantial impairment. In summarizing the recurring defects with the pickup in *Johnson v. General Motors Corp.*, 233 Kan. at 1045, the Kansas Supreme Court concluded: "(r)epairs were attempted under GMC's warranty agreement but the Johnsons had lost confidence in the truck." While only dicta, this is an indication that Kansas courts would recognize this doctrine to be an appropriate factor within the subjective element of substantial impairment and a necessary companion in concept to the seller's right to cure. This court considers the buyer's lost confidence in a product to be a relevant consideration in determining a substantial impairment in value.

6. *Nonconformities.* A nonconformity includes breaches of warranties (implied and express) as well as any failure of the seller to perform pursuant to his contractual obligation.

7. Plaintiff has sustained its burden in establishing nonconformities. The handling characteristics which created fear and apprehension in plaintiff and other experienced spray pilots were directly contrary to express representations of maneuverability and speed. There being no question that Mid-Continent is a merchant as defined at *K.S.A. 84-2-104(1)*, the Super "B" is in breach of the implied warranty of merchantability. Plaintiff has proven that the Super "B" it purchased cannot pass without objection to its handling characteristics in normal turning maneuvers in spraying fields. In a trade as hazardous as crop dusting, a pilot would not reasonably accept without objection a plane that takes some 50 hours of flight time before the pilot's unusual fears and concerns about the particular plane are allayed. This conclusion is particularly appropriate where neither the seller nor manufacturer cautions the purchaser that the particular model handles significantly different from other Ag-Cats.

9. *Substantial Impairment.* The relevant law regarding this question has been previously discussed. Plaintiff has proven a substantial impairment. His lost confidence in the Super "B" caused by its handling characteristics, which scare experienced pilots in making normal spraying maneuvers, amounts to a substantial impairment. A spray pilot's activities are considered dangerous in flying at very low altitudes and quickly maneuvering to apply sprays and to avoid obstacles. Undeniably, a spray pilot's confidence in his

plane is absolutely crucial. Mr. Dykes' endurance of his "unhappiness" and fear for the first fifty hours of flying the Super "B" does not mean that the same fears and dissatisfaction experienced by Hemmert are not a substantial impairment of value. A pilot's confidence and willingness to undertake dangerous spraying maneuvers in a plane is reasonably destroyed when the pilot consistently experiences the sensation that the plane is about to "fall out from under him" when making normal spraying turns. Similarly, it is unreasonable to expect someone to endure his fears and otherwise operate the plane in his normal spraying business for those fifty hours. A seller's subsequent assurance that the buyer need only modify his flying technique and the sensations will no longer occur is understandably ineffective in rekindling a purchaser's confidence in a plane that he believed would be more maneuverable and faster. These nonconformities substantially impair the value of the Super "B" to plaintiff. The testimony of the four spray pilots and Dykes is evidence other than plaintiff's assertion which sustains an inference that plaintiff's needs are not met by the Super "B".

10. *Acceptance under 2-608.* Another requirement is that the purchaser accepted the goods on the reasonable assumption that the nonconformities would be cured, or without discovery of the nonconformities as induced by the difficulty of discovery or seller's assurances.

Hemmert's discovery of the Super "B"'s handling characteristics was postponed until after acceptance because of the timing of delivery and weather conditions. The court does not consider the absence of the aileron servos, EGT gauge, and push-to-talk switch nor the defective spray valve to be nonconformities. Defendant has effectively and timely cured by supplying these parts and replacements. Consequently, these alleged defects do not constitute nonconformities under the terms of 2-608.

11. *Remedy.* When a buyer rightfully revokes his acceptance, he may recover pursuant to *K.S.A. 84-2-711* a refund of the purchase price paid and incidental and consequential damages, which may include expenses reasonably incurred in inspection, receipt, transportation and care and custody of goods and any other commercially reasonable charge or expense in effecting cover or caused by delay or other breach. The buyer is also entitled to prejudgment interest from the date that revocation is attempted.

IT IS THEREFORE ORDERED that judgment is entered in favor of plaintiff and against defendant, and defendant is herein ordered to pay plaintiff the sum of $159,314.14, which are those damages set forth in plaintiff's exhibit 10 modifying the prejudgment interest to commence on September 30, 1985. Upon payment of the entire judgment, plaintiff shall make the Super "B" available upon one week's notice for defendant to pick up the Super "B" at the plaintiff's place of business in Oakley, Kansas.

IT IS FURTHER ORDERED that the Clerk of the Court shall enter judgment reflecting the same.

As the court notes in *Hemmert*, on its face, the substantial impairment requirement in 2-608 is subjective—the nonconformity must substantially impair the value of the goods to the buyer revoking her acceptance. And the Comments to 2-608 tell us that's exactly what the drafters intended:

> The test is not what the seller had reason to know at the time of contracting; the question is whether the nonconformity is such as will in fact cause a substantial impairment of value to the buyer though the seller had no advance knowledge of the buyer's particular circumstances.
>
> Comment 2. 2-608.

But as *Hemmert* also explains, the courts have inferred from the same language an objective component to the substantial impairment required for revocation. The buyer's claim that the nonconformity substantially impairs her ability to use the product for her intended purposes itself must be reasonable. The buyer can claim a subjective purpose for the goods—whatever idiosyncratic use she had in mind can form the basis of her claim of substantial impairment—but the objective requirement means that her claim that the defect prevents her from using the goods for that idiosyncratic purpose must be reasonable. The buyer's reaction to the defect—she can't use the product for her intended purpose—must be a reasonable reaction to that defect under the circumstances. Requiring some quantum of objectivity is necessary to prevent buyers from turning a subsequent change of mind about the wisdom of a purchase into a basis for upsetting the settled expectations of their sellers.

Of course, the inherent contradiction in requiring that something be subjective and objective at the same time has not been lost on judges and scholars:

> The cases seem to require both subjective and objective elements. The buyer must provide objective evidence that the value of the goods was substantially impaired, but this value is to be viewed through the unique needs and circumstances of that particular buyer and not those of the average buyer. However we dress it, this concept looks goofy. How can something be objective and, at the same time, subjective? Perhaps the courts are asking us to listen to *this* buyer's complaint—but not too closely.
>
> White and Summers, Uniform Commercial Code (6th ed. 2010) at 430.

PROBLEM 7 - 9

The store ordered an automated scale to weigh meat products and label them for sale. The seller promised the scale could weigh and label twenty trays of meat per minute, which was necessary if the scale was going to keep pace with the automated wrapping machine in the butcher shop, which wrapped the trays to be weighed at a pace of nineteen per minute. The seller assembled and installed the scale in the butcher shop and trained the shop's workers how to use it. After an initial test period, during which the scale performed as expected, Rae told the seller the store would keep the scale. But within a month, the scale slowed down to only twelve trays per minute. The seller returned to the shop to make adjustments to the scale for several months, eventually getting the scale to weigh fifteen trays per minute, which was still too slow to keep up with the wrapping machine. As a result, trays stacked up on the conveyer, jamming the wrapping machine and damaging product. Rae finally called the seller and told him to come get the scale; she did not want it and was taking back her acceptance. The seller claims that, although the scale is not working exactly as promised, its performance is still better than any other product on the market, and that Rae should be thankful it works as well as it does. Can Rae revoke her acceptance if the scale is the fastest scale available? 2-608.

PROBLEM 7 - 10

The store manager ordered ten thousand quarter-bushel paper shopping bags, into which the store's carry-outs packed a customer's groceries when they checked out. Shortly after the store began using the bags, the manager noticed that many of the bags were failing—the bottom seams were opening after they were packed with groceries. The manager figured out that the glue used to hold together the seams on the bottom of the bags broke down, allowing the seams to separate and everything in the bag to fall out if the bags became damp—as they would when loaded with dairy products or frozen items. The bags worked just fine as long as they were only loaded with dry goods—cans, cereal boxes, bakery goods—but customers did not often limit their purchases to dry goods. The manager called the seller and told him he was cancelling the transaction—the seller should come pick up the bags that had not yet been used, and the store would expect a refund of the purchase price. Can the store revoke its acceptance just because the bags can't do everything the manager thought they should? 2-608.

Article 2 also requires that the revoking buyer have an excuse for not addressing his problem with the goods before he accepted the goods. What is acceptable as an excuse depends on what the buyer knew at the time of acceptance. A buyer aware of a nonconformity who accepts anyway on the "reasonable" assumption that the seller will fix (cure) is excused for not taking care of the problem before acceptance, and can revoke acceptance if it meets the other requirements of 2-608. 2-608(1)(a). In the absence of an express representation by the seller that it will fix the problem, it's not clear what would make the buyer's assumption of cure reasonable. Prior course of dealing and trade usage should justify an assumption of cure, but beyond these it's an open question. It might be possible to create a reasonable assumption of cure where the parties understand that the seller will need to adapt the goods to the buyer's particular circumstances once installed.[8]

The buyer who is not aware of the nonconformity at the time of acceptance—presumably after having had an opportunity to inspect the goods—must have an excuse for not discovering the nonconformity prior to accepting the goods. Only two excuses work: (1) the nature of the defect made it difficult to discover during the inspection process—think latent defect; or (2) the buyer did not inspect the goods or did not inspect them as thoroughly as it usually would have because the seller assured the buyer everything was all right. 2-608(1)(b). In *Carmichael & Carmichael v. Nicholstone Cos.*, the buyer had ordered customized loose-leaf binders for Volume I and Volume II of a two-volume series of cassette tapes it sold. Each volume had its own title which was to be printed, along with the volume number, on the binder covers. The first sets of binders delivered conformed to the buyer's order, but in a subsequent order of several thousand binders of each volume, the Volume I binders were labeled with the title for Volume II. The buyer did not discover the mistake until months after the binders had been delivered. When the buyer sued to revoke its acceptance, the court rejected the buyer's claim that its failure to discover the error prior to acceptance was excused by the difficulty of discovering the mislabeling—the binders had been delivered in sealed boxes—explaining:

> Latent defects are more difficult to discover than patent ones. *See* 3 William D. Hawkland, *Uniform Commercial Code Series* § 2-608:04, at 90 (1984). Thus, courts view defects in complicated machinery or in products that are already packaged as being difficult to discover prior to acceptance and payment. *In re H. P. Tool Mfg. Corp.*, 37 B.R. 885, 887 (E.D. Penn. 1984). However, the goods and the defects involved in this case do not fall into either category. The error in Volume I's title was not difficult to discover. In fact, it was readily apparent on the cover of the binders and could have been discovered simply by opening any of the cardboard boxes containing the binders and inspecting their contents. Under similar facts, the Civil Court of the City of New York found that the buyer could neither reject nor revoke its acceptance of misprinted boxes because the printing error would have been readily apparent had the boxes been inspected when they were delivered.
>
> 1992 Tenn. App. LEXIS 633.

The next case looks at how a buyer might not discover a defect because of a seller's assurances.

---

8   White and Summers, *Uniform Commercial Code* at 430.

SMITH V. PENBRIDGE ASSOCS.

SUPERIOR COURT OF PENNSYLVANIA, 1995
655 A.2D 1015

OPINION BY POPOVICH, J.:

An emu is not uncommon in Australia or as a clue in an American crossword puzzle. But, unless our research was not extensive enough, we can state that emus have never before in Pennsylvania been the subject of litigation, litigation that has herein produced a small trove of contract law principles.

This is an appeal from the order of May 31, 1994, entered in the Court of Common Pleas of Clarion County denying appellant's motion for judgment notwithstanding the verdict or, in the alternative, for new trial. Herein, we are asked to determine whether appellant should be held liable for the sale of two male emus to appellees when appellant expressly warranted to appellees that the emus were a "proven breeder pair" i.e., a male and a female.

Before delving into our analysis of the novel questions at issue, we shed informative light on this creature from "The Land Down Under". An emu is a flightless bird which originates from Australia. An mature emu typically stands at 5 1/2 feet and weighs about 125 pounds. Its features resemble those of its bigger relative, the ostrich. For breeding purposes, emus have a better temperament than ostriches. The industry of emu breeding in the United States has grown significantly within the past decade because emus adapt easily to various climates and produce rapidly on far fewer acres of land in relationship to traditional livestock. Moreover, the popularity for emu breeding has grown because an emu efficiently produces the following: red meat which is low in fat and cholesterol but high in protein; oil which is used in medicinal and cosmetic products; leather which is used for boots, briefcases, purses and clothing; feathers which are used for fashion clothing and dusters; and broken eggs which are made into jewelry. A female emu usually begins laying at age 18–30 months and will continue laying for 20–25 years.

From our view of the record, we recount the history of this contract dispute over the sale of emus as follows: In July, 1992, appellee, Donna Smith, telephoned Tomie Clark, the manager of Penbridge Farms ("appellant"), in response to an advertisement appellant had placed in the July issue of *Emu Finder Guide* concerning the sale of proven breeder pairs. A proven breeder pair of emus consists of one male and one female, which had previously bonded, successfully bred and produced fertile eggs. Upon additional telephone exchanges, appellant informed appellees that a proven breeder pair was available for purchase. In 1992, appellees sent appellant a check in the amount of $4,000.00 as a down payment for the purchase of a proven breeder pair of emus. On August 4, 1992, appellees drove from Clarion County to appellant's farm in Michigan to purchase the emus. Ms. Clark and another agent of appellant selected the pair of emus from a pen that held another emu. Donna Smith, concerned that she and her husband were properly getting the proven breeder pair, asked appellant's agents several times whether the selected emus were a male and a female and whether they were a proven breeder pair.

The gender of an emu is not discernable by mere external observation, but appellant's agents assured appellees that the pair selected had successfully produced chicks. Appellees agreed to purchase the pair of emus and paid appellant the balance of the total price of $12,500.00. Appellees then returned home that evening to their farm in Clarion County with their newly acquired birds which they named, "Andrew" and "Rachel".

Upon arrival, appellees placed the two emus alone in the same pen. In late October, 1992, during the commencement of breeding season, Donna Smith noticed for the first time that both "Andrew" and "Rachel" were "grunting". Grunting is a male trait. Donna Smith immediately telephoned appellant's agent to inform appellant of the grunting. The agent advised Donna Smith that she should "vent sex" the emus to determine their gender. The next day, appellees performed the vent sexing on the two emus. The vent sexing revealed that "Andrew" was a male. But, much to their chagrin, appellees discovered that "Rachel" was also a male. Additionally, appellees telephoned appellant's agents to notify appellant that both emus were males and to request that appellant rectify their predicament.

However, communications failed, and on December 2, 1992, appellees brought suit against appellant seeking damages on grounds that the two male emus were worth substantially less than a proven breeder pair, and appellees suffered consequential damages for not selling chicks that would have hatched from the 1992–93 breeding season. On January 26–27, 1994, the lower court held a bench trial, and on February 8, 1994, the court below entered a verdict in favor of appellees.

Appellant also maintains that appellees failed to effectuate a revocation of an acceptance of the two emus within a reasonable time. In addressing this contention, we will scrutinize appellant's second issue raised herein concurrently to determine whether notice of the breach was proper. Appellant directs our Court's attention to *13 Pa.C.S.A. §§ 2608 (b), 2607 (c)(1)*, of the Uniform Commercial Code. Those sections read as follows:

§ 2608. Revocation of acceptance in whole or part

(b) Time and notice of revocation.—Revocation of *acceptance* must occur within a *reasonable time* after the buyer discovers or should have discovered the ground for it and before any substantial change in condition of the goods which is not caused by their own defects. It is not effective until the buyer notifies the seller of it.

§ 2607. Effect of acceptance; notice of breach; burden of establishing breach after acceptance; notice of claim or litigation to person answerable over

(c) Notice of breach.—Where a tender has been accepted:

(1) the buyer must within a reasonable time after he discovers or should have discovered any breach notify the seller of breach or be barred from any remedy; ... *13 Pa.C.S.A. §§ 2608 (b), 2607 (c)(1)* (emphasis added).

"Under Pennsylvania law, what is a reasonable time after tender or delivery for rejection or revocation of defective goods is generally deemed a question of fact to be resolved by the fact finder, and no express outside time limit is set." *Ford Motor Credit Co. v. Caiazzo, 387 Pa. Super.* 561, 564 A.2d 931 (1989) (citations omitted).

Upon review, we conclude that the lower court's finding that appellees revoked their acceptance of the two male emus within a reasonable time is adequately supported by competent evidence. The record reveals that appellees ascertained that "Rachel" and "Andrew" were not a "pure breeding pair" of emus when they examined the birds internally in late October, 1992. Within two days after the sex venting, appellants were fully apprised by appellees of the breach. Appellants argue that appellees *should have* discovered the breach earlier. We disagree. Appellant rebukes appellees for not sex venting the emus on appellant's farm at the time of purchase or immediately upon their return to Pennsylvania. Appellant maintains that this procedure was easily accessible to appellees and that appellees had a responsibility of exercising it themselves. We note that appellant blindly excuses itself from undertaking that same task before selling the emus to appellees. Further, the lower court, sitting as the fact finder in this case, determined that sex venting was dangerous both to the breeding emu and the person administering it. Trial Opinion 5/31/94 at 12.[9]

---

9   Appellees presented testimony revealing that sex venting may cause an infection of the sex organs and may even cause an emu to go into shock. Trial N.T. 1/26/94 at 123-124. Further, the person administering the sex venting may become kicked or clawed by the emu. Trial N.T. 1/26/94 at 123.

Appellant expressly warranted the emus to be a "pure breeder pair" and reassured appellees that the emus were as represented. Indeed, we find that the nature of the agreement and goods at issue coupled with assurances had the effect of inducing appellees to delay an internal inspection of the emus. *See* 13 Pa.C.S.A. Comment 3 of *§ 2608,* U.C.C. (effect of assurances is that they induce the buyer to delay discovery). Upon returning to their Clarion County farm, appellees were not presented with any facts or circumstances that would reasonably lead them to question the breeding ability of the emus until Donna heard both grunting in late October, 1992. Although "Rachel" *may have looked like a female emu and walked like a female emu, it certainly did not sound like a female emu.* Thereafter, appellees promptly notified appellant of the breach. *Compare Rad Services, Inc. v. American Refining Group, Inc.,* 330 Pa. Super. 308, 479 A.2d 565 (1984) (retailer's notice of breach to distributor was timely when several months had elapsed before retailer discovered gas shortage which was attributed to distributor's faulty terminal meter). Accordingly, we find no error of law in the lower court's disposition of appellant's first and second issues raised herein.

PROBLEM 7 - 11

The produce manager convinced Rae that the department would operate more efficiently if his staff did not have to hand wrap all of the iceberg lettuce sold by the store. Rae agreed to buy a used lettuce wrapper the manager saw advertised in the local equipment journal. The seller told Rae the machine had recently been completely reconditioned and was just like new, and insisted on setting up the machine at the store and programming it for the produce department. The seller told Rae and the produce manager to leave the wrapper powered up 24/7 to avoid having to reprogram it. Several months after the wrapper was installed, a power outage at the store shut down all electric equipment, including the wrapper, for a short time. When power was restored, the wrapper rebooted itself but flashed a fault warning on the display screen indicating that the internal drive was corrupted and needed immediate replacement. The service rep sent by the manufacturer to look at the wrapper told Rae that the drive unit had been running on life support for months and needed immediate replacement. Rae now understood why the seller had been so eager to install the wrapper himself and had insisted that it never be powered off. Rae called the seller and told him she was calling the deal off—she wanted her money back because the machine obviously had never been reconditioned as represented by the seller. The seller claims the problem was not a latent defect, and therefore Rae cannot take back her acceptance. Is the seller right? 2-608.

In addition to the induced-by-assurances issue, the *Smith* case considered the timeliness of the buyer's revocation, which, under 2-608, must "occur within a reasonable time after the buyer discovers or should have discovered the ground for it." 2-608(2). Since the reasonable time requirement limits prejudice to the seller that might be caused by any deterioration in the goods, the type of goods at issue may be dispositive of whether the buyer has revoked within a reasonable time. What's reasonable for industrial equipment won't be the same as what's reasonable for perishable or seasonal goods. And although reasonableness will usually be a question of fact for the jury, "there are simply situations in which a buyer has delayed so excessively that his actions become untimely as a matter of law." *Chernick v. Casares,* 759 S.W.2d 832 (Ky. App. 1988). But where the buyer has delayed revoking because of protracted efforts by the seller to fix the problem, the time lost during the failed attempts at repair is usually not held against the buyer. If it were, buyers would have little incentive to give sellers an opportunity to save the deal and avoid the expense and disruption of litigation.

PROBLEM 7 - 12

Even if the store had an excuse for not discovering the defect before it accepted the wrapper in the last problem, shouldn't Rae or the produce manager have discovered it long before the power outage? What if the owner's manual instructed that parts of the wrapper should be removed and cleaned on a regular basis and the wrapper had to be powered down to remove the parts for cleaning? 2-608(2).

Regardless of whether the buyer's decision to revoke is made within reasonable time, a substantial change in the condition of the goods between acceptance and revocation terminates the buyer's power to revoke acceptance—but only if the change in condition is not caused by the defect on which revocation is based. The substantial change in condition requirement

> insures that post-acceptance revocation, a more extraordinary remedy as the seller may have long since considered the transaction closed, is not abused by forcing sellers to take back used or mistreated goods.

Lakawanna Leather Co. v. Martin & Stewart, 750 F.2d 1197 (8th Cir. 1984). The next case considers how the "no substantial change in condition" requirement applies when the grounds for revocation can only be discovered by altering or processing the goods for their intended use.

SCD RMA, LLC v. FARSIGHTED ENTERS., INC.
UNITED STATES DISTRICT COURT FOR THE DISTRICT OF HAWAII, 2008
REPORTER
591 F. SUPP. 2D 1131

BACKGROUND

RMA and Farsighted entered into a contract effective July 12, 2006, in which Farsighted agreed to create a die mould and produce vinyl window louvers for RMA.[10] RMA had contracted separately with HAMCO, a window installation subcontractor who would install the louvers at Waimea Canyon School in Waimea, Kauai, and with another window installation contractor, who would install the louvers in five Oahu schools as part of a renovation project contracted by the State of Hawaii Department of Education.

Farsighted manufactured the louvers based on a design submitted by James Fernando Guardia, an engineer with RMA.

Farsighted manufactured the vinyl louvers and RMA received them in three separate shipments on April 20, 2007, May 3, 2007, and July 23, 2007. The louvers were subsequently delivered to HAMCO, who then cut and installed them at Waimea Canyon School.

Shortly after receipt of the first shipment of louvers, RMA discovered certain defects, including defective vinyl or no vinyl in some of the blades. RMA informed Farsighted of these defects on May 25, 2007. According to RMA, Farsighted gave verbal assurances that it would correct the defects in later shipments. On July 26, 2007, HAMCO informed RMA that the weather strips on the louvers were detaching from the products from normal day-to-day use. The next day, RMA faxed a copy of HAMCO's email to Farsighted and informed it that the problem with the louvers could result in financial loss and harm to RMA's business reputation. On July 31, 2007, HAMCO provided RMA

---

10   Louvers are windows or blinds with horizontal slats that are angled to admit light and air but designed to keep out rain.

with a detailed description of the problems with the louvers. On August 8, 2007, RMA sent a letter to Farsighted seeking remedial measures, including replacement of all louver blades, establishment of a warranty trust fund to cover expenses relating to replacement installation, written assurances as to the quality of the other louvers, and a time-line as to the manufacture of new louvers.

Over the course of the next several months, RMA and Farsighted quarreled over the defect in the louvers and communicated often about their respective positions. Farsighted claimed that it produced the vinyl louvers in compliance with the design submitted by Guardia. RMA, relying on a site report conducted by Phil Haisley of Architectural Diagnostics, Ltd., argued that the defect was a failure of manufacturing and materials used by Farsighted.

After the State of Hawaii sent notice to RMA that it would have to replace the louvers at no cost to the schools, RMA decided to obtain replacement louvers from a different supplier. RMA filed suit on October 3, 2007 against Farsighted in the Circuit Court of the First Circuit, State of Hawaii, alleging breaches of contractual duties and implied warranties. Farsighted removed the case to this Court on October 26, 2007.

Finally, on November 7, 2007, after filing of the complaint and removal to federal court, RMA sent Farsighted a letter in which RMA specifically revoked its acceptance of the louvers and informed Farsighted that it sought costs associated with the purchase of replacement louvers and re-installation.

DISCUSSION

This case is governed by the Uniform Commercial Code ("UCC"), which was adopted by Hawaii in 1965 and codified in Chapter 490 of the Hawaii Revised Statutes. *See Haw. Rev. Stat. § 490:10-101; Haw. Rev. Stat §§ 490:1-101, et seq.* Very little State case law exists interpreting the various provisions of the Hawaii UCC. Accordingly, this Court looks to established secondary authorities and out-of-state court decisions as persuasive—though not binding—authority.

****

Finally, revocation must be accomplished prior to any substantial change in condition of the goods. *Haw. Rev. Stat. § 490:2-608(2).* This rule reflects the UCC's policy that the allegedly defective goods are to be restored to the seller in a reasonable condition. *See* Comments to *Haw. Rev. Stat. § 490:2-608(2).* It is unclear from case law, however, whether this rule applies in situations in which the buyer only discovers the alleged defect during processing of the goods. In cases such as this, where the alleged nonconformity cannot be discovered merely by looking at the louver but only after cutting and installation into a window, the question is whether RMA may still be able to revoke acceptance even though it admittedly altered the original product manufactured and delivered by Farsighted.

Farsighted cites to *Trinkle v. Schumacher Co.,* 100 Wis. 2d 13, 301 N.W.2d 255 (Wis. App. 1980), for its contention that RMA could not revoke its acceptance once HAMCO had cut the louvers and installed them into Waimea Canyon School. In *Trinkle,* the plaintiff ordered fabric from the defendant for use in making Roman shades. After delivery and during processing of the fabric into Roman shades, it was discovered that the vinyl backing was improperly applied to the fabric and therefore could not be used. According to the court, the condition was not determinable until the fabric had actually been processed into the Roman shades and cut by the plaintiff. The court, in dicta, stated that the plaintiff could not effectively revoke acceptance because "the evidence is uncontroverted that the revocation of acceptance occurred after the fabric was cut which was a 'substantial change in condition of the goods which is not caused by their own defects.'"

Later cases, however, have questioned this logic. In *Lackawanna Leather Co. v. Martin & Stewart, Ltd.,* 730 F.2d 1197, 1202-1203 (8th Cir. 1984), a manufacturer of upholstery leather purchased cattle hides from a hide supplier. After a routine visual inspection revealed no obvious defects, the plaintiff began processing the hides by chemically removing salt and hair and "splitting" them. The splitting process revealed grain and beetle damage, which rendered them unusable.

The Eighth Circuit, weighing several factors, held that the district judge was justified in submitting the plaintiff's revocation of acceptance theory to the jury. First, evidence was offered which showed that only by processing the hides could the beetle damage be discovered. Secondly, the defendants sold the hides knowing that the processing was necessary to make the hides commercially usable to the plaintiff. Given those factors, the Eighth Circuit concluded that no substantial change in condition occurs when the buyer attempts to conform the goods to their bargained-for condition.

The Fifth Circuit has also echoed the policies of *Lackawanna*. In *Deere & Co. v. Johnson,* 271 F.3d 613, 620 (5th Cir. 2001), the court noted that in almost all cases involving a dispute over a "substantial change" the buyer engaged in some activity which altered the goods. The court held, however, that "simple depreciation alone" usually does not constitute a substantial change in the condition of the good. This policy is consistent with the doctrine of revocation of acceptance because the doctrine is meant to remedy a situation in which a latent defect arises. If simple depreciation of the nonconforming good was enough to nullify the revocation of acceptance, the court explained, a buyer might never be able to revoke acceptance of a good with a latent defect.

For these reasons, this Court agrees that HAMCO's cutting and installation of the louvers did not substantially change the louvers for the purposes of revocation. As in *Lackawanna*, if the defect in the weather stripping could not be revealed upon mere visual inspection, RMA may not be barred from revoking acceptance simply because they cut and installed the louvers. Moreover, it appears Farsighted sold the louvers to RMA knowing that cutting and installation were necessary for the louvers to be commercially usable. It is for the jury to decide whether, in fact, the defect was latent and undiscoverable by RMA upon simple inspection and whether RMA effectively revoked. This Court will not bar RMA's claims as a matter of law simply because they altered the condition of the vinyl louvers in the course of installation.

A substantial change in condition that eliminates a buyer's right to revoke acceptance takes many forms and can result merely from the buyer using the goods for their intended purpose. Processing the goods (after the defect is discovered), improperly maintaining the goods, modifying the goods, reselling the goods, and installing the goods have all resulted in a disqualifying substantial change in the condition of the goods. So has depreciation—at least that which occurs during a prolonged period between acceptance and revocation. The cases cover a broad spectrum. In *Village of Mobile Homes v. Porter*, the court rejected the seller's argument that the condition of the mobile home it sold had undergone a substantial change in its condition when the buyer repainted the entire exterior of the home prior to revoking her acceptance. The court reasoned that the "no substantial change in condition" requirement in 2-608(2)

> was intended to protect the seller from changes which deteriorate or take away from the value of the goods sold. § 2.608(b), comment 6, *supra*. As stated previously, the jury found that the improvements made by appellee to the mobile home increased its value by $1,000.
>
> 716 S.W.2d 543 (Tex. App. 1986).

PROBLEM 7 - 13

Rae's father installed an automatic car wash next to the gas station at the far end of the store's parking lot. The car wash has a tunnel system design that pulls cars through a series of cleaning mechanisms inside the "tunnel." Last year, Rae had to replace the rotary top brush because the foam in the brush was so old that the brush finally disintegrated. She bought the replacement brush from the company that had originally built and installed the car wash at the store. Last week, several customers complained that their cars had been severely scratched going through the car wash. The scratches, as it turned out, were caused by the new rotary top brush—defective bearings in the shaft of the brush had, over time as it continued to be used, sheared off part of the spindle on which the brush rotated, freezing the brush in a position that scratched cars as they were pulled through it. Rae called the seller and told it she was sending the brush back and expected a full refund of the purchase price. The seller refused to take it back because the brush was useless with the spindle sheared off. Does the damage to the spindle bar Rae from revoking her acceptance? 2-608(2).

A buyer who remains in possession of the goods after revoking her acceptance—like the buyer who retains possession after rejecting the goods—must take care not to do anything with the goods that a court might later find to be inconsistent with her claim that she had put the goods back on the seller. A revoking buyer is essentially claiming that the goods now belong to the seller again, and courts have held that buyers who take any acts that are inconsistent with the seller's ownership of those goods have "reaccepted" them. Using the goods after revocation would seem to be inconsistent with the seller's ownership—we saw that it was when the buyer attempted to reject goods—but courts have tolerated some use of the goods by buyer after revocation. But when does some use become too much use? The next case looks at how we should draw that line.

DEERE & CO. V. JOHNSON

UNITED STATES COURT OF APPEALS FOR THE FIFTH CIRCUIT, 2001
271 F.3D 613

Opinion by: E. GRADY JOLLY, Circuit Judge:

Deere financed a combine its dealer, Parker Tractor & Implement Company ("Parker"), sold to Johnson. Johnson was unhappy with the combine because it would not do the job. Deere was unhappy with Johnson because he failed to make any payments on the loan. Johnson wrote Deere a letter revoking acceptance of the combine. Deere refused to take it back. Johnson continued to use the combine. Deere finally sued Johnson to collect the unpaid balance on the loan. Johnson counter-claimed against Deere, as the manufacturer of the combine, for breach of implied and express warranties, breach of the implied warranty of fitness for a particular purpose, and intentional misrepresentations. The jury returned a verdict that effectively awarded zero to both parties. The district court conformed the pleadings to the evidence and entered a quantum meruit award for Deere for the rental value of the combine while Johnson was using it.

Today's appeal addresses three issues: First, whether Johnson effectively revoked acceptance in the view of his continuing to assert ownership of the combine and failing to return it to Deere; and finally, whether Deere presented sufficient evidence of the rental value of the combine. We hold that under the circumstances of this case, Johnson effectively revoked acceptance of the combine; and that Deere presented evidence to support the jury's determination of the rental value of the combine. At the end of the day, this case is a "wash"—neither party receives anything. Accordingly, we reverse and remand for entry of a take-nothing judgment.

I

In 1994, Edward Johnson bought a combine from Parker, a retailer for Deere located in Tunica, Mississippi. Johnson made a down payment of $30,634.36. He financed the remainder of the purchase price with Deere, using the combine as security for the loan. The combine was a lemon. Throughout the harvest season of 1994, Johnson made service requests to Parker. Each time Parker sent its mechanic to Johnson's farm to repair the combine. Finally, on March 3, 1995, Johnson sent a letter to Deere, which revoked acceptance, tendered the combine, and asked for a replacement. In a letter dated May 12, 1995, Deere refused to take the combine back. It stated "Deere & Company certainly sees no reason to replace this combine and it is not willing to accept it back." Johnson continued to use the combine during the harvest season of 1995, as well as during the spring of 1996. After this lawsuit was initiated, Deere filed a replevin action, repossessed and sold the combine in July of 1997. Although Johnson used the combine from 1994 until the spring of 1996, he made no payments on the loan contract.

II

On September 26, 1995, Deere filed a complaint seeking to collect on the contract. Johnson counter-claimed. He alleged breach of contract, breach of express and implied warranties, breach of the implied warranty of fitness for a particular purpose, and intentional misrepresentations. Johnson sought lost profits, punitive and consequential damages. The jury found for Johnson on his breach of warranty claim and *against* Deere on its breach of contract claim. The jury awarded Johnson the down payment that he had made on the combine, $30,634.86, but subtracted $70,000 from this award for the fair rental value of the combine for the period of Johnson's use.

Based on the legal theory of quantum meruit—raised for the first time in Deere's post-verdict 15(b) motion—the district court amended the pleadings and entered an amended judgment for Deere. The amended judgment awarded Deere $70,000 minus Johnson's down payment and any prejudgment interest on that down payment. Notwithstanding that (1) the jury had found in favor of Johnson and against Deere, and (2) the district court had found against Deere as a matter of law on all of its asserted claims, Deere walked away from the district court with about $35,000.

Both parties now appeal.

III

We first address Deere's appeal. Deere appeals the district court's denial of its motion for judgment as a matter of law with respect to its contract claim. Deere moved for judgment as a matter of law twice—once during trial and once in its post-verdict motion.

Deere's argument is that it was entitled to collect on the loan contract for the combine because Johnson's continued use of the combine nullified his revocation of acceptance as a matter of law. The district court denied both motions.

It is not surprising that Mississippi law requires that buyers pay the contract price for any goods accepted, unless that acceptance is later effectively revoked. *MISS. CODE ANN. §§ 75-2-607(1), 75-2-608* (1999). Deere argues that because Johnson failed to revoke his acceptance of the combine, he is bound by the contract, and thus the jury erred in awarding Johnson the return of his down payment. On appeal, the question is whether, viewing the evidence in the light most favorable to Johnson, a reasonable jury could have found that Johnson revoked acceptance of the combine.

As we have noted, the Mississippi version of the UCC provides for the revocation of acceptance. A buyer revoking acceptance of goods has the same duties as a buyer rejecting a shipment of goods; in most cases, a buyer must discontinue asserting any ownership over the goods. MISS. CODE ANN. § 75-2-602(2)(a) (1999) ("after rejection any exercise of ownership by the buyer with respect to any commercial unit is wrongful as against the seller"). It is undisputed that Johnson notified Deere of his revocation in a letter of March 3, 1995. It is further undisputed that Johnson continued to use the combine after this letter of revocation. Still further, Johnson generated a tax benefit for himself by claiming depreciation of the combine on his tax forms in both 1995 and 1996. Without doubt, these two actions represent ownership activities by Johnson. The question remains: Do these activities nullify Johnson's revocation of acceptance as a matter of law?

Mississippi courts have addressed this question in several cases. In *North River Homes v. Bosarge,* 594 So. 2d 1153 (Miss. 1992) the court addressed whether a family's failure to move out of a "lemon" mobile home waived their revocation of acceptance. The court, in finding no waiver, reasoned that "[the family's] mistaken belief that North River would fulfill its assurances to repair the defects is but one reason why the Bosarges did not move out of their home. Another reason is simple and [understandable]: When you tie up all your savings into purchasing a home, you cannot take it and park it somewhere. You have got to live in it until you get the people to clear your lot so you can put another [mobile home] on it."

In a case involving a defective copier, however, the court held that the failure to return the copier did vitiate the revocation of acceptance. Nevertheless, the court noted in dicta that this might not always be true. *J.L. Teel Co., Inc. v. Houston United Sales, Inc.,* 491 So. 2d 851, 859 (Miss. 1986) (stating "without doubt, failure to surrender the copier did not per se render ineffective Houston's revocation").

Other states agree that continued use of non-conforming goods does not, in all cases, waive the revocation of acceptance. See *Wilk Paving, Inc. v. Southworth-Milton, Inc.,* 162 Vt. 552, 649 A.2d 778, 781-82 (Vt. 1994) (failure to return defective asphalt roller does not forfeit the revocation of acceptance); *McCullough v. Bill Swad Chrysler-Plymouth, Inc.,* 5 Ohio St. 3d 181, 449 N.E.2d 1289, 1291 (Ohio 1983) (failure to return automobile did not forfeit revocation); *Aubrey's R.V. Center, Inc. v. Tandy Corp.,* 46 Wn. App. 595, 731 P.2d 1124, 1129 (Wash.App.Ct. 1987) (failure to return software did not forfeit revocation).

Allowing continued use of the good is not the general rule, however. Typically, the law requires that a buyer return a non-conforming good, purchase a replacement, if necessary, and then sue for breach. MISS. CODE ANN. §§ 75-2-602, 75-2-714 (1999). The rationale is that even non-conforming goods have value, and by requiring a prompt return of the goods, the law enables a seller to resell the goods before they substantially depreciate in value. As the Mississippi Supreme Court has noted, however, a buyer, with no ability to replace the defective good, suffers substantial injury if forced to cede ownership of that good. The law thus weighs the two effects; that is, where the cost of replacement is low, the injury to the seller from the depreciation of the good outweighs the injury to the buyer that results from surrendering ownership. Thus, in such a situation the law requires the return of the non-conforming good. On the other hand, when the cost of replacement is high, the injury resulting to the buyer from returning the good outweighs the seller's injury of depreciation; hence, in this situation the cases do not penalize the buyer when he reasonably retains the non-conforming good.

As we have noted, Mississippi case law employs this principle. In North Rivers Homes, the cost to the family of giving up the trailer was high. Hence, the court held that the failure to "move-out" did not waive revocation. On the other hand, in the Teel case, the company easily could have purchased another copier, and hence, the court held that the failure to surrender the copier nullified the attempt to revoke acceptance of the copier.

Here, the evidence shows that Johnson's cost of replacement was high. Johnson's credit was adversely affected when he failed to make payments on the loan for the combine. The record reflects that Johnson was operating close to the margin; he admittedly could not make but a few of the payments. It is unlikely that any combine dealer would have either rented or sold to Johnson under these circumstances. Without a combine, Johnson's ability to farm would be severely impaired. With little farm production, he could not mitigate the damages he suffered as a result of the defective combine. Thus, as with the mobile home owners in North River Homes, the record demonstrates that the damage to Johnson from ceding ownership of the combine would have been high.

Deere also maintains that Johnson continued to use the combine, which naturally caused depreciation, and that this change of the good rendered his revocation of acceptance ineffective. Other than depreciation, Deere does not allege that Johnson damaged the combine. Deere bases its depreciation-as-change argument on the language of the statute: "Revocation must occur within a reasonable time … and before any substantial change in the condition of the goods not caused by their defects." MISS. CODE ANN. § 75-2-608(2) (1999). Deere cites no cases in which depreciation by itself was deemed a substantial change under this section of the Mississippi UCC. It seems that in almost all cases involving a "substantial change" the buyer engaged in some activity which altered the goods. See *Intervale Steel Corp. v. Borg & Beck Div., Borg-Warner Corp.*, 578 F. Supp. 1081 (E.D.Mich. 1984) (buyer broke up goods into parts), aff'd, 762 F.2d 1008 (6th Cir 1985)) [**14]; *Trinkle v. Schumacher Co.*, 100 Wis. 2d 13, 301 N.W.2d 255 (Wis.Ct.App. 1980) (buyer cut fabric); *Toyomenka (America), Inc. v. Combined Metals Corp.*, 139 Ill. App. 3d 654, 487 N.E.2d 1172, 94 Ill. Dec. 295 (Ill.App.Ct. 1985) (buyer cut goods into narrow strips).That simple depreciation alone usually does not constitute a substantial change in the condition of the good is consistent with the doctrine of revocation of acceptance because the doctrine is meant to remedy a situation in which a latent defect arises. If simple depreciation of the non-conforming good was enough to nullify the revocation of acceptance, a buyer might not be able to revoke acceptance of a good with a latent defect.

Furthermore, Deere's refusal to accept the return of the combine undermines its argument that Johnson failed to revoke acceptance as a matter of law. How does one return a combine when the dealer refuses to take it back—park it, perhaps, illegally in their lot? We find unpersuasive the premise of Deere's argument: that a seller can refuse to accept the return of a non-conforming good, and then claim that the buyer nullified his revocation by not returning the good in question.[11]

Most important for the case at hand, the issue of whether a buyer has effectively revoked acceptance is a factual one. For the reasons outlined above, we think that a reasonable jury could have concluded—despite Johnson's continued use of the combine—that he effectively revoked acceptance of the combine on March 5, 1995. The district court's denial of Deere's motion for judgment as a matter of law was thus correct.

Other courts apply a "reasonableness" test to determine when post-revocation use causes a reacceptance of the goods, using various factors to assess the reasonableness of the buyer's conduct based on the facts of the case:

> The continued reasonable use of an automobile should not as a matter of law prevent the buyer from revoking acceptance. What constitutes reasonable use is a question of fact for the jury which must be decided under the circumstances of each case. In the future, juries should be instructed that continued use, if reasonable, does not invalidate a revocation of acceptance. The jury should be further instructed that factors to consider on the issue of reasonable use are "the seller's instructions to the buyer after revocation of acceptance; the degree of economic and other hardship that the buyer would suffer if he discontinued using the defective goods; the reasonableness of the buyer's use after revocation as a method of mitigating damages; the degree of prejudice to the seller; and whether the seller acted in bad faith."

Liarikos v. Mello, 639 N.E.2d 719, (Mass. 1994). Courts are especially tolerant of post-revocation use when buyers keep the goods in order to give sellers a chance to fix the problem(s) that caused the

---

11   To be precise, Deere did demand the return of the combine after the initiation of this lawsuit. Nevertheless, up to the filling of the lawsuit in 1995, the evidence indicates that Deere would not accept the return of the combine.

buyer to revoke its acceptance. And, as we might expect, consumer buyers usually get a larger window of reasonableness than commercial parties.

Problem 7 - 14

Earlier this year, Rae replaced the old van the store had been using for home deliveries to customers with a new Ford Transit commercial van. Several weeks after the store took delivery of the van, it broke down while out on a home delivery and was never the same again. Over the next several months, the store experienced a parade of problems with the van—everything from the brakes to the cooling system to the transmission broke down at some point. Initially, the dealer was willing to resolve the problems, but as time went on and the problems continued, the dealer became less and less accommodating. Last month, Rae ordered a Nissan NV van and returned to the Ford dealer with the Ford Transit, demanding a refund of the purchase price she had paid for the van. The dealer refused to take back the van and refund Rae's payment, so she drove the Ford back to the store and has continued to use it for home deliveries until yesterday, when the Nissan was ready to be picked up. The store has put about six thousand miles on the Ford since Rae attempted to return it. Did the store, in effect, reaccept the Ford by continuing to use it after the dealer refused to take it back? 2-608.

As consumers, we tend to be more inclined to hold problems we experience with the products we buy against the manufacturer of the product rather than the local shop that sold it to us. When the Maytag washer I bought from the appliance store in town fails, I will, of course, lodge my initial complaint with the local shop. But if the problem is not resolved to my satisfaction, ultimately I'm going to want to hold Maytag responsible—after all, Maytag built the washer and put its name on it—and not the local appliance shop. If, because of its problems, I decide I cannot live with the washer any longer—I want out of the deal—can I make my revocation claim against Maytag? Can I put the washer back on Maytag and expect Maytag to refund what I paid the local shop for the washer? The following case evaluates the propriety of revoking acceptance against a manufacturer when the manufacturer was not actually a party to the sales contract.

Newmar Corp. v. McCrary

Supreme Court of Nevada, 2013
309 P.3d 1021

By the Court, CHERRY, J.[12]:

In this opinion, we consider whether a purchaser of a motor home may revoke acceptance and recover the purchase price from the motor home's manufacturer under the Uniform Commercial Code (UCC). We hold that a purchaser is entitled to revoke acceptance of the motor home against its manufacturer where, as here, privity exists between the manufacturer and the buyer because the manufacturer interjected itself into the sales process and had direct dealings with the buyer to ensure the completion of the transaction.

---

12   The Honorable Kristina Pickering, Chief Justice, voluntarily recused herself from participation in the decision of this matter.

FACTS AND PROCEDURAL HISTORY

Respondent Allison McCrary purchased a luxury motor home manufactured by appellant Newmar Corporation from Wheeler's Las Vegas RV. The purchase included Newmar's two-year express warranty for repair and service. After purchasing the motor home, McCrary let it remain in Wheeler's possession for repairs, due to some issues noticed during the test drives. A week later, McCrary returned to inspect and pick up the motor home. Noticing continued problems with the motor home during the inspection, McCrary met with a Newmar factory representative. She stated that she would not take possession of the motor home until the representative assured her that Newmar would take care of any problems and that there was a full, bumper-to-bumper warranty. After receiving the sought-after reassurances from Newmar, McCrary took possession of the motor home.

Shortly thereafter, the motor home experienced significant electrical problems, making it unsafe to drive and resulting in repeated delays and canceled vacation plans for McCrary. After numerous repairs at the Newmar factory and other repair shops, McCrary attempted to revoke her acceptance of the motor home from Newmar, but Newmar rejected the revocation. McCrary then filed the underlying action asserting, inter alia, causes of action for revocation of acceptance, breach of contract, and breach of warranty against Newmar.[13]

Prior to trial, both parties made offers of judgment. Neither offer was accepted. Following a bench trial, based on the particular facts of this case, the district court concluded that McCrary did not take possession of the motor home when she signed the contract and would not have completed the purchase and eventually taken possession except for the interactions with and assurances made by Newmar's representative to McCrary. Ultimately, the district court found in favor of McCrary and awarded her $406,500 in damages—the $385,000 purchase price for the motor home based on the revocation of acceptance, but required McCrary to return the motor home as part of the revocation, $12,500 for the cost of insuring the motor home, and $9,000 for storage fees—plus $44,251.40 in prejudgment interest and $107,581.50 in attorney fees. The court entered judgment accordingly, and these appeals followed.

DISCUSSION

We must first determine whether revocation of acceptance is an available cause of action against a manufacturer before we can reach the issues of damages and attorney fees.

Revoking acceptance from Newmar

Newmar argues that, under Nevada's applicable UCC provision, *NRS 104.2608*, a buyer can only revoke acceptance from a seller, and while it manufactured the motor home, it was not a seller of the motor home. Thus, Newmar contends that Wheeler's is the only entity from whom McCrary can revoke acceptance and that, because McCrary revoked acceptance with the wrong entity, she alone must bear the consequences of that mistake.

McCrary contends that the district court correctly determined that Newmar was a co-seller based on Newmar's exclusive warranty and its employee's participation in the sales process. McCrary asserts that Newmar should be held to its actions.

The UCC provision governing revocation of acceptance was adopted and codified in Nevada as *NRS 104.2608*. It allows a buyer to revoke her acceptance of a purchased good if the item suffers from a "nonconformity [that] substantially impairs its value to the buyer" and the buyer accepted the item on the understanding that the seller would cure the nonconformity or was induced into accepting a nonconforming item "either by the difficulty of discovery before acceptance or by the seller's assurances."

---

13   McCrary also asserted claims against Wheeler's. Wheeler's was subsequently removed from the litigation during the summary judgment stage because McCrary attempted to revoke acceptance only from Newmar.

NRS 104.2608(1)(a),(b); *see also NRS 104.2608(2)* (requiring notification to the seller of the defect and timeliness for revocation). Under the UCC, "'[s]eller' means a person who sells or contracts to sell goods." *NRS 104.2103(1)(c)*. Here, there is no question as to the motor home's nonconformity, and thus we turn directly to whether the manufacturer can be considered a "seller" under the UCC.

We have previously addressed revocation of acceptance against the immediate seller, but we have not yet determined whether revocation of acceptance is available against a manufacturer. The Legislature has given some guidance, directing our courts to liberally construe and apply the UCC to "make uniform the law among the various jurisdictions." *NRS 104.1103(1)(c)*. However, the jurisdictions are split as to whether revocation of acceptance is proper against a manufacturer, giving us the opportunity to decide the issue de novo.

In revocation of acceptance cases, the term "seller" has been restricted to the immediate seller by a majority of jurisdictions but has been inclusive of the manufacturer by a minority of jurisdictions. A majority of jurisdictions have determined that revocation is not available against a manufacturer because the manufacturer is not a "seller" under the UCC. *See, e.g., Seekings v. Jimmy GMC of Tucson, Inc.,* 130 Ariz. 596, 638 P.2d 210, 214 (Ariz. 1981) (following "the logic as well as the letter of the U.C.C." to require privity and hold that a motor home "manufacturer who does not sell to the purchaser [directly and for whom the seller was not agent] cannot be liable for revocation and attendant damages"); *Griffith v. Latham Motors, Inc.,* 128 Idaho 356, 913 P.2d 572, 577 (Idaho 1996) (determining that the manufacturer could not be liable under a revocation claim because it did not sell the vehicle to the plaintiffs); *Henderson v. Chrysler Corp.,* 191 Mich. App. 337, 477 N.W.2d 505, 507-08 (Mich. Ct. App. 1991) (rejecting revocation against non-selling manufacturer when there was no privity and leaving plaintiff with remedies under a warranty); *Neal v. SMC Corp.,* 99 S.W.3d 813, 816-18 (Tex. App. 2003) (noting that because "[t]he nature of a revocation claim logically requires privity of contract[,] ... revocation is available to the buyer only against the immediate seller"; the motor home manufacturer, "in the absence of a contractual relationship with the consumer, is not a seller" by virtue of a manufacturer's express warranty); *see generally Fedrick v. Mercedes-Benz USA, L.L.C.,* 366 F. Supp. 2d 1190, 1200 (N.D. Ga. 2005); *Conte v. Dwan Lincoln-Mercury, Inc.,* 172 Conn. 112, 374 A.2d 144, 150 (Conn. 1976); *Hardy v. Winnebago Indus., Inc.,* 120 Md. App. 261, 706 A.2d 1086, 1091 (Md. Ct. Spec. App. 1998); *Ayanru v. Gen. Motors Acceptance Corp.,* 130 Misc. 2d 440, 495 N.Y.S.2d 1018, 1023 (Civ. Ct. 1985); *Reece v. Yeager Ford Sales, Inc.,* 155 W. Va. 461, 184 S.E.2d 727, 731 (W. Va. 1971). According to these courts, revocation is not available against the manufacturer unless there is a direct contractual relationship between the manufacturer and the buyer or an agency relationship between the manufacturer and the seller. The rationale behind this position is that revocation is intended to return the buyer and seller to their original positions and that because the manufacturer does not own the goods or receive the purchase price when the goods are sold, it cannot be involved in restoring the parties to their former positions.

Conversely, a minority of states have held that revocation of acceptance can be had against entities further removed from the transaction than the immediate seller, such as the manufacturer. *See, e.g., Ford Motor Credit Co. v. Harper,* 671 F.2d 1117, 1126 (8th Cir. 1982); *Durfee v. Rod Baxter Imps., Inc.,* 262 N.W.2d 349, 357-58 (Minn. 1977); *Volkswagen of Am., Inc. v. Novak,* 418 So. 2d 801, 804 (Miss. 1982); *Fode v. Capital RV Ctr., Inc.,* 1998 ND 65, 575 N.W.2d 682, 687-88 (N.D. 1998); *Gochey v. Bombardier, Inc.,* 153 Vt. 607, 572 A.2d 921, 924 (Vt. 1990). As explained in *Gochey,* this decision is based on the viewpoint that traditional privity is not necessary, but that the relationship established based on a manufacturer's warranty is sufficient:

> "Under state law the right to revoke acceptance for defects substantially impairing the value of the product and to receive a refund of the purchase price are rights available to a buyer against a seller in privity. Where the manufacturer gives a warranty to induce the sale it is consistent to allow the same type of remedy as against that manufacturer. Only the privity

concept, which is frequently viewed as a relic these days, has interfered with a rescission-type remedy against the manufacturer of goods not purchased directly from the manufacturer. If we focus on the fact that the warranty creates a direct contractual obligation to the buyer, the reason for allowing the same remedy that is available against a direct seller becomes clear."

In assessing these two positions, we find the majority position to be too inflexible in its adoption of a strict, literal interpretation of privity and in defining what constitutes a "seller." This position ignores the UCC's mandate for liberal application. We perceive instances where, as here, revocation of acceptance against a manufacturer might be appropriate.

We also have concerns with the minority view, based on the fact that the jurisdictions taking this approach have expressly eliminated privity, enacted relevant statutory definitions, or eliminated privity from consideration. *See, e.g., Novak, 418 So. 2d at 803-04* (determining that based on the Mississippi Legislature's "abolish[ment of] privity of contract for breach of warranty claims including actions brought under the [UCC]," the sales contract and the accompanying manufacturer's warranty were "so closely linked both in time of delivery and subject matter, that they blended into a single unit at the time of sale"); *Harper, 671 F.2d at 1126* (declining to limit relief as it would be "contrary to the Code's mandate to administer its remedies liberally," even though the UCC "eliminates the defense of privity in suits for damages for breaches of warranties, [but remains] silent as to revocation of acceptance"); *Durfee, 262 N.W.2d at 357-58* (concluding that because plaintiff could have sued under a warranty theory, when "the absence of privity would not bar the suit despite the language of the pertinent Code sections [,]" the same logic should be applied to revocation as "[t]he remedies of the Code are to be liberally administered"); *Fode, 575 N.W.2d at 687-88* (determining that the buyer could revoke acceptance from a nonprivity manufacturer based on the merger of the warranty with the contract); *Gochey, 572 A.2d at 924* (concluding that an express warranty creates a contract with the ultimate buyer, pointing out that "[w]hen the manufacturer's defect results in revocation by the consumer, the manufacturer must assume the liability it incurred when it warranted the product to the ultimate user"). Our Legislature thus far has been silent on the issue of privity. As a result, we are hesitant to completely eliminate any requirement of privity, particularly because doing so may result in too broad an application of the revocation of acceptance cause of action.

While we have concerns with both positions, because of the unique circumstances of this case, we need not choose between the two at this point. The direct interactions and representations made by Newmar to McCrary expanded the relationship between the two parties and created privity. Newmar, even though it was the manufacturer, interjected itself into the sales process and through its representations assisted in the completion of the sales transaction. Under the unique facts of this case, we conclude that this direct involvement on the part of the manufacturer in the sales process created a direct relationship with the buyer sufficient to establish privity between the manufacturer and the buyer. *See Alberti v. Manufactured Homes, Inc.,* 329 N.C. 727, 407 S.E.2d 819, 824 n.4 (N.C. 1991) (stating that the prerequisite for revocation of acceptance that there be a direct contractual relationship between the parties can include the manufacturer when the buyer and manufacturer have direct dealings with each other); *Cedars of Lebanon Hosp. Corp. v. European X-Ray Distribs. of Am., Inc.,* 444 So. 2d 1068, 1072 & n.4 (Fla. Dist. Ct. App. 1984) (holding that privity can exist between the manufacturer and buyer even though there is an intermediate seller when there are direct contacts between the two parties in completing the sale). This resulting relationship is sufficient to include the manufacturer within the definition of "seller" under *NRS 104.2103(1)(c),* and, as a result, allow for revocation of acceptance against the manufacturer. When the manufacturer is ultimately responsible for the defect that resulted in the breach to the consumer and has directly involved itself in the transaction to ensure the sale, it can be the entity that is held responsible to the consumer. Accordingly, we affirm the district court's decision that McCrary was entitled to revoke acceptance from Newmar.

As the court notes in *Newmar*, the majority view is that a buyer cannot revoke its acceptance against a nonparty to the sales contract—and the statutory-construction argument in support of that position seems sound. But does the majority view lose some of its appeal (to the extent that it's also premised, explicitly or impliedly, on the concept of privity), in jurisdictions that have adopted one of the versions of 2-318 that relax to different degrees the general privity rules?

Finally, is a buyer's right to revoke its acceptance conditioned on providing the seller an opportunity to fix—to cure—the problem(s) used to justify revocation? There is no mention of cure in 2-608, but that has not stopped a minority of courts from finding one. The next case presents the arguments for and against requiring a revoking buyer to provide the seller with the opportunity to cure the nonconformities asserted as grounds for revocation.

CAR TRANSP. BROKERAGE CO. V. BLUE BIRD BODY CO.

UNITED STATES COURT OF APPEALS FOR THE ELEVENTH CIRCUIT, 2009
322 FED. APPX. 891

EDMONDSON, DUBINA, KRAVITCH, *Per Curiam.*

CAR Transportation Brokerage Company (hereinafter the "Buyer") appeals the district court's grant of summary judgment on its revocation of acceptance claim brought under *O.C.G.A. § 11-2-608(1)(b)*. At issue is whether the district court properly granted summary judgment on this claim where the Buyer of a defective motor coach provided the seller with only one opportunity to cure the defects in the coach prior to revoking acceptance.

BACKGROUND

The relevant facts of this case, as supported by the evidence construed in the light most favorable to the non-moving party, are as follows:

On December 31, 2004, the Buyer, a company located in Springdale, Arkansas, purchased 2005 Blue Bird Wanderlodge LXi motor coach (the "Coach") from John Bleakley R.V. of Douglasville, Georgia (the "Seller") for $650,000. One month prior to this sale, the Seller had discovered that the Coach's electrical system was "going haywire" and had returned the Coach to the manufacturer for repairs. After the manufacturer returned the Coach, the Seller did not confirm that the problem had been solved. The Seller did not tell the Buyer about the prior repair work performed on the Coach.

Because the Buyer did not arrive on the lot until almost five p.m. on December 31st and the Buyer was already familiar with vehicles like the Coach, the Seller did not perform its customary pre-delivery inspection and customer product orientation prior to delivering possession to the Buyer. The Seller, however, represented that the Coach was new and in working condition. The parties executed a purchase agreement, in which the Seller disclaimed all warranties, including any warranty for merchantability or for fitness for a particular purpose. The manufacturer provided a limited warranty, which the Seller gave to the Buyer pursuant to the purchase agreement. This warranty limited the manufacturer's obligation to the repair or replacement of parts, which, under normal use and service, were defective in workmanship or material.

On the day of the purchase, as the Buyer was driving back to Arkansas from Douglasville, Georgia, it noted that the Coach's low-beam headlights were not working and that the step-cover had come out. It returned the Coach to the Seller the next morning for repairs. The Seller's service technicians found and repaired several electrical issues on the Coach. On January 5th, the Buyer, accompanied by the Seller's service technician, drove the Coach approximately thirty-five miles without incident. During this drive, the Seller's service technician told the Buyer that he had no experience repairing this particular model of motor coach. The Buyer then re-took possession of the Coach and returned home to Arkansas.

Over the next two months, however, the Coach had several other problems, including other issues with its electrical system. Because the Seller's service technician had told the Buyer that he was unfamiliar with this model of motor coach, the Buyer decided to take the Coach to the manufacturer for repairs, instead of returning it to the Seller. The manufacturer returned the Coach to the Buyer on February 18, without having completely repaired the electrical system. The manufacturer told the Buyer that a "circuit board" was required to fix the defect and assured the Buyer that the required part would be ordered, but the Buyer heard nothing more from the manufacturer regarding this potential fix.

On March 22, 2005, the Buyer's attorney wrote a letter to the Seller purporting to revoke acceptance of the Coach because "the vehicle has failed to perform in the manner required for a motor coach and thus is not merchantable." The Seller did not respond to the revocation letter.

The parties do not dispute that, as early as March 2005, the manufacturer was aware that the inverters of the 450 LXi coach were defective and would cause random operation of the coach's electrical components, such as was seen in the Coach. On November 30, 2005, the manufacturer discovered an inverter that would resolve the LXi coach's defect, but it did not notify its dealers of either the defect or the solution until March 10, 2006.

On July 24, 2006, the Buyer brought suit against the Seller asserting claims for fraud, negligent misrepresentation, revocation of acceptance under *O.C.G.A. § 11-2-608(1)(b)*, breach of implied warranty of merchantability, and violations of the Georgia Fair Business Practices Act. After discovery, the Seller moved for summary judgment on all of the claims and the Buyer moved for summary judgment on the issue of revocation.

The district court granted the Seller's motion and denied the Buyer's motion. The district court found, *inter alia*, that the Buyer was not entitled to revoke its acceptance of the Coach because the "limited opportunity to cure" provided by the Buyer was insufficient to satisfy "the Georgia law that before a buyer may bring a revocation claim, it must give the seller an opportunity to cure all known defects." The Buyer appeals, challenging only the grant of summary judgment on its revocation of acceptance claim. The Buyer asserts that the district court erred in finding that it was required by statute *O.C.G.A. § 11-2-608(1)(b)* to provide the Seller with an opportunity to cure prior to revoking. In the alternative, the Buyer argues that if it was obliged to give the Seller an opportunity to repair, there is at least a jury question as to whether the Buyer satisfied this requirement.

The Seller responds that although *O.C.G.A. § 11-2-608* does not require an opportunity to cure in all situations, the district court properly found that the Buyer was required to provide the Seller with an opportunity to cure in <u>this</u> case and that the Buyer failed to satisfy this requirement. The Seller also asserts that, even if the court erred by requiring an opportunity for repair, the district court could have granted summary judgment on the alternate ground that the Buyer performed acts after the alleged revocation which were inconsistent with the Seller's ownership of the Coach.

DISCUSSION

A. Opportunity to Cure

This case hinges on whether the district court erred in finding that, under Georgia law and the facts of this case, the Buyer was required to provide the Seller with an opportunity to seasonably cure the defects in the Coach prior to revoking its acceptance. The statute governing revocation, which is within Georgia's version of the Uniform Commercial Code ("UCC"), provides:

1. The buyer may revoke his acceptance of a lot or commercial unit whose nonconformity substantially impairs its value to him if he has accepted it:

   a. On the reasonable assumption that its nonconformity would be cured and it has not been seasonably cured; *or*

   b. Without discovery of such nonconformity if his acceptance was reasonably induced either by the difficulty of discovery before acceptance or by the seller's assurances.

2. Revocation of acceptance must occur within a reasonable time after the buyer discovers or should have discovered the ground for it and before any substantial change in condition of the goods, which is not caused by their own defects. It is not effective until the buyer notifies the seller of it.

3. A buyer who so revokes has the same rights and duties with regard to the goods involved as if he had rejected them.

O.C.G.A. § 11-2-608 (emphasis added). On appeal, the Buyer asserts that because it accepted the Coach without discovery of its nonconformity and the nonconformity was not apparent, its revocation claim arose under *§ 11-2-608(1)(b)*, not *subsection (1)(a)*, and it was therefore not required to provide the Seller with an opportunity to cure prior to revoking.

On its face, the plain language of *O.C.G.A. § 11-2-608* requires a pre-revocation opportunity to cure only where a buyer knew about the nonconformity prior to acceptance and reasonably assumed that the nonconformity would be cured. Courts in a majority of jurisdictions, therefore, take the position that a seller has no right to cure nonconformities prior to revocation under *UCC § 2-608(1)(b)*, that is, where the goods are accepted by the buyer without knowledge that it fails to conform to the sales contract. See, e.g., *Preston Motor Co v. Palomares*, 133 Ariz. 245, 650 P.2d 1227, 1231 (Ariz. 1982); *Werner v. Montana*, 117 N.H. 721, 378 A.2d 1130, 1136-37 (N.H. 1977); *American Honda Motor Co., Inc. v. Boyd*, 475 So. 2d 835, 839-40 (Ala. 1985) (holding that where buyer purchased a car, believing it to be new, and in fact the car was previously damaged and repaired, and buyer did not discover this until after it had accepted car, the case fell under *UCC § 2-608(1)(b)*, and therefore, there was no right to cure); *U.S. Roofing, Inc. v. Credit Alliance Corp.*, 228 Cal. App. 3d 1431, 279 Cal. Rptr. 533, 540 (Cal. App. 3d Dist. 1991) (categorically stating that "[we] believe that the right to cure under [*UCC § 2-508*] does not apply to situations where the buyer seeks to revoke his acceptance under [*UCC § 2-608*]"); *Jensen v. Seigel Mobile Homes Group*, 105 Idaho 189, 668 P.2d 65, 69-70 (Idaho 1983) (holding that right to cure is relevant only when there has been a rejection of goods; following acceptance there is no right to cure, citing authorities for the proposition that cure is not available following the buyer's acceptance of goods); *Head v. Phillips Camper Sales & Rental, Inc.*, 234 Mich. App. 94, 593 N.W.2d 595, 600 (Mich. App. 1999) (adopting majority view that "a seller has no right to cure a defect that was not discoverable when the buyer accepted the goods"); *Bowen v. Foust*, 925 S.W.2d 211, 215 n.6 (Mo. Ct. App. S.D. 1996) (noting that this remains the majority view, although the more recent cases allow opportunity to cure more willingly following an acceptance). Accordingly, where a buyer's acceptance is as described in *UCC § 2-608(1)(b)*, the majority rule is that he may revoke the acceptance without waiting for a cure, seasonable or otherwise, by the seller.

A minority of state courts, however, interpret *UCC § 2-608* as imposing upon the buyer a duty to provide notice and an opportunity to cure in all cases of revocation. These courts point to *UCC § 2-608(3)* which provides that a purchaser revoking his acceptance "has the same rights and duties with regard to the goods involved as if he had rejected them," and note that a seller has a general right to cure nonconformities in rejected goods under *UCC § 2-508*.[14] By analogy, then, they hold

---

14   UCC § 2-508 describes the procedure a buyer must follow to reject nonconforming goods prior to acceptance. Under this section, a seller is entitled to attempt to cure any nonconformity in the rejected goods within the contract time if the time for performance has not yet expired.

that a similar duty to provide notice and opportunity to cure exists in the context of revocation. See, e.g., *Conte v. Dwan Lincoln-Mercury Inc., 172 Conn.* 112, 374 A.2d 144, 149 (Conn. 1976); *David Tunick, Inc. v. Kornfeld,* 838 F. Supp. 848, 850 (S.D. N.Y. 1993) (explaining that, through *UCC § 2-608(3),* the *UCC § 2-508(2)*'s requirement that a buyer provide notice and opportunity to cure nonconforming goods is generally applicable in the case of a revocation of acceptance); *Tucker v. Aqua Yacht Harbor Corp.,* 749 F. Supp. 142, 145 (N.D. Miss. 1990) ("Although a seller seems to have the right to cure only when the buyer rejects goods, the Mississippi Supreme Court, by analogy to *§ 75-2-508* and as a matter of public policy, has determined that before a buyer may revoke acceptance under *§ 75-2-608,* the seller must be afforded a reasonable opportunity to cure."). In these jurisdictions, revocation is only appropriate after the seller has been afforded a reasonable opportunity to cure, regardless of whether the buyer accepted the goods with or without knowledge of the nonconformity.

Georgia courts have not addressed the issue; therefore, it is not clear that the district court—which appears to have adopted the minority view—erred. We need not decide this issue, however, because, as described more fully below, the Buyer invited the alleged error or waived its right to raise the issue on appeal.

* * *

C. Sufficiency of the Opportunity to Cure

The Buyer argues that if it was required to provide the Seller with an opportunity to seasonably cure prior to revocation, there is at least a triable issue of fact as to whether it satisfied this requirement. It further asserts that even if it had returned the Coach to the Seller after the initial repairs, any further attempts at repair would have been futile because the "cure" for the electrical defect was not discovered by the manufacturer until November 2005 (nearly eight months after revocation). Accordingly, the Buyer asserts that it should be excused from the requirement of providing the Seller with another opportunity to cure because the statute should not be construed so as "to require [it] to do a futile and useless thing."

We disagree. Although the statutory opportunity to "seasonably cure" does not entitle a seller to unlimited attempts to cure a defect, it does require a buyer to provide a seller with a reasonable time in which to attempt to make repairs. *O.C.G.A. § 11-1-204(3)* (explaining that an action is taken "seasonably" when it is taken "at or within a reasonable time"). What constitutes a reasonable time in which to cure depends on the nature, purpose, and circumstances of a particular case. *O.C.G.A. § 11-1-204(2).* In this case, the evidence taken in the light most favorable to the Buyer shows that the Buyer gave the Seller one opportunity to cure after the defect in the electrical system first became apparent. After these initial repairs, the Buyer did not inform the Seller when the Coach continued to have additional problems; rather, it returned the Coach to the manufacturer for repairs. Nearly three months after acceptance, after the manufacturer also had made one failed attempt to correct the defect, the Buyer informed the Seller that it was revoking its acceptance of the Coach. Based upon this undisputed evidence, we agree with the district court that, as a matter of law, the Buyer provided the Seller with an insufficient opportunity to cure. Providing only one opportunity to repair—before the extent of the defect was truly apparent—is not reasonable, especially where the product in question is as complicated as a motor coach. See e.g., *Fedrick v. Mercedes-Benz,* 366 F. Supp. 2d 1190, 1199 (N.D. Ga. 2005) (holding, in the context of a claim for breach of warranty, that no reasonable juror could conclude that a dealership acted unreasonably where it took the dealership six attempts over six months to successfully repair the defects within the vehicle); see also *McDonald v. Mazda Motors of Am., Inc.,* 269 Ga. App. 62, 603 S.E.2d 456, 460 (Ga. Ct. App. 2004) ("When the purchaser returns the product to the dealer and makes the product available for repair, refusal to repair, unsuccessful repair, or repeated failures of the repair constitute a breach of the express warranty."). At the least, the Seller was entitled to notice of the additional problems and an opportunity to attempt to repair them at some time during the three months prior to the Buyer's purported revocation. The Buyer's failure to provide this notice and opportunity bars the revocation claim as a matter of law.

The Buyer's argument that it was excused from providing the Seller with an opportunity to cure because attempts to repair would have been futile is not supported by the evidence. Certainly, we should not read an "opportunity to cure" requirement so as to "require a party to whistle in the wind," *BDI Distribs., Inc., 501 S.E.2d at 841*, but, in this case, there is no evidence that the Buyer knew prior to revocation that the Seller would have been unable to repair the Coach. As such, the Buyer's failure to provide the Seller with another opportunity to cure was not, and could not have been, based on the perceived futility of providing such an opportunity.

Basing an absolute right to cure before revocation on the limited right of a seller to cure after rejection stretches statutory construction beyond its breaking point. As we noted earlier in this chapter, 2-508 provides for cure only after *rejection*, and then only if the statutory conditions are met. The rights and duties assumed by the revoking buyer with regard to the rejected goods are, as 2-608(2) tells us, the same as those of the rejecting buyer. But the obligations imposed on the buyer in possession after rejection are to preserve the goods—the buyer has an obligation to take care of the goods; the rejecting buyer is not obligated to preserve the relationship—to save the transaction. The right to cure is more like a personal right of the seller—not a property-based right derived from possession of the goods—and provides the seller with an opportunity to preserve the relationship, not the goods. To claim that the revoking buyer has an obligation to preserve the relationship because it has an obligation to preserve the goods requires a leap of faith a majority of the courts have been unwilling to make.

CHAPTER 8

WARRANTIES

Buyers expect the things they buy to work—to perform at some basic level based on the nature of the product. But for a long time, the law of sales gave no legal significance to a buyer's expectations about the performance of the goods she bought—caveat emptor was the law. Slowly, as the nature of sales transactions changed from face-to-face deals to mass-produced goods bought from distant sellers, the law began to assign legal significance to some of a buyer's expectations about the qualities of the goods purchased and to impose legal consequences on the seller who disappointed its buyer's expectations. Of course, once the courts recognized that buyers' expectations were entitled to protection, the question became whether all of a buyer's expectations were entitled to that protection, and if not, how they distinguish those worthy of protection from those not.

Today, protecting a buyer's expectations is what the law of warranty is all about. Warranties embody the buyer's expectations of quality—what the buyer is entitled to expect from the goods she purchased. Those expectations can be created expressly by the seller or by implication from the nature of the goods (merchantability) or, where the buyer has a special use in mind, from the purpose of the buyer if communicated to the seller (fitness). But warranties are part of a broader network of protections the law gives to buyers of goods; that network includes the law of product liability and the law of negligence. The lines separating these different protections have not been drawn as clearly as we might like, making it difficult to tell where warranty gives way to negligence or product liability. Often, the unhappy buyer gives voice to her disappointment using all three in the same case, and the overlap can make it tough sometimes to distinguish the warranty claim from the negligence claim or the product liability claim. But they are different, as the City Court for New York explained in *Rudloff v. Wendy's Restaurant*. In *Rudloff*, the plaintiff broke a tooth eating a Wendy's double cheeseburger and sued both Wendy's and the company that sold Wendy's the hamburger.

> Since each sale of a food product potentially involves three separate claims sounding in negligence, strict products liability and breach of implied warranty (UCC 2-314), one would expect to find volumes of case law on this subject. *** While all three concepts are somewhat related and often overlap, this seems to be one of those cases where the nature of the proof and the way in which the fact issues were litigated demonstrate how the causes of action can diverge and how the subtle differences and interrelations of the three theories are important.

The negligence standard in a products liability case is pretty straightforward. A defendant will be held liable if a plaintiff can show that it is reasonably certain that the product, when put to normal use, would be dangerous if it were defective. A product is defective if the defendant fails to use reasonable care in designing, making, inspecting and testing a product. In practice, this turns into an inquiry of whether or not a restaurant owner, and his or her suppliers, used ordinary care to remove from the food, as served, such harmful substance as the consumer would not ordinarily anticipate.

Under New York law, a product defect may be actionable under a strict products liability theory if the product is not reasonably safe. Liability is determined by a negligence-like risk/benefit inquiry that looks at the likelihood that the product will cause injury if not properly made, and the reasonableness of the actions (or inactions) taken by the seller/supplier/manufacturer in ensuring that the product was made safe.

In contrast, the standard under an implied warranty theory is whether the product was fit for the ordinary purposes for which such goods are used. That inquiry focuses on the reasonable expectations of the consumer for the product when used in the customary, usual and reasonably foreseeable manners, without regard to the feasibility of alternative designs or the manufacturer's or seller's reasonableness in marketing it in that unsafe condition.

Rudloff v. Wendy's Restaurant, 821 N.Y.S.2d 358 (N.Y. City Ct.)(2006).

We will read the rest of the Court's opinion later in this chapter.

Of course, there are other important differences between these overlapping claims. Damages for breach of warranty—breach of contract—are usually limited to economic loss and do not include loss based on injury to the person, which is compensable under tort law. The buyer who sues her seller for breach of warranty because the product she purchased does not perform as expected can recover costs of repair or replacement, any diminution in the value of the product, and even lost profits that result from the product's failure to perform as expected, but she cannot recover for any physical injury to herself or another (or to other property) under general contract law—losses for injury to person or property are the province of tort law. But the buyer who does seek redress for the same product failure under tort law cannot recover for economic loss.

The rationale behind the economic loss doctrine is that economic losses resulting from a defective product are best treated under the law of contracts, not tort. This is because "[t]he particular seller and purchaser are in the best position to allocate risk at the time of their sale and purchase, and this risk allocation is usually manifested in the selling price." Concordantly, when a purchaser chooses to forgo "protecting itself with UCC warranties," it "should not be permitted to fall back on tort when it has failed to preserve its remedies."

Shema Kolain-Hear Our Voices v. ProviderSoft, 832 F. Supp. 2d 194 (E.D.N.Y. 2010). The nature of the buyer's loss may ultimately determine which claims she brings or does not bring.

Warranties allocate the risk of product failure between the parties by imposing responsibility for such failures on the seller. Presumably, sellers are in a better position to evaluate the risk of product failure based on their experience selling the product—sellers likely hear from their buyers when the goods don't perform as expected and can, based on their overall sales of the product, better assess the reliability of a product and the cost of product failure over time than a buyer can. Sellers can price the product in light of the risk they assume by warranting a product, and buyers can decide how much allocating the risk of failure to the seller is worth. From the buyer's perspective, warranties can function like insurance—for a premium, the buyer can shift the cost of product failure to the seller-insurer. Most of us were probably given a similar option the last time we purchased an electronic device or appliance: for an additional contribution on our part, we could purchase an extended warranty for the product.

The parties to an Article 2 sale of goods have the option of using its warranty provisions to allocate the risk of product failure. The parties can do so by the express terms of their agreement, but, under certain circumstances, they can do so by doing nothing—Article 2 implies warranties of merchantability and fitness for a particular purpose in certain transactions if the parties do not expressly disclaim the warranties. And, as we will see in Chapter 9, Article 2 imposes a warranty that the seller has good title to the goods it transfers in all sales of goods transaction unless the parties provide otherwise.

A. IMPLIED WARRANTIES

The warranties Article 2 implies (makes part of a sale of good contract) reflect the intersection where mercantile expectations meet evolving notions of public policy. By the time Llewellyn began work on Article 2, the warranties of merchantability and fitness for a particular purpose had long been part of sales law and had been incorporated into the Uniform Sales Act. As the Comments to the 1944 draft explained, the implied warranties

> are those which rest so clearly on phases of a common situation that they have no need to be shown by any particular language or action, but, given the conditions [of the warranty sections] simply follow without more unless unmistakably negated.[1]

Both implied warranties protect a buyer's expectations about the quality of the goods purchased—merchantability (the expectations of buyers in general) and fitness (the expectations of individual buyers).

1. Merchantability

The warranty of merchantability is, at its most basic level, simply a promise by the seller that the goods sold will do what everyone expects them to do—that they "are fit for the ordinary purposes for which such goods are used." 2-314(2)(c). We expect the toaster we buy to brown bread, to warm up a Pop-Tart, and to defrost and cook frozen waffles, and if it can't do these things, it's not fit for the ordinary purposes for which toasters are used—it's not merchantable. The fact that I can't use it to dry my hair in the morning, however frustrating to me, does not make the toaster unmerchantable, because drying hair is not what people buy toasters for—not what buyers expect toasters to do. The expectations protected by the warranty of merchantability are those held by buyers in general, not the idiosyncratic expectations of a specific buyer.

The seller's promise that the goods are fit for their ordinary purpose is not a promise that the goods are perfect. Merchantability under 2-314 imposes a minimum standard, not an optimal threshold, of quality to be expected of all goods. As long as goods are not "completely worthless" or "suitable only for the junk pile," they may still be merchantable under 2-314. *See, e.g., International Petroleum Services v. S & N Well Services,* 639 P.2d 29 (Kan. 1982). The buyer who wants or needs superior performance from the goods will need to secure an express warranty to raise the standard of quality she is entitled to expect from the goods under Article 2.

But when does less than perfect become not merchantable—how do we draw the line between less than perfect and no longer fit for ordinary purposes? Courts tend to think of fitness for ordinary purposes in terms of the operability of goods, but that seems to beg the question in many cases. Is a luxury automobile fit for its ordinary purposes if the air conditioner does not work but the auto can still be used for transportation? What is the ordinary purpose of a luxury auto—a Rolls Royce? Is it different from the ordinary purpose of a Honda Civic? Is clam chowder that contains a fishbone

---

1   Kelly, *Uniform Commercial Code: Drafts,* (Rothman 1984) 163 (Comment to Section 37).

that injures a customer fit for its ordinary purpose? Is a standard-bred horse with tendinitis fit for its ordinary purpose? Is a baseball bat that cannot withstand the repeated hitting of baseballs fit for its ordinary purpose? At some point, does the burden or inconvenience caused by the less-than-perfect goods make them unfit for their ordinary purposes, or are they merchantable as long as it remains possible to use them as intended, no matter how inconvenient? The following case looks at these questions.

In re Carrier IQ, Inc., Consumer Privacy Litig.

United States District Court for the Northern District of California, 2015
2015 U.S. Dist. LEXIS 7123

CHEN, *District Judge.*

I. INTRODUCTION

Plaintiffs in this multidistrict litigation—eighteen (18) individuals from thirteen different states—have filed a second consolidated amended complaint ("SCAC" or "Complaint") against Defendant Carrier IQ, Inc. and a number of manufacturers of mobile devices. The Complaint alleges that Defendants have violated the Federal Wiretap Act as well as a number of state's privacy and consumer protection statutes through the creation and use of Carrier IQ's software on Plaintiffs' mobile devices. Plaintiffs allege that Carrier IQ designed, and the Device Manufacturers Defendants embedded, the Carrier IQ Software on their mobile devices and, once embedded, this software surreptitiously intercepted personal data and communications and transmitted this data to Carrier IQ and its customers.

II. FACTUAL & PROCEDURAL BACKGROUND

A. Plaintiffs
There are 18 plaintiffs in this action, from 13 different states. In describing each Plaintiff, the SCAC provides that "[u]pon information and belief, [the Plaintiffs] mobile device came with the Carrier IQ Software and implementing or porting software pre-installed. In addition to using his devices to make phone calls, [the Plaintiff] has used it for web browsing and text messaging, including accessing, inputting, and transmitting personal, private, confidential, and sensitive information. [The Plaintiff] would not have purchased his mobile device had he known that the Carrier IQ Software and related implementing or porting software was installed and operating on his device, and taxing his device's battery, processor, and memory, as alleged herein."

B. Defendants
The remaining defendants in this action are a number of mobile device manufacturers. Plaintiffs allege that Carrier IQ is the "designer, author, programmer, and vendor" of the IQ Agent software and provided the mobile device manufacturers the "guide or template" needed for the "related implementing or porting software known as the CIQ Interface." The IQ Agent and CIQ Interface software forms the basis of Plaintiffs' claims, as described *infra*.

The remaining Defendants are: (1) HTC America, Inc. and HTC Corporation (collectively "HTC"); (2) Huawei Device USA, Inc. ("Huawei"), (3) LG Electronics MobileComm U.S.A., Inc. and LG Electronics, Inc. (collectively "LG"); (4) Motorola Mobility LLC ("Motorola"); (5) Pantech Wireless, Inc. ("Pantech"); (6) Samsung Telecommunications America, Inc. and Samsung Electronics Co., Ltd. (collectively "Samsung"). Each Defendant is alleged to have installed the Carrier IQ Software and CIQ Interface software on at least some of their mobile device models.

C. Asserted Causes of Action

The SCAC alleges five causes of action:

* * *

- Count 5: Violation of the Implied Warranty of Merchantability: asserted on behalf of residents of the states enumerated under Count 4.

D. Carrier IQ Software Background

Carrier IQ "designed, authored, programmed, and caused the installation and activation of the Carrier IQ Software, including the so-called IQ Agent, on the devices at issue in this case." It also "designed, authored, and provided guides to the Device Manufacturers for designing, authoring, programming, installing, and activating the CIQ Interface in deployments" through the "embedded" method of installation.

Carrier IQ represents that its software is a "network diagnostics tool" for cell phone service providers. It is alleged that in reality, the software collects, and transfers, sensitive personal data off of a user's mobile device. Specifically, the CIQ Interface software is alleged to be a "wrapping or porting layer of code designed to see recognize and intercept a host of data and content, including SMS text message content and URLs containing search terms, user names, and passwords ... and to send that material down to the IQ Agent [for] further processing and possible transmittals." The SCAC alleges that the Device Manufacturers "design and program" the CIQ Interface (with Carrier IQ's aid) and then install the CIQ Interface and IQ Agent software on their mobile devices. *Id.* Once installed, the software "operates in the background," such that the typical user has no idea that it is running and cannot turn it off. Users are never given the choice of opting into or out of the Carrier IQ Software's functionality. Because it is always running, the Plaintiffs allege that it "taxes the device's battery power, processor functions, and system memory."

Plaintiffs allege that the data intercepted by the Carrier IQ Software includes the following: (1) URLs (including those which contain query strings with embedded information such as search terms, user names, passwords, and GPS-based geo-location information); (2) GPS-location information; (3) SMS text messages; (4) telephone numbers dialed and received; (5) the user's keypad presses/keystrokes; and (6) application purchases and uses. This information is intercepted as part of the Carrier IQ Software's "calls" on the device operating system for "metrics." It then stores the information in the mobile device's RAM memory on a rolling basis.

The Carrier IQ Software also has a feature referred to as "Profiles." Via Profiles, Carrier IQ customers (who are typically wireless carriers, but can also include device manufacturers) will specify which data they want from the above described "metrics." At designated times (or as requested), the Profile-specified data would then be transmitted from the mobile device to the requesting customer (the wireless carriers or device manufacturers).

The SCAC quotes from a number of letters which the various Device Manufacturers sent to Senator Al Franken in response to his inquiries regarding the Carrier IQ Software. These letters provide a glimpse into the potential scope of the Carrier IQ Software deployment. AT&T stated that Carrier IQ's Software was installed on approximately "900,000 devices, with about 575,000 of those collecting and reporting wireless and service performance information to AT&T." Sprint indicated that there were "26 million active Sprint devices that have Carrier IQ Software Installed" and stated that Sprint queried information from a fraction of those (c. 1.3 million) at any given time for diagnostic needs and that a 30,000 device subset of this 1.3 million were used for "research specific problems." T-Mobile stated that there were "approximately 450,000 T-Mobile customers [that] use devices that contain Carrier IQ's diagnostic software."

The SCAC recounts two ways where deployment of the Carrier IQ Software has resulted in "grave breaches of privacy." First, due to a "programming error," the SCAC alleges that AT&T has admitted that the "Carrier IQ Software transmitted text message content to it." *Id.* Plaintiffs use this as evidence that the Carrier IQ Software does, in fact, intercept and capture text message content. *Id.* Second, Plaintiffs state that "with some deployments, including those on HTC mobile devices and possibly on certain other devices," the data and content intercepted by the Carrier IQ Software was sent in unencrypted, human-readable form into the system logs of the affected devices. Accordingly, this information was vulnerable to anyone with access to the system logs, including to individuals with malicious intent. Further, because this information was contained in system logs, the private information improperly intercepted and stored was transmitted to Google (who is the author of the Android Operating System) as part of crash reports. Plaintiffs allege that the Carrier IQ Software continues to operate even if the consumer is using the device solely on a Wi-Fi network (as opposed to a cellular network).

III. DISCUSSION

Plaintiffs' Implied Warranty of Merchantability Claims
Plaintiffs' fifth cause of action alleges a breach of the implied warranty of merchantability under the laws of over thirty states and the District of Columbia against the Device Manufacturers. The Device Manufacturers have moved to dismiss these claims on a variety of grounds.

* * *

Finally, Defendants contend that Plaintiffs have failed to allege that their mobile devices were not "merchantable."

* * *

4. Plaintiffs Have Sufficiently Alleged that Their Mobile Devices Were Unmerchantable for Purposes of Their Implied Warranty Claims

Defendants substantively attack Plaintiffs' implied warranty of merchantability claims alleging that Plaintiffs have not—and cannot—allege that the presence and operation of the Carrier IQ Software rendered their mobile devices unmerchantable. Defendants accordingly seek dismissal of Plaintiffs' implied warranty claims arising under the laws of California, Maryland, Michigan, Mississippi, New Hampshire, Texas, and Washington. Under the laws of each of these states, the implied warranty of merchantability warrants that a purchased good is "fit for the ordinary purposes for which such goods are used." Courts across various jurisdictions have recognized that the concept of whether a product is "fit for ordinary purposes" necessarily "incorporates ... the consumer's reasonable expectations into the concept of merchantability." *Robinson v. American Honda Motor Co., Inc.*, 551 F.3d 218 (4th Cir. 2009); *see also Venezia v. Miller Brewing Co.*, 626 F.2d 188, 190 (1st Cir. 1980) ("Under Massachusetts law the question of fitness for ordinary purposes is largely one centering around reasonable consumer expectations."); *Denny v. Ford Motor Co.*, 87 N.Y.2d 248, 662 N.E.2d 730, 736, 639 N.Y.S.2d 250 (N.Y. 1995) (noting that the "fit for the ordinary purposes for which such goods are used" inquiry "focuses on the expectations for the performance of the product when used in the customary, usual and reasonably foreseeable manners").

At the same time, the implied warranty of merchantability merely guarantees that the product will perform at a "minimum level of quality." As such, the implied warranty "does not impose a general requirement that goods precisely fulfill the expectation of the buyer." Therefore, a product which "performs its ordinary function adequately does not breach the implied warranty of merchantability merely because it does not function as well as the buyer would like, or even as well as it could." Rather, the alleged defect in the product must be so fundamental as to render the product unfit for its ordinary purpose. *See Tietsworth v. Sears, Roebuck & Co.*, 720 F. Supp. 2d 1123, 1142 (N.D. Cal. 2010)

("The mere manifestation of a defect by itself does not constitute a breach of the implied warranty of merchantability. Instead, there must be a fundamental defect that renders the product unfit for its ordinary purpose.").

Defendants contend that the "ordinary purpose" of mobile devices is communication—making and receiving phone calls, text messages, facilitating internet usage, and allowing usage of apps. Because of this, Defendants argue, Plaintiffs cannot establish that the Carrier IQ Software renders their mobile devices unfit for this ordinary purpose because there are no allegations that the software rendered the devices unable to make and receive phone calls, text messages, and the like.

Defendants' definition of mobile devices' "ordinary purpose" finds some support in case law from courts in this District. Specifically, *in In re iPhone 4S Consumer Litig.*, No. C12-1227 CW, 2013 U.S. Dist. LEXIS 103058, 2013 WL 3829653 (N.D. Cal. July 23, 2013), the court stated that the "iPhone 4S's intended and ordinary use is as a smartphone, 'which the court safely presumes includes functions like making and receiving calls, sending and receiving text messages, or allowing for use of mobile applications.'" Notably, as this quote demonstrates, the court merely found that a mobile device's ordinary and intended use "includes" making and receiving calls, text messages, and the like, suggesting that the courts were not intending to provide an exhaustive definition of a mobile device's ordinary and intended use. *Cf. Dairy v. Bonham*, 2013 U.S. Dist. LEXIS 103033, (N.D. Cal. July 23, 2013) ("[U]se of the word 'including' indicates the enumerated ways ... is not exhaustive.").

Nonetheless, these courts have found that alleged defects which did not affect this core functionality did not render the mobile devices unfit for their ordinary purposes. For example, in *In re iPhone*, plaintiffs alleged that the iPhone was rendered unfit because Apple's "Siri" feature did not perform as advertised. The court, however, found that this allegation failed to state a claim for breach of the implied warranty because plaintiffs had "not alleged that the iPhone 4S is deficient" in "making and receiving calls, sending and receiving text messages, or allowing the use of mobile applications." Rather, plaintiffs had alleged that the iPhone was deficient "in providing the Siri feature to access these functions." Similarly, in *Williamson*, plaintiffs alleged that the glass on their iPhone was defective as it was easily scarred and broken, despite Apple's representations to the contrary. The court rejected plaintiff's implied warranty claim, finding that the glass defect did not render deficient the iPhone's ability to make calls, send or receive text messages, or use mobile applications. Finally, in *In re Google Phone Litig.*, 2012 U.S. Dist. LEXIS 108611, (N.D. Cal. Aug. 2, 2012), plaintiffs did allege defects which touched on the core functionality of the Google phone—specifically, they alleged, *inter alia*, that the phone's 3G data connectivity was inconsistent and the phone occasionally dropped or missed phone calls. The court found, however, that plaintiffs had failed to "demonstrate that this alleged defect is more than inconvenience" such that the phone was unfit for its ordinary purpose.

This Court finds that Defendants' argument that the Carrier IQ Software does not render Plaintiffs' mobile devices unfit for the devices' ordinary purpose simply because the devices could make and receive phone calls, text messages, use mobile apps, and access the internet is overly simplistic and under inclusive. While a defect must be "fundamental" to implicate the implied warranty, "this does not mean the alleged defect must preclude any use of the product at all." There are a number of examples of courts which have held that a defect can render a product unfit notwithstanding the fact the product at issue could, in a technical sense, perform its base function. These courts have found that the implied warranty can be breached when, although capable of performing its ordinary function, the product nonetheless fails in a significant way to perform as a reasonable consumer would expect.

Thus, in *Stearns*, plaintiffs alleged an implied warranty claim against a bed manufacturer on the basis of mold growing on its beds. The court determined that the plaintiffs had adequately alleged that the beds at issue "did not conform to expectations regarding ordinary use," and simply because "a person still may sleep on a moldy bed does not bar as a matter of law a claim for breach of the implied warranty of merchantability." Similarly, in *Long v. Graco Children's Products Inc.*, 2013 U.S. Dist. LEXIS 121227, (N.D. Cal. Aug. 26, 2013), plaintiff alleged that defendants' car seats contained a defective buckle that was "unreasonably difficult or impossible to unlatch." Even though it was not disputed that the car seat provided "adequate protective restraint" for the child, the court found plaintiffs adequately alleged the car seat was unfit. It held that "[c]onsumers do not merely expect a car seat to serve its bare-minimum purpose" but rather would expect that they "would be able to quickly unlatch the harness or buckle in case of an emergency." Finally, in *Isip v. Mercedes-Benz USA*, 65 Cal. Rptr. 3d 695 (2007), a car manufacturer argued that so long as a vehicle provided transportation from point A to point B, it necessarily was fit for its ordinary purpose. The court rejected this argument, finding it to be an "unjustified dilution" of the implied warranty. Rather, it held that a vehicle that "smells, lurches, clanks, and emits smoke over an extended period of time is not fit for its intended purpose. *Id.* at 27; *see also Fleisher v. Fiber Composites, LLC*, No. 12-1326, 2012 U.S. Dist. LEXIS 157343, 2012 WL 5381381 (E.D. Pa. Nov. 2, 2012) (plaintiffs adequately alleged outdoor deck that became discolored by mold as a result of a defect was unfit for ordinary purpose as consumers expect outdoor decks to not only provide structural support, but to also meet "a certain aesthetic expectation").

The Court concludes that in determining if a defect rises to the level of rendering a product unfit for its ordinary purpose, the Court must ask two questions. First, the defect in question must be "fundamental" in that it affects the core functionality of the product. *See, e.g., Stearns*, (requiring a "fundamental defect'). Thus defects which only affects functionality that is peripheral or tangential to the core function of the product—for example the strength of glass used in a mobile device or the effectiveness of Apple's Siri function, *see, e,g., In re iPhone*,—would be insufficient. In defining a product's core functionality, a court should not seek to reduce a product to its most basic, bare minimum purpose, but rather should take a common sense view informed by reasonable consumers' expectations about the function of the type of product in a general sense. *See Long*, (rejecting "bare-minimum" view of a car seat's purpose in light of consumer expectations); *see also Robinson*, ("This definition of merchantability incorporates trade quality standards and the consumer's reasonable expectations into the concept of merchantability."). Thus, the core function of a vehicle is not to provide transportation, it is to provide safe and reliable transportation, and the core function of a bed is not simply to provide a place on which an individual can sleep, but rather to provide a place where an individual can sleep that is free from mold. Second, just because a defect affects the core functionality of a product does not automatically mean that the product is unfit for its ordinary purposes. Rather, as discussed, the implied warranty only ensures that a product will meet a "minimum level of quality." The impairment of the core functionality must be significant enough to prevent the product from reaching a reasonably expected minimum level of quality.

On this basis, the Court finds, for purposes of the motion to dismiss, that Plaintiffs have adequately alleged that the Carrier IQ Software rendered their mobile devices unmerchantable. While there is no dispute that the Carrier IQ Software did not make it impossible for Plaintiffs to make and receive phone calls, text messages, and the like on their devices, that alone is not dispositive. Consumers have a reasonable expectation that mobile devices, in general, will allow them to communicate with others without having a third party surreptitiously intercept and transmit those communications to third parties. Stated another way, it is beyond controversy that individuals have a reasonable expectation of privacy as to the contents of communications made with their mobile devices. *Cf. Riley v. California*, 134 S. Ct. 2473, (2014) (discussing the privacy interests at stake in searches of cell phones by law enforcement and recognizing the user's expectation of privacy). Just as a consumer would likely choose not to sleep on a bed contaminated with mold, a consumer would likely choose to not use a mobile device that actively intercepted his or her private communication data and potentially shared that data with third parties.

Plaintiffs have, in the SCAC, provided sufficient factual allegations for the Court to conclude, at this stage, that the Carrier IQ Software intercepts and/or transmits personal communication data to third parties. *See, e.g.*, SCAC ¶ 65, 68 (alleging that the Carrier IQ Software intercepts and transmits to Carrier IQ and its customers data that can include URLS which contain internet search terms, user names and passwords; text messages; app purchases and uses; a user's keystrokes; numbers dialed and received; etc.). Taking all inferences in favor of the Plaintiffs, these allegations are sufficient for the Court to conclude that the Carrier IQ Software undermines consumers' reasonable expectations in privacy to such a degree so as to render their mobile devices unfit to perform their core functions. During discovery, the parties will have the opportunity to flesh out the precise way the Carrier IQ Software operates, including the degree to which Plaintiffs' personal data or communications were in fact compromised by the Carrier IQ Software. Based on development of a factual record, Carrier IQ Software may renew their argument via motion for summary judgment.

Accordingly, for the foregoing reasons, Plaintiffs have adequately alleged that their mobile devices were unmerchantable and Defendants motion to dismiss the implied warranty claims on this ground is DENIED.[2]

The *Carrier IQ* case rejects the overly simplistic view of many earlier cases under 2-314 which framed the "fitness for ordinary purpose" requirement as simply a matter of whether the goods were *capable* of performing the *basic function* they were intended to perform. *See, e.g., Mocek v. Alfa Leisure, Inc.,* 7 Cal. Rptr. 3d 546 (2003), (breach of implied warranty "means the product did not possess even the most basic degree of fitness for ordinary use.") If you could still lie on a bed, it did not matter that the bed was covered with mold. If you could still drive a car from one place to another, it did not matter whether the air conditioner worked or the transmission slipped or the engine leaked oil or the car had a propensity to roll over. Although the courts in these cases, like the court in *Carrier IQ*, recognized that fitness was based on the buyer's expectations, a buyer's reasonable expectations did not include anything beyond an expectation that the goods could be used for their most basic purpose.

But courts that reduced the fitness analysis under 2-314 to a simple mechanical test of whether the goods, even though deficient in some way, can actually be used for their intended purpose recognized that goods which are dangerous because of some defect are not fit for their ordinary purposes, even if they are able to do what the buyer expected them to do. The expectation that goods will do what they were intended to do implicitly includes an expectation that they will do it without harm to the buyer.

And more recent cases have concluded that the expectations protected by the warranty of merchantability include the buyer's expectation that goods be both safe and reliable. In *Brand v. Hyundai Motor America,* 173 Cal. Rptr 3d 454 (Cal. App. 2014), the court rejected the seller's argument that because the "spontaneous and repeated opening and closing of the sunroof" while the buyer was driving the car he had purchased from the seller did not render the car inoperable, the buyer had failed to state a claim for breach of the implied warranty of merchantability under 2-314. The Court explained that the implied warranty of merchantability ensured not only that the goods were substantially free of defects, but also that they were in a safe condition:

> This minimum guarantee in the implied warranty of merchantability protects not only the vehicle purchaser, but other motorists, passengers, pedestrians, and the public generally. Here, a reasonable jury could conclude that a vehicle sunroof that opens and closes *on its own* creates a substantial safety hazard. Brand described how on the freeway the papers in his car suddenly swirled about in the passenger compartment without notice, creating a dangerous

---

2   Plaintiffs argue that the Carrier IQ Software also renders their mobile devices unmerchantable because it depletes battery power and life, thus reducing the lifespan of their mobile device battery. The Court rejects this argument. There are no allegations that would permit the inference that the Carrier IQ Software's impact on a mobile device's battery is so significant as to render the device unfit for its ordinary purpose. See *Tomek v. Apple, Inc.,* 2:11-cv-02700-MCEDAD, 2012 U.S. Dist. LEXIA 96321, 2012 WL 2857035 (E.D. Cal. July 11, 2012) ("Plaintiff's allegations that, under unique circumstances, namely 'heavy loads' undertaken [*168] when the battery is already low, the MacBook may shut down, and that his computer shut down once over the course of a six-month period, are insufficient as a matter of law to state a claim that the MacBook is not fit for ordinary use.")

distraction.... A jury therefore reasonably could infer a multitude of similar unsafe scenarios: a driver suddenly distracted, buffeted, or even incapacitated by unexpected incoming rain, sleet, snow, dust, or blinding sun, or endangered by objects shooting through or out of the cabin.

Hyundai contends Brand's safety "argument is specious" because "[i]f open sunroofs rendered cars unfit for their ordinary purpose, then no cars would have sunroofs." The contention is itself specious, however, because it ignores the element of surprise and lack of control that differentiate a properly working sunroof and one that, as Brand describes it, spontaneously creates a gaping, "intermittent hole in your vehicle" as you are driving down the road." In minimizing the sunroof problem, Hyundai implicitly maintains that its vehicle remained roadworthy in its present condition without any repairs. But a jury reasonably could agree Brand prudently turned the vehicle in immediately because it was not safe for him to continue driving it.

Restating the "fitness for ordinary purpose" inquiry in terms of "core functionality" rather than operability, as the court did in *Carrier IQ*, recognizes that the reasonable expectations of a buyer can include not only what the product will do, but also how it will do it. The "how" can be just as important to a product's operation as the "what." The cell phones in *Carrier IQ* could make and receive calls—the app at issue did not make them inoperable—but it was not unreasonable for buyers to expect that, in making and receiving those calls, the phones would not compromise their privacy. *See also, Galitski v. Samsung Telecommunications,* 2013 U.S. Dist. LEXIS 171908 (N.D. Tex 2013)(claim for breach of 2-314 not negated because cell phone could make and receive calls where defect caused cell phone "to randomly freeze, shut down, and power off while in standby mode, thereby making it impossible to receive or deliver calls, messages or data and requiring him to remove the battery, reinsert it, and re-power the phone just for it to work again"); *Falco v. Nissan N.A.,* 2013 U.S. Dist. LEXIS 147060 (C.D. Cal. 2013)(claim for breach of 2-314 not negated because car could provide transport where car "whines, buzzes, fails to accelerate and maintain speed, experience engine failure, and ultimately requires engine repairs"); *Long v. Graco Children's Prod.,* 2013 U.S. Dist. LEXIS 121227 (N.D. Cal 2013)("Here, the mere fact that a child car seat keeps a child strapped in does not mean that it is fit for its intended purpose—reasonable consumers would also expect that they would be able to quickly unlatch the harness or buckle in case of an emergency, just as they would expect a vehicle's door to easily open in case of an emergency in addition to 'provid[ing] transportation from point A to point B.' Long adequately pleads a breach of implied warranty of merchantability under the SBCWA"); *Fleisher v. Fiber Composites,* 2012 U.S. Dist. LEXIS 157343 (E.D. Pa. 2012)(claim for breach of 2-314 based on fungal growth that caused decking materials to spot not negated where buyers do not allege they "cannot sit, walk, or entertain on their Portico decks" because reasonable "to infer that the ordinary use of outdoor decking material, and the use for which Fiber intended Portico, is in part to 'increase the aesthetic appeal' and 'enhance the outdoor enjoyment'" of buyers' properties).

We all use products in ways they were not originally intended to be used. Have you ever used a screwdriver to open a can of paint or to pry the lid off a jar of (insert object of choice)? If the screwdriver breaks or the jar shatters in the process, has the seller breached the warranty of merchantability implied by 2-314? The easy answer would seem to be "of course not," because opening containers is not the ordinary use for a screwdriver—sellers of screwdrivers intend them to be used to turn screws. But does the fact that everyone—almost everyone—has used a screwdriver to pry open a container affect the "fitness for ordinary purpose" determination? Should it? The next case considers whether the 2-314 warranty protects a buyer's misuse of the product.

VENEZIA V. MILLER BREWING CO.

UNITED STATES COURT OF APPEALS FOR THE FIRST CIRCUIT, 1980
626 F.2D 188

CAMPBELL, Circuit Judge.

Plaintiff appeals the district court's dismissal, for failure to state a claim, of the complaint filed in this diversity action. See Fed.R.Civ.P. 12(b)(6). The complaint charged Miller Brewing Company and three manufacturers of glass products with negligence, gross negligence and breach of warranty in connection with the design and manufacture of a glass bottle used as a container for Miller Beer. The complaint alleged that plaintiff, then eight years of age, was playing with friends near his home when he "found a non-returnable Miller High Life clear glass bottle" which had been "discarded by … persons unknown … ." During the course of play the "thin walled" bottle, in plaintiff's words, "came in contact with a telephone pole." Plaintiff, in his brief, has clarified this phrase, indicating that he was the party responsible for throwing the bottle against the pole. Following the impact of the glass container with the telephone pole the bottle shattered, and particles of glass entered plaintiff's eye causing severe injury. Plaintiff's basic premise is that Miller and the bottle manufacturers should have been aware of the dangers inherent in their "thin walled" "non-returnable" bottles and should have accordingly designed and marketed a product better able to safely withstand such foreseeable misuse as breakage in the course of improper handling by children.

Plaintiff's allegation of breach of warranty is based upon Mass. G.L. c. 106 § 2-314, which provides that a merchant impliedly warrants that his goods are, inter alia, "fit for the ordinary purposes for which such goods are used." The linchpin of the warranty claim (and, as will be seen, the negligence claim also) is thus the proper scope of the term ordinary purpose. While at first blush it might appear beyond dispute that throwing a glass container into a telephone pole is by no means an "ordinary" use of that product, some brief examination of recent authority relied on by plaintiff in support of the contrary view may be helpful in explaining just why the initial impression is, in fact, sound.

In *Back v. Wickes Corp.*, 375 Mass. 633, 378 N.E.2d 964 (1978), the Massachusetts Supreme Judicial Court explored the contours of section 2-314's "ordinary purpose" concept and concluded that the "ordinary purposes' contemplated by (that warranty) section include both those uses which the manufacturer intended and those which are reasonably foreseeable." "It is no more than a play on words," the court concluded, "to charge that goods must be fit for "ordinary' purposes, but not for "extraordinary' or "different' or "unusual' purposes. Such (language) fails to inform … as to whether the defendant has warranted the goods to be free from the propensity that caused the plaintiff's injuries."

Seizing on these passages and the Supreme Judicial Court's further admonition that a manufacturer must, in designing a product, "anticipate the environment in which (that) product will be used," plaintiff urges that the present defendants might reasonably be found by a jury to have broken a fitness warranty by designing and manufacturing glass bottles unable to safely withstand the arguably foreseeable product abuse that occurred here.

The weakness with plaintiff's contention, however, is that it divorces the language of the Back decision from that case's underlying facts. Back involved the question of the liability of a manufacturer of motor homes for wrongful death and personal injuries resulting when one of its vehicles exploded and burst into flames following a collision with a cable fence at the side of the highway. Plaintiffs there maintained that the manufacturer's positioning of the motor home's gasoline tank was responsible for making an otherwise minor collision fatal. The court's inquiry in *Back*, similar to that engaged in by other courts in the so-called second collision cases, *see, e. g., Turcotte v. Ford Motor Co.*, 494 F.2d 173 (1st Cir. 1974); *Larsen v. General Motors Corp.*, 391 F.2d 495 (8th Cir. 1968); *Smith v. Ariens Co.*, 375 Mass. 620, 377 N.E.2d 954 (1978), focused on the question whether the defendant's conscious design choices could be viewed as having rendered the motor home unreasonably dangerous to its users and therefore unfit for highway travel its intended use. In answering that question affirmatively and remanding the case for a new trial, we believe the Back court held only that a manufacturer's warranty of product fitness for ordinary use includes a guarantee that such product will withstand, in a reasonably safe manner, foreseeable "misuse" incident to or arising out of the product's intended use. See W. Prosser, The Law of Torts, § 96, p. 646 (1971). We think it would be stretching too far to believe that the Massachusetts courts are presently prepared to expand their definition of "ordinary purposes" to include the deliberate misuse of an otherwise reasonably safe container in a manner totally unrelated to any normal or intended use of that item. The Massachusetts Supreme Judicial Court previously has found no breach of a warranty of merchantability where a plaintiff was injured by glass breakage sustained in an attempt to pry the cover off a glass baby food jar with a beer-type can opener.[3] A fortiori, we can see no possible implied fitness warranty that an empty glass bottle discarded by unknown persons would more safely withstand being intentionally smashed against a solid stationary object. Under Massachusetts law the question of fitness for ordinary purposes is largely one centering around reasonable consumer expectations. "The propensity of glass to break under pressure is common knowledge," No reasonable consumer would expect anything but that a glass beer bottle, apparently well suited for its immediate intended use, would fail to safely withstand the type of purposeful abuse involved here. In fact, one would suspect that the present eight year old plaintiff knew well the expected result, if not the potential injury, of his conduct. What, if not the possibility of shattering the bottle, would lead him to throw it against the pole in the first place?

The seller's promise that the goods are merchantable is implied whenever the seller is a merchant—a "professional seller" who regularly deals in goods of the type involved in the sale. 2-104. Anyone selling out of inventory—who stocks the goods you buy—is a merchant. The auto-supply shop, the appliance store, the bookstore, the used car dealer, and the neighborhood bakery where you buy scones on the way to school each morning are all merchants under Article 2. But, as used in Article 2, "merchant" can also include a seller who, because of her occupation, has acquired a knowledge or expertise concerning the goods sold similar to that acquired by one who regularly sells such goods as part of its business. A plumber or electrician may be a merchant even though neither maintains an inventory of plumbing or electric supplies from which she sells to the general public; their status as professionals within a trade can give rise to expectations that any goods they provide will be fit for their intended purposes.

Remember, the implied warranty of merchantability presumes that sellers are usually in a better position than buyers to evaluate the risk of product failure based on their prior experience with that product—they know something about the product that buyers will not—but that special knowledge can be acquired from more than simply selling lots of the product.

But, a seller is not a merchant simply because she has a profession:

A person making an isolated sale of goods is not a "merchant" within the meaning of [this section] and thus no warranty of merchantability would apply.

Comment 3, 2-314. The professional musician who sells her saxophone or the professional golfer who sells his golf clubs is not a merchant for purposes of 2-314.

---

3 While the jar had included directions to open "gently," the court emphasized in reaching its decision that "glass jars are not sold, or bought, in the expectation that they will be subjected to pressures" of the sort as were in fact exerted. 151 N.E.2d at 265. If a glass container has not been warranted to withstand an attempt to open it with an improper opening device, it hardly could be warranted to safely survive impact with a telephone pole.

Warranty law has long protected purchasers of food (and drink) for human consumption, whether the food was to be consumed on the seller's premises or elsewhere—mostly as a result of legislative intervention because courts resisted treating some purchases of food for consumption as sales of goods. The guest at a restaurant did not purchase the food she was served; the price she paid was for the services provided, not the food itself. Article 2 continues this protection for buyers of food in 2-314. The serving for value of food and drink for human consumption is deemed to be a sale, making those who regularly sell such products merchants for purposes of the implied warranty of merchantability. 2-314(1). The warranty of merchantability, when applied to sales of food, promises that the food is in fact fit for human consumption. Courts initially determined that food was fit for human consumption—was merchantable—as long as it did not contain any foreign material. The warranty of merchantability was a promise that there would not be anything "unnatural" in food served for consumption. The customer injured by a fishbone in the fish chowder she had ordered did not have a claim that the chowder was unfit for human consumption, regardless of the seriousness of her injury, because fish have bones, and when you purchase chowder with fish in it, you cannot be surprised if it contains bones from those fish. But as the next case illustrates, the natural/foreign substance test for the merchantability of food purchased for human consumption has been criticized in recent years, and many jurisdictions have replaced it with a test based on the reasonable expectations of the buyers of such products.

RUDLOFF V. WENDY'S REST. OF ROCHESTER

CITY COURT OF NEW YORK, 2006
821 N.Y.S.2D 358

MANZ, *Judge.*

BACKGROUND

This is a personal injury action, wherein the plaintiff alleges that he broke a tooth while eating a double cheeseburger (herein referred to as a hamburger) at a Wendy's restaurant. Because the plaintiff claims to have swallowed the portion of the hamburger he was injured on, it is unknown whether the object that is alleged to have caused the injury was (1) a piece of bone, gristle or other substance that was "natural" to the ground beef and fat that make up a hamburger patty, (2) a "foreign" object such as a machine part that may have mistakenly gotten into the hamburger patty during its processing, (3) from some other portion of the hamburger such as the bun, cheese or condiment, or (4) not an object at all but some other condition which could have caused the plaintiff's injury such as the hamburger patty still being partially frozen at the time of consumption.

The plaintiff sued the operator of the restaurant, Wendy's Restaurant of Rochester, Inc., and the manufacturer of the hamburger patty, Moyer Packing Company, Inc., under theories of (1) negligence, and (2) strict products liability. The plaintiff then filed an amended complaint alleging breach of express and implied warranties. Wendy's and Moyer Packing each filed amended answers, which included cross claims against the other.

Wendy's is moving for summary judgment based on the following theories: (1) there was no negligence shown on the part of Wendy's in how it prepared the hamburger, and (2) the plaintiff cannot prove that the substance that caused his injury was not natural to the hamburger patty, i.e., the plaintiff cannot prove that the hamburger had a foreign object in it or was in anyway unfit for consumption; therefore there is no breach of any implied warranty.

None of the parties have addressed the plaintiff's express warranty claim, so that cause of action is not discussed by the court.

Findings of the Court

Since each sale of a food product potentially involves three separate claims sounding in negligence, strict products liability and breach of implied warranty (UCC 2-314), one would expect to find volumes of case law on this subject. However, a review of New York law shows that there is surprisingly little case law on the subject of prepared foods causing injuries to restaurant patrons, and there are no cases involving an injury caused by a hamburger.

While all three concepts are somewhat related (PJI 2:120, 2:141, 2:142) and often overlap, this seems to be one of those cases where the nature of the proof and the way in which the fact issues were litigated demonstrate how the causes of action can diverge and how the subtle differences and interrelations of the three theories are important.

The negligence standard in a products liability case is pretty straightforward. A defendant will be held liable if a plaintiff can show that it is reasonably certain that the product, when put to normal use, would be dangerous if it were defective. A product is defective if the defendant fails to use reasonable care in designing, making, inspecting and testing a product. (PJI 2:120.) In practice, this turns into an inquiry of whether or not a restaurant owner, and his or her suppliers, used ordinary care to remove from the food, as served, such harmful substance as the consumer would not ordinarily anticipate.

Under New York law, a product defect may be actionable under a strict products liability theory if the product is not reasonably safe. Liability is determined by a negligence-like risk/benefit inquiry that looks at the likelihood that the product will cause injury if not properly made, and the reasonableness of the actions (or inactions) taken by the seller/supplier/manufacturer in ensuring that the product was made safe.

In contrast, the standard under an implied warranty theory is whether the product was fit for the ordinary purposes for which such goods are used. That inquiry focuses on the reasonable expectations of the consumer for the product when used in the customary, usual and reasonably foreseeable manners, without regard to the feasibility of alternative designs or the manufacturer's or seller's reasonableness in marketing it in that unsafe condition.

As to the plaintiff's implied warranty cause of action, for almost a 100 years there has been an implied warranty accompanying all sales by a dealer of food articles for immediate use, that the food is fit for human consumption.

The consequences to the consumer resulting from consumption of articles of food sold for immediate use may be so disastrous that an obligation is placed upon the seller to see to it, at his peril, that the articles sold are fit for the purpose for which they are intended. The rule is an onerous one, but public policy as well as the public health demand such obligation should be imposed. The seller has an opportunity which the purchaser does not have of determining whether the article is in the proper condition to be immediately consumed.

In this case, the plaintiff claims that he consumed the article that caused his injury. So he cannot prove definitively what the article was. By inference, the article in question could have been a piece of bone, gristle or other substance that was "natural" to the ground beef and fat that make up a hamburger patty.

This becomes an issue because under the doctrine of implied warranty a defendant will be held liable if a product is not reasonably fit to be used for its ordinary (intended) purpose. (UCC 2-314; PJI 2:142.) However, "reasonably fit" is not defined in the statute and there is no formal test or guidelines put forth in the statute to determine how reasonably fit should be determined. (UCC 2-314.)

Wendy's urges the court to dismiss the action, based on the fact that the plaintiff cannot prove that the article that caused the injury was a foreign object. They argue that for a product to be deemed reasonably unfit, the injury-causing substance has to be foreign to the product and not a natural component of the product itself. Without proof that the injury-causing article was foreign, the plaintiff has no cause of action. This is known as the foreign/natural distinction or test.

This argument is based on the concept that there are certain "natural" hazards that occur in food which a consumer knows can be present in the food and must watch out for in order to protect him or herself. Such natural hazards do not, therefore, make the product unfit. In its crudest form the argument is basically that you can't sue for finding a bone in your steak when you order a T-bone steak.

In its more reasonable form, the argument is that since everyone knows that there are bones in fish, when you order a fish dinner you have to watch out for bones. The mere presence of an injury-causing bone in a piece of fish cannot serve as the basis for claim by a party injured while eating the fish, because there is nothing "wrong" with the fish. A piece of fish with bones in it is fit for its intended purpose.

However, the court does not agree with the defendants that the foreign/natural test is the proper test or that a finding that the substance that caused the plaintiff's injury in this case was "natural" would act as a complete bar to the plaintiff's cause of action.

Based on the *Gimenez* decision, New York courts had consistently held that a breach of implied warranty claim can be brought as a result of a deleterious *or* foreign substance contained in the food.

However, even if the foreign/natural test somehow survived New York's adoption of the Uniform Commercial Code and the use of the reasonable expectation test put forth in *Denny*, its application would not help Wendy's and would in fact call for the granting of summary judgment to the plaintiff based on the facts of this case.

If, as Wendy's argues, it could be shown that the plaintiff was injured on a piece of bone or gristle, this is not a situation where the ingredient or substance causing the injury is natural to the product or where a consumer of the product might be expected to anticipate the presence of the substance in the food. It cannot be said that the fragment of bone which may have been the cause of plaintiff's injuries is natural to a product composed of ground and processed meat and fat, or that a consumer who eats such a product ought to anticipate and be on his guard against the presence of bone.

Regardless of how courts have interpreted the foreign/natural distinction, the court agrees with the plaintiff that on a claim of implied warranty, the test in New York is now the reasonable expectation test.

We know from the Court of Appeals in *Denny* (87 NY2d 248, 256-259, 662 NE2d 730, 639 NYS2d 250 [1995]) that the focus of the inquiry is on the reasonable expectations of the consumer, without regard to negligence principles; the question then becomes how does the court apply the reasonable expectation test in the context of a motion for summary judgment? This court has been unable to find any test or guidelines put forth for a court to use on a summary judgment motion, or for a jury to use as the ultimate finder of fact, and will now attempt to formulate some guidelines.

One of the advantages of the reasonable expectation test is that it is much more flexible than any other test, because it looks at other factors besides the naturalness or origin of the injury-causing object. Therefore, it can be used in a situation like this where the origin of the injury-causing object is unknown. However, one of its downfalls in summary judgment situations is that it is much more expansive in the scope of its review.

To be clear, just because the court has refused to use any bright line foreign/natural test does not mean that the distinction between a foreign or natural object has become irrelevant to the discussion of this case as a whole. On the contrary, the origin of the injury-causing object could play an important role in determining whether the plaintiff should have expected to find it in his or her food. Yet, it should not be the sole determinant. There are many situations in which the origin of the offensive object is no more decisive than any other factor in determining the plaintiff's reasonable expectations.

Categorizing a substance as foreign or natural may have some importance in determining the degree of negligence of the processor of food, but it is not determinative of what is unfit or harmful in fact for human consumption. A bone natural to the meat can cause as much harm as a foreign substance such as a nut or a bolt. All are hazardous to teeth and likely to cause injury.

But equally as important as not using the foreign/natural test, the court cannot simply state that it is adopting a reasonable expectation test, then proceed to do a traditional negligence review of the facts. The focus should not become an inquiry of whether or not a restaurant owner used ordinary care to remove from the food, as served, such harmful substance as the consumer would not ordinarily anticipate. This is the standard for a negligence cause of action, not implied warranty.

Thus, both the nature of the object and how the food was prepared should merely be factors, and *not* the sole determining factors in considering the broader question of whether the plaintiff should have expected to find the item in his or her food.

By not limiting the focus to these two issues, the inquiry will be kept from reverting to the old foreign/natural test and/or from having the matter being an implied warranty action in name only, and in reality being a negligence action with all of the focus being on the defendant's preparation of the food.

But in order to attempt to determine the reasonable expectations of what a consumer expects to find in his or her food the court has to examine such factors as (1) the nature or size of the object, or both, (2) the type of food involved, (3) the way in which the food was inspected, processed and prepared, (4) the type of establishment where the food was purchased, (5) whether the food needed further preparation before consumption, (6) what type of opportunity the consumer had to protect himself or herself from the alleged defect (i.e., how the item is traditionally consumed), and (7) what steps, if any, must a reasonable consumer take to inspect his or her food prior to consumption.

Having put forth the factors to be considered, it is difficult for the court to conceive of how a consumer might guard against the injury complained of here, short of removing the hamburger from its bun, breaking it apart and inspecting its small components. Certainly Wendy's or its suppliers do not expect a consumer to go to such lengths, especially since a hamburger is meant to be eaten out of hand, without cutting, slicing, or even the use of a fork or knife. If one reasonably expects to find an item in his or her food then he or she guards against being injured by watching out for that item. But when one eats a hamburger he does not nibble his or her way along hunting for bones because he or she is not reasonably expecting one in his food.

Since a consumer cannot reasonably guard against this type of incident, short of not eating a hamburger in the first place, it is hard for the court to find how any consumer could reasonably expect to encounter such an object in a hamburger, which would prevent the granting of summary judgment to the plaintiff on this issue. However, the court knows that if the same question were put to some of our fair city's more senior shoppers at Buffalo's Broadway Market, the answer may be somewhat different.

Therefore, with all of the above factors to consider, it is the holding of this court that when a consumer is injured by an object in a piece of food, whether its origin is foreign, natural or unknown, the question of whether that food has been rendered unfit for consumption (i.e., should a consumer have reasonably expected the object to be in the food), except in the rarest of cases, should not be decided as a matter of law. These are all proper considerations for a jury, not a judge.

Therefore, the fact that the plaintiff cannot prove that the substance that caused his injury was not "foreign" to the hamburger patty is an insufficient basis to grant summary judgment to Wendy's and Moyer Packing on the plaintiff's implied warranty cause of action and those motions are also denied.

The court realizes that the adoption of the reasonable expectation standard puts Wendy's in a precarious position of possibly having to argue that a customer should reasonably expect to find an object in his or her hamburgers that is large enough to break a tooth. But maybe that is why there were no reported cases in New York involving a plaintiff being injured on a hamburger.

The unjustified premise of the natural/foreign substance test was illustrated by the Illinois Court of Appeals in *Jackson v. Nestle-Beich*, 569 N.E.2d 1119 (Ill. App. 1991):

> If one purchases a whole fish to bake surely he or she could 'reasonably expect' to find bones in it. However, if one purchases fish patties or fish sticks, it seems unrealistic to say he would 'reasonably expect' to find bones in the processed items. Likewise, if one purchases oysters in the shell it might be said one could 'reasonably expect' to find a pearl in one of

the oysters. However, if one purchases canned processed oysters it seems unrealistic to say he could 'reasonably expect' to find a pearl in same. Herein lies the difficulty or confusion in food cases. The *possibility* of finding a harmful substance versus the *probability* of finding a harmful substance seems the key in analyzing these cases. * * * If one 'reasonably expects' to find an item in his or her food then he guards against being injured by watching for that item. When one eats a hamburger he does not nibble his way along hunting for bones because he is not 'reasonably expecting' one in the food. Likewise, when one eats processed oysters, normally one does not gingerly graze through each oyster hunting for a pearl because he is not 'reasonably expecting' one in the food. It seems logical some consideration should be given to the manner in which the food is normally eaten in determining if a person can be said to 'reasonably expect' an item in processed food. In the present case we think the average, ordinary, reasonably prudent person eating processed oysters would eat same by way of bites and would not nibble her way through each oyster because of the possibility of finding a pearl."

We began this section by noting that warranty claims often can be restated as negligence claims. In a negligence case, the plaintiff's contributory responsibility for the harm suffered can affect the plaintiff's right to recover and/or the amount of any recovery. What effect, if any, does the buyer's conduct have on her claim for breach of the implied warranty of merchantability? The cases have noted that in a claim for breach of warranty, the seller's culpability is not an issue—if the product does not do was it was intended to do, the "innocent" seller has still breached the warranty. Should the same be true with respect to the buyer—the buyer's post-purchase conduct is not relevant to whether the product was fit for the ordinary purposes for which it was intended? Whether the toaster browns bread or it doesn't is unrelated to the buyer's IQ. The next case examines the effect of the buyer's post-purchase conduct on a claim for breach of the warranty implied under 2-314.

ERDMAN V. JOHNSON BROS. RADIO & TELEVISION CO.
COURT OF APPEALS OF MARYLAND, 1970
271 A.2D 744

FINAN, Judge.

It has been said that "the seller's warranty is a curious hybrid, born of the illicit intercourse of tort and contract, unique in the law."[4] A further reading of this opinion will show why.

On June 24, 1965, the appellants (Erdman and Pfaff) purchased a color television-radio-stereo console from the appellees (Johnson Brothers) for approximately $1,000. As events unfolded this proved to be a most unfortunate investment. The set was put into operation by one of Johnson Brothers' repairmen, and Erdman and Pfaff looked forward with great expectations to many hours of pleasant viewing. Their joy soon turned to consternation, however, as they began experiencing difficulty with the set almost from the outset. In an act of great foresight, the appellants had purchased a service policy from Johnson Brothers; they had many occasions to avail themselves of its benefits.

Approximately one month after the purchase, the set was sent back to Johnson Brothers for repairs, and was returned to the appellants' home about a week later. Sometime after that, Erdman noticed a "crackling sound" in the television; the noise was often accompanied by a "tear" in the picture. This, of course, precipitated complaints by the appellants to Johnson Brothers, and resulted

---

4   W. Prosser, *Law of Torts*, 651 (3rd Ed. 1964).

in some two dozen service calls to the appellants' house. Sometime in September, 1966, Erdman and Pfaff for the first time noticed sparks and heavy smoke shooting out of the back of the set and the smell of burning rubber, wire, or some other substance. Another complaint was made. Johnson Brothers' serviceman examined the set on September 30, 1966, and stated that whatever had happened had "fused itself together again," and that if anything serious developed he would be able to fix it.

For the next few months the television operated in its usual (cantankerous) manner and there was no difficulty serious enough to warrant another complaint, at least not until December 7, 1966, a Wednesday. On that date Erdman called Johnson Brothers and for the second time complained about having seen actual sparks and smoke emanating from the rear of the television. The person taking this complaint ventured no opinion as to the cause of the trouble, and merely noted that there would be a serviceman out to the appellants' house on Saturday, December 10, 1966. (Inasmuch as Erdman and Pfaff both worked during the week, the usual practice of the parties was to have the set serviced on Saturdays, as a matter of convenience to the appellants. The very fact that it was necessary to establish a "policy" for making service calls to the plaintiffs' residence perhaps describes the condition of the set more eloquently than this Court ever could.)

On the fateful evening of Thursday, December 8, 1966, (after the second complaint and prior to the day on which the repairs were to be performed) Erdman and Pfaff watched television from approximately 11:20 P.M. until 1:30 A.M. of Friday, December 9, 1966, at which time they observed for the third time that there were sparks and smoke coming from the set. They turned off the television, and retired for the night. About half an hour later they were awakened by the barking of one of their eleven dogs, and discovered that a fire was very much in progress in the vicinity of the television set. The fire spread rapidly, and by the dawn's early light Erdman and Pfaff saw, tragically, that their residence had been completely destroyed. The total loss in real and personal property was $67,825.91.

Suit was brought in Baltimore County, the appellants alleging in one count a breach of warranty in the sale to them of a defective unit, and in the other count a breach of the service contract and negligence. The lower court (Turnbull, J.) sitting without a jury, ruled that there was no breach of the service contract, that the appellants' use of the set was not "normal" under the circumstances, thereby negating the warranty of merchantability and, without deciding whether or not there was any primary negligence on the part of the appellees, ruled that the appellants' use of the set amounted to contributory negligence under the facts of this case. The court therefore rendered judgment for the appellees, and the appellants brought this appeal.

They urge that their conduct did not negate the warranty of fitness, that they were not contributorily negligent, and that the trial court wrongfully excluded the expert opinion testimony of two of their witnesses. In our view of the case, the key to the decision turns on the conduct of the appellants.

The Uniform Commercial Code (U.C.C.) Maryland Code (1964 Repl. Vol.) Art. 95B, governs the sale of the television in this case, and it provides that anyone who sells goods and who is a merchant with respect to that kind of goods, impliedly warrants in his contract for sale that the goods sold are "merchantable." In order for goods to be considered merchantable, they must be "fit for the ordinary purposes for which such goods are used." Code (1964 Repl. Vol.) Art. 95B (U.C.C.), § 2-314(2) (c). It would appear that Johnson Brothers most assuredly is a merchant within the meaning of the U.C.C. (§ 2-104) and that they gave an implied warranty to the appellants that the television in question was fit for the ordinary purposes to which a television might be put. The Official Comments to § 2-314 state that protection under the "fitness for ordinary purposes" aspect of the implied warranty of merchantability extends not only to a person buying for resale to the ultimate consumer (e. g. a retailer), but also, as here, to the ultimate consumer for his own use.

Section 2-714 of the U.C.C. indicates that a buyer may recover not only normal damages from a seller in case of breach, but in a "proper case" the buyer may also recover incidental and consequential damages. Section 2-715 provides that consequential damages may include any "injury to person or property proximately resulting from any breach of warranty."

The Comments to the U.C.C. speak in terms of "causation" with respect to the implied warranty of merchantability. Comment 13 to § 2-314 (implied warranty of merchantability) indicates that the buyer must show not only a breach of warranty, but also that the breach was the "proximate cause of the loss sustained." Comment 5 to § 2-715 (consequential damages) treats "proximate causation" in more explicit terms, reiterating the fact that the section allows damages for injuries resulting "proximately" from the breach of warranty. In further delineation, the Comment states that if the buyer did in fact discover a defect in the goods prior to his using them, then the injury suffered from the use of the goods would not proximately result from the breach of warranty. The U.C.C. view of the question of warranty in terms of principles of causation is in harmony with the view of the text writers who have addressed themselves to the problem.

At this juncture it is appropriate that we review the rationale upon which the trial judge predicated his opinion. Judge Turnbull stated:

> "I think the law is that there was a warranty, either expressed or implied, from Johnson to the Plaintiffs, warranty that this television set would operate safely for the general purpose for which it was intended when used in a normal manner.

> * * *

> "* * * You have a man of high intelligence, who purchased this television set, who continued to use it, even though he knew and had complained that it was arcing, smoking, with actual sparks and a burning odor. Now using a set which is in that condition is certainly not, in my opinion, a use in a normal manner. So that it is my opinion, and I so hold that, even assuming the fire came about as a result of a defect in the set, that the warranty did not extend to the point, under the circumstances of this case, of covering the Plaintiff's damages resulting from the fire. So that I find, and hold that, under the warranty, the Defendant is not responsible to the Plaintiffs.

> "* * * [I]t is inescapable to me that the Plaintiffs were guilty of contributory negligence in failing to act as an ordinarily prudent person would act under the circumstances then and there existing, in that, knowing that the set was sparking, arcing, burning or there was an odor of burning, nonetheless, they used the set for a period of, according to the testimony, somewhere in the general neighborhood of two hours, on the late evening and early morning of December 8th and December 9th. I believe that that constitutes negligence; * * *.

> "* * * So that, sitting as a trier of the facts sitting as a jury, gentlemen, I find that it is inescapable that, even if you assume primary negligence, any trier of the facts must find that there was glaring contributory negligence on the part of the plaintiffs [appellants]."

Judge Turnbull in his opinion makes it abundantly clear that he was of the opinion after hearing all the facts that the appellants used the television set after discovering the defect (when they noticed the burning and sparks and made their second complaint on December 7, 1966), and that therefore the implied warranty of merchantability did not apply.

Our reading of the U.C.C. in light of the record supports this interpretation. It would appear that an individual using a product when he had actual knowledge of a defect or knowledge of facts which were so obvious that he must have known of a defect, is either no longer relying on the seller's express or implied warranty or has interjected an intervening cause of his own, and therefore a breach of such warranty cannot be regarded as the proximate cause of the ensuing injury. Such an interpretation gives effect to the true nature of the action involved and the intention of the U.C.C. without needlessly involving the courts in a discussion of whether the implied warranty is founded in contract, tort, or both.

In fairness to the appellants it should be noted that, as was pointed out in their brief, it is somewhat unclear as to whether the trial judge based his holding of no liability on the fact that the plaintiffs, by their continued use of the television set after the discovery of the defect, were no longer relying on the seller's warranty, or on his finding that their actions amounted to contributory negligence, or on both. We should add that from the wording of his opinion he might well have found, and we think properly so, that there was a coalescence of both.

At the trial below there appears to have been no objection raised to the defense of contributory negligence in an implied warranty case; however, on appeal the appellants make the observation that, "whether or not contributory negligence is a bar to any recovery under a warranty theory remains a somewhat open question in this jurisdiction." We would think, however, that the recent decision of this Court in *Levin v. Walter Kidde & Co.*, 251 Md. 560, 561, 248 A. 2d 151 (1968), leaves little doubt but that the negligence of the plaintiff contributing to the accident, in a case involving a breach of implied warranty, would bar recovery. Before further discussing the theory of liability in the case at bar and in *Levin, supra*, it will be helpful to review the remarks of Professor Prosser in his article, *The Fall of the Citadel*, 32 *American Trial Lawyers Association Journal* 1, at 21 (1968); 50 Minn. L.R. 791, wherein he states:

> "Superficially the warranty cases, whether on direct sale to the user or without privity, are in a state of complete contradiction and confusion as to the defense of contributory negligence. It has been said in a good many of them that such negligence is always a defense to an action for breach of warranty. It has been said in almost as many that it is never a defense. This is no more than a part of the general murk that has surrounded 'warranty,' and is one more indication that this unfelicitous word is a source of trouble in the field. Actually, however, the disagreement is solely a matter of language; and if the cases are examined as to their substance, they fall into a very consistent pattern.

> "Where the negligence of the plaintiff consists only in failure to discover the danger in the product, or to take precautions against its possible existence, it has uniformly been held that it is not a bar to an action for breach of warranty. * * * But if he discovers the defect, or knows the danger arising from it, and proceeds nevertheless deliberately to encounter it by making use of the product, his conduct is the kind of contributory negligence which overlaps assumption of risk; and on either theory his recovery is barred. * * *."

Of similar import is the comment found in 1 Hursh, *American Law of Products Liability*, p. 415, § 3:9, wherein the author points out that the decisions on the application of contributory negligence in breach of warranty cases "are less than entirely harmonious." Hursh observes that, "the weight * * * which is hardly a great weight * * * of authority appears to be on the side of the view that negligence on the part of the user of the product is no defense in a breach of warranty action against the manufacturers or seller of the product." However, the author emphasizes that "liability for breach of warranty exists only where it is shown that the breach was the proximate cause of the harm for which recovery is sought, * * *" and he raises the query as to whether evidence may not properly be adduced, showing the injured person's contributory negligence, to demonstrate that the harm was caused otherwise than by breach of warranty. Hursh also makes the important caveat that:

> "It is necessary to point out that there is some authority which impliedly supports the view that contributory negligence, where established, will bar recovery for breach of warranty. Included among such cases are those which state that a breach of warranty, from which

liability for product-caused injury flows, cannot be established by evidence of a product defect of which the purchaser of the product was aware prior to the occurrence of the injury.

Note that something closely akin to the idea of contributory negligence was embodied in § 336 of the Restatement of Contracts, which states that damages are not recoverable for harm that the plaintiff 'should have foreseen and should have avoided by reasonable effort without undue risk * * *.'"

The purists among those who would not allow contributory negligence as a defense make some distinctions which we believe to be artificial. Our view is bolstered by the following comment found in 4 A.L.R.3rd 503, *Products Liability—Implied Warranty*:

"To say that contributory negligence or assumption of the risk is, or is not, available as a defense to an action for breach of implied warranty, may be deceptive. Obviously, the disallowance of one of these specific defenses would be of limited significance where the facts upon which it was based were held to constitute a different, but equally effective, defense. To illustrate, where the buyer of an article realizes that it is dangerously defective, but nevertheless proceeds to use it, a court may refuse to allow the seller to assert assumption of the risk, but hold that the buyer's actions indicate that he did not rely on the warranty, and that he is therefore barred from recovery. In such an instance, the allowance, vel non, of a given defense would be an interesting exercise in semantics, but would probably have no effect whatsoever on the outcome of the litigation."

See also 1 *Anderson, Uniform Commercial Code* (2d Ed. 1970) pg. 543.

Thus, considering the facts in the case at bar we think it no more than an exercise in semantics to quibble over whether the actions of the appellants amounted to an abandonment of their reliance on the seller's implied warranty, or contributory negligence, or indeed whether we should view the trial judge's finding of contributory negligence on the plaintiffs' part as tantamount to a finding of an abandonment by them of their reliance on the implied warranty. The important factor under either theory or an amalgam of them is that, although there may have been a breach of the warranty, that the breach is no longer considered "the proximate cause of the loss." U.C.C. § 2-314, Comment 13. That is, the defect in the set, of which the plaintiffs had knowledge, could no longer be relied upon by them as a basis for an action of breach of warranty.

A reading of the cases cited by the various authorities heretofore mentioned indicates that a defense based on the theory of contributory negligence in an action for breach of warranty was allowed in the following cases representing eight jurisdictions: *Dallison v. Sears, Roebuck & Co.,* 313 F. 2d 343 (10th Cir. 1962); *Posey v. Pensacola Tractor & Equipment Co., Inc.,* 138 So. 2d 777 (1st Dist. Ct. App., Fla. 1962); *Arnaud's Restaurant Inc. v. Cotter,* 212 F. 2d 883 (5th Cir. 1954), *cert. den.* 348 U.S. 915; *Marko v. Sears, Roebuck & Co.,* 94 A. 2d 348 (App. Div. N. J. Super. Ct. 1953); *Barefield v. LaSalle Coca-Cola Bottling Co.,* 120 N.W.2d 786 (Mich. 1963) [In this case the defense of "assumed risk" was allowed]; *Gardner v. Coca-Cola Bottling Co.,* 127 N.W.2d 557 (Minn. 1964); *Nelson v. Anderson,* 72 N.W.2d 861 (Minn. 1955); *Missouri Bag Co. v. Chemical Delinting Co.,* 58 So. 2d 71 (Miss. 1952); *Natale v. Pepsi-Cola Co.,* 182 N.Y.S.2d 404 (App. Div. 1959); *Eisenbach v. Gimbel Brothers, Inc.,* 24 N.E.2d 131 (N. Y. 1939); *Fredendall v. Abraham & Straus Inc.,* 18 N.E.2d 11 (N. Y. 1938).

In Maryland, prior to the enactment of the Uniform Commercial Code (Art. 95B of the Annotated Code of Maryland) which took effect February 1, 1964, there had been cases in which the action was based on implied warranty of the fitness of a product as limited by the common law and the Uniform Sales Act, Maryland Code (1957 Ed.) Art. 83, §§ 19-96. See *Hacker v. Shofer,* 251 Md. 672, 673, 248 A. 2d 351 (1968), and *Twombley v. Fuller Brush Co.,* 221 Md. 476, 489, 158 A. 2d 110 (1960), and cases cited therein. There have also been cases involving manufacturers' products liability bottomed on tort.

See *Babylon v. Scruton,* 215 Md. 299, 303, 138 A. 2d 375 (1958), *Kaplan v. Stein,* 198 Md. 414, 420, 84 A. 2d 81 (1951), citing *Milestone System v. Gasior,* 160 Md. 131, 152 A. 810 (1931).

Cf. also *Woolley v. Uebelhor,* 239 Md. 318, 211 A. 2d 302 (1965). Also, since the adoption of the Uniform Commercial Code there have been cases based on the breach of the manufacturer's or seller's warranty as to the fitness of a chattel for its intended use, *Myers v. Montgomery Ward & Co.,* 253 Md. 282, 252 A. 2d 855 (1969), and *Levin v. Walter Kidde & Co.,* 251 Md. 560, 248 A. 2d 151 (1968). However, in none of the above cases where the plaintiff was proceeding on the basis of an implied warranty of the manufacturer or seller as to the fitness of the product, was the Court presented with any issue regarding the defense of contributory negligence.

Actually, in *Levin, supra,* the Court assumed that the defense of contributory negligence was available to the defendant and predicated its decision in favor of the appellee on that premise. In that case the plaintiff's brother-in-law had purchased from a distributor of the manufacturer-defendant a syphon bottle for carbonated water to be used in mixing drinks, and had given it to the plaintiff as a gift. The plaintiff, while in the preparation of carbonated water, was injured when the bottle exploded in his hand. In affirming the lower court, which had directed a verdict in favor of the defendant, Judge Marbury, writing for this Court stated:

> "We conclude that under these circumstances, the lower court was correct in holding as a matter of law that the instructions constituted sufficient warning of a danger that might arise from operating a Soda King bottle. We further conclude that the appellant failed to use reasonable care in following the instructions for his own safety so that his action in manipulating the bottle constituted negligence which barred any right of recovery by him. For the above reasons, the judgment will be affirmed."

In the case at bar the trial judge did not make any finding as to primary negligence on the part of the defendant under the second count of the declaration. However, he stated that, assuming there was primary negligence, the plaintiffs were barred from recovery because of their actions. We think it should also be stated that the breach of warranty, if any there was, was not the proximate cause of the fire because of the appellants' continued use of the set after the discovery of the obvious defects. We believe that such a holding is consistent with the trial judge's characterization of the plaintiffs' conduct as contributory negligence and with the Uniform Commercial Code's Official Comment 13 to § 2-314, and Comment 5 to § 2-715. Again, we would not quarrel with those who might prefer to state it differently, i.e., that when the purchaser is guilty of actions amounting to contributory negligence in his use of the products, he is no longer relying on the implied warranty of the seller. Insofar as the issue of the liability of the defendant is concerned the end result would be the same in this case.

It may well be that a jury would have reached a decision in the case at bar contrary to the one which the lower court reluctantly reached. And, in view of the appellants' obvious ignorance of electronics and the fact that the burning symptoms complained about in December were the same as those complained about in September (at which time the appellants were apparently assured that whatever the trouble was, it was minor and had corrected itself), it is entirely possible that members of this Court would not have found any contributory negligence had they been trying the case below. However, that is of small consolation to the appellants. The fact remains, we cannot substitute our judgment for that of the trier of facts unless the findings of fact be "clearly erroneous" and we cannot rule as a matter of law that the court erred in its finding of contributory negligence in the case at bar.

Appellants' main contention with respect to the lower court's finding of contributory negligence is that their actions were not negligent because they had been assured by Johnson Brothers' serviceman in September that the situation was not serious, and that they had every right to rely on these assurances. It is true that a person may rely on assurances of safety made to him by others in a situation where an ordinarily prudent person would do so. However, such assurances do not relieve a person from the duty of caring for his own safety, and a person cannot rely on another's assurances where he is aware of the danger involved or where the danger is obvious enough that an ordinarily prudent person would not so rely.

Once again, the "reasonable man" standard must be applied, and this Court is not prepared to say that the trial court was in error in finding that an ordinarily prudent person would not have used the television on the night in question, knowing of the problems experienced only a day or two before, regardless of what he might have been told several months earlier. Likewise the fact cannot be ignored that they knew the serviceman was due within 48 hours. Also, we cannot say as a matter of law that an ordinarily prudent person would not have pulled the plug before going to bed on the night in question after having seen sparks and smoke for the third time only moments before. This is especially true in view of the fact that the television was equipped with a rather independent "instant-on" device which had been known in the past to turn on the television automatically, without aid of any discoverable human assistance (absent the presence of a poltergeist.) Accordingly, we must affirm the holding of the lower court in its finding of contributory negligence.

———————————

As the *Erdman* case illustrates, the buyer's post-purchase conduct will not affect whether the warranty of merchantability has been breached, but it can affect whether the buyer will be able to recover for that breach. Part of a buyer's claim for breach under 2-314 includes showing that the breach proximately caused the damages for which the buyer is seeking compensation. Whether we call it contributory negligence, an intervening cause, or assumption of the risk, a buyer's post-purchase conduct that severs the causal chain will bar recovery for breach of the implied warranty of merchantability under 2-314.

PROBLEM 8 - 1

Do the parties injured in the following cases have a claim against the store for breach of the implied warranty of merchantability? 2-314.

> Case 1: A two-year-old child broke one of her fingers while riding in the child's seat in one of the store's shopping carts. Her finger got caught in the nest gate hinge on the cart after her father had placed her in the cart.

> Case 2: A shopper had to be taken to the hospital to have a bone removed from his throat after swallowing a sushi sample the deli was offering as part of its "Foods from the Seas" promotion one weekend at the store.

> Case 3: A bottle of olives shattered in a shopper's hand as she was removing it from a display case to place in it in her cart. It took twenty-three stitches to close the lacerations caused by the broken glass.

PROBLEM 8 - 2

Rae ordered one pallet of sweet corn from a local farmer. The corn was packed in burlap bags, six dozen ears to a bag, one hundred bags on a pallet. When a produce worker opened the bags, she discovered that most of the ears had corn rot—a toxic fungus that makes corn inedible. Did the farmer breach the implied warranty of merchantability under 2-314?

PROBLEM 8 - 3

Determine whether the store breached the implied warranty of merchantability in the following transactions:

Transaction 1: Last month, the store unknowingly put out for sale pork products containing larval trichinella, and several shoppers who bought those products have developed trichinosis. Does it matter that the larvae are killed if pork is properly cooked—heated to 165° for at least fifteen seconds?

Transaction 2: A longtime shopper at the store has developed health problems caused by high cholesterol—which he claims resulted from his daily consumption of butter and donuts sold by the store.

Transaction 3: Last week, a shopper's home was damaged by a fire which started when the microwave oven she bought at the store shorted out while she attempted to cook a potato wrapped in foil in the oven.

Transaction 4: A shopper chipped several teeth when he bit into a roasted chicken sandwich he was served at the deli. The teeth were chipped by a chicken bone found in the sandwich. Would your answer be different if the shopper had taken the sandwich home and bitten into it there?

Transaction 5: Would your answer in Transaction 4 be different if the teeth were chipped by a nail found in the sandwich instead of a chicken bone?

Transaction 6: A shopper's child had a severe allergic reaction after eating a sandwich made with sourdough bread made in the store's bakery. The child is allergic to peanuts, and the bakery used peanut oil in its sourdough bread but did not list it as an ingredient on the label attached to the bread.

Transaction 7: A shopper suffered severe lacerations to his hand when he attempted to remove the cap from a jar of baby food with the help of a meat mallet he had purchased at the store. To loosen the cap on the jar, he tapped it with the mallet, and the jar shattered in his hand.

Transaction 8: A shopper was severely burned by hot coffee she was drinking in the deli when the handle of the mug it was served in snapped off while she was sipping it, dumping extremely hot coffee onto her lap.

PROBLEM 8 - 4

The store purchases a variety of nuts in bulk for repackaging and sale to shoppers. Rae ordered two hundred pounds of "unshelled walnuts" which were delivered to the store last week. When the bulk foods manager began repackaging the walnuts, she found some of the nuts were shelled, making them unsaleable. When Rae called the seller to complain, the seller told her that in the bulk-nuts business, an order of bulk nuts was not objectionable if it contained shelled nuts as long as the percentage of shelled nuts was not greater than 2 percent of the total nuts in the order. Are the walnuts delivered to the store merchantable, even though some of them are shelled? 2-314.

2. Fitness for a Particular Purpose

If a buyer purchases goods intending to use them for something other than their ordinary purpose, the failure of the goods to perform as expected is, obviously, not a breach of the warranty of merchantability. As we've determined, the warranty of merchantability is not a promise that the goods are fit for *any* purpose, but only that they are fit for the usual, typical, ordinary uses to which they are commonly put. The expectations of a buyer with a different use in mind are not the expectations protected under 2-314. But what if the seller knows the buyer intends to use the goods for a different purpose and encourages the buyer to go ahead with the purchase—should the seller bear some responsibility if the goods don't perform as expected by the buyer? Should we excuse the buyer for failing to investigate further the fitness of the goods for her particular purpose? Article 2's answer to these questions is provided by 2-315—the implied warranty of fitness for a particular purpose:

> Where the seller at the time of contracting has reason to know any particular purpose for which the goods are required and that the buyer is relying on the seller's skill or judgment to select or furnish suitable goods, there is unless excluded or modified under the next section an implied warranty that the goods shall be fit for such purpose.

2-315. The expectations protected under 2-315 are different from the expectations protected by 2-314:

> A "particular purpose" differs from the ordinary purpose for which the goods are used in that it envisages a specific use by the buyer which is peculiar to the nature of his business, whereas the ordinary purposes for which goods are used are those envisaged in the concept of merchantability and go to uses which are customarily made of the goods in question ... The whole point of an implied warranty of fitness for a particular purpose is that the product sold by the seller to the buyer will be suitable for the "specific purpose" which the buyer has, and any similar product which the seller may sell to the buyer which is not so suited will breach that warranty of fitness for the particular purpose.
>
> *Paper Mfrs. v. Rescuers,* 60 F. Supp. 2d 689 (N.D. Ind. 1999).

I probably don't need any help to pick out a toaster I can use to heat up my Pop-Tart every morning—even a law professor has the life experience required to make that decision. What if, instead, I'm looking for an air conditioner that has the capacity to efficiently cool my home? I could get online and try to figure it out myself, or I could enlist the help of the "expert" at Home Depot and buy the unit she recommended. If the unit does not efficiently and effectively cool my home, do I have a claim against Home Depot under 2-315?

> The implied warranty of fitness for a particular purpose requires that: (1) the purchaser have a particular purpose *outside* the scope of ordinary purposes; (2) the seller at the time of contracting has reason to know of the particular purpose; (3) the seller has reason to know that the purchaser is relying on the seller's skill or judgment to furnish appropriate goods; and (4) the purchaser must, in fact, rely upon the seller's skill or judgment.
>
> *Lorfano v. Dura Stone Steps,* 569 A.2d 195 (Me. 1990).

Ford Motor Co. v. General Accident Ins. Co.

Court of Appeals of Maryland, 2001
365 Md. 321

HARRELL, Judge.

On 5 August 1995, International Motors, Inc., trading as Montrose Towing (Montrose or Respondent), purchased a tow truck from Elzenheimer Chevrolet. The tow truck had been created by Elzenheimer by adding necessary components to a 1995 Ford F-350 base chassis cab truck that Elzenheimer had purchased from a Ford dealership. Respondent insured the truck with General Accident Insurance Company (General Accident). On 19 August 1997, the tow truck caught fire as its operator was about to tow a vehicle. As a result of the fire, General Accident determined that the truck was a total loss and paid Montrose for its value. General Accident then sought reimbursement from Ford Motor Company (Ford or Petitioner), the manufacturer of the chassis cab truck, but Ford refused.

On 5 May 1998, General Accident, on behalf of Respondent, filed a subrogation claim against Ford in the Circuit Court for Montgomery County alleging negligence, breach of warranty, and strict liability based on a manufacturing defect. The trial court, after a bench trial, entered judgment in favor of Ford on all claims. General Accident appealed. The Court of Special Appeals affirmed the Circuit Court's judgment in favor of Ford on the express warranty, negligence, and strict liability claims, but vacated that part of the Circuit's Court's judgment with regards to claims of breach of the implied warranty of merchantability and the implied warranty of fitness for a particular purpose. We granted Petitioner's petition for writ of certiorari, *Ford Motor Company, Inc. v. International Motors Inc.*, 362 Md. 34, 762 A.2d 968 (2000), to consider the following questions:

I.

On 15 March 1995, Ford sold a 1995 F-350 chassis cab truck it had manufactured to Homer Skelton Ford, Inc., a Ford dealership in Olive Branch, Mississippi.

On 16 May 1995, Elzenheimer Chevrolet, located in the State of New York, purchased the truck from Homer Skelton Ford and converted it into a tow truck. To convert the chassis cab into a tow truck, Elzenheimer Chevrolet added, among other things, a towing bar, boom tow sling, a light illumination bar on top of the pre-existing lights along the body of the truck, a strobe light in the grill, a two-way radio mounted to the dash board, a three-switch electrical panel inside the passenger cab, and a power take-off with controls on the transmission hump. On 5 August 1995, Montrose purchased the truck, as yet unused as a tow truck, from Elzenheimer and insured it with General Accident.

On 19 August 1997, the truck, now with 27,600 miles on the odometer, caught fire while its operator, Greg Blum, a Montrose employee, was preparing to tow another vehicle. Mr. Blum had responded to a routine call to Dulles Airport in Virginia to tow a limousine, which had been struck on the driver's side door by a shuttle bus. When Mr. Blum arrived, he observed that the door to the limousine was stuck in the open position. Before the vehicle could be towed safely, the door of the limousine needed to be closed. It took approximately fifteen minutes to secure the door. While working on closing the car door, Mr. Blum kept the engine of the tow truck running. This was necessary apparently because the engine must be running in order to use the power take-off to tow a vehicle. He reentered the driver's compartment of the tow truck to back the truck up to begin the actual hook-up and towing.

When Mr. Blum reentered the tow truck to begin the towing process, he noticed steam or smoke coming from under the hood of the vehicle. He checked the engine temperature gauge, but it registered normal. When Mr. Blum looked up from the gauge, he noticed flames coming from under the hood of the vehicle on the passenger side. After pulling the hood release located under the driver's side of the dashboard, he exited the cab and proceeded to the rear of the truck to retrieve a fire extinguisher. When he went to the front of the truck with the extinguisher and attempted to lift the engine hood, he found the hood too hot to touch. He aimed the fire extinguisher towards the flames and completely discharged the extinguisher.

The truck was deemed a total loss. General Accident paid Montrose for its value, stipulated to be $23,880.21. General Accident, the subrogated insurer, thereafter wrote to Ford seeking reimbursement. Ford initially responded that it needed to inspect the vehicle. General Accident voluntarily made the vehicle available to Mr. Samuel, an inspector employed by Ford. After Mr. Samuel inspected the vehicle and reported, Ford denied the claim.

On 5 May 1998, General Accident, on behalf of its insured, Montrose, filed a subrogation claim against Ford in the Circuit Court for Montgomery County. General Accident thereafter filed two amended complaints, the last of which alleged claims for negligence, breach of warranty, and strict liability based on a manufacturing defect.

At the conclusion of the trial, the judge rejected General Accident's design defect theory and entered judgment for Ford on the two remaining claims—negligence and breach of the implied warranty....

On General Accident's appeal, the Court of Special Appeals affirmed the Circuit Court's judgment in favor of Ford on the claims of breach of express warranty, negligence, and strict liability. The intermediate appellate court, however, with regard to the claims of breach of the implied warranty of merchantability, § 2-314, *supra* note 7, and the implied warranty of fitness for a particular purpose, § 2-315, *supra* note 8, vacated the trial court's judgment and remanded the case "for resolution of [the] implied warranty claims."

* * *

B. Sufficient Evidence

Petitioner alternatively argues that there was insufficient evidence to support a claim of implied warranty of fitness for a particular purpose. The Court of Special Appeals determined that, as to the implied warranty of fitness for a particular purpose, § 2-315, *supra* note 8, Respondent did not have to prove a defect in order to prevail under this theory. The intermediate appellate court surmised:

> Ford manufactures chassis cabs with knowledge that they will be modified in some form or another. Ford was aware that Elzenheimer had, in the past, purchased Ford chassis cabs for the purpose of turning them into tow trucks. Thus, Ford impliedly warranted that the truck would be fit for usage as a tow truck.

> Here, the evidence showed that Ford breached its implied warranty of fitness for a particular purpose when (1) General [Accident]'s insured was using the truck as a tow truck, and (2) the truck unexpectedly caught on fire. The circuit court was persuaded that the fire started in the engine compartment of the truck while the truck was idling. The truck was being used "normally" at that time, and trucks do not normally catch on fire while idling.

It is our view that the Court of Special Appeals improperly analyzed what the required elements of the implied warranty of fitness for a particular purpose are.

i. The Elements of § 2-315

An implied warranty of fitness for a particular purpose is conceded generally to have three affirmative elements:
1. The seller must have reason to know the buyer's particular purpose.

2. The seller must have reason to know that the buyer is relying on the seller's skill or judgment to furnish appropriate goods.

3. The buyer must, in fact, rely upon the seller's skill or judgment.

According to the Official Comment to § 2-315, a particular purpose means:

> A "particular purpose" differs from the ordinary purpose for which the goods are used in that it envisages a specific use by the buyer which is peculiar to the nature of his business whereas the ordinary purposes for which goods are used are those envisaged in the concept of merchantability and go to uses which are customarily made of the goods in question. For example, shoes are generally used for the purpose of walking upon ordinary ground, but a seller may know that a particular pair was selected to be used for climbing mountains.
>
> Md. Code (1975, 1997 Repl. Vol.), Comm. Law Art. § 2-315, Comment 2.

Explained in another manner, the particular purpose "must be distinguishable from the normal use of the goods"; "the purpose must be peculiar to the buyer as distinguished from the ordinary or general use to which the goods would be put by the ordinary buyer." *See* Clark & Smith, *supra*, P 6.02, at S6-8 (Supp. 1999) ("A 'particular purpose' under Section 2-315 contemplates a specific use of the good that is peculiar to the nature of the buyer's business, while an 'ordinary purpose' refers to use customarily made of the goods."

In addition to the particular purpose requirement, a party asserting a claim under § 2-315 must establish that the seller had reason to know, at the time of sale, that the purchaser had that particular use of the good in mind and that the purchaser was relying on the seller's expertise to select an appropriate product for that purpose. The need to establish specific knowledge on the part of the seller often may create a near requirement of direct dealing, if not actual privity, *see Wood Products, Inc. v. CMI Corp.*, 651 F. Supp. 641, 649 (D. Md. 1986) (seeking to apply Maryland law and stating that "privity is ... required in an action for breach of express warranty or an implied warranty of fitness for a particular purpose in which only economic loss is claimed"). It is often impossible for a seller to learn of a particular purpose of a buyer, and for a buyer to rely upon a seller to select the right product, without some direct dealing between such buyer and seller. As one treatise has explained:

> The warranty of fitness theory is usually not available against a remote manufacturer, who would have no reason to know of any special use to which the buyer would put the goods, even though the dealer could be liable. In other words, the absence of vertical privity removes the elements necessary to support the warranty of fitness. On this ground, the warranty of fitness sharply contrasts with the warranty of merchantability, which involves an inherent defect in the goods that existed before they left the hands of the manufacturer.
>
> Clark & Smith, *supra*, P 6.03[1], at S6-12 (Supp. 1999).

Clark and Smith also noted:

> Vertical privity would almost always be a bar against a plaintiff suing a remote link in the chain of distribution for breach of the implied warranty of fitness for a particular purpose under Section 2-315. Under this Section, a cause of action requires (1) the seller's "reason to know" the buyer's special use of the goods, and (2) the buyer's reliance upon the seller's expertise. By its very nature, [the implied warranty of fitness for a particular purpose] is a warranty embracing adjoining links in the chain. Since breach does not normally involve any inherent defect in goods, but instead arises out of the unique relationship between immediate buyer and seller, suit based upon the warranty of fitness would rarely be brought against

a remote defendant. If it were brought, the warranty of fitness would probably be dashed due to the absence of vertical privity or the absence of the requisite elements to support the theory. In short, the vertical privity defense and the warranty of fitness do not fit together in any rational way.

> Clark & Smith, *supra*, P 10.03, at 10-17 (1984).

This sentiment is echoed by Anderson:

> The elements of knowledge of the seller of the buyer's particular need and of the buyer's reliance on the seller's skill and judgment may suggest the existence of direct dealings between the seller and the buyer. This in turn would suggest that privity of contract is present and, conversely, that the lack of privity would tend to negate the existence of knowledge on the part of the seller or reliance on the part of the buyer.

> Anderson, *supra*, § 2-315:93, at 55.

Under the circumstances of the present case, a problem of proof of knowledge exists. Neither Elzenheimer Chevrolet, which transformed the cab chassis truck into a tow truck, nor Respondent was the direct purchaser of the original product from Petitioner. Because neither was the direct purchaser of the truck, it becomes more difficult to prove that Ford knew or had reason to know, when first selling the truck to Homer Skelton Ford, Inc., that Respondent would buy the converted vehicle from Elzenheimer and would use it as a tow truck, or that anyone in the chain of purchasers was relying on Ford to provide an appropriate product for that ultimate use.

Respondent responds to the privity argument by stating:

> Contrary to [Petitioner's] assertions, there is no need for a showing of privity under § 2-315. Plaintiff needs to prove that the buyer had a particular purpose known to seller ... . Indeed § 2-318 of the UCC even extends warranty protection to some third parties.

It is correct that the plaintiff only needs to prove that the buyer had a particular purpose known to seller, and that privity itself is not a required element that must be shown independently. The problem here is that, given the intermediate chain of owners, there was no proof that Ford had knowledge that the chassis cab in question would be purchased ultimately for use as a tow truck.

The only basis for the asserted breach of the implied warranty of fitness in this case is that Ford knew the chassis cab *could be* converted into a tow truck and the vehicle, so converted, caught fire while idling. This basis is insufficient, as is the Court of Special Appeals's assertion that Petitioner knew that (a) chassis cabs "will be modified in some form or another," and (b) "that Elzenheimer had, in the past, purchased Ford chassis cabs for the purpose of turning them into tow trucks." The Court of Special Appeals incorrectly determined that the particular purpose for which the tow truck was purchased was towing and that the mere happening of the fire while the tow truck was in ordinary operation constituted a breach of the warranty of fitness for the particular purpose of towing.

As far as the record of this case reveals, the customary and ordinary uses of a chassis cab after modification are not particular uses as contemplated by § 2-315, but rather are the ordinary uses of such a product. When Petitioner sold the truck to Homer Skelton Ford, Petitioner was unaware specifically how the chassis cab would be used, though it was aware of several configurations to which such trucks had been converted historically. Petitioner's expert, Mr. Elhert, testified at trial: "[Ford] did not know when this truck was shipped what it was going to be used for. It could have been used in a variety of applications. That is why we build a chassis cab." Additionally, as noted *supra* note 22, Petitioner, in an interrogatory read at trial, stated:

"Ford states that it sold the subject vehicle as an incomplete chassis cab with the anticipation that it would be or could be modified into a tow truck, dump truck, garbage truck, or any one of many other acceptable uses." Petitioner sold the chassis cab to a dealership in Mississippi, which dealer in turn sold the chassis cab (unaltered) to Elzenheimer Chevrolet, which converted it into a tow truck. There is no evidence that General Accident's insured articulated to Petitioner what particular purpose it had in mind for the chassis cab and no evidence that General Accident's insured sought to use the vehicle for other than one of its ordinary purposes.

The Court of Special Appeals reached a similar conclusion on similar reasoning in *Bond v. NIBCO*, 96 Md. App. 127, 623 A.2d 731 (1993), distinguishing between the ordinary and particular purpose of a product, i.e. faucets. In *Bond*, the plaintiff, a plumber, purchased faucets, manufactured by the defendant, from a retailer/manufacturer. *Bond*, 96 Md. App. at 131, 623 A.2d at 733. The plaintiff installed the faucets in residential townhouses. The faucets subsequently leaked. The plumber sued the defendant alleging, in part, that the manufacturer was liable for breach of the implied warranty of fitness for a particular purpose. *Id.* The Court of Special Appeals, in affirming the circuit court's grant of summary judgment in favor of the manufacturer, held that the plaintiff had failed to state a claim for breach of implied warranty of fitness because

> [plaintiff] nowhere alleged that he bought the faucets for a "particular purpose" that in any way differed from the "ordinary purpose" for which these faucets might be used, let alone that [defendant], which manufactured but did not sell these faucets to him, knew of this "particular purpose." Accordingly, [plaintiff's] complaint fails to state a claim for breach of implied warranty for a particular purpose, and so judgment was properly entered for [defendant] on this claim.
>
> *Bond*, 96 Md. App. at 137-38, 623 A.2d at 733.[5]

We conclude that there is no basis in law or fact to find any particular purpose in the present case, let alone that Petitioner had knowledge of such a purpose on Montrose's part. Because of this determination, we do not need to consider the remaining elements of § 2-315. The implied warranty of fitness for a particular purpose is inapplicable to the present case. Moreover, the chassis cab was being used for its ordinary purpose, rather than a particular purpose. Accordingly, we reverse the decision of the Court of Special Appeals and remand the case with directions to affirm the trial court's judgment.

---

5   Petitioner suggests that the Court of Special Appeals in *Thomas v. Ford Motor Credit Co.*, 48 Md. App. 617, 429 A.2d 277 (1981), incorrectly transformed the ordinary purpose of an automobile—transportation—into a particular purpose in order to bring the product under the implied warranty of fitness for a particular purpose. In *Thomas*, the Court of Special Appeals, noting that Comment 2 of § 2-315, *supra*, which differentiates between an ordinary and a particular purpose, remarked that the Comment supported Ford Motor Credit Company's contention that transportation is the ordinary purpose, not the particular purpose, of a motor vehicle. *Thomas*, 48 Md. App. at 625-26, 429 A.2d at 283. Nonetheless, the intermediate appellate court followed *Myers v. Montgomery Ward & Co.*, 253 Md. 282, 252 A.2d 855 (1969), a decision in which we quoted a treatise writer who espoused the idea that an ordinary purpose may also serve as a particular purpose. Relying on that particular passage in *Myers*, the court determined that a claim of breach of implied warranty of merchantability also constitutes a claim of breach of the implied warranty of fitness for a particular purpose. *Thomas*, 48 Md. App. at 626, 429 A.2d at 283. In *Myers*, we addressed the question of when an implied warranty of fitness for a particular purpose arises. The case involved a products liability claim against the seller and manufacturer of a lawn mower. *Myers*, 253 Md. at 285, 252 A.2d at 857. Myers was cutting grass on a slope of his lawn when he slipped and fell. *Id.* His foot "found its way under the mower," and he was severely injured by the whirling blade. *Id.* Myers sued under theories of negligence, implied warranty, and strict liability. *Id.* Defendants' demurrer was granted, and Myers appealed, arguing that implied warranties of merchantability and of fitness for a particular purpose were well plead. *Myers*, 253 Md. at 285-89, 252 A.2d at 857-59.

What if, to achieve her particular purpose for purchasing a product, the buyer has to use the product like everyone else uses it—will she not have a claim for breach under 2-315 if the product turns out not to be fit for that particular purpose? Must the buyer's use of the product be "abnormal" to trigger the implied warranty of fitness for a particular purpose? That seems to be the intent of Comment 2 to 2-315—which the Court quoted in *Ford Motor*—and most courts have required buyers claiming under 2-315 to show an idiosyncratic use for the product. But not all courts. In *Outlook Windows v. York Int'l*, 112 F. Supp. 2d 877 (D. Neb. 2000), the buyer purchased a gas-fired boiler to replace a wood-fired boiler which had been used to heat the buyer's building, based on the seller's representation that it would not cost more to heat the building using the gas-fired boiler. The cost of heating the building with the gas-fired boiler turned out to be 60 percent more than it had been with the wood-fired boiler, and the buyer sued, based on, among other things, breach of the 2-315 warranty of fitness for a particular purpose. The seller claimed that the buyer had not made out a claim under 2-315:

> [Seller] argues that there is no evidence that [buyer] purchased the gas-fired boilers for a specific use peculiar to the nature of [buyer's] business, and notes that [buyer] has not even alleged a particular use in its petition. [Seller] thus analogizes this case to *Stones*, in which the evidence indicated that a gas grill (which caused a house fire) was used for its customary purpose of grilling food, such that § 2-315 did not apply. Because the gas-fired boilers are used by [buyer] for their ordinary purpose of heating a building, [seller] concludes that the breach of warranty claim must be dismissed ... As the above cases demonstrate, it is not necessary that the buyer put the goods to an abnormal use. Because there is evidence that [seller] was aware that [buyer] wanted a heating system which would provide the same amount of heat for the same fuel cost as the old system, and that [buyer] was relying upon [seller's] expertise in making the selection, [seller's] motion for summary judgment on this breach of warranty claim will be denied.
>
> *Outlook Windows v. York Int'l*, 112 F. Supp. 2d 877 (D. Neb. 2000).

Which reading of 2-315 is more consistent with Comment 2?

Section 2-315 does not require the buyer to actually tell the seller the purpose for which she's purchasing the goods—as the *Ford Motor* Court noted, the Comments to 2-315 only require that "the circumstances are such that the seller has reason to realize the purpose intended." Comment 1, 2-315. What kind of "circumstances" give the seller a reason to realize the buyer's purpose? Can the seller "realize the reason" if there is no direct communication between the buyer and the seller? When the seller advertises that the goods are fit for a particular purpose, does the seller have "reason to realize" that the goods were bought for that purpose? Several courts have determined sellers have reason to know that their buyers purchase goods for the purpose they are advertised. *See, Filler v. Rayes Corp.*, 435 F.2d 336 (7th Cir. 1970) (sunglasses advertised as baseball sunglasses "were in truth not fit for baseball playing, the particular purpose for which they were sold" and therefore breached the warranty of fitness for a particular purpose); *Franulovic v. Coca-Cola*, 2007 U.S. Dist. LEXIS 79732 (D.N.J. 2007)(Coke "had knowledge of the particular purpose for which goods were intended [per extensive advertising regarding Enviga's weight-loss properties]"); *Durso v. Samsung Electronics America*, 2014 U.S. Dist. LEXIS 118467 (D.N.J. 2014) ("by advertising that the washers could wash king-size comforters, Samsung had reason to know that any purchaser of the washers might rely on the advertisements for the particular purpose of washing a king-size comforter"). In *Rait v. Sears, Roebuck*, 2009 U.S. Dist. LEXIS 7540 (D.N.J. 2009), the Court rejected Sears's argument that it could not have known the purpose for which the buyer purchased the product because she bought it on the Internet, explaining that Internet product advertisements "that tout specific uses may create an implied warranty of fitness for a particular purpose."

PROBLEM 8 - 5

Rae needs to build up the store's peach inventory to be ready for the annual Peach Festival that takes place in town. This year, it's become more complicated because the store does not have enough cold storage space to hold the extra peaches Rae needs. She tells the California peach broker she deals with that this year she needs a variety of peaches with an unrefrigerated shelf life equivalent to the usual shelf life of refrigerated peaches. The broker recommends a variety known as "Flavor Crest," which has an average shelf life of seventeen days at temperatures below seventy-seven degrees. Rae orders a truckload of Flavor Crest peaches, which arrives several days before the festival starts and are stacked in the dry-goods area of the main stockroom in the store. By the end of the first week of the festival, more than 75 percent of the unsold peaches are rotted and unsaleable. When Rae complains to the broker about the rotted peaches, she is told that a seventeen-day shelf life did not mean that no peaches would rot, but rather that fewer Flavor Crest peaches would rot during that time than other varietals. Does the store have a claim against the broker for breach of the implied warranty of fitness for a particular purpose? 2-315.

B. EXPRESS WARRANTIES

Sellers often make promises—what we call express warranties—about their products in order to distinguish those products from competing products. By expressly allocating some of the risk of nonperformance to themselves, sellers can make their products more appealing to buyers. A seller's assumption of risk implies that it does not expect the product to fail—that the product is of superior quality to those offered by sellers unwilling to assume any of the risks of nonperformance. A seller's express warranty also provides a form of insurance to the buyer: someone else will foot the bill in the unlikely event that the product does not perform as expected. The extra appeal provided by warranties can often be the deciding factor when buyers must choose between products that otherwise appear indistinguishable by many, if not most, attributes.

Article 2 gives effect to express warranties made by sellers that meet certain requirements—requirements that are intended to distinguish sales talk from promises or representations about the quality or performance capabilities of the product:

> Express Warranties by the seller are created as follows:
>
> any affirmation of fact or promise made by the buyer which relates to the goods and becomes part of the basis of the bargain creates an express warranty that the goods shall conform to the affirmation or promise.

2-313. An express warranty can be created without using words like "warrant or guarantee," but

> an affirmation merely of the value of the goods or a statement purporting to be merely the seller's opinion or commendation of the goods does not create a warranty.

2-313(2). A seller's description of the goods or the use by the seller of any sample or model of the goods can also create an express warranty. 2-313(1)(b) and (c).

The requirements for creating an express warranty are deceptively simple: we need (1) an affirmation of fact or promise by the seller that (2) relates to the goods and that (3) becomes part of the basis of the bargain. But in their application, they cause fear and consternation to litigants, drive courts to fits, and provide plenty of grist for the academic mill. When is a statement that looks like an affirmation of fact really an opinion or commendation by the seller that does not create an express warranty? How do we draw the line between the sales talk—the puffing you read about in your Contracts course—that is part of every negotiation and a promise about the quality of the product under discussion? Must the buyer prove that she actually made her purchase because of the seller's promise about the quality of the product—that she relied on the promise—for an express warranty to exist? These questions alone have confounded the courts, which have left us with confusing and inconsistent decisions applying 2-313.

For example, in *Sessa v. Reigle,* the court rejected the buyer's claim that the seller of a horse created an express warranty when he told the buyer that "the horse is sound," stating that it was "clear to the court that [seller's statements] were not of such a character as to give rise to express warranties under 2-313(1) but were opinion or commendation under 2-313(2)." 427 F. Supp. 760 (E.D. Pa. 1977). But in *Simpson v. Widget,* 709 A.2d 1366 (N.J. Super. 1998), seller's representation that Mighty Quinn (the horse) was a "sound horse" created an express warranty that the horse was "serviceably sound," the court noting that "the views expressed by the *Sessa* court appear unduly restrictive." Unfortunately for the buyer, the Court found that Mighty Quinn was serviceably sound, and so the warranty was not breached. It's cases like these that lead scholars to assert that "anyone who claims to be able always to tell a 'puff' from a warranty is a fool or a liar."[6]

The *Keith* case examines the threshold issue under 2-313—whether the seller has made an affirmation of fact or promise about the product.

KEITH V. BUCHANAN

COURT OF APPEAL OF CALIFORNIA, SECOND APPELLATE DISTRICT, DIVISION SIX, 1985
173 CAL. APP. 3D 13

OCHOA, Judge.

This breach of warranty case is before this court after the trial court granted defendants' motion for judgment at the close of plaintiff's case during the trial proceedings. We hold that an express warranty under section 2313 of the California Uniform Commercial Code was created in this matter, and that actual reliance on the seller's factual representation need not be shown by the buyer. The representation is presumed to be part of the basis of the bargain, and the burden is on the seller to prove that the representation was not a consideration inducing the bargain. We affirm all other aspects of the trial court's judgment but reverse in regard to its finding that no express warranty was created and remand for further proceedings consistent with this opinion.

STATEMENT OF FACTS

Plaintiff, Brian Keith, purchased a sailboat from defendants in November 1978 for a total purchase price of $75,610. Even though plaintiff belonged to the Waikiki Yacht Club, had attended a sailing school, had joined the Coast Guard Auxiliary, and had sailed on many yachts in order to ascertain his preferences, he had not previously owned a yacht. He attended a boat show in Long Beach during October 1978 and looked at a number of boats, speaking to sales representatives and obtaining advertising literature. In the literature, the sailboat which is the subject of this action, called an "Island Trader 41," was described as a seaworthy vessel. In one sales brochure, this vessel is described as "a picture of sure-footed seaworthiness." In another, it is called "a carefully well-equipped, and very seaworthy live-aboard vessel." Plaintiff testified he relied on representations in the sales brochures in regard to the purchase. Plaintiff and a sales representative also discussed plaintiff's desire for a boat which was ocean-going and would cruise long distances.

Plaintiff asked his friend, Buddy Ebsen, who was involved in a boat building enterprise, to inspect the boat. Mr. Ebsen and one of his associates, both of whom had extensive experience with sailboats, observed the boat and advised plaintiff that the vessel would suit his stated needs. A deposit was paid on

---

6   White and Summers, *Commercial Law,* (6th ed. West 2010) 454.

the boat, a purchase contract was entered into, and optional accessories for the boat were ordered. After delivery of the vessel, a dispute arose in regard to its seaworthiness.

Plaintiff filed the instant lawsuit alleging causes of action in breach of express warranty and breach of implied warranty. The trial court granted defendants' motion for judgment at the close of plaintiff's case. The court found that no express warranty was established by the evidence because none of the defendants had undertaken in writing to preserve or maintain the utility or performance of the vessel, nor to provide compensation for any failure in utility or performance. It found that the written statements produced at trial were opinions or commendations of the vessel.

DISCUSSION - EXPRESS WARRANTY

California Uniform Commercial Code section 2313 provides, inter alia, that express warranties are created by (1) any affirmation of fact or promise made by the seller to the buyer which relates to the goods and becomes part of the basis of the bargain, and (2) any description of the goods which is made part of the basis of the bargain. Formal words such as "warranty" or "guarantee" are not required to make a warranty, but the seller's affirmation of the value of the goods or an expression of opinion or commendation of the goods does not create an express warranty.

California Uniform Commercial Code section 2313, regarding express warranties, was enacted in 1963 and consists of the official text of Uniform Commercial Code section 2-313 without change. In deciding whether a statement made by a seller constitutes an express warranty under this provision, the court must deal with three fundamental issues. First, the court must determine whether the seller's statement constitutes an "affirmation of fact or promise" or "description of the goods" under California Uniform Commercial Code section 2313, subdivision (1)(a) or (b), or whether it is rather "merely the seller's opinion or commendation of the goods" under section 2313, subdivision (2). Second, assuming the court finds the language used susceptible to creation of a warranty, it must then be determined whether the statement was "part of the basis of the bargain." Third, the court must determine whether the warranty was breached.

A warranty relates to the title, character, quality, identity, or condition of the goods. The purpose of the law of warranty is to determine what it is that the seller has in essence agreed to sell. "Express warranties are chisels in the hands of buyers and sellers. With these tools, the parties to a sale sculpt a monument representing the goods. Having selected a stone, the buyer and seller may leave it almost bare, allowing considerable play in the qualities that fit its contours. Or the parties may chisel away inexactitudes until a well-defined shape emerges. The seller is bound to deliver, and the buyer to accept, goods that match the sculpted form. [Fn. omitted.)" (*Special Project: Article Two Warranties in Commercial Transactions, Express Warranties—Section 2-313* (1978–79) 64 Cornell L.Rev. 30 (hereafter cited as *Warranties in Commercial Transactions*) at pp. 43–44.)

Affirmation of fact, promise or description versus statement of opinion, commendation or value. "The determination as to whether a particular statement is an expression of opinion or an affirmation of a fact is often difficult, and frequently is dependent upon the facts and circumstances existing at the time the statement is made." Recent decisions have evidenced a trend toward narrowing the scope of representations which are considered opinion, sometimes referred to as "puffing" or "sales talk," resulting in an expansion of the liability that flows from broad statements of manufacturers or retailers as to the quality of their products. Courts have liberally construed affirmations of quality made by sellers in favor of injured consumers. It has even been suggested "that in an age of consumerism all seller's statements, except the most blatant sales pitch, may give rise to an express warranty."

Courts in other states have struggled in efforts to create a formula for distinguishing between affirmations of fact, promises, or descriptions of goods on the one hand, and value, opinion, or commendation statements on the other. The code comment indicates that the basic question is: "What statements of the seller have in the circumstances and in objective judgment become part of the basis of the bargain?" The commentators indicated that the language of subsection (2) of the code section was included because "common experience discloses that some statements or predictions cannot fairly be viewed as entering into the bargain."

Statements made by a seller during the course of negotiation over a contract are presumptively affirmations of fact unless it can be demonstrated that the buyer could only have reasonably considered the statement as a statement of the seller's opinion. Commentators have noted several factors which tend to indicate an opinion statement. These are (1) a lack of specificity in the statement made, (2) a statement that is made in an equivocal manner, or (3) a statement which reveals that the goods are experimental in nature.

It is clear that statements made by a manufacturer or retailer in an advertising brochure which is disseminated to the consuming public in order to induce sales can create express warranties. In the instant case, the vessel purchased was described in sales brochures as "a picture of sure-footed seaworthiness" and "a carefully well-equipped and very seaworthy vessel." The seller's representative was aware that appellant was looking for a vessel sufficient for long distance ocean-going cruises. The statements in the brochure are specific and unequivocal in asserting that the vessel is seaworthy. Nothing in the negotiation indicates that the vessel is experimental in nature. In fact, one sales brochure assures prospective buyers that production of the vessel was commenced "after years of careful testing." The representations regarding seaworthiness made in sales brochures regarding the Island Trader 41 were affirmations of fact relating to the quality or condition of the vessel.

Most courts addressing the threshold issue require the buyer to show that the seller's statement belongs in the "express warranty" box—that the seller made an affirmation of fact (or promise) relating to the goods. These courts have come up with different "factors" that they claim distinguish affirmations of fact from the sales talk—the puffing—that's part of negotiating a sale-of-goods transaction. Common factors include: (1) whether the statements were specific or general—the more specific the statement about the goods, the more likely it is an affirmation of fact; (2) whether the statement was hedged—the more unequivocal the statement, the more likely it is an affirmation of fact; (3) whether the product was experimental—statements about newly developed products without widespread use are more likely opinions, not affirmations of fact; (4) whether the statement was about something of which the buyer was ignorant or of which the seller had no special knowledge; (5) whether the statement was objective in nature—something that was verifiable, that could be proven either true or false—objective statements are more likely affirmations of fact; (6) whether the statements were oral or in writing—written statements are more likely affirmations than oral statements; and (7) whether the statements relate to the consequences of buying the product or to the product itself. Most courts applying a factor-based test consider the context in which the statement was made (e.g., advertisements, correspondence, invoices)—a totality-of-circumstances analysis.

PROBLEM 8 - 6

In which, if any, of the following transactions has the seller created an express warranty under 2-313?

Transaction 1: A local grower told Rae she grew the "best-tasting, most flavorful tomatoes this side of the Mississippi River."

Transaction 2: When Rae called to order bison for the store, the rancher told her his bison was the best-quality bison anyone could buy—your customers are gonna be SO happy."

Transaction 3: Rae ordered plums from an orchard in Oregon. The grower described the plums as "A-number-one plums—yummy, yummy plums."

Transaction 4: The store's produce manager just placed an order for grapes that were advertised as "100 percent seedless table grapes."

Transaction 5: When Rae bought a used bread slicer for the store's bakery, the seller told her the slicer was "in perfect condition—as good as new" and that it would "slice fifteen average-size loaves a minute."

Transaction 6: When Rae bought a new meat slicer for the deli, the seller told her that the slicing blades "would last for ninety days under normal use" and that replacement blades were "cheap and readily available."

Transaction 7: The labels on the California Merlot that was just delivered to the store read: "Alcohol content less than 14.5 percent."

Transaction 8: The lid of every tub of ice cream Rae bought from the local dairy states: "100 percent natural—no artificial ingredients."

Transaction 9: The store's beverage manager ordered twenty-five cases of "Lite Beer" from a microbrewery just up the interstate.

Transaction 10: The box containing the dietary supplement sold in the store's pharmacy proclaims: "Lose five pounds a week!"

In *Keith*, instead of requiring the buyer to show that the seller's statements about the seaworthiness of the sailboat belonged in the express-warranty box, the Court presumed they belonged in that box—an interpretation of 2-313 seemingly endorsed by the comments—and then asked whether there were grounds for removing them from the express-warranty box. Comment 8, quoted in part by the court in *Keith*, instructs:

> Concerning affirmations of value or a seller's opinion or commendation under subsection (2), the basic question remains the same: What statements of the seller have in the circumstances and in objective judgment become part of the basis of the bargain? As indicated above, all of the statements of the seller do so unless good reason is shown to the contrary. The provisions of subsection (2) are included, however, since common experience discloses that some statements or predictions cannot fairly be viewed as entering into the bargain.

Applying 2-313, as the court did in *Keith*, to presume a seller's statements are in, rather than out of, the express-warranty box is certainly, then, within the spirit of the drafters' intent as reflected by Comment 8. It also puts the burden of proof on the party that sowed the seed of future discontent—the seller controls the content of the message it communicates to the buyer. If the seller is careless with its message, the seller should have the burden of convincing the court that what it said about the product was so exaggerated, so vague and imprecise, so sensational under the circumstances, that no reasonable person could possibly believe it to be part of the agreement. Or at least the burden of showing (under the factors applied by the courts to determine whether a seller's statement belongs in the express-warranty box), that its statement should be taken out of that box.

But the *"Keith* Presumption" has never caught on, and so courts continue to use some form of a factor-based test to determine whether a seller's statement was an affirmation of fact or promise related to the goods.

The lesson for the lawyer from these cases and others like them is obvious. Only a foolish lawyer will be quick to label a seller's statement as puffs or not puffs, and only a reckless one will label a seller's statement at all without carefully examining the factors ... [7]

As the horse cases and the problems illustrated, the outcome will likely turn, in all but the most obvious cases, on the advocacy skills of the lawyers involved—their ability to persuade the court that, when applying the factors *de jour* to the particular statements of a seller, an express warranty was or was not created.

Even if a court determines that the seller made an affirmation of fact or promise that relates to the product, unless that affirmation of fact or promise became a part of the basis of the bargain between the buyer and the seller, no express warranty exists. 2-313(1)(a). The "basis of the bargain" requirement has confounded the courts since they began applying 2-313 to seller's statements about the products they sell. Prior law required a buyer's reliance on the seller's statement before the statement was considered an express warranty. Section 2-313 says nothing about reliance—instead, it uses this strange new term, "basis of the bargain"—and courts and scholars for a long time could not agree on whether basis of the bargain simply meant reliance or whether, by using the new term, the drafters intended to abandon the reliance requirement from prior law altogether. The next case looks at the competing views of the "basis of the bargain" requirement in 2-313.

KELLEHER V. MARVIN LUMBER & CEDAR CO.

SUPREME COURT OF NEW HAMPSHIRE, 2005
891 A.2D 477

GALWAY, Judge.

In these consolidated appeals, the defendant, Marvin Lumber and Cedar Company (Marvin), appeals: (1) the partial jury verdict from the Superior Court (*Brennan*, J.) in the first trial that awarded the plaintiff, John J. Kelleher, Jr., $53,676.00 in damages on his strict liability claim; (2) the jury verdict in the retrial that awarded the plaintiff $57,247.04 on his breach of express warranty and breach of the Magnuson-Moss Warranty-Federal Trade Commission Improvement Act (Magnuson-Moss Act) claims; and (3) the award of attorney's fees, at the conclusion of the retrial, in the amount of $119,898.57. The plaintiff cross-appeals the trial court's dismissal of his breach of implied warranty claim under the Act. We affirm in part, vacate in part, and remand.

The record supports the following facts and procedural history. In 1986, the plaintiff purchased and installed windows manufactured by the defendant in his newly constructed residence in Ogunquit, Maine. The plaintiff purchased the windows from John Collins, a salesman employed by Steenbeke & Son, a New Hampshire retail building materials supplier. The windows were treated with a wood preservative (PILT), which was manufactured by PPG Industries and designed to inhibit "premature, moisture-induced wood rot." Before trial, the defendant conceded that PILT is an ineffective preservative.

In 1986, the plaintiff noticed a leak in one of his living room windows. As a result of that leak, and upon the recommendation of a Marvin windows distributor, all of the newly installed windows were re-caulked. In 1993 or 1994, the plaintiff noticed that a small piece of molding on the sash of a rear window contained rot, and he had it repaired. Sometime in 1997, the plaintiff noticed that the sash of the same rear window also contained rot and the sash was replaced. Then, in 1998, the plaintiff employed a painter who found significant amounts of rot in five Marvin windows. Shortly thereafter, in August 1998, the plaintiff filed a complaint form with the defendant, thereby formally notifying it of

---

7 White and Summers, *Commercial Law,* (6th ed. West 2010) 455.

the rot damage in his windows. In response to a question on the complaint form, the plaintiff indicated that the rot problem began in "1993/'94?"

After receiving the plaintiff's complaint, a Marvin representative inspected all of the windows in the plaintiff's home and determined that seventeen windows contained rot damage. The inspector showed the plaintiff that a subtle dimpling of the surface coating of the windows was a sign that the underlying wood was rotten. On November 12, 1999, after negotiations to replace the damaged windows were unsuccessful, the plaintiff initiated the underlying lawsuit seeking damages for the replacement costs of the defective windows, loss of value of the house in which the windows were installed and costs related to repairing water damage allegedly caused by the defective windows.

During the course of this litigation, the defendant produced a one-year limited warranty (the one-year warranty), which was in effect in 1986 and allegedly accompanied the windows that were delivered to the plaintiff. This one-year warranty guaranteed the wood portion of the windows. The plaintiff alleged that an oral fifteen-year warranty was given by a Steenbeke salesman during a telephone conversation in 1998, in which the salesman represented that the windows were "guaranteed for a period of fifteen years" (the fifteen-year warranty). In addition, the defendant's catalog, which was generally available from Steenbeke when the plaintiff purchased the windows, stated that: (1) "all exterior wood is deep treated in a dry vac process with a pesticide and water repellant solution to permanently protect against rot and decay"; and (2) the pre-finish "lasts four to five times longer than paint" (the catalog warranty).

The plaintiff's writ asserted claims based upon the fifteen-year warranty but failed to identify the alleged warranty contained in the defendant's catalog. On June 23, 2000, based upon the fifteen-year warranty, the defendant moved to dismiss all of the plaintiff's claims, asserting they were barred by the applicable statutes of limitations and the economic loss doctrine. Specifically, with respect to the Magnuson-Moss and breach of express warranty claims, Marvin argued that the fifteen-year warranty was insufficient to trigger the future performance exception to the applicable statute of limitations, and, therefore, these claims were untimely. Based upon the fifteen-year warranty, the Superior Court (*Groff*, J.) denied the defendant's motion to dismiss the breach of express warranty claim, but dismissed the Magnuson-Moss claim because the fifteen-year warranty did not comply with the Magnuson-Moss Act's requirement that it be in writing. The strict liability claim also survived the motion to dismiss.

By order dated September 19, 2000, the trial court granted the plaintiff's motion to amend the writ, which ultimately resulted in both the Magnuson-Moss and breach of express warranty claims being based upon the written catalog warranty rather than the fifteen-year warranty. The defendant then moved for summary judgment, reasserting that the plaintiff's claims were untimely and, therefore, barred as a matter of law.

In October 2001, the court conducted a six-day jury trial. By way of a special verdict form, the jury returned a partial verdict for the plaintiff on the strict liability count, awarding damages in the amount of $53,676.00. However, the court declared a mistrial as to the Magnuson-Moss and breach of express warranty claims when the jury was unable to reach a verdict on them.

The defendant appealed the jury verdict ... .

While this appeal was pending and over the defendant's objection, the trial court scheduled a retrial of the breach of express warranty and Magnuson-Moss claims. We suspended the pending appeal to allow the trial court to resolve the defendant's remaining claims. Accordingly, in February 2003, the trial court conducted a three-day trial on the remaining claims.

Prior to the February 2003 trial, and contrary to its ruling in the prior trial, the trial court granted the plaintiff's motion to exclude evidence of the one-year warranty at trial. Additionally, prior to charging the jury, the trial court partially granted the plaintiff's motion for a directed verdict, ruling that the representations made in the catalog constituted a written warranty as a matter of law. The trial court then instructed the jury regarding the catalog warranty, the burden of proof, the elements of the claims, damages, and the statute of limitations. The jury returned a plaintiff's verdict in the amount of $57,247.04. The court then granted the plaintiff's motion for attorney's fees, pursuant to the Magnuson-Moss Act, in the amount of $119,898.57. Both parties timely appealed.

* * *

IV. Issues Pertaining to the Breach of Warranty and Breach of Magnuson-Moss Act Claims

The Breach of Express Warranty Claim

In addition to appealing the trial court's denial of its motions for directed verdict and JNOV, the defendant also argues the trial court erred in partially granting the plaintiff's motion for directed verdict and determining that representations contained in the catalog constituted, as a matter of law, a warranty for the purposes of the State breach of express warranty claim. The defendant asserts that the record contains evidence from which a reasonable juror could find that: (1) the defendant's sales catalog is an educational brochure and is, therefore, not a warranty; and (2) the representations in the catalog were not a part of the basis of the bargain for the windows installed in the plaintiff's home.

"A trial court may grant a motion for a directed verdict only if it determined, after considering the evidence and construing all inferences therefrom most favorably to the non-moving party, that no rational juror could conclude that the non-moving party is entitled to any relief." We uphold a trial court's ruling on a motion for directed verdict "when the record supports the conclusion that the trial court did not commit an unsustainable exercise of discretion."

RSA 382-A:2-313 provides, in pertinent part:

(1) Express warranties by the seller are created as follows:
   (a)   Any affirmation of fact or promise made by the seller to the buyer which relates to the goods and becomes part of the basis of the bargain creates an express warranty that the goods shall conform to the affirmation or promise.
   (b)   Any description of the goods which is made part of the basis of the bargain creates an express warranty that the goods shall conform to the description.

To create an express warranty, the seller is not required to use formal words, such as "warranty" or "guarantee" or have the specific intention to create a warranty. RSA 382-A:2-313(2). Further, an affirmation of the value of the goods or a statement of the seller's opinion or commendation of the goods does not create a warranty. Therefore, to create an express warranty, the promise or affirmation of fact must both relate to the goods and become part of the basis of the contractual bargain.

We first consider whether the representations in the defendant's catalog constitute an affirmation of fact relating to the windows, or whether they describe a particular feature of the windows as part of an educational brochure. The representations assert that the windows were deep treated to permanently protect against rot and decay, which we find constitutes an affirmation of fact related to the windows. When considered in combination with the additional detailed description of the exact process and solution used to treat the wood, the representations are more than a mere opinion or commendation of the goods. Accordingly, the language of the catalog warranty satisfies the first prong of the test to determine if it is an express warranty for the purposes of this claim.

We next consider whether this affirmation of fact was part of the basis of the bargain. That an affirmation is contained in a brochure, catalogue, or advertisement does not preclude a finding that it is a warranty provided it formed part of the basis of the bargain.

However, what constitutes "part of the basis of the bargain" is difficult to define. *Liberty Lincoln-Mercury, Inc. v. Ford Motor Co.*, 171 F.3d 818, 825 (3d Cir. 1999). "Ordinarily a guarantee or promise in an advertisement or other description of the goods becomes part of the basis of the bargain if it would naturally induce the purchase of the product and no particular reliance by the buyer on such statement needs to be shown." *Cipollone v. Liggett Group, Inc.*, 893 F.2d 541, 563 (3d Cir. 1990). Authorities are divided as to whether a buyer's reliance upon the affirmation is a necessary element of proving that the affirmation was part of the basis of the bargain under section 2-313 of the UCC as codified in RSA 382-A:2-313. *Id.* at 564; *see* 2 L. Frumer & M. Friedman, *Products Liability* § 9.02(2), at 9-27 (2000) (recognizing the official comments to the UCC provide little guidance to the relationship between the basis of the bargain and reliance). This is a matter of first impression for this court.

Section 2-313 does not define "part of the basis of the bargain." The UCC is an adaptation of section 12 of the Uniform Sales Act (USA) and is basically the same except for the replacement of the USA's express reliance requirement with the UCC's "part of the basis of the bargain" requirement. *Cipollone*, 893 F.2d at 565; *see* 1 J. White & R. Summers, *Uniform Commercial Code* § 9-5, at 448 (1995). Consequently, section 2-313 omits any reference to reliance; instead, it requires only that the affirmation become "part of the basis of the bargain." The extent to which the law has been changed to remove the reliance requirement is unclear.

A majority of jurisdictions continues to find that reliance is an essential element of an express warranty claim. *Cipollone*, 893 F.2d at 564; *Torres v. Northwest Eng'g Co.*, 86 Haw. 383, 949 P.2d 1004, 1013 (Haw. Ct. App. 1998); *see Frummer, supra* at 9-28 (collecting cases). A minority of jurisdictions has adopted the opposite approach, and eliminated the reliance requirement in an effort to satisfy the "part of the basis of the bargain" language in the UCC. *See Frummer, supra* at 9-28; *Torres*, 949 P.2d at 1013. This interpretation supports the underlying purpose of the law of warranty, which is to determine what it is the seller has agreed to sell, thereby making reliance irrelevant. *See* RSA 382-A:2-313 comment 4. As some jurisdictions have noted, "this interpretation drains all substantive meaning from the phrase 'basis of the bargain,'" thereby allowing the buyer to collect even if the buyer was unaware of the existence of the warranty.

Both of these positions are inconsistent with the official comments to section 2-313 of the UCC. Official Comment 3 states in pertinent part:

> In actual practice affirmations of fact made by the seller about the goods during a bargain are regarded as part of the description of those goods; *hence no particular reliance on such statements need be shown* in order to weave them into the fabric of the agreement. Rather, *any fact which is to take such affirmations, once made, out of the agreement requires clear affirmative proof.* The issue normally is one of fact.

(Emphasis added.) Furthermore, comment 8 states that "all of the statements of the seller [become part of the basis of the bargain] *unless good reason is shown to the contrary.*" (Emphasis added.) Comment 7 states that "the precise time when words of description or affirmation are made ... is not material. The sole question is whether the language ... [is] fairly to be regarded as part of the contract." Thus, the majority position that reliance is an essential element under section 2-313 is clearly contrary to the plain language of section 2-313 and comment 3. Likewise, the minority position eliminating any reliance requirement is also contrary in that it nullifies the phrase "part of the basis of the bargain," thereby allowing a buyer to recover on a breach of warranty claim without being aware of the existence of the statements when the bargain was being negotiated.

A few jurisdictions have adopted an intermediate third approach, concluding that under section 2-313, once the buyer has become aware of the affirmation of fact or promise, the statements are presumptively part of the basis of the bargain. The burden then shifts to the seller to prove, by clear affirmative proof, that the resulting bargain did not rest *at all* on the seller's statements. *Torres*, 949 P.2d at 1015; *see Cipollone*, 893 F.2d at 568; *Keith v. Buchanan*, 173 Cal. App. 3d 13, 220 Cal.Rptr. 392, 398 (Dist. Ct. App. 1985) (seller's warranty is presumptively part of the basis of the bargain, and it is the seller's burden to prove that the resulting bargain did not rest at all on the representation); *Bysom Enters. v. Peter Carlton Enters.*, 267 Ill. App. 3d 1, 641 N.E.2d 838, 843, 204 Ill. Dec. 408 (Ill. App. Ct. 1994) (warranties in a purchase agreement are *prima facie* evidence that they are part of the bargain, and the burden of disproving this is on the seller). The issue of whether the seller has proved, by clear affirmative proof, that the seller's statements were not at all part of the basis of the bargain is one of fact. *Torres*, 949 P.2d at 1014; RSA 382-A:2-313 comment 3; *see Chellman v. Saab-Scania AB*, 138 N.H. 73, 82, 637 A.2d 148 (1993) (recognizing whether advertising creates an express warranty is a question for the jury).

We adopt the intermediate approach when deciding whether representations in a catalog or brochure constitute part of the basis of the bargain in a breach of express warranty claim. We are persuaded that this approach strikes the proper balance. The plain language of section 2-313 requires that the affirmation be *part* of the basis of the bargain, and the corresponding official comments make it clear that "no particular reliance on such statements need be shown [by the buyer]." RSA 382-A:2-313 comment 3 (emphasis added). Thus, the buyer need not show that he or she would not have entered into the agreement absent the seller's statements. Nor is the buyer required to show that the seller's statements were a dominant factor inducing the agreement.

In order to become part of the basis of the bargain, the buyer must have been aware of the affirmation of fact or promise at some point in the bargaining process. To satisfy this requirement, a plaintiff claiming breach of express warranty based upon a representation in a catalog or brochure would have to prove, at a minimum, that he or she read, heard, saw or was otherwise aware of the representation in the catalog or brochure. Therefore, the dispositive issues are: whether the statements were of the type that would naturally induce the purchase of the product; and whether the buyer was aware of the statements during the negotiating process.

The presumption that a seller's statement becomes a part of the basis of the bargain can be overcome. For instance, "the buyer's actual knowledge of the true condition of the goods prior to the making of the contract may make it plain that the seller's statement was not relied upon as one of the inducements for the purchase." Additionally, a seller's statement will not be presumed to be part of the basis of the bargain when the buyer knew the statement to be false or was not influenced by it, or when the statement was not made until after the sale of the product.

In this case, the trial court determined that the representations in the catalog constituted an express warranty, pursuant to RSA 382-A:2-313, as a matter of law. The trial court reasoned that there was "no reasonable question that the catalogue ... is a catalogue that existed at the time that the plaintiff purchased his windows." The court found that the representation regarding permanent protection of the windows "becomes a part of the goods that were sold and, therefore, a part of the basis of the bargain." We affirm the trial court's determination that the representations in the catalog assert that the windows were permanently protected against rot damage. We also affirm its ruling that this representation constitutes an affirmation of fact that would qualify as an express warranty under the UCC, provided it was part of the basis of the bargain. However, whether the representation was part of the basis of the bargain is a factual determination that should have been decided by the jury.

Here, the jury heard evidence from which it could have concluded that the representations in the catalog were part of the basis of the bargain. For instance, the plaintiff testified that he relied upon representations in the catalog regarding the durability of windows manufactured by Marvin. However, he also testified that all of his paperwork pertaining to the construction of his residence was destroyed in 1987, and the catalog admitted at trial was a copy obtained from a worker involved in his home construction. While the plaintiff could not identify the exact document that he saw in 1986, he testified that he did "see what Marvin had available, and the only thing that Marvin had available was the catalog that showed each of the windows, the stock windows that were in place ... ." While this evidence could support the trial court's determination that the catalog representations were part of the basis of the bargain, given the credibility issues raised, it is not so overwhelmingly in favor of the plaintiff that no contrary verdict could stand. Therefore, we conclude that this determination is a factual one for the jury.

Accordingly, we conclude the trial court erred in directing a verdict on the question of whether the catalog representations were part of the basis of the bargain and thus constituted an express warranty pursuant to RSA 382-A:2-313. We vacate the verdict on the breach of express warranty claim, and remand for further proceedings consistent with this opinion.

The intermediate approach to the basis of the bargain" requirement adopted by the *Kelleher* Court is, as the opinion demonstrates convincingly, more firmly grounded in both the text of and Comments to 2-313 than either the reliance or no-reliance views. The trend in recent decisions is decidedly against reading a reliance requirement into 2-313, but it also recognizes, like the *Kelleher* Court, that the "basis of the bargain" requirement was intended to add something to the determination of whether an express warranty was created by a seller's statements. We won't know whether the reasoning in cases like *Kelleher* will cause courts that initially read basis of the bargain to require reliance to rethink their positions until someone—maybe you—can get the issue before them again.

Do express warranties run with the product? Can you sue Audi for breach of its manufacturer's warranty when the transmission in the Audi you bought from an uncle fails? Since you have no contractual relationship with Audi—you did not buy the car from Audi—can you still hold Audi to the promises it made to your uncle, who bought the car? The *Coleman* case examines the privity issue under 2-313.

COLEMAN V. BOSTON SCI. CORP.

UNITED STATES DISTRICT COURT FOR THE EASTERN DISTRICT OF CALIFORNIA, 2011
2011 U.S. DIST. LEXIS 96315

WANGER, District Judge.

INTRODUCTION

Pamela Coleman ("Plaintiff") proceeds with an action for damages against Boston Scientific Corporation ("Defendant") and various Doe Defendants.

FACTUAL BACKGROUND

On December 5, 2006, a physician implanted a surgical mesh device manufactured by Defendant into Plaintiff in connection with treatment of Plaintiff's stress urinary incontinence. The surgical mesh device is described as an Obtryx Transobturator Mid-Urethral Sling System ("Mesh Device") and is designed to restore normal vaginal structure secondary to pelvic organ prolapse. Plaintiff began to experience "recurrent pelvic pain, erosions, and recurrent infection of the tissue around the mesh" subsequent to implantation of the Mesh Device. From July 2007 through January 2009, Plaintiff underwent surgery, vaginal reconstruction, and mesh removal "to correct the injuries caused by the mesh."

DISCUSSION

Express Warranty Claim

"As a general rule, privity of contract is a required element of an express breach of warranty cause of action." However, privity is not an absolute requirement for express warranty claims under California law, because reliance on a seller's representations may provide the basis for an express warranty claim even absent privity. The memorandum decision dismissing Plaintiff's original complaint provides, in pertinent part:

> Defendants' contention that privity is an element of an express warranty claim is incorrect. *E.g., Evraets*, 29 Cal App. 4th 779,.34 Cal. App. 2d at 857 n.4 ("privity is not a requirement for actions based upon an express warranty"); *Fieldstone Co. v. Briggs Plumbing Products, Inc.*, 54 Cal. App. 4th 357, n.10, 62 Cal. Rptr. 2d 701 (Cal. Ct. App. 1997) ("As a general rule, privity of contract is a required element of an express breach of warranty cause of action. However, there is an exception where plaintiff's decision to purchase the product was made in reliance on the manufacturers' written representations in labels or advertising materials.") (citations omitted). However, Plaintiffs express warranty claims must be dismissed, as the complaint does not allege facts sufficient to give rise to a plausible basis to believe that Plaintiffs relied on any representations made by Defendants. *See, e.g., id.*

Plaintiffs' conclusory allegations that Defendants advertised their products as safe and effective lack even general information describing such alleged conduct. As one district court has aptly noted, conclusory allegations such as those advanced by Plaintiffs are insufficient to support a plausible basis for an express warranty claim:

> Evraets stands as clear authority that at least at the pleading stage, California law permits a claim for breach of an express warranty to go forward under circumstances [where reliance is alleged]. That said, the complaint as presently constituted fails to allege any express warranties actually made by Stryker, except in the most general and conclusory terms. Accordingly, the claim for breach of express warranty will be denied, with leave to amend.

The FAC alleges neither privity nor reliance as the basis for Plaintiff's express warranty claim. Plaintiff's argument that she need not plead reliance in order to state a cognizable breach of express warranty claim is contrary to California law and ignores the analysis provided in the memorandum decision. None of the authorities Plaintiff cites in her opposition support the erroneous proposition that reliance is not required in an express warranty action not founded on privity.

Plaintiff cites *Weinstat v. Dentsply Intern., Inc.*, 180 Cal. App. 4th 1213, 1225, 103 Cal. Rptr. 3d 614 (Cal. Ct. App. 2010) and *Keith v. Buchanan*, 173 Cal. App. 3d 13, 21, 220 Cal. Rptr. 392 (Cal. Ct. App. 1985) for the proposition that reliance is not a requirement of her express warranty claim. In *Winestat* the purchasers of dental equipment sued the seller, and the express warranty claim was based on privity. *See id.* Similarly, in *Keith*, the purchaser of a boat sued the company that sold him the boat and allegedly made express warranties antecedent to the transaction. Neither *Weinstat* nor *Keith* supports Plaintiff's erroneous contention that reliance is not required where privity is absent.

Plaintiff's invocation of California Commercial Code section 2313 is unavailing, as it does not alter the requirement that reliance (or some other substitute for privity) is required for an express warranty claim against a non-selling manufacturer of a product.

> In *Burr v. Sherwin Williams Co.* 42 Cal.2d 682, 268 P.2d 1041, (1954) the California Supreme Court held "[t]he general rule is that privity of contract is required in an action for breach of either express or implied warranty and that there is no privity between the original seller and a subsequent purchaser who is in no way a party to the original sale." *Id.* at p. 695. Burr observed that courts created exceptions to the privity rule for items such as foodstuffs, and after *Burr*, the exception was extended to drugs and pesticides. *See Windham at Carmel Mountain Ranch*, at p. 1169 & fn. 7 [observing these exceptions were created by courts before the establishment of the doctrine of strict liability in tort]; *Arnold v. Dow Chemical Co.*, at pp. 720–721. *Burr* also

recognized that "[a]nother possible exception to the general rule is found in a few cases where the purchaser of a product relied on representations made by the manufacturer in labels or advertising material, and recovery from the manufacturer was allowed on the theory of express warranty without a showing of privity." *Burr*, 42 Cal.2d at p. 696.

Since *Burr*, the California Supreme Court has made statements in cases broadly suggesting that courts no longer require privity in express warranty cases. (*See Seely v. White Motor Co.* (1965) 63 Cal.2d 9, 14, 45 Cal. Rptr. 17, 403 P.2d 145 ["Since there was an express warranty to plaintiff in the purchase order, no privity of contract was required"]; *Hauter, supra*, 14 Cal. 3d at p. 115, fn. 8 ["The fact that [plaintiff] is not in privity with defendants does not bar recovery. Privity is not required for an action based upon an express warranty"].) However, *Seely* and *Hauter* did not overrule *Burr*, and, unlike the case at hand, both cases involve written warranties similar to advertisements and labels where the plaintiffs saw and relied upon the written statements in purchasing the product at issue. (*Seely*, at p. 13 [plaintiff relied on statements in purchase order when buying a truck]; *Hauter*, at pp. 109, 117 [plaintiff read and relied on defendant's representation on the label of a shipping carton].) The broad language in *Seely* and *Hauter* narrows significantly when read in the context of those facts. Further, as indicated above, several cases decided after *Seely* reflect the continuing validity of *Burr's* privity requirement. We conclude plaintiffs' asserted "independent liability" theory under section 2313 is defeated by the fact they did not bargain with or directly purchase the products from Yihua, and were not in privity of contract with it.

Wiley v. Yihua Int'l Group, 2009 Cal. App. Unpub. LEXIS 8880.

As the court in *Kelleher* pointed out, the Comments to 2-313 state explicitly that "no particular reliance on [the seller's] statements is necessary" for the statements to create an express warranty. But the issue in *Coleman* was not whether the seller's statements created an express warranty; the issue was whether a buyer who had no actual dealings with the seller who made the warranty could recover for its breach. The court used reliance not as a bar to a claim for breach of express warranty, but rather as a surrogate for the requirement of privity that was absent because the buyer had not dealt with the seller who made the warranty. The buyer's refusal to plead reliance did not mean that no express warranty existed; rather, it meant that she had not overcome the privity requirement necessary to assert a claim for breach of warranty.

Neither the buyer nor the court in *Coleman* addressed the effect of 2-318 on the buyer's claim, probably because California was one of many states that did not include that section in the article it adopted. Article 2, as presented to the states, addressed the privity requirement in breach of warranty cases by providing three alternative privity rules for adoption by the states. The alternatives relax the general privity rule but differ in the class of beneficiaries covered. Fewer than twenty states have adopted one of the alternatives.

The reliance alternative to privity recognized by the court in *Coleman* may be of limited utility to third-party buyers. Consequential damages for a seller's breach only include loss from general or particular requirements or needs which the seller "at the time of contracting" had reason to know. 2-715(a). If the phrase "at the time of contracting" conditions the recovery of consequential damages on the existence of a contract between the party claiming them and the seller, third-party buyers would not be entitled to consequential damages for breach of express warranty, even if they had relied on the seller's express warranties. *See Beard Plumbing v. Thompson Plastics*, 491 S.E.2d 731 (Va. 1997).

Problem 8 - 7

A week after the new juice-bottling machine was installed in the produce department of the store, the seller called Rae to make sure everything was working properly. During the call, Rae expressed some disappointment at the bottling rate, which was slower than Rae had expected. The seller told Rae, "Don't worry—once the AT560 is broken in, I guarantee it will do fifty bottles an hour." It's been six months since that call, and Rae is pretty sure the bottler is broken in, but it's not doing anything close to fifty bottles an hour. Does Rae have a claim for breach of warranty based on the bottling rate guarantee the seller made after the store bought the machine? 2-313.

C. Disclaiming Warranties

A seller can control whether an express warranty becomes part of its bargain with the buyer—as long as it does not make any promises about the goods or offer samples or models for the buyer's review, an express warranty will not arise under 2-313. But if the seller is a merchant, 2-314 implies a warranty that the goods are fit for their ordinary purposes simply because the seller is a merchant. And the seller who influences the buyer's selection of a product may find herself subject to the implied warranty of fitness for a particular purpose imposed by 2-315. But what if a seller does not want to be obligated to the buyer if the product does not perform as expected—does not want to be saddled with the risk of future nonperformance? Some buyers may be unwilling to purchase goods if the seller won't stand behind them, in which case the seller, in order to make the sale, will have to assume at least some of the risk of a product's nonperformance. But other buyers, especially consumer buyers of less expensive products, will be more than willing to assume the risk of future nonperformance if the price is right. Should Article 2 prevent the parties from using their agreement to allocate the risks of nonperformance or less-than-perfect performance on their own terms?

Of course, the answer to that question is no—as we've seen throughout our examination of Article 2, Llewellyn believed sales law should, for the most part, stay out of the parties' way, and so the UCC allows the parties to change, subject to certain exceptions, the effects of its provisions by agreement. 1-302(a). And 2-316 expressly authorizes the parties to a sale-of-goods transaction to opt out of the implied warranties of merchantability and fitness for a particular purpose. But the opting-out process is subject to several conditions which courts often construe narrowly—especially in consumer transactions—to protect buyers from unknowingly or unintentionally giving up the essence of the bargain they've made.

In addition (or as an alternative) to opting out of the implied warranties imposed by Article 2, the seller may want to limit what the buyer is entitled to recover in the event of breach by the seller or to exclude damages for breach that the buyer would otherwise be entitled to claim under Article 2. And Article 2 empowers sellers to do so—again, subject to certain conditions. The seller may limit the buyer's recovery for nonperformance to replacement of the failed product or a return of its purchase price as a substitute for the buyer's right under 2-714 to recover the difference in value between the product the buyer expected to get and the value of the nonperforming product she ended up with. A seller might also want to eliminate the buyer's right to recover consequential damages for any breach by the seller—and Article 2 allows the seller to do so, although the power to do so in consumer transactions, or when the damages are based on injury to a person, are greatly limited.

Finally, regardless of the nature of a buyer's claim for breach, Article 2 requires the buyer to give timely notice of her claim for breach to the seller—or waive any right she would otherwise have to a remedy for that breach under Article 2. The timely-notice requirement furthers, in part, Article 2's goal of providing the parties to a sale-of-goods agreement with opportunities to work out their problems privately—to preserve the relationship and the agreement that embodies it. It also protects sellers from bad-faith claims by buyers who decide, after years of using the product, that it just doesn't perform as expected.

1. Warranty Disclaimers

The next case examines the requirements for a seller intending to disclaim the implied warranties imposed by 2-314 and 2-315—express warranties cannot really be disclaimed. A contract provision disclaiming express warranties is only effective to the extent that it can reasonably be construed as consistent with any express warranty made by the seller. 2-316(1). The Comments to 2-313 and 2-316 should give any court considering whether an express warranty can be reconciled with a disclaimer pause:

> "Express" warranties rest on "dickered" aspects of the individual bargain, and go so clearly to the essence of that bargain that words of disclaimer in a form are repugnant to the basic dickered terms. Comment 1, 2-313.

> [This section] seeks to protect a buyer from unexpected and unbargained language of disclaimer by denying effect to such language when inconsistent with language of express warranty ... Comment 1, 2-316.

Courts have not been friendly to sellers who try to have it both ways, and most have determined that "an attempt to both warrant and refuse to warrant goods creates an ambiguity which can only be resolved by making one term yield to the other." Since 2-316(1) requires that warranty language prevails over a disclaimer, these courts refuse to give effect to the disclaimer. *See, e.g., Wilson Trading v. David Ferguson,* 244 N.E.2d 685 (N.Y. 1968). Of course, such clauses may still benefit sellers who incorporate them into their sales agreements. The ordinary consumer, unaware that courts will not give effect to a term disclaiming an express warranty, may still be deterred by the term from pursuing a claim against the seller when the product fails to perform as promised.

HAMMOND ENTERS. V. ZPS AM. LLC

UNITED STATES DISTRICT COURT FOR THE NORTHERN DISTRICT OF CALIFORNIA, 2013
2013 U.S. DIST. LEXIS 155135

LAPORTE, Magistrate Judge.

I. BACKGROUND

This case arises out of Plaintiffs' purchase of two TMZ 642 machine lathes from Defendant ZPS America, LLC ("ZPSA") for approximately $3,000,000. Plaintiff Hammond Enterprises, Inc., manufactures and sells precision parts. Plaintiff CNC Technologies, LLC, which is managed by Hammond Enterprises' CEO, Alan Hammond, purchases machining equipment and leases it to Hammond Enterprises. Plaintiffs both operate out of the same facility in Pittsburg, California. In early 2009, Defendant Olaf Tessarzyk, the president and CEO of ZPSA, met with Alan Hammond regarding the purchase of a machine lathe. Hammond informed Tessarzyk that Plaintiffs needed a machine capable of producing 65,000 brass bodies and plugs a month due to a contract with a third party. Hammond also told Tessarzyk that each body and plug needed to be manufactured in conformance with the third party's design specifications. Tessarzyk recommended that Plaintiffs purchase a TMZ 642 machine lathe manufactured by Defendant Tajmac in the Czech Republic. According to Hammond, Tessarzyk and Defendant Tajariol, Tajmac's CEO, represented that this machine was capable of producing parts at a particular frequency ("cycle time") and that it was capable of operating a certain number of hours per day at 85% efficiency over a particular schedule ("uptime reliability"). Tessarzyk also allegedly represented that the TMZ 642 was superior to other available machine lathes and would enable Plaintiffs to meet their client's needs.

Hammond agreed to purchase a TMZ 642 machine lathe from ZPSA. In April 2009, ZPSA prepared a quote for the machine. The last page of this quote is a one-page document titled "TERMS AND CONDITIONS OF SALE ZPS AMERICA LLC." The term sheet is written in very small typeface and contains 19 paragraphs of contractual terms. Paragraph 13 sets forth a disclaimer of implied warranties in capitalized letters. On June 1, 2009, Hammond Enterprises issued a purchase order based on the first quote as amended. Tajmac delivered the machine from its facility in the Czech Republic to Plaintiffs' manufacturing facility in California in January 2010. On August 8, 2009, ZPSA prepared a quote for a second TMZ 642 machine. This quote contained the same one-page term sheet as the first quote. Plaintiffs issued a purchase order for the second machine based on this quote. The second machine was delivered to California in June 2010.

Plaintiffs allege that after installation, both machines have had "innumerable equipment failures and have been largely incapable of meeting the contractual cycle times for the body and plug, as well as incapable of meeting the required uptime and efficiency rating under the contract." Due these alleged problems, Plaintiffs state that they spent hundreds of hours attempting to keep the machines operating, that Defendants have failed to reimburse Plaintiffs for repair work that Defendants should have performed, that Plaintiffs have been forced to purchase a machine from another company to make up for the Defendants' machines' shortcomings, that defects in the machines have rendered Plaintiffs' raw materials unusable and saleable only as scrap, and that ZPSA has refused to accept return of both machines.

II. DISCUSSION

Defendants argue that Claim 5, for breach of implied warranty, fails to state a claim because the contracts for the two machines both contain conspicuous disclaimers of implied warranties. Defendants assert that Claims 6-8, which are tort claims, are barred by the economic loss rule. Plaintiffs counter that the disclaimers are not sufficiently conspicuous and that the economic loss rule does not apply due to the "other property" exception.

Breach of Implied Warranty
Plaintiffs' claim for breach of implied warranty fails to state a claim because the contracts for both machines contain conspicuous disclaimers of implied warranties. Under the California Commercial Code, disclaimers of implied warranties of merchantability and fitness must be conspicuous to be effective. The Code defines "conspicuous" as "so written, displayed, or presented that a reasonable person against whom it is to operate ought to have noticed it." *Cal. Comm. Code § 1201(b)(10).* "Whether a term is 'conspicuous' or not is a decision for the court," and conspicuous terms include "a heading in capitals equal to or greater in size than the surrounding text, or in contrasting type, font, or color to the surrounding text of the same or lesser size" and "language in the body of a record or display in larger type than the surrounding text, or in contrasting type, font, or color to the surrounding text of the same size, or set off from surrounding text of the same size by symbols or other marks that call attention to the language."

The purpose of the conspicuousness requirement is to "protect the buyer from the situation where the salesman's 'pitch,' advertising brochures, or large print in the contract, giveth, and the disclaimer clause—in fine print—taketh away." The test is whether "attention can reasonably be expected to be called to the disclaimer provision." In considering whether a disclaimer is conspicuous, relevant factors include the size of the disclaimer, color of the font, the location of the disclaimer within the document at issue, and whether there is a heading calling attention to the disclaimer. The sophistication of the parties and the circumstances of the negotiation and signing of the contract are also factors.

Here, the first and second quotes for the machines both contained an identical one-page term sheet as the last page of the document. The entire term sheet is in small typeface. Paragraph 13 of the term sheet contains a boldface, all-capitals heading stating "Warranty: Disclaimer of Implied Warranties." It is followed by a subheading A, which states, in all capitals, that

> The Warranties provided herein are the exclusive warranties made by Seller to Buyer. Seller makes no other warranties, express or implied by law or usage. Seller disclaims and Buyer waives, all express and implied warranties, including but not limited to the implied warranties of merchantability and fitness for a particular purpose. Buyer acknowledges that the description of the goods or repairs stated in Seller's purchase order is for the sole purpose of identifying the goods.

This disclaimer is sufficiently conspicuous to preclude implied warranties. Although the entire term sheet is written in small typeface, the disclaimer of implied warranties is all in capitalized letters and is introduced with a separate, bold heading, distinguishing the disclaimer from the surrounding paragraphs. Additionally, Plaintiffs are sophisticated merchants that regularly purchase machining equipment.

Plaintiffs focus on the size of the typeface and the disclaimer's location in term sheets appended at the end of the first and second quotes, but not expressly incorporated into the quotes. However, "[w]hether a disclaimer is conspicuous is not simply a matter of measuring the type size or looking at the placement of the disclaimer within the contract." Moreover, the term sheets were attached to both the first and second quotes and contained standard contractual terms absent from the body of the quotes. *See, e.g., Kowalsky v. Hewlett-Packard Co.*, 771 F. Supp. 2d 1138 (N.D. Cal. 2010) (enforcing disclaimer despite it being in a separate document on defendant's website). Plaintiffs' efforts to distance themselves from the term sheets are particularly unpersuasive because Plaintiffs allege that the term sheets are part of their contracts in Claim 4 of SAC and quote the same paragraph of the term sheet that contains the disclaimer.

Finally, although Plaintiffs cite a number of cases where disclaimers and releases were held to be unenforceable because they were inconspicuous, those cases are distinguishable. In *Dorman*, there was no heading to call the buyer's attention to the disclaimer. *46 Cal. App. 3d at 19.* In *Sierra Diesel*, the buyer was not familiar with computers or with contracts and the disclaimer was on the back of a page. 890 F.2d at 114-15. *Leon v. Family Fitness Ctr.* and *Link v. Nat'l Assoc. for Stock Car Auto Racing, Inc.*, each involved releases of liability, unsophisticated consumers, and confusing and ambiguous language, none of which are present here. *Leon*, 61 Cal. App. 4th 1227, 1230-31, 1233, 71 Cal. Rptr. 2d 923 (Cal. Ct. App. 1998); *Link*, 158 Cal. App. 3d 138, 141-42, 205 Cal. Rptr. 513 (Cal. Ct. App. 1984

PROBLEM 8 - 8

The new pallet jack Rae bought for the store last month refuses to change directions unless the operator turns it off and then restarts it, which makes it difficult, if not impossible, to maneuver large loads in tight spaces—one of the purposes for which hydraulic jacks are used. Rae has demanded that the seller-manufacturer either repair or replace the jack, but it has refused to do so unless Rae agrees to pay for the repairs, claiming it had no obligation to repair the jack even if defective because it had disclaimed all warranties. The delivery acknowledgment Rae signed when the jack arrived contained the following language on the back side:

WARRANTIES: Since we have no control over the conditions under which this equipment is used, we make no warranty, express or implied, with respect to this equipment or its fitness for any purpose. No representative of ours has any authority to waive or change this provision, which applies to all sales. IF THE PURCHASER DOES NOT ACCEPT THE EQUIPMENT ON THESE TERMS, THEY ARE TO BE RETURNED AT ONCE, UNUSED.

The receipt was attached to the delivery driver's clipboard at the time Rae signed it. Has the manufacturer-seller effectively disclaimed the implied warranties Art. 2 would otherwise impose on the Seller?

Would your answer be different if the disclaimer had mentioned "merchantability"? If merchantability was in all caps? Or if the driver had handed Rae the receipt for her signature?

PROBLEM 8 - 9

If the front page of the delivery receipt for the pallet jack in the last problem had referenced the disclaimer on the backside, would the disclaimer be effective for purposes of 2-316?

Would the seller have a better argument that the disclaimer with the pallet jack was effective if it had been on the front of the receipt instead of the reverse?

PROBLEM 8 - 10

Rae bought a used refrigerator for the store's pharmacy because certain medications require cold storage prior to dispensation. The one-page sales agreement for the refrigerator provided:

TERMS AND CONDITIONS: You understand that the product you are purchasing is used, that is, not new, and therefore will not perform as a new product might perform. You agree that you are purchasing this product "as is" and that you understand the implications of such a purchase.

A week after it was delivered, the refrigerator stopped working because of a failed condenser that needs to be replaced at a cost that exceeds the purchase price of the refrigerator. Rae wants to return the refrigerator, but the seller refuses to accept responsibility for the problem, claiming that's why it was sold "as is". Is Rae stuck with the refrigerator?

In *Hammond*, the Court noted that effectiveness of a warranty disclaimer turned in part on "the sophistication of the parties and the circumstances of the negotiation and signing of the contract." The court scoffed at the suggestion that the buyers had been disadvantaged because the disclaimer appeared only in the term sheets that were attached to the end of the price quotes submitted by the sellers: buyers "are sophisticated merchants that regularly purchase machining equipment." Would the Court have been more sympathetic to a buyer's claim that the disclaimer was insufficient under 2-316 because of its location if the buyers had been ordinary consumers presented with a standard form contract used by the seller in all of its transactions? Probably. Courts generally apply a more rigorous standard of conspicuousness when sellers are trying to enforce their disclaimers against consumers. *See, e.g., Hiigel v. General Motors Corp.,* 544 P.2d 983 (Colo. 1975); *Jensen v. Siegel Mobile Homes Group,* 668 P.2d 65 (Idaho 1983); *Louisiana Nat'l Leasing Corp. v. ADF Serv., Inc.,* 377 So.2d 92 (La. 1979); *Scientific Application, Inc. v. Delkamp,* 303 N.W.2d 71 (N.D. 1981); *Zabriskie Chevrolet, Inc. v. Smith,* 240 A.2d 195 (N.J. 1968); *Woods v. Secord,* 444 A.2d 539 (N.H. 1982); *Seibel v. Layne & Bowler, Inc.,* 641 P.2d 668 (Or. 1982); *Berg v. Stromme,* 484 P.2d 380 (Wash. 1971). These courts can point to the emphasis in the Comments to 2-316 (on protecting buyers from surprise) to justify the heightened scrutiny in consumer transactions, but there seems to be more to it than that. For some, the ability of sellers to take back under 2-316 what Article 2 gives buyers in 2-314 and 2-315 is unfathomable:

> These implied warranties, created by common-law courts long before the adoption of the U.C.C., developed to protect purchasers from losses suffered because of "the frustration of their expectations about the worth, efficacy, or desirability" of a product.   Implication of these warranties into every goods contract, without regard to the parties actual assent to their terms, served "to police, to prevent, and to remedy" unfair consumer transactions. Llewellyn, *On warranty of Quality, and Society*, 39 Colum. L. Rev. 699, 699 (1936). These implied warranties also serve other important purposes: they create incentives to produce and market higher quality products; they discourage shoddy workmanship and unethical trade practices; and they place responsibility on those who profit from the sale of goods, have the greatest control over the products, and are better able to bear the risk of loss. Section 2.316 of the U.C.C., however, subverts all of these purposes by giving sellers almost unlimited license to disclaim implied warranties.

> We live in an age when sellers of goods "saturate the marketplace and all of our senses" with the most extraordinary claims about the worth of their products. Yet, the same sellers under the *carte blanche* granted them by section 2.316 of the U.C.C. refuse to guarantee and indeed expressly disclaim that their products are merchantable or even fit for their intended purposes. Under section 2.316, not much is actually required for an effective disclaimer. To disclaim the implied warranty of merchantability the seller need only include the word "merchantability" in a conspicuous fashion. To disclaim the implied warranty of fitness the seller must use a writing and must make the disclaimer conspicuous. No particular form of words is needed to disclaim an implied warranty of fitness, nor does section 2.316 require the buyer to be actually aware of the disclaimer before it will be enforced. All implied warranties can be disclaimed by the mere inclusion of expressions like "as is" or "with all faults". Finally, as today's majority makes clear, section 2.316 does not even require the disclaimer to be conspicuous if the buyer's actual knowledge of the disclaimer can be shown.

> By establishing specific "requirements" for disclaimers, section 2.316 ostensibly "seeks to protect a buyer from unexpected and unbargained language of disclaimer." [Comment 1, 2-316]. In reality, however, section 2.316 completely undermines implied warranties. Implicitly, section 2.316 adopts the position that disclaimers should be enforced because society benefits when parties to a contract are allowed to set *all* the terms of their agreement. The problem with this position, and with section 2.316 generally, is twofold: it ignores the fact that governmental implication of protective terms into private contracts is commonplace (*e.g.* the *implied* warranties of merchantability and fitness); and, more importantly, it rests on the faulty premise that contractual disclaimers are generally freely bargained for elements of a contract.

> Freedom of contract arguments generally, and section 2.316 specifically, presuppose and are based on "the image of individuals meeting in the marketplace" on equal ground to negotiate the terms of a contract. At one time, this image may have accurately reflected marketplace realities. However, the last half of the twentieth century has witnessed "the rise of the corporation" and, increasingly, the displacement of physical persons as sellers in consumer and commercial contracts. This development has led to innumerable situations

in which consumers deal from an unequal bargaining position, the most prominent example being the ubiquitous standard form contract which is now used by most sellers of goods and which invariably contains an implied warranty disclaimer.

The great majority of buyers never read an implied warranty disclaimer found in a standard form contract. Even when implied warranty disclaimers are read, their legal significance is not generally understood. Such disclaimers include unfamiliar terminology (*e.g.* "implied warranty of merchantability"), and comprehending their legal effect requires one not only to understand what substantive rights are involved, but also to grasp that these rights have been lost via the disclaimer. [*See*] Federal Trade Commission, *Facts for Consumers* (Mar. 23, 1979) (more than 35% of those surveyed mistakenly believed that an "as is" disclaimer meant the dealer would have to pay some, if not all, costs if a car broke down within 25 days of a sale). Finally, even if a buyer reads and understands an implied warranty disclaimer, chances are he will be without power to either strike these terms or "shop around" for better ones. If the buyer attempts the former, he will likely run into an employee who is unauthorized to alter the form contract; if he attempts the latter, he will likely confront a competitor who offers substantially the same form terms. In short, the "marketplace reality" suggests that freedom of contract in the sale of goods is actually nonexistent; a buyer today can either take the contract with the disclaimer attached or leave it and go without the good.
          Cate v. Dover Corp., 790 S.W.2d 559 (Tex. 1990)(Spears, concurring).

A number of states bar warranty disclaimers in consumer transactions by statute. *See* Hart, Forms & Procedures Under the UCC, 5-2 P. 22.33 (LEXIS Law Publishing).

Another characteristic of the modern marketplace described by Justice Spears in his concurrence is the presence of intermediate sellers—very few of us purchase anything directly from the manufacturer. Target did not manufacture the toaster I bought from it last week—Westinghouse did—but even Target may not have purchased it directly from Westinghouse. Can these intermediate sellers invoke a manufacturer's disclaimer of the implied warranties if they do not expressly disclaim the warranties themselves? Can Target assert the warranty disclaimer made by Westinghouse when I sue Target for breach of the implied warranty of merchantability, even though there was no disclaimer by Target in any of the paper we exchanged when I bought the toaster? The next case addresses this question.

Gibbs Patrick Farms, Inc. v. Syngenta Seeds, Inc.

United States District Court for the Middle District of Georgia, 2008
2008 U.S. Dist. LEXIS 23923

LAWSON, Judge.

I. INTRODUCTION

In the fall planting season of 2004, disease struck the crops on Gibbs Patrick Farms ("GPF"), Lewis Taylor Farms, LTF Greenhouses ("LTF" collectively), and DL&B Enterprises ("DL&B"). In this litigation, and in a companion case also filed in this Court, the Parties attempt to assign liability for the economic damage that this incidence of disease caused. At the core of the dispute is a crop common to each farm: a variety of bell pepper plant called "Stiletto." Syngenta Seeds, Inc. ("Syngenta") produced the Stiletto seeds at issue, and R.D. Clifton Seed Company, d/b/a/ Clifton Seed Co., Georgia ("Clifton") distributed them.

The farmers assert that their crops suffered from bacterial leaf spot ("BLS"), which is caused by a bacterium called *X. campestris* pv. *vesicatoria* ("XCV"). They further claim that the Stiletto seeds carried XCV and therefore were the cause of the BLS outbreak on their farms. They seek damages associated with the destruction of their crops and lost profits.

II. FACTS

A. The Seed Purchase

Gibbs Patrick Jr. is the president of GPF, a corporation which, during the time relevant to the current dispute, grew produce for commercial sale. Patrick purchased Stiletto seed for GPF from Clifton for the fall 2004 season. He ordered the seed from George Ponder, one of Clifton's sales representatives. The men finalized the sale verbally, discussing only the variety of seed ordered, the number of units, approximate delivery, and price. Ponder agreed on behalf of Clifton to sell the seed and Patrick agreed to buy them during this conversation. There was no discussion about a disclaimer or limitation of liability, and Ponder was not authorized to negotiate these terms.

Syngenta packaged the seeds in sealed, labeled cans. Clifton purchased a complete product from Syngenta and resold it to GPF without breaking the seal on the containers. Although the cans contained no disclaimer provision on the outside of the label or any reference to a disclaimer or limit on liability, the label advised the reader to "open for additional information." Inside the fold-out label was a disclaimer of warranties and limitation on liability:

> NOTICE TO BUYER: Syngenta Seeds, Inc. warrants that all seed sold has been labeled as required under applicable state and federal seed law and that the seed conforms to the label description within recognized tolerances. THIS WARRANTY IS IN LIEU OF ALL OTHER WARRANTIES, EXPRESSED OR IMPLIED, INCLUDING WARRANTIES OF MERCHANTABILITY AND FITNESS FOR A PARTICULAR PURPOSE. THERE ARE NO WARRANTIES THAT EXTEND BEYOND THE DESCRIPTION ON THE LABEL. BUYER'S EXCLUSIVE REMEDY FOR ANY CLAIM OR LOSS RESULTING FROM BREACH OF WARRANTY, BREACH OF CONTRACT, OR NEGLIGENCE (WHICH SHALL NOT EXTEND TO INCIDENTAL OR CONSEQUENTIAL DAMAGES) SHALL BE LIMITED TO REPAYMENT OF THE PURCHASE PRICE.
>
> IMPORTANT NOTICE REGARDING SEED BORNE DISEASES
>
> Syngenta Seeds, Inc. has undertaken all reasonable precautions to identify and control seed borne pathogens on this seed. However, these precautions, which may include seed treatments cannot assure complete absence of seed borne diseases, especially if the disease is already present in the buyer's field or neighboring fields diseased from other sources. SYNGENTA SEEDS, INC. DISCLAIMS ALL WARRANTIES REGARDING SEED BORNE DISEASES, EITHER EXPRESSED OR IMPLIED, OTHER THAN THE WARRANTIES SET FORTH HEREIN. Please contact Syngenta Seeds if you would like to receive a more detailed description of the risk from seed borne diseases.

Although Patrick had purchased Stiletto and other varieties of Syngenta seed for GPF in the past, he had never read the fold-out portion of the label. Clifton did not provide any additional disclaimer or liability limitation information as a part of its sale to GPF.

B. The Discovery of BLS

In mid-June 2004, LTF noticed symptoms of disease in the bell pepper seedlings in Greenhouse 25. Greenhouse 25 contained seedlings from Stiletto green peppers, jalapeno peppers, and several varieties of tomatoes. Lewis Taylor Farms provided samples of pepper and tomato transplants to the University of Georgia ("UGA") Cooperative extension Service Disease Clinic for assessment. The extention program then shipped the samples to Dr. Ron Gitaitis's lab. A routine examination produced colonies of "xanthomonad-like" bacteria from both the tomato and pepper plants, confirming the presence of BLS. Dr. Gitaitis's research indicated, however, that the strain of the bacteria on the peppers was different from the strain found on the tomatoes.

Dr. Gitaitis's lab then learned of a BLS outbreak in Stilleto peppers on GPF. Isolations from these peppers were tested to confirm that the plants were in fact infected with BLS. Dr. Gitaitis also performed a procedure called repPCR, which confirmed that the strains of BLS in Stilletto peppers from LTF and GPF and Hungarian peppers from LTF were identical, which indicated that the same strain was involved in all three outbreaks. In contrast, peppers from different sources in Georgia that were infected with BLS were found to have different strains of the bacteria. These findings made Dr. Gitaitis suspicious that the strain was seedborne as opposed to being present in the environment.

Dr. Gitaitis then performed a race type analysis on samples of infected Stiletto peppers from different sources. The results indicated that all of the Stiletto peppers were infected with the same race of the BLS strain, another factor which indicated that the source of the bacteria was the seeds themselves.

After this testing, Dr. Gitaitis learned that GPF possessed some unopened cans of the Stiletto seeds it had purchased from Clifton. Using these seeds, Dr. Gitaitis was able to test his theory that the disease was seedborne. The cans were transported to his lab unopened and remained in that condition until the time the tests were performed.

C. The Grow-Out Test

Dr. Gitaitis chose to perform a "grow-out test," which involves planting the seedlings, allowing them to grow, observing visual signs of the presence of the disease, and then testing any visible legions to determine whether BLS is present. The grow-out test that Dr. Gitaitis designed was modeled after "sweat box" and "dome" tests, which are used to detect watermelon fruit blotch and halo blight of bean respectively.

Once the seedlings began to grow, Sanders frequently pulled samples from the trays because there was a lot of spotting on the cotyledons. As part of the effort to prevent contamination by secondary bacteria, samples were pulled as soon as legions appeared. In addition, Sanders wore latex gloves at all times when he handled the trays and samples. Dr. Gitaitis collected 65 suspected legions from cotyledons and 35 suspected legions from first true leaves. Isolations from these legions were made in a standard fashion: lesions were aseptically cut with a sterile blade, the tissue was minced in a sterile buffer, the sample was allowed to rest during which time the bacteria could swim out into the solution, and a sterile bacteriological loop was used to plate a loopful of bacteria onto the surface of a sterile petri dish containing nutrient ager. This entire process was performed under a laminar flow hood, a device that prevents contamination. The plates were then incubated in a covered incubator.

None of the cotyledon samples produced XCV; four strains were isolated from the true leaf samples, however.[8] These strains were confirmed as having the same DNA fingerprint and being of the same race as the strains in the Stiletto peppers from LTF and GPF. Based on the above observations, Dr. Gitaitis concluded that the seedlot he tested and the seedlot from LTF were the source of the inoculum of the BLS epidemic observed at the two farms.

III. SUMMARY JUDGMENT

* * *

---

8   Dr. Gitaitis speculated that the reason XCV was not detected in the cotyledons was that the presence of other bacteria could have initially masked the XCV.

D. Breach of Warranty Claim

GPF asserts a claim for breach of warranty against Clifton. Clifton has moved for summary judgment on this claim, asserting that the disclaimer on the seed containers effectively disclaimed any implied warranty and that the limitation of remedies clause prohibits GPF from recovering more than the cost of the seeds. GPF has also moved for partial summary judgment on Clifton's defenses of disclaimer and limitation of remedies. The Court finds, however, that no disclaimer or limitation of liability were applicable to Clifton. Furthermore, the application of a disclaimer or limitation of liability in this case would be unconscionable under Georgia law. These provisions therefore provide no protection to Clifton.

1. Applicability of the Written Warranty to Clifton

Clifton argues that in its prior course of dealing with GPF it has always "passed on" the disclaimer on the Syngenta seed cans to GPF, and that the disclaimer and limitation of liability on the cans were part of the Parties' contract.[9] The Court holds, however, that regardless of the prior course of dealing, the disclaimer language applies only to Syngenta. The written provisions on the seed cans therefore do not affect Clifton's liability for breach of an implied warranty.

Under Georgia law, the implied warranty of merchantability may be excluded if the disclaimer mentions merchantability and, in the case of a writing, is conspicuous. However, "a manufacturer's disclaimer of warranties does not run with the goods so as to protect any subsequent seller of them; thus, each subsequent seller must make his own independent disclaimer in order to be protected from warranty liability." 63 Am. Jur. Prods. L. § 801; *see also Clark v. DeLaval Separator Corp.,* 639 F.2d 1320, 1324 (5th Cir. 1981) (finding that seller's disclaimer was ineffective as to manufacturer); *Graham Hydraulic Power, Inc. v. Stewart & Stevenson Power, Inc.,* 797 P.2d 835, 839 (Colo. App. 1990) ("each subsequent seller must make his own independent disclaimer in order to be protected from warranty liability"); *Barazotto v. Intelligent Systs., Inc.,* 40 Ohio App. 3d 117, 532 N.E.2d 148, 149 (Ohio App. 1987) (""[T]he manufacturer's disclaimer of warranties does not run with the goods so as to protect any subsequent seller of them. To the contrary, each subsequent seller must make his own independent disclaimer in order to be protected from warranty liability."); The Law of Product Warranties § 8:14 (November 2007) ("In the usual case, a distributor or dealer must make his own disclaimer in order to be free from implied warranty liability. He cannot rely on a disclaimer used by the manufacturer even though he passes that documentation on to the ultimate buyer.").

A seller is shielded by a manufacturer's disclaimer when it provides a written disclaimer to the buyer independent of the materials that the manufacturer provides. Where the language of the disclaimer explicitly applies to the manufacturer, however, it will not effectively disclaim implied warranties that apply to the seller. *See, e.g., Stephens v. Crittenden Tractor, Co.,* 187 Ga. App. 545, 370 S.E.2d 757, 761 (Ga. App. 1988) (holding that a limitations clause that applied to the manufacturer was not effective as to the dealer). In *Stephens,* for example, the Georgia Court of Appeals held that the following language limited liability for the manufacturer, but not the dealer who sold the product: "The Company's liability, whether in contract or in tort, arising out of warranties, representations, instructions, or defects from any cause shall be limited exclusively to repairing or replacing parts ... in no event will the Company be liable for consequential damages ..." The *Stephens* court looked to the language of the manufacturer's limitation of liability to determine whether it applied to the dealer. *Id.; see also Chem Tech Finishers, Inc. v. Paul Mueller Co.,* 189 Ga. App. 433, 375 S.E.2d 881, 883 (Ga. App. 1988) (using the plain language

---

9   Clifton also contends that the disclaimer and limitations of liability are valid because they were conspicuous as required under O.C.G.A. § 11-1-201. Whether they were conspicuous, however, is irrelevant if they were never a part of the contract in the first place. *See, e.g., Bowdoin v. Showell Growers, Inc.,* 817 F.2d 1543, 1546-47 (11th Cir. 1987) ("the conspicuousness of a post-sale disclaimer is immaterial").

of the contract to determine to what products the warranty limitation applied). The contract contained explicit reference to both the manufacturer and the dealer, yet by its terms the limitation clause in the contract applied only to the manufacturer. The court therefore concluded that the limitation did not protect the dealer.

The disclaimer on the Stiletto seed container that addresses seed borne illnesses specifically states: "SYNGENTA SEEDS, INC. DISCLAIMS ALL WARRANTIES REGARDING SEED BORNE DISEASES, EITHER EXPRESSED OR IMPLIED, OTHER THAN THE WARRANTIES SET FORTH HEREIN." The general disclaimer also refers specifically to Syngenta:

> Syngenta Seeds, Inc. warrants that all seed sold has been labeled as required under applicable state and federal seed law and that the seed conforms to the label description within recognized tolerances. THIS WARRANTY IS IN LIEU OF ALL OTHER WARRANTIES, EXPRESSED OR IMPLIED, INCLUDING WARRANTIES OF MERCHANTABILITY AND FITNESS FOR A PARTICULAR PURPOSE. THERE ARE NO WARRANTIES THAT EXTEND BEYOND THE DESCRIPTION OF THIS LABEL. BUYER'S EXCLUSIVE REMEDY FOR ANY CLAIM OR LOSS RESULTING FROM BREACH OF WARRANTY … SHALL BE LIMITED TO REPAYMENT OF THE PURCHASE PRICE.

The disclaimer against seed borne illness, which is the subject of the dispute in this case, is explicitly made on Syngenta's behalf and makes no mention of dealers or secondary sellers. Even the general disclaimer and limitation of liability deal only with Syngenta. After Syngenta expressly warrants the information on the seed label, it expressly disclaims its liability for other warranties. Like the contract language in *Stephens*, the seed label in this case refers to the producer specifically instead of to a generic "seller." As a result, the disclaimer and limitations apply only to Syngenta, instead of applying to any seller of the product. In addition, like the dealer in *Stephens*, Clifton made no independent disclaimer of warranty, which it could have done by including a disclaimer in a sales contract, for example. Even if GPF had read and been aware of the terms on the seed labels, it would still not have known that Clifton, as opposed to Syngenta, had disclaimed all warranties. Applying the plain-language approach that the Georgia Court of Appeals took in *Stephens*, the Court finds that neither the disclaimer nor the liability limitation apply to Clifton by their terms. Therefore, under Georgia law, the terms of the disclaimer and the limitation of liability do not apply to Clifton and were not incorporated as a term of the contract between Clifton and Lewis Taylor Farms.

Gibbs tells us that a disclaimer does not run downstream with the product, but can a disclaimer protect an upstream seller? If Target disclaims any implied warranties on the toaster I buy, can the manufacturer, Westinghouse, rely on Target's disclaimer? If a disclaimer must be "conspicuous" to be effective under 2-316, and to be conspicuous, it must be written so that "a reasonable person against whom it is to operate ought to have noticed it," a retail seller's disclaimer of warranties would not alert the buyer to the manufacturer's intent to also disclaim any warranties. Most buyers would be surprised to learn that the retail seller's disclaimer operated to protect the manufacturer as well. *See Clark v. DeLaval Separator*, 639 F.2d 1220 (5th Cir. 1981).

As the following case illustrates, sellers can avoid the more stringent requirements of 2-316(2) and effectively disclaim implied warranties by using any language which in common understanding calls the buyer's attention to the exclusion of warranties and makes plain that there is no implied warranty.

2-316(3)(a). Expressions like "as is" or "with all faults" are expressly sanctioned as meeting the reduced standard. Comment 7 explains that such terms

> in ordinary commercial usage are understood to mean that the buyer takes the entire risk as to the quality of the goods involved.

Does "ordinary commercial usage" include consumer transactions? How likely is it that the ordinary consumer would understand that the term "as they stand" was intended to put the entire risk of future nonperformance on the buyer? As it turns out, many consumers don't fully understand the implications of the more familiar "as is" term used in countless form contracts every day. See Justice Spear dissent following Problem 8-10.

MORNINGSTAR V. HALLETT

SUPERIOR COURT OF PENNSYLVANIA, 2004
858 A.2D 125

TODD, Judge.

Sue A. Hallett appeals the March 19, 2003 order of the Franklin County Court of Common Pleas granting summary judgment in favor of Mandy Morningstar in the amount of $10,205.85. She also challenges the court's prior August 22, 2002 order precluding her counterclaims. We reverse.

The relevant facts of the instant case were summarized by the trial court as follows in its opinion in support of its order granting summary judgment:

> In August, 1999, Plaintiff Mandy Morningstar (hereinafter "Morningstar") placed an advertisement in the York Daily Record for the sale or lease of a horse that she owned, named Glissen Rhode to Pleasure (hereinafter "the horse"). Defendant Sue A. Hallett (hereinafter "Hallett") saw the advertisement and contacted Morningstar to inquire about the horse. The York Daily Record advertisement in its entirety is as follows:

> SALE OR LEASE

> Retired eventer. Lovely 11 year old thoroughbred mare. Flashy bay, 16+ hands, extension jumping & dressage, superb mover, perfect horse for any level rider. Reasonable offer considered to right home. Call [seller's phone number].

On August 18, 1999, Hallett made her first visit to examine and ride the horse at Morningstar's farm on Mentzer Gap Road where the horse was boarded. Hallett's mother, Eleanor Virginia Hallett, and an acquaintance named Jennifer Titemore, an experienced horse-rider, accompanied Hallett to Morningstar's farm. Hallett invited Jennifer Titemore to accompany her so that Hallett could observe and evaluate how the horse moved through [its] gaits under the direction of another rider, rather than make all determinations about the horse while Hallett, herself, was riding the horse. Hallett had taken her own saddle along with her to Morningstar's farm, and she and Morningstar retrieved the horse from its stall and put a bridle and Hallett's saddle on the horse. Hallett proceeded to mount the horse and walk and trot it in a small ring behind the barn where the horse had been stabled. Hallett stated that she didn't notice anything wrong with the horse as it walked, but noticed the horse was lame when she trotted it. Hallett later went to the farm again for the purpose of examining the horse a second time.

On September 2, 1999, Morningstar and Hallett entered into a contract by signing a written Sales Agreement whereby both parties covenanted that Hallett was buying the horse from Morningstar for the sum of $2,950.00. The signed Sales Agreement in its entirety is as follows:

SALES AGREEMENT

I, Mandy Morningstar in consideration of two thousand nine hundred fifty dollars ($2,950.00), hereby paid to me by Sue Hallette (sic), sell to Sue Hallette (sic) the following horse: "Glissen" Rhode to Pleasure.

Age: 11 years	Color: Bay
Breed:	Sex: Female
Height: 16+ hands	Tattoo#: R050

I hereby covenant that I am the lawful owner of said horse, that I have the right to sell the horse, and that I will warrant and defend said horse against claims and demands of all persons. There are no other warranties expressed or implied including fitness for certain purposes. The buyer is buying horse as is. (Emphasis added.) The risk of the horse's death or injury passes to the buyer as soon as the buyer takes possession of the horse. The seller has right to refuse refund for any reason. The seller may recover any and all legal fees if it becomes necessary. The seller is not liable for injury or death of a participant resulting from the inherent risk of equine activities. Said horse has been exposed to stallion and if resulting exposure produces a foal, the foal remains the property of seller. Executed this second day of September, 1999.

SELLER:	BUYER:
(Signature and address of	(Signature and address
of Mandy Morningstar)	Sue Hallett)

A short time after Hallett had tendered her check to Morningstar for the sum of $2,950.00 and had taken possession of the horse, Hallett contacted her bank and authorized a stop payment order on the check and attempted to return the horse to Morningstar. Morningstar refused return of the horse and filed a Complaint in Breach of Contract against Hallett.

On February 29, 2000, a district justice ruled in favor of Morningstar on her claim against Hallett for breach of contract. Hallett appealed the judgment to a panel of arbitrators, which, on April 26, 2000, awarded to Morningstar judgment in the amount of $6,277.03, plus attorneys' fees. On May 10, 2000, Morningstar filed a complaint against Hallett alleging breach of contract. On June 26, 2000, Hallett filed an answer with new matter and counterclaim, raising claims of fraud, misrepresentation, unfair trade practices, and mutual mistake. Hallett averred that the actual age of the horse was 16 years, and that the horse's condition, including eyesight problems and a heart murmur, rendered it incapable of significant jumping or dressage.

On July 23, 2002, Hallett filed a motion *in limine* wherein she indicated her intention to introduce at trial, *inter alia*, the newspaper advertisement placed by Morningstar and evidence of the discussions between the parties prior to Hallett's purchase of the horse. Hallett also indicated her intention to offer the testimony of veterinarian Anne Moretta. Morningstar filed an answer to Hallett's motion, and on August 22, 2002, the trial court issued an order holding that "[d]ue to the unambiguous 'as is' language in the contract as well as the 'right to refuse refund' language,

[Hallett] will not be permitted to proceed on the basis of fraud, misrepresentation, unfair trade practices or mistake claims." The trial court further indicated that "[t]he proposed testimony of Dr. Anne Moretta will not be permitted since her examination occurred after the date of entry into the contract."

Thereafter, on August 28, 2002, Morningstar filed a motion for summary judgment on the grounds that Hallett was unable to establish a *prima facie* case that Morningstar breached her contract in view of the fact that the contract stated that the horse was being sold "as is" and Morningstar had, in fact, delivered the horse to Hallett. On January 22, 2003, the trial court granted Morningstar's motion for summary judgment and attorneys' fees. On March 20, 2003, judgment was entered in favor of Morningstar in the amount of $10,205.85.

In this appeal of the trial court's grant of summary judgment, we first will consider whether the trial court erred in granting summary judgment in favor of Morningstar with respect to her breach of contract action against Hallett. Summary judgment properly is granted after the close of the relevant pleadings "whenever there is no genuine issue of any material fact as to a necessary element of the cause of action or defense which could be established by additional discovery or expert report" and the moving party is entitled to judgment as a matter of law.

In her complaint against Hallett, Morningstar argued that, pursuant to the sales agreement signed by the parties, Morningstar was required to deliver to Hallett the horse that Hallett rode and agreed to purchase for $2,950. Morningstar argued that by delivering the horse to Hallett, she complied with the terms of the contract, and that Hallett, by refusing to pay for the horse, breached the contract. Hallett, however, contends that under the contract, Morningstar was required to provide "the specific horse of the exact age noted in the Sales Agreement," and that Morningstar breached the contract by failing to do so. The trial court concluded that there was no genuine issue of material fact because:

> at no time did Hallett have the single-minded intent to set out to find and purchase a particular, certifiable eleven-year-old horse specifically identified through registration papers, reputation, or otherwise as "Glissen Rhode to Pleasure." Rather, Hallett intended to purchase for $2,950.00 the horse that she rode and examined at Morningstar's farm, and the contract reflects Hallett's intent.

As this Court previously has explained:

> The paramount goal of contractual interpretation is to ascertain and give effect to the intent of the parties. In determining the intent of the parties to a written agreement, the court looks to what they have clearly expressed, for the law does not assume that the language of the contract was chosen carelessly.

The sales agreement specifically stated that the horse being purchased was 11 years old.

With respect to the effect of the "as is" language contained in the sales agreement, Section 2316(b) and (c) of Pennsylvania's Uniform Commercial Code ("UCC") provide as follows:

> (b) Implied warranties of merchantability and fitness.—Subject to subsection (c), to exclude or modify the implied warranty of merchantability or any part of it the language must mention merchantability and in case of a writing must be conspicuous, and to exclude or modify any implied warranty of fitness the exclusion must be by a writing and conspicuous. Language to exclude all implied warranties of fitness is sufficient if it states, for example, that "there are no warranties which extend beyond the description on the face hereof."

(c) Implied warranties in general.—Notwithstanding subsection (b):

(1) Unless the circumstances indicate otherwise, all implied warranties are excluded by expressions like "as is," "with all faults" or other language which in common understanding calls the attention of the buyer to the exclusion of warranties and makes plain that there is no implied warranty.

(2) When the buyer before entering into the contract has examined the goods or the sample or model as fully as he desired or has refused to examine the goods there is no implied warranty with regard to defects which an examination ought in the circumstances to have revealed to him.

(3) An implied warranty can also be excluded or modified by course of dealing or course of performance or usage of trade.

13 Pa. C.S.A. § 2316(b) and (c).

Thus, the "as is" clause contained in the sales agreement made plain that there were no *implied* warranties with respect to the horse, and by signing the sales agreement which contained the "as is" clause, Hallett agreed to purchase the horse *in the condition* in which she found it. *See PBS Coals, Inc.*, 384 Pa. Super. at 328, 558 A.2d at 564 (when something is accepted "as is" the buyer is put on notice that there may be liabilities attendant to the purchase and the warranties which may otherwise be implied by law do not attach when the buyer agrees to accept the goods in the condition in which they are found).

However, as our Supreme Court explained in *Industrial Rayon Corp. v. Clifton Yarn Mills, Inc.*, 310 Pa. 322, 165 A. 385 (1933):

> In *W.E. Hedger Co., Inc., v. United States* (D. C.) 42 F.(2d) 553, 554, it is said that, *where the identity of articles sold is fixed, the 'as is, where is' of the bill of sale refers only to the condition of the article*. The court there relied on *Shepherd v. Caine*, 5 Barn. & Ald. 240, where the sale of an article was 'with all faults, 'and it was held that this means *all faults consistently with its being the thing described*.

Here, the horse was described in the sales agreement, *inter alia*, as being 11 years old.

We further note that Section 2316(c)(1) of the UCC pertains to disclaimers of *implied* warranties. Pursuant to Section 2313, "any description of the goods which is made part of the basis of the bargain creates an *express warranty* that the goods shall conform to the description." 13 Pa. C.S.A. § 2313(a)(2) (emphasis added). Once again, we note that the sales agreement specifically indicated that the horse being sold to Hallett was 11 years old, thereby creating an express warranty. Thus, the "as is" clause was insufficient to disclaim the express warranty that the horse was 11 years old.

Moreover, under Section 2316(a), words or conduct relevant to the creation of an express warranty and words or conduct tending to negate or limit warranty shall be construed wherever reasonable as consistent with each other; but subject to the provisions of this division on parol or extrinsic evidence (section 2202) negation or limitation is inoperative to the extent that such construction is unreasonable.

This section "seeks to protect a buyer from unexpected and unbargained language of disclaimer by denying effect to such language when inconsistent with language of express warranty." Thus, to the extent the trial court relied on the "as is" clause in finding that Morningstar did not breach the contract by failing to deliver to Hallett an 11-year-old horse, we conclude that the "as is" clause is inconsistent with the express warranty created by the description of the horse as provided in the sales agreement and hold that the "as is" language contained in the sales agreement is insufficient to disclaim the express warranty that the horse was 11 years old.

Furthermore, to the extent the trial court also relied on the language of the sales agreement which indicated that the seller had the right to refuse a refund for any reason, we conclude that this language also is insufficient to serve as a disclaimer to the express warranty created by the description of the horse as 11 years old. Rather, we find that this provision is more appropriately viewed as a contractual modification or limitation of remedy under Section 2719 of the UCC. Accordingly, for the foregoing reasons, we conclude that there is a material question of fact as to whether Morningstar breached her agreement with Hallett, and that summary judgment therefore was inappropriate in the instant case.[10]

Does the effectiveness of "as is"-type disclaimers turn on the subjective understanding of a particular buyer? Or does 2-316(3)(a) incorporate an objective standard—and if so, on what empirical basis must it rest? Most courts read 2-316 to intend an objective standard—which is outcome determinative because they then presume that most people—most consumers—know what terms like "as is" mean when used in a contract. Of course, that presumption seems questionable in light of studies like the one cited by Justice Spears in his concurring opinion in *Cote*:

> more than 35% of those surveyed mistakenly believed that an "as is" disclaimer meant the dealer would have to pay some, if not all, costs if a car broke down within 25 days of a sale.

Federal Trade Commission, *Facts for Consumers* (Mar. 23, 1979)

But a subjective standard would also have problems which would undermine any argument that consumers should be treated differently:

> [Courts] should be skeptical of any buyer's claim that the buyer did not understand words to mean what a layperson would normally understand. Remember that consumer buyers lie too; they are not different from any other contracting parties who find it convenient to deny appreciation of what they have signed.[11]

If an effective disclaimer of warranties eliminates any claim of a buyer for breach of warranty, does it also eliminate the buyer's right to revoke her acceptance? It does in Florida. In *Frank Griffin Volkswagen v. Smith*, 610 S.E.2d 597 (FL. App. 1992), the Florida Court of Appeals held that a buyer could not revoke his acceptance of a vehicle because the seller had effectively disclaimed all warranties. The Court reasoned that the seller, by effectively disclaiming all warranties, had incurred no contractual obligations it could breach, and without breach, there was no nonconformity as required for revocation by 2-608. The buyer could not show the vehicle was nonconforming because there was nothing the goods were required to conform to under the terms of the agreement. Although the Florida courts may have been the first to adopt this view of disclaimers and revocation, they are not alone. Courts in Idaho, Michigan, and Ohio, have also adopted similar positions.

The fundamental flaw in the Court's reasoning in *Frank Griffin* (and in those that have followed it) is that revocation under 2-608 and breach of warranty are separate and distinct claims; they can be based on the same facts but are independent of one another—one can exist without the other. I can bring a claim for breach of warranty if the toaster I bought last week is not fit for heating up my Pop-Tart each morning, even though I have no excuse for not discovering that nonconformity before I accepted the toaster. Without an excuse, I would not be able to revoke my acceptance. The more thoughtful courts

---

10   Significantly, the trial court did not conclude that the horse was, in fact, eleven years old, but simply held that the age of the horse was not part of the basis of the bargain.

11   White and Summers, *Commercial Law* (6th ed. West 2010) 585.

that have considered the effect of a warranty disclaimer on revocation have not followed the Florida courts.

2. Limited Remedies: Failure of Essential Purpose

Article 2's commitment to letting the parties to a sale-of-goods transaction structure a relationship on their own terms which will be respected by the law involves more than just letting them decide how much, how many, how good, and when. It allows them, among other things, to determine what happens if one of them fails to perform (breaches the agreement). The parties "are left free to shape their remedies to their particular circumstances" by limiting in whole or in part the remedies set out in Article 2 by modifying those remedies and/or by substituting their own remedies. Comment 1, 2-719. The power to supplant Article 2 remedies is not without limits—the parties can't simply leave themselves remediless, as the "very essence" of a sale-of-goods contract requires that "at least minimum adequate remedies be available." Comment 1, 2-719. The parties must provide "at least a fair quantum of remedy for breach of the obligations or duties outlined in the contract." Comment 1, 2-719. And Article 2 presumes that any additional remedy provided by the parties is cumulative to those available under Article 2 unless the parties make clear they intend otherwise. 2-719(1)(b).

Like warranties, remedies can be used by the parties to allocate the risks associated with the performance of their agreement. And, as we've seen elsewhere, how those risks get allocated will likely have something to do with the bargaining power of the parties. The seller of the iPad I bought last week doesn't want to end up in a lawsuit if the iPad does not work as expected, and, frankly, unless the defect in the iPad somehow injures me or my family, neither do I—I just want a working iPad—so the seller will offer to repair or replace the iPad if it fails to perform in exchange for my "agreement" to give up the remedies Article 2 would provide for me against a breaching seller. Of course, as the party without any real bargaining power, I have no choice, but I do want the iPad, so the seller gets what it wants—no litigation if the iPad does not work—and I get, essentially, what I want: a working iPad. And Article 2 is fine with our decision to opt out of its remedial provisions.

But what if the seller can't (or won't) fix the iPad? Article 2 would give me a claim for damages against the seller, but I gave up my Article 2 remedies when I agreed to the repair-or-replace remedy. Am I without any recourse against the seller when the remedy we agreed to does not work? The *Clarke* case illustrates how Article 2 deals with my problem.

CLARK V. INTERNATIONAL HARVESTER CO.
SUPREME COURT OF IDAHO, 1978
581 P.2D 784

BAKES, Judge.

This is a products liability case in which the plaintiffs seek to recover consequential damages for economic losses resulting from an allegedly defective tractor manufactured by defendant International Harvester Company and sold to the plaintiffs by defendant McVey's, Inc., an International Harvester Co. dealer. The plaintiffs alleged a breach of implied and express warranties and negligent design and manufacture of the tractor. Prior to trial the district court granted partial summary judgments in favor of the defendants on the warranty claims. After trial the district court, sitting without a jury, entered judgment against the defendants on the negligence claim and awarded the plaintiffs $26,950.15 in damages.

The defendant International Harvester Co. appeals from that judgment on several grounds. The plaintiffs have cross appealed from the partial summary judgments which dismissed their warranty claims.

We reverse with respect to the defendant's appeal on the negligence claims, and reverse and remand with respect to the plaintiffs' cross appeal on the denial of the warranty claims.

FACTS

Plaintiff Raymond W. Clark is a custom farmer in the Twin Falls, Idaho, area doing business as Clark's Custom Farming. Custom farmers contract to plow or preplant (a fertilizer application) farmland and are generally compensated according to the number of acres plowed or preplanted. They generally work intensive 10 to 15 hour work days, but work only during the spring and fall. In the spring of 1972 Clark first engaged in the custom farming business in the Twin Falls area, although he previously had been in the custom farming business in California.

On January 7, 1972, Clark purchased a Model 1466 International Harvester turbo-diesel tractor from McVey's, Inc. Clark took delivery of the tractor on January 28, 1972. The transmission of this tractor was equipped with a "torque amplifier" (TA). When the tractor is driven in the TA mode, as opposed to the direct or normal drive mode, the tractor develops more torque, or pulling power, at a sacrifice of speed. Clark began using the tractor in his custom farming business in March 1972. However, between April 1972, and May 1973, several breakdowns because of bent or broken push rods in the engine occurred. After each breakdown, McVey's repaired the tractor free of charge under the warranty. Because of these breakdowns Clark alleged he lost 11 1/2 days of work.

Early in the fall of 1973, more than a year and a half after he had purchased the tractor, Clark noticed a loss of power in the tractor while preplanting a field covered with potato vines, weeds and other debris. The debris in the field piled up in front of the shanks of the preplant applicator, rather than feeding back through the shanks of the applicator. Preplanting was impossible under these conditions. Clark believed this problem was caused by the inability of the tractor to pull the applicator with sufficient speed to vibrate the shanks of the applicator and thereby cause the debris to feed back through the shanks. McVey's tested the tractor on a dynamometer, a device for testing the horsepower of a tractor at the power takeoff (PTO) shaft. That test revealed no significant loss of horsepower at the PTO shaft.

Nonetheless, Clark believed the tractor was not pulling properly and concluded that the tractor was not able to plow a sufficient number of acres per hour for it to be economically practical to operate the tractor that season. Clark investigated the possibility of renting a substitute tractor for the 1973 fall season, but determined that it would be too expensive. With the exception of the first fall plowing job during which he experienced the loss of power, Clark did not do any custom farming with the tractor in the fall of 1973.

Clark testified that if the tractor had been functioning properly he would have been able to work sixty ten-hour work days that fall—approximately 40 days plowing and 20 days preplanting. Earlier in 1973, Clark had signed a three-year contract with United States Steel Farm Service for fertilizer application. A representative of that firm testified that his company could have supplied Clark with 60 days of work in the 1973 fall season.

Because field conditions were better in the spring of 1974, Clark was able to operate the tractor on a limited basis for 14 days, but at a slower speed than he had operated the tractor previously. At the trial Clark testified that he was only able to cover eight acres per hour when he felt he should have been able to cover twelve acres per hour.

In December of 1973, Clark, through his attorney, had contacted Dr. Rudolf Limpert, an associate research professor of mechanical engineering at the University of Utah. Dr. Limpert agreed to examine the tractor and try to diagnose the cause of the power loss. Over the next six months Dr. Limpert conducted several tests on the tractor. From these several tests Dr. Limpert concluded that something was slipping in the process of transmitting the power from the engine to the draw bar in the TA mode. Under Dr. Limpert's supervision the TA unit was disassembled at a tractor repair shop in Twin Falls, Idaho. Upon disassembly Dr. Limpert noted eccentric wear in a clutch shaft. Under Dr. Limpert's direction, the TA unit was replaced by the repair shop with parts obtained from McVey's. Dr. Limpert tested the tractor after repair and determined that it was performing satisfactorily.

Clark sued McVey's and International Harvester in October, 1974, alleging negligent design and manufacture and breach of implied and express warranties. McVey's cross claimed against International Harvester for indemnification.

The defendants separately moved for summary judgment alleging that when Clark purchased the tractor he signed a sales form which provided for a 12 month warranty and which limited the buyer's remedies to the repair or replacement of defective parts by the defendant and disclaimed all other warranties. The trial court granted the motion for summary judgment on the warranty claims but ruled that the disclaimer provisions in the form did not exclude liability for negligence.

CROSS APPEAL

The trial court granted summary judgments in favor of both defendants with respect to the plaintiffs' warranty claims. We reverse the partial summary judgments because on several separate legal issues there were material issues of fact.

The plaintiffs also argue in their cross appeal that even if the trial court was correct in concluding that Clark signed a sales form containing International Harvester's "New Equipment Warranty"[12] and that those warranty provisions disclaimed all implied warranties and oral express warranties in accordance with the requirements of I.C. § 28-2-316, there still remained material issues of fact whether (1) the repair or replacement remedy provided in the warranty was the exclusive remedy, and (2) even if it was exclusive, whether the limited remedy had failed of its essential purpose.

---

12   The warranty provisions on that form state:

"WARRANTY: Each item of NEW International equipment covered by this contract is sold under the regular warranty of International Harvester Company as printed hereon, and no other.

. . . .

"NEW EQUIPMENT WARRANTY

"International Harvester Company warrants to the original purchaser each item of new farm and industrial equipment bearing either the identification 'McCormick' or 'International', or a combination thereof, to be free from defects in material and workmanship under normal use and service. The obligation of the Company under this warranty is limited to repairing or replacing as the Company may elect, free of charge and without charge for installation, at the place of business of a dealer of the Company authorized to handle the equipment covered by this warranty, any parts that prove, in the Company's judgment, to be defective in material or workmanship within twelve months or 1500<*> hours of use, whichever occurs first, after delivery to the original purchaser.

. . . .

"THIS WARRANTY AND THE COMPANY'S OBLIGATION THEREUNDER IS IN LIEU OF ALL WARRANTIES, EXPRESS OR IMPLIED, INCLUDING WITHOUT LIMITATION, THE IMPLIED WARRANTIES OF MERCHANTABILITY AND FITNESS FOR A PARTICULAR PURPOSE, all other representations to the original purchaser and all other obligations or liabilities, including liability for incidental and consequential damages on the part of the Company or the seller with respect to the sale or use of the items warranted... ."

In the "New Equipment Warranty" the defendants expressly warranted that the tractor was "free from defects in material and workmanship under normal use and service," but limited their liability to the repair or replacement of parts which proved to be defective within 12 months or 1500 hours of use after delivery. Chapter 2 of the Uniform Commercial Code (UCC) which is applicable to this case, I.C. § 28-2-102, provides that the parties' agreement may limit the buyer's remedies to repair and replacement of nonconforming goods. I.C. § 28-2-719(1)(a). However, subsection (1)(b) creates a presumption that contractual clauses prescribing remedies are cumulative to other available remedies. If the parties intend the stated remedy to be the sole and exclusive remedy, that intent must be clearly expressed. I.C. § 28-2-719, Official Comment 2.

Most courts have ruled that clauses similar to the "New Equipment Warranty" are adequate expressions of the intent to limit the buyer's remedy to the repair and replacement of defective parts. However, some courts have construed such provisions very narrowly. For example, in *Ford Motor Co. v. Reid*, 250 Ark. 176, 465 S.W.2d 80 (1971), the court ruled that a clause similar to the clause in this case did not expressly state that the repair and replacement remedy was to be the exclusive remedy since the language in the clause stated that it was in lieu of other obligations and warranties, but did not state that it was in lieu of other remedies.

Although this Court is disposed to strictly construe contractual provisions purporting to limit a party's remedies, particularly those provisions printed on the back of sales forms, we are not inclined to torture the plain meaning of the language in such a clause in order to reach an interpretation different from that clearly expressed. The intent of the "New Equipment Warranty," clearly expressed by its terms, is that the purchaser's remedy is to be limited to repair or replacement of defective parts by the defendants. Even though the sales contract provides for an exclusive remedy, in certain circumstances a party may be nonetheless entitled to the general remedies of the UCC. I.C. § 28-2-719(2) provides:

> "28-2-719. CONTRACTUAL MODIFICATION OR LIMITATION OF REMEDY.— ...
> "(2) Where circumstances cause an exclusive or limited remedy to fail of its essential purpose, remedy may be had as provided in this act."

Although this Court has not considered this section in previous cases, other courts have uniformly held that where a party limits its warranty obligation to the repair and replacement of defective parts failure to fulfill that obligation, if such failure operates to deprive the other party of the substantial value of the bargain, causes the limited remedy "to fail of its essential purpose" within the meaning of that section and entitles the party to pursue the remedies otherwise available under the UCC.

In *Ehlers v. Chrysler Motor Corp.*, 226 N.W.2d 157 (S.D.1975), the plaintiff purchased an automobile which was delivered with an undersized crankshaft, a faulty transmission, and improperly installed windows. The defendant refused to repair the automobile. The court ruled:

> "By delaying for an unreasonable length of time the repair of respondent's vehicle, appellant deprived him of the 'substantial value of the bargain.' Stated otherwise, the warranty was breached causing the available remedy 'to fail of its essential purpose'. Such failure brings into play all otherwise available remedial devices, to-wit: Incidental damages from seller's breach; and Consequential damages from seller's breach."

In *Riley v. Ford Motor Co.*, 442 F.2d 670 (5th Cir. 1971), the plaintiff purchased a new automobile and received a "New Vehicle Warranty" in which his remedy was limited to the repair or replacement of defective parts. After the dealer's unsuccessful attempts to repair defects in the automobile the plaintiff sued. The Fifth Circuit Court of Appeals upheld a verdict for the buyer stating that the jury's affirmative answer to the charge to decide "whether the defendant, Ford Motor Co. has breached its warranty and [whether] they were given a reasonable opportunity to repair it and they didn't" was an implicit finding that the remedy provided in Ford's warranty did fail of its essential purpose and operated to deprive the purchaser of the "substantial value of the bargain."

In *Adams v. J. I. Case Co.*, 125 Ill.App.2d 388, 261 N.E.2d 1 (1970), the plaintiff purchased a tractor which was delivered with a defective radiator and hydraulic system. The warranty limited the purchaser's remedy for breach to repair and replacement of defective parts by the seller. The plaintiff alleged that the defendant was "wilfully dilatory" and "careless" in making needed repairs. Reversing a dismissal of the plaintiff's suit, the court stated:

> "The manufacturer and the dealer have agreed in their warranty to repair or replace defective parts while also limiting their liability to that extent. Had they reasonably complied with their agreement contained in the warranty they would be in a position to claim the benefits of their stated limited liability and to restrict plaintiff to his stated remedy."

In its "New Equipment Warranty" the defendants warranted that the plaintiffs would receive a tractor "free from defects in material and workmanship under normal use and service," but they limited their obligation for breach of that warranty to repairing or replacing defective parts. The "New Equipment Warranty" did not state the time for performance of the repair or replacement obligation. Therefore the defendants were obligated to repair or replace defective parts within a reasonable time pursuant to I.C. § 28-2-309(1).

The purpose of the exclusive repair or replacement remedy is to ensure that the purchaser receives a product which conforms to the express warranty, i. e., that the product is free from defects, and if the product proves defective within the warranty period the seller is obligated to cure the defect within a reasonable time. If, however, the seller is subsequently unable or unwilling to repair or replace a defective part within a reasonable time, the buyer is left with a defective product—not conforming to the warranty—and the limited remedy has not achieved its purpose. In such circumstances § 28-2-719(2) permits the buyer to pursue the other remedies provided by the UCC if the defect substantially affects the value of the buyer's bargain.

In some cases involving § 2-719(2) of the UCC, the purchasers have alleged dilatory and negligent conduct by the sellers in failing to repair or replace defective goods. However, proof of negligent or dilatory conduct is not necessary for that provision to apply. I.C. § 28-2-719(2) provides that the party may resort to the general remedies provided by the act "[when] circumstances cause an exclusive or limited remedy to fail of its essential purpose." That section does not specifically require the plaintiff to prove negligent or wilfully dilatory conduct. Rather, the section is to apply whenever an exclusive remedy, which may have appeared fair and reasonable at the inception of the contract, as a result of later circumstances operates to deprive a party of a substantial benefit of the bargain. Such circumstances may or may not be the result of dilatory or negligent conduct. We agree with the rule summarized by the court in *Beal v. General Motors Corp.*, 354 F.Supp. 423 (D.Del.1973):

> "The limited remedy fails of its purpose whenever the seller fails to repair the goods within a reasonable time; good faith attempts to repair might be relevant to the issue of what constitutes a reasonable time. However, since § 2-719(2) operates whenever a party is deprived of his contractual remedy there is no need for a plaintiff to prove that failure to repair was willful or negligent."

We note that I.C. § 28-1-203 imposes upon all parties an obligation of good faith in the performance of the contract. Accordingly, the plaintiffs also had a duty to act in good faith to provide the defendants with a reasonable opportunity to repair or replace any defective parts.

In sum, although the defendants may have limited their obligation under the "New Equipment Warranty" to repairing or replacing defective parts, if the tractor was defective and the defendants failed to cure those defects within a reasonable time after being afforded an opportunity to do so, the plaintiffs would be entitled to pursue their general remedies under the UCC pursuant to I.C. § 28-2-719(2).

The plaintiffs argue that there were material issues of fact whether the tractor was defective and whether the limited repair or replacement remedy had failed of its essential purpose under I.C. § 28-2-719(2) and that the summary judgments on their warranty claims were therefore improper. This argument raises a threshold question whether this issue was properly raised by the pleadings and presented to the trial court. Issues not presented to the trial court will ordinarily not be considered on appeal.

The plaintiffs' complaint did not specifically allege that the exclusive remedy provided by the "New Equipment Warranty" failed of its essential purpose, but Count Two of the complaint alleged a breach of express and implied warranties and alleged that the defendants had not "cured defects in the manufacturing and the design of the said tractor … ." Clark's affidavit submitted in opposition to the motion for summary judgment states:

"I further state that even though I consider [that] Defendant McVey's were very cooperative in attempting to discover the problems I had with the tractor, and this is what I said in my deposition, I do not feel that either Defendant McVey's or Defendant International Harvester Company made any substantial efforts to get to the root of the problem."

In view of the liberal construction in favor of the non-moving party to be given the record on a motion for summary judgment, we hold that the issue was raised in the proceedings below and therefore is properly before this Court on appeal.

The plaintiffs have alleged two distinct defects in the tractor—defective push rods and a defective TA assembly. Either alleged defect could constitute a breach of the "New Equipment Warranty" and each raises slightly different issues with respect to the alleged failure of the limited repair or replacement remedy. We therefore consider them separately and we consider issues concerning the defective push rods first.

1. There is no doubt that at the time the summary judgments were entered there was an issue of fact whether the push rods were defective at the time the tractor was delivered to Clark. Apparently the defendants finally did cure those defects, approximately a year after the problem initially developed and after four successive breakdowns—three of which followed previously unsuccessful attempts by the defendants to repair the tractor. However, we believe there was an issue of fact concerning whether the defendants had failed to cure the defect within a reasonable time, I.C. § 28-2-309(1), thereby causing the limited remedy to fail under I.C. § 28-2-719(2).

Noting these issues of fact, however, is not dispositive of the plaintiffs' argument that the summary judgments were in error. The only damages that the plaintiffs have alleged as a result of the defective push rods are consequential damages, profits lost during the periods of down time while the push rods were being repaired. However, the "New Equipment Warranty" states that it is "IN LIEU OF ALL WARRANTIES, … including liability for incidental and consequential damages …" If this exclusion of consequential damages is enforceable despite the failure of the repair or replacement remedy to achieve its purpose, the plaintiffs would not have alleged any damages for which the defendants would be liable, even if the push rods were defective and the limited remedy had failed of its essential purpose.

PROBLEM 8 - 11

Rae's uncle, a retired CPA, convinced her to let him put up a kiosk in the store offering one-hour tax preparation services to her customers while they shopped. Customers were promised completed tax forms ready for filing with the IRS one hour after they dropped off their tax information at the kiosk. Rae's uncle purchased the Quick Tax software program developed and sold by Professional Automated Support Systems ("PASS"), which promised that "basic tax preparation was now a matter of minutes rather than hours or days" because of its "proprietary cross-talk algorithms which eliminated the duplicitous calculus that slowed down the linear-based processing used by other tax-preparation software." The program delivered to the store had coding errors that prevented the program from integrating recent changes Congress had made to the Internal Revenue Code and was useless to Rae's uncle as such. Although PASS provided a number of downloadable patches intended to resolve the problem on its website, the problem was not completely resolved until after the April 15 deadline for filing tax returns had passed. As a result, Rae's uncle was not able to prepare and file tax returns for any of the store's customers this year. He has returned the Quick Tax software to PASS and demanded a refund of the purchase price of the software ($10,500). PASS has refused to take back the software and refund the purchase price, referring Rae's uncle to the provision in the purchase agreement that provides

> PASS warrants the program material to be free of coding errors when delivered. In the event coding errors are discovered after customer's acceptance, PASS's sole responsibility will be to supply corrections to the customer at no additional charge.

Since Rae's uncle had agreed to limit PASS's liability for coding errors in the purchase agreement, is he entitled to a refund (or any other relief) now that PASS has been able to correct the coding errors as promised?

Would your answer be different if Rae's uncle could show that PASS knew about the coding errors when it sold him the Quick Tax software? Would it matter if PASS could show that part of the delay in correcting the coding errors was caused in part by the virus protection program on the uncle's computer which kept identifying some of the corrections PASS supplied as threats and deleted them?

What if instead of limiting a buyer's remedies for coding errors to corrections of those errors, the purchase agreement had provided that buyers were only entitled to either replacement software or a refund of the purchase price?

Looking at International Harvester's contract from the *Clark* case, we can find examples of the different subjects we've been exploring in this chapter. First, the contract creates an express warranty:

> International Harvester Company warrants to the original purchaser each item of new farm and industrial equipment ... to be free from defects in material and workmanship under normal use and service.

The contract also disclaims all other warranties:

> THIS WARRANTY AND THE COMPANY'S OBLIGATION THEREUNDER IS IN LIEU OF ALL WARRANTIES, EXPRESS OR IMPLIED, INCLUDING WITHOUT LIMITATION, THE IMPLIED WARRANTIES OF MERCHANTABILITY AND FITNESS FOR A PARTICULAR PURPOSE

The disclaimer is set off from the other terms—it's conspicuous—and it specifically mentions the implied warranty of merchantability. It operates to allocate the risk that the equipment will not perform as expected between the parties, with IH assuming only the risk of defective parts and the buyer assuming the risk of any other cause of the failure of the equipment to perform. IH has not even promised that the equipment is fit for the ordinary purposes for which it is used.

It limits the remedy available to the buyer for any breach of the warranty it makes:

> The obligation of the Company under this warranty is limited to repairing or replacing as the Company may elect, free of charge and without charge for installation, at the place of business of a dealer of the Company authorized to handle the equipment covered by this warranty, any parts that prove, in the Company's judgment, to be defective in material or workmanship within twelve months or 1500 hours of use, whichever occurs first, after delivery to the original purchaser.

Notice the remedy is limited to defective parts—IH does not promise to replace the equipment itself, but only parts that in "its judgment" are defective in material or workmanship. And even this limited remedy is only available to the buyer for defects that arise within the earlier of twelve months from delivery or 1,500 hours of use.

Finally, the contract also excludes consequential damages. We will explore excluding damages under Article 2 in the next section, but here is an example of how a seller might attempt to exclude certain losses that the buyer might incur if the product does not perform as expected:

> THIS WARRANTY AND THE COMPANY'S OBLIGATION THEREUNDER IS IN LIEU OF ... all other representations to the original purchaser and all other obligations or liabilities, including liability for incidental and consequential damages on the part of the Company or the seller with respect to the sale or use of the items warranted.

The buyer assumes the risk that any defect in the product will result in loss beyond the value of the contract—for example, any profits the buyer might lose if she can't use the equipment because of a defective part.

It appears to be self-evident that a limited remedy promising to repair or replace fails of its essential purpose when the seller, like the seller in *Clark*, is unwilling or unable to repair or replace the defective product in a reasonable time. But is it also self-evident that a remedy limited to repair or replacement of the defective product cannot fail of its essential purpose if the seller is willing to replace the defective product. Should it matter that, because of the nature of the product's use, the consequential damages caused by its failure will greatly eclipse the price paid for the product? The next case tries to answer that question where the contract limited the buyer's remedy to a return of the purchase price.

NOMO AGROINDUSTRIAL SA DE CV v. ENZA ZADEN N. AM., INC.

UNITED STATES DISTRICT COURT FOR THE DISTRICT OF ARIZONA, 2007
492 F. SUPP. 2D 1175

ZAPATA, District Judge.

BACKGROUND

In 2004, Plaintiff Nomo Agroindustrial ("Nomo") contacted Defendant Enza Zaden ("Enza") to purchase tomato seeds. Plaintiff is a fanning company based in Mexico that grows tomatoes, cucumbers, and other vegetables to be sold in the United States. Enza is a large, international corporation that manufactures seeds. When Plaintiff contacted Enza about obtaining tomato seeds, it informed Enza of problems it had with tomato plants contracting. Tomato Spotted Wilted Virus ("TSWV"). Upon informing Enza of its concerns and needs, Enza recommended its Caiman variety tomato seed. In relation to this seed, Enza provided brochures stating that the seed was resistant to TSWV, and Enza also orally informed Plaintiff that the seeds were resistant to TSWV. Based on these assurances, and after working out the details with Enza, Plaintiff contacted a distributor, Defendant Keithly-Williams Seeds ("KWS"), to pay for and obtain the seeds. Shortly after obtaining the seeds, Plaintiff planted the seeds and they germinated into tomato plants. However, the tomato plants contracted TSWV and Plaintiff's entire Caiman tomato crop was destroyed. The litigation in this case arises from the destruction of this crop.

DISCUSSION

Plaintiff claims that Enza breached express and implied warranties because the Caiman tomato seeds purchased from Enza were not resistant to TSWV as the tomato plants grown from the seeds in question contracted TSWV and were destroyed.

The Validity of Enza's Limitation of Damages Clause

Enza argues that to the extent there was any breach of warranty, damages are limited to the purchase price of the seeds pursuant to the language in the invoice. In response, Plaintiff primarily argues that the limitation of damages clause under the circumstances of this case fails of its essential purpose and is otherwise unconscionable. The Court agrees with Plaintiff.

Pursuant to A.R.S. § 47-2719(B), a limitations of damages clause is invalid "[w]here circumstances cause an exclusive or limited remedy to fail of its essential purpose ..."

Further, A.R.S. § 47-2719(C) states that "[c]onsequential damages may be limited or excluded unless the limitation or exclusion is unconscionable." The comments to this section state: "[It is of the very essence of a sales contract that at least minimum adequate remedies be available. If the parties intend to conclude a contract for sale within this Article they must accept the legal consequence that there be at least a fair quantum of remedy for breach of the obligations or duties outlined in the contract. Thus any clause purporting to modify or limit the remedial provisions of this Article in an unconscionable manner is subject to deletion and in that event the remedies made available by this Article are applicable as if the stricken clause had never existed." *See* Comment 1 to A.R.S. § 47-2719(B); *see also Roberts v. Morgensen Motors,* 135 Ariz. 162, 166-167, 659 P.2d 1307 (Ct. App. 1992)(holding that while the seller could properly limit the remedy, "this remedy is no longer exclusive where the circumstances cause this exclusive or limited remedy to fail of its essential purpose."); *Kalil Bottling Co. v. Burroughs Corp.,* 127 Ariz. 278, 282, 619 P.2d 1055 (Ct. App. 1982). A claim of unconscionability under the UCC in Arizona can be established based on substantive unconscionability alone, "especially in cases involving ... limitations of remedies." *Maxwell v. Fidelity Financial Services,* 184 Ariz. 82, 89-91, 907 P.2d 51 (1995). "Substantive unconscionability concerns the actual terms of the contract and examines the relative fairness of the obligations assumed ... Indicative of substantive unconscionability are contract terms so one-sided as to oppress or unfairly surprise an innocent party, an overall imbalance in the obligations and rights imposed by the bargain, and significant cost-price disparity."

As Plaintiff correctly argues, unlike many products (i.e., a television, stereo, etc.) that can [sic] repaired or replaced which would actually make the buyer whole and otherwise fulfill the purpose of the contract and related warranties, simply replacing seeds or refunding the price of seeds in the agricultural context is totally inadequate. Rather, the farmer's sole purpose in purchasing seeds is to harvest a crop from those seeds. The true value of the seeds only comes from the crop yielded which is preceded by considerable time and cost expended by the farmer. A farmer's lost growing season and the accompanying loss of expected profits due to defective seeds clearly is not compensated by simply replacing or refunding the price of the defective seeds. As such, numerous courts have found that such limitation of damages provisions fail of their essential purpose and are unconscionable. In *Mullis v. Speight Seed Farms, Inc.,* the court rejected the seed manufacturer's attempt to limit damages to replacement of the defective seeds as unconscionable, and reasoned:

> [Defendant] relies on [cases pertaining to television sets, computer hardware and software, and piping] for its position that its limitation of remedy provision should be upheld as valid. However, such cases are distinguishable as they involve products such as television sets, computers, and piping, the value of which is established by the product itself, rather than agricultural seeds, the value of which is established by the plant grown from the seed. In other words, [Plaintiff] was forced to expend substantial sums of money for bed preparation, fumigation, plastic covering for the seed beds, labor, fertilizer, and irrigation, before the seed was of any benefit to him. Additionally, products such as television sets, computers, and piping are subject to repair or replacement remedies whereas a failed crop is not repaired or replaced by the original cost of the seed … In the present case, [Plaintiff] is a farmer, not a professional seed merchant. [Plaintiff] purchased the seed over the telephone during a conversation in which only the seed variety and price were discussed. [Defendant] does not negotiate warranty terms with any customers. [Plaintiff], like most farmers, was not in a position to bargain for more favorable contract terms, nor was he able to test the seed before the purchase. A crop failure is inevitable if the … seed is ineffective and to enforce the provisions here in question, which would only allow the return of the purchase price, would leave [Plaintiff] without any substantial recourse for his loss. In essence, [Plaintiff] would be left without a remedy for another's breach … [It is apparent that the allocation of risk for ineffective seeds is better shouldered by the manufacturer of the seed, rather than the consumer. The consumer does not have the ability or resources to test the seed prior to its use; however, the manufacturer does. Furthermore, the farmer is required to expend large sums of money before any defect in the seed is noticeable, and once a defect is found an entire year's crop might be worthless. Once the crop has failed, the farmer's only recourse is monetary compensation to cover his lost profit and expenditures; replacement and repair are not viable options. The manufacturer is also in a better position to allocate the cost of testing among all consumers of its product … [Defendant's] disclaimer of warranty and limitation of remedies provision is unconscionable and unenforceable …

See *Mullis,* 234 Ga. App. 27, 505 S.E.2d 818, 820-822 (Ga. Ct. App. 1999); *see also Schmaltz v. Nissen,* 431 N.W.2d 657, 662 (S.D. 1988)(finding limitation of damages to replacement cost of seed unconscionable and stating that "like most farmers, [Plaintiffs] were not in a position to bargain for more favorable contract terms, nor were they able to test the seed before their purchase. A loss of yield from an intended crop due to inferior seed is inevitable, and [Plaintiff] should not be left without a remedy."); *Latimer v. William Mueller & Son, Inc.,* 386 N.W.2d 618, 625, 149 Mich. App. 620, 637 (Mich. Ct. App. 1986)(invalidating limitation of remedies to replacement of defective seeds as unconscionable and reasoning that "where the defect could not be discovered until after the seed was planted, the remedy prescribed in the limitation of liability clause is an illusory one which represents no remedy at all . ."); *Lutz Farms v. Asgrow Seed Company,* 948 F.2d 638, 646 (10th Cir. 1991)(holding that limitation of remedies to replacement of defective seeds failed of its essential purpose and was unconscionable). While there is no Arizona authority directly addressing these issues, the Court finds the authority in question persuasive and directly applicable to the facts of this case. Accordingly, the Court finds that the limitation of damages clause at issue in this case fails of its essential purpose, is unconscionable, and is unenforceable under the circumstances of this case. Thus, Plaintiff's cross-motion for summary judgment on these issues is granted.

Did the limited remedy in *Nomo Agroindustrial* really fail of its essential purpose? The Court obviously thought it was unconscionable to limit the farmer to a return of the purchase price of the seeds under the circumstances, but does that mean the limited remedy necessarily failed its essential purpose? The court never identified the essential purpose of the return-of-purchase-price remedy, so it's unclear on what basis it concluded that the remedy failed. Is the purpose of the remedy simply to return the parties to their precontract position? If so, then maybe the remedy, to the extent that it precluded the farmer from recovering consequential damages, did fail of its essential purpose because the farmer would not have been in the same position he would have been before contracting to purchase the seed. He's still out the costs he incurred planting and growing the tomatoes. The court appeared to believe that made the limited remedy unconscionable—but alone, that would not meet the requirements of 2-302 as we've developed them.

The more likely explanation for the outcome in *Nomo Agroindustrial* is that the Court failed to distinguish limited remedies from exclusions of damages—both of which Article 2 permits. A limitation on remedies limits the form of relief available to the buyer e.g., the buyer cannot force specific performance. An exclusion of damages limits the type of loss the buyer can recover—direct damages, incidental damages, or consequential damages. Blending them together caused the Court to combine into a single analysis the distinct standards Article 2 applies to each. Limited remedies are tested under the failure-of-essential-purpose standard in 2-719(2), and exclusions of damages are tested, as we will see in the next section, under the unconscionability standard in 2-719(3).

3. Excluding Consequential Damages

The power Article 2 vests in the parties to a sale-of-goods agreement to adjust the remedies for breach to fit their particular needs includes the power to exclude (or to limit) consequential damages. 2-719(3). A seller might also try and limit its exposure when the goods it sells fail to perform (or for any other nonconformity in the seller's performance under the agreement) by taking away a buyer's right, under Part 7 of Article 2, to recover consequential damages for the seller's breach of the agreement. Since only buyers are entitled to consequential damages under the general-remedies provisions of Article 2, the power to exclude them can protect the seller in the same way a disclaimer of warranties does. Although terms disclaiming warranties and excluding damages can produce similar results—both limit a seller's exposure for delivery of nonperforming goods—how they do that is very different. A seller who effectively disclaims all warranties makes no promises about the performance of the product that can be breached if the product fails to perform, so the buyer has no claim for breach. Without a claim for breach, the buyer has no right to damages under Article 2. A seller who only excludes damages (or does not exclude all warranties) makes promises that can be breached—the buyer will have a claim for breach if the product fails to perform But the buyer will not be able to claim damages for that breach because the agreement took away the buyer's right to recover damages for the seller's breach.

But the power to exclude consequential damages is conditional; a term excluding such damages will not be given effect if it "operate[s] in an unconscionable manner." Comment 3, 2-719. In a consumer transaction, a term excluding or limiting consequential damages for personal injury is presumptively unconscionable, and the seller has the burden of convincing the court otherwise. In a commercial transaction, the buyer will have to overcome the presumption implied by 2-719(3) that such a term is not unconscionable—which has prompted commentators to opine that "findings of unconscionability should be and are rare in commercial settings."[13] But, as the next case illustrates, maybe not that rare.

Tokyo Ohka Kogyo Am., Inc. v. Huntsman Propylene Oxide LLC

United States District Court for the District of Oregon, 2014
35 F. Supp. 3d 1316

SIMON, District Judge.

Tokyo Ohka Kogyo America, Inc. ("TOK") asserts a claim for breach of contract against Huntsman Propylene Oxide LLC ("Huntsman"). TOK purchased a chemical manufactured by Huntsman and alleges that Huntsman breached its agreement to notify TOK in a timely fashion if Huntsman changed its chemical manufacturing process. The parties agreed to litigate this case in phases and further agreed that "Phase 1" of the litigation would encompass only whether the limitation of liability clause contained in Huntsman's general terms and conditions of sale that were attached to the Credit Application that TOK executed with Huntsman applies to limit TOK's potential damages in this action. The parties cross-move for summary judgment on this Phase 1 question. For the reasons stated below, the Court finds that the limitation of liability clause is not enforceable under Uniform Commercial Code ("UCC") Section 2-719 and thus does not limit TOK's damages in this lawsuit. Accordingly, TOK's motion for partial summary judgment is GRANTED, and Huntsman's motion for partial summary judgment is DENIED.

BACKGROUND

The parties stipulated to many facts for purposes of the pending cross-motions for partial summary judgment. Additional background facts are taken from the record.

TOK is in the business of sourcing, qualifying, mixing, manufacturing, selling, and delivering chemicals for use in the semiconductor manufacturing process. Huntsman makes and supplies certain chemicals. In 2008, TOK was purchasing propylene glycol ("PG"), a chemical that TOK combined with other chemicals to create a mixture that TOK then sold to its semiconductor manufacturing customer ("Customer"). The Customer was engaged in a pilot test to determine if it wished regularly to use the chemical mixture that included PG.

TOK originally sourced PG from a supplier who purchased it from Huntsman. TOK then wished to explore purchasing PG directly from Huntsman. On or about June 5, 2008, Huntsman requested that TOK sign a Credit Application with Huntsman, and TOK did so. TOK's Vice President, Michael Lindsay, and Deputy General Manager-Operations, Chris Carlson, signed Huntsman's Credit Application on behalf of TOK. Lindsay and Carlson had authority to do so.

A one-page document entitled "Huntsman General Terms and Conditions of Sale" ("Huntsman General Terms") was attached to the Credit Application signed by TOK.

The attached Huntsman General Terms include a limitation of liability clause ("Limitation Clause"), stating, in relevant part:

> LIMITATION OF LIABILITY. Seller's maximum liability for any breach of this Agreement, or any other claim related to the Product, shall be limited to the purchase price of the Product or portion thereof (as such price is set forth on the first page of Seller's invoice) to which such breach or claim pertains. IN NO EVENT SHALL SELLER BE

---

13   White and Summers, *Commercial Law* (6th ed. West 2010) 612.

LIABLE FOR ANY CONSEQUENTIAL, INCIDENTAL, SPECIAL OR PUNITIVE DAMAGES, INCLUDING BUT NOT LIMITED TO ANY DAMAGES FOR LOST PROFITS OR BUSINESS OPPORTUNITIES OR DAMAGE TO REPUTATION. (capitalization in original).

When Lindsay and Carlson signed the Credit Application, they believed that the Credit Application and its reference to general terms and conditions related to TOK's financial responsibility; they did not believe that the referenced general terms and conditions created any limitations of liability or other contractual terms governing sales that may occur at some point in the future and they did not read the Huntsman General Terms attached to the Credit Application. Carlson and Lindsay reviewed TOK's responses on the Credit Application to make sure that TOK's financial and other information as stated on the completed form was accurate, and they then signed the form. No one at Huntsman discussed with Carlson or Lindsay the Huntsman General Terms generally or the Limitation Clause specifically until after this litigation commenced.

On or about September 23, 2011, TOK and Huntsman agreed to the written Procurement Specification for E-Grade Propylene Glycol (the "2011 Procurement Specification"). The 2011 Procurement Specification contains a "Process Change Notification" clause stating:

When there is a process change in the production of the product, the supplier shall send notification. This notification will be given twelve months in advance of implementation. Shorter advance notice will require negotiated approval between the supplier and TOK AMERICA. Process changes include changes in raw material suppliers, the manufacturing process, and other significant changes affecting the quality of the product.

On or about October 9, 2012, the Customer reported to TOK that semiconductor wafers were demonstrating defects well above acceptable levels. The Customer, TOK, and Huntsman then worked together to identify the specific issue and concluded that the PG was the problem. It was then discovered by TOK that an undisclosed processing change made by Huntsman modifying temperature and pressure conditions caused an unidentifiable chemical change during the manufacture of the PG. Accordingly, although the PG met the technical specifications set forth in the 2011 Procurement Specification and was able to pass TOK's own tests, the PG used in the mixture sent by TOK to the Customer caused defects to appear in the Customer's semiconductor manufacturing process. For purposes of the pending cross-motions only, Huntsman concedes that it changed its manufacturing process and failed to comply with the Process Change Notification clause in the 2011 Procurement Specification.

As soon as the problem was identified to TOK, it stopped mixing the Huntsman-supplied PG with other chemicals and stopped ordering PG from Huntsman. By that time, however, TOK already had made a significant amount of the chemical mixture containing the defective PG and had additional, unmixed PG still in its possession. The unmixed PG was sold, and the proceeds are in Huntsman's counsel's trust account. The mixed chemicals, however, required hazardous waste disposal. TOK spent significant sums transporting the defective PG and defective chemical mixture to and from various locations, purchasing chemicals that were mixed with the defective PG and thereby rendered unusable, mixing the defective PG with other chemicals, and hiring hazardous waste disposal companies to dispose of the defective chemical mixture.

DISCUSSION

Framework for Limiting Remedies and Damages Under UCC Section 2-719

Section 2-719 of the UCC establishes that parties may agree to limit the measure of damages available for a breach of contract and may limit the available remedies, subject to certain conditions. This section provides:

> (1) Subject to the provisions of subsections (2) and (3) of this section and of the preceding section on liquidation and limitation of damages,
>
> (a) the agreement may provide for remedies in addition to or in substitution for those provided in this Article and may limit or alter the measure of damages recoverable under this Article, as by limiting the buyer's remedies to return of the goods and repayment of the price or to repair and replacement of non-conforming goods or parts; and
>
> (b) resort to a remedy as provided is optional unless the remedy is expressly agreed to be exclusive, in which case it is the sole remedy.
>
> (2) Where circumstances cause an exclusive or limited remedy to fail of its essential purpose, remedy may be had as provided in this Act.
>
> (3) Consequential damages may be limited or excluded unless the limitation or exclusion is unconscionable. Limitation of consequential damages for injury to the person in the case of consumer goods is prima facie unconscionable but limitation of damages where the loss is commercial is not.

U.C.C. § 2-719.

The official comments to this provision further clarify the ability of parties to limit remedies and the check on that ability created by Section 2-719(2)-(3), stating:

> 1. Under this section parties are left free to shape their remedies to their particular requirements and reasonable agreements limiting or modifying remedies are to be given effect.
>
> However, it is of the very essence of a sales contract that at least minimum adequate remedies be available. If the parties intend to conclude a contract for sale within this Article they must accept the legal consequence that there be at least a fair quantum of remedy for breach of the obligations or duties outlined in the contract. Thus any clause purporting to modify or limit the remedial provisions of this Article in an unconscionable manner is subject to deletion and in that event the remedies made available by this Article are applicable as if the stricken clause had never existed. Similarly, under subsection (2), where an apparently fair and reasonable clause because of circumstances fails in its purpose or operates to deprive either party of the substantial value of the bargain, it must give way to the general remedy provisions of this Article.
>
> 2. Subsection (1)(b) creates a presumption that clauses prescribing remedies are cumulative rather than exclusive. If the parties intend the term to describe the sole remedy under the contract, this must be clearly expressed.
>
> 3. Subsection (3) recognizes the validity of clauses limiting or excluding consequential damages but makes it clear that they may not operate in an unconscionable manner. Actually

such terms are merely an allocation of unknown or undeterminable risks. The seller in all cases is free to disclaim warranties in the manner provided in Section 2-316.

Consequential Damages Limitations Under UCC § 2-719(3)

In addition to limiting TOK's remedies for a breach of contract by Huntsman to only the purchase price of the PG, the Limitation Clause also contains a limitation avoiding consequential and incidental damages. TOK asserts that the limitation barring consequential and incidental damages automatically fails because the exclusive purchase price remedy fails of its essential purpose, and, in the alternative, fails because the damages limitation is unconscionable. Deciding whether a damages limitation is unconscionable is an issue of law for the Court, and the burden of proof is on the party alleging unconscionability.

Courts are divided as to whether a limitation on consequential damages is automatically unenforceable when an exclusive remedy limitation is found to fail of its essential purpose. Many courts find that if the remedy limitation fails of its essential purpose then the buyer may receive any remedy available under the UCC, including consequential damages, notwithstanding that consequential damages also may have been specifically excluded under the contract. *See, e.g., Ragen Corp. v. Kearney & Trecker Corp.*, 912 F.2d 619, 625 (3d Cir. 1990) (applying Wisconsin law); *Newmar Corp. v. McCrary*, 309 P.3d 1021, 1026 (Nev. 2013) (applying Nevada law); *Hydronic Energy, Inc. v. Rentzel Pump Mfg., LP*, 2013 Neb. App. LEXIS 189, 2013 WL 5797326, at *6 (Neb. Ct. App. Oct. 29, 2013) (applying Nebraska law); *Sutphen Towers, Inc. v. PPG Indus., Inc.*, 2005-Ohio-6207, 2005 WL 3113450, at *13 (Ohio Ct. App. 2005) (applying Ohio law and relying on *Goddard v. Gen. Motors Corp.*, 60 Ohio St. 2d 41, 396 N.E.2d 761 (Ohio 1979)). Other courts, however, find that a contractual waiver of consequential damages, particularly if it is in a separate clause from the exclusive remedy limitation, survives a remedy limitation failing of its essential purpose and requires a separate analysis of unconscionability. *See, e.g., Chatlos Sys., Inc. v. Nat'l Cash Register Corp.*, 635 F.2d 1081, 1086 (3d Cir. 1980) (applying New Jersey law); *Razor v. Hyundai Motor Am.*, 222 Ill. 2d 75, 854 N.E.2d 607, 618-19, 305 Ill. Dec. 15 (Ill. 2006) (applying Illinois law); *Schurtz v. BMW of N. Am., Inc.*, 814 P.2d 1108, 1112-13 (Utah 1991) (applying Utah law). Finally, some courts take a case-by-case approach and look at the circumstances in the particular case "to determine whether the exclusive remedy and damage exclusions are 'separable elements of risk allocation' or 'inseparable parts of a unitary package of risk-allocation.'" *Milgard*, 902 F.2d at 708 (quoting *Fiorito Bros., Inc. v. Fruehauf Corp.*, 747 F.2d 1309, 1315 (9th Cir. 1984) (applying Washington law)).

Neither Oregon nor Texas state courts have addressed the issue of whether when an exclusive remedy provision fails of its essential purpose a consequential damages exclusion also necessarily fails. There are cases in the appellate courts of each state, however, that suggest that those courts may read such clauses dependently, such that if an exclusive remedy fails of its essential purpose, consequential damages may be recovered even if otherwise excluded under the contract. *See PPG Indus., Inc. v. JMB/Houston Ctrs. Partners Ltd.*, 146 S.W. 3d 79, 101 (Tex. 2004) (holding in a case where an exclusive remedy provision also contained a waiver of consequential damages that where the remedy fails of its essential purpose "all damages provided by the UCC [become] available," without conducting a separate analysis of unconscionability on the limitation of consequential damages); *Young v. Hessel Tractor & Equip. Co.*, 99 Ore. App. 262, 782 P.2d 164, 167 (Or. Ct. App. 1989) (noting in a case where there was a separate consequential damages limitation that if a buyer could prove that the limited remedy fails of its essential purpose, then all remedies under the UCC would become available); *but see Bray Int'l, Inc. v. Computer Assocs. Int'l, Inc.*, 2005 U.S. Dist. LEXIS 48086, 2005 WL 6792280, at *10 (S.D. Tex. Sept. 30, 2005), *rev'd in part on other grounds by* 2005 U.S. Dist. LEXIS 40387, 2005 WL 3371875 (S.D. Tex. Dec. 12, 2005) (deciding as an issue of first impression under Texas law that Texas state courts would analyze exclusive remedy provisions and consequential damage waivers independently, without discussing *PPG*

Industries). The Court, however, need not reach the issue of whether Texas or Oregon would find that a consequential damages limitation automatically fails if an exclusive remedy provision fails of its essential purpose because the Court finds that under the circumstances of this case, the consequential damages limitation operates in an unconscionable manner and is unenforceable, even if it survives the exclusive remedy provision failing of its essential purpose and is analyzed independently.

Most cases analyze unconscionability under UCC Section 2-302, which expressly involves unconscionability of a contract "at the time it was made." U.C.C. § 2-302(1). UCC Section 2-719(3), however, does not include the specific language included in Section 2-302 that unconscionability under 2-719(3) be at the time the contract was made. To the contrary, Section 2-719(3) "makes it clear that [clauses limiting consequential damages] may not *operate* in an unconscionable manner." U.C.C. § 2-719 cmt. 3 (emphasis added). A provision does not "operate" in an unconscionable manner at the time of formation. Thus, for purposes of analyzing unconscionability under Section 2-719(3), the Court is not limited to evaluating the provision at the time the contract was made, but must consider how the provision operated and evaluate the provision after the contract has been breached.

Under both Texas and Oregon law, an agreement may be procedurally or substantively unconscionable. Generally speaking, procedural unconscionability refers to the circumstances surrounding the adoption of the provision at issue and substantive unconscionability concerns the fundamental fairness of the provision itself.

1. Procedural Unconscionability

Under Oregon law, procedural unconscionability focuses on the factors of oppression and surprise. *Bagley*, 310 P.3d at 702. Oregon courts explain these factors as:

> Oppression exists when there is inequality in bargaining power between the parties, resulting in no real opportunity to negotiate the terms of the contract and the absence of meaningful choice. Surprise involves the question whether the allegedly unconscionable terms were hidden from the party seeking to avoid them.

> Procedural unconscionability may also involve deception, compulsion, or genuine lack of consent.

Under Texas law, procedural unconscionability is similarly analyzed, with courts considering factors such as:

> (1) the presence of deception, overreaching, and sharp business practices by part [sic] of the stronger party; (2) the absence of a viable alternative; (3) the relative acumen, knowledge, education, and financial ability of the parties involved; (4) knowledge of the stronger party that the weaker party will be unable to receive substantial benefits from the contract; and (5) knowledge of the stronger party that the weaker party is unable reasonably to protect his interests.

> A court must consider all of the circumstances surrounding the formation of the contract with respect to the allegedly unconscionable provision, including the parties' bargaining process, the conspicuousness of the provision, whether the buyer was on notice of the limitation, and whether each party had a reasonable opportunity to understand the language at issue. *See Head v. U.S. Inspect DFW, Inc.*, 159 S.W. 3d 731, 748 (Tex. App. 2005) (a court "must consider the entire atmosphere in which the agreement was made" and "must look at the bargaining process the parties went through"); *Berge Helene, Ltd. v. GE Oil & Gas, Inc.*, 830 F. Supp. 2d 235, 271, 274 (S.D. Tex. 2011), *superseded in part on other grounds,*

896 F.Supp.2d 582 (S.D. Tex. 2012) (noting when evaluating the unconscionability of an exclusion on consequential damages that courts "must look to the circumstances surrounding the agreement," that damages limitations are generally upheld "where there is evidence that the buyer was on notice of the limitation" and that "courts often consider the degree of conspicuousness or whether a buyer had actual knowledge of a damages limitation in determining whether it is enforceable").

Here, considering the factors relevant to both Oregon and Texas's evaluation of procedural unconscionability, the Limitation Clause is unenforceable under both states' analysis.

a. The presence of deception, overreaching, or sharp business practices

This is an unusual, perhaps *sui generis* case, in which a boilerplate damages limitation is attached to a Credit Application without any bargaining or discussion, without the seller calling the buyer's attention to the clause, and after the execution of which more than two years of sample purchases and extensive testing are conducted, the manufacturing process is inspected and audited by the buyer, additional contracts are extensively negotiated, including another damages limitation clause, and the seller breaches an expressly negotiated clause in a manner that was solely within the seller's knowledge and ability to avoid the resultant harm.

Although parties to a contract are presumed to have read its terms, the Court has serious concerns about Huntsman's attaching to a Credit Application a purportedly far-reaching damages limitation clause governing all future sales between the parties without drawing TOK's attention to the clause. These concerns are compounded by the fact that Huntsman negotiated with TOK for more than two years, including specifically negotiating another damages limitation clause, and yet still failed to mention the Limitation Clause to TOK. Then, when Huntsman changed its manufacturing process that had been extensively vetted by TOK, which Huntsman knew could alter the chemical makeup of the PG and result in the chemical no longer performing as required and which Huntsman knew it was required to disclose, Huntsman failed to disclose the manufacturing change to TOK. Under the circumstances of this case, this is a sufficient presence of deception, overreaching, or sharp business practice to rise to the level of unconscionability.

Analogously, where the seller knows of a latent defect and fails to disclose it to the buyer, any limitations may be unconscionable. Here, although Huntsman did not know about the specific defect in the PG, Huntsman knew that it had changed its manufacturing process, knew that knowledge of a change in its manufacturing process was essential to TOK, and failed to disclose that manufacturing change to TOK. Under these circumstances, Huntsman's failure to disclose the known manufacturing change renders the Limitation Clause unconscionable.

b. Surprise, conspicuousness, notice, and the parties' bargaining process

Huntsman's failure meaningfully to communicate the Limitation Clause to TOK is also fatal to the enforceability of the clause in these circumstances. The Limitation Clause was inconspicuous and unfairly surprising to TOK. This aspect of the pending dispute is similar to the dispute in *Berge Helene*, in which a seller did not "meaningfully communicate" a damages limitation that was included in a data sheet provided to the buyer. 830 F. Supp. 2d at 274. As summarized by the court in the Southern District of Texas:

> Unlike in most commercial contexts where the parties expressly allocate risk and negotiate terms of the contracts containing damages limitations, there is no evidence that [buyer] and [seller] treated the [data sheet] as a contract after negotiating each of its terms. Indeed, there is no evidence whatsoever that [seller] or any person brought the disclaimer to [buyer's] attention.

Id. (denying the seller's motion for summary judgment regarding the damages limitation because there was an issue of fact as to whether the damages limitation was procedurally unconscionable). As in *Berge Helene*, TOK and Huntsman did not negotiate any of the terms of the Huntsman General Terms, including the Limitation Clause, and Huntsman did not bring the Limitation Clause to TOK's attention. Instead, Huntsman remained silent for years, and now attempts to enforce a provision to avoid paying damages for harm that only Huntsman could have avoided. In these circumstances, TOK was not provided effective notice, and enforcing the Limitation Clause would result in unfair surprise.

c. Huntsman's knowledge of TOK's inability to receive the benefit of the bargain and protect itself
Although the parties are both commercial entities with roughly equal bargaining power and business acumen, in the circumstances of this case, Huntsman was the party with the knowledge that, if the Limitation Clause is effective, TOK would not receive the benefit of its bargain in the allocation of risk and the requirement that Huntsman timely notify TOK of any manufacturing change. Huntsman also knew that TOK could not protect itself from a breach by Huntsman of its obligation timely to notify TOK of a manufacturing change if the change resulted in a latent defect in the PG. Without such notice by Huntsman and if the PG otherwise passed TOK's tests, TOK did not have the knowledge or ability to avoid the resultant harm. "If there is a type of risk allocation that should be subjected to special scrutiny, it is probably the shifting to one party of a risk that *only* the other party can avoid." Under Huntsman's argument, that would be the effect of the Limitation Clause, and such a shifting of risk fails under the scrutiny of procedural unconscionability.

d. Genuine consent
There also was no genuine consent on the part of TOK to the Limitation Clause acting as a damages limitation in the event Huntsman breached its obligation timely to notify TOK of any change in Huntsman's manufacturing process. The parties negotiated that obligation by Huntsman two years after the Credit Application was signed, and in those negotiations the parties agreed to limit Huntsman's liability for nonconforming goods for which TOK could test. There is no evidence of TOK's consent to shift the risk of harm that only Huntsman could avoid—a breach of Huntsman's obligation timely to notify TOK of any manufacturing change and a resultant undiscoverable defect.

2. Substantive Unconscionability

If the Limitation Clause were evaluated as of the time the Credit Application was executed, there is little doubt that it would not be substantively unconscionable. Commercial parties regularly limit liability for consequential damages.

Huntsman argues that for cases involving only economic damages, the Court must evaluate unconscionability for purposes of Section 2-719(3) at the time the contract was formed, and that post-formation facts are only relevant in cases involving personal injury. Huntsman's reading of Section 2-719(3) is misguided. The only difference between economic injury and personal injury in an unconscionability analysis under Section 2-719(3) is that a limitation of consequential damages where there is an injury to the person is prima facie unconscionable, whereas a limitation of damages where the loss is commercial is not prima facie unconscionable. Nothing in the language of Section 2-719(3) or its official comments supports the argument that post-formation facts are only relevant to an unconscionability analysis where there is a personal injury. The analytical difference between personal and economic injury established in Section 2-719(3) involves merely the burden of proving a prima facie case of unconscionability, not the relevant timeframe or facts that a court should consider.

Huntsman also argues generally that under Section 2-719(3) a court is constrained to only look to the facts at the time of contract formation. The genesis of Huntsman's argument is a conflation between Section 2-719(3) and Section 2-302(1), which expressly states that unconscionability under that section is considered "at the time [the contract] was made." U.C.C. § 2-302(1). Section 2-302(1) is a broad provision establishing the test for considering whether any clause in a contract is unconscionable. Section 2-719(3), however, is a specific provision applying only to a limitation of consequential damages and does not contain the requirement contained in Section 2-302(1) that the unconscionability analysis be as of the time of the contract's formation. If the requirement that unconscionability for limitations on consequential damages be analyzed at the time of contract formation was intended, the same language used in Section 2-302(1) could easily have been included in Section 2-719(3). The Court gives meaning to the difference in language between the two provisions, and to the official comment explaining that Section 2-719(3) "makes it clear" that clauses limiting or excluding consequential damages "may not operate in an unconscionable manner." U.C.C. § 2-719 cmt. 3. Huntsman's reading of Section 2-719(3) is counter to the official comment and renders meaningless the difference in language between Sections 2-719(3) and 2-302(1) and is rejected by the Court.

Huntsman cites to several cases in support of its argument. These cases either similarly conflate Section 2-719(3) and 2-302(1), or are primarily addressing other issues relating to unconscionability and comment only in dicta the timeframe for an unconscionability analysis.

Huntsman first relies on *Lindemann v. Eli Lilly & Co.*, 816 F.2d 199 (5th Cir. 1987). The Fifth Circuit in *Lindemann* held that the district court erred in its *sua sponte* finding on the eve of submitting the case to the jury that the consequential damages limitation was unconscionable because unconscionability was never raised by the plaintiff and no evidence of unconscionability was submitted by the plaintiff. *Id.* at 203. The Fifth Circuit noted that a court must have evidence of unconscionability before it can support a finding of unconscionability and that a defendant must be given fair notice that a portion of its contract will be challenged as unconscionable. *Id.* The court then went on to note that the trial court's finding of unconscionability did not comport with UCC Section 2-302(1). *Id.* The court in *Lindemann* cited to Section 2-719(3) for the proposition that a prima facie case of unconscionability is automatically found only when there is an injury to the person, and that the district court's *ad hoc* finding of facial unconscionability where only economic damages were involved was not reconcilable with the provision's distinction between personal and economic injury for facial unconscionability. Notably, the court discussed that the function of a consequential damages limitation was risk allocation, and that the limitation at issue in the case "abundantly" filled that purpose because many of the uncertainties that might cause the plaintiff to suffer damages were "uniquely within the control" of the plaintiff. *Id.* at 204. The reverse is true in this case, however, because the knowledge and uncertainty causing the risk of harm that occurred here was uniquely in control of Huntsman, the defendant.

The Court finds that in the context of Section 2-719(3), the Court is instructed by the UCC to consider whether the damages limitation *operates* in an unconscionable manner, which requires consideration of post-formation facts. Limiting TOK's damages for Huntsman's breach of its obligation timely to notify TOK of any manufacturing changes would operate in such an unconscionable manner.

Because the knowledge and ability to avoid the harm caused by a change by Huntsman in its manufacturing process was solely Huntsman's and the parties did not expressly and consciously allocate that risk to TOK, it is fundamentally unfair to enforce the Limitation Clause. Additionally, because the Court has found that a refund of the purchase price deprives TOK of the substantial value of its bargain and does not provide an adequate remedy under the specific circumstances presented, "the exclusion of incidental and consequential damages renders the available damages unconscionably low." Accordingly, the Limitation Clause, under the specific circumstances of this case, operates in a substantively unconscionable manner.

PROBLEM 8 - 12

Last fall Rae bought a commercial grade electric dryer made by Whirlpool for use at home. She always buys commercial grade appliances for her home when available because she believes that commercial grade products are better built and last longer than the typical consumer product lines. The sales agreement provided

> The exclusive remedy for any claim against Whirlpool based on this DRYER, whether for breach of our limited warranty or otherwise, shall be, at our option, replacement of the DRYER or a refund of the price paid therefore. Buyer agrees to waive, and shall not be entitled to damages, and seller shall not be liable for any damages, whether special, direct, consequential or incidental.

Two months after the dryer was delivered, the heating element shorted out while the dryer was in use and sparks from the short ignited clothes inside the dryer. Once burning, this turned the dryer into a thermal conductor that not only charred the wall next to it but also melted the linoleum floor under it and the PVC water pipes that ran behind it, flooding the basement of Rae's house. The water damage alone was over $5,000. Rae sent a letter to Whirlpool demanding reimbursement for the costs she incurred repairing all of the damage and for the price of the dryer as well. Whirlpool claims it only owes her a new dryer. If she has to sue, will Rae be able to recover damages from Whirlpool under 2-715? Would your answer be different if Rae's daughter had severely burned her hands trying to open the dryer before she realized there was a fire burning inside of it? Would it matter if Rae had bought the dryer for the store and the fire started while a deli employee was laundering the uniforms of some store employees?

In a the typical consumer transaction, the buyer cannot overcome the superior bargaining power of the seller—Target is not going to change the terms of our toaster deal because I want a better warranty—to impose its terms on the transaction. In a commercial setting, the buyer might not be so powerless, so why would a buyer agree to a term that excludes any consequential damages it might suffer if the product fails to perform? Comment 3 to 2-719 claims that exclusionary terms like the one at issue in *Tokyo Ohka* "are merely an allocation of unknown or undeterminable risks."

> Comment 3 thus recognizes that business entities may want to allocate certain risks between the parties, and under the philosophy of the UCC should be free to do so provided that such a waiver is not actually unconscionable. It often makes much commercial sense for parties to agree that the buyer will shoulder the risk of consequential losses. The seller may not be in a position to evaluate the extent or likelihood of consequential damages, since these risks are largely determined by the buyer's unique business circumstances. Likewise, a buyer may rationally agree to assume the risk of consequential losses rather than pay a higher price for the goods, a price which would necessarily include what amounts to an insurance premium for the seller's assumption of the risk of consequential losses.

Eastman Chemical v. Niro, 80 F. Supp. 2d 712 (S.D. TX 2000). The buyer usually is in a better position to control the consequences of any nonperformance, and so a clause excluding consequential damages might not be as one-sided as it may appear.

The Court in *Tokyo Ohka* noted that courts have split over the issue of whether a court can still give effect to a term excluding consequential damages if it determines that the limited remedy provided by the agreement fails of its essential purpose. The Court passed on that issue, and so it did not have to take a side on whether the clauses are dependent or independent of each other under 2-719. Early cases tended to view the clauses as dependent, but over the past twenty years, the view has shifted, and the majority view today is that the clauses are independent of one another—an exclusionary clause is enforceable unless it is unconscionable, regardless of the enforceability of a limited-remedy clause in the same agreement. *See, Razor v. Hyundai Motor America,* 854 N.E.2d 607 (IL. 2006)("We conclude that the independent approach is the better-reasoned and more in accordance with the plain language of the UCC. This conclusion is buttressed by the fact that a majority of jurisdictions to consider the issue have adopted the independent approach.... Contractual limitations or exclusions of consequential damages will be upheld unless to do so would be unconscionable, regardless of whether the contract also contains a limited remedy which fails of its essential purpose").

D. Notice of Breach

Llewellyn wanted his new sales act to provide parties to a sales transaction opportunities to work out their problems informally—to preserve their relationship and to avoid the delay and expense of litigation. Of course, in order to work things out, they need to know there's something that needs to be worked out. Because a seller can't address her buyer's disappointment with the transaction until she knows the buyer is unhappy, Article 2 requires unhappy buyers to notify their sellers if they are going to make a claim for breach against the seller:

> the buyer must within a reasonable time after he discovers or should have discovered any breach notify the seller of the breach or be barred from any remedy.

2-607(3)(a). Notice to the seller of breach is a condition precedent to any recovery by the buyer on account of that breach. Article 2's remedies are only available to a buyer claiming breach who has brought his unhappiness with the transaction to the seller's attention, and in many jurisdictions, that notice, to be effective, must be given before any legal proceeding is commenced by the buyer against the seller:

> [T]he purpose of notification under [2-607(3)] is to allow the seller an opportunity to resolve the dispute regarding an alleged breach before the buyer initiates a lawsuit. Therefore, even assuming that Defendants were aware that the fentanyl patches were defective, Defendants may not have been aware of Plaintiffs' intent to file a class action lawsuit, and were denied the opportunity to negotiate or settle this claim without judicial involvement. To "notify" under the UCC requires the affirmative act of notification, and [2-607(3)(a)] explicitly requires the buyer to "notify the seller of breach or be barred from any remedy." Plaintiffs' "constructive notice" argument does not address whether Plaintiffs ever actually and affirmatively notified Defendants of the breach, as required by [2-607(3)(a)], prior to initiating this litigation. * * * Here, the Court must also treat the [2-607(3)] reasonable notification requirement as a condition precedent to recovery, with Plaintiffs bearing the burden to prove that reasonable notification was given. As reasonable notification is a material element necessary to sustain recovery of a UCC breach of warranty claim, Plaintiffs were required to affirmatively allege that they reasonably notified Defendants. Inasmuch as [2-607(3)] bars a buyer's recovery absent the buyer providing reasonable notification of the breach, it follows that a buyer must also plead, at a minimum, in its Complaint, that it provided reasonable notification in order to state a viable claim for recovery.

FSCME v. Ortho-McNeil-Janssen Pharm, 2010 U.S. Dist. LEXIS 23181 (E.D. Pa. 2010). But this reading of 2-607(3) is not without its skeptics:

We are well aware that text writers and most decisional law treat pre-litigation notice as a condition precedent to the bringing of a civil action for breach of warranty. An examination of the authorities reveals that the only substantial reason for the requirement is the opportunity for settlement, sometimes expressed as performance or cure. This is stated in Leibson and Nowka, *Kentucky Uniform Commercial Code* (2d ed.) § 2.4(b)(2) as follows: Filing of a lawsuit should not ordinarily suffice as a section 2-607(3)(a) notification even if done within a reasonable time after the buyer discovers the breach. Even though claims are often settled after suit is filed, the underlying goal of the notice requirement of section 2-607(3)(a) is to facilitate performance or settlement. The filing of a lawsuit does not ordinarily accomplish this goal.

In our view, an opportunity for pre-litigation settlement is simply insufficient to justify holding claims for breach of warranty without pre-litigation notice to be barred, particularly when proponents of the requirement acknowledge that it could be met by a mere telephone call immediately before the suit is filed. Moreover, the views frequently expressed in legal text and decisional law naively assume that all parties to sales transactions act only in good faith. Experience teaches that some sellers of goods wish to evade answering breach of warranty claims and actually leave their place of residence to avoid service of a summons or conceal themselves so that a summons cannot be served upon them. The circumstances which prevailed here (sale of a stolen vehicle and departure from the state) might well have suggested to the purchaser that the seller would not welcome notice of the breach and that he would have resisted recovery by the purchaser. In any event, it is understandable that the purchaser may have feared that pre-litigation notice to his vendor would be to his detriment.

This Court is always reluctant to depart from the mainstream of American law, but in circumstances where the majority rule lacks convincing textual foundation and the reasons for it are unpersuasive, it is our duty to question the rule and consider whether it may be in error. With respect to [2-607], there is simply an insufficient basis in text or in logic to require peremptory application of a pre-litigation notice rule. When this is considered beside what may be good and valid reasons in a proper case to refrain from pre-litigation notice, it must follow that failure to give the notice is not fatal to a civil action for breach of warranty.

Mullens v. Wyatt, 887 S.W.2d 356 (Ky. 1994).

What should the buyer's notice communicate to the seller? 2-607(3) says the buyer is to "notify the seller of breach"; must the buyer's notice declare the seller to be in breach, or is something less than a declaration of breach sufficient? Comment 4 to 2-607 addresses the content question, but obfuscates rather than clarifies:

The content of the notification need merely be sufficient to let the seller know that the transaction is still troublesome and must be watched. There is no reason to require that the notification which saves the buyer's rights under this section must include a clear statement of all the objections that will be relied on by the buyer, as under the section covering statements of defects upon rejection (Section 2-605). Nor is there reason for requiring the notification to be a claim for damages or of any threatened litigation or other resort to a remedy. The notification which saves the buyer's rights under this Article need only be such as informs the seller that the transaction is claimed to involve a breach, and thus opens the way for normal settlement through negotiation.

Not surprisingly, courts have found support for different standards in Comment 4. In *Contech Casting v. ZF Steering Systems,* 931 F. Supp. 2d 809 (E.D. MI. 2013), the buyer, ZF, withheld several million dollars from payments it made for parts supplied by the seller (Contech) because of problems with many of the parts, including one which led to a recall of autos by BMW when a component made by ZF for BMW (which incorporated a part supplied by Contech) failed after it had been installed in almost ten thousand vehicles. Contech sued to recover the withheld payments. When ZF asserted the withholding was justified because Contech had breached, Contech contended ZF had failed to provide notice as required by 2-607(3) and therefore had waived any claims for breach. Addressing the notice issue, the court explained:

> The Court concludes, at this preliminary stage of the proceedings, that Defendant is likely barred from pursuing its breach of contract claims that are the subject of its counterclaim— with the exception of the breach relating to the BMW recall—because it failed to give Plaintiff sufficient and timely notice of those breaches.

* * *

> Two conflicting views—a so-called "lenient" view and a so-called "strict" view—have emerged regarding the sufficiency of notice required under [2-607]. The lenient view is justified by UCC comment four to this section, which states that the "content of the notification need merely be sufficient to let the seller know that the transaction is still troublesome and must be watched." The strict view is justified by other language in the same comment, which states that "[t]he notification which saves the buyer's rights ... need only be such as informs the seller that the transaction is claimed to involve a breach, and thus opens the way for normal settlement through negotiation."

> In *American Bumper,* 652 N.W.2d at 255-256, the Michigan Court of Appeals declined to adopt one view over the other, and instead analyzed whether the notice given in that case satisfied the policies underlying the UCC's notice provision. Those policies, as stated by the *American Bumper* court, are:

> (1) to prevent surprise and allow the seller the opportunity to make recommendations how to cure the nonconformance, (2) to allow the seller the fair opportunity to investigate and prepare for litigation, (3) to open the way for settlement of claims through negotiation, and (4) to protect the seller from stale claims and provide certainty in contractual arrangements.

The "lenient view" of notice suggested in Comment 4 to 2-607 is favored by many commentators:

> Under this comment, it is difficult to conceive of words which, if put in writing, would not satisfy the notice requirement of 2-607. Indeed, a letter containing anything but the most exaggerated encomiums would seem to tell that the transaction "is still troublesome and must be watched."[14]

But generally, courts seem unimpressed by such strident statements:

> Despite the fact that buyers enjoy some degree of flexibility with respect to the form of notice that must be given, ... "[T]he fact that the Code has eliminated the technical rigors of the notice requirement under [Art. 2] does not require the conclusion that any expression of

---

14 White and Summers, *UCC* (6th ed. West) at 567.

discontent by a buyer always satisfies section 2-607... . Thus, while the buyer must inform the seller that the transaction is 'still troublesome,' Comment 4 also requires that the notification 'be such as informs the seller that the transaction is claimed to involve a breach, and thus opens the way for normal settlement through negotiation."

Slack v. Suburban Propane Partners, 2010 U.S. Dist. LEXIS 135530 (D. N.J. 2010)
(quoting *Eastern Airlines v. McDonnell Douglas*, 532 F.2d 957 (5th Cir. 1976).

The buyer must give the 2-607(3) notice within a "reasonable time" after she discovers or should have discovered the breach. What is a reasonable time? The only help we get from Article 2 is the admonition in Comment 4 that what is reasonable should turn on whether the buyer is a consumer or a merchant:

"A reasonable time" for notification from a retail consumer is to be judged by different standards so that in this case it will be extended for the rule of requiring notification is designed to defeat commercial bad faith, not to deprive a good faith consumer of his remedy.

Comment 4, 2-607. Courts have resisted drawing bright lines for the timeliness of the 2-607 notice on the ground that timeliness is a question of fact that should be left to the fact finder in each case—except perhaps where the buyer offers no credible explanation for a delay that has actually prejudiced the seller. Prejudice to sellers can occur (1) where the buyer's delay in providing notice of breach deprives the seller of an opportunity to cure the breach and/or to mitigate the buyer's losses, (2) where the delay inhibits the seller's opportunity to gather exculpatory evidence—for example, where the buyer disposes of the goods prior to giving notice, (3) where delay results in the loss of claim(s) the seller might have had against the supplier of the part that caused the breach, or (4) where the seller loses the opportunity to avoid similar liability to other buyers—for example, where the breach results from a manufacturing defect that could have been corrected before additional products were sold.[15]

Courts have taken to heart Comment 4's instruction to adopt "different standards" for measuring the timeliness of notice when given by a consumer buyer, showing remarkable leniency. *See, e.g., Fiti v. Strek*, 690 N.W.2d 605 (NE 2005)(two-year delay in giving notice not unreasonable under Nebraska 2-607); *Wal-Mart Stores v. Wheeler*, 262 Ga. App. 607 (Ga. App. 2003)(notice two years and three days after injury not unreasonable as a matter of law); *Maldonado v. Creative Woodworking Concepts*, 296 Ill. App. 3d 935 (3rd Dist. 1998)(notice given three years and seven months after injury from defective door not unreasonable as a matter of law); *Maybank v. S.S. Kresge*, 273 S.E.2d 681 (N.C. 1981)(three-year delay not per se unreasonable in retail consumer personal injury case).

In *Buzadzhi v. Bexco Enterprises*, 2011 U.S. Dist. LEXIS 905 (N.D. OK 2011), the court refused to dismiss buyer's breach-of-warranty claims for untimely notice of breach where buyers gave notice two years and six months after a dresser sold by seller fell on and killed their eleven-month-old son, explaining:

[t]he court is persuaded that the "reasonable notice" requirement of Section 2-607(3)(a) should be viewed under a more relaxed standard than that expected of commercial purchasers. This is so because a retail consumer is not likely to be aware of the notice requirement, is not primarily concerned with replacement of nonconforming shipment of goods, and because there can be no issue of commercial bad faith on the part of the retail consumer. * *
* The Buzadzhis argue that even notice provided two and a half years after the breach can be reasonable in a retail consumer injury case. The Supreme Court of North Carolina analyzed

---

15   These and other factors considered by courts assessing the reasonableness of a buyer's notice are more fully discussed in Reitz, "Against Notice: A Proposal to Restrict the Notice of Claims Rule in UCC 2-607(3)(a)," 73 *Cornell L. Rev.* 534 (1988).

a provision identical to Oklahoma's and found that "[w]hen the plaintiff is a lay consumer and notification is given to the defendant by the filing of an action within the period of the statute of limitations, and when the applicable policies behind the notice requirement have been fulfilled, we hold that the plaintiff is entitled to go to [*9] the jury on the issue of seasonable notice." *Maybank v. S.S. Kresge Co.*, 273 S.E. 2d 681, 685 (N.C. 1981). The North Carolina Supreme Court held that even a three year delay in notice was not per se unreasonable in a retail consumer personal injury claim. *Id.; see also Malawy v. Richards Mfg. Co.*, 150 Ill.App. 3d 549 (Ill. App. 1986) (holding that notice can be reasonable when given three years after an injury took place if given promptly after discovering the identity of the remote seller); and *Moore v. Puget Sound Plywood*, 332 N.W. 2d 212 (NE 1983) (upholding a ruling that notice given by a consumer to a seller within two and a half years of discovering the defect was reasonable).

Can the parties, by their agreement, determine what constitutes timely notice of breach? What if the parties provide for a shorter period than the court would find to be reasonable under 2-607? Whenever the UCC requires the parties to do something within a reasonable time, 1-302(b) authorizes the parties to fix by their agreement what will constitute a reasonable time, and the time they agree to controls as long as it "is not manifestly unreasonable."

What would make a time limit for a buyer's notice of breach manifestly unreasonable? Comment 1 to 1-302 tells us that if the time fixed by agreement works to "eliminat[e] all remedy under the contract," it is unreasonable. So where the time limit for the buyer's notice of breach would expire before a buyer could reasonably be expected to discover the breach, courts have refused to enforce the contract term. For example, in a sale of tulip bulbs guaranteed to flower, if the time within which the buyer had to give notice to preserve any claims for breach was less than the time required for the bulbs to sprout and flower, a court could declare the time fixed by the parties to be manifestly unreasonable. By requiring notice of breach be given before it was possible to discover the breach (the bulbs did not flower), the contract effectively eliminated any remedy the buyer would have if the bulbs did not flower as promised. See *Q. Vandenberg & Sons v. Siter*, 204 A.2d 494 (PA 1964). But the manifestly-unreasonable limit on the power of the parties to set the time within which notice of breach must be given does not require them "to fix the most reasonable time"; it only requires that the time they fix "is not obviously unfair as judged by the time of contracting." Comment 1, 1-302. So the time fixed by the parties is not manifestly unreasonable merely because it is less than the time the court would have found reasonable under the circumstances. The buyer must still convince the court that the period provided is so limited as to be "obviously unfair" to the buyer.

PROBLEM 8 - 13

Rae purchased an American Eagle Bench Type Dough Sheeter to use in both the store's bakery and deli. The Sheeter would stretch the dough for the pizzas sold by the deli and the dough used by the bakery for the doughnuts, pastries and funnel cake it sold as part of its "Homemade" brand. Each type of dough required stretching to a specific thickness, and the machine Rae bought was supposed to be able to stretch dough at any thickness between the 1 mm needed for fine French-style pastries and the 20mm required for funnel cakes (lots of grease to absorb). But after set-up, the sheeter was not able to stretch any dough to less than 5 mm, which made it useless for pastry dough. Rae immediately called the seller about the problem and the seller sent a product specialist to address the issue. The specialist worked on the sheeter for the better part of a day, but the machine would not stretch dough to less than 4mm. Rae called the seller again to complain and was told that no further adjustments could be made to the sheeter—as the seller put it to Rae "it is, what it is." Over the next couple of months, Rae had several other bakers in town who owned sheeters look at hers but none were able to solve the problem. They all did agree that the dough Rae was using in the machine was properly prepared for its intended use.

Not having heard from the seller during this time, Rae filed suit against it for breach of warranty. The seller has moved to dismiss her suit on the grounds that she had not timely notified it of her claim for breach as required under 2-607(3). Should the court dismiss her claim?

E. ACCEPTING BUYER'S REMEDIES

The buyer does not waive its claim for breach simply by accepting a seller's nonconforming performance. A buyer with an immediate need for goods might not have the option of rejecting nonconforming goods and finding a substitute transaction. If the goods can still be used for their intended purpose despite some degree of diminished capability, the buyer might take them and deal with the seller's breach at a later, more convenient time. When the buyer accepts a nonconforming performance, though, she will have to measure her damages for the seller's breach using 2-714; the buyer's remedies we studied in Chapter 5—cover (2-712), market price (2-713), and specific performance (2-716) each presume that the buyer does not have the goods. Putting the accepting buyer in as good a position as it would have been in had the seller performed requires a measure of damages that takes into account the buyer's receipt of the goods—the fact that the buyer has the goods. If the seller's nonconforming performance gives the buyer a claim for breach of warranty, 2-714(2) measures the buyer's damages as

> the difference at the time and place of acceptance between the value of the goods accepted and the value they would have had if they had been as warranted, unless special circumstances show proximate damages of a different amount.

If the value of a toaster that browns bread, warms up Pop-Tarts, and toasts frozen waffles is thirty dollars, and that's what Ray promises the toaster he sells you for thirty dollars will do, but after using it you discover it does not toast frozen waffles, 2-714(2) gives you as damages for breach of Ray's warranty the difference between a thirty-dollar toaster (the value of the toaster as warranted) and the value of a toaster that only does two of the three things a thirty-dollar toaster does. If the value of a two-out-of-three toaster is twenty dollars, you recover ten dollars. That puts you in as good a position as you would have been in had Ray's toaster worked as warranted: you expected to get thirty dollars of value from Ray, and now you have thirty dollars—a twenty-dollar toaster and ten dollars in damages.

Measuring damages for breach of warranty looks simple—and it is, assuming we can come up with the values the measure requires. Valuing defective products is not always as easy as we made it in the toaster example; often there is not a market for defective goods, and without a market, how do we assign value to the goods? The next case illustrates how the courts have responded to the problem.

Soo L. R. Co. v. Fruehauf Corp.

UNITED STATES COURT OF APPEALS FOR THE EIGHTH CIRCUIT, 1977
547 F.2D 1365

STEPHENSON, Circuit Judge.

This appeal concerns a contract in which Fruehauf Corporation (Magor) agreed to the manufacture, sale and delivery of 500 railroad hopper cars to Soo Line Railroad Company for the approximate price of $9,750,000. Soo Line, in this diversity action initiated against Magor, claims breach of contract and negligence in the manufacture of the railcars, and the district court entered judgment based upon a jury verdict for Soo Line in the amount of $1,238,754.82. Magor appeals contending in general that the trial court erred in failing to construe certain provisions in the contract as barring recovery of damages and in allowing testimony by expert witnesses with respect to defective manufacture and resultant damages. For the reasons stated below, we affirm.

Magor and Soo Line in 1967 created the contract which provided for Magor to manufacture and deliver 500 covered hopper freight railroad cars at approximately $19,500 per car according to an agreed design and detailed written specifications.

Soo Line, a corporation that owns and operates substantial railroad lines and railroad cars, purchased the cars and utilized them pursuant to a long term net lease for public service in hauling grain and other dry bulk commodities. The cars were delivered in early 1968. It is undisputed that, despite an estimated 40-year useful life, the underframes developed serious and widespread cracks in the steel structure and welds within a few months of delivery. Following both unilateral and mutual inspection of the railcars by the parties, Soo Line concluded that the cracks resulted from structural and welding defects and accordingly requested that Magor perform its obligation to repair pursuant to the warranty. However, Magor's management, claiming that the cracking derived from construction specifications required by Soo Line, insisted it had no such responsibility. After Magor refused to repair the cars, Soo Line implemented its own remedial operation. The cost of repairs was $506,862.78, slightly more than $1,000 per car. Soo Line has contended, and the jury verdict reflects, that this expenditure did not fully restore the cars to totally acceptable operating condition.

On July 30, 1971, Soo Line filed its complaint claiming breach of express and implied warranties and negligence based on the structural failure of the railroad cars and Magor's refusal to accept responsibility for repair. Magor in its answer denied liability contending that: the railcars met contract specifications; Soo Line's failure to inspect the cars during manufacture barred recovery; damages were limited by the contract; and contributory negligence obviated liability with respect to the negligence count.

Trial commenced on August 13, 1975, and concluded on October 2, 1975, with a jury verdict in favor of Soo Line. The trial court had submitted to the jury a 24-question special verdict form. In answering these questions, the jury essentially found that the railroad cars did not conform to the contract specifications and that Magor had not performed its obligation to repair or replace defective parts. The jury found that Magor breached its express warranty, implied warranties of merchantability and fitness for a particular purpose ... The jury in its special verdicts awarded: $975,970 for the difference between the value of the cars as accepted and their value if built to conform to the contract specifications; $182,444 for revenue lost while the cars were undergoing repairs; and $10,084.93 for damages sustained in transporting the cars in connection with their repair.[16] The trial court adopted the answers in the special verdict and *inter alia* found that Soo Line had sustained $70,255.89 in damages resulting from spoiled ladings caused by water leakage through defective roofs of the cars.

* * *

III.

The third issue in this appeal is whether the district court erred in allowing the testimony of T. R. Klingel, an expert witness who testified with respect to the diminution in value of the railroad cars resulting from their structural collapse. In general, Klingel expressed the opinion that the market value of the railcars as actually constructed was approximately $1,000,000 or $2,000 per car less than the value of the cars had they been built in accordance with the contract.

Klingel, who is executive vice president of Soo Line, testified initially that the market value of the railcars had they been constructed according to the contract would have approximated their purchase price of $19,500 per car. He further expressed the opinion, over Magor's objection, that the fair market

---

16   The jury found that 95% of the negligence could be attributed to Magor and 5% to Soo Line and awarded $699,391.71 for damages sustained as a direct result of such negligence.

value of the cars as actually constructed was at the most $17,500 per car. Klingel's opinion, as to the diminution in fair market value of the railcars, basically derived from his viewpoint that a hypothetical buyer of the cars would be confronted with immediate and substantial expenditures for repair and continuation of financing costs without any concomitant receipt of revenue while the railcars were out of service being repaired, and even after the repairs the buyer would possess rebuilt and patched cars worth less than those properly constructed.

Appellant contends that the trial court erred in allowing Klingel's testimony on damages. In Magor's view, Klingel was not qualified to provide expert opinion on the necessity and cost of repair because he allegedly did not possess sufficient practical or technical knowledge. Magor asserts additionally that Klingel's prediction of future maintenance costs was speculatively improper without proof that such damages are reasonably certain to occur. Finally, Magor claims that Klingel's reliance on financing costs as a basis for damages erroneously resulted in a duplicate consequential damage award for revenue lost while the railcars were being repaired.[17]

The trial court's determination that Klingel possessed adequate qualifications, pursuant to Fed. R. Evid. 702, to testify with respect to the diminished market value of the railcars was not an abuse of discretion or clear error of law. Fed. R. Evid. 702 is not limited to experts in the strictest sense of the word but also encompasses a large group called "skilled" witnesses, such as owners, bankers, and landowners testifying on the value of property.

Klingel's responsibilities as Soo Line's executive vice president included overseeing the operations of all trains and the maintenance of all rolling stock and fixed property. He also was charged with determination of the market value of the railroad's rolling stock. Klingel was directly familiar with the railcars manufactured by Magor, and he collaborated closely with Soo Line's mechanical department and H. D. Hollis concerning the problematic conditions in the Magor-constructed railcars. In some instances, Klingel conducted personal inspections of the railcars. Klingel's knowledge was such that his opinion on valuation most likely assisted the trier of fact in arriving at the truth.

In reviewing the substance of Klingel's testimony on valuation, the measure of damages and the limits of relevancy are set by the substantive law of Minnesota. Under Minnesota law, the measure of damages applicable to breach of contract is the difference between the actual value of the cars at the time of acceptance and the value they would have had if they had been as warranted. Minn. Stat. Ann. § 336.2-714(2). The buyer is not limited to repair costs when repair does not completely restore the goods to the value which they would have had if built in conformity with the contract; remaining diminution in value may also be recovered.

Taking into consideration the structural and welding defects existing in the cars manufactured for Soo Line by Magor, Klingel expressed the opinion that the reasonable market value per car was $17,500 at the most. Klingel further opined that he would probably discount the purchase price of the cars by an additional $1,000 or $2,000, which would result in a fair market value of approximately $15,500 per car.

In formulating the diminution in fair market value of the cars, Klingel properly placed reliance on the necessity for present and future repairs and the fact that even a rebuilt patched railcar would be worth less than a correctly constructed one. The record reflects that approximately $1,000 per car in immediate repair costs was expended by Soo Line and that, even after implementation of the repairs, Soo Line had experienced continued maintenance costs beyond those expended for cars other than those manufactured by Magor.

Klingel also stated that a hypothetical buyer of the railcars would discount the purchase price because the buyer's financing costs would continue while the cars were out of service being repaired with no ability to generate revenue. Klingel testified that approximately $200,000 or $400 per car in interest payments would be lost without concomitant benefit during repairs. This statement, of course, may

---

17   In this regard, it should be noted that the jury awarded $182,444 for net loss of revenue sustained by Soo Line while the cars were undergoing repairs.

not be considered as evidence of diminution in value of the Soo Line railcars. Cost of financing is not an element of reduced market value pursuant to Minn. Stat. Ann. § 336.2-714. Nonetheless, we reject appellant's contention that this aspect of Klingel's testimony rendered inadmissible his overall opinion on the diminution in market value of the railcars. An objection that an expert's opinion is based on elements of damage not lawfully recoverable generally relates to the weight rather than the admissibility of the testimony.

In addition, the trial court carefully instructed the jury with respect to this element of damages. It stated in part as follows:

> The measure of damages is, generally speaking, the difference between the fair market value of the cars as accepted by Soo Line, and the fair market value they would have had if they had not been deficient in the particulars in which you found them deficient. This is called the difference or diminution in value approach.

* * *

> If you find that the repair of the cars restored the cars to substantially the same condition as they would have been in if properly manufactured, the difference or diminution value is the same as the reasonable cost of repairing the cars.
>
> So, if the repair costs actually restored them then the repair cost would equal the diminution in value. However, if you find that the repair of the cars did not restore them to substantially the same condition as they would have been if properly manufactured, then the difference or diminution in value is the reasonable cost of repair, plus the difference between the fair market value of the covered hopper cars if they had been manufactured without faults or defects, and the fair market value of the repairs. The total figure, however, cannot exceed the difference between the fair market value as accepted, and the fair market value in the defective condition you find.

> * * * [The court then gave an illustration.]

> Therefore, if you find that the repairs of the cars placed the cars in a better condition than they would have been at the time of acceptance if they had been properly manufactured, then the difference or diminution in value recoverable by plaintiffs is the difference between the fair market value of the covered hopper cars as accepted by Soo Line and the fair market value they would have had if Magor had manufactured them properly. So, Soo Line in this situation would not be able to recover the full amount spent for repairs.

> In the course of the charge and the special verdict you will find use of the word value. Value is described as the highest price in terms of money for which a product would have sold on the open market, the seller having a reasonable time within which to sell and being willing to sell but not forced to do so; the buyer being ready, willing and able to buy, but not forced to do so, and a full opportunity to inspect the property in question and to determine its condition, suitability for use, and all things about the property that would naturally and reasonably affect its market value.

Moreover, there is sufficient evidence in the record upon which the jury could have relied in awarding $975,970 or $1,951.94 per car, approximately 10% of their original cost, for diminution in market value of the cars. It cannot be said that the verdict constituted a shocking result.

For similar reasons, we reject appellant's assertion that Klingel's reference to "future maintenance costs" was unduly speculative and erroneous. Klingel merely expressed an opinion on the present value of the railcars at the time of acceptance in light of known risks associated with existing defects. Soo Line had already experienced increased maintenance costs with Magor cars previously repaired. Klingel's testimony overall had sufficient probative value to outweigh the danger that it would lead the jury to assess damages on an improper basis. Magor had adequate opportunity to cross-examine and refute Klingel's testimony on valuation. Under these circumstances, we conclude that the trial court did not commit an abuse of discretion in the admission of Klingel's testimony concerning the diminution in market value of the railroad cars resulting from their structural failure.

Upon full consideration of the lengthy record including over 4500 pages of testimony, hundreds of exhibits and the court's instructions to the jury, we are satisfied that no prejudicial error appears. The evidence supports the verdicts of the jury and the judgment rendered in accord therewith.

Affirmed.

Other measures courts have used to determine the value of the defective goods when measuring damages for breach under 2-714(2) are the difference between the fair-market value of the good as warranted and the salvage value of the goods, or the replacement costs of the defective goods less the value of the buyer's use of the goods up until the time of trial.

Problem 8 - 14

Rae ordered a Grindmaster 66103 Kobalto Automatic Espresso Machine with double bean and soluble hoppers for the deli. Customers had been asking for different coffee drinks for months, and she decided it was time to capitalize on the demand for designer coffee. The machine was delivered two weeks late but worked great once it was set up in the deli, and the additional revenue has exceeded even Rae's optimistic projections. She now realizes how much money the store lost during the two weeks that delivery of the machine was delayed. If the store brings a claim for breach against the seller for the late delivery, how would the court measure the store's damages, since the machine was ultimately delivered to and kept by the store? 2-714(1) and (3).

Accepting buyers can also recover incidental and consequential damages. 2-714(3). In *Irmscher Suppliers v. Schuler*, 909 N.E.2d 1040 (Ind. App. 2009), the buyers claimed a design defect in the roll screens on the thirty-two replacement windows they purchased from the defendant breached the implied warranty of merchantability. Shortly after the windows were installed, the buyers began to notice an unusually large number of bugs inside their home when the windows were open and the screens were in place:

> [Buyer] killed and cleaned up after the insects to protect their five small children from the bugs. [Buyer] observed one window for two hours and kept a log of the number of insects, recording at one point that there were thirty-three insects on the inside of the screen and nine on the outside of the screen. Kelly videotaped bugs entering her home and gave the videotape to Dan Siela, an Irmscher employee. Siela forwarded the videotape to a Pella field quality engineer, who determined the Rolscreens were defectively designed.

At the trial, the buyer presented evidence that she spent at least two hours each week in the spring and fall from 2001 to 2008 killing and cleaning up the bugs that entered the house through the gaps around the windows. The buyers prevailed on their claim for breach of warranty, and the trial court's award of consequential damages included $8,428 for the buyers' time killing and cleaning up the insects. On appeal, the seller claimed the award of consequential damages for killing and cleaning up the bugs was improper because the damages were not reasonably foreseeable. The appellate court disagreed, explaining:

> As for the time spent killing and cleaning up after insects, we agree with the trial court that it is reasonably foreseeable that a family whose home has been infiltrated with insects will spend some time and energy addressing this problem, and it is therefore proper to award some consequential damages for the insects. However, the buyer also has a duty to minimize the damages. *See* [2-715] ("Consequential damages resulting from the seller's breach include (a) any loss resulting from general or particular requirements and needs of which the seller at the time of contracting had reason to know *and which could not reasonably be prevented by cover or otherwise* ... .") (emphasis added).

> Although it is reasonable that the plaintiffs might spend some short period of time killing insects while attempting to find a solution, *seven years* is not a reasonable amount of time, especially given that the defendants offered to replace the Rolscreens with flat screens at no cost to the plaintiffs as early as March 2004.

> Because the evidence is undisputed that the Schulers could have minimized their damages due to the ingress of insects by accepting the flat screens, the trial court abused its discretion by awarding the Schulers consequential damages for seven years of killing insects. *See* [2-715] Comment 2 ("Subparagraph (2) carries forward the provisions of the prior uniform statutory provision as to consequential damages resulting from breach of warranty, but modifies the rule by requiring first that the buyer attempt to minimize his damages in good faith, either by cover or otherwise."). "A buyer cannot pile up damage by continuing to use an article when he knows that such damage will be the result and then claim that the loss is the proximate result of the breach of warranty." *Schaefer v. Fiedler*, 116 Ind. App. 226 (1945) (holding under pre-UCC law that the buyer was not entitled to consequential damages for the time required to combine his soybean crop in excess of the time required if the machine had been fit because he knew the machine's condition but used it nevertheless).

> Because the evidence shows that the Schulers failed to minimize their damages, as they were required by statute to do in order to receive consequential damages, we reduce this portion of the award to $3612 (by dividing $8428 by 7 to reach the value of one year of killing insects, and then multiplying that value by 3, which represents the three years from the Spring of 2001 to the Spring of 2004, when the Schulers received the offer to replace the screens).

Defects in the seller's performance that do not create a breach of warranty—late delivery, for example—are still breaches, and the accepting buyer has a claim for damages caused by those breaches. These claims are measured by 2-714(1):

> Where the buyer has accepted the goods ... he may recover as damages for any nonconformity of tender the loss resulting in the ordinary course of events from the seller's breach determined in any manner which is reasonable.

Early drafts of what became Article 2 measured all breach claims by an accepting buyer as the "estimated loss resulting in the ordinary course of events from the seller's failure to conform," but provided that it was "reasonable in the ordinary case" to use the difference-in-value formula to measure the "estimated loss." Llewellyn actually thought the term "warranty" should be replaced throughout the Act with "obligation for quality" in order to close off the "traditional line of thought which marked 'warranty' off as an obligation of a peculiar nature."[18] A warranty was simply another obligation of the seller, and the Act's remedies should not distinguish between nonconformities based on "time and manner of shipment or delivery, or of quality, or of quantity, or of any other nature."

Breach-of-warranty claims were eventually carved back out of the general measure for claims of an accepting buyer, and the difference-in-value formula was made the presumptive measure for those claims—absent special circumstances. 2-714(2). That leaves 2-714(1) to cover claims for breach not based on warranties and, possibly, warranty claims presenting the special circumstances noted in subsection 2. In Article 2 terms, subsection 2 measures damages when the buyer claims a defect in the quality of the goods delivered, and Subsection 1 measures damages when the buyer claims the seller's conduct did not conform to the requirements of the contract—there is no claim based on the quality of the goods delivered.

So, if the accepting buyer is not claiming that the goods are defective, then 2-714(1) will apply to measure the damages. Problems with delivery—untimely delivery, delivery to the wrong place, delivery under incorrect documents—will give the seller a claim for breach and a right to any damages caused by the breach. But how do we actually measure those damages? 2-714 tells us we measure them under Subsection 1 but, unlike most of the other remedies provisions of Article 2, 2-714(1) does not give us a formula to use. Reading 2-714(1) and 1-305 together, most courts have adapted some form of an expectancy measure to calculate damages under 2-714(1) intended to give the buyer the benefit of its bargain.

---

18   Comment to Section 67-A, *Revised Uniform Sales Act,* Second Draft, I Kelly, *Uniform Commercial Code: Drafts,* (Rothman 1984) 562.

CHAPTER 9

TITLE

When we walk out of the local electronics store with the latest iThing we've purchased, we assume the little gadget is all ours—we've paid for it (or at least we've committed VISA to pay for it), and no one can take it away from us. Buyers of goods don't expect their right to treat the goods as their own to be challenged later—we don't anticipate having to defend our right to keep and use the thing against an attack by someone claiming a superior right to it. But what if someone does come along and claim our little gadget? If the claim succeeds, we lose our iThing, even though we paid for it. And even if the claim does not succeed, we've suffered, at a minimum, the expense and inconvenience of having to defend our right to keep it. Do buyers assume the risk that they are getting less than they are expecting to get? Should they? Caveat emptor, after all. As between the buyer and the seller, which is in the better position to know the pedigree of the goods? To protect against third-party claims to the goods?

Early common law left buyers to fend for themselves; buyers assumed the risk that the seller did not have title to the goods or had defective title. Caveat emptor was really the law. By the time the Uniform Sales Act was ready for adoption by the states in the early 1900s, courts were implying in sales of personal property a representation by the seller that it had the power and the right to transfer the property—a warranty of title.

The Sales Act incorporated the different species of this warranty of title that had evolved at common law into a uniform provision providing that, unless a contrary intent appeared in the contract, the seller warranted that he had a right to sell the goods. When Llewellyn got to work drafting Article 2, the seller's warranty of title was a well-established part of sales law that had to be part of the new Code.

> Article 2 provides that, subject to its modification or exclusion by the contract, (1) there is in a contract for sale a warranty by the seller that
>
> (a) the title conveyed shall be good, and its transfer rightful; and
>
> (b) the goods shall be delivered free from any security interest or other lien or encumbrance of which the buyer at the time of contracting has no knowledge.

2-312. There is no requirement that the seller be aware of any problems with the title to the goods she sells, and courts have not required a buyer claiming under 2-312 to show that the seller knew of or had notice of a problem with title. Why impose what amounts to strict liability on sellers who sell goods with title problems? The Comments explain that 2-312

> makes provision for a buyer's basic needs in respect to a title which he in good faith expects to acquire by his purchase, namely, that he receive a good, clean title transferred to him also in a rightful manner so that he will not be exposed to a lawsuit in order to protect it.

Comment 1, 2-312. Do the "needs" of buyers require shifting all risk to the seller—even the innocent seller? As we saw in the chapter on warranties, Article 2 assumes that sellers know more about the goods they are selling—or at least are in a better position to know more about the goods—than the buyer at the time of contracting.

Superior knowledge can also influence resource allocation, and when it does, the case for placing the risk on the party with superior knowledge is more compelling.

> Article 2's warranty provisions do reflect, in the main, the efficiency calculation underlying the strict liability principle. For example, the seller is closer than any other party to situations that would raise questions about good title. Any search of title by the buyer must include inquiry into the seller's authority to sell. The seller starts out with that knowledge and therefore need expend resources only to check the authority of prior parties in the chain of distribution. Accordingly, § 2-312 provides that the seller warrants to the buyer that "the title conveyed shall be good, and its transfer rightful."[1]

Of course, sellers can avoid the strict liability imposed by 2-312 by opting out of it, just as they can opt out of the implied warranties of merchantability and fitness for a particular purpose by disclaiming the warranty of title in their contracts. To the extent that liability under 2-312 is strict, then, it would seem to be a self-inflicted risk.

How do we determine whether a seller has breached the warranty of title—how do we determine whether a seller has title to the goods it sold? The next case examines the passing of title under Article 2.

MIDWAY AUTO SALES, INC. V. CLARKSON

COURT OF APPEALS OF ARKANSAS, DIVISION FOUR, 2000
REPORTER
29 S.W.3D 788

OPINION

John B. Robbins, Chief Judge. Appellant Midway Auto Sales, Inc., sued appellee Mike Clarkson for breach of title after a 1986 Corvette it had bought from Clarkson was confiscated as a stolen vehicle by the Washington County Sheriff's office. Appellee then filed a third-party complaint against Larry Bowen, who had sold the car to him. At some time before April 1, 1998, Jimmy Haddock purchased the car with an open title from an individual in Oklahoma with a computer-generated check on a nonexistent bank account. On April 1, 1998, Mr. Haddock entered into negotiations to sell the Corvette to Mr. Bowen on an open title in exchange for a pickup truck, a camper trailer, and $1,000 in cash. Before consummating the sale, Mr. Bowen checked with the Oklahoma licensing agency and was informed that the car's title was free of encumbrances. He did not register the car. On June 11, 1998, Mr. Bowen sold the

---

1   White and Summers, *Commercial Law* 501.

Corvette with the open Oklahoma title to appellee for $5,500. Clarkson also did not register the car. He sold it to Midway for $6,000 with the same open title on July 18, 1998. On July 24, 1998, the Corvette was confiscated by the sheriff's department as a stolen vehicle and was later released to the original seller.

In his letter opinion, the circuit judge said that the original seller had the opportunity to void the sale and the certificate of title so that they did not pass into the hands of bona fide purchasers, which he found Clarkson and Mr. Bowen to be. He recognized the hardship to Midway but stated that Midway must take its recourse against someone other than the bona fide purchasers. Midway has appealed from the order of dismissal.

Midway argues that Clarkson breached his warranty of title because the Corvette was confiscated as a stolen vehicle by the sheriff. According to *Ark. Code Ann. § 4-2-312 (1)(a)* (Repl. 1991), in a contract for sale, there is a warranty by the seller that the title conveyed is good and its transfer rightful. Clarkson relies on *Ark. Code Ann. § 4-2-403* (Repl. 1991), which recognizes the legal distinction between a sale of stolen goods and a sale of goods procured through fraud. Absent exigent circumstances, one who purchases from a thief acquires no title as against the true owner. However, under *section 4-2-403*, the result is different when property obtained by fraud is conveyed to a bona fide purchaser:

> (1) A purchaser of goods acquires all title which his transferor had or had power to transfer except that a purchaser of a limited interest acquires rights only to the extent of the interest purchased. A person with voidable title has power to transfer a good title to a good faith purchaser for value. When goods have been delivered under a transaction of purchase the purchaser has such power even though:
>
> ....
>
> (b) The delivery was in exchange for a check which is later dishonored; or
>
> ....
>
> (d) The delivery was procured through fraud punishable as larcenous under the criminal law.

This section of the Uniform Commercial Code has been explained as follows:

> Under 2-403, voidable title should be distinguished from void title. A thief, for example, "gets" only void title and without more cannot pass any title to a good faith purchaser. "Voidable title" is a murky concept. The Code does not define the phrase. The comments do not even discuss it. Subsections (1)(a)-(d) of 2-403 clarify the law as to particular transactions which were "troublesome under prior law." Beyond these, we must look to non-Code state law. In general voidable title passes to those who lie in the middle of the spectrum that runs from best faith buyer at one end to robber at the other. These are buyers who commit fraud, or are otherwise guilty of naughty acts (bounced checks), but who conform to the appearance of a voluntary transaction; they would never pull a gun or crawl in through a second story window. Presumably these fraudulent buyers get voidable title from their targets, but second story men get only void title because the targets of fraud are themselves more culpable than the targets of burglary.

Subsection (1)(b) of 2-403 deals with a more common occurrence: the "rubber check." Even when Bert Buyer pays Sam Seller with a check that returns to Sam marked "NSF," a good faith purchaser from Bert takes good title.

Subsection (1)(d) of 2-403 provides that even where delivery was procured through criminal fraud, voidable title passes. Thus if Bert acquired goods from Sam with a forged check, a good faith purchaser from Bert would obtain good title.

James J. White and Robert S. Summers, *Uniform Commercial Code*
§ 3-12 at 187-89 (4th ed. 1995).

In his letter opinion, the circuit judge relied on *Pingleton v. Shepherd, 219 Ark. 473, 242 S.W.2d 971 (1951),* which was decided before the Uniform Commercial Code was enacted. There, it was held that the appellee, who had purchased an automobile in good faith from an individual who had given the appellant a worthless check, had good title. In so holding, the court relied upon a provision of the Uniform Sales Act, Ark. Stat. Ann. § 68-1424, which stated:

> Where the seller of goods has a voidable title thereto, but his title has not been avoided at the time of the sale, the buyer acquires a good title to the goods, provided he buys them in good faith, for value, and without notice of the seller's defect of title.

The court held that a fraudulent purchase of personal property accompanied with delivery is not void, but only voidable at the election of the seller; until it is avoided by the seller, the buyer has power to make a valid sale of the goods to a bona fide purchaser who has no notice of the fraud.

Section 4-2-403 is consistent with the court's decision in *Pingleton v. Shepherd.* Therefore, it follows that: (1) Mr. Haddock obtained a voidable title from the original seller, with whom he entered into a voluntary transaction of purchase; (2) until the sale was avoided by the original seller, Mr. Haddock had the power to transfer good title to a good-faith purchaser; (3) if Mr. Bowen was a good-faith purchaser, he had good title to convey to Clarkson, who would have conveyed good title to Midway; and, (4) if the title Clarkson conveyed to Midway was good, the warranty of title was not breached. Therefore, the issue is whether Mr. Bowen and Mr. Clarkson were good-faith purchasers.

"Good faith" is defined at *Ark. Code Ann. § 4-1-201(19)* (Supp. 1999) as "honesty in fact in the conduct or transaction concerned." Generally speaking, whether a party has acted in good faith in a commercial transaction is a question of fact. In bench trials, the standard of review on appeal is whether the judge's findings were clearly erroneous or clearly against the preponderance of the evidence. *Smith v. Russ, supra.* Mr. Bowen testified that, before consummating his purchase, he contacted the Oklahoma licensing agency and was informed that the Corvette's title was good. Mr. Clarkson testified that Mr. Bowen related this information to him.

Relying on *Acklin v. Manhattan Credit Corporation, supra,* Midway argues that an individual cannot be a good-faith purchaser unless the vehicle is titled in the name of the seller. There, a certificate of title based upon a bill of sale, issued to the borrower, was held to be sufficient reason to assign innocent third-party status to the lender that had relied upon it. The case does not, however, hold that one cannot be a bona fide purchaser without a certificate of title in the name of the seller. Although it would have been obvious to Midway when it purchased the vehicle, Midway now makes much of the fact that neither Mr. Bowen nor Mr. Clarkson registered the vehicle; however, it has provided no citation to authority holding that this failure will prevent one's buyer from acquiring bona-fide-purchaser status. We hold that the circuit judge's finding that Mr. Clarkson and Mr. Bowen were good-faith purchasers is not clearly erroneous. Accordingly, Clarkson did not breach the warranty of title.

Affirmed.

PROBLEM 9 - 1

Rae purchased a used golf cart for the store. She intended to use it to transport senior shoppers from their cars to the store and then back again to their cars. She purchased the cart from a motor-sports shop in town that had taken the cart as a trade-in on a new ATV it sold. The ATV buyer bought the cart from a craigslist seller who had stolen the cart from a golfing club in the next town up the interstate. The golfing club has traced the cart to Rae and has demanded its return. As between Rae and the golfing club, which has the superior claim to the cart? 2-403.

PROBLEM 9 - 2

Would your answer to Problem 9 - 1 be different if the ATV buyer had purchased the golf cart at an estate sale with a check that was later dishonored and it was the estate agent demanding that Rae return the golf cart?

PROBLEM 9 - 3

Would your answer to Problem 9 - 1 be different if the ATV buyer had borrowed the golf cart from his neighbor and it was the neighbor demanding that Rae return the golf cart?

PROBLEM 9 - 4

Rae dropped off one of the powered shopping carts she had purchased at the local repair shop for reconditioning. When several weeks had passed and she had not heard anything about the cart, she stopped by the repair shop, only to find the building empty and boarded up. As it turned out, the shop had gone out of business, and all property in its possession had been sold at an auction a few days after Rae had dropped off the shopping cart. Rae located the party that bought her cart and has demanded its return. As between Rae and the buyer at the auction, which has the superior claim to the shopping cart? 2-403. See 1-201(9).

So, what does the seller promise when it warrants "good title?" As the Court noted in *Midway Auto*, Article 2 does not define the term "good title," and the courts have had to develop a working definition of the term when assessing claims that a seller breached the warranty of title in 2-312. *Midway Auto* implies that the promise of "good title" is simply a promise that the goods can't be taken away by another. With "good title" comes security—the security of knowing that no one has a better claim to the goods than the buyer—so, as long as no one ultimately succeeds in permanently depriving the buyer of the goods, no breach of the warranty of title has been committed.

That will be some comfort to the buyer, but what about the interference with the buyer's use of the goods that is likely a part of any ownership dispute? The worry, inconvenience, and expense that are part of a title dispute are not simply erased if the buyer ultimately prevails. The comments to 2-312 suggest the seller is promising more, and as the next case illustrates, courts have read the warranty of title to be more than a promise that the buyer will win any lawsuit disputing title.

Saber v. Dan Angelone Chevrolet

Supreme Court of Rhode Island
2002
Reporter
811 A.2d 644

OPINION

Williams, Chief Justice. In this case, the defendant, Dan Angelone Chevrolet, Inc. (defendant), appeals from a Superior Court judgment, challenging several rulings made by the trial justice. Before closing arguments, the trial justice determined as a matter of law that the defendant, a Rhode Island corporation, breached the warranty of title of a car sold to the plaintiff, George Saber (plaintiff), a resident of the Commonwealth of Massachusetts. The jury found that the plaintiff provided the defendant with sufficient notice of the breach and awarded the plaintiff damages in the amount of $14,900. On appeal, the defendant alleges that the trial justice committed a variety of errors. For the reasons set out below, we deny and dismiss the defendant's appeal and affirm the trial justice's rulings.

I. Facts and Travel

On February 7, 1990, plaintiff bought a used 1985 Chevrolet Corvette (Corvette or car), from defendant for $14,900. The Corvette was red, had an automatic transmission, and its odometer said 34,744 miles. At that time plaintiff also purchased an extended warranty to cover certain problems that might arise with the car. Between March 1990 and April 1992, plaintiff experienced several mechanical problems with the car and brought it to defendant for service. Because of the series of problems he was experiencing, plaintiff decided to research the car's history. In conducting a title search on the car, he discovered that a title application for the Corvette described it as black and equipped with a manual transmission. In light of his discovery, plaintiff, through an attorney, contacted the Massachusetts State Police (state police).

In response to plaintiff's call, state police Lieutenant Joseph Costa (Lt. Costa) examined the Corvette and discovered some discrepancies with respect to its vehicle identification number (VIN) and major components. The plate located on the window downpost, which contained the VIN, was blistered and painted over. Additionally, derivative identification numbers on the car's frame, engine and transmission did not correspond to the VIN on the window downpost. Further, a Mylar sticker, which is typically located on the door of the car and also has the same VIN as the window downpost, was missing. Finally, the Corvette was equipped with a third brake light, which was manufactured one year after the car supposedly was manufactured. Based on those observations, Lt. Costa believed that some of the car parts were stolen.

After the inspection, plaintiff drove the Corvette home. The next day, plaintiff drove the car to the North Dartmouth barracks of the state police. There, he voluntarily left the car in the parking lot, dropped off the keys and took a ride home from an employee. Lieutenant Costa testified that the car was impounded and that plaintiff could not have it back.

Later, the Corvette was delivered to Danny's Autobody, a privately owned business located in New Bedford, Massachusetts, that the state police used as an impound facility. A subsequent investigation revealed that the Corvette was neither stolen nor composed of stolen parts. Rather, according to defendant's brief, the Corvette was destroyed in a fire and subsequently rebuilt using parts from various other cars. The frame was replaced with one from an "identical type" car, the motor was replaced, the engine block was taken from a Chevrolet Camaro and the car was painted red. According to defendant, it received the Corvette in its current, refurbished condition as a trade-in and later sold it to plaintiff. None of those facts were disclosed to plaintiff when he purchased the car, and it is not clear whether defendant was aware of them when it sold the Corvette to plaintiff.

In 1992, plaintiff filed a lawsuit against defendant in Massachusetts District Court, which later was dismissed for lack of jurisdiction. In 1995, plaintiff filed the instant action in Superior Court seeking damages for negligence and breach of contract. The plaintiff's amended complaint added counts for deceptive trade practices, misrepresentation, revocation of acceptance, and violations of the Magnuson Moss Warranty Act, *15 U.S.C. §§ 2301-2312*, but did not expressly allege breach of warranty of title. To support his claim for negligence, however, plaintiff alleged in his complaint that he was not given good title to the car.

The trial began in April 2000. At the close of plaintiff's case, defendant moved for judgment as a matter of law, arguing that there could be no breach of the warranty of title because the car was not stolen. The trial justice, however, denied defendant's motion, stating that the warranty of title may be breached by law enforcement impoundment. Before closing arguments, both parties moved for judgment as a matter of law. The trial justice determined that, based on Lt. Costa's testimony, the car was impounded and because of that impoundment, defendant breached the warranty of title owed to plaintiff. The trial justice granted plaintiff's motion on that issue.

II. Impoundment

Next, defendant argues that the trial justice erred in finding that the Corvette was impounded. A car is impounded if it is placed "in the custody of the police or the court." Black's Law Dictionary 760(7th ed. 1999).

The trial justice found it undisputed that "law enforcement authorities of the Commonwealth of Massachusetts * * * impounded [the Corvette]." At trial, Lt. Costa testified that after he inspected the car, he suspected that it was composed of stolen parts. Lieutenant Costa further testified that, based on his suspicion, the car was seized and impounded and that plaintiff could not have it back.

According to defendant, because plaintiff voluntarily relinquished custody of the Corvette to the state police, the car never was impounded. We deem that argument unpersuasive. Lieutenant Costa testified that plaintiff's consent was irrelevant to the impoundment. We agree that plaintiff's failure to oppose the impoundment in this case should have no impact on the trial justice's finding. The defendant did not offer any testimony to contest the fact that plaintiff was dispossessed of the car by the state police. In fact, the state police still possessed the car at the time of the trial. Based on the facts presented at trial, there was no dispute that the car was impounded and the trial justice did not err in so finding.

C. Breach as a Matter of Law

Under *§ 6A-2-312(1)* of the Rhode Island Uniform Commercial Code (UCC), "there is in a contract for sale a warranty by the seller that: (a) the title conveyed shall be good, and its transfer rightful." The UCC does not define "good title." Thus, to determine what is required of a seller to convey "good title" under *§ 6A-2-312(1)(a)*, we apply our well settled canons of statutory construction.

> "'Generally when a statute expresses a clear and unambiguous meaning, the task of interpretation is at an end and this Court will apply the plain and ordinary meaning of the words set forth in the statute.' *State v. Bryant*, 670 A.2d 776, 779 (R.I. 1996). However, when the statutory language is ambiguous, 'the primary object of the Court is to ascertain the legislative intention from a consideration of the legislation in its entirety, viewing the language used therein in the light, nature, and purpose of the enactment thereof.' *770 A.2d 867, 871 (R.I. 2001).*

The term "good title" as it is used in *§ 6A-2-312(1)(a)* is ambiguous. The UCC does not provide whether a seller's obligation under *§ 6A-2-312(1)(a)* is limited to transferring legally valid title or whether "good title" assumes some other associated qualities.

Unlike most other statutory enactments, the UCC is accompanied by official commentary. "While these comments are not controlling authority and may not be used to vary the plain language of the [UCC], * * *" they are useful for determining the purpose of its provisions and ascertaining the intent of its drafters. Official comment 1 to § 6A-2-312 declares that one of the purposes of the warranty of title is to provide "for a buyer's basic needs in respect to a title which he in good faith expects to acquire by his purchase, namely, that he receive a good, clean title transferred to him * * * so that he will not be exposed to a lawsuit in order to protect it." That comment goes on to state that the warranty of quiet possession is abolished, but that a "disturbance of quiet possession *** is one way, among many, in which the breach of the warranty of title may be established."

The language in official comment 1 evidences the General Assembly's intent to allow a buyer to establish a breach of warranty of title even if a seller did indeed deliver legally valid title. Without ruling on the official comment's abolition of the warranty of quiet possession, we do adopt its position that a buyer may establish a breach of warranty of title by showing a disturbance of quiet possession. After reading the official comment we conclude that disturbance of quiet possession does not depend on a buyer's ability to show that a seller transferred legally invalid title. Were we to limit the scope of § 6A-2-312 to those situations where title lawfully rested in a third party, buyers would be attempting to *establish*, rather than *protect*, their title and the language in official comment 1 would be rendered nugatory. Thus, the General Assembly apparently intended to "provide a remedy for the buyer who successfully defends a title suit." James J. White & Robert S. Summers, *Uniform Commercial Code*, § 9-12 at 536 (4th ed. 1995).

There is, however a split of authority concerning the scope of the warranty of title. *C.f. Jefferson*, 408 A.2d at 1039-40 (holding that proof of superior title in third party is not required to establish breach of warranty of title); *American Container Corp. v. Hanley Trucking Corp.*, 111 N.J. Super. 322, 268 A.2d 313, 318 (N.J. Super. Ct. 1970) ("The mere casting of a substantial shadow over his title, regardless of the ultimate outcome, is sufficient to violate a warranty of good title."); *Colton v. Decker*, 540 N.W.2d 172, 176 (S.D. 1995) (holding that a seller breached its warranty of title by selling buyer a truck with conflicting vehicle identification numbers that was seized by the police under the mistaken belief that it was stolen) *with C.F. Sales. Inc. v. Amfert, Inc.*, 344 N.W.2d 543, 555 (Iowa 1983) (holding that warranty of title is not breached unless superior title is established in a third party). We conclude that we are giving effect to the General Assembly's stated intention by aligning ourselves with those jurisdictions that allow a buyer to establish breach of warranty of title if a substantial shadow is cast over a title, even if the buyer's title ultimately is proven to be legally valid.

By adopting this position, we do acknowledge that "there is some point at which [a] third party's claim against the goods becomes so attenuated that we should not regard it as an interference against which the seller has warranted." White & Summers, § 9-12 at 537. Here, the car and its parts were not stolen and defendant did indeed have and deliver a legally valid title to plaintiff. We are satisfied, however, that under the facts in this case, the claim made against plaintiffs car—the state police's impoundment—was not too far attenuated. Lieutenant Costa's inspection of the Corvette revealed that it had contradicting VINs and a missing Mylar sticker. Based on those facts Lt. Costa reasonably, albeit mistakenly, believed that the car was composed of stolen parts, and therefore impounded it. By doing so, the state police called plaintiffs ownership into question, thereby "casting * * * a substantial shadow over his title."

The Corvette in this case reminds us of a passage attributed to Abraham Lincoln when he asked, "how many legs does a dog have if you count his tail as a leg? Four. You can call a tail a leg if you want to, but that doesn't make it a leg." Just as a dog's tail is not a leg, this car is not a typical 1985 Corvette. Although defendant argues that the car is a 1985 Corvette, the car has several "unique" qualities that distinguish it from most other 1985 Corvettes. Without knowing the colorful past associated with this car, plaintiff could not get the benefit of his bargain when he made his purchase. The Corvette was rebuilt after having previously been declared a total loss because of fire damage. Various parts were replaced from an assortment of other vehicles. Vehicle identification numbers embossed on certain parts did not correspond to one another. We conclude that those distinctive characteristics associated with the car and its title would lower its value in the eyes of a reasonably prudent purchaser. By imposing liability for breach of warranty of title in this scenario, the trial justice allayed buyers' fears of encountering a similar situation. Thus, we uphold the trial justice's ruling that defendant breached the warranty of title.

Most courts, as the Court noted in *Saber*, have not read 2-312 to require—as the common law had—proof of superior title in a third party to establish a breach of the seller's promise of good title. These courts recognize that the buyer's peace of mind protected by 2-312 is shattered long before a court enters judgment in a title dispute, and that the buyer who successfully defends her title has still endured the interference with her use and enjoyment of the goods that necessarily follows when ownership is challenged.

So something less than losing the goods to another can result in a breach of the seller's promise of good title, but when is that "less" still enough for purposes of 2-312? Any challenge to the buyer's title, in theory, would undermine the buyer's expectations that through the sale she acquired unfettered use and enjoyment of the goods; is the seller's promise of good title a promise that no one will ever question the buyer's right to the goods?

The law of real property has been sorting out title disputes for centuries, and many courts grappling with the issue of when is less enough have borrowed from it when applying 2-312. The "substantial shadow" test used in *Saber* is the equivalent of the "cloud on title" doctrine from real-property law. But "substantial shadow" is hardly a bright-line standard—the *Saber* Court acknowledges it's just a continuum along which at some point we leave the shadows and see sunlight. When is a challenge to the buyer's title "so attenuated"—translate, frivolous—that we cannot reasonably hold it against the seller as a breach of her promise of good title? Should the "baseless anxiety of the hypersensitive purchaser regarding the validity of his title" give rise to a claim under 2-312? Courts, again borrowing from real-property law, have relied on terms like "colorable" and "spurious" to interject an element of objectiveness into the shadow test—the buyer is protected from colorable claims but not from spurious claims. One person's colorable claim, though, is usually perceived as spurious by the target, and a spurious claim can still undermine a buyer's confidence in the transaction. Ultimately, whether a claim casts a substantial-enough shadow over the buyer's title is going to turn on the facts of each case and the ability of buyer's counsel to convince the court that the buyer hasn't seen the sun since the challenge to title arose.

Instead of trying to define the scope of the seller's promise of good title by analogy to real-property law, a court could simply "hold a seller liable for expenses incurred in successfully defending against an inferior claim only if the seller knew or had reason to know that such a claim was likely to be asserted."[2] The exact reach of the seller's promise would be less critical if the seller's liability, as we move toward the outer limits, turned on its awareness of possible problems at the time of sale. A seller concerned about such exposure could disclaim the warranty; a seller aware that others could contest title and who does not disclaim the warranty only has herself to blame if the buyer later asserts a claim for compensation based on 2-312.[3]

Regardless of how broadly a court defines the seller's promise of good title under 2-312, buyers who find their title to the goods challenged may have recourse against the seller outside of 2-312. Both the common law and the Uniform Sales Act recognized the right of a buyer to put the defense of her title on

---

2   White and Summers, *Commercial Law* 501.

3   The Comments to 2-312 note that the warranty of title is not an implied warranty, the significance of which for our purposes is that the methods for disclaiming Article 2 implied warranties in 2-316 do not apply to the 2-312 warranty of title.

the seller and to recover for breach of the warranty of title if the seller refused to defend and the buyer ultimately lost the title dispute.[4] Article 2 appears to preserve this "practice of voucher to defend" for all breach of warranty claims. Comment 7, 2-607.

PROBLEM 9 - 5

Could the motor-sports shop that sold Rae the golf cart have protected itself against a claim by Rae for breach of the warranty of title under 2-312 by including an "as is" clause in the sales agreement? 2-312, Comment 6.

If the seller is a merchant, the seller also promises that the goods she delivers are free of the rightful claim of any third person by way of infringement or the like. The Comments to 2-312 explain that the seller's duty when the goods sold are part of its "normal stock" and sold in the ordinary course of its business, is

> to see that no claim of infringement of a patent or a trademark by a third party will mar the buyer's title.

Comment 3, 2-312. As with the seller's promise of good title, the courts have been left to define the scope of the seller's warranty against infringement, and have not always agreed with one another when required to do so.

The "rightful claim" that creates a breach of the seller's duty under 2-312(3) is as much a mystery as the claim that casts a "substantial shadow" over the buyer's right to good title under 2-312(1). "Rightful" implies, at the very least, that a claim of infringement cannot be frivolous—but does it also imply that the warranty can only be breached if the infringement claim is successfully litigated? Or does a "rightful" claim fall somewhere on a continuum between these two extremes—beyond frivolous, but before court adjudication? And if so, how far beyond frivolous or how close to court adjudication must it be to create a breach of the seller's promise under 2-312(3)?

The next case addresses the basic scope question in the context of deciding between competing visions for 2-312(3) as reflected in the arguments of the parties.

CREATION SUPPLY, INC. V. ALPHA ART MATERIALS, CO., LTD.
UNITED STATES DISTRICT COURT FOR THE DISTRICT OF OREGON, 2013
2013 U.S. DIST. LEXIS 151292

BROWN, Judge.

This matter comes before the Court on Plaintiff's Motion (#68) for Summary Judgment on Count I of its Complaint. For the reasons that follow, the Court DENIES Plaintiff's Motion.

BACKGROUND

Plaintiff Creation Supply, Inc. (CSI) is an Illinois corporation. Defendant Alpha Art Materials, Co., Ltd., is a Korean corporation. CSI and Alpha entered into a Memorandum of Understanding (MOU) on approximately April 1, 2011. Pursuant to the MOU, CSI had the exclusive right to purchase Mepxy markers from Alpha and to sell them in certain territories in the United States. Accordingly, CSI purchased Mepxy markers from Alpha and sold Mepxy markers in the United States.

---

4   See White and Summers, *Commercial Law* at 502.

On April 25, 2012, CSI was sued in the District of Oregon in *Too Marker Products, Inc., and Imagination International, Inc. v. Creation Supply, Inc., and John Gragg,* 911 F. Supp. 2d 1114 (the Too Marker lawsuit). The Too Marker lawsuit included Too Marker's assertion that, among other things, CSI's sale of Mepxy markers infringes Too Marker's registered trade dress. On or about July 26, 2013, Too Marker and Imagination International, Inc., accepted Alpha's Offer of Judgment (#91), and on August 19, 2013, a Settlement Order (#92) was entered dismissing without prejudice all claims asserted by Too Marker and Imagination International against CSI as well as the counterclaims that CSI asserted against Too Marker and Imagination International. The only claims remaining in the Too Marker lawsuit are the third-party claims of CSI against Alpha.

On July 11, 2012, CSI filed this action in the Northern District of Illinois, Eastern Division, which transferred this action *sua sponte* to the District of Oregon on June 19, 2013. In this action CSI asserts Alpha breached the Warranty of Title and Against Infringement (Count I) and Implied Indemnity (Count II), and, as noted, CSI's instant Motion seeks summary judgment on Count I.

DISCUSSION

I. The Law

The MOU provides, and the parties agree that Illinois law governs the MOU: "This MOU will be governed by and construed in accordance with the laws of the State of Illinois. The interpretation and validity of this document will be according to the Laws of the State of Illinois."

Title *810 ILCS 5/2-312* provides:
Warranty of title and against infringement; buyer's obligation against infringement.

***

(3) *Unless otherwise agreed a seller who is a merchant regularly dealing in goods of the kind warrants that the goods shall be delivered free of the rightful claim of any third person by way of infringement or the like* but a buyer who furnishes specification to the seller must hold the seller harmless against any such claim which arises out of compliance with the specifications.

Emphasis added.
The elements of breach of an implied warranty against infringement are: (1) the seller was a merchant regularly dealing in goods of the kind warranted, (2) the goods were subject to a *rightful claim* of infringement by a third party upon delivery, (3) the buyer did not furnish specifications to the seller, and (4) the parties did not form another agreement.

II. Analysis

Alpha contends summary judgment is not available on Count I because there are genuine disputes of material fact concerning elements (2), (3), and (4) that preclude summary judgment. Alpha first asserts the Too Marker lawsuit does not contain a *rightful claim* of trade-dress infringement because Too Marker's claims for trade-dress infringement in the Too Marker lawsuit were exceptionally weak and, therefore, not "rightful." Alpha, however, does not cite to nor can the Court find an Illinois case on point to support Alpha's position.

CSI, in turn, argues it is entitled to summary judgment on its claim against Alpha for the breach of implied warranty of noninfringement and contends there are not any genuine disputes of material fact. CSI relies on *Pacific Sunwear of California, Inc. v. Olaes Enterprises, Inc.,* 167 Cal. App. 4th 466, 84 Cal. Rptr. 3d 182 (Cal. Ct. App. 2008), to support its position. In *Pacific Sunwear* a clothing retailer sued a t-shirt supplier for breaching a statutory warranty similar to *ICLS § 5/2-312(3).* The underlying case for trademark infringement was settled under seal. On the ground that the buyer's remedy arises immediately upon notice of infringement (*i.e.*, well before resolution of the claim), the court found any "significant claim of infringement—whether or not ultimately meritorious—triggers the … warranty." After considering the official commentary to an analogous provision of the *Uniform Commercial Code (U.C.C.) § 2-312* (amended 2011), the statutory scheme, and public policy, the California court concluded "the warranty against rightful claims applies to all claims of infringement that have any significant and adverse effect on the buyer's ability to make use of the purchased goods, excepting only frivolous claims that are completely devoid of merit." The court reversed the trial court's grant of summary judgment on the ground that there was "at least a 'triable issue of material fact' as to whether SNCL's infringement claim was a rightful claim."

The analysis in *Pacific Sunwear* was also applied in *Phoenix Solutions, Inc. v. Sony Electronics, Inc.*, 637 F. Supp. 2d, 683 (N.D. Cal. 2009). Therein the court found Sony met its burden of asserting a "rightful" claim and survived a summary-judgment motion on the ground that the infringement claims against Sony had a significant and adverse effect on Sony's ability to make use of the purchased computer system. "Although Phoenix and Sony entered into a settlement early in the litigation, the case advanced beyond more than the mere filing of an action. The settlement terms, provided to the court under seal, indicate an evaluative inquiry was made into the merits of the underlying claim itself."

Here, however, Alpha argues whether a claim is "rightful" requires a substantive investigation of the underlying infringement claims that allegedly give rise to the indemnity obligation. Alpha relies on *84 Lumber Co. v. MRK Techs., Ltd.*, 145 F. Supp. 2d 675 (W.D. Pa. 2001), to support its position. The court in *84 Lumber Co.* determined it had subject-matter jurisdiction over a warranty-against-infringement claim because plaintiff's claims could not be addressed without inquiring into the nature of the underlying infringement claims. The court noted if claims of patent infringement are seen as marks on a continuum, "whatever a 'rightful claim' is would fall somewhere between purely frivolous claims, at one end, and claims where liability has been proven, at the other." "We must have some indicia that Lemelson's claim that the defendants infringed his patents had merit. We cannot impose liability on the defendants based solely upon the plaintiff's subjective belief and representation that it thought Lemelson was likely to win."

Alpha also relies on *EZ Tag Corp. v. Casio America, Inc.*, 861 F. Supp. 2d 181 (S.D.N.Y. 2012), to support its position. The *EZ Tag* court granted a motion to dismiss under the New York Uniform Commercial Code in an action brought by EZ Tag "for attorney's fees and costs incurred in defense of a patent infringement action brought by Raylon LLC" in Texas. The *Raylon* court granted summary judgment to EZ Tag and Casio and found there was not a patent infringement. The *EZ Tag* court noted the definition of the term "rightful" was a question of first impression in that circuit and that no court in that circuit had determined that a claim was "rightful" following an affirmative adjudication of noninfringement. The *EZ Tag* court found a "claim of infringement must have some merit beyond being 'nonfrivolous' for Rule 11 purposes to support a breach of warranty claim." The *EZ Tag* court concluded Raylon's claims were not so frivolous as to be sanctionable, but its claims "were not so substantial as to impose a significant and adverse effect on EZ Tag's ability to make use of the goods."

As noted, CSI argues in this case that Too Marker's claims against Alpha are "rightful" as demonstrated by Too Marker's acceptance of Alpha's $40,000 Offer of Judgment as to Too Marker's trade-dress infringement claims, but Alpha asserts Too Marker's claims were "exceptionally weak" and, therefore, do not give rise to a "rightful" claim. These contradictory positions as to the "rightfulness" of Too Marker's claims against Alpha are not solely questions of law, but require resolution of the factual dispute at least as to the "rightfulness" of that claim as Alpha contends. Accordingly, the Court concludes whether the settlement between Too Marker and Alpha settled a "rightful claim" within the meaning of *Title 810 ICLS 5/2-312(3)* is a question of fact. Based on the foregoing, the Court denies CSI's Motion for Summary Judgment.

Courts have applied the "substantial shadow" test from 2-312(1) to claims that the seller breached its warranty against infringement under 2-312(3), arriving at the same place we did with our assessment of the test under the warranty of title: it's a fact-intensive inquiry, the outcome of which will turn on the particular facts of each case.

> This "substantial shadow" description is as apt as any other in describing what constitutes a "rightful" claim of infringement by a third party, and ... its application in a warranty against infringement dispute will doubtless often require resolution by the factfinder after weighing the nature and facts of the third party's claim.

****

> We agree that a frivolous infringement claim does not generate a breach of the warranty described in *N.J.S.A.* 12A:2-312(3) any more than a buyer is obligated to prove the seller's liability for infringement to succeed in demonstrating a breach of this warranty. A third party's claim of infringement—to be "rightful" within the meaning of *N.J.S.A.* 12A:2-312(3)—must cast a "substantial shadow" on the buyer's ability to make use of the goods in question, in order to constitute a breach of the warranty against infringement. In this context, we agree with the holding in *84 Lumber* that resolution of this question requires the factfinder's analysis of the patent and the claim of infringement. Again, this does not mean that [buyer] would have to actually prove the validity of the infringement claim to succeed on this warranty argument, only that CCL's claim had sufficient substance to unduly disturb [buyer's] ownership and disposition of the goods in question. In other words, to prove that a seller breached a warranty because goods were the subject of a third party's rightful claim of infringement, a buyer must establish that the infringement claim is of a substantial nature that is reasonably likely to subject the buyer to litigation, and has a significant and adverse effect on the buyer's ability to make use of the goods in question. The uncertainty about the substance of CCL's claim was not so free from question as to permit the disposition of this contention by the judge as a matter of law. As a result, we conclude that, in light of the record presented at trial, the judge correctly denied [buyer's] motions and permitted the matter to be decided by the jury.
>
> *Sun Coast Merchandise v. Myron*, 922 A.2d 782 (N.J. App. 2007).

Section 2-312 limits the buyer's right to claim infringement when the infringement results from the seller's use of specifications provided by the buyer. If the goods are made to order based on specifications supplied by the buyer, and if by complying with the buyer's specifications the seller infringes the rights of another who brings a claim against the buyer, the buyer will not have a claim against the seller for breach of the warranty against infringement. If the infringement claim is asserted against the seller, then, according to the Comments, the buyer must indemnify the seller for any loss suffered from the infringement claim. As the Comments explain:

> when the buyer orders goods to be assembled, prepared or manufactured to his own specifications ... If ... the resulting product infringes a patent or trademark, the liability will run from buyer to seller. There is, under such circumstances, a tacit representation on the part of the buyer that the seller will be safe in manufacturing according to the specifications, and the buyer is under an obligation of good faith to indemnify him for any loss suffered.

Comment 3, 2-312. So, 2-312(3) really creates two warranties—one by the seller against infringement, and one by the buyer in the event that the buyer is the source of an infringement.

Finally, sellers who do not want to warrant the transfer of good title must do more than merely disclaim the warranty under 2-316. Instead, they must "exclude" the warranty by using "specific language"—terms which "in common understanding" would alert the buyer to the seller's intention to exclude warranties are not sufficient to exclude the warranty of title. A sale of goods "as is" might negate the warranties of merchantability or fitness for a particular purpose, but they will not "exclude" the warranty of title. How "specific" must the language excluding the warranty of title be in order to have the effect intended by the seller? It has to be more specific than "seller transfers only such right, title and interest as seller may have," or that "seller is making no warranties of any kind," or that "all warranties are hereby excluded from this transaction," or that "no representations or warranties of any kind are made with respect to the property to be sold," each of which has been found insufficient to exclude the warranty of good title.

> The warranty of title is also excluded
>
> by circumstances which would give the buyer reason to know that the person selling does not claim title in himself or that he is purporting to sell only such right or title as he or a third person may have.

What kind of "circumstances" would put the buyer on notice that the seller does not claim to have title to the goods that she can transfer to the buyer? The comments note that certain sales

> may be so out of the ordinary commercial course that their peculiar character is immediately apparent to the buyer ...

Comment 5, 2-312. Sales by sheriffs, executors, foreclosing lienors, and "persons similarly situated" should put the buyer on notice that the seller is not claiming to transfer title to the goods.

CPSIA information can be obtained
at www.ICGtesting.com
Printed in the USA
FSHW022138051119
63787FS